ANALECTA BIBLICA
INVESTIGATIONES SCIENTIFICAE IN RES BIBLICAS
108

Institution and Narrative

Collected Essays

ROMAE
E PONTIFICIO INSTITUTO BIBLICO
1985

† DENNIS J. McCARTHY S.J.

Institution and Narrative
Collected Essays

ROME
BIBLICAL INSTITUTE PRESS
1985

Published with the assistance of a grant
from the Wisconsin Province of the Society of Jesus.

ISBN 88-7653-108-4

PRINTED IN ITALY

Gregorian University Press
Biblical Institute Press
Piazza della Pilotta, 35 - 00187 Rome, Italy

Preface

A professor dead at 58 seems to us a professor *manqué*. His life has been cut off in full flower with senseless finality — "a man's years are seventy." Even though we know that death is the beginning of true life, we miss the life which was his presence among us. But someone who has given himself to teaching can stay alive in his writings. He can live on in the pages which we read, though these pages, like their author's life, have reached completion.

We the colleagues, friends, and fellow religious of Dennis McCarthy wish to extend his career by publishing in this volume his collected essays. Some of these essays are rigorously technical, with footnotes; others are a type of personal reflection which some call *haute vulgarisation*. There are two types of readers, then, which are addressed.

We tend to think of a professor in terms of his field of specialization, perhaps in terms of his most influential book or most notable success. As though he were a dead butterfly on exhibit or a tree labeled in Latin. The professor usually provides a reason for such simplification, but he also usually breaks out of too facile a categorization. Thus McCarthy evokes the term "covenant." This was the subject of his basic work: *Treaty and Covenant. A Study in Form in the Ancient Oriental Documents and in the Old Testament.* And this is the subject of eight articles in the present work.

But this book does not end with covenant. McCarthy views covenant as the relation between man and God. Connected with covenant are other institutions of the Old Testament world — the Holy War, the rite of installation, leadership, monarchy, the role of blood in sacrifice. God is the subject of a number of articles: Love of God, Word of God, Presence of God, Wrath of God, God the Prisoner, Creation, Law. God is clearly at the center of McCarthy's scholarly concern.

As professor and as private individual McCarthy took a special interest in literature. He did not look on literature as a form of ornamentation but as a means of expression and communication: "Literature is the Word of God" he says in one article. He was a voracious reader and for a while led a circle of students in the informal reading and commenting of short stories, poems, and plays in English. He directed a number of doctoral candidates to studies of this sort. He delighted to move in the world of imagery and symbolism and allusions and the point of view of a narrator.

Human experience was a basic given in McCarthy's thought — human experience which he felt could be captured in its essential aspects and conveyed in words. This human experience for him culminated in the experience of God.

All this did not prevent him from concerning himself with such current issues as academic freedom and human rights.

All the articles in this book are reproduced as they originally appeared except for two: "Hero and Anti-Hero in 1 Sam 13,2 – 14,46" and "Human Rights and the Old Testament."

Rome
November 16, 1984

LUIS ALONSO SCHÖKEL, S.J.
Editor, Analecta Biblica

Editorial Note

The two articles which are here published for the first time have different editorial histories. "Human Rights and the Old Testament" is presented exactly as I found it in the typescript except for a few minor changes of wording which Fr. McCarthy introduced in his own hand and except for the addition of a few commas by myself for aid in reading. "Hero and Anti-Hero in 1 Sam 13,2 – 14,46," on the other hand, was retouched considerably by Fr. McCarthy in the typescript which I have used for publication. I have incorporated all his changes which bear the mark of final thinking. One or two suggestions in the margin added with an obvious view to further development I have not incorporated. This article is being published by *Journal of Biblical Literature* and I am unfamiliar with the typescript on which their version is based. The explanation given above will clarify any differences in the two versions.

The abbreviations used in this volume are those of the publications in which the contributions originally appeared. In case of doubt the reader may consult such standard lists of abbreviations as those given in the *Elenchus bibliographicus biblicus*, *Biblica*, and *Catholic Biblical Quarterly*.

Rome
November 20, 1984

JAMES SWETNAM, S.J.
Managing Editor, Analecta Biblica

Table of Contents

Part I

Covenant Studies

Reprinted from the Catholic Biblical Quarterly, Vol. XXVI, No. 2, pp. 179-189, April 1964

THREE COVENANTS IN GENESIS

This inquiry is concerned with three passages, Gn 21,22-24; 26,26-33 and 31,49-54 about whose components there is general agreement among scholars, even though their structure is sufficiently complex. In Gn 21,22-34 the story of a covenant made between Abraham and Abimelek, King of Gerar, at Beersheba is made up from the Pentateuch strand called E in 22-24, 27 and 31 and a form of that designated J in 25-26, 28-30 and 32-34.[1] There is another J version of the events at Beersheba in chapter 26, but here it is Isaac with whom Abimelek deals. The general object is the same, namely to account for the covenant with the Gerarites and for the place-name Beersheba. However, not only the actors are different in this version, but the explanation of the name implied in 21,28-30, "Well of Seven," is different from the "Well of Oath" in 26,31.

The third passage, Gn 31,44-54, is like the first complex. There are certainly two accounts of covenant making, even if the delineation of the parts belonging to J and E is not clear to the last detail. I take verses 46 and 51-53a to belong to J, with the mention of the *maṣṣēbâ* in 51 and 52 to be omitted as a harmonizing addition.[2] Verses 44-45, 49-50 and 53b-54 would stem from E.[3] These accounts of a marriage covenant (E) and a

[1] G. Holscher, *Geschichtsschreibung in Israel* (Lund, 1952) 282-283, still follows H. Holzinger, *Genesis. Kurzer Handkommentar zum Alten Testament* I/1 (Freiburg i.B., 1898) and attributes the whole passage to E, but in view of divine names, the association of Abraham with the Philistines (never elsewhere in E) and the different explanations of the name Beersheba implied in 28-30 and in 31, the division given in the text must be maintained.

[2] Verse 47 is commonly admitted to be a learned gloss. H. Gunkel, *Genesis. Göttinger Handkommentar zum Alten Testament* I/1 (Göttingen, 1910) suggests that 48 originally belonged at the end of the J passage. It is surely connected with J (cf. the use of *gāl* where E has *maṣṣēbâ,* and the *gāl*-witness as in v. 52) but why the displacement? Is it not rather a fragment from another J story explaining the name Gilead? Its double Beersheba traditions show that J could have more than one version of such a thing.

[3] Often 44b is separated from 44a because the feminine noun "covenant" has a masculine verb if the two halves are taken together. However, a feminine often has a masculine complement if separated from the latter (cf. G. R. Driver, "Hebrew Studies," *Journal of the Royal Asiatic Society* 71 [1948] 164-176) so there is no reason to separate the half verses. In 49 read *'elōhîm* with LXX (*theos*); in addition to the reasons given in the commentaries, the emphasis on God as guardian in the absence of a human overseer fits E's marriage covenant far better than J's frontier pact. With Laban the natural guardian returning to Aram and Jacob crossing into Palestine, there is no one to look out for Laban's daughters. A violation of the frontiers would normally be discovered and avenged by men.

covenant fixing a frontier (J) add two more pieces of evidence to the dossier on ancient covenant making. This gives us five witnesses, and as the study of antiquity goes, that is considerable evidence. More, it is very old evidence, for the fact that the Beersheba and Gilead covenants appear in both J and E indicates that they belonged to a stage antedating both these traditions. Also, these covenants are marked by nomadic traits which were not those of the normative Israelite tradition after the Conquest.

Covenant and Oath

What do these sources have to teach about the nature of covenant making? One point of interest is the relation of covenant and oath and particularly the question of an oath taken by the more powerful of the parties to the covenant. It has been a common opinion that the most ancient covenant was a pure grant from the superior with no place for an oath on anyone's part. More recently, after the discovery in Israel of a covenant in the form of the ancient vassal treaty, a new element has been brought into the argument, for this type of pact demanded an oath from the inferior but not, usually, from the superior party. If, then, Israel used this form we might expect the oath-taking to follow this pattern. This would be true even though our Gn covenants are not vassal arrangements in the formal sense, that is, they do not establish a relation of lord and underling, but rather regulate certain specific details. The great king did not bind himself by oath in the fundamental agreement which established his relationship to the vassal; much less would he do so when arranging matters of lesser import. This is demonstrated again and again in the international documents from Ugarit, where the Hittite overlord regulates even such important matters as boundaries and tribute by decree. Thus the societies which made use of the vassal treaty were consistent; they did not demand an oath from the superior in dealings with an inferior.

Now, there can be no doubt that our Gn texts do insist on the fact of an oath. This is a little clearer in E, which actually uses the verb *šbʿ* in both its accounts of covenant making: 21,23-4 & 31; 31,53b. Indeed, in its account of Abimelek's dealings at Beersheba the oath is all-important. His concern is explicitly and precisely to get Abraham to swear an oath. On the other hand, J does not use the root *šbʿ* so often. In fact one almost has the impression that it is avoided, for it appears only in 26,31, and there it is demanded by an extrinsic factor, since the name Beersheba is to be explained and this commands the use of the root. Otherwise the J story in chapter 26 has Abimelek's demand for an *ʾālâ,* "curse, oath, agreement,"[4]

[4] The usage of *ʾālâ* in this passage, somewhat unusual in Hebrew, reappears in an inscription in the Phoenician dialect: see T. H. Gaster, "A Canaanite Magical Text,"

and it has the traditional *krt b^e rît* where the E parallel has *šbʿ*. In chapter 31 once again J avoids the word, but it has the thing: 52b is an anacoluthon oath which contains the covenant terms. Once more, E uses *šbʿ* in 53b.

The precise use of this verb in our passages is worth some notice. It is used absolutely, never with a direct object. "To swear" taken by itself is enough to imply a covenant. There is no need to say "swear a covenant" even though the phrase is perfectly possible,[5] and the verb appears parallel to "cutting a covenant," particularly in the sequence 21,27 & 31, but virtually in 31,44 & 53b and in J in 26,28 & 31. A similar formulation occurs also in Jos 9,15: "Joshua made peace with them, and he made them a covenant that they might live, and the heads of the community swore them an oath." The formula is very old; in the Akkadian treaty of Abba-AN of Yamkhad with Yarimlim found at Alalakh and dating from the 18-17th century B.C. we read that "Abba-AN swore an oath and cut the throat of a sheep."[6] The point is that though taking an oath is part of covenant making, it is kept separate from the process of "cutting a covenant." At this early stage one swears an oath and also[7] cuts a covenant; one does not swear a covenant. The careful separation involved in the terminology appears to imply an original distinction between covenant by oath and covenant by rite, a distinction still reflected in Gn, but beginning to be glossed over in Dt, where God can swear a covenant.[8]

Nevertheless, our passages from Gn do know of the relation between covenant and oath. Who takes the oath? Most often it is a reciprocal thing. This is clearest in J, for in c. 26 Abimelek's speech calls for an oath between Isaac and his people, and the pericope concludes with the notice that Isaac and Abimelek "swore an oath each to the other." So also in 31,52 both Jacob and Laban swear to respect the frontier. E is less straightforward. In 21,31 Abraham and Abimelek both swear an oath, but the opening verses are entirely concerned with Abimelek's getting Abraham to swear an oath for Abimelek. This almost makes v. 31 look like an attempt to improve

Orientalia N.S. 11 (1942) 44. Is there a hint of the Canaanite coastal dialect in the "Philistine" Abimelek's speech?

5 Cf. Dt 4,31; 7,11.

6 D. J. Wiseman, "Abban and Alalah," *JCS* 12 (1957) 126, lines 39-41.

7 In the Akkadian text cited the conjunction is coordinating *u*, not the subordinating *-ma*. Note also *AT* 54,16, where the cutting of a lamb's throat is enough by itself to confirm a contract. The rite is therefore separable from the oath and efficacious without it.

8 The distinction between the covenant based on ritual and the covenant based on the pledged word is developed in the writer's *Treaty and Covenant: A Study in Form in the Ancient Oriental Documents and in the Old Testament. Analecta Biblica* 21 (Rome, 1963), c. 13.

the picture, to make the agreement mutual lest the Patriarch be in the humiliating position of binding himself to the gentile king. However, v. 27 has already introduced the idea of reciprocity, and, as we shall see, Abraham's giving gifts, which is found there, need not be taken to mean he is a humble petitioner but relatively superior. Hence there is no need to posit an editorial addition to save the patriarchal dignity. In fact, even in the opening verses it is Abimelek who is on the defensive. He wants the pact, he pleads for it in sufficiently abject terms. He is sure of his own disposition, and his problem is to arouse something similar in Abraham. Hence the emphasis on persuading Abraham to take an oath.

As for E in c. 31, there is no question of reciprocity. Laban proposes the covenant in 31,44 and sets the terms in 31,50. These affect Jacob alone, and only he swears an oath in 53b. However, this is a result of the situation and the subject matter of the covenant, which is a marriage agreement, and as presented one with an especially narrow object: the protection of the wives. It is for the son-in-law to give the necessary assurances and there is nothing which the father-in-law can do to reciprocate.

These passages of Gn, then, present covenants involving an oath by both parties as far as the subject matter allows, and the mutual oath is typical of the treaty between equals though not of the vassal treaty. Must we conclude from the analogy of the so-called parity treaty that these are covenants among equals? It seems rather that the texts themselves point to a situation in which one party is clearly superior and yet takes an oath. Thus, in the account of the dealings with Abimelek at Beersheba it is the Hebrew patriarchs, Abraham (E, J) and Isaac (J), who are superior. This is counter to the etiological interpretation of the incidents current since Gunkel. In his view the stories have to explain why Israelites in the days of their relative power still respected the feebler Gerarites. The reason offered is that in the time of Israelite weakness, that is, when Abraham or Isaac was not yet a nation but a small group of family and retainers, a covenant was made with the more powerful Gerarites and it was still binding even though the balance of strength had changed. The signs of the supposed weakness of the patriarchs are these: Abraham gives gifts to Abimelek, Isaac fled Gerar,[9] Abimelek dictates terms.

These hardly make a conclusive argument. It is true that a weaker power could offer gifts to tempt a stronger into alliance as Asa of Judah did to Damascus and Ahaz to Assyria.[10] This looks much like a bribe, and it was in fact used to buy off an enemy.[11] However, the more important figure

[9] Holzinger, *Genesis. KHAT* I/1, *in loc.*

[10] 1 Kgs 15,18-19; 2 Kgs 18,14-15.

[11] 2 Kgs 16,8; Jacob and Esau in Gn 32,21.

could also offer gifts to the lesser as the king of Babylon did to Hezekiah.[12] These were all cases of international diplomacy, where a "gift" was a useful means to open negotiations demonstrating that there was something in it for the power being solicited.[13] More apt would be the comparison of the more homely gift to cement a pact of friendship. Often enough in simpler societies it is the superior who binds people to him by gifts, and this is true in particular of the bedouin, Semitic nomads like Abraham.[14] But perhaps the best illustration is in our texts themselves in the variant J version of the events at Beersheba. Abraham is making demands on Abimelek, who is obviously uncomfortable about it all. He is definitely suspicious of Abraham's gift, as 21,29 shows. Why else except that he realizes accepting a gift will mean he submits to the other's will?

As far as Isaac's fleeing Gerar goes, this may be the realistic interpretation of the episodes in Gn 26, but it is not that of the text itself. Initially thought weak and robbed of his wife, Isaac is proved strong in the eyes of the Gerarites because he was seen to have divine protection. This is emphasized in 26,10-14, and it is the express motive for Abimelek's seeking a covenant. It was fear of Isaac that led to his leaving and to his being asked terms. Gerar probably had the bigger battalions, but they were not about to march against divine power.

This leaves the problem of the imposition of terms. Can we call the words of Abimelek in 21,23-24 and 26,28-29 imposing terms? It is more like asking for concessions. He is making a plea for good treatment. He asks for nothing except not to be harmed. Contrast, within our pericopes, Laban's calm words in 31,50: here is a real imposition of limits. Or Abraham's words to Abimelek in 21,25-26: these show what it sounds like to impose terms rather than ask a favor. The patriarch forces what he wants from Abimelek.

In the case of the covenants between Jacob and Laban the question of relative superiority is somewhat different. In the frontier pact which comes from J we have mutual oaths, but is one party treated as more important than the other? The terms are perfectly equal so that we can decide nothing from them. It is Laban who proposes them, and while we have seen that this is not an automatic sign of superiority, the situation is different from that of Abimelek. Laban is not appealing to Jacob to grant him something, he is taking the lead in solving their problem. Moreover, Laban is represented as the active party throughout the episode. He erects the stone pile

12 2 Kgs 20,12.
13 Jonathan and David in 1 Sm 18,3-4.
14 Cf. J. Pedersen, *Der Eid bei den Semiten* (Strassburg, 1914) 25.

and fixes the terms. All in all, he seems to be represented as the leading figure; yet he too takes an oath.

In the other covenant in Gn 31, E's account of a marriage agreement, once again Laban proposes the covenant which binds Jacob alone. He definitely acts as the predominant party, though we have seen that this may be due to the subject matter in this case. The only thing which might indicate that Jacob is superior is that he offers the sacrifice in v. 54, and we would normally expect the sacrificer to be the one in the more dignified position. However, this was not always the case: in Ex 24,5 it is not the leaders but the young men who perform the sacrifice. Further, E is sensitive about the exclusivism of the cult of Yahweh and so could not be expected to allow a patriarch to take part in a sacrifice offered by the gentile Laban. Thus the E tradition did not have any choice in the matter, and once more circumstances other than the nature of covenant making itself can explain the roles of Jacob and Laban.

We have, then, in these Gn texts several representations of covenant in which the superior as well as the inferior binds himself by oath: Abraham in 21,24 & 31 (E), Isaac in 26,31 (J), perhaps Laban in 31,52b (J). In one J account, 21,25-25 & 21,28-30, taking an oath is simply not mentioned. Only in the E portion of c. 31 is the oath confined to the seemingly lesser party, as in a necessarily unilateral affair it would have to be. Thus there is good testimony to the fact that, when an oath was involved in covenant making and the case permitted, Israel knew a form demanding a mutual taking of an oath from early times.

This evidence is all the more pertinent for the fact that this form is used in regard to matter such as frontiers and aggression which are a primary concern of the vassal treaty, a form of covenant which did not normally involve an oath on the part of the greater king. Even the manner of formulating the terms recalls certain aspects of the treaty literature. The stipulation, that is, the obligation imposed, is formulated as an oath, a conditional self-cursing, just as there is in the vassal treaties of Esarhaddon. The adjuration to do good just as one has received good in Gn 21,23; 26,29 is frequently paralleled in the Hittite treaties. Yet in handling familiar matter in familiar terms Gn departs from the familiar in its demand for an oath from the superior.

Covenant and Sacrificial Meal

A further point of interest in these pericopes is the element of the covenant meal, a rite which in itself has little connection with contract under oath represented by the treaty. There are two clear instances of such a meal: Isaac feeds Abimelek in 26,30 and Jacob eats with Laban in 31,46.

There is also a common meal in 31,54, but in this passage the element of sacrifice has been added. The meal alone as part of covenant making is therefore confined to J.

This custom of forming a union by taking bread together is widespread; doubtless it is based on the idea that it is the family group which eats together so that admission to the meal implies admission to the family. The practice is attested in ancient non-Biblical texts as well as among Semitic nomads;[15] once more Israelite practice reflects its historical environment. However, we need not seek outside the Bible to grasp its meaning and importance, for in Israel itself a "salt" covenant is especially binding to the extent that the phrase is equivalent to saying unbreakable covenant.[16] The implications are that sharing a meal could by itself be an effective means of constituting a covenant. It seems less than likely that an auxiliary rite, a mere adjunct, would give its name to an especially lasting union. More, such a union must have been conceived of in terms of a family bond.

This concept of covenant making is especially associated with J in the passages under study. In the one passage from E which can be cited there is an added element, the sacrifice, which changes the meaning as we will see. The meal alone as part of covenant making belongs to J. Here one must note the order in which the actions involved in validating the pact are presented. The covenant meal precedes the taking of an oath in 26,30-31; 31,46 & 52. The oath comes after a union has been formed and serves to define its extent, its terms.

But can we validly deny E a use of the covenant meal? It does present the allies as eating together in 31,54. However, here the meal is not a sharing of a familial repast through which one party admits the other to his family circle. It is not a rite which is the first, constitutive step in making a covenant. It is a sacrificial repast. Doubtless joining together at the same divine table implies unity among the participants, but this is not the first meaning. The rite aims directly at communion with the divine and not at a union within a family. This seems to be verified in E's account where the covenant has already been made by an oath when the sacrificial meal is offered. The shared sacrifice is at most a reinforcement of the covenant already defined and sworn.

Covenant and Witness

A further important element in these Genesis covenants is the role of the witness, the *'ēd*. In 21,30 (J) the seven sheep are to be taken by Abimelek

15 Cf. D. J. Wiseman, *The Vassal Treaties of Esarhaddon* (London, 1958), 1. 154; J. Pedersen, *Israel. Its Life and Culture* (Copenhagen, 1926), I-II, 305-306.

16 2 Chr 13,15; in 2 Sm 3,20 it is eating together that ratifies Abner's alliance with David.

to be a witness to the agreement about the wells.[17] In 31,52 (J) the stone pile, the *gāl,* is a witness, apparently to the oaths that follow.[18] For J, then, the witness is something material and at least relatively permanent. The stone pile is almost indestructible, and the seven strange sheep in the flock would be recognized as such as long as they lived and so remind the new owner of their origin and the agreement involved. I should think this is the way we must conceive of the material witness. It is a sort of monument which serves as a reminder of the important event, the covenant, which is its origin.[19] We might call it a document in the French sense of the word, although our English term implies written text.

However, this inarticulate sort of document presents a difficulty. It helps safeguard the memory of the event, but the connection between the material document and the matter of the agreement is arbitrary. If the latter should be forgotten or distorted the monument would serve as a reminder that something had happened, but it could not preserve information as to exactly what it was. Hence we may look upon it as something of an advance when in 31,44 E calls the covenant itself an *'ēd.* As a text[20] formulated, agreed upon and conserved—whether in writing or memory is immaterial—it can be cited as a witness in the sense that it can be referred to as a means to show whether and in what way one or the other party is out of line if dispute should arise.

Though once more exhibiting a kind of witness which is more effective than a dumb monument, the idea of God as witness in 31,50 is somewhat different again. This is a way of saying that the covenant is made under

[17] According to A. W. Falk, "Forms of Testimony," *VT* 11 (1961) 90, it is the act of acceptance which is the witness, but the specification that the sheep are ewes means they are to be kept so that they would be there to recall the act and the covenant it instituted.

[18] 31,48 is probably another testimony to the function of the stone pile which belongs to J. It brings out nothing not contained in the texts already cited.

[19] The Canaanite *maṣṣēbôt* could also function as memorials of events and of heroes as well as grave stones and religious symbols (cf. L. H. Vincent, "La notion biblique du haut-lieu," *RB* 55 [1948] 271, 275; W. F. Albright, "The High Place in Ancient Palestine," *VTS* IV [Leiden, 1957] 244, 253). In 1 Sm 13,3-4 a column (*neṣîb*) is a mark of Philistine sovereignty.

If the connection between monument and covenant could thus be original there is no need to explain our texts as etiologies made to account for pre-existing monuments, as for instance G. von Rad, *Das erste Buch Mose. Das Alte Testament Deutsch* 2-4. (Göttingen, 1958), does for the covenant of Jacob Laban.

[20] It is difficult to find the proper term here. "Text" implies writing, "discourse" speaking. By "text" I mean organized discourse whether written or oral, as we speak of a Biblical text or the text of Homer without meaning either as written or as spoken but simply the words in the structure the author gave them.

oath, just as in our own language we define an oath as the calling upon God to witness to the speaker's sincerity. But how is God to function as witness? We could hardly expect Him to give testimony in regard to the exact terms of alliance or to an accused perjurer before some sort of human court, though we can by no means exclude some sort of judgment by ordeal or lot which in effect calls to God to testify in a dispute and which was well enough known in Israel. However, the context in Gn emphasizes that God is a witness who is also a sanctioning agent, one who will infallibly assure the punishment of a perjurer, for this is the meaning of Laban's admonition in 31,49 that God will see to the keeping of the covenant even when the parties are separated and no human judgment and sanction is possible.

The various sorts of witnesses represented here are not confined to Gn. A material thing, an altar, appears as a witness in Jos 22,27-31. Here the idea of monument-document as reminder is quite explicit. The Transjordanian tribes put up an altar which is designated not for sacrifices but for a witness, a sign that these tribes are faithful followers of Yahweh. It is no objection here to say that this designation is an attempt to explain what was originally a regular altar of sacrifice in a way which would bring it into accord with the sort of centralist ideas which appear in Dt. Even if this were so the point is that the concept of monument as witness was familiar in Israel.

A stele is brought into relation with covenant as a witness in Jos 24,27. Though it is not explicit, the twelve stones which Moses raises up as part of a covenant ceremony in Ex 24,4 are also related to the tradition of the material witness, and the stones are tenaciously fixed in the covenant tradition since they reappear in another form in Dt 27,2-3 in connection with a covenant ceremony. However, there has been an added development. In Dt the stones alone are not a document. They serve to hold a copy of the law, in other words a public and permanent record of a covenanted text. This practice reappears in Jos 8,32. These monuments, it is true, are not explicitly called witnesses, but there is no doubt that this is a development of the old connection between covenant and monument in stone as seen in Gn 31,45 & 51; Jos 24,27, and the development is in the direction of making the monument a more satisfactory witness by providing it with a text.[21] This is a step on the way to what we find in E, where the covenant text itself has become the witness to the covenant. This also has its parallel, for in Dt 31,19

[21] The Aramaic treaties on steles from Sfiré (A. Dupont-Sommer, *Les inscriptions araméennes de Sfiré* [Paris, 1958]) may illustrate the development. The steles are not called witnesses but in effect they are, and they are not thought of as passive objects to be read. They are *bty' lhy'* (II, C, 11. 2,7,9) with an active power to make known the texts inscribed on them (I,B,1. 8).

the Song of Moses is to be written down and preserved as a witness against Israel and in 31,26 there are directions to do the same thing with the law. Here the function of the text-witness is clear: it is a norm against which the people's conduct can be judged.

These latter texts come from relatively more recent sources, and they seem to show the effects of reflection, the effort to give the old, numinous monument a clearer, more effective role. In so far as it seems to reflect this development of the idea of the witness to covenant, E shows the greater refinement of theological thought which has been recognized in other areas as characteristic of this source. In this connection it is worth remarking that in 21,23-24 E makes use of a vocabulary which is characteristic of more sophisticated covenant thinking. There is the urgency of the demand for an oath which is a feature of the form of covenant best attested in Deuteronomic writings.[22] Then Abraham is asked not to treat Abimelek falsely. *šqr* as here used is not just "trick" in a general sense. It means precisely to break covenanted faith.[23] Finally, *ḥesed* appears, and it represents a concept which is properly covenantal, as is well known. This use of a fuller covenant terminology would seem to confirm the more developed character of E.

Conclusion

To conclude, we shall try to relate the data drawn from the covenants in Genesis with the rest of the Pentateuch. First, passages from both J and E in Genesis present solid evidence that the superior and not just the inferior, binds himself to a covenant by oath. This is in accord with an ancient tradition of covenant making attested at Alalakh. In the 18th century treaty of Abba-AN, he, the master, binds himself by oath along with the subordinate, and in the 14th century treaty of Niqmepa with Ir-IM of Tunip there are reciprocal oaths even though the document as a whole is so concerned with securing advantages to Ir-IM that it cannot be considered an agreement between equals. Thus we have biblical and extra-biblical evidence for a kind of covenant making which diverges from the more common form with its oath by the lesser party alone. The form with a double oath is not confined to Genesis. It reappears in Dt 26,17, where it is somewhat alien in a document which otherwise parallels the ancient vassal treaty closely. This would seem to represent an old tradition tenaciously held in Israel.

[22] Cf. the writer's *Treaty and Covenant,* cc. 9, 13.

[23] Cf. Ps 44,18; Is 63,8. *šqr* is also the standard designation for the violation of the covenant in the 8th century B.C. Aramaic Treaty from Sfiré.

Secondly, in Gn 31 E relates a *maṣṣēbâ* to treaty making. This taken together with the fact that J alone has a covenant meal may throw some light on the difficult analysis of Ex 24. E's stele is closer to the twelve stones of 24,4 than the stone pile of J since the twelve stones must be large individual stones, in effect stelae. On the other hand the covenant meal of 24,11 is more like J. These are small indications, but they add weight to the evidence for assigning 24,3-8 to E and 24,1-2,9-11 to J.

Thirdly, in J, that is in Gn 26,26-33 and 31,46 & 52, the sequence is covenant meal followed by the ceremony of the word, the oath, which surely was concerned with the exact definition of the matter of the covenant. This order of ceremonies enables us to assign Ex 24,11 and c. 34 of Ex to J without assuming that a redactor has altered the original order of the text to bring the ceremony of the covenant meal, which originally stood after the rites described in c. 34, into connection with the ceremonies in 24,3-8.[24]

Finally, E shows an affinity to certain aspects of the Deuteronomic writings. It has a sacrifice followed by a ritual repast, and this reappears in Dt 27,7. It calls the covenant a witness and the only parallels are Dt 31,19 & 26, where a song and a collection of laws are described as witnesses. It places emphasis on the oath in covenant making, and the roll of the pledge, the word, is particularly important in the Deuteronomic form of covenant. These coincidences are all the more striking in that they are now woven into the Deuteronomic corpus, but they are largely related to materials, rubrics and the Song of Moses, which preserved elements from the oldest traditions. Thus there is evidence for a relationship between E and Deuteronomy which is not a mere dependence of one on the other but rather a matter of representing a common ancient tradition.

DENNIS J. MCCARTHY, S.J.
St. Mary's College, Kansas

[24] This is the assumption of G. von Rad, "Das Formgeschichtliche Problem des Hexateuch," in his *Gesamelte Studien zum alten Testament* (Munich, 1958) 29.

HOSEA XII 2: COVENANT BY OIL

The lines

Ephraim pastures upon the wind
and chases the east-wind all the day long:
they multiply falsity and violence,
they make a covenant with Assyria,
and oil is brought to Egypt.

are hardly a *crux*. Chiastic parallelism makes clear that the bringing of oil to Egypt implies some sort of double-dealing on the part of Assyria's vassal, Israel. Bringing oil, then, must mean something of the same nature as *ûbᵉrît* . . . *yikrōtû* in the first part of the half verse, just as the wind and the east-wind of the first half-verse share the same nature. Nonetheless, it is worthwhile to find a more precise meaning for the act of bringing oil, if this be possible. The text itself relates it somehow to covenant. Can we specify more exactly why and how?

Is it merely a matter of commercial relations which somehow violated the Assyrian overlord's rights? Are we to think of a gift aimed at inducing Egypt to become protector of Israel? Is it tribute signifying that the vassal relationship has already been made? Rather, this article attempts to show that oil is mentioned because it by itself would be recognized as a customary element in one kind of covenant making. One could "swear an oath by oil", and Hosea's *w šemen* . . . *yûbāl* in the last half verse is a direct allusion to a form of covenant making and thus a complete, explicit parallel to the first half, so that we need no inferences or explanations to arrive at the parallelism obviously intended. Parallelism does not force a meaning on a rather recalcitrant subject matter it is there explicitly.

There are, of course, interpretations content to treat the matter as a purely commercial affair [1]), but there is no evidence that the vassal relationship in the ancient Near East forbade normal commercial activity on the vassal's part, even though this meant trade with a rival power. It seems that an Israel sworn to fealty to Assyria could continue to export the olive oil which Egypt itself did not produce without meriting the reproach of faithlessness. The mere fact of trade is not enough to complete the meaning of the text.

Is it enough to treat the oil as a gift designed to induce the Pharaoh to enter into alliance with Israel against Assyria? [2]) A priori such a procedure is not unlikely; indeed, it was inevitable if Israel sought such an alliance, and it is in fact attested by texts like Is. xxx 1-7. Such gifts must not be confused with tribute. Tribute, commonly expressed by *minḥâ* in Hebrew, is a tax levied on vassal *as a consequence*

---

1) So, for instance, *New American Catholic Edition*: *The Holy Bible*, New York 1961, *in loc.*; T. K. CHEYNE, *The Book of Hosea*, Cambridge, 1913, p. 113.

2) So K. MARTI, *Das Dodekapropheton*, *KHAT XIII*, Tübingen, 1904, p. 93; W. R. HARPER, *Amos and Hosea*, *ICC*, New York, 1915, p. 378; M. SCHUMPP, *Das Buch der zwölf Propheten*, *Herder-Bibel*, X/2, Freiburg i. B., 1950, p. 57; E. DHORME, *La Bible* II, *L'Ancien Testament*, 2, Paris, 1959, p. 716.

of the relationship established by a vassal alliance. The sort of gift suggested in this interpretation aims at disposing a power to join the petitioner; it *precedes* the alliance. We might call it a bribe, and in fact in Hebrew it is called *šōḥād* in 1 K. xv 19; 2 K. xvi 8. These texts are important. They are the only detailed Biblical accounts of this kind of thing, and the bribe is made up of silver and gold. Frankly, one is inclined to think such gifts would be more impressive than the best of oils; at any rate, they are the only ones explicitly mentioned. This points up the question: Why does the prophet single out oil, if we decide that he is describing such dealings?

As noted, the question of tribute proper is somewhat different. It is a consequence of vassalhood, a sign of the already constituted relationship to the overlord. If we have to do with tribute, as many commentators state [1]), then the bringing of oil to Egypt is an explicit but indirect reference to an existing alliance with this country. In this regard, it would be of value to know the actual materials involved in tribute paid from Palestine. Is oil actually a factor here? What do the texts say? Old Testament texts concerning tribute of this sort are not numerous, but such as exist, 2 K. xv 19-20; xviii 14-16; xxiii 33-35, mention again the precious metals, not produce. Now, these are all real tribute, levies paid to an overlord already recognized as such. Booty is something else again. The golden calf of the northern kingdom—once more precious metal—is mentioned as a *minḥâ* for Assyria in Hos. x 6. This might be tribute, but the context of the chapter seems to threaten more complete ruin, so that the thing sounds like booty. In any case, Shishak—I suppose the price necessary to keep his army away from Judah itself may fairly be classified under booty—and Nebuchadnezzar took all the treasures of the palace and temple [2]). We know that these treasures included fine oil which was displayed to foreign ambassadors [3]), but one wonders if an army on the march would bother to carry off such an item.

Even so, may we assume that what the mighty kings may have taken as booty they wanted as tribute so that, if the fine oil of Palestine

---

[1]) G. A. F. Knight, *Hosea, Torch Bible*, London, 1960, p. 112; H. W. Wolff, *Dodekapropheton* 1, *Hosea*, *BKAT* XIV/1, Neukirchen, 1961, p. 273; A. Weiser, *Das Buch der zwölf Kleinen Propheten* 1, *ATD*, Göttingen, 1956, p. 89; T. H. Robinson u. F. Horst, *Die Zwölf Kleinen Propheten*, [2] *HAT* I/14, Tübingen, 1954, p. 46.

[2]) 1 K. xiv 25-26; 2 K. xxiv 12-13.

[3]) 2 K. xx 12-19.

were prized as booty, it would be abnormal element of tribute, so normal that the mere mention of it would evoke the idea of tribute and its cause, covenant? Two difficulties arise here. First, why are precious metals the only materials named specifically as tribute if other things such as oil were so important an element in it? Secondly, why does oil have so small a place in the lists of materials Egypt received from its Asiatic tributaries, a place so small as scarcely to matter?

As early as Pepi I it is slaves who are prized, and this is still true in the New Kingdom [1]). Oil is indeed mentioned as tribute from the Asiatic subjects of the Pharaoh, especially in the extensive annals of Thutmose III [2]). However, this is not material brought down to Egypt; it is supplied on the spot in Asia as part of the provision for the Pharaoh and his retinue levied on the subject localities. None of this should be taken to deny that realia ever were given as tribute. They were, as 2 Chron. xvii 11 attests in other circumstances. Further, oil was certainly imported into Egypt: witness the mention of "Syrian oil" in the lists of temple income under Ramses III [3]). It is even called tribute in a tomb inscription, even though it appears as one of the products brought in from the trading expedition to Punt [4]). This is a warning as to semantics: everything turned over to so great a figure as the Pharaoh was tribute, even if he paid for it! The more objective observer must call it trade, so we have no explicit link between tribute and oil *brought to Egypt* which might explain how our text would be a self-evident reference to covenant for Hosea's audience. We are left with the problem: why does the prophet single out the statement "oil is brought to Egypt" to parallel "they make a covenant with Assyria?"

Some have suggested that, since kings were anointed, to supply the oil for this ceremony was tantamount to recognizing the overlordship of the king whose anointing was thus provided for [5]). This is an attractive idea, but there is no textual evidence for it, and

---

[1]) Pepi I: Victory Hymn (*ANET* [all references to *ANET* are to the 2nd ed.], p. 228); Ahmose: tomb inscription of a certain Ahmose *not* the Pharaoh (*ib.*, p. 233-34); Amenhotep II: Memphis and Karnak Steles (*ib.*, p. 247); Seti I: Beth-shan Stele (*ib.*, p. 255).

[2]) Cf. J. H. Breasted, *Ancient Records of Egypt* II, Chicago, 1927, nos. 472-73; 482-83; 509-10; 518-19.

[3]) Cf. *ANET*, p. 261.

[4]) Breasted, *ARE* II, p. 750.

[5]) D. Deden, *De kleine Propheten*, Roermond, 1953, p. 71; E. Sellin, *Das Zwölfprophetenbuch*, [3] *KAT* XII/1, Leipzig, 1929, p. 119.

the answer must remain in the realm of interesting speculation.

On the other hand, we have explicit extra-Biblical information which is pertinent to the idea of oil and covenant. While we do not have the details, though it seems clearly to have nothing to do with anointing a king, there was in the ancient Near East a method of covenant making in which oil played an effective role, the symbol perhaps and certainly the means by which a covenant was produced. The data come from Assyrian texts. In a prism of Esarhaddon we read: "The people of Assyria had sworn an oath by oil and water to preserve my kingship" [1]). Substantially the same thing occurs in a fragment of the Babylonian creation epic when the gods swear to exalt Marduk to the head of the pantheon [2]). Finally, the Esarhaddon vassal treaties forbid the vassals to join insurgents: "You shall not make a treaty by means of a common meal, by drinking from a cup, by kindling fire, by water, by oil, by touching breasts" [3]). Some of these covenant making activities, the sharing of a meal, for instance, are well known and it is certain that their binding force required nothing outside themselves. Performing the act made the covenant, and the covenant making by oil is on a par with them.

The vassal treaties are important in showing that oil alone could be a means of covenant making: the omission of the conjunction found in the other texts shows that oil and water could be separate means. It may be that the omission of the mention of oil in several versions of the treaty texts confirms this. If this is not merely the result of scribal error, it shows clearly that one element was enough for the covenant making rite.

It is unfortunate that we have as yet no information as to how the oil functioned in covenanting, information which might enable use to understand somewhat the thinking involved; at any rate the fact is clear. Oil could be used in a rite of covenant making, and by reference to it in xii 2 Hosea implies the alliance which completes the parallelism of his lines.

The direct allusion to covenant making supported as yet only from Accadian texts, is strengthened by the religious connotations of the rare (in Hebrew) verbal root *ybl* used in the phrase "oil is

---

[1]) R. C. Thompson, *The Prisms of Esarhaddon and Ashurbanipal*, London, 1931, p. 11, lines 50-51.

[2]) O. R. Gurney, *Anatolian Studies* II 1952, p. 33, lines 95-98; Translation in *ANET*, p. 514.

[3]) D. J. Wiseman, *Esarhaddon's Vassal Treaties*, London, 1958, lines 153-56.

brought to Egypt". The root has been said to imply tribute [1]), that is, the consequence of a covenant between unequals, not covenant making itself. The Accadian cognate, *biltu*, certainly carries the meaning tribute often enough, but it is hard to show that the root has the required connotation in the Old Testament. It occurs but seventeen times, and in two instances, Ps. xlv 15-16 and Job xxi 30 (?)-32, we have a repeated use so bound into a unified context that the extra appearances scarcely count. In effect we have fifteen separate uses of *ybl*. How often do these point to tribute pure and simple, an "offering" induced or commanded by political dependency? Except for Hos. x 6, where golden calf is to be brought as a gift to the king of Assyria, there is not much evidence for this. In fact, apart from Is. xxiii 7, where we are told that Tyre's feet have carried her afar, the root always appears in context where it has religious overtones.

True, Ps. xlv celebrates a royal marriage, but we need not go so far as the idea of a *hieros gamos* to realize that marriage, like all else relating to the mysterious gift of fertility, was not a purely secular matter, and never less so than in the psalm. Here we have a prophetic oracle (cf. v. 2) about the marriage of the king, the representative of God's people whose marriage was even more meaningful in that he carried the promise made to Israel in the person of David [2]). The "bringing" of the bride and retinue to this marriage is far indeed from a mere secular matter. Again, the uses of *ybl* in Ps. lx 11 and Job x 18-19; xxi 32, while not referring to *functions* which were religious in character in Israel, occur in *texts* of a religious character. All these instances are laments or supplications, poems which are prayers, in sum, religious contexts. I do not, of course, claim that every word which occurs in religious texts must always carry a religious tone; this is as obviously untrue of Hebrew as of other languages. However, it is significant when a word is practically confined to religious contexts. In this case it does have the religious tone, as, for instance, "amen" does in English.

However, the case is clearest in the other uses of *ybl*. Four times it is used to describe the bringing of gifts to Yahweh, in Ps. lxxvi 12, the gifts by which His people acknowledge His providence and power; in Ps. lxviii 30; Is. xviii 7; Zeph. iii 10, those by which the Gentiles

---

[1]) G. Rinaldi, *I profeti minori 2*, *La Sacra Bibbia*, Turin, 1959, p. 108.

[2]) Cf. vv. 3, 7, 17. For the interpretation of the psalm see H. J. Kraus, *Psalmen*, *BKAT* XV/1, pp. 332ff.

finally acknowledge His unique supremacy [1]). This might be called tribute—Zepheniah even calls it *minḥâ*—but it is not tribute to an earthly king. It is something religious, a gift to symbolize submission to Israel's God. A special verb is used to speak of a special, religious tribute. If we say that Hosea's verb implies submission and tribute, we must accept that there is a religious color to this. *ybl* is used elsewhere: in Jer. xi 19 and Is. liii 7 the prophet and the Servant respectively are given over to the tormentor just as a lamb is led *yûbāl*) to slaughter. The texts are not directly sacrificial; the emphasis is on meekness. Still, both prophet and Servant are figures with special, divine vocations whose every act and suffering has a religious meaning. Moreover, the fate of the Servant is expressly that of a sin-offering (lii 10), that is, quasi-ritual and entirely religious.

Finally, *ybl* is used for the return of the People from the Exile in Jer. xxxi 9 and Is. lv 12. Each text emphasizes the miraculous nature of the return, the manifestations which recall the focal point of Old Testament salvation history, the Exodus and Sinai. Note especially in this respect Jer. xxi 9a and Is. lv 12a.

This religious color to the root *ybl* reinforces the reference to covenant implied by the mention of oil, for to the ancients covenant making was always a religious act, whether the contract was made before the gods as was usually the case, or with God, as is the case with Israel's alliance with Yahweh. Verb and noun together in Hosea make an unmistakable statement of a kind of covenant making, a different kind of covenant making from the *krt b^e^rît* of the first half verse, a perfect example of Semitic poetic parallelism. In the one member he names the action; in the other he refers to a known means of covenant making.

St. Marys, Kansas, U.S.A. Dennis J. McCarthy

---

[1]) This reading of Zepheniah involves dropping the words *ʿ^ea^thārai bat-pūsai* with LXX. If MT is kept the text must be classed with Ps lxxvi 12. The decision one way or the other does not affect the argument here.

B^e^rît AND COVENANT IN THE DEUTERONOMISTIC HISTORY

BY

DENNIS J. McCARTHY
Rome

From the point of view of the experience which gives its words their connotations, religious vocabulary can be divided into two classes; (1) terms directly religious in their associations, and (2) those primarily associated with everyday experience. For us (or for me) the first sort is largely connected with cult, a realm of experience consciously connected with religion and religion alone. Thus an example of it in English would be "sacrament." The word has deep meaning and rich associations, but they are religious, and in any context it will introduce a religious coloration. An example of the second sort would be "father." It is deeply rooted in the scriptural religious tradition, but no matter how a person meets this tradition, he normally meets it with rich associations already tied to the word from experience not thought of as specifically religious, and these associations will always be present in the religious context.

Hebrew *b^e^rît* belongs to the second class. It was experienced in society in a context larger than the explicitly and exclusively religious. Men made *b^e^rîtôt*[1] among themselves, as Jonathan did with David, or David with the northern tribes. Moreover, the word does not seem to have achieved an important position in the Old Testament religious vocabulary until rather late.[2] In other words, *b^e^rît* was not merely

[1] The use of this odd plural points up a problem of discussion in this area. The traditional translation, "covenant *(Bund)*," has been called into serious question: cf. E. Kutsch, "Gesetz und Gnade. Probleme des alttestamentlichen Bundesbegriffs," *ZAW*. 79 (1967), pp. 18-35; "Der Begriff ברית in vordeuteronomischer Zeit," *Rost Festschrift*. *BZAW*. 105, Berlin 1967, pp. 133-143; "Von ברית zu 'Bund'," *Kerygma und Dogma* 14 (1968), pp. 159-182; *THAT* I, cols. 339-352, insisting that the word should be translated by "obligation" *(Verpflichtung)* or the like. To avoid the appearance of prejudging the case I have avoided any translation and used *b^e^rît* in the body of this article.

[2] On the rise to prominence of *b^e^rît* in the theological vocabulary of the Deuteronomic school see L. Perlitt, *Bundestheologie im Alten Testament*. WMANT 26, Neukirchen 1969, but note that despite Perlitt *b^e^rît* was not the exclusive

experienced in a secular context *along with* a religious; historically it had been experienced there for a long time *before* it appeared in the religious context in an important way.

This means that, when it became important in religious vocabulary, it will have carried over connotations it had acquired in its primary context. Hence it is important to study the phenomenon of the secular [1] *berît*, or more exactly *berît*-making, for *berît* was first of all an act (see below, n. 23) to see what associations it has, since these will color its use in religious contexts. This study will deal directly with the reports of secular *berît*-making in the Deuteronomistic History. For one reason, most mentions of such *berît*-making occur here or can be dealt with indirectly in relation to texts from the History.[2] Simply in quantitative terms these examples determine the general connotations of the word. Even more important, *berît* is applied to religious phenomena primarily in the Deuteronomic school, and surely the word so applied carried with it the connotations familiar to that school from the history with which it concerned itself.

A final preliminary note is in order. The modern debate about *berît* has been posed largely in terms of the questions: Who obliges whom in a *berît*, and, What kind of obligations are involved in *berît*, unilateral or multilateral? [3] This study is not aimed directly at these questions.

---

property of that school and its successors. It was used in a modest way at least in religious contexts before Deuteronomy: see my review article in *Biblica* 53 (1972), pp. 110-121.

[1] "Secular" is a problematic word, of course. *berît* was made "before Yahweh" or under oath, and so was connected with religion at least *in obliquo*, as every aspect of ancient life seems to have been. But *in recto* it could concern connections among men, things apart from the specifically religious sphere of cult and things thought to be primarily an aspect of relations with God. There is a real distinction between these two aspects of *berît* so that "secular" seems a valid as well as convenient designation of the second.

[2] In fact 17 of 21 (or 22) examples. There are thirteen mentions of *berît*-making in Dtr: Jos. ix 1-x 1; 1 Sam. xi 1-3; xviii 1-4; xx 5-8; xx 10-17; xxii 8; xxiii 16-8; 2 Sam. iii 12-21; iii 21; v 1-3; 1 Kings v 26; xv 18-19; xx 32-34; 2 Kings xi 4; xi 17. Each of this set of texts is eparate evidence of the connotations of *krt berît* because it deals with a different *berît* or represents a different report of a *berît* from that presented in another text. The five texts: Ezek. xvii 11-21; Hos. ix 4; xii 2b; 2 Chron. xxiii 1; xxiii 3 can be dealt with in connection with the texts in Dtr.

This leaves only three texts: Gen. xxi 22-32; xxvi 22-33; xxxi 23-xxxii 3 (or 4, if one were to treat separately the J and E elements in xxi 22-32, as he probably should). On these see provisionally D. J. McCarthy, "Three Covenants in Genesis," *CBQ*. 26 (1964), pp. 179-189. They deserve further study, but there is no space for it here. It will be seen, however, that they confirm the major conclusions from the Deuteronomistic evidence.

[3] See J. Begrich, "Berît. Ein Beitrag zur Erfassung einer alttestamentlichen

It is concerned simply to find out what the texts associate with *krt berît*. However, one cannot and should not ignore the *Zeitgeist*, and it will be evident that much that is said relates to these questions.

I. Israel and the Gibeonites (Jos. ix 1-x 1).[1] Joshua *wayya'aś lāhem šālôm wayyikrot lāhem berît leḥayyôtām*, and the leaders of Israel *wayyiššābe'û lāhem* (ix 15). The agents of Israel are presented as the sole actors in the *berît*-making. The text describes negotiations. The Gibeonites propose a *berît*, justifying this by the fact that they are from afar. Israel objects, and the Gibeonites answer with persuasion: they are Israel's servants. Their identity is questioned anew, and the Gibeonites reassert their points: they are strangers and servants. It is on this understanding that they are given a *berît* granting them life.[2] *Berît* is correlative with the words and acts connected with its making. What follows shows this. When Gibeon is found actually to be nearby, only one of the elements involved in the negotiations is altered. Servitude remains in new conditions. The result is not an end of *berît* and its obligations, but alteration of them. The relation of servitude is still there, and Gibeon can appeal to it (x 6).

Thus the obligations actually involved in this *berît* turn out to be effectively bilateral. Israel guarantees Gibeon and Gibeon serves Israel, even though Israel's representatives are presented as the sole actors in the actual *berît*-making. But, in fact, the text does not stick quite consistently to this view of the action. x 1b says: *hišlîmû yošbê gib'ôn 'et-yiśrā'ēl*. That is, the Gibeonites did just exactly what ix 15a presents Joshua as doing alone in making the *berît!* It may well be that x 1b is a memory of a tradition which presented the Gibeonite *berît* as an

Denkform," *ZAW*. 60 (1944), pp. 1-11; A. Jepsen, "Berith. Ein Beitrag zur Theologie der Exilzeit," *Rudolph Festschrift*, Tübingen 1961, pp. 161-179; and the articles of E. Kutsch mentioned in n. 1.

[1] For the text see M. Noth, *Josua*, *HAT* I-7, pp. 53-60: it is a combination of traditions which cannot be analyzed into parallel sources. The present combination of traditions is pre-Deuteronomic and it gives a coherent view of *berît*-making. It is, therefore, valid evidence for the connotations of *berît* at a relatively early date. J. Liver, "The Literary History of Joshua IX," *JSS* 8 (1963), 227-243, analyzes the text into an ancient tradition of friendship with Gibeon altered to give it an anti-Gibeonite cast during Saul's efforts to destroy Canaanite enclaves such as Gibeon. One may not accept his reconstruction in detail, but he makes some important points. One, relevant here, is his recognition of the bilateral character of the *berît* (pp. 227, 235).

[2] The grant of life is associated with ancient treaties. See J. Wijngaards, "Death and resurrection in Covenantal Context (Hos. vi 2)," *VT*. 17 (1967), pp. 226-239. It is associated with *berît* in Jos. ix 15; 1 Kings xx 32; and, apparently, 1 Sam. xx 14, and implied in *berît* contexts in 1 Sam. xi 1-3 and xx 7-8 (see below, p. 70, n. 3).

explicitly two-sided affair.[1] This may allow interesting historical speculation, but the present form of the text is significant in itself for the connotations of *b^e^rît*. It shows that a relatively early form of the tradition could already ascribe a *b^e^rît*-making to Joshua alone and then calmly present the same action as the Gibeonites' work. The terminology, in other words, is not very rigid. What it asserts in any given place should not be pressed *in sensu negante* without further ado. The text can pass from attributing the act to one party to attributing it to another without embarrassment.

Conclusions from the report of the Gibeonite *b^e^rît:* 1) There is an extensive report of negotiations which work out bilateral obligations. 2) There is no explicit statement defining these obligations. 3) Joshua is the only subject of the phrase *krt b^e^rît*, but x 1b has the Gibeonites performing what is in fact the same action.

II. Jabesh-Gilead and Nahash (1 Sam. xi 1-3). The men of Jabesh-Gilead make a proposal: with a *b^e^rît* they will serve Nahash. He does not reject this entirely, but he adds cruel and humiliating terms. Even in his contempt he allows a counter-proposal.

Conclusions from this report: 1) There are negotiations involving service and implying that this is a condition for a grant of life. 2) There is not explicit statement of the *b^e^rît* obligations. 3) Nahash is the subject requested to *krt b^e^rît*.

III. Jonathan and David, 1 (1 Sam. xviii 1-4; xx 5-8). It is generally accepted that in this first *b^e^rît* involving the heroes Jonathan is the agent. He binds himself to David by a symbolic gift of clothes and weapons. He is granting fellowship.[2] No doubt, but in clause actually mentioning *b^e^rît* both Jonathan and David are agents, both subjects of the verb *wayyikrot*.[3] In the midst of a description of *b^e^rît*-making where all the emphasis is on what Jonathan feels and does the text

[1] On the history of the Gibeonite *b^e^rît* see J. Blenkinsopp, "Are There Traces of the Gibeonite Covenant in Deuteronomy?", *CBQ*. 28 (1966), pp. 207-219, and J. M. Grintz, "The Treaty of Joshua and the Gibeonites," *JAOS*. 86 (1966), pp. 113-126. It is true that *šlm* relates x 1b to ix 15a, not *krt b^e^rît*, but in ix 15 "make peace" is perfectly parallel with two other expressions for creating an obligation. It is not credible that the Gibeonites could be thought of as subjects of one member of the triad and not the others. Further, *šlm* is integral to *b^e^rît:* cf. 1 Kings v 26; Gen. xxvi 28-30.

[2] *Lebensgemeinschaft*. So Begrich, *ZAW*. 60 (1944), p. 1; A. Jepsen, *Rudolph Festschrift*, p. 163; E. Kutsch, *ZAW*. 79 (1967), p. 26, n. 29; *Rost Festschrift*, p. 135, n. 12.

[3] The singular verb with a double subject in xviii 3a is perfectly acceptable grammar, and the text needs no emendation. For the construction see Gen. ix 23; discussed in Joüon, *Grammaire de l'hebreu biblique*, 150q.

still takes the action as somehow attributable to David as well as Jonathan. One can conceive of explanations of this as some sort of correction of the history. E.g., the writer may not wish to leave the great David in an interior position. This simply means that for him *b^erît* and *b^erît*-making are such that he is free to write in this way. There is nothing fixed in the process or vocabulary to prohibit him from making David subject of the *krt b^erît* phrase when he wishes, even though all else point to a *b^erît* simply granted to him. The *b^erît* is not totally one-sided. The all-important initial act at least is attributable to both parties.

This is even clearer in 2 Sam. xx 8, where David says that Jonathan has "brought him into a *b^erît*" *(bib^erît yhwh hēbē'tā 'et-'abd^ekā)*. This does not prove that David acted in the *b^erît*-making. The usage is figurative, and the hifil could be declarative. Theoretically the sentence could simply mean that Jonathan has affirmed that David is within the figurative area of his *b^erît*. An English paraphrase could be: "thou hast brought thy servant under thy protection." However, actual usage is against this interpretation. Ezek. xvii 13 says that Nebuchnadnezzar *wayyābē'* Zedekiah *b^e'ālâ*. This stands in synonymous parallelism with *wayyikrot 'ittô b^erît*. And xvii 18 equates the oath and *b^erît* with giving one's hand, i.e., with the *act* signifying assent. *Hēbî'*, then, in the context of *b^erît*, is not just declarative. It means to cause one to do something which commits him to the *b^erît*. This is not to create a state of *b^erît* by unilateral fiat. It means one move the other to do something.[1] He may not be entirely eager to do it, but he does it.

In our case there is no reason to doubt David's willingness to go into the *b^erît*. In any case, he is active. He follows Jonathan's lead. 1 Sam. xx 8 thus shows that the use of *krt b^erît* in xvii 3 is correct. It is not a rather careless generalizing expression. It describes what

[1] Ezekiel's use of the root *bô'* in relation to *b^erît* shows this and more. In xvi 8 *wā'ābô bib^erît 'et-* describes Yahweh's entering into *b^erît* with Jerusalem. His act realizes the *b^erît*. This use of the kal stem is the correlative of the use of the hifil in xvii 13, and the correlatives produce a picture. The more powerful person simply acts. The weaker is acted upon. He is made to do something, and yet he also does something. This is complex, but it is realistic. The more forceful of several persons involved together usually is more active in determining the nature of a connection. In the first moment, the weaker undergoes the influence of the stronger but he too must *act* under this influence. There is no leading without following. The use of the Hebrew verb thus conforms to experience. But experience also shows that influence is two-sided. The weaker can move the stronger, and this is accounted for in Hebrew usage too: cf. 1 Sam. xx 17 (MT) where a troubled Jonathan makes David swear *(hašbîa')*.

b^e^rît-making involved here, a two-sided activity, with Jonathan leading, perhaps, and David following, but both acting.

The *b^e^rît* obligation might still be unilateral though the act of *b^e^rît*-making was not. But consider xx 8 again. David appeals to the *b^e^rît*. It obliges Jonathan to show *ḥesed*, to protect faithfully his partner. This might be an appeal to an obligation incumbent on Jonathan alone, but there is more. David appeals as Jonathan's *'ebed*. He puts himself in a subordinate relationship to Jonathan, and this is as closely associated with the *b^e^rît* as is *ḥesed*. Indeed, it is only here, in an explicit appeal to *b^e^rît*, that David styles himself Jonathan's *'ebed!* It is the retainer who has a right to the lord's protection.[1]

Moreover, 2 Sam. xviii 1-4 puts much emphasis on Jonathan's *'ah^ae^bâ* for David. This means love, to be sure, but it is a love which is associated with treaty and covenantal contexts. This means, as Moran has shown,[2] that the love which is the basis of the first Jonathan-David *b^e^rît*, whatever else it may include, has two major implications. It involves loyalty *(ḥesed)* and service (cf. *'ebed*), the very things appealed to in connection with *b^e^rît* in 2 Sam. xx 7-8. This confirms the close connection between the two as they appear there, and more probably, their correlation. The love on which the Jonathan-David *b^e^rît* is based implies what David makes explicit: reciprocal obligations.

Thus much of the vocabulary of this *b^e^rît* is attached to biblical tradition. Still, one can hardly fail to notice a special atmosphere about it. It is a fellowship of warriors. It is a very personal relationship—note the emphasis on love. The lord is a gift-giver. The retainer commits his very life into the lord's hands.[3] It involves obligations one can appeal to, but these are in no way made explicit in the *b^e^rît*-making. This combination of factors is unique in Old Testament *b^e^rîtôt*, but it is by no means without parallel. It is, in fact, an example of the heroic friendship.

Such associations of heroes are part of the heroic tradition from Gilgamesh and Enkidu through Roland and Oliver down to its imitation in stories like Fennimore Cooper's *Leatherstocking Tales!* They have fairly definite and consistent characteristics and a natural setting in a specific stage of society. Typically they involve a lord and a

[1] Though JEPSEN, *Rudolph Festschrift*, p. 163, interprets this in just the opposite sense.

[2] "The Ancient Near Eastern Background of the Love of God in Deuteronomy," *CBQ* 25 (1963), pp. 77-87, especially p. 82, n. 33.

[3] Note xx 7b, where David puts his life in Jonathan's hands. He returns it to the lord who, in the convention, grants life with *b^e^rît*.

favorite member of his *comitatus*. The lord is a gift-giver, correlative duties of protection and service are taken for granted, life itself is committed to the association, and the friendship involved is indeed a love surpassing the love of women. Such associations are normally described in the literature of the so-called heroic ages, and these are usually ages when a nomadic group is beginning to come to terms with settled life in an invaded land but has not forgotten its tribal past.[1] In this setting certain familial and personal aspects of relationship are emphasized over more political and impersonal ones. And all this is exactly the situation of Israel under Saul. The *b^erît* of Jonathan and David, then, describes a heroic friendship in its proper setting. The special connotations which this adds to the word *b^erît* must be remembered if we are to feel its full resonance.

Conclusions from the report of the first Jonathan-David *b^erît:* 1) There were no negotiations, but Jonathan had come to love David before the *b^erît* was made. 2) There is no explicit statement of *b^erît* obligations, but these were taken for granted and so could be explicitly appealed to. They were bilateral. 3) Both parties are subjects of the phrase *krt b^erît*. 4) The special features of the *b^erît* mark it as the unique biblical example of a heroic friendship.

IV. Jonathan and David, 2 (1 Sam. xx 11-17; xxiii 16-18). The first passage certainly deals with a formal connection between Jonathan and David, but the text is a problem. In 14-16 Jonathan's troubles and desires are not clearly expressed, and at the crucial point, the oath in 17, MT has Jonathan making David swear while LXX has Jonathan doing the swearing. Must we then reject MT? Many do so, and for two principle reasons. First, the text is supposed to be concerned with

[1] The term *comitatus* comes, of course, from Tacitus' classic description of the heroic band in the *Germania*. Old Germanic poetry, e.g., in Anglo-Saxon, *Beowulf*, *The Seafarer*, *Finnsburg Fragment*, is another indispensable source for the background of heroic society and its literature which are reflected in many elements of the David story besides the Jonathan *b^erît*. See also C. M. Bowra, *Heroic Poetry*, London 1961, pp. 65, 476-507. H. J. Stoebe, "Gedenken zur Heldensage in den Samuelbüchern," *Rost Festschrift*, 208-218, sees the matter rather differently. He seems to take the Jonathan-David association as described in 1 Sam. xviii 1-4 to be altered by more popular, unheroic elements. However, it is difficult to accept exact distinctions between heroic saga, popular *(bauerlich)* saga etc. in such a small sample of literature as Samuel, and indeed the Bible, offers. Neither does the distinction itself allow for the variety within the strict heroic tradition itself. It concentrates too much on the aristocratic element, while Bowra has shown that there are primitive and proletarian traditions that may properly be called heroic. In any case, the friendship of Jonathan and David is paralled in the heroic tradition even in its most limited sense.

David's need for help. Hence it is more appropriate that Jonathan swear to stand by him. Secondly, the appeal to love (17b) is a motive for Jonathan to act, not David.[1] The first argument seems to miss the point. 12-13 show Jonathan's willingness to help David, but the next verses show him as a man troubled by the danger which David's rise presents to him and his. He wants reassurance in return for his help and so it is fitting that he adjure David. As for the love, as we have seen, it is connected with *b^erît*, and it implies fidelity and service. This is a proper basis for an appeal for reassurance in a new situation with the positions of the parties reversed. This is the more fitting in that xviii 1 shows that the disposition, the love, is larger than the act which formally ratifies it. It exists before that act.

Thus it is hardly necessary to turn to LXX. MT remains problematic in details, but it gives a picture sufficiently complete and coherent. Jonathan binds David by oath to an obligation defined by his pleas for himself and his family. And he binds him *again (wayyôsep)*. In the text this "again" can only refer back to xviii 3-4. No other *b^erît* has been reported. That is, MT 1 Sam. xx 16-17 assumes that the first Jonathan-David *b^erît* involved a binding oath on David's part. So it confirms our analysis of xviii 1-4; xx 7-8: Jonathan appears as the chief mover of the *b^erît*-making, but David had his part in the action.

In fact MT xx 10-17 may well reveal the steps involved in the process of *b^erît*-making. Jonathan urges the action. The expression *wayyikrot ʿim* taken by itself might even mean "imposed a *b^erît* on" David or the like. However, the continuation of the process rules this out. It is no simple, one-sided act. David is made to do something, to take an oath.[2] One might describe the process in parliamentary

[1] The arguments are given in detail in H. P. Smith, *Samuel. ICC*, Edinburgh 1899, pp. 187-189, and S. R. Driver, *Notes on the Hebrew Text of the Books of Samuel*,[2] Oxford 1913; W. Caspari, *Die Samuelbücher. KAT* VII, Leipzig 1926, p. 259, adopts the LXX reading but insists that the oath is *gegenseitig;* cf. pp. 251-252, 258. MT 16a *wayyikrot y^ehônātān ʿim-bêt dāwid* is a standard ellipsis for *krt b^erît* (cf. 1 Sam. xi 2; xxii 8). LXX has no reference to *diathēkē*. This is not an argument for preferring the MT text, but it means that only MT is directly relevant to a discussion of the connotation of *b^erît*. It shows what Hebrew could connect with it. LXX refers only to an oath, which is not necessarily identified with *b^erît* at all.

[2] The close parallel to 16a in xxii 8a (or perhaps reference: n.b. the ellipsis of *b^erît* and the allusion to David's family, not to David directly, in both texts) is a further argument. Saul complains about Jonathan's initiatives with David: his making *b^erît* is parallel to stirring him up! He has made David do something (on the emphasis on David's *action* here see A. Weiser, "Die Legitimation des Königs David," *VT*. 16 (1966), 332). Note the use of the hifil in xx 17a also; like Ezekiel's *hēbîʾ* it implies a complex action with two subjects.

language. Jonathan moves a *b^e^rît* and David accepts it. The mutuality is confirmed by 1 Sam. xx 42 where Jonathan says that both he and David have sworn. The only thing in the text this can refer to is the account in xx 20-17. The pattern resembles the earlier *b^e^rît*. The action is complex, not one-sided. One side may do more than the other, but both are agants.

There is also an element of definition. Jonathan's speech tells what it is all about. Mutual obligations are adumbrated. Jonathan will keep David informed as long as he is in danger, and David will protect Jonathan when he has come to power.

The other report of a Jonathan-David *b^e^rît*, 1 Sam. xxiii 16-18 seems to be a tradition parallel to that in xx 10-17. The circumstances are the same. Jonathan comes to David who is in hiding. He proposes a *b^e^rît*, and his proposal covers the same points: Jonathan alludes to David's danger but admits his coming supremacy and calls for respect for his own position. The act of *b^e^rît*-making is reported more simply, but clearly both parties are agents: *wayyikretû š^e^nêhem berît.*[1]

The whole report is clear and succinct. One might imagine an editor tidying up the disorder of xx 10-17. But if that were the case, why did he not do something in that text itself? And why repeat it here in a position where it is rather out of place? Surely we have here an alternate tradition of the affair. In any case, whether as a parallel or, less likely, a re-interpretation, 1 Sam. xxiii 16-18 confirms the view that emerges from MT xx 10-17. Hebrew tradition saw the later Jonathan-David *b^e^rît* as a bilateral thing both in its making and in its content.

Conclusions from the second Jonathan-David *b^e^rît:* 1) Strictly speaking there are no negotiations, but the urgency of Jonathan's language in 1 Sam. xx 12-15 accords with the tradition associating persuasion and so negotiation of a kind with *b^e^rît*. 2) There is a statement defining mutual *b^e^rît* obligations. 3) Both parties act in the *b^e^rît*-making, and in 1 Sam. xxiii 18 both are subjects of the phrase *krt b^e^rît.*

V. David and Israel (2 Sam. iii 21; v 1-3). Both texts mention *b^e^rît* in connection with David's accession to kingship over the northern tribes. It is a single act seen from different points of view.[2]

---

[1] Perhaps a technical phrase for mutual *b^e^rît*-making. It recurs for the *b^e^rît* between the equal and friendly sovereigns Solomon and Hiram: 1 Kings v 26. The tradition of mutual *b^e^rît* with Tyre is alluded to again in Am. i 9: *b^e^rît 'aḥîm. 'aḥ* was the normal way allied kings of equal status described themselves in the ancient near east.

[2] Not the points of view of different historians but of a single tradition. 2 Sam. iii 21 and v 3 belong to the same strand (cf. L. Rost, "Die Überlieferung von der

Each party is represented as acting: in iii 21 all Israel *wayyikr^{e}tû b^{e}rît 'itt^{e}kā*, i.e., with David, and in v 3 David *wayyikrot lahem b^{e}rît*. Perhaps these correlatives indicate that Israel imposes an obligation on David and he formally accepts it, for, it is said, *krt b^{e}rît* with *'et* or *'im* means "impose an obligation on" *(verpflichten)* and with *l^e*-, "accept *(übernehmen)* an obligation." [1] This might be, but the case is complicated. Even though one were to grant that the obligation involved was one-sided,[2] the repetition of the phrases reporting the act means that things were not entirely one-sided. Both parties were agents, active *b^{e}rît*-makers, though their activities may have been different. At least the act of *b^{e}rît*-making, which produces and conditions all that follows, was bipartite.

However, there is a problem even with the obligation involved. No doubt in actual fact David undertook express obligations to respect the liberties of Israel. The theory of the *Kônigsvertrag* is pertinent, and it would justify the assumption that David really undertook to foster Israel's "Heil, Frieden, Wohlstand, Leben." [3] But this

Thronnachfolge Davids," *Das kleine Credo*, Heidelberg 1965, p. 238; not even CASPARI, *KAT* VII, who has a most detailed source analysis, separates these verses).

[1] The normal usage for mutual *b^{e}rît* would have been *bên... ûbên*. This description of the use of the prepositions is given by E. KUTSCH, *THAT* I, cols. 343-346; *ZAW*. 79 (1967), p. 24, n. 26. However, A. JEPSEN, *Rudolph Festschrift*, 172, asserts that there is no differentiation in the use of the prepositions. J. MAIER, "Urim und Tummim," *Kairos* 11 (1969), pp. 23-24, thinks that *l^e*- is used when one "...eine Verpflichtung gegenüber einem anderen eingeht," that is, he agrees with KUTSCH to this extent, but finds the use of *'im*- and *'et*- neutral. In fact, it is difficult to maintain distinctions, at least in the materials under discussion in this article, and MAIER himself says that in 2 Sam. v 3 *krt b^{e}rît l^e*- concerns a "...Vertrag... in dem wohl Rechte und Pflichten des Königs festgelegt waren." Thus the ties are two-sided, and this is surely the correct interpretation of the text, as we shall see.

[2] So A. JEPSEN, *Rudolph Festschrift*, pp. 163-164, and E. KUTSCH, *THAT* I, col. 343. In *ZAW*. 79 (1967), p. 26, n. 33 KUTSCH took the two passages together as a possible exception to his rules for the use of *'et*- and *l^e*- in that they would express bilateral *b^{e}rît* with these prepositions, but he already was leaning to JEPSEN's view.

[3] Quoted from A. JEPSEN, *Rudolph Festschrift*, p. 164. But the *Königsvertrag* cannot be understood simply as a one-sided obligation imposed on the king to limit his power. In the *Vertrag* the people had to submit to the royal power except as limited by the specific agreement. Thus, the total context of the classic case, 1 Sam. x 17-25, includes 1 Sam. viii. The people subject themselves to a king who can tax, carry out public works, make war and peace, even though only within the limits defined by the "constitution" alluded to in x 25. Hos. ix 4 might be further evidence that Israel's royal *b^{e}rît* was bilateral both in the content of its obligations and in the act which realized it. The text is cryptic—it could be no more than a reflection on perjury as a common crime—but mention of the king in ix 3 inclines one to think of the *Königsvertrag* (cf. H. W. WOLFF, *Hosea. BKAT* XIV-1, p. 227). If this the reference it indicates that in the *Vertrag* the people of Israel bound

is not what the text of Sam. actually associates with *krt b^e^rît* here. The act is the conclusion of lively negotiations. The terms which give the obligation under oath [1] a concrete content have been hammered out. The outlines of the process are simplified but clear. Abner, on David's behalf, deals with the tribes (2 Sam. iii 17-18). This results in a readiness to make a *b^e^rît*. Two things are explicit: readiness for the *b^e^rît*-making, and admission of David's supremacy (iii 21). When the *b^e^rît* is actually made it is accompanied by the statement summing up the results of the negotiations (vlb-2). The emphasis is entirely on David's power. Israel accepts him as king and war-leader (v 2; cf. iii 17) and recognizes his divine election (2 Sam. v 2; cf. iii 18). This may not reflect the total historical reality, but it is what colors *b^e^rît* as it stands in the text. David is taking over mastery over Israel. David's "obligation" is to rule and guide!

Thus the posited normal usage of *krt b^e^rît 'et-* and *l^e^-* is actually reversed: Israel comes to David who reigns when it makes a *b^e^rît* with (*'et-*) him, and he becomes their shepherd and leader when he makes a *b^e^rît* for (*l^e^-*) them. This may be the result of development. Perhaps the terminology reflects an earlier stage when the roles were more or less reversed. One can imagine an accord in which Israel was presented as imposing limiting obligations on David's power and he acknowledging the limits. This might have been expressed in precise

---

themselves to something (*d^e^bārîm* surely indicates the contents, the things sworn to; cf. the semantic parallels *awātu* and *memiyaš* in Akkadian and Hittite treaties), and they were subjects of the phrase *krt b^e^rît*. Thus the people had a part in the *b^e^rît* exactly parallel to that presumed for the king. See also J. MAIER, *Kairos* 11 (1969), pp. 25, 30, on the royal *b^e^rît* as a conferral of power which, though it might be limited, was still related to divine powers. On the *Königsvertrag* in general sed G. FOHRER, "Der Vertrag zwischen König und Volk in Israel," *ZAW*. 71 (1959), pp. 1-22. Concerning the actual historical basis of the picture of kingship, and particularly that of David, see A. WEISER, *VT*. 16 (1966), pp. 335-337, 349-350: passages like 2 Sam. v 2 which emphasize the divine origin of royal power are the work of the author of the history put into the mouths of his characters. They serve to justify the claims of the Davidids. Weiser places this interpretation of history in the time of Solomon. He is no doubt correct in seeing interpretation and not historical reporting at work—though the interpretation doubtless had a solid basis in history—and his dating is persuasive. Even if the interpretation is later than Solomonic times, it is pre-Deuteronomic, and once more offers evidence for connotations of *b^e^rît* in an early era.

[1] Even though oath (*nšb'*) is not mentioned, *krt b^e^rît* by itself signifies an especially solemn oath. Originally it seems to have been a ritual, "acted-out" conditional curse on oneself (cf. D. J. MCCARTHY, *Treaty and Covenant. Analecta biblica* 21, Rome 1963, pp. 52-57; E. KUTSCH, *ZAW*. 79 [1967], pp. 20-21), but it came to mean a solemn act of commitment even when there was no such rite, as in 1 Sam. xviii 3; xx 16 etc.

terminology with *krt* b^e*rît* *'et-* and *l*^{e}*-* attributed to the appropriate subjects. Even so, one should note, each of the parties would be an active subject of the phrase *krt* b^e*rît*. But this, though perhaps probable, is not the way *krt* b^e*rît* is used in the text. The writer actually reverses the usage. For him b^e*rît*-making no longer involved a precisely fixed vocabulary, if it ever had.[1]

Conclusions from the David-Israel b^e*rît:* 1) It was prepared for by negotiations. Presumably each party conceded something, but in the text everything is in David's favor. 2) The statement summing up the negotiations defines the b^e*rît* obligations. It is an affirmation of David's supremacy. 3) Both parties are subjects of the phrase *krt* b^e*rît*.

VI. Ahab and Ben-Hadad (1 Kings xx 31-34). According to this report Ahab has defeated Ben-Hadad and the latter sues for peace. His ministers offer his submission: *'abd*^{e}*kā ben-ḥ*^{ae}*dad*, and plead for his life: *t*^{e}*ḥî-na' napšî*. Ahab responds generously: Ben-Hadad is not his servant but his brother. Encouraged by this, Ben-Hadad himself appears and proposes terms. Ahab accepts them and grants a b^e*rît*.[2]

[1] 1 Kings xv 19 is another example of the fluidity of the terminology. The text uses *bên... ûbên* of a bilateral b^e*rît* in 19a and then slips into b^e*rît 'et-* in 19b for the connection between Israel and Damascus which was even more certainly two-sided than the b^e*rît* between insignificant Judah and Damascus mentioned in 19a. On the actual situation see A. Jepsen, "Israel und Damascus," *AfO*. 14 (1941-44), 153-172, especially p. 154.

[2] It is not necessary to alter the text here, reading *t*^{e}*šall*^{e}*ḥēnî* for MT *'*^{ae}*šall*^{e}*ḥekā*, as suggested (but not preferred) by A. Jepsen, *Rudolph Festschrift*, p. 164, and accepted by E. Kutsch, *Rost Festschrift*, p. 135. A. S. van der Woude, "I Reg XX 34," *ZAW*. 76 (1964), pp. 188-191, has shown that *šlḥ* can mean "give," and on this basis he can translate 34aβ-b with Ben-Hadad remaining the subject: "Ich will (sie; scl. die Städte und Basare) dir unter feierlicher Zusicherung *(babb*^{e}*rît)* schenken,' und er die feierliche Zusage gab und (sie) ihm schenkte." This avoids the problems of the unannounced changes of subject which plague the verse in all other interpretations without violence to the text. Even the ellipsis of the direct object of *šlḥ* (understanding as the object what has just been mentioned) is paralleled with *šlḥ*, "give," in Ugaritic texts cited by van der Woude. This interpretation leaves the weaker party tying himself to the stronger by *krt* b^e*rît l*^{e}*-*, but it should be noted that the obligations involved are still bilateral. Differently P. A. H. de Boer in *Hebräische Wortforschung. Festschrift W. Banmgartner*, SVT 16 (1967), p. 28, who translates: "ich will dich freilassen auf Verpflichtung, (bedingt)," conditionally. The example of the weaker making the b^e*rît* is paralled in Hos. xii 2b. There Ephraim *yikrotû* b^e*rît 'im-aššûr*. However, the prophetic text raises another problem with the use of the prepositions because it certainly means that Ephraim put itself under obligation to Assyria, and *krt 'im* is supposed to mean "put an obligation on" another. Hosea's text, of course, implies diplomatic dealings (cf. D. J. McCarthy, Hosea xii 2: Covenant by Oil, *VT*. 14 [1964], pp. 215-221), but the prophet is concerned with what Ephraim has done, not how it did it, and there is little more about the connotations of b^e*rît*, e.g., about the unilaterality or bilaterality of the obligations involved, to be gained from the explicit information

This is a miniature picture of the way such things must have worked. Negotiations were needed, as is normal when two persons are settling something important involving them both. There is some technical language. As we have seen, the grant of life is part of the tradition. *ʿebed* designates the inferior party (cf. David in 1 Sam. xx 7-8), and *ʾaḥ* an approximate equal (e.g., Israel and Tyre; cf. above, n. 18). That is, in formal terms Ben-Hadad acknowledges defeat and Ahab accepts reality: a single defeat is not the end of a power like Damascus. These negotiations result in a definite statement of the obligations accepted by each party. Ben-Hadad restores territory and makes commercial concessions, and in return Ahab frees him to rule his kingdom. Unlike any of the examples we have examined previously, there is no indication that more than one party acts in the *berît*-making. Ahab makes it for Ben-Hadad.

Conclusions from the report of the Ahab—Ben-Hadad *berît:* 1) The text describes, in technical vocabulary, the negotiations in which obligations were formulated. 2) There is a statement defining the obligations, which affect both parties. 3) Only one party is the subject of the phrase *krt berît.*

VII. JEHOIADA AND JOASH (2 Kings xi; 2 Chron. xxiii).

There are two *berîtôt* described here, but we can avoid repetition in the comparison of Kings and Chronicles by treating them together. 2 Kings xi 4b simply says that Jehoiada *wayyikrot lahem berît wayyašbaʿ ʾotām*. Is this perfectly synonymous parallelism? It is possible. Passages like Jos. ix 14-15; Gen. xx 31-32; and xxvi 28 show a tendency to multiply expressions for the action by which men establish an obligation. However, the contexts of these passages are not exact equivalents of the verse in Kings. They are stories concerned with *berît*-making as such. Periphrasis in describing the matter of central interest is natural. In Kings the *berît*-making is but an incident in an account of violent action directly concerned with something else. The priest decides on a coup, summons the guard officers to the temple, *krt lahem berît*, causes them to take an oath, and reveals the king.

The story hurries forward. There is no pausing. There is no time for pleonasm. Every clause moves the action forward—unless the author forgets and repeats himself in 4b. Why should he? It fits the style and the occasion to read *krt berît* as being a step in the action different from the oath. What might it be? We have found negotiations

in the text. One assumes that the benefits accrued largely to Assyria, but this is an assumption.

normal procedure in connection with *berît*. Perhaps here *krt berît* is metonymy referring to this element. One might translate "came to terms with," or, with *NEB*, "made an agreement with." This is surely what did take place. Jehoiada made a deal with the "colonels" which was to their advantage and fostered his plan. Such is the way of conspiracies. This seems the most natural interpretation of the text, and it would imply that the officers' oath obliged them to the mutually advantageous deal they had worked out. Or one might take *wayyikrot lahem berît* to refer to Jehoiada's counter-commitment to the officers' oaths. He binds himself to them as they to him.[1] Again, as a simple matter of fact, this the way it must have been, however it may have been described. In either interpretation the *berît* is not one-sided. A deal on mutual advantageous terms is part of the picture, or each party joins as subject in the complex act which ratifies a commitment.

In xx 17b the *berît* is *bên hammelek ûbên hā'ām*. The *berît*-maker, the subject of the phrase *krt berît*, is the priest, Jehoiada. The text makes no statement about the obligations involved, but if *bên... ûbên* has its common meaning, they are incumbent on both parties. This is meager information, but perhaps Chronicles can add to it.

2 Chron. xxiii 1 begins like 2 Kings xi 4a: "In the seventh year Jehoiada took the officers," but at this point it takes a new direction with "...into a *berît* with himself." xxiii 2 is new material describing the extension of the conspiracy into Judah, but 3 returns to the parallel in 2 Kings xi 4b with *wayyikrot berît*. But the Chronicler has already put Jehoiada's *berît* with the officers into his first verse so that at this point he puts in the *berît* between the people and Joash. Having described this *berît* here, when his story reaches the point parallel with 2 Kings xi 17b, he omits further mention of it.[2]

In the course of all this the Chronicler makes clear that the first *berît* is a conspiracy. Jehoiada takes the officers into it with himself. This is as clear a description of *berît* as a relationship as one could wish, the more striking in that by the Chronicler's time *berît* had become closely identified with law. The second *berît* is differently described too. The congregation itself, not the priest makes the *berît* with *('im)* the king, and there is a statement about the king immedi-

[1] Differently E. Kutsch, *ZAW*. 79 (1967), p. 24, because of the parallel with *wayyašba'*. Our version saves the "probability rule" that *le*- points to an obligation the subject takes on himself toward another.

[2] Hence its omission in xxiii 16 is no argument against the authenticity of the clause in Kings, a fact already widely accepted on other grounds.

ately after the mention of *berît*-making. Such a statement has been connected with *berît* so often that it is not surprising here. The only unusual thing is that it follows the report of the action rather than precedes. The Chronicler inverts the usual order because he is following the text of 2 Kings xi 4 so closely. There, naturally, Jehoiada is said to wait until he has made *berît* and bound the officers by oath; then "he showed them the king's son..." Chronicler models his statement: "Behold the king's son..." on this clause so that his statement follows the mention of *berît* itself.

The content of the statement recalls that in 2 Sam. iii 21 and v 2 in its emphasis on the royal power: "he shall reign as Yahweh promised to David's family." Royal power and divine election: this *berît* covers the same ground as that of David with Israel. It goes beyond 2 Kings xi 17b: for the Chronicler, the *berît* between the people and the king leaves the latter clearly and explicitly overlord.[1] Is this simply because he wishes to insist on the supremacy of the house of his hero, David? Or did *berît*, even one which establishes a king who is of David's house and the object of Yahweh's promise, self-evidently include limits on the power it conferred? Perhaps both factors, and others as well were at work. In any event, the writer could use *'im* in the place of *bên... ûbên*, and he could use it of a *berît* implying relations of lordship and subjection. Neither the conception nor the terminology of *berît* was so fixed as to prevent him from such a change.[2]

Conclusions from the report of *berîtôt* in 2 Kings xi:

A. Jehoiada and the officers: 1) Negotiations are indicated in 4b, (an interpretation confirmed by 2 Chron. xxiii 1. 2) There is no statement of any obligation (though the negotiations must have involved a *quid pro quo*). 3) Jehoiada is the subject of the phrase *krt berît*, but the officers take an oath. Both parties, then, are active.

B. Joash and the people: 1) No negotiations are mentioned. 2) There is no definition of *berît* obligations (but 2 Chron. xxiii 3b describes them in terms of traditional royal power. 3) The subject of

[1] Differently E. Kutsch, *THAT* I, col. 344, no. 5.

[2] Probably the Chronicler's report is simply an elaboration of his source in Kings: see J. M. Myers, *II Chronicles. Anchor Bible* 13, New York, p. 131. The way his variations grow out of details in the text of Kings seems to confirm this. If it is so, his interpretation is noteworthy not so much because of its antiquity but because of its presenting *berît* in terms of a two-sided relationship (which is what the text of Kings points to in our opinion) when the habit of his time would have led him to turn it into law.

the phrase *krt b^e^rît* is Jehoiada (but 2 Chron. xxiii 3a changes this to the congregation).

VIII. Abner and David (2 Sam. iii 12-21). The report of the *b^e^rît* is incomplete. It is the only one of any length which lacks a direct affirmation the "he-they made a *b^e^rît*." Nor is there any summary statement defining the major *b^e^rît* obligations. These lacunae may occur because the story is interested in David and Israel, and Abner enters only in relation to this central interest. Still, we have something. Abner asks David to make him a *b^e^rît*. Then, there are negotiations, which all seem to work to David's benefit. This seems very one-sided. David is the sole subject of the phrase *krt b^e^rît*. He takes on no obligations explicitly mentioned. Perhaps he is simply taking Abner into his service.[1]

Now, it is clear that this leaves out a great deal. Abner was negotiating from strength. He was the power in Israel, and he knew it.[2] An able condottiere will have used such a position to his advantage. His price surely included the command of David's army, this was surely granted, and it led the displaced Joab to murder him.[3] But this is deduction. It is what we can reasonably see as the history behind the text. The problem is: Was talk about *b^e^rît*-making inevitably associated with things that would bring like ideas to the mind of the writer and his audience? In other words, did *b^e^rît*-making accompanied by bargaining necessarily imply a *quid pro quo?* On the evidence of the texts examined before this one, it would seem that it did. That is, the general character of *b^e^rît*-making as it appears in Dtr supports the conclusions which historical probability induce us to draw from this text. But the text is not explicit in the matter.

A final point: it is unusual that there is not report that *b^e^rît* was made. However, the banquet in iii 20 seems to be the equivalent.[4]

---

[1] E. Kutsch, *Rost Festschrift*, p. 136: "...er (David) ihn in Pflicht nimmt."

[2] This is apparent in his ironic question in iii 12: "to whom does a country belong?" I.e., to the shadow king or real commander of its forces? He can bring Israel to David. He and David know it, and his immediate success show they are right.

[3] So H. W. Hertzberg, *I and II Samuel*, Philadelphia 1964, pp. 258, 260.

[4] See the affirmation of the act: he-they made *b^e^rît* in Jos. ix 15; 1 Sam. xviii 3; xx 16-17; xxiii 18; 2 Sam. v 3; 1 Kings xx 34 (and note 2 Chron. xxiii 3, where the allusion in 2 Kings xi 17 has been turned unto a report with the affirmation; the report in 1 Sam. xi 1-3 has no affirmation of the fact, but the act never took place!). See also Gen. xxi 27, 32; in xxvi 30 and xxxi 53b-54 the act is reported through an equivalent expression. Hence the quasi-certainty that 2 Sam. iii 20b is an allusion to the action which formally realized *b^e^rît*.

Immediately it is done Abner sets out to bring Israel under David's sway. This is his *b^{e}rît* obligation and it is now in force. We have seen synonyms used along with *krt b^{e}rît* to affirm the *b^{e}rît*-making. Here one seems to be substituted. This is interesting in itself, and the symbolism of the equivalent used is important. David has taken Abner into his family for his service *and* for his protection.

Summary

I. *Type of source:* We have seen six reports of *b^{e}rît*-making as such, that is, stories which are entirely concerned with the process as their central theme. We have six texts which speak of *b^{e}rît*-making as part of another theme which is the central interest. Other references are more or less passing allusions. It is worth noting these distinctions because they condition the kind and the quantity of information we can expect. The direct reports are the most important, and must be noticed as such.[1]

II. *Elements characteristically associated with* b^{e}rît-*making:*

A. *Negotiations:* elements of persuasion, proposal, and counter-proposal are characteristic. These are found in all the regular reports except the first Jonathan-David *b^{e}rît*, a personal association where negotiation was unneeded and indeed out of place, and 1 Sam. xxiii 16-18, a succinct report paralleling xx 10-17 which does imply the negotiations. Note that all the reports of *b^{e}rît*-making in Genesis have negotiations.[2]

B. *Terms:* 1) *formulations* which state what one or both parties were to do as a result of the negotiations are common.[3] Again, the feature is paralleled in the Genesis reports.

2) However, the terms may be left *unformulated* in this strict. sense. However, they appear clearly in the course of the negotiations (Jos.

[1] Direct reports: Jos. ix 1-x 1; 1 Sam. xviii 1-4 (with xx 6-8); xx 10-17; xxiii 16-16; 2 Sam. iii 21; v 1-3; 1 Kings xx 32-34; incidental in other reports: 1 Sam. xi 1-3; 2 Sam. iii 12-21 (about the rise of Saul and David respectively); 1 Kings v 26 (about Solomon's greatness); 1 Kings xv 18-19 (incident in a war report); 2 Kings xi 4, 17 (incidents in the report of the restoration of the Davidids; 2 Chron. xxiii 1-3 turns these into reports); allusion: 1 Sam. xxii 8; Hos. ix 4 (in a prophetic reflection); Hos. xii 12b, and Ezek. xvii 11-21 (in prophetic reproaches).

[2] Gen. xxi 22-32; xxvi 22-33; xxxi 23-xxxii 3.

[3] Cf. 1 Sam. xx 12-15; xxiii 17; 2 Sam. v 2 (cf. iii 17-18); 1 Kings xx 34. 1 Kings xv 18-19 shows that the parties knew clearly what was expected of one another; 2 Chron. xxiii 3 provides a formulation for the incident in 2 Kings xi 17, showing how oppropriate the feature was felt to be.

ix 6-13; 1 Sam. xi 1-2), in appeals to the *b^e^rît* (1 Sam. xx 7-8; cf. 1 Kings xv 18-19), in the equality of the parties (1 Kings v 26; 2 Kings xi 17—though 2 Chron. xxiii 3 formulates the terms and removes the parity here), or in the kind of association involved (2 Kings xi 4: fellow conspirators; cf. the interpretation in 2 Chron. xxiii 1-2). The prophetic texts, Hos. ix 4 and Ezek. xvii 11-21, complain of broken obligations, but only Ezekiel gives any concrete content to this. Hos. xii 2b reproaches the *fact* of *b^e^rît*-making, not the terms involved, so that the conclusion that they were a one-sided obligation on Ephraim is a deduction.

3) The terms, whether formulated or alluded to, are *usually bilateral*, that is, they indicate duties incumbent in some way or another on both parties (service in return for the grant of life, service in return for protection, help in war in return for payment etc.).[1] So too in Gen. xxi 22-32 and xxxi 32-xxxii 3 the *b^e^rîtôt* are explicitly bilateral. This is implicit in Gen. xxvi 22-33.

4) *Occasionally obligations are unilateral*, that is, they empower or tie but one party: in 2 Sam. v 3 David assumes leadership over Israel (compare 2 Chron. xxiii 3: the enthronement *b^e^rît* seems to concern divinely-ordained sovereignty), in 2 Sam. iii 12-21 Abner submits to David (if we discount implications of mutuality in 20), and in Ezek. xvii 11-21 Zedekiah is Nebuchadnezzar's vassal. Possibly also in Hos. ix 4, but the prophet is reproving one party and simply says nothing about another, and in Hos. xii 12b, and Ephraim's obligation must be deduced (see number 3 above).

C. *Relationships: b^e^rît*-making usually occurs when a relationship already exists. Jonathan already loves David, David is already the destined head of Israel (note 1 Sam. xx 13, 15; xxiii 17, as well as 2 Sam. iii 18; v 2), or a state of inferiority already exists and is accepted by Gibeon, by Jabesh-Gilead, and by Ben-Hadad. The pre-existent relationship is characteristic of the Genesis reports also: Gen. xxi 23 and xxvi 29 insist on the peace and good relations already in force; Gen. xxxi 43 on family connections.

D. *Social usage:* in certain situations the terms seem to have been self-evident. A hopeless or a defeated party was to serve in return for

[1] This is true of all *b^e^rîtôt* reported except the David-Israel example (2 Sam. v 3), all noticed incidentally except that of David with Abner (2 Sam. iii 12-21, and here 20 may imply the mutual obligations of a *paterfamilias* and a retainer admitted to the *familia* in a formal meal); and of Joash and the people (2 Kings xi 17) *as (re)interpreted in* 2 Chron. xxiii 3 (for the distinctions: reports, incidental reports, and allusions, see above, p. 81, n. 1).

the grant of life (Jos. ix 1-x 1; 1 Sam. xi 1-2; 1 Kings xx 32). The heroic friendship also involved service and life but in a very different atmosphere.

E. *The act* of *b^e^rît*-making: the report regularly states that the act took place (see above, p. 80, n. 4).

F. *Variety of agents:* this is simply bewildering. There can be a third party agent (2 Kings xi 17), one agent (1 Sam. xi 1; 2 Sam. iii 12—but both of these are proposals to make *b^e^rît*, not real affirmations of the act itself; 1 Kings xx 34), one apparent agent with the other party finally involved (Jos. ix 15; x 1; 1 Kings xi 4), two parties seem to have approximately equal roles (1 Sam. xxiii 18; 2 Sam. iii 21; v 3; 1 Kings v 26), or two parties, one of whom seems to do more than the other (1 Sam. xviii 3-4 [cf. xx 8]; xx 17-18; Ezek. xvii 11-21—note that a hifil is usually used). This becomes even more complex if one tries to relate agancy to unilaterality and multilaterality. There is no correlation! There are bilateral *b^e^rîtôt* with one agent (1 Sam. xi 1; 1 Kings xx 34), with two (1 Sam. xxiii 18; 1 Kings v 26) with two agents, one more active than the other (1 Sam. xviii 3-4; xx 16-17), with a third party as agent (2 Kings xi 17), or with an apparent single agent who turns out to have a partner (Jos. ix 15-x 1; 2 Kings xi 4). Then there are unilateral *b^e^rîtôt* with but one agent—though none of the examples is conclusive—(Hos. ix 4; xii 2b; 2 Sam. iii 12-21), with two agents (2 Sam. iii 21-v 3), or with two agents, one more active than the other (Ezek. xvii 11-21). Among other things, this complexity means that in the cases treated there is no rule about the primary agent of *b^e^rît*. He need not be more or less powerful than the other party, and in any case he does not act alone. It is interesting that the move toward *b^e^rît*-making usually comes from the inferior, but not always: cf. 1 Sam. xviii 1-4 and 2 Kings xi 4. These are special cases, and indeed the complex character of *b^e^rît*-making cannot be understood unless we observe the great variety in kinds of *b^e^rît* and in the situations in which it is made. This deserves a special study in itself.

If the reader finds this obscure and confusing, this is because it is so.[1] The texts simply do not concern themselves with relating unilateral terms to single agents, or with any other consistent combination of these factors.[2] This is important for the question of unilaterality.

[1] The only way to make the situation clear is to put it on a graph with lines for one party, two-party etc. crossing those for unilateral etc. This does not lend itself to print, and what it makes clear is that there is no clarity.

[2] This confusion or indifference accounts for the irregular use of the preposi-

No bᵉrît *is one-sided unless the obligation is incumbent on one party and one party makes the* bᵉrît. The first point needs no explanation. The second is clear when we reflect that the act realizes and so conditions the obligation. Even if it is incumbent on but one party, there is no *bᵉrît* obligation unless there is a *bᵉrît* act, and as long as the latter involves both parties the obligation is somehow dependent on them both.

Conclusions. krt bᵉrît originally referred to a specific act, but it came to mean a solemn commitment in general. The reports concerning such commitments normally start from the fact of a relationship. They normally include a record of negotiations, formulation of terms, and a statement that the act of making *bᵉrît* was actually performed. Thus the negotiations end with a solemn ratification of the terms. The terms normally apply to both parties, and the act is commonly the work of both. Indeed, even unilateral terms could depend on a common act. In these circumstances it seems impossible that *bᵉrît* not acquire an association with ideas of relationship. It is tied up with a complex of recognized relationships, active relations (negotiations), terms which relate one party to another, and a common act. The word *bᵉrît* carries these overtones. It is relational.

This is confirmed by some of the parallels with the act in the texts studied. It is paired with *šālôm* (cf. above, n. 8). That is, it is paired with a state of "peace," "unity," "completion." *šālôm* is hard to translate, but it is relational. The act is also paired with kingship (1 Sam. iii 5). David makes *bᵉrît* and becomes king. He acquires an enduring status which is a relationship: one is king *of* something. *A pari*, the *bᵉrît* made is enduring and relational. Another kind of *bᵉrît* involves the relation of love, and *bᵉrît* can make one a servant or a brother, that is, put one in a state of enduring relationship. So one appeals to the servant relationship (Jos. x 6). Again, one is *in* a *bᵉrît*, and he appeals to this, to the relationship in which the obligations obtain (1 Sam. xx 7-8).

Secular *bᵉrît*, then, as described in Dtr (and in Genesis) is as clearly tied to relation as to obligation. Indeed, the two are inseparable. Obligation is a relational word too. With regard to translation, then:

---

tions. If there is no concern to coordinate agent and obligation, then it is no wonder that *krt bᵉrît lᵉ-/ʿim-/ʾet-* show no consistent differentiation in their use in this sample (see comments on 1 Sam. xx 16; xxii 8; 2 Sam. iii 21; v 3; 1 Kings xx 34, for ex.). Even *bên... ûbên*, the most firm fixed prepositional usage, is equated with *ʾet-* in 1 Kings xv 19 (and with *ʿim* if we compare 2 Kings xi 17 with 2 Chron. xxiii 3). The sample, of course, is too small to establish tules for probable useage, but it does indicate exceptions.

relation and obligation, commitment and action, these are what we mean by covenant.[1] The traditional translation can stand. With regard to its religious use: *b^erît*, when applied to the relation of man to God, must carry some of its rich associations with complex relationships with it. These were surely modified and others added, but they cannot have been lost.

---

[1] See *The Oxford English Dictionary:* "covenant" means, in addition to "agreement," "undertaking, pledge or promise of one of the parties," "an agreement... or promise of legal validity," "a clause of such an agreement," and, in older usage, "vow" and "matter agreed upon... or promised." Thus, as well as the *relation* itself, it can mean the *action* of undertaking it or the *content* (obligation) undertaken. It can be *multilateral:* "agreement," or *unilateral* "promise or undertaking of one party." This range of meaning, which is not due to theological usage, is very close to that of secular *b^erît*. I do not presume to judge definitively whether this is true of the traditional translations in other languages, e.g., *Bund*, *alliance*. They do seem, to an outsider, to concern rather more the aspect of relation than that of content or action, but this study would seem to indicate that a substitute should not on this account overemphasize these other aspects at the expense of the relational.

RES BIBLIOGRAPHICAE

berît in Old Testament History and Theology (*)

Dennis J. McCarthy - Rome

Given the great interest in covenant in the Old Testament during the past decade and more, and especially the enthusiasm and the broad claims of some students of the problem, a book like this was surely inevitable. It is exciting because it is a direct attack on much of the received wisdom concerning covenant. In truth, one must have reservations about many of the author's presuppositions; ideas about the nature of historical study, the value of the study of literary structures, the place of investigation of cultic and sociological settings of texts, and logical procedures, among others (1). It is also unfortunate that his judgments on the work of other scholars are sometimes couched in language which makes them sound much harsher than one imagines he intended. Still, the writing and the argumentation are brilliant, and what Perlitt has to say demands careful consideration. In so far as we accept it we will have to revise much of our basic ideas about covenant. But what does he say, and how far does it compel acceptance?

Most striking, perhaps, is the flat rejection of the parallel between covenant and treaty which has become almost a commonplace. However, the larger, positive side of Perlitt's work is the more important. For one thing, Hebrew *berît* is given a meaning different from the conventional translation "covenant" (German *Bund*). Following E. Kutsch's work (2), Perlitt asserts that *berît* refers basically not to a relationship (*Verhältnis*) as our translations suggest; rather the basic meaning is "obligation" (*Verpflichtung*), which one may take on oneself or impose on another. Particularly, any idea of reciprocal obligation, while possible, is secondary to *berît*. Hence *berît* as a theological term means either Yahweh's commitment to Israel, often, in Deuteronomic

(*) Review article on Lothar Perlitt, *Bundestheologie im Alten Testament* (Wissenschaftliche Monographien zum Alten und Neuen Testament, 36). VIII-300 S. 23,5 × 15,5. Neukirchen-Vluyn 1969. Neukirchner Verlag. Ln. DM 44,—; brosch. DM 42,—.

(1) See the review by M. J. Buss, *JBL* 90 (1971) 211, for some sound criticism of this aspect of the book.

(2) See "Gesetz und Gnade", *ZAW* 79 (1967) 18-35; "Der Begriff ברית in vordeuteronomischer Zeit", *Rost Festschrift* (BZAW 105; Berlin 1967) 133-143; "Von ברית zu 'Bund' ", *KerDo* 14 (1968) 159-182.

terminology, his oath, or Israel's obligation to Yahweh, that is, obedience or, concretely, the law. (In view of the questions thus raised about the meaning of *b^{e}rît* I have preferred to avoid translations and to retain the Hebrew word in transcription wherever possible in this article).

So much for the definition or translation of *b^{e}rît*. Perlitt goes on to propose a history of *b^{e}rît* as a theological concept in the Old Testament. When was *b^{e}rît* introduced into this theology? With the patriarchal stories? With Sinai? With the Davidic claims? No. With and by the Deuteronomic school! All significant uses of the word are said to belong to this school. This is argued as it should be: from a close study of the relevant texts in which Perlitt tries to show that any apparent exceptions to this rule are actually Deuteronomic interpolations into older contexts. Neither are the accounts of ceremonies in which a *b^{e}rît* is said to have been made with or before Yahweh reflections of an authentically ancient Israelite (or Judean) tradition. Where this seems to be the case we are actually dealing with reflections of the desire to support the claims of the Deuteronomic law by representing it as having been promulgated by the highest public authorities.

These exegetical arguments are buttressed by over-all historical considerations. The eighth and seventh centuries, the formative era of the Deuteronomic school, are the perfect setting for the development of the *b^{e}rît* theology. The point is that the idea of parallel obligations, Yahweh's commitment to Israel by promise or oath and Israel's duty to obey the law, can be expressed by *b^{e}rît*, and this idea offered a chance to explain the circumstances of the time. A people threatened in its identity as Yahweh's own favorite needed the reassurance of an explicit promise from Yahweh guaranteeing its position. At the same time, this insecurity of the people called for explanation, and this could be found in the implications of the demand for obedience and the threats attached to the failure to give it. *b^{e}rît* enabled the Deuteronomic school to develop a complex theological idea perfectly adapted to the exigencies of the situation.

This argument is important, but I am not sure that it will bear all the weight which Perlitt puts upon it. He often seems to be saying that the Deuteronomic era is the *only* conceivable setting for an idea, when, in fact, the most that can be said is that it is *a* good setting. Other settings can never be excluded on the basis of such general considerations.

In any event, it will be seen that in many ways Perlitt's argument refurbishes the Wellhausenian scheme: a progression from older conceptions of a connection with Yahweh in terms of natural relationships, through the prophets with their ethical demands, to a moralistic and legalistic idea of *b^{e}rît* characteristic of the Deuteronomic school and later strata of the Old Testament. In fact, Perlitt actually goes farther than Wellhausen. The latter saw a complete change of concepts in the course of the development of Old Testament theology, but at least this was covered by the common name, "covenant". Perlitt will not allow even this continuity in name. The very word *b^{e}rît* came only with the Deuteronomic school.

Neither the reminiscence of Wellhausen nor the radical low dating of *b^e^rît* is objectionable in itself. On the contrary, there is much to applaud here. For instance, even if one were not to deny that any reference at all to *b^e^rît* can be found in the oldest strata of the Sinai narratives, there is no doubt that these strata put their heaviest emphasis on theophany. On the other hand, there is equally little doubt that the concept of the conditional *b^e^rît* with all its consequences comes to the fore with the Deuteronomic school. I have long insisted that this is what the texts say.

However, can we leave it at this? I think not. Perlitt himself emphasizes that the Sinai theophany, for instance, is *gezielt*. It has an end, a purpose. Is this entirely unrelated to what has been traditionally subsumed under the name "covenant?" This is quite doubtful, and it introduces a basic query which one must put to Perlitt's conclusions. Was there no evolution of the *b^e^rît* concept? Not, was there no development of ideas which ended in a new concept and/or new name, *b^e^rît* (Perlitt would admit this), but, was there no development of the idea of *b^e^rît* itself (which Perlitt hardly allows for)? In other words, was *b^e^rît* a theological novelty, practically an invention of the Deuteronomic school? Was there nothing in history which prepared the word and the idea of *b^e^rît* for its role in the Deuteronomic writings? Without doubting for a moment the creativity of the Deuteronomists, I do wonder whether they produced things *ex nihilo sui et subjecti*.

Nor is it entirely satisfactory to say with Wellhausen, as Perlitt does, that the *b^e^rît* idea as used in the Deuteronomistic writings had its origins in an impulse from prophetism. The prophets do not favor the word *b^e^rît*, and authors like Perlitt emphasize the problem which this fact raised for the view that prophetic thought was much influenced by *b^e^rît* ideas. True, but surely it works both ways. This is equally an argument against the claim that a prophetism to which *b^e^rît* was alien was the seedbed in which *b^e^rît* and related concepts developed. It seems much more likely that the stream of development included some explicit *b^e^rît* elements, even if these must be sought outside of prophetism. Or, if we are to grant that in this case it is simply a matter of similarity of ideas, that prophetic ideas were so like those subsumed under *b^e^rît* that the name is almost an accidental appendage to a well-established block of ideas, and that later *b^e^rît* ideas and prophetic morality were so alike that we have to admit a connection, we should be ready to admit that this sort of argument is valid in other cases. A set of ideas may exist and be identifiable in cases where a common word fails. I have in mind the meal of the elders in Ex 24,11. Particularly if we are to read this passage in connection with Ex 18,12 it seems impossible to avoid the thought of the covenant meal of the nomads even though the word *b^e^rît* does not occur. In other words, a primitive passage has already introduced covenant thinking into the description of Israel's encounter with Yahweh. This is a method which does allow us to trace ways of thinking related to covenant in Old Testament strata older than the prophets. An overly rigid insistence that the word must occur before one can admit the presence of the concept is questionable. However, it is true that Ex 24,11 is a particularly clear case, and the mode of argumentation is in general delicate. It must be pursued in a detail impossible here, and so I shall make no more of the point. But it is something which should not be neglected in further studies. Right now it is better to look to more concrete points.

One of these is the occurrence of the very word *b^{e}rît*. Perlitt insists that the word is applied to Yahweh and Israel only in documents of the Deuteronomic age and later. Is this the case? The crucial texts in the search for an answer to this question are Hos 6,7 and 8,1; Gn 15,18; Ex 19,5; 24,7.8; 34,10.27.28; and 2 Sm 23,5. According to Perlitt the first text from Hosea does not refer to a *b^{e}rît* involving Yahweh and Israel; all the others are Deuteronomic or later. If this is so, there is no case for a pre-Deuteronomic use of *b^{e}rît* for Yahweh–Israel connection. But is it so?

In Hos 6,7 it is true that *b^{e}rît*, if it means the *b^{e}rît* with Yahweh, is unusual. In normal prose it would be *b^{e}rîtî*. One trouble is that the normal prose in this connection is Deuteronomic, and we are asking about the possibility of antecedents to Deuteronomic usage. To treat the normal prose usage as an iron law is to prejudge the case. Must Hosea have conformed to (later) normal usage and said *b^{e}rîtî*? I cannot escape the feeling that Perlitt would confidently assert that the passage is a Deuteronomizing interpolation, if this were the case. In other words, the appeal to normal prose usage to argue that *b^{e}rît* here cannot refer to a Yahweh *b^{e}rît* is in danger of begging the question.

Moreover, we are not dealing with normal prose. This is poetry in which the weight of imagery and of parallelism must be respected. "Behold, they have walked over the covenant like dirt; lo, they have betrayed me!" (1). The figure is vivid and concrete in the first half-verse, and there is no reason to doubt that this is true in the second. "Betrayed" is no generality to be interpreted in the light of parallel passages. It is concrete. It means transgression of the *b^{e}rît* so that one must think of the *b^{e}rît* as "my *b^{e}rît*" since to transgress it is to "betray me". It is no argument against this that *bgd* in other contexts is used of sexual infidelity (e.g., Hos 5,7; Jer 3,8) or generically (e.g., Jer 5,11; 12,1). That is what the parallelism in these other passages indicates. Here we have a different bit of poetry which demands interpretation according to its own individual structure. In the light of this passage we must give *bgd* a new nuance and not impoverish the passage to make it conform to others. And so we have an argument that Hosea does indeed speak of a *b^{e}rît* which is Yahweh's.

If anything, this is even clearer in Hos 8,1. Not that the details of its meaning are clear in every respect, but it is at least certain that 1b equates transgression of "my *b^{e}rît*" with violation of "my *tôrâ*" in a Yahweh speech. This usage, of course, is immediately suspect. If the

(1) For the translation, especially *k^{e}'ādām*, "like dirt", see M. J. Dahood, "Zacharia 9,1 *'ên 'Ādam*", *CBQ* 25 (1963) 123-124.

suffix with *bᵉrît* and especially the equating of *bᵉrît* and *tôrâ* are ineluctably Deuteronomic, then the passage is a post-Hosean interpolation. But once again there is danger of taking what is to be proved as the means of proof. The context should support the claim that *bᵉrîtî* is a sure sign of a Deuteronomistic hand. Otherwise we are reduced to saying that *bᵉrîtî* is Deuteronomistic because *bᵉrîtî* is Deuteronomistic. Now, in Hos 8,1, there is hardly question of a Deuteronomistic context. Deuteronomistic writers, whatever else they were, tended to be clear, and Hos 8,1 is notably obscure. It is easier to imagine traditionists garbling a difficult poetic passage than it is to imagine a Deuteronomistic interpolator composing gibberish or indulging in obscurantist poetry. As Perlitt himself says in another context (speaking of Ex 24,1): "ein Ergänzer hätte es besser gekonnt".

One might also remark that a willingness to consider the possibilities of interpreting *bᵉrît* in the light of wider biblical and ancient oriental usage could help in the understanding of this difficult passage. The "colorless" expression *ṭôb* in 8,3 is not really a rather empty generality unworthy of the prophet-poet. The root is one which is characteristic of treaty contexts, where it refers to something like comity or good relations between the parties (1). Hosea knew precisely what Israel had cast off: its special relationship to Yahweh. One cannot avoid the conclusion that Hosea knew of a Yahweh *bᵉrît*. This does not mean that Deuteronomistic writers, influenced though they were by Hosean ideas, did not develop the *bᵉrît* concept further, but it does mean that they were working out of a tradition and that the history of *bᵉrît* in Old Testament theology was really an evolution of a concept. The Hosean passage, with its variant terminology and similar ideas, is a clear step in this evolution.

Perhaps the case is less clear with the passages from the Pentateuch. They do have elements which relate to Deuteronomistic usage. But it is surely over-facile to classify them as Deuteronomistic for this reason, for they also have elements which are wholly uncharacteristic of Deuteronomistic usage. If we have to choose one horn of the dilemma or another, Deuteronomistic or non-Deuteronomistic, we could as reasonably choose the latter as the former. But it is surely more reasonable to recognize the peculiar character of these passages. They are Deuteronomistic and un-Deuteronomistic. Where should we expect such a combination? Why not in pre-Deuteronomistic passages where neither the language nor the thought has reached the purity of later developments? Once more, there are indications that *bᵉrît* theology did not spring full-armed from Deuteronomistic brains. It was a complex thing which had a history much older than its Deuteronomistic expression. Let us look at the pertinent passages.

(1) See W. L. MORAN, "A Note on the Treaty Terminology of the Sefire Stelas", *JNES* 22 (1963) 173-176, and D. Hillers, "A Note on Some Treaty Terminology in the Old Testament", *BASOR* 176 (1964) 46-47.

First Gen 15,18, which has commonly been attributed to J. Given the problems with the analysis of the chapter, however, one would not wish to insist over-much on this attribution. The way, then, is open to another attribution. In our case, according to Perlitt everything comes down to the probable dating of the *b^erît* ritual which comes to a climax in verse 18, and the point is well taken. Perlitt sees the ritual as parallel to that described in Jer 34 and similar to that mentioned in the treaty between Mati-ilu of Arpad and Assyria in the 8th century B.C. This parallelism would seem to indicate that far from being primitive, *uralt*, the rite is characteristic of the 1st millennium. However, it is not clear that this conclusion takes due regard of all the details involved, for, since there is no doubt that oath ceremonies involving the slaughter of animals were practiced in the second millennium as well as the first, a dating through parallelism is only valid if it establishes that the rite described has properties peculiar to a particular era. Thus it must be shown that the characteristic details of the rite described in Gen 15 and the mentality behind it are those of the 1st millennium. Now, the Mati-ilu text hardly proves anything. It does not deal explicitly with a precise ritual involving passing through the parts of the slaughtered beasts. Rather it establishes the general fact of a belief in ritual or magic identification which is surely not the peculiar property of the 1st millennium. This is a timeless idea operative in the 2nd as well as the 1st millennium and still alive today.

As for the ritual in Jer 34, it does involve the practice of passing between the parts of the animals. The trouble is, the details are not quite the same as those in Gen 15. In Jeremiah's rite it is a case of passing between the halves of animals cut in two. In Gen 15 they are cut into three parts, or, less likely, severed in three places to produce four parts (1). This may seem an unimportant difference, and the symbolism of mixing with the carcasses may be the same in either case. However, given the extreme importance of detail in the practice of ritual, it is not safe to assume so without further thought. In fact, such is the nature of ritual belief that a seemingly minor variation in a meaningful gesture can mean a significant change in the ritual. Nor is this the only point to notice. In Jer 34, as in the Mati-ilu treaty, the meaning of the ritual is made explicit. Not so in Gen 15. The rite is presented as though its meaning were self-evident. Its efficacity needs no explanation. And of course the stage at which a rite is accepted as effective without explanation is generally older than that in which it needs some sort of verbal explanation.

There is another factor which seems to point to the relative antiquity of the rite as described in Gen 15. This is its anthropomorphism. In itself there is no problem with Yahweh's passing symbolically among the slaughtered beasts and provisionally identifying himself with their fate. This is no more — but no less — illogical than ascribing a verbal

(1) See H. CAZELLES, "Connexions et structure de Gen. XV", *RB* 69 (1962) 321-349.

oath with its conditional self-curse to Yahweh. However, the vivid imagery does raise something of a problem. A mind that can accept the verbal anthropomorphism because its meaning is veiled by familiarity will still notice the oddity of a pictorial representation of the same thing. Now, it is actually possible to see the description of the firebrand and furnace passing among the chopped-up parts of the animals in Gen 15 as a step away from anthropomorphism. At least Yahweh does something different from what a man would do in the circumstances: pass among several parts rather than between two, and he does it not in human shape but symbolically. His act is not quite human, but is it the sort of thing Deuteronomists would imagine? They are not keen on ritual. Why picture such an odd rite at such an important juncture? And is it really possible that the Deuteronomic school, after experiencing the process of demythologization which has left its traces in 1 Kgs 19, for example, would be the ones to identify Yahweh with torch and furnace and make him act parallel to the way a man would? Someone did this, but hardly a true Deuteronomist. This may not demonstrate that Gen 15,18 is older than the Deuteronomic school, but it does argue that the passage must be ascribed to another source, and there are signs that it is older. More, the sources for the patriarchal stories are generally much older than Deuteronomy. The burden of proof would seem to be on one who wished to take this one important passage as an exception to the rule. Gn 15 is a non-Deuteronomic reference to a Yahweh *b^erît*, and probably an ancient one. Theology must consider this in any effort to understand the *b^erît* concept over its whole range.

Another key text is Ex 19,5. Without a doubt the actual distich, "hear my voice and keep my *b^erît*", sounds thoroughly Deuteronomistic. So also the basic idea of the whole passage, 19,3-8, which must be considered as a whole. This is, of course, the idea of a reward conditioned on obedience. Still, there is much in the passage that does not sound Deuteronomistic. Expressions like "house of Jacob and sons of Israel", "what I did to Egypt", "brought you to me", and "a kingdom of priests and a holy people" are very unusual or in some cases unique. This argues strongly for a separation from the highly stereotyped language of the Deuteronomic school which had regular but different expressions for what is said in these phrases. To say that these latter are almost like something Deuteronomistic is actually to emphasize their divergence from the normal Deuteronomistic ways of writing. Simply as an exercise in literary criticism, assigning the passage to a Deuteronomistic source without further ado is to over-simplify. If we go beyond criticism to interpretation, ignoring the singular elements of a highly poetic passage like this and treating it as another example of a stereotype means we will miss the richness of meaning which it has to offer. Certainly a complete theology of *b^erît* in the Old Testament will have to take account of the special nuances which a passage like this adds to the concept. Simply to reduce it to its Deuteronomistic elements is to impoverish the theology which we build on it. This is true even if one were to deny that poetic passages of this sort have every chance of being the sort of thing from which Deuteronomistic theology developed and so represent a stage of evolution older than the Deuteronomistic, as I believe. In any case, they are something more than Deuteronomistic, and a complete theology of *b^e^rît* will have to cover this added factor.

In Ex 24,7 and 8 Perlitt argues that the first is a Deuteronomistic interpretation of the ritual scene, and that the second is an even later addition to the pericope seeking to tie verse 7 more closely to 6 and to complete the picture of the ceremony. This is ingenious, but it is not entirely convincing. Perhaps 7 is an interpolation, but surely 8 is the natural sequel to 6. In it the ceremony is completed as it should be, by the proper use of the rest of the blood, the half that was not applied to the altar. It is really hard to believe that this second half of the symbolic blood had no role in the ritual even though its conservation in the vessels is so carefully noted. This seems to be confirmed by the language. *seper habb^e^rît* in 7 does sound like the Deuteronomic school, as we might expect in an interpolation, but on the other hand *dam habb^e^rît* in 8 sounds very un-Deuteronomic. The phrase is unusual, and its ritualism and mysticism is very far from characteristic of the Deuteronomic school. If 24,7 is a comment marked by a Deuteronomistic vocabulary, 24,8 is not, and we are up against what may well be called a key text for *b^e^rît* theology. Here the concept which sees *b^e^rît* as essentially a matter of law and obedience is face to face with another and older concept which sees *b^e^rît* in ritual and mystic terms. I have argued elsewhere and I would repeat that these are not mutually exclusive views. Seen in proper order, they complement one another and demand a complex view of *b^e^rît*. A full theology of *b^e^rît* will not suppress the difference but include it. The result may be a rather more cumbersome picture, a less systematic whole, than we can achieve by confining *b^e^rît* to the Deuteronomistic view of it, but that is the price of completeness.

Ex 34 is a harder case. The analysis is extraordinarily difficult, and there are elements which do recall the Deuteronomic school. This may be true of the emphasis on a written *b^e^rît* in 34,37 and 28, though one does wonder if the tablets are a Deuteronomistic conception. Be this as it may, the theophany resists reduction to a Deuteronomistic hand. Even the epithets given to Yahweh in 34,7, though perhaps not part of the primitive *mise en scène* with the simple proclamation of the divine name, are not Deuteronomistic (see A. Jepsen, *ZAW* 79 [1967] 289), and at least 10a: "Behold, I am making a covenant", has every chance of being a continuation of that proclamation. At least one is justified in having suspicions of an analysis in which every decision in the difficult process falls against the possibility of a non-Deuteronomistic origin of a phrase mentioning *b^e^rît*.

In 2 Sam 23,5 we move from the Pentateuch to an entirely different literature which offers a surer case in a different doctrinal area. This is royal ideology. Now, it may be that the reference to *b^e^rît* in verse 5 is an interpolation within an ancient poem. However, the sequence of thought and images does not demand this conclusion. The reference fits the context well. The real reason for doubting its authenticity is that elsewhere *berît ʿôlām* is found in later contexts. Does this prove that the passage is a late addition to the poem, or is this the sort of context in which the idea and the phrase *berît ʿôlām* arose? I submit that the royal ideology is an obvious place in which the idea and the name could have developed. This ideology emphasized the permanence of the royal prerogatives on the basis of Yahweh's favor, as the royal psalms amply demonstrate. How is this better summed up than in the phrase *berît ʿôlām*, "enduring commitment?". Surely, when a phrase fits its immediate literary context as this one does, and when the idea it expresses is natural to the world to which that context belongs as it is here, it is dubious method to resort to the hypothesis of interpolation. It is far more likely that this is evidence for another element in *berît* theology, an element tying it to royal ideology. Once more that theology is seen to be more complex and richer.

The texts, then, resist the attempt to attribute every allusion to a Yahweh *berît* to a Deuteronomistic hand. They demand that we take account of the *berît* idea in relation to Abraham, to Sinai, to David, and in Hosea. This is what the evidence points to, and it is a more satisfactory state of affairs than the claim that *berît* is exclusive to the Deuteronomic school. It is easier to believe that a relatively unused concept already in existence was developed by later thinkers than that one was made up out of whole cloth.

The same thing is true in the case of ceremonies involving *berît*. I yield to no one in my scepticism about the existence of an elaborate "covenant cult" at the center of ancient Israelite religious practice. The explicit evidence simply indicates that other things were at the center of that practice. However, this does not mean that one should reject the importance of the cult out of hand. It may not have been something exclusive to Israel, but it was central to Israelite religion from the first, and, as in all religious traditions in history, it had a profound influence on Israelite thought and expression. Israel went to school to the liturgy as well as to the wisemen and the prophets. The fact that scholars have overvalued the cultic influence does not justify our undervaluing it, and I fear that this is what Perlitt does (See *Bundestheologie*, 128, which is paraphrased here). Rightly rejecting exaggerated claims for the place of a study of the cult in reconstructing the history of Old Testament theology, claims based usually on hypothetical reconstructions of a cult which is not directly described, he fails to notice the possibilities which are opened by the study of the limited but concrete data about Israelite religious usage which the texts do provide.

Specifically, an aversion to excessive claims for a covenant cult should not close our eyes to the evidence for a modest but real place for *berît* ceremonies in the public religious life of Israel. Perlitt has to deny this, for, if *berît* is to be a purely Deuteronomistic idea in the religious sphere, it cannot have belonged to the regular exercises of religion which are older than Deuteronomy. As for that, I can only repeat: it is antecedently more likely that the Deuteronomic school used a religious concept it found rather than that it imposed a new one. But apart from what seems likely, what do the texts say?

Here 2 Kgs 23,1-3 is crucial for Perlitt. He thinks that in this text "hat Dtr dem Dt den Makel des Nichtoffizielles der vorexilischen dt Predigt genommen" in giving "der Gehalt der dt Predigt einer Institutionalisierung" (p. 11). This was achieved by picturing the very king of Judah in the act of imposing the Deuteronomic Code. All other similar scenes will have been modelled on this. The central point is the commitment to keep the law., and this has an exact parallel, for instance, in Neh 8 – 10, where we find a sworn acceptance of the obligation to keep the law. The parallel is revealing. No doubt the action described in Neh 8 – 10, like that in Ex 10, was stimulated by the record of Josiah's *b^e^rît*. But the parallel is not quite exact, *pace* Wellhausen. In Nehemiah the people enter into a written contract to observe a known law code. The contractual formality is alien to older *b^e^rît* usage (1). Nor is this the only difference in the details of the scenes. In Nehemiah the whole people represented by a large number of leaders literally subscribe to a contract to keep the law (notice that there is no mention of *b^e^rît*). They do this under oath, but there is no mention of Yahweh by name. The scene in Ezra is much the same, though *b^e^rît* is mentioned: law, oath, active cooperation by the people. In 2 Kgs 23 one leader imposes a law in the presence of many notables but without there being any sign of the group's entering actively into the process. There is no mention of oath, but the king's act is done "before Yahweh". In the one case acceptance, in the other imposition; in the one, group action, in the other individual action; in the one an explicit oath, in the other not; in the one, no mention of Yahweh, in the other explicit mention. The law seems a little different in the two cases also. In Nehemiah it is something familiar. One regrets not having lived by it and pledges a reform. There is no need for an authoritative imposition, nor is there anyone who imposes. In Kings the law is unfamiliar, and someone has to impose it. *b^e^rît* is given a new interpretation in detail and from above. All things considered, the two scenes are similar but not identical.

This can be explained, but it is to be explained historically. Notice the action. In 2 Kgs 23 Josiah is presented as exercising a power. He may be redefining the *b^e^rît*, but he has an accepted power to impose it. Where is this paralleled? Not in Nehemiah, but in 2 Kgs 11,17, where a single leader, the high-priest, makes a *b^e^rît* for the people. There is no oath, but Yahweh is mentioned. The modalities are those of Josiah's action, an authoritative imposition on a passive people. The difference in the earlier scene from Kings is in the relatively unspecified *b^e^rît*. It is not yet something as concrete and detailed as the law.

All this constitutes a coherent historical tradition about public *b^e^rît* ceremonies. There was development as the structure of society

(1) See Gene M. TUCKER, "Covenant Forms and Contract Forms", *VT* 15 (1965) 487-503.

changed. The role of authority shrank as time went on and the community took an active role. The concept of *berît* also changed. It meant a generalized obligation, then a detailed law that was still an innovation, and finally a code which was not a new regulation but a timeless absolute to which one renewed allegiance. This is the way historical institutions develop. It shows that making a *berît* with Yahweh was part of the religious experience and the religious vocabulary of Judah.

Thus the evidence of religious practice marches with the testimony of the texts to pre-Deuteronomic uses of *berît* in relation to Yahweh. *berît* may not have been ubiquitous, but it did have a place in religious life as well as religious literature. Hence it was available for theological development. It did not need to be invented.

A final point seems to be relevant to this question of over-reaction to possible exaggerations. There has, of course, been a great deal of writing based on the supposed analogy between Old Testament *berît* and the ancient treaty. No doubt too much has been claimed for the analogy, and, especially, illegitimate historical conclusions have been drawn from it. Still, this does not invalidate such evidence as there is for the analogy, nor does it justify a claim that the "...Sitz eines religösen Textes im Leben ist vollkommen uninteressant ohne ... Beachtung der geschichtlichen Erstreckung... dieses 'Lebens'" (p. 83). This is too absolute. We can never neglect the historical dimension, but there are many cases in which it is impossible to determine the historical context of a passage or even of a genre. It may still be possible to discern a sociological setting, and this can be a valuable instrument of interpretation. One thinks of Gerstenberger's explanation of "apodictic law" in terms of the timeless wisdom of the clans (1). I believe that the treaty analogy could be a similar case, even though it were impossible to date the era in which the treaty concept began to exercise a large influence. In fact, the treaty concept will be found to have been at work particularly in the Deuteronomic era, but even apart from this historical aspect of the matter, recognizing the treaty analogy is a useful aid to interpretation.

This must be demonstrated in the actual practice of exegesis, but one can point to some of the more obvious examples. We have already seen that recognition of the treaty analogy reveals the fuller significance of the supposedly colorless *ṭôb* in Hos 8,3. It gives a more accurate and meaningful content to *'hb*, "love", in the Deuteronomistic writings. It must be considered in interpreting Dt 29,24-28 and the context, for these verses are practically a quotation from an inscription of Ashurbanipal describing the effects of violating a treaty. And surely Dt 28,1-2.15 at least must be read in the light of the exact parallels in the treaty literature as indicating, if not a relationship to Yahweh conceived as a treaty, a conditional possession of the land which is scarcely di-

(1) E. Gerstenberger, *Wesen und Herkunft des "Apodiktischen Rechts"* (WMANT 20; Neukirchen 1965).

stinguishable from an important aspect of the treaty idea. The parallels along with the rhythmic form of the verses do not *prove* that the verses and the idea they embody are older than the Deuteronomic school — *proof* in matters of this sort is always a will-o'-the-wisp — but they point in this direction. They can hardly be treated as a Deuteronomistic invention without further ado, and this means that we cannot too quickly claim that Israel's conditioned possession of the land is a purely Deuteronomistic idea (as Perlitt does: p. 34).

Apart from details, recognition of the treaty character of the Deuteronomistic view of the connections between Israel, Yahweh, and the land helps us to realize the poignancy of the complex of theological ideas and historical situation. Here was a vassal people in the Assyrian empire who knew from the experience of daily life, not just from religious theory, what loyalty to the lord demanded and how fearful could be the consequences of disloyalty. The explanation which the Deuteronomic school offered of Israel's obligations, of its dependence on its lord, of the reasons for the threat to the people's very existence had the solidity and vividness of vital experience. Once again, accepting an added connotation of *b^e^rît* will complicate our theology, but that is the price of completeness and richness.

To conclude: one will agree with Perlitt so far as he insists that the widespread and repeated use of *b^e^rît* as an interpretative category in Old Testament theology, and particularly the use of *b^e^rît* to point up the law and obedience as conditions for being the people of Yahweh, is a later element characteristic of the Deuteronomic school. However, this does not exhaust the history of *b^e^rît* in Old Testament thought, nor does it exhaust the content of the concept. In earlier stages it is true that *b^e^rît* was just one of a number of theological concepts and not necessarily the most important. It existed without being all-pervading and all-explaining. This existence, modest though it may have been, must be taken into account. The Sinai accounts point to a ritual, mystic element in the *b^e^rît* concept that forbids merely equating it with law and obligation. 2 Sam 23,5 connects it with the royal tradition. Hos 8,3 may well make explicit use of treaty terminology. In view of this evidence Perlitt's view of the history of *b^e^rît* as a theological concept must be judged incomplete because it fails to include the pre-Deuteronomic levels.

As for the content of the concept, the Deuteronomic school's emphasis on law and obedience is important, but it does not exhaust the concept. In view of the treaty analogy and its influence on the thought of the school, this is true even of the use of *b^e^rît* in Deuteronomistic writings. Here, but even more in other strata, we have to take account of the aspects of love and loyalty, rite and mystic union. As with the history, so with the meaning of *b^e^rît*. The last word has not been said.

Covenant-relationships

Covenant[1] was a public thing. As something designed to regulate relations among men, it had to be. It was a point of reference, a reminder of obligations, and a norm to which to appeal in the face of wrongs. A thing like this will normally have a relatively fixed formula. Society establishes fixed ways of making contracts and the like so that they may be accessible to all to whom they pertain. One needs to know exactly what to do to make one validly, and what to look for in order to judge whether someone has fulfilled his obligations.[2] Further, making a covenant was a secular activity. To be sure, it was not without a religious aspect (what part of ancient life was not ?) because it involved an oath and so the gods. However, it can properly be called secular because it was directly concerned with relations among men and not with things of the gods such as the cult. It was, then, as something known from secular experience and as something with a well-defined profile that covenant came to be applied to the religious purpose of describing and explaining the relation between Israel and Yahweh.

If we wish to understand the basic meaning and especially the connotations, the " feel " of covenant, we should look for descriptions of its basic secular form. And it would be desirable to give special attention to any texts which reveal something of the formal structure which

1. " Covenant " is used here for *b^erît* although this translation (or its German equivalent, *Bund*) has been questioned for putting too much emphasis on relational ideas when *b^erît* means essentially " obligation " : See E. Kutsch, *Gesetz un Gnade. Probleme des alttestamentlichen Bundesgriffs*, ZAW 79 (1967) 18-35 ; "*Der Begriff* bryt *in vordeuteronomischer Zeit*", *Rost Festschrift*, (BZAW 105), Berlin, 1967, 133-143 ; " *Von* bryt *zu ' Bund '*, " Kerygma und Dogma 14 (1968) 159-182 ; THAT I, cols. 339-352. However, I believe that " covenant " remains the best translation and retain it here. For discussion see D. J. McCarthy, S.J., " Berît *and Covenant in the Deuteronomistic History* ", *VTSuppl.* 21. Leiden, 1972, 74-75.

2. Because it was stylized, publically known, and enforcable, covenant may properly be called a legal matter. Thus I am extending the use of " legal " beyond what G. M. Tucker allows in his demonstration that covenant was not formally a contract according to the categories of ancient law (*Covenant Forms and Contract Forms*, VT 15 (1965) 487-503). However, this is to restrict the legal to a particular aspect of law (largely that concerned with property), when, in fact, it is something much broader than this.

covenant-making as a public activity must have had. In fact, there is evidence which meets these requirements in the reports of covenant-making scattered through Genesis and the Deuteronomistic History. They give a unified picture of an activity with settled elements and procedure which are presented as understood by the actors in the process and intelligible to the authors' intended audience. And surely these were things current in the society which produced them, not peculiar to some coterie, because they appear in traditions from various parts of that society. We can supplement this picture from the passing references to covenant-making which occur in the deuteronomistic material and the prophets. However, in part because they deal *ex professo* with covenant-making and in part because they give a convincing picture of a complete and ordered activity, it is the reports which must guide our understanding of the other material. For example, a passing reference to covenant will usually ignore the negotiations which the reports show to have been a regular feature of covenant-making.

It is the purpose of this paper to examine some of these reports in detail and then see what this examination reveals about covenant in general. The first part will concentrate on the reports of covenant-making in Genesis, since I have already studied the complex and important material from the Deuteronomistic History elsewhere. [3] In the second part devoted to some of the problems about covenant which recur in recent literature we will use the results of the analysis of all the material.

I. The Reports in Genesis

As the text of Genesis now stands there are three full reports of covenant-making : *Gen.*, 21,22-34 ; 26,23-33 ; and 31,25-32,3. However, consideration of the sources behind these texts reveals that they contain elements of several more reports so that the extent of our evidence is appreciably increased. Thus, in *Gen.*, 21 we have a J form of the story, verses 25-26,28-30,32-34, and an E form, verses 22-24,27,31. [4] *Gen.*, 26,23-33 is all J, but *Gen.*, 31,25-32.3 is again composite. This latter text,

3. See *VTSuppl.* 21 (1972) 55-75.

4. The assignment to J and E follows Gunkel with the agreement of many commentators. G. von Rad, ATD 2/5 believes that there are two E traditions here. This seems less likely, but even if it were true it would leave us with two reports of covenant-making. M. Noth, *A History of Pentateuchal Traditions*, N.J., 1972, 35, n. 131, thinks that there is an E tradition glossed from *Gen.*, 26,15ff., but this does not really do justice to the completeness of the two descriptions of the covenant-making.

however, is a difficult case for source analysis, and its problems demand more extended notice.

There clearly are different parallel traditions of the covenant between Jacob and Laban, but how are they to be divided from one another, and to what sources are the various parallel accounts to be assigned ? The only clear connections within the passage are between the stone-heap (*gāl*) in 31,46 and 51-52, and the only really exclusive doublets are the meals which occur at different points in the proceedings (31,46 and 54). Beyond this the possibilities multiply. Are the three monument-signs, the stone-heap, the pillar (*maṣṣēbâ*), and the watchtower (*miṣpâ*) marks of three traditions ? Or are we to identify the pillar and the watchtower on the basis of the assonance of the Hebrew names as Gunkel suggests in his Genesis commentary ? This is plausible but not demonstrative. Or are we to take the word *miṣpâ* as a proper name for the stone-heap ? Then, what part of the report uses Elohim and what Yahweh ? Are we to keep Yahweh with the MT in verse 49, or read Elohim with the LXX ?

These are some of the more obvious alternatives which the text poses for the analyst. In themselves and especially in combination with one another and with other data they open the way to a bewildering variety of possibilities in the reconstruction of sources. [5] Discretion is surely indicated. But perhaps with care we can reach some conclusions which, though they must remain incomplete, allow us to build on something more than mere hypothesis. For this it helps to keep in mind that the problem here is not to reconstruct the historical order among the texts but simply to discern whatever different clues to the nature of covenant we can. In this line, we can at least be sure that the doublets and inconsistencies demonstrate the existence of several independent reports of the Jacob-Laban covenant. Moreover, no matter how one selects verses as belonging to sources or what sources he attributes them to, the reconstructions produce at least two similar pictures of covenant-making. There are always negotiations and the construction of a monument-sign which occasions a formulation of terms. It is unsatisfactory not

5. There is no agreement among the commentators : e.g., in the verses which principally concern us Gunkel divides 44,46,48.51-53a (J) and 45.49-50.53b-54 (E) ; Proksch 45.49-50.51b.53b-54 (J) and 44.46-48.51a.52-53a (E) ; Wellhausen 46.48a. 50a (J) and 45.51-54 (E). This is not divergence, it is contradiction ! I find Gunkel's analysis convincing, but one can hardly say that it has been demonstrated to be true. Basing an argument on a particular analysis in a case like this is to restrict oneself to hypothesis. However, it is not necessary to do this when one is not dealing with history of tradition or of sources. Here we clearly have multiple data relevant to covenant-making, and we will find that these data have a common structure and content. This evidence is independent of detailed assignment to sources.

to be able to go beyond this to a sure, simple reconstruction of sources, but it is all the more striking that amid so much obscurity and confusion a repeated pattern does occur. *Gen.*, 31,25-32,3, then, offers multiple evidence, wherever it may have come from, for a structure in reports of covenant-making. With our other Genesis texts it makes a total of at least five originally separate reports of covenant-making available to us.

In these five reports certain formal elements, means of expression, topics, and structural relations among the parts of the process, recur. To look first at this last element, we find that the larger structure of the report of covenant-making is clear and simple. Once the parties have been brought together there are negotiations. That is, some kind of give-and-take aimed at clarifying the situation is introduced. Then there is an action which is itself a sign or which at least produces a sign related to the covenant. In most instances this relation appears in the fact that the terms, which are always stated, are formulated as an explanation of the meaning of the sign. Finally, the report concludes with a notice that a covenant has been made.

This is the over-all structure. It is so organized that one can call it stylized, and the same can be said for many details within it. The negotiations involve an explicit challenge and a response. This can take the form of a question. [6] Or there can be a protest. [7] Or there can be an imperative or cohortative : " Swear, " or " Let us make a covenant ! " or the like. [8] This is functional stylization. It poses a problem, clarifies its solution, and brings out what is involved for the several parties to the covenant. It would appear that covenant-making, or at least the literary representation of covenant-making, which after all is what concerns us, followed an established procedure with a recognized syntax which covered the presentation of the negotiations as part of the whole process. This appears too in the comparative formulations used in the negotiations reported in *Gen.*, 21,23 and 26,28 : as you received good from us, so be good to us. This usage also occurs in ancient legal forms related to covenant. The treaties call for loyalty in similar terms, and the same thing recurs in royal decrees, documents from the same mold as the treaties. [9] Not only is the language of covenant-making stylized, then, but the stylization reflects firmly established legal traditions of the ancient near eastern world.

6. *Gen.*, 26,27 ; 31,26-44 where two sources are combined, each of which makes extensive use of questions.

7. *Gen.*, 21,25. Note the technical legal expression *hôkîah.*

8. *Gen.*, 21,23 ; 26,28 ; 31,44.

9. For example, from outside Israel see A. GOETZE, *Kizzuwatna*, New Haven, 1939, 27-30 : a royal decree establishing a priesthood and tying it to the king.

Another regular feature connected with the negotiations reported in our texts is the role of the sign. In 21,28 (J) the gift of some ewes occasions an explanation in which the terms of the covenant are given an exact formulation. In *Gen.*, 31 we have two and perhaps three signs in the stone-heap, the pillar, and the watchtower, which may or may not have been originally identified with one of the other signs. In any event, the important thing here is that the signs receive an explanation which constitutes the formal statement of the terms of the covenant : in one case, a guarantee of the rights of Laban's daughters as Jacob's wives, in the other, a border guarantee. This seems to establish the role of a visible sign in covenant-making. It helps us to interpret less clear cases. In *Gen.*, 21.27 (E) there is a gift of cattle, the function of which is not explained. In the light of the other examples surely this feature of the report must be interpreted as a relic of a functional sign in the story of the covenant. If a sign was thus normal in covenant-making as reported in Genesis, this would explain the occurence of a formal meal in several of our texts : 26,30 ; 31,46 ; and 31,54. Like the gift the meal was a recognized sign of covenant, and we may see the meals in the Genesis reports as elements integral to the covenant-making process. [10]

The last element in the reports of covenant-making proper is the final notice that " they made a covenant " or that " he/they swore " [11]. This obviously has a formal function. It concludes the report, and after it the action goes on to other things. In itself it serves to affirm and record the fact that a covenant has been completed. It sums up the result of the action. It seems doubtful that in addition to this it is intended to present a separate action or at least a separate element in the total action. It is not as though something in addition to the negotiations, the sign and the rest were required. Thus, the J section of *Gen.*, 21 clearly implies that the setting apart of the gift-sign settles things. The gift lambs are themselves the surety that Abraham has the right to the well, and their acceptance is Abimelek's acknowledgment of this right. There is no need for an added ceremony, and the concluding notice stands as a summary for the whole. Now, as we have seen, all the reports have some kind of sign, a material thing or an action. That is, they contain an element strictly parallel to the functional sign in 21,27-30. In this text this is what constitutes the covenant, and the concluding notice is a formal element. One would assume the same in the parallel

10. On the function of gifts etc. in ancient near eastern law dealing with agreements see M. WEINFELD, *Deuteronomy and the Deuteronomic History*. Oxford, 1972, 102 (with references). On the covenant meal see D. J. McCARTHY, S.J., *Three Covenants in Genesis*, CBQ, 26 (1964) 184-185 ; W. McCREE, *The Covenant Meal in the OT*, JBL 45 (1926), 120-128.

11. *Gen.*, 21,27 (E) ; 21,32 (J) ; 26,31 ; 31,53b.

cases. The notice of covenant-making, then, would be a statement affirming the validity of the transaction, a usage not without its parallels.[12]

Finally, some notes about vocabulary. The notices of covenant-making alternate *krt bᵉrît* and *nšbʿ*. Nor is the equivalence of *krt bᵉrît* and taking an oath merely a matter of parallels in different texts which might reflect usage in different traditions or the like rather than real synonyms. In both *Gen.*, 26,28-31 and 31,44-53 a proposal to *krt bᵉrît* is concluded by the statement that an *oath* was taken. [13] That is, an explicit demand for " cutting a covenant " is satisfied by an oath. However, oath and covenant are not to be treated as simply identical. In *Gen.*, 26,28 we have " oath " (*'ālâ*) and *bᵉrît* used together to describe the thing that Abimelek seeks from Isaac. This is a hendiadys which is paralleled in other ancient near eastern languages. " Oath and tie " together designate a treaty by combining its two chief features. They are different features of the whole, even though now one, now the other can stand for the whole or for one another (cf. *Deut.*, 29,12-27 for examples), and they should not simply be identified. Covenant implies oath ; it is not simply an oath. [14]

There is a last feature of these reports of covenant-making which needs attention from a formal point of view. They are among other things name etiologies. They are not this in the sense of being stories made up to explain a name. The stories are too complete and too important and too independent of any particular name for that. The naming seems rather a mnemonic device for the sake of the story rather than the story's being for the sake of the name. One is reminded of the possibility that monuments, shrines and material " witnesses, " may have been used to recall important events like significant covenants involving a clan or tribe. [15] In any case, the naming element does tie the covenants in two of our reports to a shrine important in the patriarchal traditions. Nor is this connection peculiar to the texts which involve monuments. There are other links in these reports between covenant-making and holy places. *Gen.*, 21 ends with a notice of Abraham's stay at Beersheba centered on the planting of a (sacred) tree and the naming of the place *yahweh 'ēl 'ôlām*. In *Gen.*, 26 the covenant report is preceded by a notice of Isaac's stay at Beersheba. This notice turns about a theophany, a

12. Note the function of the affirmation in sacrificial law : G. VON RAD, *Old Testament Theology* I, New York, 1962, 260-262.

13. This, of course, may be true only of the final redacted text, depending on how one assigns 31,44 and 53b to sources, but it remains true that the combination stands in the text.

14. See H. BRICHTO, *The Problem of " Curse " in the Hebrew Bible.* (JBL Monograph 13), Philadelphia, 1963, 30-31 ; G. M. TUCKER, VT 15 (1965) 487-503.

15. See D. J. MCCARTHY, S.J., *CBQ* 26 (1964) 186, with references to Albright and Vincent.

shrine foundation, and a naming. In *Gen.*, 32 the E narrative continues from chapter 31 with a "theophany" (actually, *mal'aekê 'ĕlohîm* are involved, but formally this is a theophany), and a naming. This is not placed at the same locality where the covenant was made as is done in the other examples, but nevertheless both in E and in our final text it constitutes the immediate literary context of the covenant-making. It seems, then, that the tendency was to associate the covenant reports with sacral places and events. Why ? For one thing, there is the fact that the priests were concerned with traditional law, necessarily so in an undifferentiated society. [16] This probably was especially true in the case of covenant law because covenant, made by oath and under divine protection, involved the divine. A connection with sacred places, then, is natural. And this too connects with the larger near eastern tradition for it is well known that the treaty documents were kept in sanctuaries where, in fact, treaties may often have been made. [17]

The formal characteristics of the reports of covenant-making reveal a number of things. Their uniformity and the precision of their language confirm the hypothesis that covenant-making, a public activity, would conform to a settled pattern. This reflects a setting in society, a legal tradition which made it clear that a covenant obligation had been created by dictating a procedure suited to the purpose and known to be such. There are, in fact, explicit ties to such a tradition. The use of a sign, the comparative formulation of terms, the hendiadys "oath and tie", and the association with a sacred place, are all elements paralleled in ancient legal tradition, specifically that which appears most often in the treaties. This is not to claim that our texts are formally treaties, but merely to note the fact that they belong to a tradition which came to expression in one way in the covenants and in an analogous way in the treaties. Making a covenant was a complex thing rooted in a firm setting. The determination of the whole significance of covenant must take into account the connotations which all this gives the word.

This should have something to say to the problems which are raised in contemporary discussions of covenant. One thing leaps to the eye. In our texts covenant-making is always tied to negotiations. This seems

---

16. See the traditions of priestly responsibility for the Torah and especially *Deut.*, 17,8-13 where even the "secularizing" deuteronomist allots an important judicial role to the priests.

17. This may have been more than mere custom and convenience of storage. Was there some feeling that there was an intrinsic connection between certain covenants and the numinous ? This would appear in the desire to share the blessings of the divinely favored person, the succesful party, be he patriarch or Great King. For this desire see *Gen.*, 21,22 and 31,42 (E) and 26,28 (J) (see on this G. von Rad, ATD 2/5 at *Gen.*, 21,22) and *I Sam.*, 20,15 (Jonathan and David) and *2 Sam.*, 3.18 and 52 (David and Israel).

to rule out any idea that covenant is one-sided in the sense that it is simply imposed by one party without any consideration of the other. The point of the negotiations is to arrive at some kind of agreement, something acceptable in some way to both parties. Of course, negotiations arrive at a compromise, something not completely the wish of either party, but it is still something acceptable relative to other possibilities. Indeed, even when a report of negotiations is a pure formality, when there is not real give and take, it is significant that the formality is required. It is felt that something of the sort is necessarily tied to covenant.

Another striking thing is the way all the negotiations reported presuppose a relationship which already exists. Thus, the negotiations concern *ḥesed* (21,23) and *šalôm* (26,29). These are relational things, and they already exist between the parties in fact. The problem is to define them and to assure their continuation. This is emphasized by the use of comparatives in speaking of these things. Abimelek wants *ḥesed* and *šalôm* to obtain from the patriarch to himself just as they already obtain from him to the patriarch. Clearly the dealings take place in a context of relationships which already exist. The same thing is true in other cases, though they are expressed differently. Abraham asserts that he has rights to the well at Beersheba which Abimelek is already bound to respect, and Abimelek accepts this existing fact. Again, the negotiations in *Gen.*, 31 seek recognition of rights that already exist and are to be respected, rights of marriage, of fatherhood, of property. The point is not to create a connection but to define and confirm one.

And what of the content of the terms at which the negotiations arrive ? Do they affect only one party ? Are they unilateral, or can they be bilateral ? In some cases they are clearly unilateral. Abimelek is to respect Abraham's rights to the well at Beersheba without a return being demanded from Abraham, and Jacob's power over his wives, Laban's daughters, is restricted without his receiving anything explicit in return. Other examples are not really so clear. Abraham is asked to wear *ḥesed* and Isaac *šalôm* to Abimelek. Abimelek makes no explicit commitment. The direct object of the covenants, then, seems to be to tie one party to the other without a return. But this is hardly the whole story. There is surely an obligation on the second party, though this is implied in the situation, not stated. The patriarchs are to treat Abimelek as he them. This comparative formulation surely means that the patriarchal obligations were in fact conditional. If Abimelek's good conduct should cease, the basis of their obligation would fail. This means that the obligation here is really mutual. The last example, the border pact between Jacob and Laban, is explicitly bilateral in its terms. So far as our examples go, then, a covenant may be unilateral or bilateral. Whether it is one or the other is not determined by the simple fact that there is a covenant but by the particular nature of a given covenant. However, the more or less hidden mutuality in two of our examples emphasizes a further point. One must always consider the social context. Covenant was made within a well-defined framework of social usage, and this means that some things did not need to be made explicit. The implications of things like relational expressions and comparative formulations must be remembered. But there is especially the fact that the whole process of setting up a covenant took place within the framework of established relationships. Though the concern may be to emphasize the role of one only of the parties to the covenant so that his obligations are brought to the fore, this is always against the background of the total, multi-sided relationship which is not denied nor abrogated.

Another question often asked about covenant concerns the agent who makes a covenant. Who is represented as the author of a covenant ? Is it the work of one party imposed on or accepted for another ? This question is commonly asked in terms of inferior and superior. Can any party, stronger or weaker, greater or less, take the first steps ? In these Genesis texts it is not easy to decide who is thought of as the superior party, though it seems to me clear enough that the tradition would always have maintained the superiority of the patriarch. [18] But in regard to one aspect of agency, namely the question : who initiates covenant-making as a whole, this need not be determined since any party can make the beginning. In 21,22 (E) Abimelek opens the proceedings, but in the J parallel, 21,25, Abraham does so. In 26,26 Abimelek makes the first move, though Isaac is actually represented as speaking first. In 31,26 Laban seeks out Jacob as Abimelek had Isaac, but then he goes on to speak first as well. Thus we need not decide whether the patriarch or his partner is held to be the superior. The tradition allows either party to begin things. It is indifferent who begins covenant-making, and this observation corresponds to the indications of the reports of covenant-making in the Deuteronomistic History. [19]

But there is another way in which one may ask about the agent in covenant-making. Perhaps anyone can ask for a covenant. But who is actually said to make a covenant when all is said and done ? In fact, in three of the four notices of covenant-making which occur in our Genesis reports both parties are said to " cut " the covenant or to swear. What is notable here is the lack of correlation between this fact and the direction of apparent obligation. That is, the terms may seem unilateral, binding only Abimelek or Abraham or Isaac, as the case may be, but still the making of the covenant is said to depend on both. Both are responsible for the covenant. In such circumstances one cannot speack of a merely

18. See D. J. McCarthy, S.J., CBQ 26 (1964) 183-184.
19. VTSuppl. 21 (1972) 73-74.

unilateral covenant simply because the terms are one-sided. As long as the covenant is made by both parties it depends on the will of each. It is not imposed but accepted. Of course, this fact may simply confirm our earlier observation that the covenants involved are really bilateral even though the terms are apparently unilateral. The notice of covenant-making may simply make explicit the reality behind the situation, the responsibility of all parties.

However, this exactness in the usage is not confirmed by the last example. The pact between Jacob and Laban is, of course, a complicated literary problem. Given the uncertainty about source divisions, it is hazardous to affirm too strongly what terms were originally tied to the notice that Jacob took an oath (31,53b) which serves as the notice of covenant-making. I am inclined to think that this is to be coupled with the unilateral marriage pact in verse 50 and assigned to E. However, this is subject to argument, and for present purposes it is not necessary to insist on it. The point is that in the final redacted text this notice is coupled with a summons to a mutual covenant-making action (31,44: " Let *us* make a covenant ") and with bilateral terms in verses 51-52. That is to say, it was perfectly possible for the compiler to describe a covenant involving two-sided obligations as the work of only one of the parties. He may have done this for reasons not directly connected with the concept of covenant, e.g., as many commentators suggest, to magnify Jacob's role. The point is that he could do this without its being too incongruous in a procedure which had a well-established contour. No doubt it was easier to do this because this concluding notice is largely a formal element. Perhaps too the urge to retain the maximum from the sources helped override formal exactness. In any event, the ability to do this at all points to a certain freedom in covenant-making (or in describing it, which for us who must deal only with the descriptions comes to the same thing) which warns us against being too apodictic in asserting what covenant could and could not involve. And we will find that this freedom exists in the deuteronomistic material as well.

II. Summary

It may be helpful to draw together some central points which we have discovered about covenant-making. At the same time I shall note how these relate to the results of the study of the Deuteronomistic History. [20] First some elements characteristically associated with it will be listed.

20. Detailed summaries of these results will be found in VTSuppl. 21 (1972) 71-73, II.A-F.

1. Negotiations

Challenge and response, a give and take involving both sides, is part of all the covenant-making reported in Genesis. This is true of all the reports in the Deuteronomistic History but one. [21] We may conclude that mutual activity aimed at producing some meeting of minds was an ordinary part of the covenant-making process.

2. Terms

A. *Formulation of terms*

The Genesis reports all show the negotiations arriving at a precise formulation of terms. This is not unexpected in an established legal procedure. In view of this, it is interesting that the deuteronomistic material sometimes leaves the terms without explicit definition. They are left to be understood from the negotiations or the social context. One might imagine at first that the deuteronomistic reports reflect less concern with legal niceties. However, notice the matter of these reports. They deal with vassal subjection, relations between a hero and his *comitatus*, or the covenant between the king and the people. These are situations where social usage provides a definition of the relationship so fixed and clear that it need not be expressed in full in a report of the transaction. Of course, this conforms to the evidence for the force of social usage already found in Genesis.

B. *Unilateral or bilateral ?*

In Genesis the explicit terms are more often unilateral. Once in the sources (31,51) they are bilateral. In two of the texts as they now stand the combination of the sources has turned apparently unilateral covenants into explicitly bilateral ones. Clearly covenant in itself allows either unilateral or bilateral terms. This is evident when we add the data from

21. The force of social usage and the danger of ignoring it when discussing covenant may be illustrated from another text outside the reports of covenant-making. *Deut.*, 7,2 which forbids making covenant with Canaanites (*lo'-tikrot lahem b^e^rît*). This has been taken to mean "grant (i.e., unilaterally) no covenant." However, the subject matter of the covenant in question is connubium (an important matter often dealt with along recognized lines in ancient pacts ; cf. C. H. W. Brekelmans OTS 10 (1954) 223), and this was no one-sided thing. It implied negotiations and mutual concessions as in *Gen.*, 34 (and note the implications of mutual influence even in *Deut.*, 7,3-4). We must not forget a recognized context like this simply because it is not mentioned in a passing allusion to covenant made for purposes other than describing a covenant.

the deuteronomistic texts, for there the terms are the opposite of the apparent terms of the Genesis examples : normally bilateral.

3. Relationships

Covenant-making occurs when a relationship already exists. The point is to define and affirm the connection. This is the case in all the examples in Genesis ; it is usually so in the deuteronomistic examples as well.

4. Social usage

The fact of relationship is based on accepted usage. For example, good treatment of a specific kind calls for a specific kind of return. The force of social usage is even clearer in the Deuteronomistic History. Some aspects of covenant relationships were so well known that they could be assumed without needing explicit statement (see 2. A above).

5. Variety of agent

In Genesis the act of making the covenant is usually attributed to both parties. In the Deuteronomistic History there is no uniformity and there are no apparent rules. The fact of making a covenant is regularly affirmed, but this is attributed now to one, then to the several parties to the covenant without apparent concern for other circumstances.

In conclusion we may note that this has a good deal to say to the problems which are raised in contemporary discussions of covenant. It is fair to say that these center on the nature and direction of the covenant relationship. It is a one-sided thing, or is it mutual ? Or, even if it should be indifferently unilateral or bilateral in itself, can it be one or the other at the will of one of the parties to covenant-making, and ideally should it be so ? Or should both parties be concerned ? Or should we ask about relationship at all ? Does our translation, " covenant " (or *alliance* or *Bund*), mislead us by implying something of agreement, of mutuality, while *b^e^rît* actually looks in another direction ? Then there are questions, perhaps less exercised but nonetheless real. Is *b^e^rît* properly the action which establishes a lasting relation and not the relation ? Or is *b^e^rît* merely more or less a synonym for " oath ? " [22] Such are the

22. For the discussion of these matters see E. Kutsch cited in n. 1 on the translation of *b^e^rît* ; J. Begrich, *Berit. Ein Beitrag zur Erfassung einer alttestamentlichen Denkform*, ZAW 60 (1944) 1-11, on covenant as grant ; A. Jepsen, *Berith. Ein Beitrag sur Theologie der Exilzeit, Rudolph Festschrift*, Tübingen, 1961, 161-179, on

questions. They approach covenant from the point of view of the act, the circumstances and the effect of the act, and the agent. We can respond according to these categories.

Covenant (*b^erît*) can indeed be equated with the act of taking an oath, but it denotes and connotes a good deal more than merely taking an oath. As a totality involving an action, a thing done or made, it regularly implicates all the parties involved in it. This is clear in the negotiations which aim at defining some aspect of a relationship or relationships which include all the parties and which already exist. That is, it does not create a connection but presupposes one. Thus it is understood only as something between parties, as part of a complex relation which involves all. This can usually be seen in the terms which no matter how expressed really implicate all parties. Covenant is made within a framework of relations which it fixes in a recognized form. Moreover, however terms may be phrased, the several parties are said to have "made (cut) a covenant" or to have "sworn," that is, covenant depends on the wills of all involved. Again, this is confirmed in the negotiations : anyone may begin this first step toward covenant, but the others must respond.

Covenant-making, then, is a complex action, and so is its result. As an amalgam of negotiations, of relationships specified, of signs relating to all parties, covenant cannot be reduced to any one element in the whole nor to any aspect of its total meaning, however important that aspect may be in a given case. It is not simply the act, nor the obligation on one party which results from the act, nor anything else so simple. One will expect it to involve all parties both as a relationship and as an act. It cannot usually come about unless all join in making it, and it means nothing unless all are somehow involved in it, even tied by it. No doubt this can be changed in a particular case, but this is its basic character, and it is doubtful whether these connotations are usually lost in any context or even whether they can be lost completely in a very special context.

Via della Pilotta 25
Roma 00187 (Italie)

D. J. McCarthy

covenant as act ; N. Lohfink, *Die Landesverheissung als Eid*, (Stuttgarter Bibelstudien 28.) Stuttgart, 1967, on covenant as oath.

ANIMADVERSIONES

Ebla, ὅρκια τέμνειν, *ṭb*, *šlm*: Addenda to *Treaty and Covenant*²

In a review of material pertaining to any major biblical question such as that attempted in the revised and enlarged edition of *Treaty and Covenant* (¹) lacunae are inevitable. Given the amount of material, an exhaustive survey is scarcely possible, and it would seem nugatory to try to fill the lacunae with a never-ending series of addenda. However, primary evidence from the ancient texts as opposed to secondary literature seems to have a special importance which justifies the attempt to rectify omissions. Hence this article.

*Treaty and Covenant*² 34 calls attention to "an agreement with a foreign ruler" from Ebla which uses language and concepts pertinent to the treaty tradition (²). To this the text of a letter from the same place should be added. It too uses the language and concepts of the treaties so that it is worth citing for its own sake. In addition a full transcription may be of interest as giving an idea of the actual state of the language and orthography in these third millenium B.C. Ebla tablets (³). The text is composed in five columns with a single word in each line of the columns.

(I, 1) *en–ma* (2) *ì–bù–bu*$_6$ (3) agrig (4) é (5) en (6) *lì–na* (7) sukkal.du$_8$ (8) *an–tá* (9) šeš (10) *ù* (II, 1) *an–na* (2) šeš (3) lú.šeš (4) *mi–ni–ma* (5)

(¹) D. J. McCarthy, *Treaty and Covenant: A Study in Form in the Ancient Oriental Documents and in the Old Testament.* New edition completely rewritten. (AnBib 21A; Rome ²1978).

(²) From the preliminary report by the epigrapher of the Ebla expedition, G. Pettinato, "The Royal Archives of Tell-Mardikh-Ebla", *BA* 39 (1976) 48.

(³) Cf. G. Pettinato, "Gli archivi reali de Tell Mardikh-Ebla", *RBibIt* 25 (1977) 238-242, with transcription, translation and discussion of the language and setting. Pettinato's fuller treatment will appear in *Archives archéologiques arabes syriennes* (Damascus). For a photograph of the tablet and an English version see *1978 Nature/Science Annual* (Time/Life Books, Alexandria, Va.) "The Lost Empire of Ebla", 40.

Conventions used in the transcription are: *italic* for Eblaite written in clear, lower case for Sumerograms whose value in the Ebla syllabary is established, upper case for Sumerograms not so fully established (the Sumerograms, of course, were *read* not as Sumerian but in their Semitic equivalent: e.g., "en" was read *maliku*, "king").

al.du$_{11}$.ga (6) *ṣi* (7) ka (8) *an–na* (9) in.na–sum (10) *ù* (III, 1) *an–tá* (2) al.du$_{11}$.ga (3) *ṣi* (4) ì.na.sum (5) BAR^{IL}. ŠA$_{6}$ (6) ḫi.mu.túm (7) *an–tá* (8) šeš (9) *ù* (10) *an–na* (11) šeš (IV, 1) 10^{giš}. EŠ (2) 2^{giš} ašud.EŠ (3) *ī–bù–bu*$_{6}$ (4) in.na.sum (5) sukkal.du$_{8}$ (6) *ir–kab–da–mu* (7) en (8) *eb–la*^{ki} (9) šeš (10) ZI.ZI (V, 1) en (2) *ḫa–ma–zi–im* (3) ZI.ZI (4) en (5) *ḫa–ma–zi–im* (6) šeš (7) *ir–kab–da–mu* (8) en (VI, 1) *eb–la*^{ki} (2) *ù* (3) *en–ma* (4) *ti–ra–il* (5) dub.šar (6) [*i*]*k–tub* (7) *lí–na* (8) sukkal.du$_{8}$ (9) ⟨ZI.ZI⟩ (Verso, I, 1) ì.na.sum.

(I,1) Greetings ([4]) (2) from Ibubu, (3) the superintendent (4) of the palace (5) of the king ([5]) (6) to (7) the ambassador: (8) "Thou (9) art (my/our) brother, (10) and (II, 1) I am (2) (thy) brother, (3) a man and a brother(?). (4) Whatever (5) wish (6) comes forth (7) from (thy) mouth (8) I (9) shall grant, (10) and (III, 1) thou (4) shalt grant (2) a wish (3) coming forth (from my mouth). (6) Send (5) soldiers(?)/equids(?)! (7) Thou art (8) (my/our) brother (9) and (10) I (11) am (thy) brother. (IV, 1) Ten pieces of woodwork (2) (and) two wooden ornaments (3) Ibubu (4) grants (5) the ambassador. (6) Irkab-Damu, (7) king (8) of Ebla (9) is a brother (10) to ZIZI ([6]) (V, 1) king (2) of Hamazi (3) (and) ZIZI, (4) king (5) of Hamazi (6) is a brother (7) of Irkab-Damu, (8) king (VI, 1) of Ebla. (2) And (3) these greetings (4) Tirail (5) the scribe (6) has written down (7) (and) to (8) the ambassador (9) ⟨of ZIZI⟩ (Verso, I, 1) given (them).

This is treaty language: the partners are "brothers", aid (men or animals) is requested, and a counter-payment for it is made. This is the very voice of Asa of Judah making a treaty with Damascus (1 Kgs 15,18-19) or Ahaz with Assyria (2 Kgs 16,7-9) two millenia later. The legal traditions of Coelo-Syria show a remarkable continuity.

The letter also shows subordinates explicitly making or administering a treaty. This must have been the case in most or all treaty activity. Personal diplomacy among heads of state themselves had hardly yet made its appearance in those days of difficult and dangerous travel. However, the treaties and the references to them which have come into our hands until now retain the convention that the ambassadors and ministers involved were mere mouthpieces of the kings, and the treaty is presented as the king's own word. Not so in this Ebla letter: it shows the actual working-out of diplomatic matters between Syrian Ebla and a faraway kingdom of Kurdistan by subordinates. An assumption about the way the actual administration of treaties worked is explicitly confirmed by a text which also shows a developed treaty tradition well back in the third millenium B.C.

([4]) Following the suggestion of my colleague, Mitchell Dahood, that *enma* is *en*, "grace, blessing" (cf. Hebrew *ḥēn* and its Semitic parallels) with enclitic *–ma* in a construct chain with Ibubu, forming a stylized letter opening such as is found at Ugarit. This avoids reading an odd form of the Akkadian style *umma*, "thus says".

([5]) In Eblaite the Sumerogram en is read *maliku*, "king", and not *bel*(*bāʿāl*), "lord", as in Akkadian.

([6]) ZIZI: the name is uncertain. It could be a Sumerogram or a non-Semitic personal name spelled out.

A second point concerns the parallels between ancient near eastern usage and the Classical tradition in the matter of treaties (cf. *Treaty and Covenant*², 105 with notes 62 and 63). References here should be expanded. In the Maccabean era Hellenistic society continued to use the Greek equivalents of technical vocabulary from the older Semitic and Hittite tradition: "peace, friendship, brotherhood, mutual defensive agreement" (εἰρήνη, φιλία, ἀδελφότης, συμμαχία) (⁷). Other striking examples come from all over the Classical world: "friendship oath" (ὅρκοι καὶ φιλίαι), "friendship and peace" (φιλία καὶ εἰρήνη), "friendship and mutual defense" (φιλία καὶ συμμαχία), and the like (⁸). This common use of hendiadys is noteworthy because it is typical of the ancient near eastern vocabulary too. Again, Greeks and Romans "entered into a pact" (εἰσέλθειν εἰς σπονδάς, *in amicitiam venire*): compare the Akkadian *ina adē erēbu* (⁹).

However, the Greek ὅρκια τέμνειν and Latin *foedus ferire/icere*, exact parallels of the Semitic expressions where "'cutting' a pact" means "making a pact" (cf. *Treaty and Covenant*², 91 with notes 16-18 and page 105), are surely the most important of these parallels. So odd an idiom could hardly arise independently in such diverse languages. It is the strongest evidence for a common origin. Moreover, if we could penetrate its meaning adequately, it would surely reveal more about the psychology behind treaty making and the force of the bond made. All the more valuable, then, material related to the usage, and we can add to that mentioned in *Treaty and Covenant*², 91-96, 105, the passage of Plato emphasizing the solemnity of the final election of leaders for the ideal state described in the *Laws*. The electors are to pass between the severed parts of animals as evidence of their sincerity (¹⁰). This is a very solemn form of oath recognized in Greek culture (cf. Liddell and Scott *sub verbo* τόμιος). It was surely thought of as an acted out curse. In view of the Greek attitude toward such bloody business it can have meant nothing

(⁷) A. PENNA, "διαθήκη nei Libri dei Maccabei", *Bib* 46 (1965) 149-180.

(⁸) Cf. H. H. SCHMITT, *Die Staatsverträge des Altertums III: Die Verträge der griechisch-römischen Welt von 338 bis 200 vor Christus*. General editor, H. BENGSTON (Munich 1969) indices.

(⁹) For a fuller discussion of Greek and Latin parallels to ancient near eastern treaty language see M. WEINFELD, "Covenant Terminology in the Ancient Near East and Its Influence in the West", *JAOS* 93 (1973) 190-199 (already cited in *Treaty and Covenant*², 105 note 63) and "Bond and Grace—Covenantal Expressions in the Bible and the Ancient World—A Common Heritage", *Lěšonénu* 36 (1971) 85-105 (with unpaged English summary). Weinfeld's studies are most useful, but his assumption that the ancient near eastern vocabulary "*penetrated* the Greek political milieu" and was "*adopted* by the Romans" (italics mine), i.e., that the vocabulary and practices developed mostly in Asia and spread thence through the Mediterranean world is by no means a sure explanation of the phenomenon of community. This may be another example of the common heritage behind certain aspects of life in the northeastern and eastern Mediterranean world, as in vocabulary (*bāmâ*—βωμός, Aramaic *ktn*—χιτών); sacrificial usages, etc.

(¹⁰) *Laws* 753d: διὰ τομίων πορευόμενος.

but the devotion of a possible perjurer to the powers of darkness ([11]). Of course, Plato is not dealing with treaty-making, but the fact that so sophisticated a writer could feel the power of the rite helps us to understand how such a vivid conditional self-curse could be effective in ancient treaty making.

A third point: there is much evidence to show that "good(ness)" (Akkadian *ṭūbtu, ṭābūtu*; Aramaic *ṭbt'*; Hebrew *ṭôbâ, ṭôb*) was a technical word for "proper, useful relationship; friendship," in treaty and covenant contexts. For the extra-biblical evidence the basic article is W. L. MORAN, "A Note on the Treaty Terminology of the Sefire Stelas" ([12]). For the Hebrew itself there are a number of references to be added to those in *Treaty and Covenant*² 171 note 28. A. Malamat seems to have been earliest in the field ([13]). In addition to 1 Kgs 12,7 he cites 2 Sm 7,28: *ṭôbâ* refers to Nathan's promise, already called a covenant (*bᵉrît*) in an ancient poem (2 Sm 23,5); 2 Sm 3,19: Abner urges *kôl–'ăšer–ṭôb bᵉ'ênê yiśrā'ēl* on David, where the fixed phrase (syntagma), *ṭôb bᵉ'ênê*, "choices, decisions," may have been selected in place of an equivalent so that the covenantal connotation of *ṭob* (here the terms) might sound early though the *bᵉrit* as such is reported only in 2 Sm 5,3; and 2 Chron 24,16: Jehoiada's *ṭobâ* may well be his fidelity to his obligations under his *Königsvertrag*. He also cites 2 Kgs 25,28 and Jr 33,9, though these passages may have another interpretation. In the first Evil-merodach speaks *ṭōbôt* to Jehoiachin: this might signify some sort of vassal treaty, but in fact there is nothing said about Evilmerodach's restoring Jehoiachin to actual rulership, and the phrase may simply denote "speak kindly" or the like as part of the general good treatment shown the dethroned king. The passage from Jeremiah could indeed refer to a restored divine covenant, but it might mean simply a renewal of favor and fulfilment of promises in general.

Shortly thereafter D. R. Hillers called attention to Dt 23,7, where *ṭôbâ*(standing parallel to *šālôm*) between Israel and Moab or Edom is forbidden, certainly an hendiadys for the *bᵉrît* which general law prohibits between Israel and the natives of the promised land (cf. Dt 7,2; Ex 34,12), and to 2 Sam 2,6, where David surely uses *ṭôbâ* to hint at a political alliance with Jabesh-Gilead ([14]).

In 1971 M. Weinfeld returned to 1 Kgs 12,7 and explained the *dᵉbārîm ṭôbîm* there as referring to the freedoms given the people by royal grant which he equates with covenant ([15]). However this equation

([11]) Blood was tied to death and malediction in Greek ritual: cf. D. J. MCCARTHY, "Further Notes on the Symbolism of Blood and Sacrifice", *JBL* 92 (1973) 208-209, and *IDBSuppl.* 115.

([12]) *JNES* 22 (1962-63) 173-176.

([13]) "Organs of Statecraft in the Israelite Monarchy", *BA Reader* 3 (Garden City, N.Y. 1970) 196-197 (= *BA* 28 [1965] 34-64, but already delivered as a conference in 1963).

([14]) "A Note on Some Treaty Terminology in the Old Testament", *BASOR* 176 (1964) 46-47.

([15]) "King-People Relationship in the Light of 1 Kgs 12", *Lĕšonénu* 36 (1971) 1-13 (with unpaged English summary); for the covenant and

is questionable: the grant was a decree valid in se (or at least if properly witnessed by human testimony), the covenant or treaty a decree *with a difference.* It had divine witnesses called into the matter by the oath which was the response to the decree which validated it and was recorded in it (cf. *Treaty and Covenant*², 38-39, 73, 119). Formally and conceptually the two things were very different, though as far as it goes the grant has a structure like that of the treaty and it is that of the royal decree. The trouble is that this does not go far enough: the oath and its consequences turn the treaty or covenant into something very different. Rather 1 Kgs 12,7, if it is covenantal, must refer to the covenant between king and people, the *Königsvertrag,* as Malamat had pointed out in his original work. Weinfeld would also add 1 Sm 25,30 where it is indeed possible that *haṭṭōbâ* does refer to the oath or covenant made by the LORD for David but only mentioned specifically in later passages (2 Sm 3,9.18). Finally, he points to Jr 33,14, but like 33,9 the passage need refer nothing more specific that general promises of salvation.

In the prophets, *ṭôb* in Hos 8,3 would seem to refer to covenant (16). It is in a context which parallels the word with *bᵉrît* as well as *tôrâ* (covenant obligations) and which also uses the covenant word *yd'*, "recognize (a lord or vassal": cf. *Treaty and Covenant*² 167, note 22). *ṭôb* in Hos 3,5 may also be tied to covenant: it is connected here with language used of covenant in other passages (17), and the return spoken of is parallel to the renewed relationship described in Hos 2 (marriage imagery which might imply a covenant; cf. *bᵉrît* for the marriage relation in Mal 2,14).

Finally, there is the root *šlm* which furnishes important elements for the treaty vocabulary in different languages. For these the references in *Treaty and Covenant*² 35, note 15, and 289, note 31, concerned mostly with Mari as they are, should be augmented. *šulmu* is used for "treaty" (e.g., in the phrase *šulmu epēšu,* "make a treaty") in chronicles and in the Amarna letters, and *sulummû* is a characteristic treaty word throughout the tradition in Mesopotamia (18), while for the Hittites the word

---

grant see M. WEINFELD, "The Covenant by Grant in the Old Testament and in the Ancient Near East", *JAOS* 90 (1970) 184-203; ibid. 92 (1972) 168-169. Cf. also "Bond and Grace" (above, n. 9).

(16). D. J. MCCARTHY, "*bᵉrît* in Old Testament History and Theology", *Bib* 53 (1972) 114; also M. FOX, "*ṭôb* as Covenantal Terminology", *BASOR* 209 (1973) 44.

(17) FOX, "*ṭôb*" 43; Fox also notices Jr 33,9, already discussed above, and Jr 12,6. This latter is a problem: some of the language in the context might be associated with covenant, but the text seems to be dealing with a contract, a very different matter (cf. *Treaty and Covenant*² 119 with note 42).

(18) Cf. MORAN, "Treaty Terminology", *JNES* 22, 174, and R. FRANKENA, "The Vassal Treaties of Esarhaddon and the Dating of Deuteronomy", *OTS* 14 (1965) 135-136. H. HUFFMON also treated Mari and the Bible in a paper, "*Salîmu, s/šalāmu* and *šālôm*: An Investigation of Treaty Terminology," given at the meeting of the American Oriental Society, New Haven, Conn., March 21, 1967, noting that *salêmum* and *šālôm* respectively can be used to refer to the resolution of political and

meant at once *paix* and *traité* (19). The verbal form occurs in Hatti too: Goetze (*ANET* 203) quite properly renders *ki šālmuma šalīm* "as he was bound by treaty, he remained bound by treaty," for the context concerns serious national obligations and not mere personal goodwill. Again, at Ugarit on the Levantine littoral we have in Akkadian *u itti šalmiya lū šalmāta*, "you are to be the ally of my ally," (20) and in the language of Ugarit itself *'mn šp[š.mlk.rb]/ b'lh šlm*, "he remained an ally of the Su[n, his lord]" (21). That is to say, the entire treaty tradition, Akkadian, Hittite, Syrian, used elements from the root *šlm* to express central aspects of the treaty relationship: "union, amity," and in the concrete "ally, comrade".

Thus, when the Shechemites think they have made an agreement guaranteeing coexistence, connubium, and trading privileges (Gn 34,9-10.16), the very stuff of so many treaties, with the sons of Jacob and then say "these men are our allies (*šᵉlēmîm*)," they use an age-old affirmation effecting a treaty, making another power ally and partner. Then, the noun *šālôm* is clearly connected with treaties in Hebrew: cf. 1 Kgs 5,22, where *šālom* with Tyre is cemented by Solomon's treaty (*bᵉrît*), or Dt 23,7, where *sᵉlōmām wᵉṭōbātām* — note the characteristic hendiadys (22) — form the equivalent of *bᵉrît* in Dt 7,2, or Ps 55,21 speaking of

---

other problems by pact. Particularly striking was his observation that favor encountering a proper disposition can produce such a state: cf. 1 Chron 12,18, where a disposition to alliance (*bā' bᵉšālôm*) is met with favor (*yihyeh lî 'ălēkem lēbāb*), and this in a context heavy with juridical languages. It sounds very much like thė formal establishment of an alliance.

A particularly clear example of the Hittite Use of *sulummū* to denote "amicable relationship" as the object of treaty-making occurs in the Ramses II – Hattusilis III treaty: cf. E. Weidner, *Politische Dokumente aus Kleinasien. Die Staatsverträge in akkadischer Sprache aus dem Archiv von Boghazkoi* (Boghazkoi Studien 8-9: Leipzig 1923) No. 9, line 14-16: ᴹ*Reamašeša māi* ᴰ*Amana...ītepuš ina rikilti.../qadu* ᴹ*Hattušili...ana nadāni sulummā damqa aḫḫūta damiqta /ina berinni adi dārīti*, "Rea-mashesha mai Amana...has entered into a treaty... /with Hattusilis...to establish true peace (and) true brotherhood /between them forever" (note the characteristic piling up of expressions, "peace, good, brotherhood," to express the object of the treaty: a solid relationship).

(19) J. Nougayrol, "Guerre et paix à Ugarit", *Iraq* 25 (1963) 110.

(20) RS 17.353, line 13; cf. *Palais royal d'Ugarit* IV (Paris 1956) 89.

(21) RS 11.772, lines 10-11; ibid. 45. The text is a letter about international relationships, not a treaty itself. The Ugaritic texts were discussed by Y. Muffs in a paper, "Some Comparative Notes on Ras Shamra Akkadian," also given at the meeting of the American Oriental Society, New Haven, Conn., March 21, 1967.

(22) Forms of *ṭb* and *šlm* occur in parallel already in Akkadian from the time of Shamshi-Adad I in a call for a formal ratification of peace. The writer of a letter admits that the enemy Lullum are still disorderly, but he still begs the addressee to accept their proposals and make a pact because the defending army is without support (cf. the neat translation of G. Buccellati, "accetta le loro (proposte di) alleanza (*ṭābatišunu ṣabat*) e accogli le loro (proposte di) pace (*salīmšunu liqī*): "2 Sam. 2,2-7", *BibOr* 4 (1962) 233. For the text see J. Laesøe, *The Shemshara Tablets*

the desert tribes which destroy *šālôm* and despise *bᵉrît*, that is, they break their agreements, attack their allies (23), and so creates disorder.

A striking use of the verb is found in 2 Sm 10,19: the Aramaeans *wayyašlimû 'et–yiśrā'ēl wayya'abᵉdûm*, which must mean "made a treaty to serve Israel," i.e., made a vassal treaty, for the idea is perfectly parallel with 8,2 and 6 where Moab and other Aramaeans "become servants bearing tribute," a technical phrase for being subjected to a vassal treaty (cf. *Treaty and Covenant*² 161, note 6; 287, note 22). Hebrew usage thus fits snugly into the treaty/covenant tradition, and the connotations which this tradition gives the root form one facet to be considered in the interpretation of this many-sided, central root in the biblical lexicon.

Pont. Ist. Biblico; Via della Pilotta 25
I-00187 Roma

Dennis J. McCarthy

(Copenhagen 1959) SH 812 1,24-36. An exemplary case of treaty and covenant making: the situation is far from perfect, one cannot get all that one wants but takes the best possible. There is freedom, but it is relative.

(23) Cf. the version in the *Nueva Biblia Española*: "Levantan la mano contra su aliado, violando los pactos".

Compact and Kingship: Stimuli for Hebrew Covenant Thinking

DENNIS J. MCCARTHY, S.J.
Pontifical Biblical Institute, Rome

When Yahwist religion takes on reality for us in the biblical record it is covenantal. As understood here this means not the natural, inevitable religion inherited by tribe, city, or other social group, nor mere over-whelming awe before the numinous, but rather a personal and social commitment to the God who presented himself. The old Sinai traditions of a self-presentation of and response to the deity, though rather simple in content, were complicated as ritual: the people (a mix of races and nation, not a community with its religion given in the nature of things) met God and proclaimed allegiance to him with word, sacrifice, and sacred meal. This is already covenant, but the representation of covenant(-making) moved from cultic and rather undefined tradition, as in Exod 24:1, 9-11 and 4b, 5-6, 8,[1] to the elaborate deuteronomic treaty covenant with introduction, detailed obligations, and conditional blessings and curse.[2] Thus biblical covenant may be described as a single species expressed in variant forms, not a unique form. Here Dr. Jörn Halbe (in a personal communication) raises a pertinent question: given the development, how are we to picture the transitions in concrete historical terms?

This paper argues that qualities of Hebrew monarchy, especially that monarchy as presented in the era of transition from loose tribal life to royal nation state, are one plausible stimulus to the development. I say "stimulus" because, if it is hardly possible to show that one thing was the model or the logically necessary antecedent for the other, the likeness of certain

---

[1]Source analysis according to W. H. Schmidt, *Alttestamentlicher Glaube in seiner Geschichte* (Neukirchener Studienbücher 6; 3d ed., 1979) 45-47.

[2]So, covenant is not a late (deuteronomic) idea, apparently without antecedents (*contra* L. Perlitt, *Bundestheologie im Alten Testament* [WMANT 36, 1969]); nor is covenant a misnomer implying relationship for what shoud be (usually one sided) "duty" (*contra* E. Kutsch, *Verheissung und Gesetz* [BZAW 131, 1973]). Discussed in D. J. McCarthy, "*bᵉrît* and Covenant in Old Testament History and Theology," *Bib* 53 (1972) 110-21; *Treaty and Covenant* (AnBib 21A; 2d ed., 1978) 16-24, 277-93 (and accepted, e.g., by B. Childs, *Introduction to the Old Testament as Scripture* [London, 1979] 44), and M. Weinfeld, "ברית," *TWAT* 1 (1970-73) 781-808; J. Barr ("Some Semantic Notes on the Covenant," *Beiträge zur alttestamentlichen Theologie. Festschrift W. Zimmerli* [eds. H. Donner et al.; Göttingen, 1977] 23-38), though unwontedly diffident, cannot quite agree with Perlitt and Kutsch.

aspects of covenant making and kingship to the classic deuteronomic religious covenant is so close that it is unrealistic to separate them entirely. It is common that a highly visible fact stimulates parallels. For example, writing has been "re-invented" more than once not because someone learned an older system but because he was stirred to invention by seeing it in use. In modern times secular ritual from freemasonry to communist weddings is shaped by the stimulus of church rites. In old Israel, memory of kingship encouraged priestly anointing in later times, and one may suppose that the inviolability of the Holy of Holies in the Canaanite-style Temple affected ideas about the complete otherness of the divine.

The key elements in the influence of the early monarchical era on covenant thinking are (1) formal compacts used to structure societies, and (2) the special sanctity of the kingship.[3] I use "compact" (as a temporary measure for the argument) to avoid fixed concepts or genres implied by usual words like "contract," "treaty," or "covenant." It refers to deliberately created, enduring social structures (often not yet defined in a technical terminology) as opposed to casual and transitory meetings and combinations on the one hand and on the other to natural social forms not defined by a more or less free choice, like family or class.

Such structures are needed because there will be friction when social units accepted without reflection like the independent clan or village meet each other. The new social factor met needs to be integrated, its relation to the familiar defined, for mere contact with the alien, even without competition, arouses suspicion which must be allayed.[4] It is this definition which I am calling "compact." This is the way mankind regularly expands natural groupings. The jealously independent Greek states tried to organize themselves by a system of oaths fixing rights and duties, Roman law dealt with graded rights and duties with its allies, Herodotus testifies to rites for

---

[3]Redaction analysis questions the historicity of much in the early monarchical story, assigning it to exilic editors, Dtr^{P} and Dtr^{N} (T. Veijola, *Die ewige Dynastie* [Helsinki, 1975] and *Das Königtum in der Beurteilung der deuteronomistischen Historiographie* [Helsinki, 1977], with full bibliographies). However, techniques like repetition here point to unity, not "sources," and limit the value of the analysis (R. Carlson, "Élie à Horeb; I Rois xviii-xix," *VT* 19 [1969] 416-39; "Élisée—le successeur d'Élie: II Rois ii, 1-25," *VT* 20 [1970] 385-405; D. M. Gunn, *The Story of King David. Genre and Interpretation* [JSOT SupS 6, 1978] 24-26). Gunn (ibid.) cites oral story-telling techniques and artistic construction to argue an interest in the story for its own sake without historical referents. This confuses the artistic "syntax" used to *tell* a story with its *content*. Art, oral or written (on writing art in 2 Samuel see C. Conroy, *Absalom! Absalom!* [AnBib 81, 1978]), is quite compatible with serious history, as the tradition from Herodotus to Churchill attests (some discussion of this problem in J. Levenson, "1 Samuel 25 as Literature and as History," *CBQ* 40 [1978] 11-28). In any case, our argument is based on customs and ideas older than Israel itself and tales do record real social forms, if not always events; see S. De Vries' review of H. Schulte, *Die Entstehung der Geschichtsschreibung im Alten Israel* (BZAW 128, 1972) in *BO* 31 (1974) 100-101.

[4]George Eliot's *Silas Marner* (Chap. 1) describes from personal experience the friction the alien brings to a pre-industrial hamlet. "Alien" includes unfamiliar, remote "family" (Jacob-Laban) or the alienated "natural unity" (Jacob-Esau [David-Israel?]).

compacts among Arabs, Scythians, and Persians.[5] Ancient Germans organized an artificial "family" in the chief's *comitatus*, which still echoed in the feudal oath, an essential tie among the fragmented societies of Europe's Dark Ages.[6] Among Amerinds the legendary Hiawatha united by compact five warring Iroquois tribes into a power lasting for centuries.[7]

The records also confirm the making of compacts in the ancient Near East. In the 3rd millennium Sumerian cities and Semitic Ebla made pacts. In the early 2nd millennium the Shemshara and Mari tablets show rulers dealing with alien tribes by compact. Chiefs in Syro-Palestine "do good" (technical treaty language!) to the Egyptian Sinuhe in ways like later bedouin covenant and ancient treaty making.[8] Late in the 2nd millennium there are compacts (or references to them) from Alalakh, Ugarit, Hatti, Assyria, Babylonia, and Egypt.[9] These compacts could be formal treaties, or they might have other forms. They all witness to the need to stabilize relations among diverse social units. The need and answer continued, though for later times evidence is spotty but plentiful enough. The Egyptian Wenamon's troubles in 12th-century Phoenicia are those of the stranger in a society where he has no agreed position. Later evidence comes from Assyria, Syria, and the Bible itself, as well as the classical data noted.[10]

The compact, then, meeting a primary social need, is a widespread instrument. The formalities vary but in the ancient Near Eastern and Mediterranean worlds the data cited give special importance to the oath: invocation of the gods or self-imprecation. Thus, the compact was protected by the gods as distinguished from the contract protected by mere human witnesses. Such compacts covered everything from complex perma-

---

[5]General Data: M. Weinfeld, "Covenant Terminology in the Ancient Near East and Its Influence in the West," *JAOS* 93 (1973) 190-99; McCarthy, *Treaty and Covenant*, 105, and "Ebla, ὅρκια τέμνειν, *ṭb*, *šlm*: Addenda to *Treaty and Covenant*[2]," *Bib* 60 (1979) 249-50; Greece: C. M. Bowra, *Periclean-Athens* (Harmondsworth, 1974) 86 (Original, 1971); Rome: *Kleine Pauly, s.v. foedus*, and *The Oxford Classical Dictionary, s.v. socii* (bibliography); Arabs, Scythians: Herodotus, *Historiae*, 1.74; 4.70; Persians: ibid., 3.8, and Xenophon, *Anabasis*, 2.2,9 (discussed in D. J. McCarthy, "Further Notes on the Symbolism of Blood and Sacrifice," *JBL* 92 [1973] 207-208).

[6]Tacitus, *Germania*, 13-14; the *Chanson du Guillaume* illustrates the medieval sequel: unsworn knights may not join Lord Vivien even for safety against the common paynim enemy, so inconceivable is unity apart from family or pact!

[7]See *Encyclopedia Americana, s.vv.* Hiawatha, Iroquois. Further useful facts (not the often dated interpretations) under "Brotherhood (Artificial)," Hastings, *Encyclopedia of Religion and Ethics.*

[8]For *ṭôbâ*, cognates and parallels: McCarthy, *Treaty and Covenant*, 171; *Bib* 60, 250-51 (bibliography). Hebrew טוב ("good treatment," Gen 26:29) may have preceded more abstract טובה introduced from treaty usage, but David already uses טובה in an annalistic report (2 Sam 2:6). For Sinuhe, see *ANET*, 19; D. J. McCarthy, "Semitic 'Good' in an Egyptian Text," *BASOR* (in press).

[9]References: McCarthy, *Treaty and Covenant*, chaps. 2-8; *Bib* 60, 248-49.

[10]For Wenamon, see *ANET*, 29; the rest, McCarthy, *Treaty and Covenant*, Chap. 6, and pp. 383-89 (and cf. n. 5, above).

nent treaty organizations to problems of small trade. The biblical "covenant report," used regularly to describe compact making, gives an excellent picture of what was concretely involved. It notes: (1) negotiations based on existing contacts; (2) clearer definition of the relation; (3) symbolic affirmation; (4) notice of covenant making (oath); (5) association with a shrine.[11] So the situation: strangers in contact mean conflict (e.g., Abimelech's men attack Isaac's, or Abraham's: Gen 26:20; 21:25) or tension (e.g., will good will continue?: Gen 21:23; 26:29). The situation is resolved by clear definition of obligations (often customary). Further, men need to signify assent, or who is to know of it? Hence the reports record symbol(ic actions) and oath (normally with נשבע or כרת ברית). Then, the compact must be remembered if it is to define a lasting relationship. Hence the association with shrines, focal points for traditions. All this is very important: a social need so strong as to develop a sturdy literary genre and a focus of tradition to maintain it. Rarely do we find a *Sitz im Leben* so clearly the real source of a genre. It is also very old, older than J and E.[12] This is something basic, a real response to a real need.

Moreover, the tradition was still alive at the beginning of monarchy. Joshua 8 shows genre and setting in full before deuteronomistic hands had touched the text,[13] and the hoary tale in 2 Sam 21:1-14 shows the old tradition working under the first kings. Then, there is the conspiracy between Abimelech and the lords of Shechem. Surely it meant a compact dividing the spoils of the plot, the powers of the king, and the privileges of his new subjects. Such cabals are truly social situations requiring definition. Rebels do not expose themselves without reassurances. It requires a compact, a ברית, to bring palace guards over to revolution (2 Kgs 11:4), and Abimelech too must have had a compact with his minions: it is not for nothing that they are associated with Baal- or El-Berith. Again, it matters not what comes from story teller, what from event. Either way, the story reveals the realities of its milieu.[14] Again, the citizens of Jabesh-gilead seek to resolve a conflict with Ammonite Nahash by compact. He is willing, if they mark themselves his subjects by an enduring sign of humiliation (1 Sam 11:12a).

---

[11]References: McCarthy, *Treaty and Covenant*, 18-22. The genre declines later, naturally, as the nation states learned to regulate social friction by means other than *ad hoc* compacts.

[12]Found in J (Gen 21:25-26, 28-31; 26:26-31; 31:*44-32:3) and E (Gen 21:22-24, 27, 32; 31:*44-32:3) and so from older common tradition. J. van Seters (*Abraham in History and Tradition* [New Haven, 1975] 190): the Abraham stories reflect late claims to Philistia, but see H. Cazelles' critique in *VT* 28 (1978) 241-45.

[13]J. Blenkinsopp (*Gibeon and Israel: The Role of Gibeon and the Gibeonites in the Political and Religious History of Early Israel* [SOTS MS 2, 1972]: Chap. 2 a *Forschungsbericht*); J. Halbe ("Gibeon und Israel: Art, Veränderung und Ort der Deutung ihres Verhältnisses in Jos ix," *VT* 25 [1975] 613-41); and B. Halpern ("Gibeon: Israelite Diplomacy in the Conquest Era," *CBQ* 27 [1975] 303-15) agree on a solid pre-deuteronomistic basis in Joshua 8.

[14]See R. Boling, *Judges* (AB 6A, 1975) 170; full discussion in P. Kalluveetil, *Declaration Formulae in Old Testament Secular Covenants* (PBI Diss., 1980) 60, 86-87.

These examples already involve kings, and David, seeking kingship in Israel (2 Sam 2:5-6), congratulates the Jabeshites on their fidelity (חסד) to Saul. Noting that he too is now a king, he offers them solid relations, טובה. Thus, he neatly hints at protection for the exposed city in return for חסד. An offer of a compact is part of the power game. When disillusioned with his protégé Ishbaal, Abner offers to deal with David (כרת ברית: 2 Sam 2:12). Details are murky, but at least Abner is to bring the northern tribes over to David (3:17-19) in return for a favored position in the new situation. He eats at the royal table (3:20), a possible covenant rite, and he departs with "peace" (בשלום: 3:21), a covenant word. Probably he was offered the supreme command, to judge by the general Joab's murderous reaction and the parallel case of Amasa (3:27; 20:10-11a). Surely the family feud over Asahel's death had a role in Abner's case, but just as surely a hardened soldier-plotter did not simply give himself up to David and his men. He had a position as military leader to bargain for new power by compact, and he surely did so—until Joab altered things irregularly but drastically. Still the ברית arranged by Abner betwen Israel and David (3:21) was ratified when the northern tribes did accept David as king (5:3).[15] This is explicitly connected with the LORD's promise that David shall rule and protect Israel (n.b.: the heart of compact, status and duties, granted by the LORD himself: 2 Sam 5:2b) already cited by Abner (3:9b, 18b). We are already in touch with the sacral, but our present concern is the importance of compacts in the society where monarchy began, especially any relation of king and compact. So, for the moment, we pass on to more political evidence, David's apparent compacts creating vassals as described in the style of ancient royal records: 2 Sam 8:2, 6; 10:19.[16]

Finally, monarchy began in the Hebrew Heroic Age (see n. 16). This provides a setting emphasizing personal loyalty, the formation of heroic friendships and so of faithful groups of retainers. So, we have David's friendship with Jonathan.[17] Based on affection (1 Sam 18:1), it becomes a ברית (18:3; 20:8, etc.) in which Jonathan arms his friends (shades of Achilles and Patroclus and the "gold giver" chiefs of Nordic saga!), and each is sworn to protect the other in all things (20:42). David carries out the obligation with Jonathan's crippled son Mephibaal (2 Samuel 9; but see 19:25-31). Thus the compact of heroic friendship. Saul took the classic means to engage a loyal group: grant of land in return for service, the way of generous kings (1 Sam 8:11-12:14; 22:7).

---

[15]*If* a story teller's addition (see Gunn, *King David*, 70-76, with bibliography), 5:3 imitates reality: see the parallel annalistic report in 2:4b-7 and David, Joab, and Abner, typical figures from a heroic age like the monarchy's beginnings (full discussion in H. M. Chadwick and N. K. Chadwick, *The Growth of Literature* 2 [Cambridge, 1936] 629-82).

[16]Parallels in McCarthy, *Treaty and Covenant*, 161; *Bib* 60, 253.

[17]J. Thompson ("The Significance of the Word *love* in the David—Jonathan Narratives in I Samuel," *VT* 24 [1974] 334-38; P. Ackroyd ("The verb love—ʾĀHĒB in the David-Jonathan Narratives—A Footnote," *VT* 25 [1975] 213-14): 1 Samuel 17-20 articulates the transition

Thus the society of the early monarchy was quite familiar with formal compacts, public, (Gibeon, Abimelech, Jabesh-gilead and Nahash, David and Israel), personal (David and Jonathan, Saul and his retainers) secret (David's dealings with Jabesh-gilead and Abner will surely have been *sub rosa*), as a structuring factor. Furthermore, it is tied to the actual institution of monarchy. One element which might stimulate thought about religious covenant is clearly in evidence.

For the other element, the special sanctity of the king, we have the anointing. Samuel's anointing of Saul (1 Sam 9:16; 10:1) and of David (16:1-13) are usually held to be later accretions,[18] but the notices of the elders of Judah and of Israel anointing David king are dry annalistic reports of events (2 Sam 2:4; 5:3). Moreover, they report something probably very old in itself, for anointing to kingship was not normal ancient usage. It is documented only for Hittite kings. Egyptians used it to rub a bit of Pharaoh's numinous power into officials, not on Pharaoh himself. Later non-Israelite powers seem not to have had the rite. That is, there were no contemporary potentates, Hittite or Assyrian kings or, after the 12th century B.C., Egyptian governors, whose anointing one could imitate. Why then anoint a "king like all the nations?"[19] Surely it was

---

from personal attachment to recognition of David as the LORD's chosen by the use of אהב (and contrary קשר). D. Jobling (*The Sense of Biblical Narrative: Three Structural Analyses of the Old Testament* [JSOT SupS 7, 1978] 4-25) explains more fully how Jonathan's story with its compact(s) mediates theologically the transfer of Saul's kingship to David. This is correct, but a little oversimplified: Jonathan does *not* simply cede his succession rights in taking David as a follower (H. J. Stoebe, *Das erste Buch Samuelis* [KAT 8/1, 1973] 348), nor does heroic gift necessarily pass from lower to higher person (see next paragraph in the text and the story of Sinuhe: n. 8). Jobling does show well the complex dialectic of such narrative: the symbolic transfer of rights *is* complex in a story of much time and many vicissitudes. So, after 18:1-5 David is properly Jonathan's עבד (20:5) who bows to his lord (20:41), though David's future greatness is accepted (20:12-17): "thesis" and "antithesis" are finally *aufgehoben*! Earlier reflection had already given the simple tales of Jonathan's exploits (14:*4-14) an all-Israel Holy War dimension: F. Schicklberger,"Jonatans Heldentat: Textlinguistische Beobachtungen zu I Sam xiv, 1-23a," *VT* 24 (1974) 324-33. These sample moves from story to reflection on its meaning are analogous to the process from the fact of kingship to conceptualizations of covenant.

[18] See the commentaries and T. N. D. Mettinger (*King and Messiah: The Civil and Sacral Legitimation of Israelite Kings* [CB OTS 8, 1976] 174-79, 309): the story of Saul's anointing imitates David's, itself old but not original, and so is an early tale influenced by prophetic ideas, as often held; L. Schmidt, *Menschlicher Erfolg und Jahwes Initiativ* (WMANT 38, 1970) 58-102; B. C. Birch, *The Rise of the Israelite Monarchy: The Growth and Development of I Samuel 7-15* (SBL DS 27, 1976) 35-37, 39; V. Fritz, "Die Deutungen des Königtums Sauls in der Überlieferung seiner Entstehung 1 Sam 9-11," *ZAW* 88 (1976) 346-62. Z. Weisman ("Anointing as a Motif in the Making of a Charismatic King," *Bib* 57 [1976] 378-98) uses typology to separate anointing as civil acceptance (old in Israel) from that of giving "divinity" (e.g., 2 Sam 10:1) which may reflect prophetic and/or "magic" ideas (not necessarily old). However, Habel's basic study ("The Form and Significance of the Call Narratives," *ZAW* 77 [1965] 297-323) finds the divine call for various offices pre-prophetic; see also W. Richter, *Die sogenannten vorprophetischen Berufsgeschichte* (FRLANT 101, 1970) 29, 51, 55.

[19] 1 Sam 8:5, 20—old whatever the context's date, for here Israel seeks to oppose 11th-10th century Philistine unity with the only form of centralized society it knew.

because the obsequious Canaanite princelings seen in the Amarna letters had imitated their Egyptian masters. They sought power, and anointing gave it to Pharaoh's officials. They may well even have sought the very infusion of the numinous. It suited kings who had special religious duties anyway.[20] And, once a rite has been introduced it remains. Canaanite kings after the decline of Egyptian hegemony will still have been anointed. When the Hebrews imitated these nations they made a king by anointing—and stressed his religious powers. It may be that these later Canaanite monarchies were practical oligarchies, the king barely *primus inter pares*.[21] No matter: typically in such situations it was the religious role which remained to the king. Thus the βασιλεύς and the *rex* remained religious figures in Greece and Rome long after the states had become "republics." The Canaanite king, whatever his political power, would be a religious figure.

Further, we do not merely argue by analogy to the religious office of the Hebrew king. He acted as one empowered by the divine. David brought the ancient palladium, the Ark,[22] to Jerusalem. The king, that is, commanded an object of worship which held its power even beyond political barriers (1 Kgs 12:26-33). The Temple contributed to this: even its ruins attracted non-Judean pilgrims (Jer 41:4-5). But then, the king had created this focal point, seen to its design and building, and maintained it.[23] Thus, he produced massive results in the religious sphere.

---

[20]Egyptian influence and sacral anointing: R. de Vaux, "Le roi d'Israël: vassal de Yahvé," *Mélanges Eugène, Cardinal Tisserant* 1 (Vatican City, 1964) 119-33. Mettinger (*King and Messiah*, 185-232) rightly criticizes de Vaux, over-influenced by the vassal treaty genre, for insisting that anointing made a subordinate king; rather it created an official. Mettinger also treats early anointing as secular (cf. E. Kutsch, *Salbung als Rechtsakt in Alten Testament und im Alten Orient* [BZAW 87, 1963]) with a development to a sacral meaning, but his development has occurred by Rehoboam's time, quite early enough to be a royal element influencing covenant thought. Mettinger also doubts Egyptian influence on the concept as opposed to mere external imitation of the rite. Indeed, without contemporary texts that say so, one cannot prove that ideas were assimilated, but surely strange rites communicated awe, if not understanding, and this is what is in question here, and what Canaanite princelings hankered for. As for secularity, did the relatively undifferentiated 11th-10th century Hebrew society feel any crucial rite as "purely civil"? H. Seebass ("Zur Teilung der Herrschaft Salomos nach 1 Reg 11:29-39," *ZAW* 88 [1976] 361-76) emphasizes the early need for sacral confirmation; surely parvenu kings would press all symbols of authority like anointing: cf. T. Ishida, *The Royal Dynasties in Ancient Israel* (BZAW 142 [1977] 75-77).

One might also note holiness given by the divine spirit (1 Sam 11:6 [and 10:6, 10?]), but the former old tradition is *ad hoc*, showing Saul a fit successor to the judges at the moment, and the latter may not be positive value. The "secondhand" charism of the Davidic dynasty which forms Nathan's promise was more effective (hinted at by David's non-ecstatic spirit, 1 Sam 16:13: a power lived, not exhausted in an energy outburst?).

[21]R. de Vaux, *Historie ancienne d'Israël: Les Origines* (Paris, 1971) 137; J. Gray, "Canaanite Kingship in Theory and Practice," *VT* 2 (1952) 193-220; "Sacral Kingship in Ugarit," *Ugaritica* 6 (1969) 298-302.

[22]Num 10:35-36; H.-J. Zobel, "ארון," TWAT 1 (1970-73) 391-404.

[23]2 Samuel 6; 1 Kgs 5:15-7:51; 2 Kgs 12:4-15; 23:3-7; and the great legend of David in 1 Chronicles 23-28, a hierophile source!

Nor was he merely a patron, not directly part of the sacral. Taking over a pre-Israelite model for the great shrine, along with its sacrificial rites and its psalmody, he emphasized the intrinsically religious role of the king. The psalms make him God's "son" empowered to rule nations (Pss 2:7b-8; 89:28). So close to the numinous was he that his maintenance of social order was coincident with the maintenance of the natural order of crops and life (Psalm 72). Naturally, such a figure and his family served as priests (2 Sam 8:18b) and offered sacrifice (2 Sam 24:25; 1 Kgs 8:64). His own family apart, the king made and unmade priests: Solomon removed Abiathar with his priestly lineage for the parvenu Zadok.[24] Even the apostate Ahaz has his way with so holy a thing as sacrifice (2 Kgs 16:10-16). This was anathema to late Aaronid orthodoxy, but when kings still were objects of hope and necessary leaders they could not avoid the religious character of their office.

The case of the Gibeonites in 2 Samuel 21 points this up admirably. With its blood guilt, curse, and expiation it is the very stuff of religion, the numinous at work and the problem of dealing with it. Here no one turns to priest or elder or seer, functionaries of the religious society some suppose to have run parallel to the political kingdom.[25] Israel as a people is involved in the religious guilt of a violated oath, and the king presides, turns to the oracle, receives an answer, and acts to turn away the curse. He is supreme agent in most urgent religious matters. The arcane (to us) ideas of Psalm 72 take on sharper outlines. Keeping order in society and nature involves mysterious and often harsh realities. The sacral twines the spheres together and a king must know how to act where they mix. There is no pre-established harmony keeping two orders flowing parallel. One must recognize the impingement of the numinous on both and have the power to meet it as needed. This belonged to that figure of awe, the king, whom one did not even lightly touch (1 Sam 24:4; 28:9; 2 Sam 1:14, 16; 19:22). Indeed, he was "like a מלאך אלהים," the embodiment of the divine power to discern good and evil (2 Sam 14:17, 20; 19:28). Perhaps a bit of this is *Hofstil* (cf. 1 Sam 29:9), but solid reality stands behind it. The king was expected to give judgments of more than human wisdom.[26] So Absalom based his

---

[24]On the early monarchical organization: T. N. D. Mettinger, *Solomonic State Officials* (CB OTS 5, 1971); on priests especially: E. von Nordheim, "König und Tempel. Der Hintergrund des Tempelverbotes in 2 Samuel vii," *VT* 27 (1977) 434-53. Of course conflicts arose between kings and priests (e.g. 2 Kgs 12:13-16); the kings selected among men who had their own priestly traditions, and history shows opposition between civil and priestly traditions almost inevitable. Each makes absolute claims in separate but overlapping spheres, and overlapping absolutes mean conflict.

[25]So M. Noth, "The Laws in the Pentateuch," *The Laws in the Pentateuch and Other Studies* (Edinburgh/London, 1966) 28-49 (German original, 1940).

[26]N. W. Porteous, "Royal Wisdom," *Wisdom in Israel and Ancient Near East* (VTSup 3, 1955) 247-49; right judgment is divine: Psalm 82; the מלאך is the *alter ego* of his principle: R. Fischer, "מלאך," *Theolgisches Handwörterbuch zum Alten Testament* 1 (eds. E. Jenni and C. Westerman; München/Zürich, 1971) 907.

rebellion in part on the need for a true royal judge, and the tradition made Solomon wisest of judges. Even the Chronicler has Jehoshaphat extending the judicial system (2 Chr 19:8-11), though he himself knew only priests or elders as judges in a hierocratic society. All the more significant that the tradition of a special royal power of judgment persisted through changes which had diminished royalty's prestige.

Hebrew kings, then, were as much involved in the sacral as in compacts. This mere juxtaposition in a conspicuous figure might suffice to turn thought toward a connection between the compact and the sacral and so provide the stimulus toward the development of the classic deuteronomic treaty covenant we seek. However, this remains a suggestion. Is it expressed concretely? Or, can we find an explicit tie between royal compact and sacrality, an adumbration at least of the ultimate deuteronomic expression of the covenant with God?

One must note points which raise problems, if not insuperable objections. Hebrew kingship was sacral, but with limitations. As a novelty, not a timeless, unquestioned customary institution "come down from heaven," the people who sought it for their defense would pay for it, but, as its (partial) source, they would have their say in it. Hence, the need for acceptance of the king, apparently by acclamation vividly illustrated by its refusal to Rehoboam.[27] The king, the defender of the people, must accept the definition they gave his power. One cannot isolate this from the משפט המלכה of Saul (1 Sam 10:25) with its properties associated with compacts and other *res juridica*: it was a written instrument and it was deposited in a holy place. Its contents remain unstated, but we can deduce something of their character from the demands made on Rehoboam and especially from the משפט המלך quoted in 1 Sam 8:11-17. Samuel's speech in chap. 8 is heavy with irony, but irony must travesty reality, not deny it.[28] The king must have the right to levies, the power to tax, punish, and reward if he is to do his job, organize and defend a people against the modern organization of Philistia; 22:7 indicates Saul's acting accordingly. Kings may demand too much and no one likes taxes, even necessary defense taxes, especially when they seem to succeed and the enemy threat recedes, let

[27] 1 Kings 12: discussed in A. Malamat, "Organs of Statecraft in the Israelite Monarchy" (1965) *BAR* 3 (1970) 163-96; M. Weinfeld, "King-People Relationship in the Light of 1 Kings 12," *Lešonénu* 36 (1971) 1-13 (Hebrew, with unpaged English summary), and "The Loyalty Oath in the Ancient Near East," *UF* 8 (1976) 379-414. The latter offers valuable observations and comparative texts, but without good distinction of genres: the ancient treaty/convenant was a genre unto itself *externally* like a "decree (grant)" plus a "loyalty oath," but *separate* decrees or oaths are different genres from this, not to be called covenants. Note also I. Plein ("Erwägungen zur Überlieferung von 1 Reg 11:26-14:20," *ZAW* 78 [1966] 10): Israel, rejecting Rehoboam, formally rejected a covenant.

[28] Stoebe, *Das erste Buch Samuelis*, 186-87; R. E. Clements ("The Deuteronomistic Interpretation of the Founding of the Monarchy in I Sam viii," *VT* 24 [1974] 398-410) defends the antiquity of the basic ideas in 8:11-17 without distinguishing fact and polemic.

alone those which seem only to augment royal pomp. Hence, the irony in describing the king's *necessary* powers. Nor were these all the king's powers. How much was spelled out in documents we cannot tell. Any society must leave much to customary definition, or "the world itself could not contain the books that should be written" trying to create instruments to record them.

What we have so far may properly be labelled compact: status (kingship) with defined duties and privileges regarding another party (the people), but it is all secular. Has not the royal compact actually put a further distance between the king and the sacred? Not entirely. The duty of military service continues old Hebrew tradition with a religious tone: going to war for the people was to act for the LORD (Judges 5; 1 Samuel 15; and cf. David's use of the priestly oracle in 2 Samuel 5), and this was now the business of the king. A self-evident result of the situation demanding a king, it may not have called attention to itself. Still, it is a link joining royal compact with a religious tradition. Further, the ברית making David king over Israel is tied to a divine oath (5:2b-3 and 3:18: אמר; 3:9: נשבע). The ברית must have defined usual mutual obligations, service from the subjects and defense by the monarch, but it has a basis in a divine word. With no record of this word itself one may always think the reference is later Davidic propaganda, but already when Israel accepted him David's success had demonstrated his blessing, divine choice, and this in the mode of early thought is merely made explicit as the effect of power, the LORD's word. This ברית had a strong religious element.

Further, we are seeking a stimulus to thought, and the novelty of kingship, the introduction of a strange institution, would call attention to it and invite reaction and reflection. Ways and fields of action become custom are so habitual as not to raise questions. Who asks why we keep to the right (or left) of the road? So, novelty can be a stimulus. So, also, ideals set before the king were perhaps more important from our point of view than what they did. Ideals are already things of the mind and will, not mere externals, and so that step to stimulating new thinking. Now, the ideal king had pledged himself to foster justice and put down the wicked (Psalm 101),[29] to guard the poor, the defenceless, to be the security for those the economic and social order by-passed (Ps 72:4, 12-14). All this merely echoes the proclaimed concerns of ancient kings in general,[30] but the Hebrew king was doing something the others were not in any clear way. He was making himself *especially* responsible for duties which *religious* direction imposed on every Hebrew: direct help for the indigent: Exod 22:21; 23:6; Lev 25:35; Deut 15:7-8; regular provision for the dispossessed: Lev 19:9-10; 23:22; Deut 24:19-22 (the gleaning restrictions); protection for the

[29] H. Kenik, "Code of Conduct for a King: Psalm 101," *JBL* 95 (1976) 391-403.

[30] J. Eaton, *Kingship and the Psalms* (SBT 2/32, 1975) 135: references to the ideal from Hammurabi to Jeremiah.

classless: Exod 22:21, 22; 23:9; Lev 19:33-34; Deut 24:14. These are ancient ideals carried through the whole Torah tradition and always valid, only needing application to new circumstances, as the gleaning laws in Deuteronomy and Leviticus protect the classless in what has become an agricultural community. Thus, the king took over ideals making him the Yahwist *en grand.* He did not merely judge others, he was to embody Torah, that basic element in Hebrew self-identity.[31] Thus, he was a highly visible figure calling attention to obedience freely given, not subjection through fear or habit, that is, the moral element present in all religion but especially Hebrew religion with its emphasis on the correlation between status and performance.

Further, comparison of Psalm 101 with the entrance liturgies, Psalms 15 and 24, reveals a society much like those based on compacts.[32] The would-be worshipper may join the congregation if he keeps his community obligations: status, fellowship in worship, comes in return for stipulated performance. Now, though we have no ancient "entrance liturgies" especially for kings, for whom would they have been so appropriate? In fact, an ancient hymn does tell us that he, who had consciously undertaken to embody the community's basic ideals, was received by God when he lived out his undertaking (Ps 18:21-27). Surely the first *full* realization of the relationship of status in the community to performance sanctioned by God came in regard to the highly visible kings. So, the rejections in Kings are not all arbitrary *ex post facto* judgment but sharper statements of a fact first vaguely intuited: the king was responsible before God for self and people (2 Sam 12:1-13; Psalm 72).

The claims made here about Hebrew kingship do draw on psalms and Torah in what may be late expressions, but I do not think this invalidates the claims. Dating psalms is indeed tricky, and if there is anything like a consensus, it puts the royal psalms late, a consequence of and not a stimulus to change in covenant thought. I myself doubt that anyone hymned kingship as it failed, but be this as it may, Psalms 18 and 72 with their ancient ideas are about enough to make our case. Further, whatever the date of particular expressions of Torah or the royal ideal, the content we are using, concern for justice, protection for the weak, the sacrality of royalty, is as old as Yahwism and older than Hebrew monarchy. Nor need we be hesitant about particulars. There are conceptual correspondences we have noted between the "coronation pledge" in Psalm 101 and the ancient Psalm 18. Then, too, Psalm 101 uses wisdom, a timeless idiom known in Israel before the kings. If Psalm 101 itself is not early, its ideas and language show continuity with old material.[33]

---

[31]J. Halbe (*Das Privilegrecht Jahwes* [FRLANT 114, 1975]) shows how ancient in Israel was cultic proclamation of obligations: they were known and accepted.

[32]Kenik, *JBL* 95, 396 with n. 19.

Further, it appears from the beginning that the dependence of the king's special status, even his life, on his observance of the ideals he espoused was to be enforced by the LORD. The evidence begins with Nathan's dynastic promise (2 Sam 7:1-17). For our purposes we need not choose any as the original form of the promise from the infinite variety proposed.[34] All reconstructions seem to admit a promise giving the Davidides special status. Dating is more important, but no real problem. There is a consensus, if not unanimity, for an early date. Indeed, the idea should come from the early days when the Davidids were pressing a claim to "rebel" Israel, not from a later time when the division of the kingdoms was a pragmatically accepted fact and which would not allow much scope for the complex development evident in the present 2 Samuel 7. The claim that the promise is Josianic founders on the text's nondeuteronomistic language, as does the idea that it is an exilic construct to reassure the people after the implimentation of the unconditional deuteronomic covenant. Anyway, the idea misreads the deuteronomic covenant which always allows and even quietly urges repentance and return.[35]

Further, a prophetic support for the new dynasty is proper to the times. Prophecy was old, as the Mari texts show, and it is no accident that it appears in the Bible at the beginning of the royal era (1 Samuel 10), for it was undergoing a renaissance in the general cultural milieu of the time. Prophets were accepted forces in courts at Byblos, at Hamath, in Tyre and Israel, in later Philistia and throughout Phoenicia and Transjordania (Jer 27:2, 9: Tyre, Edom, Moab, Ammon).[36] At least until the penetration of

---

[33] Kenik, ibid., 399-402; for the antiquity of Psalm 18, F. M. Cross and D. N. Freedman, "A Royal Psalm of Thanksgiving: II Sam 22 = Psalm 18," *JBL* 72 (1953) 16-20. For wisdom, note the Succoth lad writing for Gideon (Judg 8:14) and the abecedary from a 12th century Israelite settlement (M. Kochavi, "An Ostracon from the Period of the Judges from ᶜIzbet Sartah," *Tel Aviv* 4 [1977] 1-13): scribal schools, primary but not unique carriers of wisdom, taught writing in early Israelite times. Wisdom was not necessarily for the "intellectual"—see a farmer's wisdom (Isa 28:23-29), and the proverbs, fables, etc., indigenous to peasant culture as that of modern African agriculturalists or of 19th century Sicilian peasants illustrated in G. Verga's novel, *I Malavoglia*. R. N. Whybray discusses the ubiquity of wisdom in this volume: "Wisdom Literature in the Reigns of David and Solomon."

[34] T. Veijola, *Das ewige Dynastie*, 68-79 (bibliography). Some important analyses: L. Rost (1926)—7:1-4a, 11b, 16 original; S. Herrmann (1953/54)— an early, unitary *Königsnovelle* on the Egyptian model; Veijola himself—two old oracles: vv. 1a, 2-5, 7 and vv. 8a, 9, 10, 12, 14, 15, 17 combined in Dtr^{G} into a divine guarantee of Solomon's succession; Mettinger, *King and Messiah*, 48-63—a Solomonic: vv. 1a, 2-7, 12-14a, 17, and a dynastic promise: vv. 3, 8, 11b, 14b-15, *16, 18-22a, 27-29, from "shortly after the death of Solomon." F. M. Cross (*Canaanite Myth and Hebrew Epic* [Cambridge, MA/London, 1973] 241-65) takes 2 Samuel 7 as deuteronomistic but it has no significant amount of the school's language (see the forthcoming PBI Diss. by Sr. Alice Laffey, R. S. M.).

[35] D. J. McCarthy, "The Wrath of Yahweh and the Structural Unity of the Deuteronomistic History," *Essays in Old Testament Ethics: J. P. Hyatt in Memoriam* (eds. J. L. Crenshaw and J. T. Willis; New York, 1974) 97-110; "2 Kgs 13:4-6," *Bib* 54 (1973) 409-10.

[36] For Mari: H. Huffmon, "Prophecy in the Mari Letters" (1968) *BAR* 3 (1970) 199-224; W. L. Moran, "New Evidence from Mari on the History of Prophecy," *Bib* 50 (1969) 15-56;

Hellenism prophetism was a normal working factor in ancient Near Eastern politics. Surely the new Hebrew monarchy looked to the recognized instrument for support. Then, David's response to the oracle (7:28, generally accepted as old) speaks of הטובה הזאת, that is, covenanted relationship (see above, n. 9, for the language). The technical language of compact is applied to the Davidic office.

Our next step involves another prophetic intervention, 2 Sam 12:1-7a, 13-15a (at least, concisely formulated in traditional style, unexpected and against the king, without deuteronomistic language, these verses are old, whatever may have been added to them).[37] The promise turns out not to be quite so unconditional as usually claimed. Like all relations that were created by it, it had its limits, its definition, spelled out by custom, not by stipulation. It often must be so. A thing is so well understood that it needs no explicit definition, or it cannot support one: "friends" carefully defining the limits of their friendship make a contract, not friendship. Or, the definition is too long and complex for formal expression. At any rate, David is not left free, the LORD's protected no matter what he does. He is bound by the usages of his people and of mankind. No adultery, no murder! David was to be the ideal king, the model of justice and mercy, whether this was made explicit or left implicit. Oppressing the weaker, he went directly against the key points in the ideal. He must pay for this, though repentance mitigates the penalty. Mitigation or not, we now have the element balancing the Davidic status: performance. Only the promise plus the condemnation in chap. 12 gives the full picture. There is no really unconditional relation; there is promise of favor within the framework of fundamental customary responsibilities. The Davidic "promise" turns out to be very like a compact involving the LORD and a family, with obligations on both sides. This is not yet the expressly conditional form with spelled-out obligations of the treaty covenant, but there is more than the mere juxtaposition of religion and compact in the person of the king with which we began. The two elements are intertwined so that one practically is the other: David is the LORD's chosen, holy, but his performance must match his status, protecting and observing the "law," the ideals the hymns proclaim and the All Holy sanctions.

An explict link between religion, compact, and king is finally found in the so-called Last Words of David (2 Sam 23:1b-7). Heavy, sententious gnomic poetry like this is typical of heroic and post-heroic society like the

---

for Byblos, the Wenamon story, *ANET*, 26; Hamath, the Zakir inscription, *ANET*, 655; Tyre and contemporary Israel: Jezebel and her rivals, 1 Kings 18-19; Philistia, the local *muḫḫū* who urged submission to Assyria and saved his lord: J. Gray, "The Period and Office of Isaiah in the Light of a New Assyrian Tablet," *ExpTim* 63 (1951-53) 263-65. An exhaustive study of non-Israelite prophecy: L. Ramlot, "Prophétisme," *DBSup* 8 (1972) 812-903.

[37] For the antiquity of the heart of 2 Samuel 12 see Rost, n. 35, and the general arguments in n. 3.

ages of David and Solomon.[38] The style is heavy with images and tropes. It opens straightforwardly: the king is the mouthpiece of the LORD (vv. 1b-3a). A pair of simple proverbs follows (v. 3b), but the king's relation to nature, civil order assuring natural order, is put metaphorically. Then the contrast between just king and worthless men (Belial, v. 6) hints at diverse fates for good and bad kings (vv. 5-7). The hint is broad enough, but still it is partly figurative and so subject to various interpretations. Still, do the contrasting figures not remind one of the contrasting blessings and curses formulated in the treaty covenant? Behind the dense expression is all that concerns us: the king is sacred for he is the voice of the LORD, he has numinous attributes, for his justice means order and plenty in the land, but most of all his status, his success or failure and with him that of the people, is tied to performance, ruling justly. We have the sacred and something very like the two elements of the compact, and the set-up is explicitly called a ברית at last (23:5b).

Our final evidence is Samuel's reconciliation speech concluding the introduction of monarchy (1 Samuel 12), and it may be the most important of all. The speech is usually dismissed as deuteronomistic, but careful reading shows that the Deuteronomist built his scenes (Samuel's vindication, vv. 1-5; paranesis, vv. 6-15; reconciliation, vv. 16-25) around a core of older material. This includes (1) the confession-vindication liturgy in vv. 2-5 (probably); (2) the introductory legal adjuration in v. 7abA (probably); (3) and argument from history justifying the LORD's actions: v. 8a, bC—"going into Egypt" is a formula available to any biblical writer, and מקום for the Land, not the Temple is not deuteronomistic usage; vv. 9b-11a—the list of enemies and of judges is not that of the deuteronomistic Book of Judges; v. 12—the reason for needing a king is not of this same book; (4) some form of grant of a king—v. 13 may not be a

---

[38]The poem is gnomic both because it is aphoristic and because it is very intricate, with a weighty series of synonymous parallelisms (vv. 1b-3), synthetic parallelism (v. 4), interwoven synthetic (v. 5a-bAB)-synonymous (v. 5bA-B)-synthetic (v. 5bAB-C) parallelisms within an inclusion (v. 5a=bD) containing the climax: David's ברית, and another interweaving of antithetic parallelism (vv. 6a-b7a)—synonymous parallelism (v. 7aA-B)—synthetic parallelism (v. 7a-b) to contrast with the climax in v. 5 and the metaphor in v. 4. Further, the image of growing things links the final three, more complex sections (v. 4: דשא מארץ; v. 5b: יצמיח; v. 6: קוץ [v. 7a: עץ?]). On gnomic form and milieu: Chadwick and Chadwick, *Growth of Literature* 1, 377-403. So "baroque" form argues for antiquity as well as for lateness, while the gnomic is ancient wisdom suited to the age (*contra* common opinion summarized in S. Mowinckel, " 'Die Letzten Worte Davids:' II Sam 23:1-7," *ZAW* 45 [1927] 30-58). As for language, see "late" נאם in the ancient Balaam oracles, and, while ברית עולם may be a P phrase (Mettinger, *King and Messiah*, 257, 279-80); in P it refers to the patriarchal not the Davidic covenant. In any case, the phrase is too little used to provide a solid basis for comparative dating. H. N. Richardson ("The Last Words of David: Some Notes on II Samuel 23:1-7," *JBL* 90 [1971] 257-66) and D. N. Freedman ("II Samuel 23:4," *JBL* 90 [1971] 339-40) show the ancient language and syntax of the poem's original form. A study of content and structure without reference to the Gnomic: T. N. D. Mettinger, " 'The Last Words of David:' A Study of Structure and Meaning in II Samuel 23:1-7," *SEÅ* 41-42 (1976-77) 147-56.

particularly old expression, but vv. 14-15 show that it gives the substance of what did stand here;[39] (5) a blessing and curse in vv. 14-15—v. 14 is not corrupt or an example of aposiopesis, for v. 14b is a complete apodosis: "you and the king who reigns over you will truly be the LORD's," the greatest blessing imaginable; (6) the miracle and the people's repentance in vv. *16-20 (and elements in vv. 21-25 less important for us).

The confession-vindication need not concern us in detail, but note that it does make kingship a part of the ongoing institutions of Hebrew society, the successor to the judgeship introduced with solemn liturgical form. The rest of the old material is very significant. The summons in v. 7abA puts us in an official context. We have a historical introduction, to keep the legal flavor, perhaps "plea." We have a grant clause. We have a blessing and a curse conditioned on fidelity. Even the repentance scene fits well with all this. It is a sort of "enabling act" making the sinful people parties to a compact with the holy God. For a sinful partner-to-be repentance is the equivalent to ratification in normal biblical covenant usage.[40] If there were a proper stipulation instead of a grant (remember, grants are *not* covenants), the text would have the form of a full treaty covenant. As it is, we are but a step away in this old royal material.

As for dating, we begin by noting that the present text is pre-deuteronomistic precisely because it is *not quite* deuteronomistic. Its language is *almost* deuteronomistic, an all-important point. So firm a style as the deuteronomistic knows exactly how to express things. There are no near misses. A phrase not *exactly* deuteronomistic must simply be non-deuteronomistic, for example, "dwell in safety (v. 11b: בטח)" for deuteronomistic "quiet (שקט)," "*making* a people for Yourself (v. 22b)" for deuteronomistic "be a people . . .," or מקום for "land" (v. 8b) and not deuteronomistic "Temple." Such material, then, cannot be dismissed simply as deuteronomistic.

---

[39]Verses 14-15 refer expressly back to *king and people* (v. 13), now a God-granted unity. The presence of a king is no more a sin but part of God's plan for the people: see D. J. McCarthy, "The Inauguration of Monarchy in Israel: A Form-Critical Study of 1 Sam 8-12," *Int* 27 (1973) 401-12 (bibliography); "The Wrath of Yahweh and the Structural Unity of the Deuteronomistic History," 97-110. For the apodosis in v. 14: אתם . . . אחר יהוה, "be in the retinue of, truly belong to," see McCarthy, *Treaty and Covenant*, 215 with n. 10 (bibliography). All this departs from the commonplace that 1 Samuel 12 is anti-monarchical (e.g., T. Veijola, *Das Königtum*, 83-99—bibliography). For the positive attitude of 1 Samuel 12: McCarthy, *Treaty and Covenant*, 206-21; *Int* 27, 401-12; Jobling, *Sense of Biblical Narrative*, 5, 17; J. R. Vannoy, *Covenant Renewal at Gilgal* (Cherry Hill, NJ, 1978), good synthesis and philology, too insistent on detailed historicity; A. D. H. Hayes, "The Rise of the Israelite Monarchy," *ZAW* 90 (1978) 1-20, but thinks the chapter deuteronomistic; Z. Ben-Barak, "The Mizpah Covenant (1 Sam 10:25)—The Source of the Israelite Monarchic Covenant," *ZAW* 91 (1979) 30-43, but elicits more detail than the text will bear.

[40]For the doctrine see, e.g., Deut 4:29-31; 30. Exodus 32-34 shows it in action: the repentant people are receptive and so ratify covenant as it is promulgated; see McCarthy, *Treaty and Covenant*, 126-29, 216-17, 298 (bibliography).

The text as a whole, then, is pre-deuteronomistic (and pre-deuteronomic: the language is no more deuteronomic than it is deuteronomistic). Why pre- and not post-deuteronomic? A major reason is the link of such material (other examples Exod 19:3b-8; 23:20-33; Josh 24:2-24, [28]) to the "pre-writing" prophets recognized by classic source criticism.[41] But, we need not and should not stop with the text in itself, old as it may be. Its core fragments go back even farther: old legal formulae uncharacteristic of later practice, a variant tradition of the judges era naming a forgotten hero, Bedan, an affirmation of belonging to a retinue not normal to later times, and all this in a cultic-*cum*-juridical context. Here are links with very old forms, tales, and institutions. Is it presumptuous to suggest that some of this nucleus goes back to the beginnings of monarchy? After all, they had their משפט המלך/המלכה (1 Sam 8:11; 10:25) and ברית (2 Sam 5:3; 23:5): king, people, and God in 1 Samuel 12, are involved in compacts with some feature of the treaty covenant. This links with notices in 2 Kgs 11:17: the priest makes a covenant between God, king, and people, and in 2 Kgs 23:3: the king himelf makes the covenant. King, people, and covenant were a full part of the liturgy.

Here was a carrier and adapter of the traditions, with new coronations, new circumstances, new and more adequate expressions of the royal office in relation to God and people were worked out. This assumes a sacral renewal or at least reiteration of the royal covenant at normal coronations in Judah and, surely, Israel (1 Kings 12 points to covenant as an essential part of legitimation in the north). Renewal is explicit in one crisis: restoration of David's dynasty after Athaliah's attempt at usurpation (2 Kings 11). Surely it was needed in other crises with less obvious priestly involvement when ceremonies receive less attention, for example, the palace intrigues with murder of the reigning monarch frustrated by the עם הארץ insisting on dynastic continuity (2 Kgs 12:20; 14:19-21; 21:23-24). However, as long as monarchy as such retains its "charism," the mystique it can certainly hold, *any* royal death is a crisis. There is a chance of an interregnum, with the danger that, the keystone gone, the arch of society will topple, and with it, in the ancient world at least, the very order of nature. Hence, the high probability that all coronations renewed or reiterated covenant to show that the crisis was met and normal order assured.[42]

[41]For the pre-/proto-deuteronomistic style leading to the "almost deuteronom(ist)ic" concept: C. Brekelmans, "Éléments deutéronomiques dans le Pentateuque,' *RechBib* 8 (1967) 77-91; applied in detail to 1 Samuel 12 in McCarthy, *Treaty and Covenant*, 206-13. For the pre-, not post-deuteronomistic nature of this vigorous, original style: J. Muilenburg, "The Form Structure of the Covenantal Formulations," *VT* 9 (1959) 346-51.

[42]Other evidence for repetition of royal covenant: a covenant specifically with Hezekiah and so not simply the dynastic promise continued, with Jehu (argued by P. Kalluveetil, *Declaration Formulae*, 190, 195-235). Royal covenant renewal in general: G. Fohrer, "Der Vertrag zwischen König und Volk in Israel," *ZAW* 71 (1959) 1-22; G. von Rad, "The Royal Ritual in Judah," *The Problem of the Hexateuch and Other Essays*, (New York, 1966) 222-31 (German original, 1948).

But, even granting, solely for the sake of argument, that covenant renewal or reiteration was rare, the liturgy is a key. The special nearness of the king to God, his status and responsibilities, that is, a *de facto* compact, were kept to the fore from of old in the Temple liturgy where royalty was the object of song, where it controlled, directed, and presided from Solomon to Josiah. This is enough. The liturgy is not dumbshow. It must be meaningful to evoke a reaction, and this demands response to problems and new situations. So, the Temple liturgy reflected especially in the Psalms celebrated the king's, the Temple's (Zion) and the people's relation to God with continuity, true, but not in stasis. There was development as circumstances altered and understanding changed and deepened.

Perhaps we have met our aim? Compact and holiness came together in the king and stimulated development of a religion expressed in covenant terms. The Bible even adumbrates this when Isa 55:3 extends the Davidic covenant to the whole people,[43] expressing actual intellectual development (though it would not recognize this terminology) as well as stating a theological idea. The development may be summarized. (1) Hebrew kingship began in a society familiar with compacts, the beginnings of kingship actually being associated with them. (2) The king was a sacred figure in whom the compactual and the sacral met *de facto*. (3) Nathan's promise and judgment oracle (2 Sam 7:12) express this early, practically defining a compact giving the king status before God based on responsibility before God, and 2 Sam 23:5 actually speaks of a royal ברית. (4) All Hebrews must observe certain ideals of conduct if they as individuals are to belong to the religious community, but the king's observance affects the very community itself (Psalm 72). This is a key: the king manifests in himself the more or less explicit ideals of the community and the relation between them and his status and the community's. If he lives them, he and the people are God's community, otherwise not. All the features of Hebrew covenantal religion are highly visible in this if one looked at it. (5) The king's and people's tie to the LORD was early expressed in a compact with most of the elements of the full treaty covenant (core of 1 Samuel 12). (6) The tie was continually re-expressed in a developing liturgy. (7) This material is explored and developed in pre-deuteronomic circles. (8) Ur-deuteronomy finally expresses the relationship to God in the full treaty covenant form. The obligations emphasized for the king and his status near to God really involve the whole people. The status is theirs if they choose, for the obligations, the honorable and honored definitions of a life specially related to God, are theirs too. The logic of the development is clear, and there is concrete evidence supporting each step in it. The royal association of compact and sacrality does seem to have stimulated the growth of the concept of covenant religion.

---

[43] O. Eissfeldt, "The Promise of Grace to David in Isaiah 55:1-5," *Israel's Prophetic Heritage. Essays in Honor of J. Muilenburg* (eds. B. W. Anderson and W. Harrelson [New York, 1962]) 196-207.

A final note about dates: the long-continued working of the royal stimulus prohibits fixing *a* date for its effect. The basic elements, compact and sacral kingship, antedate Israel itself, but their direct, combined influence on Hebrew religious thought hardly preceded their actual presence and impact together in the king. They *need* not have been so visible as to have marked effect under David and Solomon. Still, the problem in the *history of ideas* remains. Covenant did change in its form of presentation. Change implies stimulus. It suffices that key points (for example, Davidic promise and responsibility, psalmody) come enough before the "pre-writing" prophets to allow the two influences to fuse in the pre-deuteronomic texts. If everything is late (deuteronomic, exilic), there is no time or mechanism to explain change. On the other hand, the story of kingship provides time and stimulus for development to pre-deuteronomistic passages, to Urdeuteronomy and the Deuteronomistic History. Tying biblical matters to more particular times (and places) than this is often imprudent. The relative chronology is meaningful, the data are insufficient for more precision.[44]

[44] J. Levenson, "The Davidic Covenant in Modern Interpretation," *CBQ* 41 (1979) 205-19, unavailable for this paper, though wrongly connecting treaty covenant and Sinai, grant and covenant, properly separates Davidic from Sinaitic covenant: one did not grow from or into the expression of the other but did affect the other as diverse theologies will. Hence our insistence on stimulus, influence without identification or derivation.

Covenant and Law in Chronicles-Nehemiah

DENNIS J. McCARTHY, S.J.
Pontifical Biblical Institute
I-00187 Rome, Italy

THIS PAPER will treat Chronicles-Nehemiah, starting from the consensus that the material as we have it is postexilic and constitutes some sort of unity as a position, not beginning with an attempt at source analyses or exact datings of passages.[1] This procedure is possible because we are dealing with a set of passages which reflect a common form and ideology, not differences which make sources significant immediately. They are descriptions of covenant-renewal in a form which points to a West Semitic setting, and they imply a particular concept of law. In truth, all this does have something to say about the date and reliability of Chronicles, for the form in question is demonstrably preexilic in extrabiblical literature. It also speaks to the unity of Chronicles-Nehemiah, for there is a shift in the relevant form and related vocabulary, though not a total abandonment of the form in Ezra-Nehemiah. However, to repeat, while our data are open to historical and source-critical applications, we are concerned with the study of forms and ideas which, whatever their origins, came to the fore in later OT literature, since the problem of the basis and nature of law in this literature is a real one in the history of ideas worth attention for its own sake.

1 For a recent study, see F. M. Cross, "A Reconstruction of the Judean Restoration," *JBL* 94 (1975) 4-18. A survey in R. W. Klein, "Ezra and Nehemiah in Recent Studies," *Magnalia Dei: The Mighty Acts of God: Essays on the Bible and Archaeology in Memory of G. Ernest Wright* (eds. F. M. Cross et al.; Garden City, NY: Doubleday, 1976) 361-76.

Covenant and/or Law

A pair of contrasting texts points up the problem. In Deut 26:17-19 God and the people exchange pledges: "Today you have accepted the LORD's word that he will be your God . . . and the LORD has accepted your word to follow all his commands. . . ."[2] Nehemiah 8-10 has a reading of the whole law, a parenetic section, the people's pledge to a particular action, and the carrying out of it. In Deuteronomy the first step is a pledge whose object is a personal relationship, the law a guide for living out that relationship. In Nehemiah the law itself is the object of the pledge. The commitment seems to be to the law, not to a person who guides a relationship by directives or "laws." Martin Noth, in *The Laws in the Pentateuch*, reflects a widespread opinion when he sees this last as making the law a self-subsistent reality (*absolute Grösse*) independent of covenant and personal relations. Yet Chronicles-Nehemiah speaks regularly of covenant. Does the word have any specific meaning? Especially, does it have any significant relation to law?

A quick answer is tempting. The Chronicler substituted the Davidic covenant for the Mosaic but kept the latter's stipulations simply as laws by themselves. So he divorced law from covenant (and also avoided a problem which bothers many moderns, that of the relation between the two covenants, because he has but one).[3] But what, then, is the basis for the Chronicler's laws? Are they truly simply given? Or mere usage? Or perhaps royal decrees? Indeed, Chronicles does emphasize the Davidids and their powers. For example, it changes its *Vorlage* (2 Sam 5:3) and the clandestine anointing in 1 Sam 16:13, so that David is openly anointed at God's direction (*kidĕbar yhwh bĕyad-šĕmûʾēl*; 1 Chr 11:3). David's kingdom is not just his but equally God's (*malkûtî* in 1 Chr 17:14 for *mamlaktĕkā* in 2 Sam 7:16). David's house is not so much his dynasty as the LORD's temple (*bêtî* in 1 Chr 17:14, where it takes precedence over mention of the kingdom, for *bêtĕkā* in 2 Sam 7:16). Such seemingly slight changes emphasize a theology of the temple and royal responsibility for it and its community. Does this give royal decrees the force of divine law as did revelation to Moses in the pentateuchal theory?

Further, 1 Chronicles 17—2 Chronicles 7 goes to much greater length than Samuel-Kings to show that building and furnishing the temple fulfills the divine covenant with David. (True, the word *bĕrît* is not applied to this

[2] For the verses and an explanation of the translation, see T. C. Vriezen, "Das Hiphil von *ʾāmar* in Deut. 26, 17. 18," *JEOL* 17 (1963) 207-10; N. Lofink, "Dt 26, 17-19 und die 'Bundesformel,'" *ZKT* 91 (1969) 534-35.

[3] See J. D. Levenson, "The Davidic Covenant and Its Modern Interpreters," *CBQ* 41 (1979) 205-19 on the problems of "integrationists" who assimilate the two covenants and "separationists" who insist that the twain shall never meet.

relationship, but the practical synomym *haṭṭôbâ hazzōʾt* [17:26] is, and 2 Chr 7:18 has *krt* with *bĕrît* the understood object, a frequent abbreviation, whereas 13:5 speaks of David's *bĕrît* outside of the promise-fulfillment story of the temple in the earlier chapters.) David's vision of the angel at Arauna's threshing floor is interpreted as revealing the awesome site of the altar and not just as a vision of the Destroyer (1 Chr 21:30 with 2 Chr 3:1; contrast 2 Sam 24:17). David is the complete liturgist ordering the roles of the Chronicler's favorite levites (1 Chronicles 23-26). God gives him the temple-plan which is in writing (1 Chr 28:19).[4] Therefore 1 Chr 22:9 refers to the promise in speaking of the temple-building, and Solomon[5] can call the temple the fulfillment of the LORD's words to David (2 Chr 6:4), and God's choice of David is on a par with the choice of Zion (6:6). David's fidelity (*ḥasdê dāwîd*, 6:42)[6] and his covenant (7:18 significantly changes the simple *dibbartî* of the *Vorlage* [1 Kgs 9:5] to the covenantal *kārattî*) are strong motives for lasting confidence.[7] The Chronicler's covenant thus binds together king and temple and so ties together the LORD's demands on king, cult, and worshipping community. The saving commitment is the LORD's, but the saving covenant and its (levitical) cult are David's (2 Chr 13:5, 9). The Davidic covenant is thus given a very wide application, just as in late prophetic passages it is the hope for *all* the people (cf. Isa 55:3; Zech 12:8).[8]

Now, this description of the saving link of Davidic covenant with the cult is rich with expressions for law from the deuteronomic (Mosaic) form of covenant: *miṣwōt*, *ᶜēdôt*, *ḥuqqîm* (e.g., 1 Chr 29:19; 2 Chr 7:19), and the Chronicler makes frequent use of the whole range of deuteronom(ist)ic legal language: *šāmar*/*ᶜāśâ* *tôrâ*/*ḥuqqîm*/*mišpaṭîm*/*miṣwōt*/*ᶜēdôt* (e.g., 1 Chr 22:13-14; 28:7-8; 29:19; 2 Chr 14:3; 19:10; 24:20; 33:8; 34:31; 35:26); *bĕmiṣwô-*

[4] Verse 19 is variously interpreted; but MT *ᶜālay* is to be retained, "All this is in writing from the hand of Yahweh upon me, causing me to understand all the works of the pattern"; cf. E. L. Curtis and A. A. Madsen, *The Books of Chronicles* (ICC; Edinburgh: Clark, 1910) 299, with references for *yad yhwh* meaning inspiration. For the hand of God and prophetic inspiration, see J. J. M. Roberts, "The Hand of Yahwe," *VT* 21 (1971) 244-51; W. T. In der Smitten, "Die Gründe für die Aufnahme der Nehemiaschrift in das chronistische Geschichtswerk," *BZ* 16 (1972) 207-21, esp. p. 209.

[5] Such speeches also enhance Solomon and his role in the covenant; for the process in general, see R. L. Braun, "Solomonic Apologetic in Chronicles," *JBL* 92 (1973) 503-16; but it remains David's covenant.

[6] For *ḥesed* and covenant in this literature, see Ezra 3:4; Neh 1:5, 9:32.

[7] For a connection of David with a covenant in the standard treaty-form and peculiar to Chronicles, see 1 Chr 12:18-19: the covenant word *šālôm* repeated, divine witness, and office for the vassal. Chronicles does not use the treaty-covenant, but its elements were known to the author.

[8] Fuller discussion of 1 Chronicles 17-2 Chronicles 7: J. Goldingay, "The Chronicler as a Theologian," *BTB* (1975) 114-16.

taw hālak (2 Chr 17:4), *sēper tôrat yhwh* (2 Chr 17:7, 9), and *kātûb battôrâ bĕsēper* (25:4; 35:26), law written so that priests can teach it (15:5). In spite of all this, one cannot simply assume deuteronom(ist)ic (or pentateuchal) law and its centrality in creating community for the Chronicler.[9] For example, David, not Moses, receives the command giving the plan of the temple (1 Chr 28:19 *contra* Exodus 25-40). Then, some of the prophetic admonitions so frequent in Chronicles show a feeling of brotherhood for the kingdom of Israel (despite the normal stance ignoring the north!) or an abhorrence of foreign alliances closer to the older prophets than to the spirit of the Pentateuch. Finally, there is a clear distinction between civil and religious law. Jehoshaphat confides "every royal matter" to an officer, "every divine matter" to a priest for judgment (2 Chr 19:11). Whatever one may hold about the historicity of Jehoshaphat's supposed institution, the fact of the distinction of the two spheres in the Chronicler's mind stands clear, and it is a distinction very hard indeed to draw from Deuteronomy, let alone reconcile with that book. Clearly the Chronicler was free to handle the details of law as he liked, whatever "the law" in general may have meant for him.

Thus the Chronicler's free use of deuteronom(ist)ic legal language does not warrant a deduction that he derived law from covenant, as did Deuteronomy. He adapts, he does not parrot its language. For fuller data to back any conclusions we must consider not just the legal vocabulary and the great covenant made and fulfilled under David and Solomon, but also the other examples of covenant-making, or more exactly covenant-renewal,[10] characteristic of these texts and the vocabulary associated with them. We note that those kings, who the Books of Kings say "did right like David their father,"

[9] Cf. R. W. Klein, "Ezra and Nehemiah," *Magnalia Dei*, 266-68; H. Lusseau, "Les autres hagiographes," *Introduction à la Bible: Edition nouvelle*, vol. 2 (ed. H. Cazelles: Paris: Desclée, 1973) 665; B. S. Childs, *Introduction to the Old Testament as Scripture* (London: SCM, 1979) 647-48, for discussion of the law as understood in Chronicles-Nehemiah and its relation to the laws in the Pentateuch.

[10] According to a common opinion the mere mention of covenant-renewal should eliminate any possible reference to Deuteronomy. That included a covenant irrevocably ended by the curses automatically actuated by infidelity. Even for the "promissory" covenant of David, unconditioned and unending, there could only be a sort of shoring up, a reminder of something always really in force. However, treaties could be and were renewed after their rupture because they were not contracts but pledges of loyalty that could be renewed by personal appeal to the lord by the incriminated defector, as later Israel knew: cf. Lev 26:40-42, 44-45; Deut 4:29-31; 30:1-10; Zech 8:13, contrasting *qĕlālâ* and *bĕrākâ*. See P. Buis, *La notion de l'alliance* (LD 88; Paris: Cerf, 1976) 189; D. J. McCarthy, *Treaty and Covenant* (AnBib 22A; 2d ed.; Rome: Biblical Institute, 1978) 127-28, 132. Nor was the Davidic covenant really without conditions; see D. J. McCarthy, "Compact and Kingship: Stimuli for Hebrew Covenant Thinking," *The International Symposium for Biblical Studies, Tokyo, Dec. 5-7, 1979: Proceedings* (Tokyo: in press).

Asa (1 Kgs 15:11), Hezekiah (2 Kgs 18: 3), and Josiah (22:2), renewed covenant. That is, every fourth or fifth king in the line did so. Is there some ritual periodicity here? Did being like David call for involvement with covenant? Or did flagrant infidelity demand it? The last seems likely. Asa repaired the gross infidelities of Rehoboam (the intervening reign of Abijam is too short to matter), Hezekiah those of Ahaz, Josiah those of Manasseh (again, Amon's short reign hardly counts).

The renewal of covenant begins with a prophet, Azariah (2 Chr 15:1—or Oded, 15:8!) or a king, Hezekiah, speaking as a prophet in the levitical sermon which Chronicles uses for the prophets (29:5:11).[11] The mere mention of the proclamation of the new-found law replaces the "sermon" only in the renewal under Josiah (34:30=2 Kgs 23:3). Apparently the writer found his *Vorlage* sufficient without his familiar sermon. In fact, if the law concerned was some form of Deuteronomy for him as it is usually thought to be by us, it applies the OT's most effective sermon to the renewal. After the exhortation the people are brought into the covenant by action of the leader, the king (29:10), and especially in 34:31-32, ". . . the king . . . made a covenant (*wayyikrōt ʾet-habbĕrît*) before the LORD, to walk after the LORD . . ., to perform all the words of the covenant. . . . Then he caused all . . . to adhere (*wayyaʿămēd*) to the covenant" (*An American Translation*). The last sentence varies the *Vorlage* of Kings to make the king the active agent of the people's commitment. Even when the text says that the people came into the covenant (15:12, *wayyābōʾû babbĕrît*), it is because the king has brought them together for this. Chronicles insists that the king brought the people into the covenant, just as in the classic vassal treaty the lord granted covenant to underlings. Once the covenant is made, the community destroys the idols which mark their infidelity (all examples), offers sacrifices (Asa, Hezekiah) with cultic rejoicing: shofar and trumpets (Asa, Hezekiah) and a new Passover (Hezekiah, Josiah). There is a certain similarity to the *Vorlage* describing Josiah's covenant in 1 Kings 23, but the differences are striking, particularly the emphasis on parenesis, on sacrifices, not only Passover, and explicity rejoicing, not merely that implied in Passover. 2 Kings 23 is but a sketch of the full form.

One result of the change is to make liturgy central to the covenant-renewals. The people leave false gods and rejoice as the LORD's worshipping community, a structured community with three principal leadership ele-

[11] See J. D. Newsome, Jr., "Toward a New Understanding of the Chronicler and His Purposes," *JBL* 94 (1975) 201-17, esp. pp. 203-4, 212. He analyzes the structure thus: (1) Summons to attention; (2) The word (warning, reproach); (3) Call to act rightly with renewed vigor. The transition from the word (parenesis) to command uses *wĕʿattâ*, giving a structure like J. Muilenburg's "covenant-formulation"; see "The Form and Structure of the Covenantal Formulations," *VT* 9 (1959) 347-65.

ments: king, prophets, levites. The prophets, some of whom are cult officials (1 Chr 25:3-4), some raised up at need, are emphasized. Chronicles has fourteen more prophets than Kings. They are God's ambassadors who might have saved Judah (2 Chronicles 24; 36:15-16). These prophets are themselves the guides to salvation, not reminders of God's word at work in history by pointing out a constant scheme of word and fulfillments, as in the deuteronomistic history. So Uzziah prospered when he followed Zechariah *hammēbîn birʾōt hāʾĕlōhîm* (2 Chr 26:5). Chenaniah had useful "understanding of divine things" (1 Chr 15:22), and many other prophets gave exact directions which were for the good.[12]

So one scholar even calls the prophets very gods for the kings,[13] but the kings themselves are at least equal to the prophets (1 Chr 16:25). David had God's word as a prophet (e.g., 1 Chr 28:19; 2 Chr 29:25), and four other kings act as prophets, six if we include non-Jews.[14] It is kings whom God leads to build and maintain the temple (2 Chr 24:4; 34:8-12), the center without which the community of worship cannot exist, the assurance of God's presence and protection,[15] and the prophetic nature of this is explicit: Solomon's temple is accepted with the same sign as Elijah's sacrifice (2 Chr 7:1-3; cf. 1 Kings 8). Even the second temple depends on the Persian king's will (*ṭaʿam*) in exact parallelism with God's (Ezra 6:14). Our books find kings like Fitzgerald's rich: "There's something different about them." They are different from prophets, as important and more important than they, the top of the tripartite leadership of the community.

The third leadership group is the priest or, better, the levites. This is obvious if the temple they serve is central to the Davidic covenant. Moreover, in the covenant-renewals repentance and purificatory rites and sacrifices are essential so that the group exclusively charged with these cultic acts must come to the fore. Still, they are directed by kings in general (1 Chronicles 23-25) and in particular (2 Chr 29:4; 31:2; 35:2). It is these three groups which must work together, with the king holding pride of place, to keep the temple-community a whole, for, when covenant renewal

[12] Shemaiah stops an Israelite-Judean war (2 Chr 12:2-4); Azariah/Oded proposes a covenant (2 Chronicles 15); Hanani, Jehu, and Eliezer condemn foreign alliances (16:4; 19:2; 20:37); Oded frees Judeans captive in Samaria (28:9-15).

[13] T. Willi, *Die Chronik als Auslegung* (FRLANT 106; Göttingen: Vandenhoeck & Ruprecht, 1972) 223, 227-29.

[14] For Solomon, Abijah, and Hezekiah, see J. D. Newsome, Jr., "A New Understanding," 203-4. Hezekiah also intercedes like a prophet or even replaces one (compare 2 Chr 32:20, 24 with 2 Kgs 19:15; Isa 37:15 and 20:1; 38:1). God speaks to the reprobate Manasseh (2 Chr 33:10) and even to pagan kings, Necho (35:22) and Darius (Ezra 1:1).

[15] See also the Psalm of Jonah 2:5, 8: the temple is the place to meet God and be heard by Him.

is needed, it is the coherence of that community, the community defined by exclusive service of the LORD, which has been put in question because of infidelity.

This social structure with defined duties for king, prophet, and priest at the head of the people is unlike anything hinted at in the deuteronomistic history or deuteronomic covenant-making. Moreover, Chronicles, despite its borrowing from traditional legal language, develops not just a structure for covenant-renewal but its own precise vocabulary to express its ideas. There is the fundamental *dāraš*, "strive for, seek eagerly," which occurs 29 times in Chronicles. It is used 137 times elsewhere, usually for seeking guidance from a prophet or a magician or the law, not as in Chronicles for striving to cleave to the LORD directly (27 times) and not through the word of a seer or the law (2 times only). This is very personal, and it is reciprocal: "If you seek him earnestly, he will be found of you." The LORD is ready to meet those who turn to him. This implies "rightness of heart," firmness of commitment to the service of the LORD (1 Chr 29:17-19, a cultic context). It calls for "humility": king and people must "bow before" (*kānaᶜ*) the demands of the LORD (cf. 2 Chr 7:14 on the need for penitence and humility in the temple). Even the model Hezekiah must be humbled when he takes too much upon himself. So *kānaᶜ* becomes another technical word for the Chronicler; he has 17 out of 32 biblical uses of the word, and in other places the reference is to a subject's submission to an earthly lord, not to humility before the LORD.

This is the positive vocabulary. There is a parallel negative one in which the basic dictum is, "Forsake the LORD, and he will forsake you" (2 Chr 12:5; 15:2; 24:3; and cf. Ezra 8:22 and the variant formulations in 1 Chr 28:8; 2 Chr 7:22; 15:4). With the aid of this reciprocal formulation, the verb *ᶜāzab*, an emotional word implying not so much indifference as rejection, when used even by itself becomes technical language, a powerful warning to Judah. So also *māᶜal*, "rebel wantonly," another emotional word for estrangement from God and characteristic of this material (15 out of 35 uses, and many of the other uses are not theological). Hence the urgency of covenant-renewals to get back to God, before it is too late and rebellion and consequent rejection become final. Thus this special vocabulary marks the covenant-makings and covenant-renewals. So David urges Solomon to "seek" the LORD and not to "forsake" him in the speech officially commissioning him to build the temple in 1 Chronicles 28.[16] The verbs *ᶜāzab* and *dāraš* are central in Asa's renewal, *ᶜāzab* and *māᶜal* in Hezekiah's. The law is doubtless important, but the very personal concern not to "rebel" or "for-

[16] On commissioning, see D. J. McCarthy, "An Installation Genre?," *JBL* 90 (1971) 31-41.

sake" and so "be forsaken" but rather to "seek earnestly after" and be "humbly submissive" to God is urgent.[17]

The Chronicler, then, with all his deuteronom(ist)ic language, has his own idea of the relation to God. He does not just take over the pledges of Deut 26:17-19. This is a brief liturgical action amidst a mass of exhortation and law not in itself essentially cultic. Chronicles is almost entirely cultic, dealing with a total liturgical relationship. When the community worshipped as it should, it and its members were one with God. Hence the covenant-renewals: their thrust is to revalidate cult, make it pure so that God *can* be there with his people. Hence the rejoicing: the community feels itself again what it should be. An odd example of Holy War illustrates this. The Chronicler knows the theory, and a trusting Judah generally wins (2 Chronicles 14; 25:7-13), but he really lets himself go with Jehoshaphat against the easterners (20:1-30). The war is a formal liturgy even to the chants (vv. 18-19, 21-22) and the festal joy (vv. 27-28). In the right frame of mind the worshipping community will get anything from its God.[18] So it must have the temple pure and well-maintained, for God is especially present in it and so in the land. Look at Jonah escaping from the place to escape God (Jonah 1:3)! Maintaining the temple was on a par with keeping the commandments (1 Chr 29:19; 2 Chr 32:21), while a faithless king can see it profaned by foreign entry and plundering (2 Chr 12:5-9).

In Ezra-Nehemiah the focus changes somewhat. A king is still a necessary, even an inspired, supporter of the temple and cult by decree (Ezra 6:14) and material aid, but he is a pagan outsider working through intermediaries. Prophetic influence is perfunctory: the LORD stirs Cyrus' spirit (Ezra 1:1), his hand is on Ezra (7:6-9, 28; 8:18, 22), Haggai and Zechariah get honorable mention (5:1-2; 6:14), and false prophets try to block Nehemiah (6:7, 12), but prophetic speeches are not the first step in covenant-renewal itself. Still, the point is always building and purifying the temple, which continues Chronicles' emphasis on cult purity but without its technical vocabulary of rebellion, forsaking, and seeking the LORD humbly. The Torah, which is from the prophets (Ezra 8:11; 9:10-11; see Zech 1:6), is more to the fore. It demands the temple (Ezra 3:2; 7:23). The same factors, kings, prophets, cult functionaries, and fidelity, are at work, but the mix is now different.

Naturally this produces varied descriptions of covenant-renewal. Ezra 9-10 is a ceremony directed against mixed marriages. The opening exhortation is expanded: the priest-scribe confesses the people's sin (9:5-9), moves,

[17] Note that technical *dāraš* and *kānaᶜ* in all uses and *ᶜāzab* and *māᶜal* in all but two appear in Chronicles; Ezra-Nehemiah tends to use *dāraš* for "study" (of the law) and *māᶜal* for "marrying foreign wives."

[18] See J. Goldingay, "*The Chronicler,*" 108.

with a transitional *wĕᶜattâ* (9:10) into a tirade using the past (deuteronomic law, Israel's sins, and their punishment, God's displays of goodness and justice) to motivate avoidance of the dangerous marriages. The genre of the speech is difficult to define. It is a sermon, a confession, a call for new resolution. Structurally, it is a "covenantal formulation" on its way to becoming liturgical prayer,[19] but the covenantal form still gives it a general context. After the speech the people on their own, not directed by the leaders as in Chronicles, bemoan their sins (10:1-2) and resolve on a covenant (*nikrāt bĕrît*, 10:3) with their *wĕᶜattâ* serving to link their resolve and Ezra's oratory. Ezra proceeds to "put under oath (*wayyašbaᶜ*) the leading priests (and) levites and all Israel to do what had been said" (10:5). Though an individual expresses the resolve to reform, the community and *the* leader, Ezra, remain the true protagonists. Note the language: though common (cf. Gen 26:28, 31; 31:44, 54; 2 Chr 15:11, 14), the addition of *hišbîaᶜ* (v. 5) to *kārat bĕrît* (v. 3) is unnecessary. *Kārat bĕrît* itself signifies a most solemn oath,[20] but here the pleonasm has a precise function: it returns the action to Ezra and involves the community. He is lord of the common covenant as in the old traditions. This point established, all is ready for the final step. It is familiar in covenant-renewals, but not as the final step: there is purification. We miss the sacrifices and rejoicings of Chronicles. And, of course, all this does not directly renew covenant as a whole but only commitment to one stipulation, though one necessary to protect the total fidelity of the community.

Neh 5:8-13 is similar, if simpler. An opening charge against usurers (vv. 8-11) leads to their repentance (their action again: 12a). Then Nehemiah administers an oath (*wāʾašbîᶜēm*) before priests (12b). He also shakes out his lap, praying God to "shake out" of the community any who violate the oath (13a). This sort of thing is a novelty in this literature, but as an acted-out curse it goes to the very heart of covenant ritual. *Kārat bĕrît* and its analogues in other languages originally referred to just such an acted-out curse, variations of which fill first millennium B.C. treaties. Further, Nehemiah, like Ezra in 10:5, has resumed the initiative in the ceremony, as is normal for the leader. Finally, there is a distant echo of the joy emphasized in Chronicles' renewals; though there are no sacrifices, the sacral assembly (*qāhāl*) solemnly agrees and praises the LORD (13b). However, once again the object is not covenant as a whole but a single stipulation which touches a social, not a cultic duty, not even indirectly, but closely like the problem of mixed marriages which mislead people into the service of false gods.

[19] See J. Muilenburg, "The Form," n. 11.

[20] N. Lohfink, *Die Landesverheissung als Eid* (SBS 28; Stuttgart: Katholisches Bibelwerk, 1967); D. J. McCarthy, *Treaty and Covenant*, 92-96.

The last reported covenant-renewal, Nehemiah 8-10, is even more complex in its final structure, let alone possible sources, but it is still the final form which concerns us. In all its complexity it, not possible and divergent antecedents, shows what the postexilic author thought covenant-renewal should be like.[21] First, Ezra reads out the law, and the people must be told not to grieve at hearing God's word (8:8-11). Later and bitter experience inhibits the joys of the days of Asa and Hezekiah. Then, there is a review of Israel's history with a confessional flavor (9:6-31) which turns with *wĕʿattâ* again into a penitential prayer/admonition. The whole is the mixed genre with its covenantal flavor as in Ezra 9:6-15. Then the people, not the leader, "make a covenant written on a sealed document," 10:1. (The rough Hebrew may mark a join between sources, but this does not diminish the important fact: the chapters *are* joined.[22] On the contrary, the struggle to put two sections together shows that the compiler—if any—found the sequence so necessary to his idea of covenant-renewal that he paid the price of clumsiness to express it).[23] The names of the signers of the document follow and then the common people enter in the covenant: *bāʾîm bĕʾālâ ûbišĕbûʿâ*.[24] Here the leader never really reassumes the initiative, though Nehemiah does sign first. The objects of the renewed covenant are avoidance of mixed marriages, observance of the sabbath, and support of worship, all points indirectly or directly tied to cult. Though broader than Ezra 9-10 or Neh 5:8-13, once again the pledge is to particular stipulations, not to the relationship with a person as such.[25]

Such, then, is the shift in the view of covenant-renewal in Ezra-Nehemiah: more emphasis on an opening exhortation which has no particu-

21 Even if, as many think, Nehemiah 8-10 is mere imitation of Ezra 9-10, the passage is solid evidence for the writer's concept of covenant-renewal, if not a report of events, for he found the model fitted the idea of the rite he wished to portray.

22 On the problem of the join, see, e.g., J. W. Myers, *Ezra, Nehemiah* (AB 14; Garden City, NY: Doubleday, 1965) 174. The solution in our translation depends partly on L. W. Batten, *The Books of Ezra and Nehemiah* (ICC; Edinburgh: Clark, 1913) 373-74, with its idea of a sealed document, though it avoids his false idea that *kārat* alone cannot mean "make covenant"—*ʾămānâ* is an excellent surrogate for the usual *bĕrît*, but the noun could even be unexpressed and the verb alone carry the meaning.

23 The objection, based on the demand for an "historical" prologue, that Nehemiah 9 and Ezra 9 are calls to conversion, not covenant-renewal (P. Buis, *La notion d'alliance*, 179; W. T. In der Smitten, "Die Gründe," 218) is pointless. Most history should be confession! Anyway, the "historical" prologue is really parenesis, and covenant-renewal is conversion.

24 On the hendiadys with *ʾālâ* to mean "covenant," see H. C. Brichto, *The Problem of 'Curse' in the Hebrew Bible* (SBLMS 13; Philadelphia: SBL, 1963).

25 See P. Ackroyd, "God and People in the Chronicler's Presentation of Ezra," *La notion biblique de Dieu* (BETL 41; ed. J. Coppens; Gembloux: Duculot; Leuven: Leuven University, 1976) 160.

larly prophetic characteristics, a more active role for the "congregation," less emphasis on rejoicing, stress on particular rules of conduct. Further, there is a somewhat different conceptual background reflected in the vocabulary of the books. Chronicles' essential words, *dāraš*, *kānaᶜ*, *ᶜāzab*, *māᶜal*, are not characteristic of Ezra-Nehemiah.

Rather there is emphasis on a written law. This is not alien to Chronicles, but the change of emphasis is notable. The Chronicler honored "the book of the law," but it is at the very heart of Ezra-Nehemiah. This is the object of Ezra's "eager search" (*dāraš*) and not *hāʾĕlōhîm* as in Chronicles. This is the guide to true life; Ezra's study of it made him a ready teacher.[26] This teaching aspect was very real to the contemporary audience (Neh 8:7-9). Ceremonies like those described in Ezra 9-10, Neh 5:8-13 or 8-10 brought to life in cultic action parts of the rich collection, but the *whole* was there to *learn.* In Nehemiah 8, indeed, reading the law opens a rite, but the author narrows this down to some specifics in chap. 10, and reading the whole cannot reflect a regular liturgical occasion. So detailed and so various collections as the possible forms of later Hebrew law can hardly be heard as a whole in any case, and are far too long for reading in normal rituals. Naturally, therefore, renewal concentrated on important parts, endangered parts, especially those affecting cult.

This emphasis on law down to its detailed expression is an important factor in giving the renewal-rites of Ezra-Nehemiah their different cast from those in Chronicles. The latter are concerned with cultic life *in globo*, the very life of the community, but with that life as it radiated out from the people-as-worshipping, and not with particular exigencies. The difference is real, but it is a matter of shading. There is a continuity. In Ezra-Nehemiah renewal might center on particular, pressing needs, but it is still sought in order to strengthen the temple-community, to assure its remaining God's proper worshippers. The need for something like this was, if anything, graver than ever. Subjects of a foreign empire and hated by its neighbors, the community had to preserve its identity for a new day, which meant constantly reminding itself of what it was, constant renewal.[27]

Covenant Renewal and Loyalty Oath

This continuity, I think, enables us to appeal to all the examples of covenant-renewal we have studied as evidence for a dominant structure:

[26] For the nature of Ezra's work, see F. Vattioni, "Esdra, scriba o lettore?," *Studi storici* (ed. C. Colafemmina; Molfetta: Seminario Regionale, 1974) 11-26.

[27] For a study of recoil and renewal as a central motif in all this material, see R. Mosis, *Untersuchungen zur Theologie des chronistischen Geschichtswerkes* (Freiburger theologische

(1) parenesis, used here as a general word for various kinds of exhortation; (2) covenant-making; (3) purification of land and people; (4) renewed cult. The force of these structural elements can vary with the context. One can make a covenant to continue purification which has already had some beginning, as in Ezra-Nehemiah, or as a basis for beginning purificatory action. One can concentrate the cult-reference on sacrifice, the center from which all particulars followed, or on a great feast like Passover, or narrow it down to a few vital aspects. One can have the community act as a whole by offering covenant as a response to the parenesis or divide the community-response according to classes, though most often the leader continues his urging with the actual bringing of the people into the covenant. However, these are changes in detail, responses to circumstances or problems of expression. The essential structure remains the same. Yet, oddly, it fits none of the formal covenant-structures usually proposed for biblical covenants, though these books were hardly unaware of such structures after the use of the deuteronomistic history, which is full of them. Still Chronicles-Nehemiah uses yet another form for its covenantal-renewal scenes, a form which seems to go back to a West Semitic prototype attested in the Assyrian *adû* and, in name at least, Aramaic *ʿdn* (*ʿdy*, *ʿdyʾ*).

The *ʿdn*/*adû* explains the features peculiar to the covenant-renewals in Chronicles-Nehemiah. This can be shown most clearly by considering societal function. The renewal ties the community together with an oath administered by a king or his surrogate. The basic demand, which assures this unity, is fidelity to the LORD who is Israel's real king from of old,[28] i.e., one must worship ("serve") him alone. Hence a weak or wavering community must purify itself, put aside other gods, and honor him alone. However, it cannot stop with this. He is LORD of the worshipping *community*, and this calls for many particular directions to keep the community together.

We know nothing of Aramaic *ʿdn* and their function within national or city-state societies, for the word appears only to designate an international treaty at Sefire, but we can say something about the *adû* as used in internal Assyrian administration. They were made under oath,[29] administered by a god through a royal personage or his delegate[30] to unite the community. The

Studien 22; Freiburg im B.: Herder, 1973). The renewal and pause at the end of Nehemiah is part of the rhythm by which this theology pointed to the future (*contra* W. T. In der Smitten, "Die Gründe," 214.

[28] For the antiquity of the claim in 1 Sam 8:7, see A. R. Johnson, *Sacral Kingship in Ancient Israel* (2d ed.; Cardiff: University of Wales, 1967) 38 n. 5; F. M. Cross, *Canaanite Myth and Hebrew Epic* (Cambridge, MA: Harvard University, 1973) 91.

[29] E.g., *niš ilāni* (M. Streck, *Assurbanipal* [Vorderasiatische Bibliotek 7; Leipzig: Hinrichs, 1916] 4. I, 21).

[30] *CAD* I/1; R. Borger, *Die Inschriften Asarhaddons Königs von Assyrien* (AfO Bei-

first demand was loyalty to the king; the primary defection was rebellion.[31] *Adû* even provided for smaller social units. They organized guilds of experts under the larger community, defining their duties and corresponding rights (even a closed shop),[32] but always emphasizing the prime factor, loyalty to the leader. Thus the societal functions of Mesopotamian *adû* and covenant-renewals according to Chronicles-Nehemiah are identical: unity of the community assured by total fidelity to the community's central figure plus attention to the smaller details essential if the larger community is to function smoothly.

Besides this functional identity the ceremonies for the two, *adû* and covenant-renewal, are similar. Both are presided over by royalty or its representatives. Each formulates a concern with fundamental loyalty. Rebellion, the Chronicler's *mā*ᶜ*al* and the Assyrian *in libbi adē ḫaṭû*, is the fundamental sin. Deference, prostration before the mighty lord, the Chronicler's *kāna*ᶜ, is the fundamental attitude of the subject in Israel and in Assyria. Finally, it is an oath which guarantees renewal of covenant and *adû*. In fact, "loyalty oath" is the natural translation of the latter; *adû* means first of all "oath." Von Soden's *AHW* actually gives this as the only meaning (but it comes to mean by synecdoche the object and content of oath-taking as well). So also the Hebrew root *šāba*ᶜ, in both the niphal and hiphil stems in which it appears, means "take an oath" or "cause to take an oath," and it is often associated with covenant-renewals, whereas the basic phrase, *kārat bĕrît*, as we have noted, is a reference to a particularly strong and vivid oath. The only variant is the biblical insistence on purification, for the sacrifices associated with covenant-renewal are the basic element in the service of the LORD and so simply concrete expressions of the basic theme of renewal (and *adû*). The biblical purifications are demanded by the absolute need for ritual purity in those who are involved in sacrifice. The divergence has a further societal cause. The *adû*, though it calls on the gods seriously, is primarily a political or economic instrument. The covenant renewal is also basic to the structure of a human society, but the temple of the LORD is the central constituent of that society so that it is primarily religious. The renewal, therefore, is in the realm of the sacral, the holy and the unholy, where one expects a concern for purity, particularly since the ceremony is a renewal

hefte 9; Graz: Ernst Weidner, 1956) 43, line 50; Zakuti (Naqiʾa): R. F. Harper, *Assyrian and Babylonian Letters* (14 vols.; Chicago: University of Chicago, 1892-1914) nos. 1105, 1239; M. Streck, *Assurbanipal,* 4.I,21.

[31] R. Borger, *Asarhaddon*, 41, line 80.

[32] R. F. Harper, *Assyrian and Babylonian Letters*, no. 33, line 13; D. B. Weisberg, *Guild Structure and Political Allegiance in Early Achaemenid Mesopotamia* (Yale Near Eastern Studies 1; New Haven, CT: Yale University, 1967).

after a falling away. It takes place, by definition, when the subject party is "soiled" and wants purification. Such *adû* as we have by contrast are new acts, beginnings, and so details are dictated not merely by their emphasis on politics and economy but also by the fact that they are beginning from a clean slate.

Further, there is linguistic evidence pointing to a connection between *ᶜdn*, *adû*, and covenant renewal. This is so even though Israel with its memory of its ancient Aramean connection (e.g., Genesis 24; Deut 26:5; Josh 24:2) and its constant contact with Syrian Aram kept its own name for the ceremony, whereas *adû* simply replaced Akkadian *māmītu* in Neo-Assyrian and Neo-Babylonian as the Arameans with their *ᶜdn* were occupying Mesopotamia. One supposes that *kārat bĕrît* was a consecrated phrase, too embedded in religious and legal language (cf. Jeremiah 34) to be displaced. However, Hebrew does have forms from **ᶜd* in other contexts with meanings belonging to the semantic field of *ᶜdn* and *adû*; *ᶜēdôt* and its variant forms mean "covenant-obligations." The Hebrew base is plural so that Hebrew conforms even in its grammatical number to the Aramaic and Assyrian forms. Then, we find the phrase *hēᶜîd ᶜēdôt* (cf. Neh 9:34), "stipulate covenant-stipulations," to retain the etymological figure in a clumsy translation.[33] Even by itself in at least 19 out of 35 OT uses *hēᶜîd* means something like "impose from on high," which is exactly the king's function in *adû* or covenant-renewal ceremonies. Striking examples are Deut 32:46: "the demands which I (Moses, *the* covenant mediator) bind on you (*mēᶜîd bākem*) today for you to command (*tĕṣawwum*) to your children," where *hēᶜîd* is parallel to *ṣwh* and so can hardly have a weak meaning like "witness to" (for Moses, see also Exod 19:21, 23); 1 Kgs 2:42: "I made you swear . . . and bound (*wāʾāᶜid*) you;" Zech 3:6-7: "The messenger of the LORD bound Joshua (*wayyāᶜad . . . bîhôšuaᶜ*), 'If you walk in my ways . . . , then (*wĕgam*) you shall rule my temple. . . .' " Ps 81:7-11 could be a miniature covenant-renewal: (1) parenesis: I saved you from slavery and the desert (vv. 7-8); (2) covenant-renewal: (*NEB*) "Listen, my people, while I give thee solemn charge—do but listen to me (*šĕmaᶜ ᶜammî wĕʾāᶜîdâ bāk yiśrāʾēl ʾim-tišmaᶜ lî*: v. 9);" (3) purification: "There shall be no strange god among you . . ." (v. 10); (4) cult: "I am the LORD thy God" (cultic self-presentation: v. 11). Thus Hebrew has verbs as well as nouns whose meaning fits well with *ᶜdn* and the Assyrian loan word, *adû*. This is hardly a mere accident in a strongly covenant context.[34] It is solid indication of a relation, a com-

[33] For the demonstration of the meaning of the nouns, see B. Volkwein, "Masoretisches ᶜēdût, ᶜēdwōt, ᶜēdôt—'Zeugnis' oder 'Bundesbestimmungen'?," *BZ* 13 (1969) 18-40; of the verb, see T. Veijola, "Zu Ableitung und Bedeutung von *hēᶜîd* im Hebräischen," *UF* 8 (1976) 343-51.

[34] The psalm verses are part of a prophetic call to renewal; see H.-J. Kraus, *Psalmen*

mon background within a tradition hinted at in Aramaic and expressed in Assyrian.

There is, then, linguistic evidence, *ᶜdn* from Sefire in the middle of the 8th century, for a procedure which was taken over in Assyria by the beginning of the 7th century as the *adû*, a technique for holding societies together. Israelite covenant-renewals show elements of the form in describing Josiah's reform efforts ca. 623. A common social purpose, ceremonial structure, and language all point back to this West Semitic origin.

The arguments for a common heritage are reinforced by an atmosphere evident in late Babylonian inscriptions, texts about royal prophecy and devotion from the "Chaldean" (West-Semitic-influenced) milieu which attracted and yet repelled the Hebrew exiles (cf. Deutero-Isaiah). Nabonidus is made to claim revealed knowledge: "I have seen se[cret things], the god Ilteri has made me a vision (*ušabrû* ᵈ*Ilteʾri*, i.e., made me a seer—*barû*)."[35] Even the revealing god is West Semitic. Of course, this text from orthodox priestly circles is propaganda hostile to the upstart king, but like all good satire, it is realistic, catching the tone of the man's special religiosity. A direct command from Marduk also determines Cyrus' Babylonian campaign: *ana âlišu Babili alākšu iqbi*, "He commanded his (Cyrus's) going to his city, Babylon," and his restoration of shrines in Sumer and Akkad: *ilāni . . . ina qibīti* ᵈ*Marduk bēli rabî ina salimtim ina maštakišunu ušēšib šubat ṭūb*,[36] "I set up the gods at the command of Marduk, the great lord, in peace in their lovely dwelling-places." The content is in the tradition of the royal annal. Assyrian kings acted for Asshur, and they saw visions, but generally these claims are somewhat standardized. Their mission was less a personal duty than a general one self-evident in the doctrine of Asshur's right to world rule. The urgency and directness of Nabonidus' and Cyrus' claims to personal divine guidance is new and it is closely akin to Chronicles-Nehemiah seeing pagan kings as prophets.

(BKAT XV/2; 2d ed.; Neukirchen-Vluyn: Neukirchner-V., 1961), 2. 563; E. Gerstenberger, K. Jutzler and H. J. Boecker, *Psalmen in der Sprache unserer Zeit* (Neukirchen-Vluyn: Neukirchener-V./Zürich: Benziger, 1972) 134. Verses 10-11 are, of course, clichés from covenant-settings; S. Mowinckel, *The Psalms in Israel's Worship* (New York/Nashville: Abingdon, 1967), 1. 156-61.

[35] "Verse Account of Nabonidus," col. 5:10-11. Translations and discussions: B. Landsberger and T. Bauer, "Zu neuveroffentlichten Geschichtsquellen der Zeit von Asarhaddon bis Nabonid," *ZA* 37 (1926-27) 92; *ANET*, 314. In the restricted circumstances in which the first version of this paper was written material of this sort could not be checked, and I wish to thank Prof. H. Tadmor of Jerusalem for calling my attention to the material behind nn. 35-37. However, responsibility for the specific texts used and their interpretation is mine, not his.

[36] *Cyrus Cylinder, 15:33-34*. Translations and discussion: F. H. Weissbach, *Die Keilinschriften der Achämeniden* (Leipzig: Hinrichs, 1911) 2, 4, 6; *ANET*, 315-16.

Again, Nabonidus' own inscription tells how he sought out gods.[37] Mostly this sounds like ordinary pilgrimage, but he really seeks after his gods. He took trouble to make his way to the god MAḪ: *âlu ᵈMAḪ itēt-tuqia.* Nabonidus is not proceeding to visit his shrine, he is eagerly seeking his person—something of an equivalent of Hebrew *dāraš*. Emphasis on interior feeling, on personal devotion, is not characteristic of earlier records, just as it is not characteristic of older Hebrew. Thus emphasis on intentionality appears in the cuneiform records along with emphasis on the king's prophetic experience in the age when the *ądû* replaced the *māmītu*, just as similar emphasis comes in the OT when it begins to emphasize covenant-renewals with their structural similarities to the *ᶜdn/adû*. It is not just the form which is shared but the ideology of nearness to the divine which came to surround it.

Law the Expression of Loyalty

All this, the form and the attitudes surrounding it, is wonderfully adapted to expressing the basic religious concepts of Chronicles-Nehemiah. The concentration on loyalty to a society's lord was admirably fitted to a society which the LORD had made and wished to keep his very own. His earthly representative was the Davidic king, and this representative bound the society to the LORD by oath in covenant-renewal, though in need another authority could substitute. *The* expression of the society's unity with its LORD was in worship, the service of the LORD alone. Hence arose the concern not just for loyalty in general but for proper worship and the rules, including those of moral purity, to be kept by those who would join in the worship. This is the significance of the case in Neh 5:8-13. It attacks the usurers who accumulate property and slaves through their loans, the chronic problem of peasant societies from Egypt (cf. Gen 47:13-26) to modern India as well as in the Middle East in the fifth century B.C. The community of worshippers, all responsible to the LORD, could not tolerate such injustice for it meant the disintegration of the very community. The have-nots would be driven out of the group. Hence the emphasis on such social duties with their relationship to the integrity of the worshipping community as community.

All this is obviously relevant to our question about the relation of law and covenant or better, we now know, covenant-renewal in Chronicles-

[37] Nabonidus' Basalt Stela, col. 9:55, a partly broken and difficult context in which we miss much information which might be useful. For us the significant word is the Gtn of *etēqu*, for in New Babylonian the form always refers to journeys made in the face of obstacles (see *AHW*, 262). For translations and discussions see L. Messerschmidt, "Die Inschrift der Stele Nabunaʾids Königs von Babylon," *MVAG* 1/1 (1896) 37; *ANET*, 311.

Nehemiah. Under the aegis of the king the leaders of the worshipping community commit that community to fidelity to its LORD. The basic demand is that central to the very being of the community, undividedly loyal service of the LORD. However, the community could be endangered not just by direct attack on the center. Other evils might threaten the integrity of the community, and so its ability to serve. Hence emphasis on particular aspects of loyalty, the prohibition of mixed marriages or of usury in the covenant-renewals of Ezra and Nehemiah. One might guess that in their time the conditions necessary for service were better codified or at least realized in detail. So their want would be more evident, and they could easily become the object of covenant-renewal. The demand for fidelity stands; the form for renewing it is the same; only the means of living that fidelity changes, becomes more specific, to give the covenant renewals in these books their own special color.

The whole picture of covenant-renewal does *not* point to law as a self-existent thing standing by itself in a realm of ideas. Its heart is commitment to a person in community. The laws merely assure that the community as such can serve him. This is personal devotion, not subjection to rules. In fact, it hardly fits the more common, much less Platonic or Kantian, ideas of law. It is not in itself mere *usage*, obligatory because it has always been done so; nor *natural law* deduced from the proper essences of mankind and the cosmos; nor mere *belonging*, as a born Roman or Athenian belonged, had rights and duties which a foreigner did not, for one who fails to seek the LORD no longer belongs despite birth (2 Chr 15:13). It is certainly no Rousseau's *general will*, a concept not easily compatible with a highly personal Providence, nor mere *power maintaining itself* as in Marxist theory (though its agents may have abused their position by fraud etc., as one can always imagine and seldom prove). The LORD is indeed power, but power to serve and save, not to crush people. Finally normal *utilitarianism* has never listed humble worship of the LORD very high among "the greatest goods of the greatest number."

To repeat, the main thing is not general rules but a personal attitude, fidelity and repentant humility, a "listening heart," so that the people may enjoy unity with God in worship. So the law of Chronicles-Nehemiah is no independent preformed category or Platonic idea. It is a means to relate to God. The change from Deuteronomy is not toward the impersonal but toward a realization and admission of failure and the consequent need of regular renewal of fidelity within the convenanted community.

Suggestions about Date and Authorship

So our primary question is answered, but the investigation has thrown light on date relative to other questions about Chronicles-Nehemiah, and it is worth our while to conclude with a short excursus on them. There is the question of dating (as a biblical genre) the form we have discussed. Is the covenant-renewal a late idea among the Hebrews formed under the influence of the realization of sin which grew in the exile and of the Mesopotamian *adû* experienced during that time? Then there is the relation of Chronicles to Ezra-Nehemiah. Are the four books the work of one hand or one redaction? Or have at least two produced two significantly different works.

First, the question of date. The renewal as we have seen it is so suitable to the fundamental form of Hebrew religion and not just to ideas peculiar to the age of Chronicles-Nehemiah that it is difficult to believe that it was a novelty imposed on the Hebrews by late Aramean or Mesopotamian influence. In terms of influence one might argue that the Arameans of Damascus, etc. must have had their *ᶜdn*, and these peoples influenced the Hebrews from the time that David brought the two nations into contact. In rebuttal one might say that the early Aramaic *ᶜdn* material is too exiguous. Its real influence can only have come when Arameans so dominated the Middle East as to change Akkadian *māmītu* to *adû*, *inter alia*, ca. 700 B.C. However, the Hebrews themselves belonged to the West Semitic tradition. They need not have waited for Aramaic influence. Indeed, the independent development of **ᶜd* in their language confirms an early and autonomous connection with the circle of ideas tied to it which allowed the development of a vocabulary based on the root divergent from the Aramaic norm.

Further, as noted, the ritual was well adapted to basic Hebrew religion. Quite apart from the normal ancient Near Eastern king's concern for cult—see David's bringing of the ark to Jerusalem—the Davidids had that peculiar Hebrew relation to God, a special covenant. I have proposed that this involvement in covenant (secular as well as religious) plus concern for cult by the highly visible king was the stimulus for the development of the covenant concept toward its complete expression under the influence of the treaty-form in the elaborate treaty-covenant which is Deuteronomy.[38] The importance of the king in the covenant-renewal would be another specific way in which the royal role in cult stimulated thinking about covenant. Of course, this implies with Chronicles-Nehemiah against Kings that covenant-renewal was regular under the Davidids, and it probably was. Any serious profanation of the temple like Shishak's plundering or Ahaz's pagan altar would call for reconsecration, covenant-renewal.[39] So too the death of a Davidic king.

[38] D. J. McCarthy, *International Symposium, Tokyo* (n. 10).

[39] So a major issue in Josiah's renewal was restoration of a profaned cult. Is the renewal also a late *preexilic* example of covenant renewal? The description in 2 Kings 23 can be read so as to include the major points of Chronicles' renewal-structure: exhortation (the law read was

When monarchy is a live social form, "a certain divinity doeth hedge a king."[40] His death is an incursion of disorder only a proper new king can repel. The traditional cry, "The king is dead, long live the king," was not mere politics (let my party prevail!) nor flattery. It was a plea from the heart that order not be interrupted. Psalm 72 prays for this. The new king acts with God to this end (Psalm 101). The nature of Hebrew kingship, Hebrew religion, and West Semitic origins, then, all seem to argue that Chronicles-Nehemiah has preserved an ancient form and not imported a new one of more or less exilic date.[41]

There is also the question of unity of origin for Chronciles-Nehemiah. We can touch only on the aspect opened by this particular study. We have seen that the four books use a common structure to present covenant-renewals with emphasis on the royal role, a ritual leader and oath. However, significant differences appear within the over-all similarity. Ezra-Nehemiah makes the community itself and even various groups organized within the community more active in entering covenant. Chronicles has the king as agent, and the community is treated as an undifferentiated whole from this point of view. Ezra-Nehemiah emphasizes the penitential and the historical-hortatory in its introductory calls to renewal, Chronicles the simpler prophetic summons. Ezra-Nehemiah is more concerned with particular directives, Chronicles with cultic purity and sacrifices in general. There is much more rejoicing in the renewals of Chronicles. Formally Ezra-Nehemiah tends to expand the presentation of a renewal. Particularly the opening ex-

God's commanding word) covenant-making, purification, and sacrifice along with rejoicing (in the passover). But is the role of the law a retrojection of later practice? The purification was long and much scattered through the land. Can it be part of a renewal-rite? And the passover is a feast in its own right (as it was even for Hezekiah: 2 Chronicles 30, the passover, follows the completion of the covenant-renewal in chap. 29). So the picture of Josiah's renewal would be a pastiche with no inner relation to the structure of the covenant-renewal. On the other hand, if covenant-renewal were an ancient and well-known practice, the record which touches only on the points important to the author would be a fully intelligible unity to an audience which was familiar with the practice alluded to. In other words, Josiah's act definitely establishes a connection between profanation and need for renewal. It is our oldest concrete example of formal renewal.

40 Brilliantly expressed in *Hamlet*, Act 3, Scene 3, lines 11-22 and *Troilus and Cressida*, Acts 1, Scene 3, lines 75-137 from an author and time sensitive to the mystique of full kingship.

41 But does not the new attitude of humility analogous to the new demands of Chronicles found in late Babylonian inscriptions point to a late date for the ideological complex? Perhaps this is so for the attitude in Mesopotamia because it was connected with western influence like the *adû*. However, the sixth century was a new era of a more interiorized religion throughout the Near East. Thus the emphasis on it for kings or covenant-making with the LORD would be an insight into the meaning of an office or a rite due to the spirit of the age, not to the date of influences, office, or rite.

hortation and the description of entering into covenant are much expanded and more complex, while the transitions between the formal elements are not so smooth.

One can explain these differences in various ways. Ezra-Nehemiah is dealing with a chastised community, not the confident Judean monarchy of Chronicles. Ezra-Nehemiah seems to have a law more realized in its details, a fact reflected in its emphasis on "the book of the law" compared to Chronicles. In the new community there was no native king. Ezra and Nehemiah acted as representatives of an alien monarch and so had less authority. They had to take real account of the various power-groups within the community. Formally, it is natural that a genre expand and also loosen its structure over time, and Ezra-Nehemiah's renewals are much later than those in Chronicles. Thus new circumstances can be adduced to explain the divergences of the covenant-renewals in Ezra-Nehemiah from those in Chronicles.

However, the differences are accompanied by a basic divergence in technical vocabulary. Chronicles emphasizes the need to "seek earnestly" (*dāraš*) after and "be humble" (*kānaᶜ*) before God and not to "rebel contemptuously" (*māᶜal*) and "forsake" (*ᶜāzab*) him lest he forsake the community. Ezra-Nehemiah looks more to studying, learning, and teaching the book of the law and so, perhaps, is led to concentrate more on particular demands. Even these differences may be explained by new circumstances in the new era represented by Ezra and Nehemiah. Language certainly does change with time and circumstance. One might even hold that Ezra-Nehemiah is dealing with a form it did not really undersand well and so did not express well; but I for one am more than dubious of a claim that an ancient writer understood his material less well than we. Nevertheless, the differences are there. It is particularly hard to see why an author who deals honestly with documents and events which are of a type but which had altered with time and circumstances, in sum, is content to picture the variations in covenant-renewals as they came to him, would have to abandon the technical vocabulary he used not so much to record the type as to expound its meaning and consequences. Surely it was still valid for interpreting the variant forms of the type. The unity is there, but it is stretched very thin by variation in structure, ideas, and especially in language where it is unnecessary. Does this point to different origins? Different authors? At best, a school? It would be a school which dealt so differently with climactic points as to stretch the concept of a single school so thin that it seems to lose any real meaning.

PART II

Exegetical Studies

Reprinted from the CATHOLIC BIBLICAL QUARTERLY, Vol. XXVII, No. 4, pp. 336-347, October 1965

MOSES' DEALINGS WITH PHARAOH: EX 7,8—10,27

There is no doubt about the unity of Exodus 5 to 15 in some sense. These chapters deal with Moses' negotiations with Pharaoh, his initial frustrations, and his final success in leading Israel out of Egypt. Thus they progress to a climax. Yet they are not an entire unity, constructed as though one piece from one hand in every sense of the phrase. Doublets, inconsistency, stylistic variations, all the classical criteria of source criticism, occur so that the discernment of the various literary strata in these chapters is certain. This discernment has in fact been the focus of the interest of commentators. One recent writer,[1] indeed, feels the need to defend the primary value of the search for sources against the current interest in the final redaction. The latter may be a skillful cento; nevertheless for him the chief value lies in its preservation of bits of the old sources. It is easy enough to understand this attitude if we remember that he is thinking of the cult tradition theories of Pedersen and others. Aside from this I find little evidence for a need of such a protest in regard to these chapters of Exodus, whatever may be the case in OT studies in general. In the latest extensive commentaries we find careful attention to source criticism; Rylaarsdam,[2] for instance, is much concerned with the theological dimension but he devotes careful notice to the sources, and Noth,[3] though an advocate of a modified cult tradition origin for the plague narratives, offers very detailed source criticism.

In fact, even the historical-traditional school which considers Exodus 1 to 15 to be a unit developed from the Passover liturgy has failed to devote sufficient attention to the final form of the text, the form which the believer takes to be inspired and which in any case is the unique source of our knowledge both of underlying oral and literary traditions and historical events. A careful assessment of the structure of the final text and the intention this reveals must be of value and interest when the redactor's text is a real unit. This is so even though source criticism and tradition-historical analysis reveal different structures and intentions in the materials which have been used to make up the final text, for this text is a literary datum in its own right. In addition such literary analysis can often help us in our assessment of the use of sources and the direction of the tradition, that is,

1 G. Fohrer, *Überlieferung und Geschichte des Exodus* (BZAW 91; Berlin, 1964) 5.
2 "Exodus," *Interpreter's Bible* (New York and Nashville, 1952) 1, 831-1099.
3 *Exodus* (Old Testament Library; London, 1962).

in our view of the actual process of tradition and redaction. It is the contention of this paper that there is a clear, meaningful structure in the story of the so-called plagues. They are presented in an elaborate literary structure, a structure which includes the episode of the wand and serpents (Ex 7,8-13) but not the death of the first born of Egypt (Ex 11-12). And this must lead us to question the ordinary, somewhat uncritical thesis that the "plagues" as they stand are the development of a ritual *legenda* for the Passover, a *legenda* recounting the death of the first-born of Egypt and the Exodus.[4]

We may begin with a question: Why do we have the plagues we find in MT and not others? We can exclude the claim that the account in Exodus is a literal history of a succession of natural phenomena.[5] This assumption is disproved by the simple fact that Psalms 78 and 105 vary the order of the plagues, which along with Ex itself, shows that literary and other factors and not the desire to mirror reality point for point govern the sequence of these episodes. The various stories of the plagues are surely the result of a long oral and literary development around the basic fact of the escape from Egypt.

Neither does the evidence indicate that we are dealing with a logically ordered collection of all possible plague stories, that is, that a desire to be exhaustive governed the collection of the plague stories in Exodus. This is proved by the fact that some doublets from various sources have been kept; "gnats" and "flies," murrain and the "boils" are found, but other variants have been suppressed. The story of the pollution of the Nile clearly combines two elements in one version: the death of the fish making the water undrinkable, and the waters turning to blood.[6] The doublets show that the redactor was not motivated by a desire to construct a perfectly smooth logical sequence; the combination means that some features have been suppressed so that we know he was not driven by an antiquarian's urge to conserve every scrap of the old data.

[4] The standard treatment is J. Pedersen, *Israel* III-IV (London and Copenhagen, 1940) 384-415, 728-737. A modified version is found in M. Noth, *Überlieferung und Geschichte des Pentateuch* (Stuttgart, 1948), 70-77, which perhaps takes more account of the problems actually raised by the texts. A telling criticism of the failure of the cult *legenda* theory to take into account the inconcinnities in the actual text will be found in S. Mowinckel, "Die vermeintliche 'Passahlegende' Ex. 1-15 in Bezug auf die Frage: Lituraturkritik und Traditionskritik," *Studia Thcologica* 5 (1951) 66-88, but the author stops short with traditional source criticism.

[5] There is of course a great deal of literature on this. The best up-to-date survey and critique is to be found in G. Fohrer, *ibid.*, 75-79.

[6] Probably there is evidence for a collation of *three* versions: death of the fish, pollution of the Nile, and pollution of all the waters of Egypt; see G. Fohrer, *ibid.*, 63, 71.

If these were not his motives, was he governed by the desire to produce as dramatic a sequence as possible? The situation does indeed develop, but this is not really a function of the plagues. They have not been so selected and arranged that there is a regular increase in severity and impressiveness. To be sure, there is progress from the magician's trick in Ex 7,8-13 through four evils visited upon the Egyptians which produced discomfort, then through four which endanger health, to the numinous fear cast by the plague of darkness.[7] However, this progress is not verified in detail; the pollution of the waters is really as bad as any of the following plagues, in fact, worse, while the sequence of "gnats" and "flies" or hail and locusts hardly shows an increase of discomfort or danger.

No, neither a dramatic sense nor an antiquarian catch-all drive nor a simple yen to report can serve to explain entirely the choice or sequence of the plagues in MT. I suggest that the governing device is a complex concentric literary scheme, the recognition of which points to important conclusions concerning the structure, aims and origins of significant parts of the pericope Ex 5 to 15. A discussion of all this involves an amount of material far too extensive for a single article. Here I shall confine myself to presenting the analysis of the plague narratives themselves. A further article to appear soon will deal with the problems of connections with the context in Ex 5 to 15 and of the implications of all this for source criticism and tradition history.

Division of the Text

The first problem in dealing with the plague narratives is the correct division of the text. I have already mentioned that such a division does not show a literary unit beginning with the pollution of the waters of Egypt (Ex 7,14-25) and including as its climax the threat against the first born of Egypt and its execution (Ex 11-12), nor even the threat alone in chapter 11. This sequence, pollution of the waters through the blow against Egypt's first born, is indeed the customary grouping of most commentaries and of most other literature. However, though this sequence is logical in that it finishes with what is clearly the climactic event conceptually, the formal characteristics of the literary text do not bear it out. From the purely for-

[7] So D. M. G. Stalker, "Exodus," *Peake's Commentary on the Bible* (London, 1963) 182h, quoting *A Catholic Commentary on Holy Scripture.* A proper understanding of the force of the rather innocuous-seeming plague of darkness depends upon recognizing it as a terrifying numinous experience, an aspect developed in Wisdom 17,1—18,23. Rylaarsdam (*Interpreter's Bible* 1, 913) points out the special terror darkness held for the Egyptians with their belief that the monster Apophis threatened the life-giving sun during each period of darkness.

mal literary point of view the affair of the first born is separate and the preceding episodes beginning with the trick with the rod and the serpent, not with the pollution of the Nile, form an independent unit, Ex 7,8—10,27. Martin Noth has recognized this in the organization of his commentary.[8] However, the German scholar has not developed the insight in detail; in fact he seems to abandon it. For instance, he treats the "gnats" and the "flies" (Ex 8,12-28) as a single unit, which does violence to the formal structure. Probably this occurs because in the end he is primarily concerned with source criticism and these episodes are in fact doublets from P and J. Thus source criticism obscures literary analysis, a not unusual event.

As a matter of fact the procedure to be seen in Exodus 7,8—10,27 is rather unusual. The sources have been broken up and the *disjecta membra* reorganized into a new whole.[9] The resulting construction excludes the account of the stroke against the first-born of Egypt from the literary unit so formed. Chapter 11 is clearly set off from the preceding episodes in its formal literary characteristics. It is different in structure and especially in style from the episodes recounted in Ex 7,8—10,27. The difference is clear, whatever may be its origins and significance.[10] The opening verse of chapter 11 is indeed the standard one. In form and vocabulary it is just like that of the other plague narratives but it goes on in a wildly different manner. The image of the divorce[11] is in a new spirit and the verb *gāraš* is not part of the vocabulary of the plague stories, though it does occur in Ex 6,1. The theme of tricking the Egyptians out of their goods (11,2) is entirely new in the plague context, though its basic idea, the slyboots, belongs to the world of folklore which has been heavily drawn upon in the earlier plague stories.[12] The notice in 11,3 that Israel enjoyed great favor in Egyptian eyes is of course nonsense after the plagues. A people shown to

[8] *Exodus,* 62-84. Rylaarsdam, *ibid.,* 839-895, notices the careful, highly stylized construction of the plagues narrative, but he retains the customary division, while G. Fohrer, *Überlieferung . . . des Exodus,* 62, remarks that the earlier plagues can seem at first to be a formal unity, but that this impression is deceiving.

[9] M. Noth, *op. cit.,* 269 (with n. 648) claims that this procedure is unusual, but there is no doubt that it does occur here; cf. Rylaarsdam, *ibid.,* 838.

[10] The alien character of the account of the stroke against the firstborn of Egypt has not escaped notice. P. Zerafa, O.P., "Passover and Unleavened Bread," *Angelicum* 41 (1964) 240 thinks that there may have been a decomposition of a unit originally similar to the rest of the plague stories; see also M. Noth, *Exodus,* 68-69.

[11] For the proper translation of 11,1b: "As one letteth go a slave-wife shall he surely expel you hence," see D. Daube, *The Exodus Pattern in the Bible* (All Soul's Studies 2; London, 1963) 58.

[12] For the folklore elements see F. Dumermuth, "Folkloristisches in der Erzählung von den Ägyptischen Plagen," *ZAW* 76 (1964) 323-325.

be under the protection of so powerful a deity would receive a terrified respect but never favor![13] Again, the odd figurative language of verse 7 deals with a familiar theme, Israel's exemption and Egypt's suffering, but in a new manner. This same verse uses a clause, "that you may know," which is familiar from the earlier plague stories. The trouble is, this use leads one to expect the customary continuation, something like "I am Yahweh." Here in 11,7 the so very different sequel is a jolt. Then there are the sudden leaps and the disjointed structure. For example, why the mention of Moses' reputation in 11,3, and to whom is Moses speaking in verse 4? This is quite unlike the earlier stories which have their inconsistencies but which keep the action clear and show a structure of almost Alexandrian nicety.

Here I submit that the use of language and of ideas which are *almost* like those of another body of writing and yet quite different is a striking criterion of diversity. Neutral, i.e., simply different language and ideas can be worked into a context; language and ideas which arouse the expectation that they will be similar to a given context, only to turn into something very different, make it almost impossible to fit them into that context. They force attention to their divergence as though deliberately to emphasize that one has to do with very different views of a subject. For example, a tale about a more or less colorless Renaissance student might well be worked into the story of Hamlet; a tale about a violent thug called the "black-hearted Denmarker" who thirsted for his family's blood could not.

And so it goes; if we forget *our* logical conviction that the affair of the death of the first born of Egypt is the climax of the plague narrative and examine the plague narrative as narrative, that is, purely as literary structure, if we examine the textual evidence in this light, we must be struck by the profound dissimilarity of this text concerning the death of the first born from the foregoing stories. Thus an attentive study of Ex 11 has shown that it diverges in many ways from the structure and the style and the ideas of Ex 7,8—10,27. This negative evidence supports the claim that the proper division of the literary unit is Ex 7,8—10,27, not the usual 7,14—11,10 (or even—13,15).

However, this is better shown by demonstrating positively that the pericope Ex 7,8—10,27 is a relatively closed unit. Custom dictates that we speak of plagues here, and I have done so and shall continue to do so. However, the opening episode is not really a plague in the sense of something damaging. Still, the change from *nāḥāš*, "serpent" used in Ex 4,2-4,

[13] The probable reaction to such a display of divine power on behalf of strangers is well illustrated by the behaviour of the people of Gerar to Isaac in Gn 26.

where the theme of the staff and serpent is introduced, and repeated in Ex 8,15, to *tannîn,* "reptilian monster," is probably significant. Doubtless the author wanted to make the episode more impressive as an introduction to the real plagues,[14] but the alteration is especially appropriate in giving a harmless bit of mystification a sinister cast. Still, it does not make the episode a material blow against Egypt like the other plagues so that we should probably better title the whole pericope "Moses' Dealings with Pharaoh."

A look at the various accounts of these dealings beginning with Ex 7,8 reveals that there is a general structure which shows up in each of the episodes: Yahweh announces a plague to Moses, it is carried out, the effects are noted, and the conclusion about Pharaoh's hard heart is given.[15] However, there is a good deal of variation in detail. Sometimes Aaron appears, sometimes not; sometimes we have an elaborate report of Yahweh's words, sometimes not; sometimes the narrative is long, sometimes not, etc. It is the strict order in the appearance of these variations which shows the concentric structure of the whole.

Thus, if we divide the tales into two groups of five, the first including the trick with the rod and running through the plague of "flies" (Ex 7,8—8,28), the second including the murrain and running through the strange darkness (Ex 9,1—10,27), we find that each member of the group shares certain formal characteristics with its opposite number in the other group. Thus the second event, the pollution of the waters of Egypt, has in addition to the opening words of Yahweh to Moses (an opening shared with all the plague stories) a second command from Yahweh to Moses, in this case to be relayed to Aaron. It also speaks of the hardening of Pharaoh's heart at its beginning as well as its ending (where all the stories mention this). Further, Moses uses the prophetic formula, "thus says Yahweh," and says explicitly, that Israel "must go and serve Yahweh." Exactly the same collection of items in exactly the same sequence occurs in the account of the plague of locusts (Ex 10,1-20), the ninth episode, and so corresponding in its group (the second from the end) to the second plague, and only there. In the third episode, that of the frogs, we find the second command, the formula "thus says Yahweh," and the explicit "go and serve Yahweh." Exactly these features appear in the eighth episode, that of the hail, the structural parallel to number three. In the fourth plague, that of the "gnats," the first command to Moses is for Aaron. The only similar case is in the opposite number of this plague, the seventh, the "boils." Finally,

[14] G. Fohrer, *ibid.,* 59.

[15] G. Fohrer, *ibid.,* 63-68, gives detailed outlines of the plague stories.

plague number five, the "flies" has the explicit request to serve Yahweh and the prophetic formula, as does the sixth episode, its opposite, the murrain. The whole scheme is seen most clearly when outlined in parallel columns:

I. 7,8-13: 5 vv. with introductory and closing formulae.	X. 10,21-27 (29): 6 vv. with introductory and closing formulae.
II. 7,14-22 (25): 7 vv. with hardening of Pharaoh's heart at beginning and end; prophetic formula with specific request; second command to Moses.	IX. 10,1-20: 20 vv. with hardening of Pharaoh's heart at beginning and end; prophetic formula with specific request; second command to Moses.
III. 7,26—8,11: 14 vv. with second command to Moses; prophetic formula and specific request to serve Yahweh.	VIII. 9,13-35: 22 vv. with second command to Moses; prophetic formula and specific request to serve Yahweh.
IV. 8,12-15: 3 vv. in which the opening formula is a command to Moses for Aaron.	VII. 9,8-12: 4 vv. in which the opening formula is a command to Moses for Aaron.
V. 8,16-28: 12 vv. with prophetic formula and specific request to serve Yahweh.	VI. 9,1-7: 7 vv. with prophetic formula and specific request to serve Yahweh.

Thus, within a similar general framework for each unit there are variations in the formula, variations which mark the unit off from the others and set it apart along with its opposite number. By this formal device a perfect correspondence between each pair of episodes is achieved and so between the first set of five plagues and the second.

I would also draw attention to the fact that the concentric scheme as outlined so far depends upon the careful use of certain key phrases. In fact, it is constructed by means of variations on the forms in which essential concepts of the whole pericope are expressed. The structure is not a matter of manipulating secondary elements, nor of adding little touches. In great part the composer works with his main motifs. Thus we have the essential assertion that Yahweh has communicated with Moses, *wayyō'mer YHWH 'el mōšeh,* which supplies the formula marking the opening of each plague story. Its repetition within some stories gives a special mark to certain pairs of stories within the whole. Then there is the presentation of Moses as a prophet achieved by putting the prophetic formula, *kōh 'āmar YHWH,* in his mouth; again the clause is used to set off certain pairs of plague stories. Finally, the closing formula for each plague story is the notice that Pharaoh has refused to be enlightened: his heart is hard (*ḥzq, kbd*), and the repetition of this formula in some episodes is used to form certain of the pairs.[16] Of all the thematic ideas and phases of Exodus 7,8—10,27 only the expressed purpose of all Yahweh's dealings, namely, that he be acknowledged as supreme god[17] is not used in a way which reinforces the concentric structure. Surely this use of primary formal and conceptual elements to set up the concentric structure emphasizes that structure. In its turn this structure serves to give greater weight to these key themes.

Another formal element apart from this use of thematic expressions is the alteration between longer and shorter stories. Variations in length of subordinate units is certainly a formal literary element.[18] In the plague narratives we have a distinctive sequence of longer and shorter stories which is identical in each of the sets of five stories. The sequence from plagues I to V is: longer, longer, shorter, longer; so also from X to VI.

So much exact correspondence in detail between pairs of plague stories and so between the two sets of five cannot be gratuitous. It must have been planned and carefully worked out so as to produce this concentric structure of the whole series of ten episodes from Ex 7,8 to 10,27. The probability that this is so is surely increased by the fact that this sort of concentric arrangement is an important element in the rhetoric of OT authors.[19]

There is, then, a carefully articulated concentric structure in the account of Moses' dealings with Pharaoh in Ex 7,8—10,27. The ten individual units fit together into a whole which is complete in itself. This fact calls for investigation in various directions. First of all, it confirms the alien character of the account of the death of the first born of Egypt which begins in Chapter 11. Whatever its conceptual connection with the foregoing narrative of the plagues, on the literary plane this event stands apart. Further, we should expect any continuation of so elaborate a literary device as the story of Moses' dealings with Pharaoh in the ten episodes of the plagues to show itself to be a similarly careful, even elaborate piece of writing.

[16] Oddly, the use of now *ḥzq,* now *kbd,* is not woven into the concentric pattern. I do not know why, but of course not everything need be forced into the pattern so that this fact hardly argues against the general structure confirmed by so many factors.

[17] Expressed through variations on the basic sentence *yd' kî 'aenî YHWH* in Ex 7,17; 8,6; 8,18; 9,14; 9,29, with different expressions of the same idea in 8,15 (the magicians recognize the finger of God) and 9,16 (Yahweh's name is to be spoken everywhere in the country).

[18] This is demonstrated in the study of N. Lohfink, "Der Bundesschluss im Land Moab," *Biblische Zeitschrift* 6 (1962) 32-56.

[19] See L. Alonso-Schökel, *Estudios de poética hebrea* (Barcelona, 1963) 317, 370.

This is matter for a further article. The first task must remain the investigation of the plagues pericope in itself. For one thing, such a device as concentric structure is open to easy abuse. A fascination with purely external, formal elements brings the danger of preciosity and lack of content. Further, the concentric form can easily tend to the static. Such is not the case in Ex 7,8—10,27. The concentric literary scheme, of course, is there for its own sake in a way. It is an element of style which structures the passage, gives it harmony and so pleases the reader. It thus performs the function of any such rhetorical device, but it does not stultify. For one thing, the type of concentrism used helps avoid the tendency to the formation of a static and isolated unit. In one type of concentrism a unit is given a prologue and a corresponding epilogue. The central unit is thus set apart and given great emphasis. In Ex 7,8—10,27 there is no such solid central block. We really have a narrowing set of inclusions where the first and last episodes correspond, then the second and the penultimate, and so forth. Concentrism in this form allows the author to carry things forward more easily even while marking off a step in his literary scheme because it does not focus on an element in the center of its own literary unit.

In fact, there is considerable progress through the ten plague episodes so that, though they bring no definitive result themselves, they do prepare the reader for something more, something beyond themselves. By the end we know a great deal more about the confrontation of Moses and Pharaoh, really a confrontation of Yahweh with Egypt's gods, and its meaning, and we understand much better the characters of those involved in the confrontation. Thus there is a definite tension between the basic formal element, the concentric structure with its static tendency, and the real progress in the narrative and its ideas, a tension which gives vitality to the whole unit.

The elements in which the progress appears are clear enough. The earlier episodes still reflect a more primitive and popular, a more or less magical concept of the proceedings. The magician's wand operates. There is a contest with the magicians representing the gods of Egypt,[20] in which for a time these latter are able to hold their own without disgrace. Finally, they are discomfited and Yahweh and his agents dominate the scenes. This is definite progress and it is no objection to say that it results from the disappearance of the P source in the later episodes. This is indeed the case,

20 The exact character of the *ḥarṭumîm* has often been discussed, but J. Vergote, *Joseph in Egypte* (Orientalia et biblica lovaniensia 3; Louvain, 1959) 66-72 seems to have established that they were originally religious functionaries, scribes who kept the ritual texts, hence the words of power, spells.

but the point is that the sources have been combined with conscious art so as to achieve this element of increased seriousness.

Besides this negative process, the removal of a primitive factor, there is a positive progression. The dignity of Yahweh's human representatives increases in that Moses works alone without Aaron in the later plague stories. To be sure, one point of view in our OT sources tends to make Aaron Moses' equal, but there is no denying that the dominant tradition emphasizes the unique status of Moses so that his emergence as a sole human agent of Yahweh gives greater importance to the later episodes. Beyond the human actors it should be noted that, though it is clear that all the events are brought about by Yahweh, in the earlier plagues Moses and Aaron are the immediate agents. At most we are informed that they act through the power of Yahweh who thus is brought in at second hand, as it were. From the fifth plague on it is Yahweh himself who strikes Egypt immediately. Likewise, it is only in the later plagues (VII: 9,8-12; IX: 10,1-20; X: 10,21-27) that Yahweh hardens Pharaoh's heart. Once more the dignity of the agent increases, this time immeasurably, and so the import of the whole.

Again, though the plagues do not attain what seems to be their object, the freeing of Israel from Egypt, they are effective in attaining another important object as they go on. Pharaoh advances from a grudging assent permitting sacrifices in Egypt (8,21) or nearby (8,24) to greater, if still insufficient acquiescence, along with a confession of sin (9,27-28; 10,8. 16-17), surely a notable admission from a living god. In this the plagues come close to achieving Yahweh's expressed intention to produce a conversion in Pharaoh, to teach him that "I am Yahweh." This is the purpose of the plagues as expressed in the text (cf. 8,6. 18; 9,16. 29 where *l^ema'an* introduces the demand that Pharaoh "know that I am Yahweh") and surely we must respect this information. Strikingly the working of "signs and wonders" is of no importance in Ex 7,8—10,27, contrary to the claim that the multiplication of signs and wonders is the reason for multiplying the plagues.[21] In fact, there is no reference to this in the plague stories themselves, where the phrase "signs and wonders" never occurs. "Sign" (*'ōt*) is used, once in Pharaoh's request for an amusing bit of magic, and only once and there in passing in the words of Yahweh and Moses. It hardly seems correct to draw from this a basic purpose of the story, much less an anticipatory connection with the Passover.[22] The "signs and wonders" belong

[21] So, v.g., M. Noth, *Exodus,* 69.
[22] *Ibid.,* 67.

to a rather different spirit from the plague stories, as they certainly belong to a different literary unit.

In fact, the expressed aim of the plagues in Ex 7,8—10,27 is to produce an almost cultic recognition of Yahweh, for the liturgical provenance of the key demand, *yd' kî 'ani YHWH* is well known.[23] This demand is thematic, and it is repeated in a manner giving it increasing emphasis and meaning. In the second plague a simple confession is demanded (7,17); in the third this is to be an exclusive confession (8,6); in the fifth recognition in *Egypt* is demanded (8,19: the point is that the apparent local dominion of Yahweh over the desert is seen to include Egypt as well); in the seventh plague this recognition is to be exclusive and to include expressed admission that Yahweh is lord of Egypt. (9,14.16.19). This is a gradual revelation of the divine nature which will eventually be acknowledged even in Egypt.[24] Correlative with this broadening of the claim on Pharaoh's conscience or perhaps better his religious sense is the development of Yahweh's demand for his people; by the plague of darkness it has become absolute. No restrictions, no conditions are allowed. Thus the demands put forward by Yahweh through Moses are another element which makes for progress within the concentric structure of the plague narratives.

We must, then, recognize a definite forward movement in the account of Moses' dealings with Pharaoh in Ex 7,8—10,27, and this extends beyond the observation that the plagues do not attain their principal object. Though there is an elaborate, detailed concentric structure in the pericope, this does not mean that, tightly knit unit though it be, it is closed within itself. We must look beyond it since the progression within it does not come to term. We must seek its continuation, but such seeking must be done with the literary character of the unit in mind. With its concentric form it is at least a subdivision which in so far as it is set forth is a satisfactory unit in itself. Its continuation must leave this intact. We should expect this continuation to display the developed instinct for structure revealed in Ex 7,8—10,27 and to use the thematic ideas developed but not completed there. All these literary facts must be taken into consideration in our thinking about Exodus. Further, the mosaic-like way in which various sources have been fitted together to form an intricate concentric pattern reveals a good deal, or perhaps, better raises important questions about the way sources were used in constructing the Pentateuch. Finally, the special, relatively

23 See W. Zimmerli, "Ich bin Jahwe," *Alt Festschrift* (Tübingen, 1953) 179-209 (=*Gottes Offenbarung* [Munich, 1963] 11-40).

24 See Y. Kaufmann, *The Religion of Israel* (Chicago, 1960) 164 on the fact that Egypt somehow came to know Yahweh.

closed character of Ex 7,8—10,27 and the failure of this unit to mesh with Chapter 11 (and the rules for the Passover in Chh. 12-13) surely have something to say about the relation of much of Exodus chh. 5 to 15 to the Passover liturgy, and consequently about the tradition-history involved.

DENNIS J. MCCARTHY, S.J.
Saint Mary's College
St. Marys, Kansas

II SAMUEL 7 AND THE STRUCTURE OF THE DEUTERONOMIC HISTORY

DENNIS J. McCARTHY, S.J.
ST. MARY'S COLLEGE, KANSAS

IN HIS *Überlieferungsgeschichtliche Studien* Martin Noth points out a number of passages which are used to tie the complex deuteronomic history together. Where possible, these take the form of speeches attributed to leading actors in the history (Josh 1 11–15; Josh 23; I Sam 12; I Kings 8 14–61). Where this is inconvenient, the writer offers his own reflections (Josh 12; Judg 2 11–23; II Kings 17 7–23). In the one case as in the other the content is a kind of meditation on Israel's history. The past is considered, the future scanned, and the sequence of events explained so as to give a practical guide for man's activity.[1] These passages stand at the turning points of Israel's history: the beginning and the end of the conquest, of the era of the judges, and of the monarchy. They call attention to the significant changes in Israel's circumstances and serve to explain how these things have come to be. It is the contention of this paper that the passages which Noth has singled out are indeed important. They do serve as major articulations in the deuteronomic scheme of Israel's history. However, another passage should be included in the list: Nathan's promise to David in II Sam 7. This famous passage fills the same function as the key passages picked out by Noth; more, in conjunction with the others it sets in relief a carefully worked out over-all structure in the deuteronomic history as a whole.

In an argument of this type the analysis of possible literary sources for the present form of II Sam 7 is not essential. As a matter of fact, the chapter seems to be a unity in form and content, and it does show the marks of the deuteronomic hand.[2] But whatever the origins and the history of the growth of the text, whatever its possible composite character, it is the actual text as it stands in the deuteronomic history which matters. This is the text which functions as an integral part of the literary complex. The problem here is to show this function. To do

[1] M. Noth, *Überlieferungsgeschichtliche Studien*, p. 5.

[2] So M. Noth, "David und Israel in II Samuel, 7," *Mélanges Robert*, pp. 122–30. See also J. McKenzie, S.J., "The Dynastic Oracle: II Samuel 7," *Theological Studies*, 8 (1948), pp. 187–218, and H. van den Bussche, "Le texte de la prophétie de Nathan sur la dynastie davidique," *Ephemerides Theologicae Lovanienses*, 24 (1948), pp. 355–94.

this, I shall try to show that the text operates with ideas that are important and special to the deuteronomic work, that it is closely integrated into its immediate literary context, and finally that, in part in virtue of the very foregoing factors, it has a key position in the scheme of the whole massive work which extends from Deuteronomy to Kings.

We may begin with a significant phrase applied by Yahweh to David: "my servant David." The only other occurence of this precise phrase, "my servant N.," in the whole of the deuteronomic work is "my servant Moses" in the words of Yahweh to Joshua when he takes over the leadership of Israel.[3] Not even Joshua himself merits the title; besides Moses only David does. This calls attention to David's importance — he merits comparison with Moses — and the important new thing, the institution of the Davidic monarchy, which begins with him.

Another point: twice in II Sam 7 we are told that Yahweh has given David rest from his enemies.[4] The word is the hiphil הֵנִיחַ which, of course, is practically a technical term in the deuteronomic writings for Yahweh's ultimate blessing on Israel: rest from the enemies in the promised land.[5] The realization of the ancient hope of Israel in and through David is thus indicated, and the people's destinies are tied to his. In this regard we should note the way the people are brought into the picture explicitly. The author does not state directly that the people are blessed in and through David. They are simply juxtaposed with him. In the midst of a proclamation about David's office (vss. 7, 9b) and the grace which Yahweh will show him in giving him rest from his enemies (9b, 11b) the author inserts a notice that the people have been given a place in which to dwell in peace (10–11a). It is obvious that the two are connected, that the people's position depends on that of the king and his line. Now, exactly this same technique is used elsewhere in the deuteronomic corpus: in Deut 31 1–6 we find the divine commissioning of Joshua with a similar commission to the people inserted within it.[6] Again, there is no explicit relating of the two, but the connection and dependence of one on the other is obvious. Apparently what is being done is this: it is put beyond a shadow of a doubt that a commission and a promise to a properly constituted leader ex-

[3] Josh 1 2, 7.

[4] II Sam 7 1, 11.

[5] See G. von Rad, *Theologie des Alten Testaments*, I, p. 233. הֵנִיחַ in this sense of giving rest from troubles is peculiar to the deuteronomic writings and the Chronicles except for one instance in Exod 33 14 (the source of the usage?). In Chronicles its use is obviously dependent on the deuteronomic usage; very often it occurs in direct references to the promise to David and in relation to the temple.

[6] Joshua (1–4, 6b); the people (5–6a). The latter verses in the plural cannot refer to Joshua, for, while it is possible that a text address the people now in the plural, now in the singular, since they are at once a collection of individuals and a moral unity, there is no reason to speak to one man in the plural.

tends to all the people, and in the deuteronomic writings this is done by this simple technique of juxtaposing the two.

A further link between the promise and an earlier portion of the deuteronomic history is the reference to and contrast with the era of the judges in vss. 7, 10–11.[7] The concept of the judges as official leaders of all Israel and the picture of their era as a time of regularly recurring troubles is, according to Noth, specifically deuteronomic. These ideas form the background for the reference in II Sam 7, and David and his line are presented as the true successors of the judges who will bring on the lasting rest from Israel's enemies which the earlier leaders were unable to achieve.[8]

II Sam 7, then, operates with terms and concepts familiar to the deuteronomic world, and this is not a matter of mere minor stylistic points. The passage calls attention to itself because of the major themes which appear in the promise: David is compared with Moses and given a key position in the progress of salvation history, precisely as it is seen by the deuteronomic school. It is at least suitable that a proclamation of such importance function as a key member in the articulation of the whole history.

The next step must be to show from literary considerations how the chapter is fitted into or, better, made the central element of its immediate context, the story of the decline of Saul and the accession of David. As soon as the account of Saul's rejection and the consequent gradual decline of his power begins in I Sam 13, we begin to find allusions to his eventual successor, allusions which look forward to Nathan's promise to David. Not merely is there a hint of a successor, but the fact that his family will hold the throne enduringly — an idea proper to Nathan's promise — is certainly implied in the contrast between the faithless Saul, who loses his chance at a kingship for ever (עַד־עוֹלָם), and the successor who is after God's own heart.[9] As the story progresses, the successor is identified as David, and his future prospects are given in terms which recall the words and ideas of the promise. His throne will endure, and Yahweh will cut off his enemies.[10] He will have a "sure house."[11] He will succeed the judges and successfully fulfill their mis-

[7] In vs. 7 read שֹׁפְטֵי with Chron for שִׁבְטֵי.

[8] See M. Noth, *Überlieferungsgeschichtliche Studien*, pp. 20–21, 53 on the deuteronomic character of the structure which is given to the era of the judges. In *Mélanges Robert*, pp. 125–26, Noth shows how the promise of Nathan is concerned to link David with the Hebrew *Heilsgeschichte* in general; the connection with the judges is but a specific instance of this.

[9] I Sam 13 13–14.

[10] I Sam 20 15.

[11] בַּיִת נֶאֱמָן (I Sam 25 28). The phrase occurs only here and in II Sam 7 16; I Sam 2 35 (the last instance of the priestly house which will succeed that of Eli; in view of the connection between the house of Zadok taking over the high priesthood

sion.[12] He will be a shepherd of God's people.[13] In view of all this there is no reason to doubt that other passages which look forward to the enduring Davidic kingship are intended to evoke the promise, even if they are couched in more general terms.[14] Thus, as the story of David's taking over from Saul progresses, the promise is continually called to our attention so that the episode with Nathan comes as a climax to the narrative.

As for what follows upon the promise, its effects are apparent in the account of the latter days of David's reign and in the story of Solomon. It is universally recognized that I Kings 2 3–4 and I Kings 8 are direct allusions to the promise. Further, the account of Solomon's reign is so structured as to come to a climax in I Kings 8, that is, in the completion of the temple, at once the fulfillment and the guarantee of the promise.[15] The promise, therefore, provides the literary framework for the account of the events which followed upon it. It is at once the climax of the narrative which precedes it and the program for what follows; in a word, it is central to its immediate context.

Can we show that this passage is one of the key elements in the deuteronomic history, one of the passages which give structure to the whole? To show this we must begin with I Sam 12, which is said to mark the transition from the era of the judges to the era of the monarchy.[16] This may be so, but it can hardly be said that the kingship as it has begun with Saul is accepted without cavil. It has generally been accepted and it is true that I Sam 12, at least in Samuel's speech beginning in vs. 6, is basically antimonarchical. At best Samuel, who speaks for Yahweh, gives a grudging consent to the kingship. The whole business has a negative tone. The historical section of Samuel's speech is unusual in the emphasis it lays on the era of the judges with its accent on Israel's failure — compare the structurally similar speeches in Josh 23 and 24, where Israel's history is given with no mention of them. The people's motive for demanding a king (vs. 12) is put on a level with the sins of the era of the judges, sins caused by Israel's readiness to turn to the ways of the gentiles, for, if they seek a king to defend them against Nahash the Ammonite, this is surely in large part because they consider the alien institution to be effective and so worth

---

and Solomon's succession as the child of the promise it is probable that the phrase was applied to the house of Zadok under the influence of Nathan's promise) and I Kings 11 38 (Nathan's promise repeated by Ahijah). It seems clear that the phrase was special to the complex of ideas about the promise.

[12] II Sam 3 18.

[13] II Sam 5 2.

[14] I Sam 24 21–22; 28 17–18; II Sam 3 9–10; 5 12; 6 21.

[15] Noth, *Überlieferungsgeschichtliche Studien*, pp. 68–70.

[16] *Ibid.*, pp. 4, 53–60.

imitating. In any case, Samuel sees fit to reprove the demand as a rejection of Yahweh. The demand for the kingship, in fact, seems almost the climactic sin of the era of the judges. The negative cast of the speech is carried over into its conclusion: in vs. 14 we expect a hopeful apodosis to the condition as is normal in the construction and indicated by the parallel in vs. 15. The deliberate omission of this blessing upon fidelity calls attention to itself and serves as an effective rhetorical device to emphasize the sinister cast of vs. 15.

As though this verse were not enough, Samuel concludes with the explicit statement that the demand for a king that led to Saul's coronation was a sin, and he elicits an express, miraculous confirmation of this judgment from Yahweh. Now I submit that if this is the transition from the judgeship to kingship, the transition is not at all smooth and is by no means complete. It ends in a rejection, not an acceptance of kingship, at least as it has appeared so far in the history of Israel. It is true, however, that the chapter ends with a reconciliation; in vss. 20–25 Yahweh through Samuel accepts the people's repentance and promises to stand by them. The trouble is, this acceptance makes no mention of the king and in the context this omission is striking and surely deliberate. Yahweh accepts the people who want a king but he has deliberately refrained from accepting the kingship itself. In sum, I Sam 12 is much more a conclusion to an unhappy era than the beginning of a new one.

This position of Saul's monarchy, ambiguous at the least, becomes clearer as we turn back to the historical narrative. Immediately in ch. 13 comes the explicit rejection of Saul and the first of the numerous adumbrations of the promise to David which we have seen. The monarchy which arose from Israel's sin, the creation of its own will rather than Yahweh's will, is passing and something new is on the way. The change comes slowly in the detailed account of Saul's decline and David's accession, but it moves steadily to its climax in the taking of Jerusalem, the moving of the ark thither, and, finally, Nathan's promise. Here, obviously, the monarchy is judged positively. The sin at the very root of the first attempt at monarchy, self-will, is avoided. A conscious reworking of the more primitive form of Nathan's promise changes the old relationship: David protected the ark; therefore he is rewarded with a promise that his line will endure. Now it is the reverse: David's line may build a temple precisely because it has Yahweh's promise given in entire freedom.[17]

There may even be an explicit link between the aspect of reconciliation of I Sam 12 and II Sam 7 in the concept of the divine name. In

[17] See H. Gese, "Der Davidsbund und die Zionserwählung," *Zeitschrift für Theologie und Kirche*, 61 (1964), pp. 10–26.

I Sam 12 22 Yahweh forgives Israel for his name's sake; in II Sam 7 26 the glory of his name is tied to David's line.[18] The first instance is general: reconciliation with no details as to how; the second specifies this: the reconciliation takes place in and through the Davidic monarchy. However, references to the divine name in the deuteronomic writings is so common that it is impossible to prove that this link is intended.

The presumptions of the sequence here postulated: sin, repentance, renewal in a new subject, are deuteronomic. The overriding theological principle is that Yahweh's word is infallible.[19] Even though it be frustrated in a given instance, it will eventually be fulfilled. The same principle is at work in Deut 1, where the desert generation sins and is denied the promised land (vs. 35) but the succeeding generation is assured possession of the land (vs. 39) because the promise to the patriarchs is still valid as is apparent even in vs. 35.[20] One might even ask if the disappearance of Saul and his family, the concrete embodiment of Israel's sinful self-will, is not thought of as a parallel with the death of the desert generation leaving the way open for the guiltless successor.

Note that this apparent equating of the promise to David with the promise to Israel through the patriarchs brings it into the complex of ideas relating to the covenant. As a matter of fact it has often been stated that the Davidic covenant tends to absorb the older one.[21] If we are right in holding that a number of important ideas about Israel's special relation to Yahweh — the ideas of "rest," of Moses as Yahweh's special mediating servant, etc. — are taken up and applied to David, this does not seem strange. However, in view of this whole complex it seems inaccurate to think of the Davidic covenant as displacing the older covenant between Yahweh and Israel, as is often done. Rather, for the D writer, the Davidic covenant continues and specifies the older one. David's covenant does not compete with the people's covenant as an independent, parallel means to Yahweh's grace; rather, through David the whole people receives the divine favor. The continuity is brought out among other ways in the unembarrassed application of old covenant terminology to David, as, for instance, in I Kings 8 24, which of course depends on the promise by Nathan.

In any event, gathering so many basic ideas as it does, II Sam 7 is eminently fitted to be a renewal, a program for the future. David's

[18] See Noth, *Mélanges Robert*, pp. 124–25, on the central importance of Yahweh's name in Nathan's promise.

[19] See II Sam 7 21 and often in the references to David's accession between I Sam 12 and II Sam 7. Yahweh's favor to Israel through David is given because of his word.

[20] See N. Lohfink, S.J., "Darstellungskunst und Theologie in Dtn 1, 6–3, 29," *Biblica*, 41 (1960), p. 127.

[21] E. g., A. Alt, *Kleine Schriften* II, p. 133; J. McKenzie, *Myths and Realities*, p. 207.

line has a lasting destiny bound up with the temple, the proper center for worship of Yahweh. As noted already, the working out of the promise is the explicit source for the structure of the account of Solomon's reign culminating in the building of the temple. More, the grace of Yahweh promised to David continues to work in the destinies of the kings of Judah. Surely the deuteronomist's preoccupation with the kings' attitudes to worship arises in part out of the connection of the house of David with the temple which is based on Nathan's promise. In the deuteronomist's eyes the very "constitution" of the kingship makes the proper worship of Yahweh the king's great duty and great glory.

Now I believe it can be shown that this use of the promise of Nathan as a new beginning, related to the past but essentially a program for the future, fits into the scheme of the deuteronomic history as a whole and gives that block of literature a symmetric form. The passages which Noth has pointed out do stand at turning points in Israel's history. They do indeed sum up the past and look to the future, but in addition there is a clear relationship among the passages and certain other key parts of the deuteronomic writings themselves. They do not stand on the same level. Briefly, what the deuteronomic writer has done is to provide three programmatic passages and then to use six of his key passages to show how these programs worked or failed in subsequent history. We can put this schematically as follows:

A. Moses commands the conquest and distribution of the land (Deut 31)	A^1. Joshua undertakes the conquest (Josh 2)
	A^2. Joshua conquers and prepares the distribution (Josh 11–13)
B. Joshua commands the בְּרִית, the program for life in the land (Josh 23)	B^1. The people break the בְּרִית (Judg 2)
	B^2. The people reject Yahweh for a human king (I Sam 12)
C. Nathan's Promise (II Sam 7)	C^1. The promise fulfilled in Solomon (I Kings 8)
	C^2. Final failure of the kingship (II Kings 17)

It is generally recognized that Deuteronomy itself is the program for the history which follows this book: it provides the norm by which Israel's history is judged and its success or failure explained. However, there is a more precise relationship than this between parts of Deuteronomy and the key passages in Josh 1 and 12. In Deut 31 we have an extended presentation of the commissioning of Joshua by Moses (Deut 31 7–9) and by Yahweh (Deut 31 14–23), a commission to which the passages of the Book of Joshua certainly refer as is shown by the way they pick up the language of Deuteronomy in this regard. In fact, what we have here is first the program, the commission given to Joshua which has two parts: leading the conquest and distributing the Promised Land, and then the introduction to the carrying out of now the one part of this program (Josh 1), now the other part (Josh 12).[22]

In the next set of key passages (Josh 23, Judg 2 and I Sam 12) we can see the same relationship. Josh 23 "formulates the principal demands governing the way of life in the conquered land."[23] Thus it is a program for future living, and its programmatic character is emphasized by its form which is surely intended as an allusion to the covenant.[24] Judg 2 and I Sam 12 are related to this, but in a negative manner. They attest the failure to live up to the program. As was pointed out earlier, I Sam 12 actually sees Saul's monarchy as the culminating sin of the period of the judges, and while there is certain reconciliation in vss. 20–25, the monarchy is excluded from this. Thus in the complex Josh 23+Judg 2+I Sam 12 we have this structure: program plus a double affirmation of its failure, a structure which is the negative double of that in Deut 31+Josh 1+Josh 12.

The last key passages conform to the same scheme if we include II Sam 7. That section provides the program, and the next two, I Kings 8 and II Kings 17, show its working out. The first is hopeful: Solomon has built the temple, and the promise to David is working out to good; but the second is negative: the kingship and with it the people have come to grief, and this precisely because of its relation to the cult, the heart of the program of Nathan's promise. Thus the final section of the deuteronomic history reproduces the structure of the first two sections, and it even takes up and combines the peculiar aspects of each of the first two: in part it is positive like the working out of Joshua's commission, in part negative like the era of the judges.

[22] Josh 12 not only sums up the conquest; it also establishes the necessary basis for the distribution of the land which is then immediately commanded (Josh 13 7). For a detailed study of the relation of Deut 31 to Josh 1 and 12 see N. Lohfink, "Die deuteronomische Darstellung des Übergangs der Führung Israels von Moses auf Josue," *Scholastik*, 37 (1962), pp. 32–44.

[23] M. Noth, *Überlieferungsgeschichtliche Studien*, p. 5.

[24] See D. J. McCarthy, S.J., *Treaty and Covenant*, p. 139.

PLAGUES AND SEA OF REEDS: EXODUS 5–14

DENNIS J. McCARTHY, S.J.
ST. MARY'S COLLEGE

AN ATTENTIVE reading of the book of Exodus in the form in which the tradition presents it to us, that is, the present text of the Bible, reveals that the so-called plague stories are not properly united to the account of the death of the first-born of Egypt which begins in ch. 11, for the formal literary elements of the text show that the stroke against the first-born does not belong to the literary unit properly designated "Moses' Dealings with Pharaoh."[1] That is to say, the customary treatment of the sequence Exod 7 14—11 10, beginning with the pollution of the waters of Egypt and including the announcement of the attack on the first-born of Egypt, needs reconsideration. In truth, the last episode of this series is *conceptually* the climax. It is the most terrible and impressive of the blows struck against Egypt, and with it begins the attainment of the apparent object of all of Yahweh's dealings with Egypt through Moses: because of it Pharaoh releases the Israelites. Thus the final position of the stroke against the first-born in the series of plagues as well as the nature of the event itself does indeed emphasize it, and Exod 7 14—11 10 forms a logical unit. Purely in terms of what is said, ch. 11 fits into its present position. The final redaction of Exodus has a real organization and dramatic progress up to this point. However, as long as the connection remains at this level, as long as it is an affair of content only, we are not assured that the connection is older than this final redaction since it is clear that the redactor used various independent sources to construct his stories, but, because the materials in these sources all concerned the same general subject, there is no reason why parts of one could not be combined with those of another to yield a new, coherent, and even dramatic whole. In view of this, mere coherence, logical sequence between parts of a pericope, is simply not enough to show a connection antecedent to the final redaction.

[1] Such a designation is more accurate than the customary "Plagues" (cf. D. J. McCarthy, "Moses' Dealings with Pharaoh: Ex 7 8 — 10 27," *CBQ*, 27 [1965], pp. 336–47), but the latter name is customary and will be used in this paper. It always refers to the ten episodes in Exod 7 8–10 27.

Therefore, in searching out the prehistory of apparent units of the final redaction we must rely on literary criteria — as we should in any case when dealing with a literary phenomenon. Granted that any extensive literary whole has subordinate units, we may ask whether formal literary elements indicate any special links among some of these units. If certain of them share special features while others show positive divergences from these, the links on the one hand and the differences on the other surely point to some special unity among the units sharing special features. In fact, these principles are commonly recognized in the practice of source criticism. We argue for separate sources behind the Pentateuch on the basis of literary criteria which show connections among certain subordinate parts of the present whole and set them off from other parts marked by divergent vocabulary and so on, even though these various units are fitted together now to produce a more or less coherent narrative whole. We must use the same procedure in the face of the same phenomena when they direct attention to a different kind of analysis.

From this point of view, then, it is clear that the ten episodes beginning not with the pollution of the waters of Egypt but with the business of the wand and the serpents (7 8–13) and ending with the numinous darkness (10 21–27) form a closed, tightly knit concentric unit.[2] The essential technique used to construct this concentric unit is a series of inclusions in which the first episode (wand and serpent) corresponds formally with the tenth episode (the darkness), the second episode (the pollution of the waters) with the ninth episode (the locusts), and so forth. The structures of the stories in each of the corresponding pairs are exactly like one another and unlike all the others in significant points of detail even though all the plague stories are in general similar in construction. This variation within unity is achieved mostly by the manipulation of important thematic elements: for instance, repetition of Yahweh's direct communication with Moses in the second and the ninth episodes, a varied form of such communication in the fourth and the seventh episodes, the use of the prophetic formula, "thus says Yahweh" in the second, third, fifth and the ninth, eighth, sixth episodes, and so forth. Such a literary construction obviously tends to be a unit closed and complete within itself. This is the positive evidence for the need to separate Exod 11 from the immediately preceding chapters. This evidence is substantiated by a comparison of the two pericopes which shows them to be divergent in vocabulary and in the literary skill displayed and to be positively incompatible with one another in their concepts of the total action of the exodus. I shall develop this later in the discussion of the relations of the plagues narrative with its immediate

[2] *CBQ*, 27 (1965), pp. 338–43.

context, but first it is necessary to justify the search for such relations in view of the fact that this plagues narrative is formally so self-contained a literary unit that one might find it difficult to believe that it has such relations from the formal point of view.

Despite this self-contained character there is clearly progress in the action. For instance, the more primitive, quasi-magic concept of the wand disappears, Yahweh acts more directly in the later episodes, Pharaoh comes to recognize Yahweh and confess his sins, and so forth.[3] Even so, the story does not come to its term. The problem, then, is to find the proper relation of this pericope with its context, the relation which offers the resolution of its unanswered problems, and to do this through a study of the text as a literary phenomenon.[4]

We may begin by seeking out the significant phrases, certain regular expressions of basic ideas, which are characteristic of the plagues narrative.[5] Among these are the recurring introduction, ויאמֶר יהוה אֶל־משֶׁה, and conclusion in which Pharaoh's heart is "hard" (חזק) or "stubborn" (כבד) — the English equivalents are given for the sake of indicating that different Hebrew words are involved and do not claim to be more. Then there is the prophetic formula, "thus says Yahweh."[6] There is the expressed demand for liberty, the demand that the people be set free (שׁלח) to serve (עבד) Yahweh. There is the instrument through which again and again Yahweh brings the plagues about, the upraised (הרים) or outstretched (נטה) arm or staff (מַטֶּה). Finally, there is the demand that one confess Yahweh (ידע כי אני יהוה). All these elements are important both because of the frequency with which they occur in the unit and because they express its essential motifs.[7] Where else do they occur in the immediate context?

[3] *CBQ*, 27 (1965), pp. 344–46.

[4] Note that this is in no way a question of source criticism. Exod 7 8–10 27 uses two or three of the classic pentateuchal sources, as do the surrounding chapters, so that elements from each source in the one set of chapters are related to corresponding source elements in the other. Here we are concerned with the relations of the characteristic elements of a complex as a whole, not those of its components.

[5] See *CBQ*, 27 (1965), pp. 342–43, on certain of these as elements of Exod 7 8–10 27 which are thematic because they involve ideas which are important to the pericope *and* are presented in expressions which themselves function in its structure. Not all characteristic forms are thematic in this sense; e. g., the "arm/staff" motif is certainly characteristic, and it involves an important idea, namely, that Yahweh has given Moses (and Aaron) special powers, but this particular expression of the idea has as such no clear function in the formal literary structure.

[6] W. Richter (*Die Bearbeitung des "Retterbuches" in der deuteronomischen Epoche*, p. 101) notes that the prophetic formula is a *Rahmung* for the plague episodes. It is, but it is not the only one; rather it is but a part of a more complex organizing scheme.

[7] Note that the argumentation is based on formal characteristics, not on ideas as such but on distinctive expressions of ideas. For instance, in all the plague episodes the aim is clearly to bring about Israel's release to serve Yahweh, but this receives a

We might study all the opening chapters of the book of Exodus to find the answer. Chs. 1–4 and 5–14 are certainly part of an organized whole. However, they are different acts in the drama, the first chapters being devoted to the introduction and preparation of the chief actors. For the major Israelite actors this action really is private, between them and their God, and in any case the conflict has not begun. There is, of course, an attack by Pharaoh on Israel in the opening chapters, but this does not create real conflict. Israel, lacking a champion, is a mere passive sufferer. For these reasons the public action, the dealings with Pharaoh, and the conflict beginning with ch. 5 are a new step in the action which is clearly marked off from the preceding. Hence we may accept this separation and confine ourselves to the account of the struggle which begins in Exod 5.

The passage between Pharaoh and his Israelite subjects described in this chapter is not entirely of a piece with what follows, as is well known. There is, however, an important change from the situation in the first act, that is, chs. 1–4. Here at least Israel takes the initiative; it no longer passively suffers Pharaoh's oppression. Hence, though the action does not conform perfectly to the conception of the action in the following chapters, ch. 5 belongs to this new act. It shares in the over-all concept dominating this new action in that Israel requests Pharaoh's permission to go serve Yahweh, even though its details differ markedly from the following chapters.

The most striking difference is the importance of the Israelite leaders, the elders of the people. They rather than Moses are the protagonists, though Moses must egg them on so that he does play a significant rôle in the action. Further, the subservient attitude of these leaders, even when goaded by Moses, is far different from that of the imperious Moses who later confronts Pharaoh. Finally, the action described is very different. No pressure is brought to bear on Pharaoh; rather he is the one who brings pressure to bear on Israel, while Yahweh seems to do nothing. All this constitutes a very different view of the Israelite-Egyptian conflict, a fact which has been duly noted and used to establish, surely correctly, that ch. 5, while essentially J, represents a variant tradition in that source.[8]

At first glance it seems that this is the same situation as that in ch. 11. The chapter has common ground with Exod 7 8–10 27, but this is simply a matter of contents which are governed by so different an idea of the

---

characteristic expression and function so as to become a formal element only in the second (pollution of the waters) and ninth (locusts), the third (frogs) and eighth (hail), and the fifth ("flies") and sixth (murrain) plagues.

[8] M. Noth, *Exodus*, pp. 52–56; G. Fohrer, *Überlieferung und Geschichte des Exodus*, pp. 57–58, presents a different view.

proceedings that the two pericopes can hardly be said to represent a single scheme. However, the problem is not really the same here as in ch. 11. For instance, unlike Exod 11, Exod 5 is not a nearly incoherent hodgepodge. Even though it is not all from one source, the narrative flows quite smoothly. We always know who is speaking to whom, and no violent saltus appear in the action. Further, the conflicts in conception are not impossible as in ch. 11. Further, and most important, ch. 5 does in fact introduce most of the great themes of the following plague stories along with their expression, and it does so without distorting them. In this it is quite unlike ch. 11 which does recall some of the familiar themes of the plague stories but in a most alien way. In ch. 5 there is Yahweh's message for Moses, there is the prophetic "thus says Yahweh," there is the explicit demand to be allowed to serve Yahweh, there is the overriding aim that Yahweh be recognized by Israel and even by Egypt. If we could count the appearance of the root כבד in 5 9 as a punning allusion to its frequent use later in a different sense, i. e., to describe Pharaoh's hard heart — and I would so count it without insisting on the point[9] — we have all the important thematic phrases introduced in this chapter. Thus, despite the undeniable differences between ch. 5 and the account of the plagues themselves, ch. 5 seems to fit into a whole along with the ten plagues. It works with the key elements of these episodes and it has an important function organically connected with them. It is formally an introduction. Thus it meets the essential criteria; it has a logical function in the whole *and* it is linked to this whole by formal literary means in that it works with the same thematic phrases.

Indeed, it functions precisely as introduction in bringing these thematic elements before us in a block so that they will surely be noticed in the later chapters. More, it serves to set the scene: Pharaoh's unreasonable tyranny, Israel's terror before him, and its need to learn that Yahweh is indeed its effective god. Thus the chapter gives us the thematic elements of the plague episodes, it introduces the chief actors in those episodes, and it shows the experiential and emotional background against which they act.

In addition, this introductory chapter is the one that exposes most clearly the important idea that the whole episode is more than an attack on the alien Egyptian to make him release Israel. It is a necessary step

[9] It is extremely difficult for us to evaluate the use of puns in the OT correctly because of our conviction that words are simply conventional signs. For the ancient Semite the word, i. e., the sound or the writing, was very much the thing. Hence, puns were not merely word play; their being referred to by the same word meant that things distinct (to us) were somehow connected. For examples besides the present use of כבד see J. De Fraine, "Jeux des mots dans le récit de la chute," *Mélanges Robert*, pp. 47–59, and A. Guillaume, *Prophétie et divination chez les Sémites*, pp. 146–64, 182–84 (the English original was not available to me at the time of writing).

in the education of God's chosen people, a step which will have to be repeated again and again, since the people lose heart and murmur (14 10, 15) until finally they do learn to believe after a fashion (14 31)[10]

If ch. 5 can thus be seen to fulfill an essential function in the whole Egyptian episode, and if it uses language which fits it formally into the narrative of the plagues, the same cannot be said for the rest of the introductory material which appears in Exod 6 2–7 7. The source critics have, of course, recognized that the original parts of these verses — as is generally agreed, they are not a unity even from the source critical viewpoint — are a doublet, P's version of the call of Moses and so forth which are described in Exod 1–4 on a basis of J and E. This is doubtless correct. These verses serve no particular purpose in their present context. In fact, they retrogress in that they present the commissioning of Moses, already taken care of in the first four chapters of Exodus, and then prepare the way for the dealings with Pharaoh, dealings which have in fact already begun with ch. 5. Moreover, they have their own quite special vocabulary. This is the place where the multiplication of "signs and wonders" is the expressed object of the dealings with Pharaoh (7 3), an idea found again in 11 9.[11] Only here (7 3) is קשה used to describe the hardening of Pharaoh's heart. In 6 26 and 7 4 the Israelites are the "host" (צְבָאוֹת). This recurs in 12 17, 41, 54 but never in the section running from 7 8 to 10 27 where the expression is regularly "people" (עַם). Again the striking word "mighty judgments" (שְׁפָטִים גְּדֹלִים) occurs in 6 6 and 7 4 and (without גְּדֹלִים) in 12 12, but never in the plagues narrative. Finally and perhaps most important, there is the concept of Yahweh's bringing Israel out of Egypt (הוציא) in 6 26 and 7 4. Again, the expression is characteristic of chs. 11–13 (indeed, the liturgical formula in 13 14 surely exposes its *Sitz im Leben*) but the pericope Exod 7 8–10 27 does not use it. In it the characteristic word is שלח. Pharaoh is to set the people free, and though in fact Yahweh is thus "sending out" the people, this is not expressed by the hifil of יצא as it is in chs. 6 2–7 7 and 11–13.

It is this special vocabulary added to the fact that 6 2–7 7 doubles the function of the preceding chapters which establishes that the basic

[10] Despite the idealization of the generation of the exodus and desert wanderings seen, e. g., in Hosea, the tradition of the "murmuring," reluctant people who needed again and again to be brought to Yahweh was very strong: see the classic expression of this in Deut 1 (and note even Hos 11 1–3). This general background lends greater weight to the hints of Israel's need to be converted in Exod 5 and 14 31 (on this conversion see Y. Kaufmann, *The Religion of Israel*, pp. 223–31).

[11] This is hardly a motif at all, let alone an important one in the plagues narrative; cf. *CBQ*, 27 (1965), pp. 345–46; and add to the evidence for an Egyptian "conversion" as an object of the dealings the remarks in J. Scharbert, *Heilsmittler im Alten Testament und im alten Orient*, pp. 72–73, 166.

elements in this section belong to the P source.[12] However, once more analysis may not stop with this. The P tradition appears also in Exod 7 8–10 27, but in such a way that these characteristic ideas and expressions do not appear there. Thus they serve as literary criteria distinguishing one section from the other and so are further evidence that the plagues pericope is a deliberately separate unity. It uses P, but in a fashion different from Exod 6 2–7 7.

The special language of these latter chapters does more than mark them off from the immediately succeeding stories of Moses' dealings with Pharaoh. As noted, language characteristic of this special introductory unit does recur, not in the plagues narrative, but in the following account of the Passover. This is important evidence for the next step of the argument, the search for formal literary sequels to the plagues narrative.

In the course of this search we must note the obvious fact that there are two climactic events in the exodus complex, the destruction of Egypt's first-born and the consequent freeing of Israel, and the spectacular miracle of the Sea of Reeds, each of which was originally the subject of its own tradition.[12] Even in their present combined form it is clear that the two episodes are differently conceived, and they have disparate vocabularies and style. These apparent diversities at once call forth the question: Can we find any literary links between the accounts of the two climactic events and the several units which we have found in the preceding chapters? Concretely, is there any hint of a special connection between the plagues complex (Exod 5 1–6 2+7 8–10 27) or the P introduction (Exod 6 2–7 7) and the Passover complex or the Sea of Reeds miracle, a connection beyond their present juxtaposition in the final redaction of the book of Exodus and yet not mere community of source?

First we may look at the complicated account of the first Passover night as it is presented in Exod 11–13. Once again, simply as external sequel, that is, merely through postposition, this story and especially ch. 11 is unmistakably intended to be the climax of the plagues. From the point of view of content it serves this purpose admirably in that it is a striking episode which actually produces the result aimed at from the first. Still, all this is on the conceptual plane; we see and recognize the meaning and importance of the event in relation to what has gone before. We still face the question: How is the "last act" tied to the earlier scenes from the formal literary point of view?

There is, as a matter of fact, strong negative evidence in regard to this. Thus, the closed structure of Exod 7 8–10 27 makes it difficult to see the episode in ch. 11, though it is superficially similar to the plague stories, as the proper continuation of these stories. The tightly knit

[12] Cf. M. Noth, *Überlieferungsgeschichte des Pentateuch*, pp. 70–77; *Exodus*, pp. 104–05.

character of the concentric structure in the plagues narrative surely indicates that this particular technique, the plague story, has been finished with. In view of this, the fact that the account of the attack on the first-born of Egypt beginning in Exod 11 is the same generic kind of thing as the plagues — a blow against Egypt while Israel is exempted — does not establish that it is the original literary sequel. On the contrary, the fact that an episode so like the plague stories is placed after and outside so highly organized a ten-part structure as Exod 7 8–10 27 calls attention to its separateness. Of its very nature it should have been worked entirely into the plague unit and yet it has not been. Upon close scrutiny, therefore, its being placed next to this tight unit calls attention to its strangeness.

Analogously the story about the first-born in ch. 11 uses a different vocabulary from that of the plagues narrative in a way which emphasizes the differences. It uses familiar bits of language which lead one to expect the phrases to which one has become accustomed, but then these bits are continued in a different way.[13] This seems a deliberate affirmation of difference, for it makes it far more noticeable than would a merely variant vocabulary. Thus like the structure the similar but different vocabulary of ch. 11 draws attention to its divergence from the earlier plague stories.

Further, the conception of Israel's relation to the Egyptians in ch. 11 is incompatible with what has gone before. According to 11 3 Israel enjoys the favor of Egypt, a thing which is simply impossible after Israel has brought the horrors of the plagues upon the country. Finally, the obscure and disordered construction of the chapter — the saltus from vs. 3 to 4 or 6 to 7 are surely enough to document this — clashes with the careful structuring of the plagues narrative. With all these incongruities the chapter can hardly be the original formal literary continuation of the plagues narrative, for all the logic of its climactic position.

Thus far the argumentation has merely been negative. I have given the evidence for important formal dissimilarities between Exod 11–13 and Exod 7 8–10 27. There are, of course, positive connections. The climactic position already noted is one. Then we may note the developing elements in the plagues narrative, the decline of the magic motif, the increased dignity of the actors, the growing power of Moses' work,

[13] E. g., 11 1, 6, 7; cf. *CBQ*, 27 (1965), pp. 339–40, and add to the data there cited the fact that the designation of what is done to the Egyptians as "plague" or "stroke" (נגע, נגף) is peculiar to chs. 11–12 and does not occur in Exod 7 8–10 10. Perhaps it should be noted also that the meeting between Moses and Pharaoh in Exod 11–12 is evidently impossible after 10 28–29, but this affects the argument only if these verses belong to the original plagues complex. I believe they do, but this can be shown only at a further stage of the argument.

the added inclusiveness of the demand to confess Yahweh and the actual increasing recognition of him and his servant on the part of Pharaoh. Most of these are continued in chs. 11–13, even to the Egyptian's explicit acceptance of Yahweh's overwhelming power in Egypt (12 32b–33). However, all this is necessarily derived from the situation and so does not carry us beyond the factor of conceptual connection. At the formal literary level we still need to find the links. These might be varied, key words and phrases, structural elements, perhaps even similarity of structure as a whole. Thus, I suppose one would consider a repetition of the concentric structure so elaborately worked out in 7 8–10 27 as a sign of some kind of literary relationship. Unfortunately I can find no evidence of this in the account of the Passover.[14] However, the case is somewhat different with certain of the structural elements.

Before discussing this, however, one must deal with an obvious objection. The matter of chs. 11–13 is so extensive that it is more difficult to see the scheme there than it is in the compact plague story. The incongruities in the later chapters are indeed monumental, but in part at least this is because these chapters contain blocks of matter, the ritual laws, which are extremely hard to integrate with other elements. They are inserted as speeches giving directions governing the following action, but they are so special in their manner and so self-contained in their matter that they must seem to interrupt rather than carry on the action.[15] Nevertheless, fascination with source criticism or tradition history, i. e., the drive to get behind the actual text in one way or another, has often obscured the fact that such difficult items can be integrated into larger wholes.[16] The recalcitrant nature of the ritual laws means that we cannot look for much adaption within these texts themselves. The matter was sacred enough to make tampering difficult.[17] More, the authors probably felt it to be supremely important. If there must be adaption, from their point of view other things would likely be fitted to these. Thus we should first look for integration through function, that is, through making the relatively unchangeable blocks of

[14] According to L. Alonso-Schökel (*Estudios de poëtica hebrea*, Barcelona, 1963), pp. 317–18, E. Galbiati, *La struttura letteraria dell'Esodo*, in *Scrinium theologicum*, 3 (1965), has found a complex concentric structure in the story of the first Passover night. Unfortunately Galbiati's work was unavailable and the scheme summarized by Alonso-Schökel is not apparent to me in Exod 11–13.

[15] So Rylaarsdam, "Exodus," *IB*, 1, p. 915, remarks that 12 1–13 are "... as it were, an interruption" before the climax.

[16] See the analyses of such structures in N. Lohfink, "Der Bundesschluss im Land Moab," *Biblische Zeitschrift*, n.s. 6 (1962), pp. 32–56, and D. J. McCarthy, *Treaty and Covenant* (*Analecta Biblica*, 21), pp. 131–40.

[17] So the ritual of the מַצּוֹת is left separate from the rite of the paschal lamb even though a combination would make a better structure and accord better with the ritual of later times.

matter serve as parts of a characteristic scheme. Is there any evidence of this?

In fact, it is easy enough to find the basic elements of the scheme used for the plague story in the first section of the Passover material, ch. 11. There is God's command to Moses, the request and threat, their transmission to Pharaoh, the effects of this, and the concluding formula. All are there and they function. The opening in 11 1 is standard: God speaks to Moses to give him a message for others. 11 2–8 gives us the directions for Israel and Pharaoh, unusual in their details but functionally the proper sequence to "and God said to Moses." Vss. 9–10 echo the closing formula — note the reference to the hardening of Pharaoh's heart in 9 as well as 10. The formula is not, strictly speaking, in place here since it is not final. It does not follow the request, the execution of the plague, and its effects as in the regular form; but the special circumstances of the episode explain this. In fact the execution of the plague in this instance came later and did soften Pharaoh. Again 12 1–28 can fit into the plague story form, for these verses represent the renewed instructions to Moses (and Aaron) preceding the execution of the action, an element which is found in four of the plague narratives.[18] Here, of course, the instructions are much extended, as in the nature of the case they must be. However, the proper sequence, instruction and then notice of obedience, that is, the execution on the part of Israel (12 27b–28), is clear. Even the complex sequence in chs. 11 and 12, unsuccessful dealings followed by repeated instructions and their execution, is paralleled in the plague stories (Exod 9 13—10 20). In ch. 12 the notice of the effects of the plague (12 29) and Egypt's response (12 30–32) is handled in the manner of the plague story with the formula, "Pharaoh called to Moses."[19] There follows the effect of the whole episode, here not the confirmation of Pharaoh's obstinacy as in the plague story, but Israel's escape. Obviously the customary closing formula cannot be used here.

Thus the basic elements of the typical plague story do appear quite clearly in Exod 11 1—12 42, strikingly so in view of the recalcitrance of much of the material used. In large outline we find: 1. Yahweh speaking to Moses (11 1); 2. the word to be conveyed (11 2–3a) and its conveyance (11 4–8); 3. the "closing formula," Pharaoh's hard heart (11 9–10); 4. Yahweh's speaking to Moses anew (12 1); 5. the word (now of command: 12 2–27); 6. its execution (12 27b–29); 7. its effect, that is, the human response to the events (12 30–42). However, when we look more closely at all this, there are serious problems. One of these is stylistic, perhaps even structural. There are inconsistencies in chs. 7 8—10 29. Indeed this is what makes source criticism possible there.

[18] Exod 7 19–20; 8 1–2; 9 22–26; 10 12–13.

[19] קרא אֶל־/לְ משֶׁה: (8 4, 21; 9 27; 10 16, 24).

However, these inconsistencies are minor from the literary point of view since they hardly effect the flow of narrative or the over-all structure and meaning, so careful is the construction. This is not the case in the parts of chs. 11 and 12 under discussion.

For one thing, ch. 11 expresses a view of the proceedings which is foreign to the earlier plague stories. In them the idea of a contest between Yahweh and Egypt in the persons of their representatives, Moses and Pharaoh (with his magicians), is important, as is also the drive to convince even Pharaoh that Yahweh is God and so in a sense to convert him. In any event, there is a struggle, an effort to persuade Pharaoh and so to save Egypt from trouble. There is none of this in ch. 11 or 12. Egypt's ruin is simply proclaimed, with nothing offered as a means to ward it off. This cannot be explained away with pleas that the previous failures have rendered such ideas nugatory. From this point of view the only possibility is indeed to crush Egyptian resistence, but 11 2–3 is ignorant of this background. It proclaims the direct contrary. Israel is said to enjoy favor and prestige in Egypt, surely a condition favorable to the aim of persuasion and of achieving recognition, not one that renders it impossible! Thus ch. 11 conflicts with the basic concepts of the former plague narratives.

More, it has its own peculiar view of the matter. The theme of the despoiling of Egypt by a sly trick (11 2–3; 12 35–36) is entirely alien to the earlier stories. The idea that Israel is looked upon with favor by Egypt is, as we have seen, positively ludicrous if it is to be taken as part of the climax of the events Exod 7 8–27. Finally, less telling but significant, the action in 11 8, in which Pharaoh's servants come to deal with Moses, is contrary to the unchanging picture in the plague stories where Pharaoh always summons Moses (and Aaron) and deals with him directly.

Further, the strange ideas of chs. 11 and 12 are introduced with relatively little literary skill. They appear without introduction or explanation. This fits with the rough construction of these chapters in general, all of which seems to indicate that the resemblance of Exod 11–12 to a standard plague story is a superficial and secondary construct. In regard to this, it should be noted that even though vss. 1–8 of ch. 11 are usually assigned to J,[20] they are not really all of a piece. First of all, there is the obvious break between vss. 3 and 4: the present sequence cannot be original,[21] but the problem goes deeper than a mere

[20] The strange language and ideas of Exod 11 1–8 raise a problem with the usual attribution to the J source. The whole can only represent a variant tradition within that complex (M. Noth, *Exodus*, p. 88).

[21] Rylaarsdam, *IB*, 1, p. 911, proposes an original sequence of 10 27+11 1–3+10 28–29+11 4–8.

change in the original sequence within a document or source or tradition. Vss. 4–8 must be secondary elements within J, for not merely do they come with a jolt after 1–3, but they perform no function essential in the J narrative.[22] This leaves us with a primal view of the stroke against the first-born of Egypt, that presented in 11 1–3, which in no wise coincides with the earlier plagues since there is no mention of the proclamation to Pharaoh which was an essential element in the typical plague story. 11 4–8 will have been added in an effort to remedy this inconsistency. However, the ineptness with which this has been done contrasts sharply with the skill shown in the construction of the plagues narrative. Hence, though it is correct that the composite character of Exod 11–12 does not of itself set off the section from Exod 7 8–10 27 since the latter is also a cento, the manner and quality of this composition does mark it off.

This failure of the oldest material in the story about the first-born (11 1–3) to mention any dealings with Pharaoh is significant from more than a stylistic point of view. In the previous plague episodes the idea of dealings with Pharaoh has been expanded by the careful weaving in of material which develops the plague concept, but the idea itself of dealings comes always from the oldest source, from J, the source also of the primary material in Exod 11.[23] Thus, in a manner which reverses exactly the procedure in the plagues narrative, the idea of dealing with Pharaoh has had to be added to the oldest source in ch. 11. This means that the primal conception of the stroke against the first-born as recorded in Exod 11 differed from that of the previous plagues. It was a blow delivered without warning, not a punishment upon one who rejected Yahweh's command. Far from being the model from which the others grew and around which they clustered, the text indicates that the episode in ch. 11 has had to be doctored to bring it into conformity with the scheme of the other plagues.

A further difficulty with the connection between the account of the Passover night and the preceding plagues is the odd vocabulary which, as has already been remarked concerning ch. 11, calls attention to itself by its tantalizing difference-in-similarity to the vocabulary of the plagues narrative. In this matter ch. 12 merely continues ch. 11, to which it is joined by verbal links, the shout that goes up in 12 29 and the motif of "favor" in 12 35–36. In fact, the characteristic phrases of Exod 7 8–10 29 are strangers to ch. 12. The only one of them we find is a single "I am Yahweh" in 12 12, where it is used in a way very

[22] M. Noth, *Exodus*, pp. 92–93.

[23] For the source criticism of Exod 7–10 see the commentaries and most recently Fohrer, *Überlieferung . . . des Exodus*, pp. 61–79. No one disputes the attribution to J of the verses where Moses deals with Pharaoh. In the plagues which are wholly from P (Exod 8 12–15 and 9 8–12) Moses does not speak directly to Pharaoh. If there is anything from E in the plagues narrative, it shows no evidence of this either.

different from the demand in the plague stories that Yahweh be recognized.

Indeed, in itself ch. 12 has an even more exotic vocabulary from the point of view of the plague stories than ch. 11. To be sure, we would not expect that cultic laws would use the vocabulary of narrative, but this observation does not entirely settle the question, since the "rubrical" texts in ch. 13 can reflect the deuteronomic vocabulary. The real problem is that the influence should be in the other direction. If the Passover *legenda* were the seed from which Exod 1–15 grew,[24] surely we would expect these passages to have influenced the vocabulary of the plague stories as a whole, as, for example, a vocabulary related to the laws of Deuteronomy has in fact influenced the narrative in the deuteronomic history. Thus the thing in itself is perfectly conceivable. It simply has not taken place in the book of Exodus. Exod 12 attaches to ch. 11, itself an exotic. Beyond that the significant attachments are with Exod 6 2–7 7, with which the Passover material shares the use of צְבָאוֹת, שְׁפָטִים, הוֹצִיא, as we have seen. Thus there is not merely the negative fact that Exod 11 1–12 42[25] lacks almost all the characteristic materials of Exod 7 8–10 27; the pericope is linked positively with Exod 6 2–7 7, which has been intruded between the introductory ch. 5 and the narrative of the ten plagues.

Thus, despite the undeniable appropriateness of the substance of chs. 11 and 12 in the position of climax to the plagues narrative, and despite their use of elements of the scheme of the typical plague story, it is hard to see them as an originally integral part of a literary whole which included the introduction in ch. 5 and the stories of the plagues in chs. 7 8–10 27 with their special structure and vocabulary. The difference in vocabulary and outlook in the chapters concerning the Passover gives them too different a cast. On this literary level — characteristic vocabulary and phraseology — Passover and plagues are separate. More, on this level the Passover material has its own special link with foregoing chapters, but this is with 6 2–7 7, not with the story of the plagues. Serious effort has been made to fit the two pericopes, plagues and Passover, together but it is hard to see that this has produced more than a secondary and rather superficial unity of the two. Where, then, is the follow-up on the plagues narrative?

[24] J. Pedersen, *Israel*, III–IV, pp. 384–415, 728–37; M. Noth, *Überlieferungsgeschichte des Pentateuch*, pp. 70–77. Often, even those who deny that the plague stories developed out of cultic *legenda* admit that they developed out of the story of the exodus and the death of the first-born of Egypt carried in some other tradition (so, e. g., Fohrer, *Überlieferung . . . des Exodus*, pp. 96–97, 118). There is the same problem with this as with the cult *legenda* theory of origin and development.

[25] Exod 12 43–13 16 is generally and correctly held to be secondary even within the Passover complex. If it were included, it would merely reinforce the arguments I have drawn from Exod 11 1–12 42.

The attempt to answer questions like this must again begin with the primary considerations, the literary, rather than the study of the geography of the itinerary in chs. 12–14. The account of the exodus is governed by literary and religious considerations, not by topographical ones. A close reading reveals at once that most of the characteristic phrases of chs. 7 8–10 29 which were so notably missing in Exod 11–13 reappear in force in Exod 14. The command of Yahweh to Moses (14 1, 15, 26), the hardening of Pharaoh's heart (14 4, 5, 8, 17), the acknowledgment of Yahweh (14 4, 18, 31), the upraised arm and outstretched wand (14 8, 16, 21, 26–27, 31) — all these are back again. Further, in ch. 14 the construction is again quite a bit smoother, and in this also it recalls the plagues narrative. The harsh incongruities of chs. 11–13 are not imitated here.

However, it is perhaps the return to the basic rhythm of command, execution, effect, and result which is most striking. Of course, these elements, unlike the themes, had not disappeared entirely, but in Exod 14 they recur in a number of subordinate units which makes for a definite rhythmic sequence recalling the plagues. It is this and not their mere presence which seems significant.

The commands are threefold: 14 1, 15, 26. Each is followed by a notice of its execution and the effects of this. In the first instance this is not so readily noticeable since it is no more than a fragment, 14 4b ("and they did so"), but it is there nevertheless. The other two cases correspond to the fuller expression of the scheme with their solemn announcements of Moses' action in 14 21 and 27 and their fuller description of the effects which Yahweh's word always has. Thus the first command leads Pharaoh to set out after Israel. In the second case the effect of Yahweh's word is to bring Israel safely across the sea, while his final command turns Egypt's pursuit into its own ruin and Israel's salvation. In turn these things result in fear in Israel, fear in Egypt, and finally faith and awe in Israel. In the plagues narrative the important instance of this latter sort of result, the human reaction to the event, was always the same, stubbornness on the part of Pharaoh, so that it could be expressed in a final formula. Here this element varies so that a formula is impossible, but the thing itself is there. Besides these similarities to Exod 7 8–10 27 in language and structural elements, we should notice the emphatic return to the same purpose as that which largely governs the complex of the plague stories. As there, so here a principal aim is the due recognition of Yahweh (cf. 14 4, 18, 31).

All these elements have been built into a thoroughly structured unit.[26] The structure, moreover, is largely built on these basic elements

[26] This is true despite the apparent irregularities; the evidence for an intention to give a structure to the materials is too strong. The principle is admitted in most literary analysis. Thus, for example, M. Noth (*Exodus*, p. 118) finds variant elements in the J picture of the Sea of Reeds miracle, but he has no hesitation in assigning them

which are shared with Exod 7 8–10 27. In ch. 14 the fundamental construction involves two corresponding blocks of material and two sets of phrases which mark off the two halves into which it is divided. The first of these elements, the corresponding blocks of material, involve the sequence: pursuit plus fear. In the first instance Egypt pursues Israel (14 7–9) and causes it to be afraid (14 10); in the second Egypt is still the pursuer (14 23), but the consequence now is its own panic (14 25). Thus the two blocks balance one another, and this is surely intended, for the wish to introduce the element of fear led the composer to turn to a tradition which does not follow the conception of the event at the Sea of Reeds as an awesome miracle involving its waters, the conception which he has made the basis of his narrative. Rather, in 14 24 he uses a form of the story in which Yahweh arouses a panic among the Egyptians, not by means of the Sea but directly and mysteriously.[27]

In addition to this, the two parts of the chapter are marked by decided differences in the occurrence of certain important words which thus emphasize its bipartite structure. חזק and כבד occur three times in the earlier verses (4, 8) and never after 18. The words strike one because of their frequency and their importance earlier in the plagues narrative so that their repeated use and sudden disappearance definitely mark a turning.[28] The second half of the chapter has its own double leitmotif, the phrases רֶכֶב וּפָרָשִׁים and נטה יָד. The first, indeed, appears already in vs. 9, but it becomes emphatic only when repeated three times in 23, 26, and 28. The might of Egypt is stressed so that its fall is all the more remarkable. The second phrase is noticeable first of all because it is characteristic of the plague stories, but again it is marked by triple repetition in vss. 21, 26, and 27.

A further use of key words calls attention to a further structural

---

all to J because of the wider evidence of unity, and, in another instance, Rylaarsdam (*IB*, 1, p. 924) finds Exod 12 31–32 contradicting 10 29 but nonetheless attributes both verses to J. S. Mowinckel ("Die vermeintliche 'Passahlegende' Ex 1–15 in Bezug auf die Frage: Literaturkritik und Traditionskritik," *Studia Theologica*, 5 (1951), p. 76) points out that the collectors and redactors of Israel's traditions were dealing with sacred and so relatively fixed materials. They could and did order these into patterned wholes, centos, but they were not free to change entirely the traditional views and modes of expression.

[27] In 24, 25b. Even 25a involves marshy ground which traps the chariots, not the mighty waters of the tradition taken as the base for ch. 14 (on 25a see L. S. Hay, "What Really Happened at the Sea of Reeds?" *JBL*, 83 [1964], pp. 397–403). In itself this move to marshy ground in 25a is not incompatible with 24, for we might take it that the panic led the Egyptians to fly blindly onto marshy ground, but 25b seems to continue 24 directly so that 25a is an intrusion, a fragment from yet another tradition (cf. H. Holzinger, *Exodus*, *KHAT*, 2, p. 24; M. Noth, *Exodus*, pp. 105–06; G. Fohrer, *Überlieferung . . . des Exodus*, p. 100).

[28] כבד is used in a new sense in Exod 14, but it occurs in close proximity to חזק, which makes the punning reference to the standard use in Exod 7 8–10 27 certain; on the force of puns in the OT see above, n. 9.

element. There are clusters of characteristic elements: "raise the wand and stretch out the arm" (חזק and כבד *bis*) "chariots and horsemen" (*bis*), "recognize Yahweh," in 14 16–18. This, of course, is in the central of the three major scenes into which the chapter is divided by Yahweh's commands to Moses (14 1, 15, 26). In the first scene Yahweh led Pharaoh on by means of Moses and the Israelites. Now the reversal sets in. Moses, Yahweh's agent, is revealed as Egypt's nemesis and Israel's savior. The dramatic turning is marked by the heaping up of key phrases just noticed and so made a central point on which the narrative hinges.

Thus far the formal literary elements of Exod 14 which have been considered are those which serve in one way or another to set the first half of the chapter off from the second. Obviously, this is not the whole of the matter. The very concentration of key themes in the central point marks it as a hinge, that is, a point of change and yet a linkage. In addition, a set of inclusions is used to connect and yet in a way contrast the two halves of the chapter. There is a correspondence between certain important elements: recognition of Yahweh in 14 4 and 31,[29] Yahweh's mighty arm in 8 and 31, Yahweh's salvation in 13 and 30, and Yahweh's fighting on Israel's behalf in 14 and 25. As inclusions these are a linking element, but as announcement and fulfillment they are also contrasts.

Perhaps a schematic presentation such as the following will help to make all this clearer:

INCLUSIONS:	(4)	וְיָדְעוּ . . . כִּי־אֲנִי יהוה	
	(8)	בְּיָד רָמָה	PURSUIT and FEAR (7–9);
	(13)	יְשׁוּעַת יהוה	LEITMOTIFS: (4, 8) חזק, כבד
	(14)	יהוה יִלָּחֵם לָכֶם	
TURNING:	(16)	הָרֵם־מַטְּךָ וּנְטֵה אֶת־יָדְךָ	
	(17–18)	חזק, כבד	
	(17–18)	בְּרִכְבּוֹ וּבְפָרָשָׁיו	
	(18)	וְיָדְעוּ . . . כִּי־אֲנִי יהוה	
INCLUSIONS:	(25)	יהוה נִלְחָם לָהֶם	
	(30)	וַיּוֹשַׁע יהוה	PURSUIT and FEAR (23, 24–25);
	(31)	הַיָּד הַגְּדֹלָה	LEITMOTIFS: (23, 26, 28) רֶכֶב וּפָרָשִׁים
	(31)	וַיַּאֲמִינוּ ביהוה	(21, 26, 28) נטה אֶת־יָד

[29] 14 4, 18 use the standard ידע; 14 31 introduces a different verb, האמין. This assymmetry is not accidental. It emphasizes the resolution of the action; Egypt has come to know Yahweh in terror and is lost; Israel is saved and learns of Yahweh's fidelity. It also links the finale with the beginning of the whole story by repeating Exod 4 31.

So balanced a construction recalls, yet differs from, the concentric form of Exod 7 8–10 27 in that the balanced halves hinge on an emphatic central point rather than displaying a simple parallelism between themselves.[30] The central point, be it noted, is emphatic, but not climactic. Here the story turns and begins to move toward its high point. As in the plagues narrative, balance does not deny progress within the whole unit. Once again, we have a vital tension between balanced form and forward movement. The movement — escape, pursuit, salvation — is obvious. Here the contrasting halves with their emphasis on Yahweh's glory in the first half and Egypt's powerful army in the second and their announcement and accomplishment of Egypt's ruin and Israel's salvation heighten the tension and point up the ultimate resolution of the whole exodus episode in Israel's salvation and confession of Yahweh.

To conclude this discussion of Exod 14: it seems to be of a piece with Exod 7 8–10 27. It uses the vocabulary and the key themes of those chapters. It represents the same concept of Israel's escape from Egypt; it is a blow which causes suffering to Egyptians and salvation to Israel; and it does not confuse the issue with variant traditions, for instance, of the favor which Israel enjoyed in Egypt. It uses the same structural sequence: command, execution, result, and effect. It is a well-constructed balanced unit just as the plague stories are.[31] In all these ways it fits far better than Exod 11–13 with the plague stories of Exod 7 8–10 27.

Finally, the fact that Exod 14 shows no influence from the account of the blow against Egypt's first-born is remarkable. For instance, Pharaoh's readiness to pursue Israel cries for explanation after the event of Exod 12 29 and Pharaoh's response to it. Further, it is hard to understand the fears of the Israelites if they have just seen what Yahweh can do. Again, in 14 5a Pharaoh does not even know that Israel is gone while in 12 30–32 he has with full awareness sent them away. If the plague stories developed out of the story about Egypt's first-born, we should expect their literary pendant, Exod 14, also to show some influence from that direction. However we may explain away the fact that the plague stories hardly reflect the first-born story or the Passover in any literary way, it is impossible that an element like the Sea of Reeds miracle be narrated after the Passover complex and yet show no marks of this source, which in fact must have governed it if the hypothe-

[30] Once again, L. Alonso-Schökel (*Poética hebrea*, p. 318) reports an analysis by E. Galbiati in *La struttura letteraria dell'Esodo* which reveals also an elaborate concentric structure in Exod 14. As reported it appears somewhat assymmetrical.

[31] In itself balance or concentrism is a standard rhetorical figure and hence does not prove that the two belong to a single literary whole. Still, it does no harm to the argument for such a unity, and the shared concern for structural niceties is even suggestive.

sis that the story of the stroke against the first-born is the source of the plague stories is correct.

In conclusion, then, there is good reason to believe that Exod 14 is independent of the story of the Passover, but that it has a special literary connection with the plagues narrative. It is a well-constructed unit linked to Exod 7 8–10 27 by common concepts and expressions. In it the tensions of the latter are resolved and its aims achieved. Israel has come to confess Yahweh, and even Egypt must recognize his terrible power. Israel is freed and Moses is vindicated. His hand works terrible miracles; his word is fulfilled; and he is seen to be close to Yahweh, a prophet and more. Thus we have a climactic conclusion to the plague story, one thoroughly integrated with it in vocabulary and concept, not one needing to be doctored to fit.

However, it would be foolish to pretend that Exod 14 was intended to follow immediately upon Exod 10 27, and that Exod 11–13 has simply been intruded between the two parts of the original literary whole. The situation is more complex. The movement from the plagues to the events at the Sea of Reeds would be too abrupt. We would move from a series of inconclusive encounters between Pharaoh and a Moses seeking Israel's release to a story about what happened *after* Israel's escape. How did Israel get away in the first place? In the present text there is no explanation or description of this event which shows the special literary characteristics of the complex of the plagues narrative and the miracle at the Sea of Reeds.

How is this to be accounted for? First we should notice important hints about the nature of Israel's escape as it must have been in order to fit into the plagues–Sea of Reeds complex. For one thing, Moses' dealings with Pharaoh are a closed unit. They are finished with the episode of the miraculous darkness in Exod 10 21–27, but Moses' and Yahweh's object has not been obtained. Israel has not achieved freedom; yet there can be no more negotiations with Pharaoh whose assent would be essential if there was to be a release. This fits perfectly with the datum of Exod 14 5a, where it is clear that Israel has escaped from Egypt to the desert by some sort of surprise move so that Pharaoh did not know of the departure. This, indeed, seems to be contradicted in 5b, where שלח seems to imply that he does know of Israel's escape. Surely, we think, those who "let someone go" know of the journey. However, שלח as used in the story of the exodus has a special sense. It refers specifically to the release of persons held in slavery in foreign lands. Hence it can and should be taken here not as "sent away" but as "allowed to go free." One can do this without knowing that the escape is occurring or has occurred, for instance, by failing to keep a proper guard on the persons involved. In fact, the root שלח does allow this meaning of unsupervised and unnoticed action, of roaming.[32] In

[32] On the technical meaning of שלח in the exodus stories see D. Daube, *The Exodus*

this way 14 5b is reconciled with 5a, and there is nothing in all of ch. 14 to indicate that Pharaoh or Egypt knew of Israel's flight.[33]

That is to say, the literary complex under study conceived the actual departure from Egypt as a sneak escape, not, as in the two actually preserved conceptions of the departure, either as some sort of confidence trick or as a release forced upon Egypt by the tremendous blow of the death of its first-born. A further relic of the account of some sort of surreptitious escape is to be found in Exod 10 28–29, where it is emphasized that Moses saw Pharaoh no more.

Such a conception of the exodus as a stealthy escape is of course incompatible with the picture of the exodus actually preserved in chs. 11–13. Hence it is a reasonable hypothesis that the story of the actual "going out" in the literary complex which also included the ten plagues and the story of the Sea of Reeds miracle as described in ch. 14 was dropped to make room for the different account of Israel's departure connected with the Passover.[34] It is easy enough to understand why such a substitution would have seemed desirable. The ultimate importance of the Passover in Israel's liturgy and life would naturally make that account of the exodus which was connected with it most interesting.

All this has important consequences in several directions. One regards the source theory. If the literary analyses carried out here are valid to any significant degree, they indicate that there are in the all-important pericope, Exod 5–15, literary organizations on a level between that of the sources and the final redaction. There is one complex which includes in one way or another Exod 5 1–6 1+7 8–10 27+14 1–31, and another complex which includes Exod 6 2–7 7+11 1–12 42. These

---

Pattern in the Bible, especially pp. 29–30. In Prov 29 15 the pual of שלח is used of a child left untended; in Isa 32 20 the piel, of cattle allowed to roam free — uses which confirm the interpretation given. The idea that Exod 14 1–4 represents a calculated strategem to avoid a dangerous pursuit (Rylaarsdam, *IB* 1, p. 933) would fit well with the concept of a surreptitious flight. M. Noth (*Überlieferungsgeschichte des Pent.*, pp. 75–76) indeed, finds that the secret flight connected with the story of the Sea of Reeds miracle in Exod 14 creates a certain opposition (*Spannung*) to the plagues narrative, but this seems to be based finally on the conviction that the plagues grew out of the Passover rite. If the secret escape grows out of the fact that the dealings with Pharaoh (the "plagues") were inconclusive and all contact between him and Moses was cut off, rather than contradicting the conception in the plagues narrative, it is the logical result of the impasse in which that pericope terminates.

[33] This use of "flee," ברח, in 14 5a is also significant. It is found only here in this sense in this Exodus context, and it seems to indicate a view of the events which did not involve a "release" from Pharaoh. Perhaps, according to M. Noth (*Exodus*, pp. 111–12), this is a very ancient tradition preserved by E.

[34] The geographical indications in 14 2 could be a remnant of the description of the route of Israel's secret flight or an adaptation to fit the Sea of Reeds story into the redacted text.

two complexes are set off from one another in that each has its own characteristic phrases and its own conception of the why and the how of the exodus; yet each is by general admission not simply an independent composition in its own right but is made up of material drawn from the classical sources of J, E, and P (and even, in ch. 13, deuteronomic material!). Thus the situation is that these two accounts of the exodus, each using the several sources, have been combined by the insertion of Exod 6 2–7 7 after the introduction in Exod 5 1–6 6 and by the substitution of chs. 11–13[35] for the account of a secret flight from Egypt which must have stood between the events which finish in Exod 10 and those which are recounted in Exod 14.

How are we to conceive this? It has been customary to hold that J and E had already been combined when P was added in postexilic times to produce the final redaction.[36] The trouble is that here we have two independent literary combinations in which P is included along with J E, combinations, which have been themselves combined to form the final text. Clearly, the original combinations must have antedated the final redaction. That is to say, some important elements of the P traditions had been worked into intricate literary structures with J E well before the final redaction of the exodus story into the present pentateuchal form. This is a further argument for separating the composition of P from a final postexilic redaction of the Pentateuch and, therefore, for dating it earlier than the 5/4th-century date of classical source criticism. At the very least, if one insists on a close association between some form of P and R, he must hold that important elements of the P traditions had existed and been joined much earlier to the main stream of Hebrew tradition to become along with J and E an object of the continuous work of collecting, editing, and collating which was a major effort of that tradition. This means a more carefully nuanced view of the joining of material related to P to the other traditions. This could scarcely have been a single operation in which two ready-to-hand blocks of material were fitted together. Rather, elements of the P traditions must have been absorbed in a gradual process over a considerable period of time.[37]

[35] The literary character of these chapters is of course far more complex than this statement suggests, but the problem of their internal structure, both from a literary and a source critical point of view, does not affect their character as units within the present redacted composition.

[36] The standard view assigns P to the postexilic period and considers that it was combined with JE soon after its composition (see, for example, C. A. Simpson, *IB*, 1, pp. 198–200); in his excellent survey "Pentateuchal Criticism" (*The OT and Modern Study*, Oxford, 1951), p. 81, C. R. North puts the composition of P earlier, but still holds to the late date for the compilation with JE (as also D. N. Freedman, *Interpreter's Dictionary of the Bible*, 3, p. 717).

[37] At present the best description and explanation of this process is H. Cazelles, "Pentateuch," *SDB*, 7, cols. 812, 843–46; see also S. Mowinckel, "Erwägungen zur

The second important consequence of a careful study of the complex literary phenomena of Exod 5–15 involves the tradition-historical aspect. According to the standard analysis, from this point of view the several stories of the plagues developed out of the *Urplage*, the killing of the first-born of Egypt, which was an element of the cult *legenda* of the Passover festival.[38] Since in fact the attack on the first-born and the ten plagues belong to different literary complexes set off sharply from one another, one can hardly accept this without further discussion. In the abstract it is easy to imagine that the natural urge to develop a striking story led to the addition of more and more details, more and more plagues, and to their arrangement so as to work toward a climax. However, in the concrete, why do the supposed developments, the ten plagues, not use the verbal themes and the concepts of the story of the first-born? Looked at in detail, it is hardly credible that these stories have developed from this story; they belong to separate literary units and they contradict one another. In fact, if there is any influence, it seems to be from the ten plagues in ch. 11, which section, as we have seen, has been roughly adapted to the standard concept of the dealings with Pharaoh.

Of course one might argue that this is true only of the present text

---

Pentateuchquellenfrage," *Norsk teologisk Tidsshrift*, 65 (1964), esp. p. 15. O. Eissfeldt (*Einleitung*^{3}, pp. 279–82) also acknowledges the gradual process by which the sources must have been combined, but he does not treat the problem of P in any detail. In the abstract one can imagine an alternative explanation to that proposed here, namely, that the careful cento of the introduction+plagues+Sea of Reeds was worked out and that at the same time the P introduction was connected with the Passover material and this complex inserted into the other, perhaps because of the urge to conserve as much material as possible. But this would have involved a scarcely conceivable combination of fineness and clumsiness if one author were involved. And do we have any right to assume several contemporary major redactors?

[38] The word *Urplage* is from M. Noth, *Überlieferungsgeschichte des Pentateuch*, p. 71; G. Fohrer (*Überlieferung . . . des Exodus*, pp. 96–97) also considers the story of the first-born of Egypt the germ of the whole although he rejects the idea of a development of it from cultic *legenda*. Further references in note 24. Here the question of the date of the Passover as an *important* element in the cult is relevant. It has often been placed late; cf. G. Fohrer, *Überlieferung . . . des Exodus*, pp. 92–93. J. B. Segal, *The Hebrew Passover*, pp. 78–113, has a well-documented survey of the problem of the date and nature of the Passover (he himself holds for a very early date on the basis of rather unconvincing analogies with the supposed form of the New Year's festival in the ancient Near East). In regard to this problem of the date of Passover, the relatively unformed character of the complex Exod 6 2–7 7 (a kind of introduction)+ Exod 11–12 (Passover and exodus) is not unimportant. It is limited in scope; it is carelessly connected in comparison with the plagues-Sea of Reeds complex; it has suffered free interpolation. This looser structure may be a reflection of the fact that the materials acquired major importance relatively late, so that there was less time for development. If this is so, there is even less reason to suppose a development from the story of the death of the first-born to the plagues. Would there have been time for it

of Exodus and that this latter is the result of secondary literary manipulation of originally related material. This is quite possible, but the argument has no concrete literary basis in our single source of information, the text. This source points in a different direction, and one must be reluctant to contradict it on the basis of a priori arguments about the ancient cult and the stories or texts connected with it.

As far as the evidence of the text goes in terms of vocabulary, structure, and ideas, that is, in literary terms, the real connection of the plagues narrative in Exod 7 8–10 27 is with the story of the miracle at the Sea of Reeds as told in ch. 14. Since the two pericopes share vocabularies and viewpoints, it is much easier to see the former as an expansion of the latter than of anything which we find Exod 11–13. And why not? If we are to see the locus in which traditions were preserved and developed as the cult — and this much of the traditio-historical approach is certainly correct — we must look closely at cult and text to find out what in Israelite cult was the probable locus of a given tradition and text.

From this point of view the connection between the story of the plagues and that of the Sea of Reeds miracle is significant since the Sea of Reeds probably gives us a cultic locus. The tradition about the events at the Sea of Reeds was certainly originally distinct from that of the Passover, and these events were celebrated in the cult, as is shown, among other things, by the existence of a liturgical poem about it in Exod 15 1–18.[39] Why could the *legenda* for this liturgy not have been the nucleus around which the elaborate story of Moses' dealings with Pharaoh, the story of the plagues, grew? The stories would serve the same purpose as they are supposed to have served in relation to the Passover *legenda*, the purpose which they do serve in the final redaction of Exodus. They would satisfy the desire for more detail in the narration, and they would build up to the climax: the ultimate demonstration of Yahweh's power which ruined Egypt and saved Israel, leading the latter to a true belief in Yahweh.

[39] On the original separateness of the Sea of Reeds tradition see M. Noth, *Überlieferungsgeschichte des Pentateuch*, pp. 55, 70, and G. von Rad, *Theology of the Old Testament*, 1, pp. 22, 177–81. Noth (*Exodus*, pp. 104–5) points out the original importance of the Sea of Reeds miracle and its place in hymns. For more on the liturgical character of Exod 15 1–18 see G. Auzou, *De la servitude au service*. Paris, 1961, p. 205, and K. Galling, *Die Erwählungstraditionen Israels*, pp. 5–7. F. M. Cross and D. N. Freedman ("The Song of Miriam," *JNES*, 14 (1955), p. 240) show that the poem uses motifs from Canaanite cultic texts, a fact which puts the song very close to the Israelite cult in its early stages since so many of its forms came from this source.

Reprinted from the CATHOLIC BIBLICAL QUARTERLY, Vol. XXIX, No. 3, pp. 87-100 (393-406), July 1967

"CREATION" MOTIFS IN ANCIENT HEBREW POETRY

The OT scholar should be surprised when he finds that Ugaritologists ordinarily deny that anything like a creation story has been found at Ras Shamra.[1] It may well be true that nothing like the various Egyptian cosmogonies, the Babylonian *enuma eliš,* or Hesiod's *Theogony* have turned up in Ugaritic literature, and it is a limitation of the definition of a creation story to this kind of thing which brings about the reservations of the Ugaritologists. However, there is a great deal about the struggle of the beneficent weather god, Hadd (mostly designated by his title, Baal), to (re-)establish a proper order of things which means assuring sovereignty for Baal and fertility for the earth. This is exactly the sort of thing which we have taken for granted to be creation myth since at least Hermann Gunkel's *Urzeit und Endzeit.*

We deal with a picture of a divine struggle against chaotic forces represented usually by the sea or the "waters," and we assume that this is a creation story of a kind. This sort of story, which we may call a *Chaoskampf,* is generally held to have three basic themes: (1) the fight against chaos often represented by or personified as a monster of the waters; (2) the conquest of this monstrous force by a god who is consequently acclaimed king; (3) the giving of a palace (temple) to the divine king. In fact, despite the doubts of so many students of the Ugaritic texts about the occurrence of creation ideas in them, these discoveries have actually confirmed most of us who are primarily concerned with the OT in the conviction that some such picture of creation was part of Canaan's legacy to Israel.[2] Perhaps the

[1] For discussion and references see Loren R. Fisher, "Creation at Ugarit and in the Old Testament," *VT* 15 (1965) 313-324, and "From Chaos to Cosmos," *Encounter* 26 (1965) 183-197. Fisher suggests that we distinguish between *theogony* and *cosmogony* and that we can find the latter in Ugaritic texts. He would call this creation because it is the typical thing we call *Chaoskampf* here, a struggle of a young god, Baal, against hostile waters (Yam, the sea god) leading to his acclamation as divine king. This calls for more discussion than can be given here. It must suffice to notice that the struggle is between adversaries for control of an apparently organized world, and that there is no hint that the winner constructs a new order as Marduk does in *enuma eliš*: this hardly conforms to what are usually considered creation or even cosmogonic ideas in the ancient Near East.

[2] For a recent study in this sense see Lucien Legrand, "La création, triomphe cosmique de Yahvé," *NRT* 83 (1961), 449-470 (*TD* 11 [1963] 154-158), who feels that the creation theme was so inviting and dangerous because of its Canaanite origin that it was allowed into the canonical writings only in late times. We shall see that this reservation is hardly correct.

problem the Ugaritologists find in identifying this sort of thing as creation is a good omen. It should give us pause. Are we so sure that the *Chaoskampf* with all its attendant themes is really a story of creation in any meaningful sense?

Perhaps we are asking the wrong questions of our texts. In fact, when it comes to creation we seem fated to do this in one way or another. The Christian is familiar with the firm teaching of the Church that God made everything without using any pre-existent materials. We tend to forget that the explicit and official formulation of this teaching has been governed by the actual situations which the Church has had to face. It has addressed itself to specific problems, particularly the recurrent challenge of gnostic dualism and the need to distinguish the trinitarian processions from the process of creation.[3] Hence the rightful insistence on *creatio ex nihilo* which denies both the existence of some sort of matter independent of God and the formation of the world as something which emanated (in the Plotinian sense) from God. However, apart from John,[4] dualism is not a biblical problem, and nowhere in the Bible are the special questions of developed trinitarian theology a concern. Addressing the scriptures directly (their implications are something else, but they are not the immediate concern of the exegete in this matter) for answers to questions not their own turns out to be fruitless, and yet we have asked our texts about *creatio ex nihilo* as though this was the concern of them and their authors.

Still, without going so far as the technical meaning expressed in terms drawn from philosophy, for us the word creation in its normal context must mean some sort of absolute beginning of our world, or we equivocate. Can we really say that this is what the *Chaoskampf* and all it implies is usually concerned with? In other words, when we speak of these things as creation motifs, are we in danger of introducing foreign elements, our own common sense notions even if not technical ones, into the understanding of the texts just as we do when we seek philosophy in them? It seems to me that in fact we are. In the OT the so-called creation motifs are intro-

[3] The classic official Catholic text is the decree of the 4th Lateran Council (1215 A.D.) condemning the dualism of the Cathari (*DS* 800); on the Fathers and the problem of procession and creation see H. A. Wolfson, "The Meaning of *ex nihilo* in the Church Fathers, Arabic and Hebrew Philosophy, and St. Thomas," *Ford Festschrift: Medieval Studies* (edd. U. T. Holmes, Jr., and A. J. Denomy, C.S.B.; Cambridge, Mass., 1948) 355-367.

[4] The concern with the gnostic dualist crisis in John is most recently affirmed by Frederick C. Grant, *JBL* 86 (1967) 92-93 in reviewing *The Jerusalem Bible,* ed. by Alexander Jones.

duced in function of something else, and we must wonder whether we are safe in speaking of creation here at all.[5]

The questions which bring out the motifs in the OT are various. There is the question of where salvation lies. There is question of an orderly world of men (and secondarily of nature).[6] There is question of identifying the true god (Deutero-Isaiah; 2 Mc 7,28). There is question of the proper cult (P). But where is the question of absolute origins as such?

Obviously, all of this is matter for many papers; we can deal only with restricted aspects here. We shall take only the first point: salvation and so-called creation imagery. This probably seems to be a commonplace. It is such, and one can find reference to it anywhere.[7] However, it is often rewarding to review the commonplace from the proper viewpoint. We may begin by noting the most influential study of the relation between the origin of things and salvation: Gerhard von Rad's brilliant analysis of the form of the Hexateuch and his conclusion that the primeval history is the genial addition of J as a kind of cosmic prologue for salvation history.[8] It is not without interest, then, that von Rad, following Hartmut Gese, now admits that the primeval history must have been part of Israel's basic account of itself even before J. This conclusion is based on the fact that the literary form of this account called for such a prologue.[9] Of course, if the primeval history was a given part of the genre rather than an addition to the basic historical credo by J as von Rad argued, it is harder to show that it is a brilliant stroke relating creation and grace as never before. Still, it can be shown that the genre has been adapted to a new purpose. Borrowed from

[5] As implied in the first note, I believe that the Ugaritic materials show that the so-called creation motifs borrowed from Canaan are also in this class. Not only do they not speak of creation by progressive emanation from some primordial thing (Fisher's theogony), but they do not really tell of a struggle against chaos and the formation of an ordered world consequent on victory over that enemy. At most they speak of a struggle for control of the world and its organization. This, however, is matter for another article hopefully to appear soon.

[6] This is characteristic of much in the Psalter, where the laments imply that sin creates disorder and the royal psalms (note especially Ps 72,1-7) see the king's justice (right order) as being in the same line as and even the cause of right order in nature.

[7] For example and more or less at random: T. Boman, "The Biblical Doctrine of Creation," *CQR* 165 (1964) 140-151; A. Jepsen, "The Scientific Study of the Old Testament," *Essays in Old Testament Hermeneutics* (edd. Cl. Westermann and J. L. Mays; Richmond, Va., 1963) 280.

[8] "Das formgeschichtliche Problem des Hexateuch," *Gesammelte Studien zum Alten Testament* (Theologische Bücherei 8; Munich, 1958) 71-75.

[9] *Int* 16 (1962) 21.

tradition, it has been changed radically to provide a deepened understanding of God's dealings with his people.[10]

However, when we look at the texts from the special point of view we are adopting here, it is extremely difficult to speak of creation as being in them in a meaningful sense. In the Yahwist parts of the primeval history, the only ones which interest us, there is no real concern for the origin of the world. All the interest is directed toward its good ordering. This is not *creatio ex nihilo* of course, but equally it has nothing to do with the *Chaoskampf* theme either. The order depends upon watering (rain) and man (cultivation): "When Yahweh God made heaven and earth no plant had yet sprung up in the fields because neither Yahweh God had brought rain to the earth nor had man worked the ground" (Gn 2,4b-5). The familiar motif of the waters is there, but in unfamiliar guise. They are no force to be fought or contained. They are simply God's instrument, his contribution to an orderly world. Even in the flood story the waters are no raging monster; they are released to do their task quietly enough.[11] In all the talk of the struggle against a watery chaos which is supposed to have been of the essence of the *Chaoskampf* type of creation story, as far as is known to me there is no attention paid to the fact that in the only instances when the waters do get out of hand (and remember that they are supposed to threaten this yearly!)[12] they do so not as a force opposed to the divine but rather as the passive instrument of divine punishment. In the OT version, in fact, they are used to overcome disorder, moral disorder it is true, but for the OT moral and natural order or disorder are a continuity,[13] and in any case we shall see that *Chaoskampf* motifs are commonly linked to

[10] See H. Gese, "Geschichtliches Denken im alten Orient und im Alten Testament," *ZTK* 55 (1958) 127-147: the literary form called for a "Golden Age" at the beginning of things but J has made it a time of sin; this is developed in detail elsewhere by me, cf. "The Word of God and 'Literary Embellishment,'" *RRel* 24 (1965) 771-784.

[11] It is not surprising that the waters are not represented as a personal monster in Gn, but the same thing is true of the Babylonian deluge story where, if the *Chaoskampf* idea were as ubiquitous as is often claimed, we should expect something different. This is another of the bits of evidence calling for a review of our ideas of ancient cosmogonies and cosmologies in general.

[12] This, of course, is the basic idea behind the *Chaoskampf* concept: the representation of the annual vegetation cycle in the guise of a divine battle against the ruin which threatens when the vegetation dies: see T. H. Gaster, *Thespis* (Anchor Books; Garden City, N.Y., ²1961) for a study of the ancient Near Eastern Material from this point of view; more general: Mircea Eliade, *Cosmos and History: The Myth of the Eternal Return* (Harper Torchbooks; New York, 1959).

[13] See above, note 6.

moral or social order in the OT. The flood at least is there to purify, not pollute. The conclusion must be that the center of attention is the order of things, not their origins, in this use of the theme of the raging waters. In J, then, rather than speak of creation or cosmogony as the background for the OT drama of sin and grace one should speak of the order of things, cosmology in the root sense, if one will.

Thus the familiar struggle element is entirely absent from J. At most it gives us very early evidence (older than the document itself!) for an interest in the beginnings of the order of things, particularly the moral order. There is no mark of the mythic *Chaoskampf,* but then this section of Genesis has never been part of the argument for the occurrence and importance of the *Chaoskampf* theme in the OT. It is rather the poetry of the Hebrew Bible which has shown the creation struggle imagery.

In view of this, it is remarkable that the poetry which is identifiably oldest does not seem to have been studied systematically from this point of view. Yet much is gained if we can characterize the attitude to these most ancient texts. It may be that the forms found in later poetry, the kingship of Yahweh psalms for instance, are older as forms, for they surely antedate Israel itself. However, as we have them they are hymns modified by later use. They do not bear the linguistic marks of antiquity which other poems do, for example. If these latter tell us something about the use of the *Chaoskampt* theme in early days in Israel, about the meaning of the imagery borrowed from it and the purposes to which it was put, this direct evidence will show more clearly the meaning of the theme in Israel in the vital formative stages of Israelite religion than any extrapolation from later texts, even though this latter is integrated into a view of the theme as it was supposed to have existed outside Israel in earliest times.

The ancient poetry in question can be found in Gn 49; Ex 15,2-18; Dt 32,1-43; Dt 33; Jgs 5; 2 Sm 22,2-51; and Psalms 29 and 68, materials which bring us back close to Israel's beginnings. Rather than take the older and relevant parts of these texts one by one in exegesis we shall address three basic questions to them. (1) What does God do in them which can be related to creation? This will come down to a discussion of certain basic vocabulary, the verbs used. Are they in fact ones also used of creation? (2) How does God act? Is the imagery used that associated with creation? (3) Why does he do it? This is crucial, for the purpose of an action will often reveal whether it is creation or not, and in what sense.

When we turn to the first question: what does God do, we find at once that certain of the predicates attributed to him in these old texts are associated with creation or at least production both in the Bible and at Ras

Shamra. Among these are *qnh* (Ugaritic *qny*) and *kwn*.[14] In the ancient victory hymn in Ex 15,2-18, verse 16b reads *'am-zû qanîtā*, "the people which thou hast gotten." In another old text, Dt 32,6b, we have: *hălô'-hû' 'ābîkā qānekā*, "Is he not thy father (who) got thee?"[15] It is well to retain here the double meaning in the rather old fashioned use of "get," for, though the root seems to mean "form" in a general sense, "acquire," or "be master of,"[16] the myths of Ugarit certainly demonstrate that it has the sense of "produce" and "procreate."[17] This Ugaritic evidence points up the sexual overtones of the root *qny/qnh* as opposed to some more general note like produce or the like.

The other root, *kwn*, on the other hand, does not have this sort of overtone: the basic meaning is to "make firm," and so, among other things, "form," and "found."[18] This is clearly the case in Dt 32,6, where it is part of a passage describing Yahweh's founding of Israel as a special instance of his universal activity of "setting the boundaries of the peoples, assigning them to the various sons of God."[19] Yahweh has formed a social order with each people given a proper place and guide.

These verbs do not exhaust the vocabulary pertinent to our investigation. On the contrary, though the ancient Israelite poems avoid a favorite word of the Ugaritic texts relating to origins, *bny* (Hebrew *bnh*), which is so

[14] On these roots in Ugaritic and "creation" see M. H. Pope, *El in the Ugaritic Texts* (*VTS* 2; Leiden, 1955) 50-54, though it is hard to follow him in emphasizing the sexual aspects of the roots. *qny* certainly has this aspect, but not always; see I Aqhat 220: *d yqny ddm*, "who possesses/owns (i.e., is master of) fields." *kwn* is certainly neutral, though it may have a sexual sense in context. Its basic meaning is established by the new text in *PRU* II, 188 (RS 15.128), lines 6 and 9, where it is a question of *establishing* guarantees.

[15] For the antiquity of the poem in Dt 32 see O. Eissfeldt, *Das Lied Moses, Deuteronomium 32,1-43 und das Lehrgedicht Asaphs Psalm 78 samt einer Analyse der Umgebung des Mose-Liedes* (Verhändlungen der säch. Akad. zu Leipzig, Phil.-hist. Klasse, 104/5; Berlin, 1958); W. F. Albright, "Some Remarks on the Song of Moses in Deuteronomy XXXII," *VT* 9 (1959) 339-346; G. E. Wright, "The Lawsuit of God: A Form-Critical Study of Deuteronomy 32," *Muilenburg Festschrift: Israel's Prophetic Heritage* (edd. B. W. Anderson and W. Harrelson; New York, 1962) 26-67. The first two opt for a date as early as the 11th century B.C.; Wright sees later redaction of earlier material, but the texts which concern us belong to this older material (see below, note 21).

[16-17] On *qnh* see above, note 14, and add, for the meaning "create," F. M. Cross and D. N. Freedman, "The Song of Miriam," *JNES* 14 (1955) 249, n. 57 with references, and F. M. Cross, "Yahweh and the God of the Patriarchs," *HTR* 55 (1962) 240, note 70.

[18] See above, note 14.

[19] Reading in 8b *b^e^nê 'ĕlōhîm* with LXX for MT *b^e^nê yiśrā'ēl*, a reading confirmed from Qumrân; see G. E. Wright, *Muilenburg Festschrift* 28, note 8.

common as an epithet of the high god El, *bny bnwt,* "creator of creatures," and do not apply its Hebrew cognate to Yahweh, they use what would seem a far less likely verb, *yld,* "bear a child." At Ras Shamra this was a cosmogonic or better theogonic word. For instance, goddesses bear a divinized Dawn and Dusk to El.[20] In Dt 32, 18 Yahweh himself is "the Rock (who) bore thee . . . , the God who was in travail with thee." The imagery is strong: "bore thee" (*yᵉlādkā*) is parallel to *mᵉḥollekā,* "writhe in the pangs of childbirth" literally, surely at first sight as extreme an anthropomorphism as one could imagine. But, of course, it is precisely a freedom from the basic anthropomorphic view of the divine current in the ancient Near East which permits this. A pantheon preserves the distinct sexual functions with its gods and goddesses. The one God of Israel is beyond anything like this, so far beyond that the poet can freely use the image of childbirth to emphasize the affective aspect, the love of Yahweh for his people, a love which like a mother's is unearned and even more intense for the weakling among her children, since the poet uses this image to introduce the section on the faithlessness of Israel which deserves and gets parental punishment.[21] This makes the usage here all the more poignant, for verse 18 resumes verse 6 with a new note. In the earlier verse we have to do with a section concerning the special marking out of Israel for Yahweh's favor among the nations, but the verbs used, *qnh* and *kwn,* though significant, are not especially colorful. The repetition of the title Rock (32,4) as well as the parallel in ideas between 32,6 and 32,18 form a kind of inclusion which brings us back to the earlier, happier situation, but by the change in tone also points forward to the judgment scene which continues the poem in verses 19ff. Hence the highly emotional figures; the measure of Yahweh's love and favor is the measure of Israel's guilt and punishment. This is the mood of Hos 11, but in archaic form.

The conclusion at this point is clear. Yahweh is indeed spoken of in terms which, in one way or another, refer to the coming to be of things, and this vocabulary is the same as that of the Ugaritic texts when they speak of origins. However, the OT gives the words a particular focus. It uses the

20 C. H. Gordon, *Ugaritic Textbook* (Analecta orientalia 38; Rome, 1965) Text 52, called by Gaster, *Thespis,* 418-435, "Poem of the Gracious Gods." Gaster points out, probably rightly, that there is a burlesque element in it as we have it. This, though, implies something serious to be burlesqued. Insofar as this deals with natural phenomena we might speak of a cosmogony; insofar as they are personified and deified, a theogony. This ambiguity seems inevitable in the ancient stories of origins.

21 V. 18 is evidently old: witness the ancient title, Rock, and El (not Elohim), the lack of connectives and of the article. We may assume that the less colorful parallel, v. 6, which also lacks some connectives, is also ancient.

vocabulary to speak of Yahweh's favors to his people, his marking them out and making them a people (Dt 32,6: *qnh, kwn;* Ex 15,16: *qnh*) with emphasis on the love shown in all of this (Dt 32,18: *yld*). Even at Ugarit these expressions were mostly used for the origins of man and the gods (though the latter may well be personified natural phenomena), of a kind of social order or at least of social beings rather than of a cosmos. Still there is nothing there about the formation of a god's people, nor of his loving and judging them. Israel seems to have done something quite new in applying these "creation" words to the description of its position as a saved and chosen people among peoples all under God's guidance.[22] What is "created" is a social or political order. In Ex 15 Israel is constituted a nation at Egypt's expense. In Dt 32 all nations have their place and their guides assigned them; a whole social order is brought into being.[23] We can and do call this sort of thing creative, but it is scarcely creation in any technical sense since it does not touch at all upon absolute beginnings of a whole world.

We find thus far that what Yahweh is described as doing when "creation" verbs are predicated of him is something quite different from what the divinity does in the supposed *Chaoskampf* creation myth. It is somewhat different when we turn to the *how* of things. The poetry makes ready use of the motifs associated with the *Chaoskampf*. This is obvious in Ex 15. We have a battle in which the raging waters do indeed figure, the victorious god gains a temple, and he is acclaimed king. This is the very stuff of the creation myth in its classic formulation in *enuma eliš*. But here it is demythologized.[24] The waters are not the enemy but the weapon of God, and his temple is his own work. He is not subject to approval from on high, nor does he need a motion from the floor in a divine assembly.[25]

This use of terms related to the *Chaoskampf* is not confined to this passage. The psalm in 2 Sm 22 turns the imagery to a different purpose:

[22] Perhaps we should add to the "creation" words the very name Yahweh if, as has been persuasively argued, it is a causative of the verb "to be" and so means "he makes to be." See F. M. Cross, *HTR* 55 (1962) 252-254. Note 123 is important for showing through parallel forms that the idea was not too "abstract" and "metaphysical" for the ancients.

[23] This is not a common OT idea, but it does occur in another form in Am 9,7. Does Amos' insight into Yahweh's universal love and providence depend somehow on the view couched in more mythic terms in Dt? The idea is very old, as it occurs in the 14th century Egyptian hymn to Aton (see *ANET* 370b) where, as here, it is entirely disassociated from any *Chaoskampf* motifs.

[24] See on this Cross and Freedman, *JNES* 14 (1955) 239-240.

[25] As did Baal at Ugarit: Text 51, IV-V (*ANET* 133), and Marduk at Babylon: *enuma eliš,* VI, 49ff. (*ANET* 68).

"breakers of death" and "torrents" surround the afflicted king (22,6), but Yahweh the Warrior appears to confound and turn back the enemy (22,16). The imagery of the mighty sea is the same, but its function is different. Now it is not Yahweh's weapon as in Exodus but the symbol of the adversary he so easily puts down. Early in its history Israel is so free from seeing any reality in the *Chaoskampf* theme that it has become a mere source for figures of speech. Its language can be used now one way, now another as seems useful in a given literary situation, something hardly possible if it were felt to be a description of reality, for then the use of the language would have to be controlled by the reality behind it. The only consistency is the end to which the imagery is directed. Always it tells how Yahweh saved by producing or restoring order, whether it is by means of the waters or by saving from the waters which symbolize evil. The "creation" motifs have become images of salvation, and, of course, this became a tradition in Israel. In the psalms of lamentation, for example, the waters are a cliché for evil, and we shall find them appearing again as a weapon in God's hands. The point is that this turn was given to the imagery very early. Indeed, from its very first recorded use in Israel this is so.

One further instance of the imagery of the waters is worth noting. This motif from the *Chaoskampf* theme appears in Gn 49,25 (= Dt 33,13): *birkôt tᵉhôm rōbeṣet tāḥat,* "blessings from Deep lying in wait below."[26] The note of threat, even of recalcitrance, echoes faintly in that "lying in wait," a hint of an evil will in the waters, a hint all the more striking because it seems unconscious. It is just there. It serves no figurative purpose, it has no reason to be there except it be some traditional phrase or the like. The most one might say is that it emphasizes Yahweh's control even over difficult things, but this will hardly do in a context where there is no hint of any difficulties or opposition. This is as close as one comes to "rebellious waters" in the earliest poems, and it seems to be a case where the phrase is so trite it has lost any figurative meaning and its participle has become so colorless as to be equivalent of "being" or the like, even with the mild poetic figure of a personified Deep. Once more no battle, once more the waters are Yahweh's instrument, not enemy, and they are as mild as the brooklets they refer to, the blessings of springs in a dry country. So here too, in the realm of nature, the emphasis is on order for the benefit of God's people.

[26] On the date of this text see H.-J. Zobel, *Stamesspruch und Geschichte* (*BZAW* 95; Berlin, 1965) 59-61, and F. M. Cross, *Studies in Ancient Yahwistic Poetry* (Baltimore, 1950) 226-227. The translation in the text here of course takes *tᵉhôm* to be personified as is indicated by the primitive ideas in the phrase. On this see F. M. Cross and D. N. Freedman, "The Blessing of Moses," *JBL* 67 (1948) 206, note 44. This, of course, refers to the entirely parallel text of Dt 33,13.

This same emphasis on order in society comes out in the motif of Yahweh the Warrior (Ex 15,3) inseparable from much in the ancient poems. Now, obviously the idea of the *Chaoskampf* implies (a) warrior god(s), but nonetheless the divine warrior idea had its own independent and important place in Israel's traditions. In many ways it was the holy war led by Yahweh, God of armies, which made the people of Israel.[27] It would seem that this was combined with the other theme. The warrior god (*'îš milḥāmâ*) is described in images borrowed from the *Chaoskampf* theme, as is clear in Ex 15, but especially in 2 Sm 22 where the God who pushes back the waters and bares the foundations of the earth (10-16) is the one who trains the king to fight (33-37).

The same relationship appears in Jgs 5,20-21, where the very elements, the stars and the rain, are the weapons of Yahweh in the holy war against Sisera. This is not precisely the imagery of the *Chaoskampf,* as in the case of Ex 15, but rather of the Lord of nature and man making use of the resources of his domain on behalf of his people.

This again brings us to a new theme. This is the god of the storm. Very early the description of the storm god's power was applied to Yahweh. Already in Ps 68,5 Yahweh is the cloud-rider, an epithet of Baal at Ugarit, and in 2 Sm 22,11b-15 he moves on the wind with thunder and lightning.[28] However, the *locus classicus* here is Ps 29. Yahweh shows his dominance through the storm. The emphasis is on the awesome power displayed in the thunder, the lightning, the blasts of the wind capable of smashing the mightiest giants of the forest. Awesomeness calls forth awe, and this terrible God receives it from the "sons of God" (29,1) as well as from men, and he receives it in his palace. Thus the result of the storm god's appearance at once ties into the complex of motifs associated with the *Chaoskampf.* The conqueror god receives homage and temple, but once again as in Ex 15 the means are different. There the means was not any conquest of chaos but the formation of a people through the defeat of Egypt, but at least the imagery describing this defeat was borrowed in part from the traditions of the *Chaoskampf.* Here in Ps 29 even the imagery is different. In a sense it is true that the picture is closer to the *Chaoskampf* in that the storm is real and

27 The basic work on this idea has been that of R. Smend, *Jahwekrieg und Stammebund* (*FRLANT* 84; Göttingen, 1963), and *Die Bundesformel* (Theologische Studien 68; Zurich, 1963).

28 For the dates of 2 Sm 22 (Ps 18) and Ps 68 see H. J. Kraus, *Psalmen* (*BKAT* 15/1; Neukirchen, [2]1961) 136-151, 464-477, with extensive references to the literature. The basic study of 2 Sm 22 remains F. M. Cross and D. N. Freedman, "A Royal Song of Thanksgiving: II Samuel 22, Psalm 18," *JBL* 72 (1953) 15-34; see also D. N. Freedman, "Archaic Forms in Early Hebrew Poetry," *ZAW* 72 (1960) 103.

belongs to the realm of nature, not merely figurative and pertaining to society as in Ex 15. But this general connection proves nothing. The explicit topic of the psalm is the terrible power which the divinity shows in the storm. To be sure, the rainstorm could be beneficent. It was essential to the economy of Syro-Phoenicia, but this is not what the poet chooses to emphasize.

In the accepted analysis of the supposedly ubiquitous *Chaoskampf* theme this would be impossible. Such destruction wrought by water is not the manifestation and instrument of the divinity who will be king but of his monstrous opponent. Yet there it is; the storm god is acclaimed king, and this is in a hymn taken over almost without change from pre-Israelite sources.[29] This might be significant in several ways. It attests an attribution of kingship to the god of the storm by acclamation of the divine council, something which as far as we know Ugaritic mythology allowed only to El.[30] It shows that the waters, even in their destructive aspect, could be a divine instrument and bring a god to supremacy. If this is because of the concern with a rain economy as so often and persuasively argued by C. H. Gordon, it shows a concern with the order of things, an order maintained by violent divine power but not in any way which resembles the workings of the so-called creation myth. In any case, what matters is the maintenance of the world of Syro-Phoenicia, not its origins. Granted that this psalm is a direct borrowing from Canaan, we have here an antecedent to some of the things which we have found in the ancient Hebrew texts we have examined. There is the use of the waters, natural phenomena, as divine weapons instead of making them symbols of inimical chaotic forces. There is the connection of this altered or new motif with the divine kingship.

Finally, to complete the survey of the means by which Yahweh is represented as achieving his purposes in our texts, the answer to our second question about how Yahweh acts, we must look at a further set of images commonly used. Regularly he is associated with mountains. He is the "One of Sinai," the one who "goes forth from Seir" (Jgs 5,4-5; Dt 33,2). He comes with smoke and fire (2 Sm 22,9; Dt 32,22-25), and at his coming the earth is shaken to its foundations (Jgs 5,4-5; 2 Sm 22,8). This calls to mind at once the account of the events on Sinai, especially Ex 19, and the tradition associating Yahweh with mountains was constant (1 Kgs 19; Psalms of Zion; Na 1,5-6). What is pertinent here is that the manifesta-

29 On this see most recently M. Dahood S.J., *Psalms I: 1-50* (The Anchor Bible; Garden City, N.Y., 1966) 175-180, with extensive references.

30 See W. Schmidt, *Königtum Gottes in Ugarit und Israel* (*BZAW* 80; Berlin, 1961) 20-21, and "Jerusalemer El-Traditionen bei Jesaja," *Zeitschrift für Religions- und Geistesgeschichte* 16 (1964) 308.

tions of the god from the mountain, fire and the rest, are the instruments, the weapons with which he achieves his purposes. He destroys Israel's enemies (Jgs 5; 2 Sm 22) or he punishes his disloyal people (Dt 32,22-25). This is the same figure as that of the waters in Ex 15 or the storm in Ps 29.

Probably Dt 32 and 2 Sm 22 are most important here since the fire of the mountain god merges with the raging storm, and everything seems to have cosmic meaning. The foundations of the earth are consumed, the breakers of death turned back. So many motifs are crowded together here: mountain god, storm god, warrior god, *Chaoskampf*; but they are all symbolic, impressive figures of speech and thought for picturing the way Yahweh controls events among men. The point is always political or social order.[31]

We have not yet turned explicitly to our third question about the *why* of Yahweh's activities as depicted in our texts. Since the answer is so bound up with what he does and how he does it, in fact we have dealt with much of the answer. It is double: one object of it all is that Yahweh be acknowledged supreme, acclaimed king, the other that order be established for his people.

As for the first, we have seen Yahweh reigning in Ex 15; Ps 29; Ps 82; Dt 32,2-3 and possibly Dt 32,43.[32] The ancient Israelites saw no difficulty in picturing Yahweh as reigning in a divine council, since we must take a picture of him amid the sons of God in Dt 32 as somehow real if his special choice of Israel is to mean something. If it is a mere figure of speech, then the contrast between his taking Israel and the others' taking the other nations loses its force and election disappears. What appears to be unusual is the source of his reign. It is not the conquest of chaos in the

[31] We might note that this mixture of motifs is not peculiar to Israel. Apart from the kingship in the divine council and the mountain god aspects they are all applied to Baal in Ugaritic literature. He is even associated with a mountain (Schmidt, *Königtum Gottes,* 23-27), but this is the seat of kingship, and he manifests none of the fiery attributes of the God who comes from the mountain in the OT. Even so, we should note this pre-Israelite mixture of motifs. Such mixing of literary phenomena is generally held to be part of the declining stage of a form, and this should call our attention to the fact that we should not assume pure forms at the start of OT literature. The Hebrews borrowed wholesale from an advanced culture, and this example shows what is evident anyway: much that they borrowed was far past the stage of pure forms. This is borne out by the mixed state we find in the forms of the oldest Israelite texts.

[32] On the reconstruction of Dt 32,43 in this sense see G. E. Wright, *Muilenburg Festschrift,* 33. On Ps 82 see, besides the commentaries, G. E. Wright, *The Old Testament against Its Environment* (*SBT* 2; London, 1950) 30-41.

manner of a Marduk in *enuma eliš*. It is simply his overwhelming power. This may be affirmed in violent imagery as in Ex 15 or Ps 29. However, in another image he is absolute ruler who orders society and its guardians as he will (Dt 32,7-9) or nature and its powers as he wishes (Gn 49,25). This is quiet superiority, but still total power. Once more the total expression cannot be simply subsumed under one head but the basic aim is clear amid the many images: Yahweh is absolute king of all.

If anything the other object of Yahweh's activities in our texts is even clearer. With imagery borrowed from almost any source at hand including the *Chaoskampf* theme, they affirm that God controls events among men for the benefit of his chosen people.

In itself this is no very startling conclusion. The longing for order in human and natural affairs is characteristic of the laments of the ancient world, including Israel, and the praise of it rings in the Psalter (e.g., Pss 8; 19). Here Ps 104 is informative. In part very old, it has the special feature of uniting a *Chaoskampf* motif (putting down the rebellious waters: 5-9) with quiet praise of the order of nature (10ff.). However, the union is not quite smooth and organic. One feels the abrupt change from the mythic imagery to the *Listenwissenschaft* of the ancient Near Eastern wisdom tradition.[33] Evidently it is not this wisdom tradition even united with hymns based on *Chaoskampf* motifs which is the original locus of Israel's articulated and (to it) self-evident concept of Yahweh as orderer. Neither did it grow out of a gradual "demythologizing" of a primitive *Chaoskampf* concept fully held in earliest Israel.

Rather, the study of the ancient poems scattered in various books of the OT has shown them concerned with the events of Israel's historical relationship with Yahweh and points in another direction. Israel was thoroughly at home in the imagery of the *Chaoskampf* from the earliest evidence for it in Israel. This ease with mythic imagery seems to come precisely because it was seen as having nothing to do with a story of real, ultimate origins. The origins which counted for Israel were political and social, ultimately religious because these things were not separated, and these origins were seen to be the mighty work of Yahweh in choosing and saving Israel, protecting it, and punishing it if proper order called for it. Connected with this was the proper allotment of places to the other nations. All this could be and was described in the imagery of battles involving nature, especially the waters, which could symbolize Yahweh's enemy or instrument involved in the real task, bringing about the desired order

[33] See W. Schmidt, *Die Schöpfungsgeschichte der Priesterschrift* (*WMANT* 16; *Neukirchen,* 1964) 42; H. J. Kraus, *Psalmen* II, 709.

among men. Other imagery could be and was used; the divine warrior, the storm of God, the God of the mountain, the divine king who could and did extend his order to the "sons of God," the guides of nations, and thus all mankind. What we have here is not evidence for any real belief in a *Chaoskampf* with its attendant pantheon, forces on the same plane as God. Quite the contrary, as was mentioned earlier, the freedom in using *Chaoskampf* imagery in different, even contradictory, ways shows that there was little feeling of a reality behind it. Rather it was simply a convenient source of tropes.

This is borne out by the complex mixing of motifs which we have found. Warrior, mountain, and storm gods motifs are all used along with those from the *Chaoskampf*. This sort of mixing is usually seen as representing the break-down of a form. Be that as it may, the fact confirms the point already made: there is little or no effort to use all these ideas and images as consistent, independent wholes. Rather they are merely sources for means to describe what is important, and this once again is the proper ordering of the world of men.

Thus the evidence hardly indicates a need for demythologizing in the sense of a working away from a belief in the *Chaoskampf* and all its characteristic apparatus. The evidence is that such "demythologization" was there from the first because Israel was interested in historical, not cosmic origins, and so it could use the mythic themes without hazard.

Once more, if we ask the proper questions, it would seem that we get answers. We should not ask about creation as such from these texts. It may be that there are relics in them left over from myths about absolute origins, though it seems to me that this idea forces the meaning even of the supposed myths. The problem arises because we assume the myths and assume their meaning, a meaning they sometimes had indeed; but do we not extend this meaning to all the myths because there is always for us the question of absolute origins? In fact, the ancient Israelite poems we have looked at do indeed contain material usually associated with the *Chaoskampf*. However, because the poems speak not of absolute origins but rather of the origins of the social order as Israel found it and understood it, these relics do not speak of world origins. They speak of God's saving Israel, and it may be misleading to seek more from them.

DENNIS J. MCCARTHY, S.J.
St. Louis University
St. Louis, Missouri

THE SYMBOLISM OF BLOOD AND SACRIFICE

DENNIS J. McCARTHY, S.J.

ST. LOUIS UNIVERSITY DIVINITY SCHOOL

BLOOD rites are so common that the student of religion must ask about their meaning. Is there a basic, common meaning, or are there several not reducible to a single one? One common answer is to attribute a special power to blood: It is a "divine sanguinary substance" which revivifies the divinity and so gives force to rites.[1] But that blood rites are widespread is not enough to justify such a claim. Blood impresses the imagination. Its loss means weakness and death. It can, therefore, easily be identified with strength. But blood also arouses fear and repulsion. It can be a sign of illness and death. Just what motive accounts for its presence in rites must be matter for careful study of the individual cases.

Since Wellhausen and W. Robertson Smith a prime base for the claim that blood is divine and so is used in ritual has been the assertion that the ancient Semitic world generally held that "in the blood is life," or at least that this was characteristic of the West Semites.[2] The purpose of this paper is to study the extrabiblical evidence to see whether it confirms the doctrine of Gen 9 4, Lev 17 11, and Deut 12 23. This means careful study of what is largely indirect evidence. We have descriptions of or allusions to the rites, not explanations of their meaning.

Turning to the evidence, we might expect that the ancient cultural leader, Mesopotamia, would attribute a divine character to blood, for blood, or at least human blood, was from the gods. They had created man by vivifying clay with the blood of a god slain for rebellion,[3] but no conclusions for the cult seem to have been drawn from this. The Mesopotamian sacrifice was essentially a meal served to the gods, a ritual undoubtedly influenced by the Sumerians, who, as far as we

[1] E. g., E. O. James, *Sacrifice and Sacrament*, pp. 27, 60–61, 136. One main source for the idea is B. Spencer and F. J. Gillen (*The Native Tribes of Central Australia*, p. 206), noting that blood "drives out" the spirits of game from their hiding places and so increases the available supply. But "drive out" does not seem to imply "impart power" so much as frighten or the like. We shall probably never know the exact force of that "drive out," but it is an admonition to care in using our sources.

[2] A. L. Oppenheim (*Ancient Mesopotamia*, p. 192) avoids the earlier generalization, but speaks of ". . . the 'blood consciousness' of the West. . ."

[3] Cf. *enuma eliš* VI, 5–34; *KAR* 4, 26.

know, did not associate blood with the clay of creation.[4] To argue that this extrinsic influence changed the basic character of ritual among the Mesopotamian Semites does not seem possible. This might account for the concept of the sacrifice as banquet, but it leaves unexplained the unimportance of blood in their numerous purificatory and dedicatory rituals. This contrasts sharply with Hebrew practice, where blood was the universal purifier and consecrator. If this stems from a primitive Semitic belief in the divine nature of blood, an idea not unknown in Mesopotamia, it is difficult to understand how the Akkadians and their Semitic successors could have stopped using so powerful a substance for ritual, if they had originally so done.

Of course, since Akkadian *naqû* ("pour") is the ordinary word for "offer sacrifice," it is argued that the pouring out of a victim's blood was so central as to denominate the whole sacrificial process. However, there is no positive evidence for the ritual manipulation of blood, drink offering was an important element in the banquet offering, and the act of libation was certainly designated by *naqû*. Given the overriding conception of sacrifice as a meal, surely it is most likely that the drink offering, not an unattested use of blood, gave the name to the whole ritual.[5]

Hittite civilization offers an instructive parallel. Since the verb *šipand-* ("pour") also designated sacrificing, some conclude that blood had a central rôle in sacrifice. Once again, the texts are remarkably reticent about the use of blood. To establish its rôle one must fall back on interpreting ritual scenes on the monuments which do depict libations, but not necessarily of blood.[6] In fact, as in Mesopotamia, the concept of sacrifice was that of offering the gods needed food and drink.[7]

The same is true in the other great center of early civilization in the eastern Mediterranean basin. Egyptian religion was not one where the blood of sacrifice played a significant rôle. Once more, the offerings

[4] So generally; references in Oppenheim, *Ancient Mesopotamia*, pp. 182–98, and R. Schmid, *Das Bundesopfer in Israel*, pp. 51–54. For the Sumerians, see S. N. Kramer, *The Sumerians*, p. 150.

[5] For a discussion of *naqû* use E. Dhorme, *Les religions de Babylonie et d'Assyrie*, pp. 224–25, 252. The prevalence of the word is all the more significant in that *ziqû* (Heb. *zbḥ*) implying bloody offerings was in the language from Amorite times (cf. Codex Hammurabi iv, 22) but never prevailed as *the* ritual word.

[6] For blood in Hittite ritual see A. Goetze, *Kleinasien*^{2}, p. 164, and R. Dussaud, *Les religions des Hittites et des Hourrites, des Phéniciens, et des Syriens*, pp. 428–29, which depends upon the work of G. Furlani; but Furlani himself ("La religione degli Hittiti," in G. Castellani, ed., *Storia delle religione* I^{5}, Turin, 1962, pp. 460–61) is careful to avoid mention of blood, which, of course, cannot be shown to be the substance of the libations depicted.

[7] A. Goetze, *op. cit.*, pp. 162–64; H. Otten, "Das Hethiterreich," in H. Schmökel, *Kulturgeschichte des alten Orient*, pp. 428–29.

were essentially royal meals for the gods.[8] Man must maintain temples and festal meals to see to the care and feeding of the gods. The gods depended upon his offerings, but this support was not a "divine sanguinary substance"; it was simple food and drink. Thus the basic concept of sacrifice in the major centers of the more ancient civilizations, for all their diversity, is remarkably unitary. Sacrifice is offering food to the gods, and blood as such had no special, explicit part in it.

In fact, since Robertson Smith the parade example of the ritual use of blood among ancient Semites has been the religion of ancient central Arabia. We are told that the tribes of the region anointed the horns of their altars and poured out the blood of sacrifice in a special place connected with the altar. This sounds like familiar Israelite ritual, and that is the trouble. The information still seems to come from the Christian Nilus' report on the tribe which captured him, and Nilus was an unreliable reporter.[9] Even if he were reliable, his evidence comes from the sixth century of our era when Jewish (and Christian) ideas had thoroughly penetrated Arabia. It is hardly solid, independent testimony for primeval practice and belief.

There is another class of rites, purification and apotropaic rituals, perhaps not strictly sacrificial, but certainly not sharply distinguished from religious rites by the ancients themselves, if they made any distinction at all. Hence such rituals may be sources of evidence for beliefs about blood.

Once again, our evidence is complex. In Mesopotamia propitiatory rites and the like were inextricably mixed up with magic. Without getting into a discussion of the relation of magic to religion we can ask whether these rites treated blood as somehow divine and so efficacious. The *Chicago Assyrian Dictionary* gives no references to *dāmu* in incantation texts and the like. Furlani does refer to two apotropaic rites using blood.[10] It also appears in omen texts, but as a mere physical sign on a par with lines on the liver, not as having a special meaning in its own right. Considering the mass of propitiatory texts and the like which are preserved, this infrequent mention of blood as such surely indicates that it had little importance in ritual.

Red wool does play a part in some of the *šurpu* purificatory rites,[11]

[8] References in Schmid, *Bundesopfer*, pp. 47–51.

[9] The latest treatment gives no other reference: see G. Ryckmans, "Les religions arabes préislamiques," in *Histoire général des religions* III, pp. 202–03, followed by R. de Vaux, *Studies in Old Testament Sacrifice*, p. 16. On Nilus' unreliability see Gaster, *IntDB*, 4, p. 151.

[10] See G. Furlani, *Il sacrificio nella religione dei Semiti di Babilonia e Assiria. Memoria della accademia dei lincei. Classe di scienze morali*. . . VI/IV/III. Rome, 1932, p. 352.

[11] E. Reiner, *Šurpu: A Collection of Sumerian and Akkadian Incantations*, *AfO Beiheft* 11, I, lines 14, 14', V–VI, lines 93–102, 113–22.

and this is assumed sometimes to be a surrogate for blood, indicating its power. However, the manipulation of red wool takes away curses, hexes, and the like, as well as bodily pain. It is aimed at evil in general and therefore is not even sympathetic magic for trouble associated with blood and so life symbolized by blood. The text does not specify blood, nor does it give red pride of place. A Hittite substitution rite adds to our knowledge of this kind of thing. To protect the king an animal substitute for him is adorned with flocks of varicolored wool. These symbolize diseases, and we might assume that the red signifies blood or blood-red spots or the like. Perhaps so, but it is on a level with green, black, and white. Red or blood has no special place or meaning in the Hittite ritual, nor, presumably, its Mesopotamian prototype.[12]

Still, it is sometimes said that there was a special purificatory power in blood because Akkadian *kuppuru*, like Hebrew *kāppēr*, means "purify with blood" on the basis of the Babylonian New Year ritual text, where a slaughtered sheep is used to purify the temple.[13] But line 354 says, "The incantation priest shall purify (*ukappar*) the temple with the corpse (*ina pagri*) of the sheep." The body, not the blood, purifies, and even it does not confer purity like the blood in Lev 16. Rather it absorbs impurities, becoming so contaminated that it and the men who handled it were cast out of the holy precincts, carrying away impurity.[14]

The typical purificatory rite in Mesopotamian practice was washing or rubbing with water or oil or milk or the like, not with blood as in Israel. In fact, the Hittite ritual of Papanikri is unusual in cuneiform literature because it uses blood to purify. Blood was smeared on a building contaminated by bloodshed, and the removal of the new blood took away the contamination of the old.[15] This is simple imitative magic. Blood is blood, and removing the new takes away the old. It is a specific for problems related to blood, not something specially and generally powerful in its own right.

Thus, to say the least, there is little concrete evidence that blood is purificatory. Where are the parallels to Lev 17 11: blood is life given by God and so it has purifying power? It is rash to extrapolate this

[12] Cf. H. M. Kümmel, *Ersatzrituale für den hethitischen König. Studien zu den Boğazköy-Texten* 3. Wiesbaden, 1967, who demonstrates the Mesopotamian source of the ritual (cf. pp. 6, 112, 124, 188–98). M. Vieyra, "Rites de purification hittites," *RHR*, 119 (1939), pp. 141–42, points out that similar decoration of men or animals may be simply imitation of royal regalia.

[13] Kümmel, *ibid.*, p. 193.

[14] Materially, this is like the removal of the remains of the sin offering, Lev 7 12, but the meaning is quite different. The remains are too pure to keep, the sheep and the men in Babylon too impure. This is very clear from the normal use of the Akkadian verb to mean "purify (by wiping) with bread or dough," i. e., substances which literally absorbed impurities.

[15] See F. Sommer and H. Eheloff, *Boghazköi-Studien*, 10, Leipzig, 1924.

isolated theory into an explanation on the meaning of blood in rite and sacrifice in the ancient Near Eastern world, let alone relgion in general.

However, there is still more evidence to be examined. There was another view (or method) of sacrifice in the ancient world. The rituals of Canaan and Greece shared some remarkable practices. Both had holocausts which, whatever their exact meaning, represent a different conception from that of the divine banquet. The **θυσία** and *šlmm* offerings with their peculiar allocation of parts of the victim to the god and the communal meal again show a different conception.[16] Doubtless burning the divine portion represents feeding the god, but in a way not to be subsumed under one concept with laying the god's table. But for us the question is whether the rituals common to the Aegean and Levant give blood a special rôle.

Of the two, Greek ritual is better documented. In fact, ordinary Greek sacrifice did not bother about the blood. It did not belong to the gods. Men ate it, e. g., *Odyssey* xviii, 44–49, and we know this attitude aroused revulsion among Jews later. Most important, the cult of the dead and the netherworld did stress blood. In other words, blood is connected with death, not life. This needs following up, but it will be postponed until we finish the survey of other evidence.

In western Asia we know that Ugarit had burnt offerings and "peace offerings" (*šrp wšlmm*). The parallel with Israel is all the more striking when a sacrificial tariff combines them with an offering of two birds.[17] This simply confirms the commonly accepted fact that Israelite rubrics were borrowed from the Syro-Phoenician environment. But the Ugaritic texts show no special concern for blood in ritual. King Keret washes and reddens (*wy'adm*) his arms ritually, but this is *preparation* for sacrifice. Whatever the purpose of this, what is significant for our context is precisely that it is not sacrificial blood which is used.[18]

Until recently the sacrificial tariff just noted might have come into our question. Its opening line, [ ]*t slḥ npš t' w*[x x x]*bdm*, might have been taken to mean ". . . absolution of a person, and offering . . . with blood." This could hardly mean anything but a connection of a blood rite and purification. However, the restoration of the latter part of the tablet rules this out, for line 13 has *kbd* and line 16 *kbdm* listed among offerings. Instead of a reference to *dm* ("blood") then, in line 1

[16] On the community between Greek and Levantine sacrificial ritual see D. Gill, "*Thysia* and *šᵉlamîm*: Questions to R. Schmid's *Das Bundesopfer in Israel*," *Biblica*, 47 (1966), pp. 255–61; R. de Vaux, *Studies in OT Sacrifice*, pp. 48–50.

[17] Cf. A. Herdner, *Corpus des tablettes en cunéiforms alphabétiques. Mission de Ras Shamra*, x. Paris, 1963, text 36 with *addenda* from RS24, 253, and Lev 1 14–17, 12 8, 14 22, 30–31; for Ugaritic *šrp* as holocaust, cf. A. DeGuglielmo, "Sacrifice in the Ugaritic Texts," *CBQ*, 17 (1955), p. 204.

[18] DeGuglielmo, *op. cit.*, p. 203.

we must assume one to *kbdm* offerings, which are otherwise unexplained but which are not connected with blood in our texts.[19]

The psalms themselves give some evidence for popular belief about blood and sacrifice in the Levant. Ps 50 13, "Do I eat the flesh of bulls, or drink the blood of goats?" is directed against a people contaminated by Canaanite ideas. Does the reproof misinterpret alien practice, as is common in Judeo-Christian polemic?[20] Or was Yahweh indeed popularly thought to be like the gods of the netherworld who, as we shall see, did drink blood? In any event, the text is an ironical question implying that those reproved knew that the answer was no. Such irony is no basis for a serious theory of sacrifice. Ps 16 4 is more difficult, and it is to be understood in a special context, as we shall see later.[21]

For completeness we may mention our meager South Arabian information. The word for altar is *mdhbḥ*, there was burnt offering (*mṣrb*), and animal offerings were important.[22] However, there is nothing explicit about the meaning or use of blood. Thus the Levant and South Arabia shared some ritual words and concepts, but the texts do not take us beyond this to a special meaning for blood in general.

This is not to say that ritual use of blood is unmentioned outside Israel. It is, in rituals pertaining to the dead or to the gods of death. This is found in the standard Babylonian form of the story of Etana (*Marsh Tablet*, lines 34–36):

> Daily Etana beseeches Shamash:
> "Thou hast eaten, O Shamash, the fat of my sheep,

[19] *slḥ* in line 1 may mean "sprinkle" or "forgive," reminding one of the place of blood in Israelite purifications, but the word is a hapax in Ugaritic and so no solid base for a theory of sacrifice. Besides, the context of *npš* in line 16 implies a cult object, probably a stela (for parallels cf. C. Gordon, *Ugaritic Textbook*, p. 446), which might be purified with blood (pure assumption!), but in the tariff much more likely is the object of offerings.

[20] As in Deutero-Isaiah's caricature of the function of idols, or *Epistle of Diognetus* 2 8, which sees Greek sacrifice in Jewish terms.

[21] It should be noted that even the common Punic expression *mlk 'dm* has been referred to blood offerings by taking the aleph as prosthetic, leaving the root *dm* (J.–C., Février, *RHR*, 143 (1953), p. 11). Were this correct, it need refer to no more than animal sacrifice, but the prosthetic aleph is not normal in Punic (J. Friedrich, *Phönisch-Punische Grammatik*, Rome, 1951, no. 95); the suggestion should be rejected. For a discussion of *mlk 'dm* from other aspects, see de Vaux, *Studies in OT Sacrifice*, pp. 77–78.

[22] For South Arabia see G. Ryckmans, "Les religions arabe préislamiques," p. 217 (see n. 9 *supra*). The Levantine Semites and South Arabians also shared a common form of nomenclature (M. Noth, *Die israelitischen Personennamen im Rahmen der gemeinsemitischen Namengebung. BWANT*, III, 10, pp. 52–54). Note too that Hebrew, South Arabic, Phoenician, Punic, and Aramaic share a name for altar based on the root *ḏbḥ* with mem prefixed; but they share the idea, not the name, of whole or burnt offering: Ugaritic, *šrp*; Heb. and bibl. Aram., *'lh*; S. Ar. *mṣrb*; Punic, *kll* (or, late, *'lt*).

the netherworld has drunk the blood of my lambs;
the gods I have honored,
the ghosts (*eṭimmu*) I have revered."

Blood belongs to the lower regions. If it revived its ghosts (we are not told), this would recall the idea that "in the blood is life," though not in the biblical sense. Essentially blood belongs to the gods of death, not life.

Other religious practices relate blood to the underworld. Indeed, *Iliad* XIV, 518 and XVII, 86 even equate blood with soul and life, but in a figure of speech based on the common observation that blood and life go together. In ritual, blood was used in the cult of the dead. The oldest evidence is *Odyssey* x–xi, where the "strengthless dead" attain a semblance of life by drinking blood from the offerings, but all remains brooding and sinister (contrast *Iliad* XXIII, 34: "Everywhere about the body blood ran by the cupful," which is merely an expression of Achilles' heroic bounty at Patroclus' funeral feast). This sinister aspect of the ritual use of blood appears in the very vocabulary of Greek. In the Boeotian dialect death rites were called "pourings of blood" (αἱμακουρίαι) but in standard Greek ἐναγίσματα, a noun built on the phrase ἐν ἄγει, "under a curse." These things were horrors, as in Euripedes' picture of Death personified skulking about the tomb to suck the "gory clots" of blood. This picture is verified by Athenian vase paintings of the era.[23] The older poem could still have the blood revivify the dead temporarily, the later brings out the feeling involved more vividly. Perhaps in the old idea there is something of blood as life, but it is eerie, partial, and at the opposite pole of true life.

There is further evidence associating blood with sinister, if different, gods. The Hittite war god was drawn to blood.[24] This attraction characterizes also the Canaanite Anat, a classic example of the combined war-love goddess, who glories in gore and drinks her brother's blood.[25] Rather than blood being representative of life and so of the beneficent divine in the ancient Semitic-Aegean world generally, such evidence as we have associates blood with death and its divinities.

The Bible also associates blood with rites for the dead. Lev 19 28 and Deut 14 1 prohibit gashing oneself in mourning to keep Yahweh's people from shedding blood in rites like those of their gentile neighbors. The theory that drought was connected with the death of the rain god

[23] *Alcestis* 837–56; for the vase paintings see L. Weber, *Euripedes Alkestis*. Leipzig, 1930, *in loc.*

[24] Goetze, *Kleinasien*, p. 160.

[25] Anat II, lines 5–34, and M. Astour, "Un texte d'Ugarit récemment découvert et ses rapports avec l'origine des cultes bachiques grecs," *RHR*, 164 (1963), pp. 4–5, and *Helleno-semitica*, Leiden, 1965, p. 180. Plutarch, *de Iside* 46 (ed. F. Dübner, p. 432) describes a "Zoroastrianism" where blood is offered to Hades and darkness.

explains the actions of the Baalist prophets in I Kings 18 28 in this light. Blood is connected with death. It has already been suggested that Ps 50 13 condemns a popular misconception of the God of Israel as one of these gods who liked or needed blood, and this may explain the very difficult text, Ps 16 4:

ירבו עצבותם
אחר מהרו
בל־אסיך נסכיהם מדם
ובל־אשא את־שמותם על־שפתי

The "libations of blood" in bα is hardly a metaphor for bloodshed as is often suggested, for bβ, "names on my lips," surely refers to a magic or ritual invocation and calls for a parallel action in the first half-line. The suggestion that we read *middēm*, northern dialect for "from (my) hands," in bα[26] is tempting, but it avoids the question of the kind of rite involved. Admittedly the first part of the verse is disturbed, but aα is clear enough: "They multiply their aches." But who were "they?" Apparently those seeking relief from present pain (they multiply, not begin it) from the wrong source, for the psalmist is contrasting his Yahwist piety with their impiety. That is, they turn to the kind of god who liked "libations of blood," that is, the gods of wounds and death, as we have seen.[27]

We are left with but one important piece of evidence, the apotropaic rites of Arabs like that of the Passover. Modern observers attest the anointing of doors, tents, animals with blood to ward off evil spirits.[28] This might be subject to the objection that such late evidence may stem from some remnant of influence from Jewish ritual. Possibly it may, but the rites are not so like the Jewish in detail that one senses an influence from that direction on them (or on their description), as in Nilus. Moreover, these rites are especially characteristic of nomadic Arabs and not entirely in accord with their Mohammedism. In view of this and of the fact that the Passover rite was in a sense extra-Israelite, in being an old nomadic rite taken into Yahwism,[29] it is not unreasonable to see this blood rite as part of the culture of proto-Semitic nomads

[26] M. Dahood, *The Psalms* I., pp. 88–89.

[27] This argues for reading or understanding אל (Kraus, Weiser) at the beginning of 4aβ, for indeed "they multiply their pains who seek another *god*," Resheph or the like, with "libations of blood" and incantations.

[28] References in de Vaux, *Studies in OT Sacrifice*, pp. 7–8. The claim that blood rites are common to all hunters and their herdsmen successors, hence to the primitive Semites, goes too far. For discussion see R. J. Thompson, *Penitence and Sacrifice in Early Israel*, pp. 35–38.

[29] Cf. R. de Vaux, *Les institutions de l'Ancien Testament*, II, pp. 389–90, and *Studies in OT Sacrifice*, pp. 2–12.

or seminomads. Even so, we are not back at our starting point, the claim that blood was generally considered divine and life-giving and so the basis of sacrificial ritual. The blood of Passover and analogous rites does protect life, but it does not communicate it. It wards off the Destroyer because it is a protective sign. One might speculate that the power of the sign lay in the Destroyer's aversion to the divine element, but this is not said and it is not a necessary conclusion. Destructive powers were attracted, not repelled, by blood, as we have seen. It might even be that the sign worked because it showed that the Destroyer had been given his bloody due.

In fact, the peculiar efficacity of blood is not really explained in this rite. Need we assume that it was spelled out in terms of life or horror or anything else? The rite was simply accepted as potent in accord with the common phenomenon of sacral action coming well before its explanatory verbalization. Passoverlike blood rites may well have been in the ritual of the earliest nomads of the Near East, but the intrinsic meaning of blood is still not spelled out, and the explicit claim that blood is life and so divine remains isolated to Israel.

Finally, we may note that representations of Mithras' slaughter of a bull left by the cult popular in the later Roman army sometimes show the blood of the bull springing immediately into grain, a clear equation of blood with fertility and so life, but this does not seem to have been a very old idea. The original Mithras protected contracts and befriended cattle, and his proper sacrifice in ancient India was milk, butter, and grain.[30] Even if Mithraism has appropriated an old myth, it is not simply blood but any part of the sacred bull which produces plant life.[31] The same picture of blood as seed of life appears in the Attis cult,[32] which eventually produced the taurobolium. The Attis cult had ancient antecedents in Asia Minor, and the bull was a widespread symbol of fertility, but the question is what part blood played in this in the early stages. The bull's evident male power made him a symbol. Even in the Attis myth it is the blood of his castration which yields life. Is it the blood or the male member which really signifies life? The second view is supported by the myth of Uranus and the birth of Aphrodite. On the other hand, the blood of Attis' beloved, Ia, also springs up into an almond tree when she kills herself upon news of his death. However,

[30] A. Hillebrandt, *Vedische Mythologie* II, p. 49.

[31] See illustration 28 and discussion on pp. 128, 130, in R. C. Zaehner, *The Dawn and Twilight of Zoroastrianism*. See also M. J. Vermaseren, *Mithras, the Secret God*, pp. 67–68.

[32] For the aspects of the Attis myth discussed, see H. Hepding, *Attis: seine Mythen und sein Kult*, pp. 106–07, 119. Note that even the ancients sometimes interpreted the blood rites of the Attis cult as funereal mourning rites, expressions of regret having nothing to do with giving new life: *ibid.*, pp. 43, 158, 160.

this touch sounds like the widespread folklore motif of plants from the graves of star-crossed lovers (as Barbry Allen) and not like basic myth. On balance, in the orientalizing religions we seem to be dealing with later developments, not basic, universal belief in the power of blood.

This survey of the actual data from the Mediterranean and Near Eastern world does not offer any real support for a theory of sacrifice based on the sharing of a divine substance, blood. In fact, it shows a complexity hard to reduce to any common denominator.

1) There were two general concepts of offerings to the gods prevalent in the area. One, Hittite, Mesopotamian, and Egyptian saw them as simply provisioning the deities. The other, Greek, Levantine, and perhaps South Arabian, burned the god's share. Seemingly the gods needed this portion too, but the basic idea is quite different from laying a table and waiting for the god to consume the food. Further and to our purpose, neither concept generally attributes importance to blood as such.

2) Blood is attractive to certain powers, but these are associated with unpleasantness, war, and death. The meaning of blood in this sphere is ambiguous. It may temporarily revivify, but in an eerie way. Blood is associated not with true life, but with its pale and ghostly counterpart. This concept of the power of blood crosses the lines of the different concepts of sacrifice we have seen, for it appears in Mesopotamia as well as in Greece and the Levant.

3) The apotropaic use of blood seems to be a practice of Semitic nomads. Its meaning in this use is not self-evident. Does it give life or show that the powers of darkness have had their share?

4) Hebrew ritual is much concerned with blood. It must be reserved to God, and it is a purifying agent. This is explained by the fact that "in the blood is life"; so blood belongs to the divine sphere. The explicit statement of this doctrine comes in deuteronomic and priestly documents, but they are explaining a ritual much older than they.

5) Can we give any explanation of this peculiar concern for blood in the Hebrew ritual? An answer must be highly speculative. We do know that the primitive Passover emphasized the use of blood. May this not have been added to a ritual largely borrowed from Canaan in its details? Such mixings of rituals were acceptable enough. For instance, though Hebrew ritual was essentially of the burnt-offering type, it took over without embarrassment aspects of the banquet concept.[33] Later theologizing would explain the hybrid ritual in a rather sophisticated manner. The developments in the Mithras and Attis cults might be analogies illustrating this process of theological reflection. From the sacrifice of

[33] Compare the shewbread, the boiling of the sacrificial meat in I Sam, and the daily ritual at Uruk (*ANET*, p. 344b)

the bull, the symbol of fertility, came the idea that its blood was a source of new life. So in Israel the old apotropaic rite would be generalized, and, from a mere sign, the blood would become a vehicle of divine purification and life.

Another possibility is opened by Rendtorff's form- and traditio-historical study of Israelite sacrifice.[34] He finds that originally the manipulation of blood had no rôle in עלה or זבח. It did have a purificatory function in the חטאת and a public, ritual function in the שלמים which closed off the עלות. This is especially significant because older Levantine people (Ugarit) had the sequence *šrp wšlmm*. Did this also include blood rites which Israel borrowed along with the ritual of the area? Once more, it is tempting to think so, and it is entirely possible; but once again we must emphasize that we do not know. In any case, blood rites came to be part of all Israelite sacrifice in a process culminating shortly after Josiah's reform. Thus, even though the *šlmm* were the source of the ritual use of blood, the *general* explanation of sacrifice in terms of blood as life and so somehow divine would still be relatively late and specifically Israelite. We must, then, conclude that the evidence from the ancient Semitic and Aegean areas does not show a general belief outside Israel in blood as a divine element which served as the basic reason or explanation for sacrifice. As far as we know, the reservation of blood to God because it was life and so divine is specifically Israelite.

[34] R. Rendtorff, *Studien zur Geschichte des Opfers im alten Israel*, *WMANT*, 24. On חטאת see pp. 205–06, 231–32; on עלות and שלמים, pp. 119–32; on the spread of the blood rites, pp. 97–101, 156–57, 247.

AN INSTALLATION GENRE?

DENNIS J. McCARTHY, S.J.

PONTIFICAL BIBLICAL INSTITUTE, ROME

I. *The Texts*

THE most important block of material which concerns us is the deuteronomistic introduction and conclusion to Deuteronomy and its continuation in the Book of Joshua. In studying the transfer of power from Moses to Joshua described in these chapters, N. Lohfink has distinguished a genre (*Gattung*) which he calls an *Amtseinsetzung*, which I translate as "installation genre."[1] The elements of the genre are clear and simple: I. Encouragement Formula (Hebrew, *ḥ^{a}zaq we^{ʾe}meṣ*), II. Description of the Task, and III. Assistance Formula (Hebrew, *Yhwh ^{c}imm^{e}kā*). Doubtlessly Deut 31:23 illustrates the genre in its simplest shape, complete but unencumbered by deuteronomistic or other expansions. Lohfink shows how the Deuteronomists took this and developed it into a literary and theological framework which links the Book of Joshua to Deuteronomy and gives shape to the former. Briefly, Joshua is assured of divine assistance and encouraged to stand to his task both by Moses and by Yahweh himself.[2] This task is twofold: to conquer the promised land and to distribute it among the tribes. Allusions in the deuteronomistic introduction to Deuteronomy prepare the way for this.[3] Yahweh's commands to Joshua in Joshua 1 lead to the carrying out of the first part of the task, the conquest, and the commands in Josh 13:1, 7 to the second, the distribution of the land.[4]

This analysis reveals a meaningful structure linking Deuteronomy and the Book of Joshua as well as telling us something about the deuteronomistic theology of leadership. However, it does not complete the study of the genre itself. In fact it seems to make that study more difficult for two reasons. First, since it reduces the instances of the formula *ḥ^{a}zaq we^{ʾe}meṣ* from Deut 1 to Josh 10 to redactional developments from the single original formula in Deut 31:23, it effectively

[1] "Die deuteronomistische Darstellung des Übergangs der Führung Israels von Moses auf Josue," *Scholastik*, 37 (1962), pp. 32–44.

[2] Deut 31:7–8 (Moses), 23 (Yahweh).

[3] Deut 1:38; 3:28.

[4] In the remainder of this paper this block of material will be referred to by the abbreviation Deut–Josh.

reduces the number of examples of it from fourteen to six.[5] This seriously limits the possibility of tracing a background and development of the genre insofar as it may be tied to the formula. Secondly, the analysis creates a problem for form-critical investigation because it shows the formula performing a wide variety of functions. In the examples in these chapters the formula occurs as an instruction to Moses, and as a word of encouragement from Yahweh, from the superior, and from inferiors.[6] Such variety in the use of a formula is hardly characteristic of an element in a genre when the genre is in firm shape.

Still, it is possible to do something with the material. It will help toward this to fix some definitions. I use formula to designate a fixed set of words as in the classic messenger formula, "thus says Yahweh." A genre may use formulae, but it need not. It can be made up of elements, that is, parts which regularly enter into its composition though not expressed in a fixed set of words. If we concentrate on the elements rather than on formulae, we may find texts which fulfill the same function and yet allow more freedom than do formulae. In our specific case the overall function of the genre is to describe installation in an office, the commissioning of a task. Are there examples of texts which are of this genre and made up of elements corresponding in function to Lohfink's formulae? These would be simply described: I. Encouragement, II. Description of the Task, and III. Assurance of Divine Aid.[7] Attention to function rather than to forms of expression is of considerable importance. As we have just noted about the passages in Deut–Josh, the function of a fixed expression can vary. Sometimes this can wholly alter its force and change the genre of discourse. On the other hand, a similar function can be performed by a varied set of expressions. As long as the function remains the same, the genre will not change.

To return to the concrete, the example most like those in Deut–Josh is in II Chron 32:6–8. The form is complete: I. "be brave and of stout heart (v. 7), II. job description: generals (v. 6), III. assurance of divine assistance (v. 8). There is no reason to doubt that Hezekiah appointed generals for the Assyrian war, nor that he did it in proper form. Here the genre is somewhat expanded, but in a clear way. The encouragement

[5] Deut 3:28; 31:6, 7; Josh 1:6, 7, 9, 18 and 10:25 would all be redactional uses based on Deut 31:23 and so not independent witnesses to the formula. Other occurrences of the formula are Amos 2:14; Pss 27:14; 31:25; I Chron 22:13; and II Chron 32:7. In this paper I shall refer to the formula by the translation "be brave and of stout heart."

[6] Instruction: Deut 1:38; 3:28; word of a superior: Deut 31:6, 7 (Moses); Josh 10:25 (Joshua); of Yahweh: Deut 31:23; Josh 1:6, 7, 9; of inferiors: Josh 1:18 (Transjordanian tribesmen to Joshua).

[7] The numbering is arbitrary since the order of elements is not fixed. Even in Deut–Josh they appear in various sequences.

is negative, "fear not," as well as positive, and the divine assistance is emphasized by repetition and contrast. Something similar is found in Joshua 1, but the likeness is rather generic. "Fear not" is not expressed in exactly the same way, and the emphasis is on the divine assistance as a continuation of that given to Moses, not in contrast to the force on which the enemy relies as in Chronicles. In other words, the expansions of the elements are quite natural, and there is no reason to see a dependence of Chronicles on the means of expression used in Joshua.[8]

II Chron 19:5–7 offers another clear example of the genre. This text describes Jehoshaphat's appointment of new Judges. There is a little expansion in describing the judicial duties, but the functional elements are easily seen. The task is named: the men are to be "judges over the land;" the assistance of Yahweh is affirmed; and the appointees are encouraged: "keep your eyes open and be active" (*šimᵉrû waᶜᵃśû*). There are few things more to be encouraged in judges than awareness and an industry which will keep the docket clean. Once again, this is an appeal to late material in that it is found in Chronicles but not in Kings, but there is no reason to doubt that Jehoshaphat did institute judicial reforms.[9]

Another concise example occurs in I Chron 28:10. The speech in vss. 2–9 complicates it, but only extrinsically. Vs. 10 is easily separated from it and is complete in itself. Yahweh's assistance is assured (he has chosen Solomon), the task is stated (build the temple), and the encouragement given, "be brave and active" (*ḥᵃzaq waᶜᵃśēh*). Once more, all the elements are there and in language fitted to the occasion. The theology of the king and temple, the relation between Yahweh and Solomon as stated in II Samuel 7 and repeated by the Chronicler, is precisely that of being chosen for the work of building the temple. The commissioning of David's successor is exact in theological terms.

There are other texts which seem to be related to the installation form, but they are not so clearly constructed. One is Hag 2:4. Yahweh speaks, assuring his assistance (*ʾᵃnî ʾittᵉkem*) and giving encouragement:

[8] II Chron 32 almost corresponds to Lohfink's formulae. It has "be brave and of stout heart." The job description does not have the introduction *kî ʾattāh*, but this is hardly a formula in any case. The divine assistance is assured in the phrase *wᵉᶜimmānū Yhwh*, which is very close to *wᵉᶜimmākem Yhwh* which would be the formulaic equivalent, since the king is addressing not individuals but several new generals. In any case the formula is broken, if only slightly. Perhaps this is an allusion to the Isaian Emmanuel prophecy (cf. J. Myers, *II Chronicles* [Garden City, N. Y., 1965], p. 187), but even if this is so it does not show that the expression itself goes back to Isaiah's time. The present form of the text could be a change dictated by intervening tradition.

[9] The deuteronomistic historian looked with some favor on Jehoshaphat and records Elisha's respect for him, which may argue for the probability of his being a reformer. Cf. Myers, *ibid.*, p. 108.

"be brave . . . and active." However, "be brave" is repeated three times with three subjects, Zerubbabel, Joshua the high priest, and the people, while *ʿśh* appears once in the plural with all three together as subject. Finally, the task, the building of the second temple, is clear enough, but it is mentioned apart from the other elements in vss. 7 and 9. The elements are there, but the genre as a whole is very freely constructed. It might be noticed, however, that in itself the inclusion of the leaders and the people is not unheard of. In Deut 31:5–8 first the people and then the leader is each given the same task, just as in the prophet, but in the latter the commission is compressed into a single, complex formulation which allows him to emphasize "be brave" by rhythmic repetition. In Deuteronomy there is a complete, separate expression of the form for each, first for the people, then for Joshua.

Elements of the genre also occur in David's last instructions to Solomon in I Kings 2. The situation is suitable: the succession of a new leader. Solomon is given a twofold task: to observe the Law and so be assured of the divine assistance, and to carry out vengeance on David's remaining enemies. Here is the description of a job and mention of divine help, but this latter is twisted from an assurance of divine help toward fulfilling the task into something to be gained by fulfilling one part of the task: obeying the Law. Finally, there are the words of encouragement. Solomon is to "be brave and play the man" (*wᵉhāyîtā lᵉʾîš*), once more, the common term "be brave" accompanied by a special term. This is actually in accord with the function of the genre, for it makes it more expressive in that the language conforms to the task required. What more suitable encouragement than "play the man" could be given to one called on to carry out the family's blood-feuds?

A last reminiscence of the genre appears in Ezra 10:4. Ezra has a duty (*dābār*); he is encouraged to "be brave and active," but instead of the divine assistance the motive for this is that the people are with him (*ʾᵃnaḥnû ʿimmāk*). This interesting variation looks very much like an alteration playing with a familiar form of expression.

II. *Vocabulary*

We may list some preliminary conclusions about these texts. "Be brave" almost always occurs in these contexts — II Chronicles 19 is the only exception — but "be of stout heart" appears only in Deut–Josh and in II Chronicles 32. In both these examples there is question of war. Joshua is sent on a campaign of conquest, and Hezekiah is appointing generals. In other instances *ʿśh* replaces *ʾmṣ*, and in these cases the task is civil-religious (the hyphenated word being necessary because we distinguish the two areas where the ancient world did not). In one case Solomon is encouraged to "play the man" in carrying out his task of blood vengeance. The vocabulary is flexible, then, adapting itself to the task which is being given. A similar flexibility appears in expressing the divine assistance, particularly when it is emphasized that this comes from Yahweh's special choice.

In view of this I doubt that we should speak of formulae in connection with the genre. Since Deut 31:23 appears to explain the use of "be strong and of stout heart" in the rest of Deut–Josh, this is the equivalent of one example of the sentence used with the other elements of the genre. It also occurs in II Chron 32:7 as part of a complete example of the genre which has every chance of being original. On the other hand, I Chron 22:13 is surely derivative, and the genre can be reconstructed only by seeking its elements within a drawn-out speech. Other occurrences of *ḥzq* and *ʾmṣ* together, in Pss 27:14 and 31:25, do not belong to the genre. Indeed, they relate not to a specific office but to the confidence of the sufferer in his God. Amos 2:4 also has the two words, but not in the form of an exhortation and not in connection with other elements of the genre.

On the other hand, there are several examples of texts which display all the elements of the genre without this exact formula. *ḥzq* is normally found, but *ʿśh* replaces *ʾmṣ* in civil-religious contexts and, possibly, "play the man" in the context of the blood feud. With so few examples of the supposed formula and so many varied expressions which fulfill the function of encouragement, it seems better to speak of encouragement itself as an element in the genre, not of a particular way of putting it as a formula necessary to the genre. The same is true of the assurance of divine assistance; the substance is the same, the expression varied. It is an element, not a formula.

III. *The Use of the Texts*

We have already seen this in the Deut–Josh complex. There is a double moment in the over-all structure. First, Joshua is given his twofold task; then he carries out one part after the other in immediate response to a divine command which repeats or alludes to elements of the genre.

There are echoes of this double moment in II Chronicles 19 and 32. First, the kings of Judah appoint their officials. Then, in a second step they publicly set them to their tasks. In these instances, unlike Deut–Josh, the separate moments are not marked by repeated full statements, each using the full genre. However, this simplicity seems natural. The Chronicler is reporting simple events, not creating an elaborate structure designed to tie together important historical events and theological concepts. The fact of the two moments, appointment and then putting to work, is clear enough, and the elaboration of expression in Deut–Josh is best explained as adaption by the deuteronomistic writer. The double moment natural to the genre has been emphasized for theological purposes. It makes clear that Joshua is the new Moses and that this is arranged and confirmed by Yahweh himself.

Another case almost gives the impression that the Chronicler has studied Deut–Josh with great care, but it may well be that his overloaded texts reflect an actual tradition. The sequence between I Chronicles 22 and I Chronicles 28 is like that between Deuteronomy 31 and Joshua 1 and 13. In ch. 22 David commissions (*ṣwh*, cf. vs. 6) Solomon to build the temple in what seems to be a private audience. Then he publicly commands the fulfilment of the task in ch. 28. There are differences from Deut–Josh, of course, for with Joshua it is Yahweh who commands and even repeats the commission to conquer Canaan (Deut 31:23), though only Moses gives the complete task of conquest and allotment of the land. Still, the sequence of the commission fully expressed and of the command to begin action seems more significant than the differences. Given the Chronicler's attitude toward his hero, David, one would expect him to emphasize his dignity by making him the mouthpiece of both commission and command, especially in anything having to do with the temple. After all, his main object in this whole section of his history is to show that to all intents and purposes the temple is due to David. Solomon only puts together what David has arranged, rather like the constructor of a pre-fabricated house.

It is probably this latter emphasis of the Chronicler which explains the complexity of I Chronicles 22. As we have seen, all the elements of the installation genre are found in 28:10. They can be pieced together in ch. 22. Solomon, the man of peace, is being commissioned to do what his warrior father could not do: build the temple. However, the description of David's preparations is so elaborate that one almost forgets this. Amid all the accounts of David's activities, then, we are a long way from a simple statement of installation in office. Still, the elements are there. Encouragement is repeated: in vs. 13 there is "be brave and of stout heart," the standard phrase, but just a little out of place in this contrast between war, with which it is associated, and peace, to which it is applied; and in vs. 16 there is "be up (*qûm*) and doing," the latter a return to the presumed civil-religious term. The element of assurance of divine help, while stated in the standard words, *Yhwh ʿimmākem* is also altered both in itself and in its context. The phrase is subtly changed because the verb form *wîhî*, used with it, turns it into a prayer that the divine aid be given rather than a simple affirmation. To be sure, for the Chronicler a prayer of David was as good as an affirmation, but nonetheless the formulation has been altered. Even more significant is the color the context throws on the element. It dwells on the duty of obeying the Law and so on the conditioned nature of Yahweh's support of Solomon and David's dynasty. Fidelity conditions Yahweh's help for their governing and especially — the conclusion is inescapable — their looking after the temple.

Repetition and the inclusion of extra elements confuse the clear outline of the genre here, but one should not overemphasize the impression of disorder. What goes on is clear enough. David arranges for labor and material for the temple (22:1–5), then explains why he cannot build the temple but his son must (6–10); he admonishes Solomon to keep the Law (11–13) and add to his own preparations (14–16), and he finally encourages the men of Israel to aid Solomon in his task (17–19). In this way David gets as much credit as possible for the temple, and the connection of leadership and the Law is emphasized. At the same time the fact that Solomon is being commissioned is kept before us by the use of elements from the installation genre. All this rather muddles the genre but carries the author's conceptions accurately. In fact, it looks as though all this has grown out of I Chron 28:10. The mention of Yahweh's choice there opens the way for the development of the Solomon-for-David theme. The use of *ʿśh* may be characteristic of the civil-religious context. The complications come not from the form itself but from the need to define David's position and to bring the Law into prominence.

From this point of view I Chronicles 22 and 28 parallel the construction of Deut–Josh. These chapters have taken an originally simple example of the installation genre and used it to express a rather complex theological conception. This elaboration was made the easier by the fact that the texts often reflect a double movement in the genre, commissioning and then setting in action.

Finally, a word as to the designation of the form as an installation genre. This is not merely a convenient translation of Lohfink's *Amtseinsetzung*. One could speak of a commissioning, but the genre seems really to be generic. It covers related but separate cases. Most often it is used to describe a legitimate commissioning by a competent power. However, Hezekiah's generals, Jehoshaphat's judges, and the builders of the second temple are not succeeding others in office; they are taking up new duties. In Deut–Josh, on the other hand, the genre is used to describe a legitimate succession of one leader of all Israel for another, and in I Chronicles a succession to an important office. Thus the installation which is described in the genre can be either a commission to a new office or a succession to one already existing.

IV. *Tradition-History*

First of all, it is not sufficient to relate the genre to the Holy War and its ideology or to link it to a deuteronomic turn of style,[10] and then go no farther. True, the formula "be brave and of stout heart" may be connected with war, but it need not be. This is shown by Pss 27:14 and 31:25, complex forms involving both lament and thanksgiving, but hardly connected with war. Even within the Joshua passages the task of allotting the land has no intrinsic connection with war. As for the deuteronomistic style, the use of the sentence in imperative form in the Psalter, as well as the allusion to it in the indicative in Amos 2:14, show that it cannot simply be reduced to a mark of deuteronomistic redaction. This is not to say that it is totally unconnected with war or that the deuteronomistic school did not make good use of it. The way in which it has been made into a structural element in Deut–Josh is enough to show how well the school could use it.

As for war, there is that clause in Amos 2:14, "and his strength will not give force (*ʾmṣ*) to the brave (*ḥāzāq*)." This is Amos' favorite device of irony. Just as he turns the divine choice (3:2) and the day of Yahweh (5:18–20) against the faithless people, so here he mocks their confidence that Yahweh is at their side in battle. To be effective, such irony must play on a usage whose positive meaning is well known.

This is an argument moving back from a rather sophisticated bit of poetry. One feels closer to a primitive sociological situation in II Sam 10:12 when in the face of a successful Aramean attack Joab cries, "Be brave, and let us show courage (*ntḥzq*) on behalf of our people and the cities of our God! And let Yahweh do what is right." Since this is a rallying cry, we can hardly understand the last sentence to advocate resignation; rather it asserts a firm trust. Perhaps this is not the sort of thing actually said in the midst of battle, but it is a natural speech on the occasion of a difficult encounter. This is the sort of thing which can be formalized in rite and word to meet a recurring situation. It is the sort of natural reaction to events which lies at the basis of most formalized means of expression. It is, then, reasonable to accept a connection between war waged with Yahweh's help and the use of *ḥzq*; and since such war, indeed all war in early Israel, was sacral, it is fair to speak of Holy War here.[11] However, it will not do to trace

[10] G. von Rad, *Deuteronomy* (Philadelphia, 1966), p. 189: Holy War; J. Gray, *Joshua, Judges and Ruth* (London, 1967), p. 50: "a feature of the hortatory style of the Deuteronomic introduction."

[11] On the sacral character of all war in earliest Israel, see R. de Vaux, *Ancient Israel* (New York, 1961), pp. 258–263.

Apart from the passages mentioned in the text Josh 10:25 sounds most natural. It could almost be a part of a war narrative used by the historian because it fitted

the usage to Holy War vocabulary without further ado. The evidence is too complex.

For one thing, there is another formal connection of Joshua himself with the Holy War. In Num 27:17–18 he is appointed war-leader of Israel, and this is expressed in technical terms. He is to lead the armed forces out (*yṣ*ʾ) and bring them back (*bô*ʾ), and he is invested with the office by the laying on of hands. The passage is attributed to P, but the terms "lead out" and "bring back" belong to the original vocabulary of war. The vocabulary, therefore, is old, and so too, probably, the rite connected with it for the commissioning of a war-leader.

This does not prove that a different tradition could not express the same thing differently or that the full rite and vocabulary did not include more than what is recorded in Num 27. However, the installation genre still remains a possible alternative to, as well as a complement of, the rite in Numbers, and we have seen that this genre need have nothing to do with war. It could equally well be used of installing in an office directed toward peaceful pursuits. In the circumstances it is well to ask whether the genre had to have its origins in the Holy War. Might it not be a more general form applied to war-leaders as well as to other officials?

There are two peculiar texts which strengthen the argument for disassociating the genre from the Holy War. One is Ezra 10:4 where we have seen that the motive for encouragement is not the assurance of divine assistance but of popular support. This is not quite so clear in Josh 1:18, but still the implication is that Joshua should "be brave and of stout heart" because the men of the Transjordanian tribes will be with him. Nothing could be farther from Holy War theory than these assurances of human aid. One might object that these passages are late, one deuteronomistic, one due to the Chronicler. To be sure, the Holy War was not really a living institution when they were written, but equally surely this was the era when its theory was most jealously guarded. Would these late writers produce texts at variance with a theology they cherished? This is very unlikely. Of course, they may have failed to appreciate the Holy War aspects of the genre, but this seems unlikely in theoreticians of the Holy War unless, in fact, the genre was not closely associated with war.

Apart from all this, there is the connection of the genre with civil-

---

into his scheme rather than a fragment composed by him to elaborate that scheme. However, it is generally regarded as redaction (e.g., M. Noth, *Joshua*, p. 66; though one wonders whether this does not rest on the assumption that "be brave and of stout heart" is a deuteronomistic invention, which it is not; note that Gray, *Joshua, Judges and Ruth*, p. 112, while mentioning the deuteronomistic possibility, recognizes that we may be dealing with "an ancient oracle-form"); but it is not necessary to rely on this disputed case. Even without it *ḥzq* is clearly associated with war.

religious functions. But perhaps most important of all, there is the appearance of the sentence "be brave and of stout heart" in the concluding verses of Psalms 27 and 31. It is not easy to define the genre of these psalms, as a glance at the commentaries such as those of Kraus and Weiser will confirm. Moreover, it is hard to date these psalms. Still, they locate the sentence in a cultic context. Further, they put it in the position of a response to lamentation and gratitude. Whatever the circumstances, one must rely on Yahweh. This is the message of these verses, whether they are oracles or priests or cult-prophets responding to the preceding prayers, or a kind of concluding meditation in which the psalmist encourages himself.[12] However it was communicated, this is encouragement.

This reminds us of the frequency of other hortatory usages in connection with the genre. We have noted "fear not," variously expressed, an expression usually associated with the Holy War but also at home in the context of the theophany and of cultic awe in general. In addition there are frequent imperatives, and one should note the relative frequency of "be up (and doing)" (*qûm*),[13] all in connection with the installation genre.

Considering all the factors, we may suggest a setting for the genre. First, it is hortatory and connected with the cult. This is shown by the Psalms and Hag 2:4, and possibly I Chronicles with its concern for the building of the temple. Secondly, in most examples it is connected with the Davidic monarchy. In fact, remembering the connection of Hag 2:4 with the Davidic heirs through Zerubbabel, we find that this is true of all the texts except those in Deut–Josh and Ezra 10:4. Since the monarchy and the temple cult are but reverse sides of one coin, they explain much about the genre: its elements, its association with kings, and its developments.

For the first point, Psalms 27 and 31 imply the elements which become explicit and formalized in the genre. They insist on fidelity to one's duty to Yahweh in general terms, and this would easily be refined to a statement of particular duties. They are hortatory in their concluding verses, even supplying examples of the key sentence, "be brave and of stout heart." Once again, this could be made more precise in relation to specific duties. Hence the different uses of the sentence itself (see n. 6) and the various ways of expressing encouragement. Finally, the psalms supply motives for encouragement: Yahweh is with

[12] However one conceives the details, it seems better to look on these verses as exhortations directly aimed at others, not self-encouragement, even of a fictive sort really designed to elicit acts of faith in others, because "be brave and of stout heart" and its relatives in their other uses are always explicitly directed to a second party.

[13] Josh 1:2; Ezra 10:4; I Chron 22:16, 19.

his faithful ones. As for the monarchical element, the kings will simply have used certain things from the cult to express the legitimacy of their own powers, including the power of delegation to others. The urge, or rather the necessity, of doing something like this is explained easily if we accept the suggestion that the monarchical idea had to struggle for acceptance among the people of Yahweh. By associating its duties and offices with a cult connected with the ark, it made an emphatic claim to legitimacy.

This is not to assert that Psalms 27 and 31 are themselves so old as to be the sources of the installation genre. It is rather a matter of the attitudes which they embody (fidelity to duty, trust in Yahweh because of his assured help) as well as certain particulars of expression which are not necessarily of the same date as the psalms in their present forms. These attitudes are as old as Israelite religious poetry, and I suggest that their concrete expression in the cult as carried on in the royal temple was the matrix in which the genre was formed.

The argument is supported by the fact that it explains certain secondary aspects of the genre and its development. There is the atmosphere of encouraging exhortation which so often accompanies it. This is easily explained if the genre developed from cultic responses which assured Yahweh's help to those who trusted in him and were faithful. Such responses had a rich vocabulary of encouragement, and it is not surprising that some of this eventually carried over into the contexts in which the installation genre occurs, though they do not make up part of its elements in the strict sense.

Again, there is the persistent intrusion of the Law into the context of the genre. We find it in Joshua 1, I Kings 2, and I Chronicles 22 and 28. Doubtless this reflects deuteronomistic thought, but the point is that the genre easily lent itself to this development. This does not mean that reference to the Law could be worked into the structure of the genre with ease. It could not, for the structure is too simple and compact. However, if it was related to a larger cultic context which emphasized fidelity as a condition of Yahweh's help, it was natural to couple the genre with exhortations to observe the Law when the latter became the chief object, test, and expression of fidelity. Finally, this same emphasis on fidelity as a condition of divine assistance is the simplest explanation of those odd texts which offer popular help as a motive of confidence and encouragement to action. A faithful people were an assurance of divine help. Thus we have an answer to the problem which the Holy War theory as the origin of the genre can overcome only with difficulty.

The Theology of Leadership in Joshua 1 - 9

Dennis J. McCarthy - Rome

The Book of Joshua is a prime example of the way our preoccupations tend to control our interpretations even at a gross level long before we come to the subtleties of hermeneutic theory. A survey of modern literature on the subject shows that there are just two basic lines of approach, and they are not entirely different from one another. The one looks for possible historical and topographical content. This line of inquiry is dominated by the work of Alt and Noth who found the first eleven chapters to be essentially a collection of etiologies giving an idealized and simplified picture of the Conquest. Even the most important replies to Alt and Noth meet them on their terms. That is, they contest the total or almost total devaluation of the etiology as a source of historical information, but the question is still one of history and etiology (1).

The second line of research is also concerned with the sources from which the book was constructed, but rather than seeing in them a collection of scattered stories it looks for continuations of the Pentateuchal source documents. The *Introductions* of Eissfeldt and Fohrer take this line, and it shows also in Langlamet's study of chapters 3 - 4 (2). The effort to trace cultic elements behind the stories claims to be the antithesis of such interests, but like any good antithesis, it is on the same line. It is seeking the sources in some sort of continuous tradition (3).

(1) So J. Bright, *Early Israel in Recent History Writing* (London 1956). Noth himself later admitted that etiologies must be studied individually and that this might reveal a real connection between the fact and the tradition as well as illuminate the way a tradition grows. Cf. "Der Beitrag der Archäologie zur Geschichte Israels", *Congress Volume, Oxford 1959* (VTS 7; Leiden 1960) 262-282, especially 278.

(2) F. Langlamet, *Gilgal et les récits de la traversée du Jourdain.* (Cahiers de la Revue Biblique 11; Paris 1969).

(3) E.g., J. A. Wilcoxen, "Narrative Structure and Cult Legend: A Study of Joshua 1 - 6", in J. Coert Rylaarsdam, ed., *Transitions in*

All these are legitimate interests, but Noth himself has shown that the Deuteronomistic History is a carefully constructed work [1]. Like any self-respecting history it has a point of view and it has to be selective. This would seem to point to the possibility of asking some different questions. What is the point of view in this particular section of the work? Why were these stories chosen to express it? Do they have any special message in themselves? Since the point of view of the history in question is, of course, strictly theological, this might sound like a call for a return to the attitude which finds in a Rahab a model of faith, Heb 11,31, or of good works, Jas 2,25, and an ancestress of Jesus, Mt 1,5. This is not the case, though I think a study of such interpretive methods might be profitable. But who is equipped to do it? Really my questions are aimed at something more modest, something for which our training has equipped most of us. It is simply to look at the material in the light of the context which is primary to us, that is, the form in which we meet it first, which is that of an integral part of a literary whole. Rather than looking behind the text for historical, geographical, or liturgical information, perhaps we can look at the text in itself, as a verbal structure.

The trouble is the vagaries of literary interpretation. The practice is hard, and the explanation of the practice harder still. Still, two questions seem basic and simple enough to get us started. One:

Biblical Scholarship (Chicago 1968) 43-70, trying to show that the sequence of events in Jos 1 – 6 follows that of a liturgical ceremony.

(1) In *Überlieferungsgeschichtliche Studien*, I² (Tübingen 1957). G. von Rad and H. W. Wolff have devoted attention to the theology of the deuteronomistic history with valuable results, but their work looks more to the whole as described by Noth and less to the theological detail which interests me here.

There is an explicit study of the theology of the Joshua material in N. Lohfink, "Die deuteronomische Darstellung des Übergangs der Führung Israels von Moses auf Josue", *Scholastik* 37 (1962) 32-44. He shows that the shape of the Book of Joshua is largely governed by an *Amtseinsetzung* genre. This is marked by the formula of encouragement, *ḥazaq weʾemaṣ*, assurance that Yahweh is with the leader, and a description of the leader's task. Here this is twofold: the conquest of the land and then its distribution. The conquest is carried out at Yahweh's order given in Jos 1, the distribution at his order given in 13,1.7. This formal structure is surely correct, and it is enlightening. My aim is to fill it out with more content concerning the conquest, particularly in terms of Joshua's role as the moving factor in the process, even down to details.

What was the writer (here understood as the redactor who gave the fundamental structure to the text, not earlier collectors or later annotators) aiming at? Two: How did he set about achieving his aim? However, the simplicity here is only on the surface. Aims can be complex. A writer might wish to record a liturgy because it glorified an important historical event. Or his interest might turn directly to the history and the liturgy be only a convenient means of expression. And so on; the possible combinations and variations are countless. But at least we can try to see the aim of the text and not be governed by our antecedent interests. As for the question of the writer's means, that too can only be answered from his text. What were his means of expression: the literary forms he used, his tricks of style, and so on.

This brings us to the first point which it seems anyone interested in this material must touch upon: the problem of etiologies. Often enough a text is called an etiology as though this identified its literary form. It may possibly be so, but actually only in rather rare instances, usually in the etymological etiologies (1). These, however, are not of much importance in our material. Far more important is the explanation supposed to be identified as an etiology by the expression "until this very day", *ʿad hayyôm hazzeh.* In a very general sense this is meaningful. The expression implies some sort of explanation which ties a past phenomenon to something present (to the writer). However, Childs has subjected the formula to exhaustive study (2). He finds that the form of which it may originally have been a part has largely suffered a breakdown because it is attached to a specific historical, not a universalized subject, that the verb has become a simple past (aorist) instead of a frequentative, that the explanatory clause does not give the *cause* of the present phenomenon, and that the phrase "until this very day" no longer

(1) The formulae are: I. *wayyiqrāʾ ʾet-šᵉmô* ... *kî ʾāmār* ..., with the *kî* clause giving the explanation of the name. II. The explanation followed by *ʿal-kēn qārāʾ šᵉmô* .... Cf. J. Fichtner, " Die etymologische Ätiologie in den Namengebungen der geschichtlichen Bücher des Alten Testaments", *VT* 6 (1956) 372-396, and Burke O. Long, *The Problem of Etiological Narrative in the Old Testament* (BZAW 108; Berlin 1968). The latter finds that etiologies in these forms scarcely generate stories of any importance.

(2) B. Childs, "A Study of the Formula 'Until this Day' ", *JBL* 82 (1963) 279-292.

modifies a verb (1). That is, the story no longer explains why people *in general regularly say* or *do* something *even now.* This is a change not just in form but in meaning. It will be found that the important etiologies of Jos 1 – 11 belong to this "broken down" category.

Without any really fixed and distinguishing techniques of this kind it is hard to call etiologies literary forms in any real sense. By the use of the phrase "until this very day" any tale can be attached externally to something so as to explain it. In fact, I suggest that it is usually the story which matters. People are not terribly interested, for instance, in how some feature of the landscape got its name. They are interested in a good story. For example, in *Christ Stopped at Eboli* Carlo Levi speaks of the Cliff of the Bersagliere, a cliff whence a local bandit tossed a Piedmontese soldier in the 1860's. In that little southern Italian town the bandits were still popular heroes, the Piedmontese the symbol of the eternal enemy, Those-In-Power. So the peasants liked the story and remembered it. There were many other cliffs in the town from which men had been pushed. No one cared. Here the popularity of the story preserves the name. And in that eroded country the mudcliff may disappear, or may already have done so. If so, one can expect that another cliff will get the name, or there will appear a Tree of the Bersagliere where the bandit hanged the stranger, or something of the sort.

This is a real etiology. It is history which explains a current name. One can quote modern, false etiologies. For instance, the Sioux Indians of South Dakota have a Council Hill to which the planning of their memorable wars, hunts, and so on is attached. The stories are usually true enough; the connection with the hill is not, since it came into Sioux ken only when their history was over and they were forced into the reservation. I submit that in either case what really matters is not the explanation of the place name but the fact that the stories are satisfying to the tellers. At a deeper level, it is not the fact that matters either, whether it be the name or whatnot explained or the factual truth of the stories involved; it is the general social attitudes revealed in the stories.

The principle is certainly true when the formality of an etiology is lacking. For example, Jos 6 is usually treated as an explanation of the tell at Jericho, though it has no formal mark of the etiology. In any case, it is the story that counts, and it is all turmoil. It is never clear who blows how many trumpets how often, despite the

(1) Ibid. 284.

fact that many verses are devoted to the subject. Most commentators are struck with this, and they discuss the contrast between the repetitions about the trumpets, the Levites, the ark and the rest, and the single, simple statement in v. 20 of the all-important fact that the walls came tumbling down. One is supposed to feel that something is out of kilter. But is it? When we stand back, forget about sources and the like, and look at the story as such, we find that it is memorable, one of those which everyone remembers. And the technique, suspense built up over a more or less lengthy story until we get to the short punch line has been effective from biblical writers to Aesop to O. Henry! Or to return to a story with an external mark of the etiology, Jos 2, is it or was it really of primary importance to anyone that Rahab's Canaanite clan "dwelt in Israel until this very day"? What strikes the reader is that the harlot saves the men of Israel. Here the universal element is not an obvious technique, though the chapter is well put together, but a favorite theme: the prostitute with the heart of gold, which may account for the effectiveness.

There are a number of things about Jos 2 which make it a useful test case for an investigation of the possibilities of asking new questions of our text. For one thing, it is strange in its immediate context, which certainly is loaded with the paraphernalia of the cult: shofar and ark, processions, circumcisions, and priestly activities. There is none of this in Jos 2. Even if we accept the speculative proposal that Rahab was a cult prostitute, the whole tone of the story is different from its immediate surroundings (1). Then, its claim to be an etiology is even feebler that that of most of the stories in the opening chapters of the book. According to Childs it is no real etiology, for its conclusion in 6,17.22-23.25 with its "until this very day" is a redactional addition, a personal testimony of the historian to his tale (2). This formal observation is borne out strongly by a study of the vocabulary. There are departures from the usage of chapter 2. There the spies are always *hā'anāšîm*, here in chapter 6 they are *hammal'ākîm* (twice) or *hanne'ārîm*. In chapter 2 the verbs for hide are *ṣāpan* and *ṭāman*, here *ḥābā'* (twice). Finally, instead of "looking at (*rā'āh*)" the place or "digging up information (*ḥāpar*)", they frankly

(1) Commentators do not take much note of this, but cf. S. MOWINCKEL, *Tetrateuch-Pentateuch-Hexateuch* (BZAW 90; Berlin 1964) 13, noting that the chapter stands "im krassesten Gegensatz zu den heiligen Legenden" which surround it.

(2) "A Study...", 286, 292.

spy (*raggēl*). In a total of only four verses this is a significant variation hardly consistent with the view that the verses are fragments from an original conclusion to the matter of chapter 2.

One can see some reasons why the redactor altered the vocabulary in the direction he did. It glorifies Joshua. The spies become his messengers or subordinates ("young men"), and they have an explicitly military mission. Even the formula, "until this very day", may have meant more to the redactor than a simple reference to the truth of the tradition of the existence of a Rahabite tribe. By emphasizing the survival it points up the effectiveness of Joshua's directions, and, of course, it does tie the two chapters together. Whatever values chapter 2 may have are recalled, and the whole Jericho tradition in 2-6 is tied together and made ready for its continuation in the following chapters. But of this more in a moment.

I have argued that almost any etiology of the "until this very day" type has to be considered as a story in its own right. In Jos 2, an etiology only by the most external of attributions, this is even more true. In fact, the story is a closed whole without the etiological information in chapter 6. In chapter 2, v. 1 sets the scene, and v. 24 closes it. The story between has a clear outline:

I. Report of the Mission of the Spies (v. 1)

II. Folk-Tale: Rahab and the Spies (vv. 2-21).
  A. Dialogue: Rahab and the King's Men (vv. 2-5).
  B. Report of Israelite and Canaanite Activities (vv. 6-8).
  C. Dialogue: Rahab and the Spies (vv. 9-14).
  D. Report of the Spies' Escape (vv. 15)
  C. Further Dialogue: Conditions of the Oath (vv. 16-21)

III. Narrative of the Spies' Return (vv. 22-24).

Still, it is supposed to have its inconsistencies and doublets. The sequence of events is difficult: the spies come, are hidden twice, converse with Rahab, escape, and then resume the talk in improbable conditions. Then, how did the king learn of the spies' entry into Jericho? It can sound very confusing. One approach is to admit the confusion and attribute it to a rather haphazard conglomeration of sources or fragments.

But is this the most revealing approach? Often one wonders, if these things were fitted together like jig-saw puzzles, why the fitting is so rough. In fact, it is possible to eliminate some of the inconsistencies by looking at the tenses of the key verbs. If verses 4 and

6 have "pluperfects", "she had hidden" and "she had led (them) up", if v. 15 has an inchoative (*futurum instans*), "she was about to let (them) down" and if v. 17 has a "future perfect", "(The rope with which) you will have let (us) down", the temporal sequence is saved. The grammars allow these meanings for the various forms involved, but all this implies an exactness in our knowledge of the Hebrew " tenses" which seems to me less than certain. In any case, they leave us with a complex telling of what is essentially a simple story. Why the complexity?

It may indeed be an indifference to logical details characteristic of Hebrew story telling (1), but this answer avoids the issue. Is there something gained by the seeming inconsistencies? Do they function in the story-telling? One can argue that they do. For one thing, there is a series of verbal structures in the chapter which give it a pattern which, if not governed by logic, has rhetorical force (2).

Then there is the question of the kind of material the story deals with. In sum, though the question does not seem to be asked often (this is an etiology *e basta*): what kind of literary form or forms are involved? Clearly there are many elements of the popular tale and marks of the oral style. The latter can explain much of the repetitiveness. As for the former, there is the interest in the slyness by which the weaker outdoes the stronger (Rahab and the king) and a fascination with legalities (in the oath scenes). The first is a universal folk theme; the second is well documented in Germanic folk literature, among others, Finally, there is the dialogue (3) with the immediacy of its frequent use of *hinneh*, *ʿattâ*, and the imperative. This is the realm of the folktale (4).

(1) So, e.g., H. W. HERTZBERG, *Die Bücher Joshua, Richter, Ruth* (ATD 9; Göttingen 1953) 2a.

(2) W. L. MORAN, "The Repose of Rahab's Israelite Guests", *Studi sull'Oriente e la Bibbia* (Rinaldi Festschrift; Genoa 1967) 273-284. The structures are the sevenfold use of *y/tōʾmer(û)* in verses 4, 9, 14, 16, 17, 21, and 24, and concentric patterns in verses 6-8 with *ʿālāh* in 6 and 8, and *ʾanāšîm* in 7 taken up by *hēmmâ* in 8, and in verses 9-21: 9-13, Rahab speaks, 14, the spies, 16, Rahab, 17-20, the spies, 21a, Rahab.

(3) On this form, cf. E. SELLIN – G. FOHRER, *Einleitung in das Alte Testament*[10] (Heidelberg 1965) 87-88, where Fohrer calls it "Gespräche"

(4) Briefly discussed in O. EISSFELDT, *Einleitung in das Alte Testament*[3] (Tübingen 1964) 49-50. Most discussions of folk literature in relation to the Old Testament suffer from the artificial classification into fairy-tale, novella, anecdote, and saga, which usually seem to be in-

This does not mean artless. This is a well told story, and not just because of tricks of style like concentric structures. The rule is: get on with the story and keep it interesting. Among other things this means omitting all but the essentials and sticking to action, not explanations. Let us look at this at work in Jos 2. The men put themselves in the hands of the harlot, always interesting and in the situation suspenseful. The king knows they are there — we are not told how, but then kings just do know all sorts of things. Will Rahab betray the men? Ah, no, but how can she protect them? By her sly answers. But now, though the men are hidden and the enemy put off the scent, we have a problem. How are they to get out of the locked-up city? And we have a new factor. Rahab has become an interesting and sympathetic figure. What are her motives, and what is to become of her? Forgetting about sources, historical or cultic possibilities, and similar distractions, I think we can see these interests, these responses arising from the complex series of flash-backs (or prolepses) in verses 2-8. Now we begin to get answers.

First there is Rahab's great declaration of faith, embellished by the deuteronomistic writer, but the center of the tale before him. It is a religious document, but it is also a proud affirmation of the greatness of the nation, Israel, the sort of thing which is usually popular in both the senses of "from the folk", and "well received". In response there is the oath which assures Rahab's safety. Then another trick enables the men to escape. Even the final scene may not be without its parallels in folklore. I would not insist on it as a parallel, but it is a fact that popular tales are full of dialogues between women in towers and men below. We expect the dialogue to be romantic, but romance is a medieval development. It is a common scene for dialogue (perhaps reflecting social conditions in which women, even harlots, kept more to the house), and for a popular audience concerned with realities and for whom law is a great reality, why should the subject not be legalistic?

Perhaps this sketchy outline will help to appreciate something of the flow and the bite of the story. The story line and the form

---

distinguishable or inadequate. Folk literature may well be too protean to categorize, but its formal elements and favorite themes can be studied even if they appear in such varied combinations that we cannot do more than speak of folk-tale in general.

elements, particularly those of the dialogue, cut across all projected source analyses, emphasizing the fact that the point is to tell a good story. Other elements are subordinate to this. Of course, this is not art for art's sake. The story is good, but it is given to us for more reasons than that. For instance, it includes a great confession of faith, and it shows Yahweh taking care of a singularly incompetent set of spies. One can rely on him. So there is religious teaching involved.

Still, from one point of view this may seem irrelevant. This is the one which sees the account of the Conquest dominated by the Benjaminite traditions centered on Gilgal. Thus we have the stories we have less because of their intrinsic values than simply because all these traditions have been used. This may be true, but it should lead to another question. Why this set of traditions? It is hard to believe that only Gilgal had a significant set of Conquest traditions over against a shrine like Hebron in the south and perhaps Tabor in the north. In fact, we all know that there were traditions in Judah of an entry from the south, and there are bits of this material in the stories of Joshua's forays into the south, while the north is represented by the attack on Hazor. Still it is the Jericho–Ai axis which dominates. Why? We know that the historians selected, and Noth has shown that elsewhere in the deuteronomistic history they were governed by theological conceptions. Thus in Kings much is ignored, but nothing touching the important theological themes of prophecy and temple (1). The usual answer applied to the Joshua material is to say that the selection of the Benjaminite traditions was made in order to expound the theory of a single, swift conquest. This is true enough, but I do not believe that it comes close to exhausting the theology involved.

We may begin with the climax of the tale of Rahab and the spies, that is, her confession and their escape with the desired information. There is much here, but for our purposes the most revealing is the holy war element. The behavior of the spies is an excellent example of man's part in the holy war. They are saved and their mission accomplished because of Rahab's intervention inspired by faith in Yahweh. They are entirely passive, the classic situation illustrating that Yahweh and not men wins wars. Further, Rahab's

(1) For an example of theological selection and adaptation closer to our material cf. CHILDS, "A Study...", 287, on Jos 14.

speech is loaded with holy war vocabulary: fear is upon the enemy, their hearts melt, they have no spirit, for they know that Yahweh has given the land into Israel's hand. That is, panic, the essential weapon of the holy war, has already accomplished its purpose. The war is virtually finished. The essential is done and all that really remains is that Israel take over what is already its own. There is some confirmation of this idea in Jos 24,11-13, which reflects a tradition that the whole conquest was accomplished physically at Jericho. There is more, I believe, in Jos 2 itself, for apart from the limping addition of "and Jericho" in v. 2, all the action and all the information explicitly concern not Jericho but "the land". The spies find not simply that the city but the whole country is in their hands.

And in fact what follows this chapter is largely the picture of this occupation. Crossing the Jordan opens the way, the action at Jericho begins the work, and actuates what follows. The conquest of Ai is no more of a problem than that of Jericho when the people act properly, and it is the fall of the great cities which sets the last act of the war in motion according to 9,1. The whole land is in motion against Israel, but it is the helpless twitching of the moribund, for the people of the land, according to the testimony of one of their own, melt away before the very name of Israel and its God.

As noted, there are conditions on this. The basic one is that Israel give itself entirely into the hands of Yahweh and give him what is his. The failure to do this, to observe the ban, on the part of one man is enough to hold off the fall of Ai. We may note that the only acceptable way to avoid the ban is to make a covenant with Israel. This can be done openly (Rahab) or by a trick (Gibeon), but it always joins a portion of the people of the land to Israel in some way and so saves it. These traditions are predeuteronomistic, and show the redactor's respect for the traditions he uses since these allow something which the deuteronomic theory of the Conquest forbids. It also surely reflects an actual situation, and one that perdured, for Israel did not in fact occupy a desert. It was joined by many inhabitants of the promised land, and the process lasted a long time since it was still going on under David. Further, there was a recognized means for effecting this joining, an oath given by Israel to the inhabitants.

So far our texts might be seen as sources for the theology of the holy war, and so they are, but there is a special aspect which deserves emphasis. This is the role of Joshua. However he may have gotten into the tradition, as things now stand he has a central position in the theological view being expounded. The spying is done at his command, and it sets everything in motion, or better, reveals that the essential is already in hand. The Jordan crossing is subject to his direction so that he may be confirmed as the new Moses and be "made great" or "exalted" (*gādal*) (1). He directs the Jericho operation and his fame fills the land (2). All this is not simply "creating an image". It is operative in the holy war theology of the conquest. The marvelous events augment the panic in the land (3), and this is the operative element in the conquest destroying the spirit of the inhabitants and giving their land over to Israel.

Thus Joshua becomes the instrument through whom Yahweh continues the work of Moses. Moses' marvelous feats at the Sea of Reeds and in the Transjordan had begun the panic fear which made the land virtually Israel's. Now Joshua directs the holding back of the waters, destroys cities and kings, and works wonders by his outstretched arm and javelin at Ai. His "fame in all the land" cannot but add to the panic and give extra assurance of the result.

This gives us two intertwined unifying themes in the first chapters of the Book of Joshua: the Jericho operation which inaugurates and virtually accomplishes the taking of the land, and the figure of Joshua who as Yahweh's chosen leader is the means by which this is done. So, returning to the opening question, the emphasis is not on historical or geographical details. There is the familiar lesson of the holy war: total trust in Yahweh. But there is added emphasis on the element of leadership. Yahweh accomplishes his designs through a leader he chooses and sustains. If you will, this is a theology of legitimate leadership, and the problem of leadership is one which will confront the deuteronomistic historian throughout his story. Nor is it without interest for theology in general. Perhaps closer attention to what the Bible has to say about it would be profitable (4).

(1) 3,7; 4,14.

(2) 6,27.

(3) 5,1; 9,1.

(4) I should point out that I realize no one actually thinks Joshua is simply geography or history, but many seem to treat it as though it were no more. Nor, in looking for a theological "plus" in it, must one deny any value to the historical or topographical content. Much historical and geographical information may lie behind the stories. Cf. WILCOXEN, in *Transitions in Biblical Scholarship*, 70, n. 38.

Reprinted from the CATHOLIC BIBLICAL QUARTERLY, Vol. XXXIII, No. 2, pp. 228-230, April 1971

SOME HOLY WAR VOCABULARY IN JOSHUA 2

There is no need to emphasize the importance of the war theme, whether under the aspect of the holy war or of the divine warrior in the theology of the Old Testament.[1] However, in spite of the interest in the theme we have no thorough study of the vocabulary associated with it. This note discussing a few of the words pertinent to it which occur in Jos 2 is no more than an adumbration of what might be done. There is no doubt that the chapter in question does reflect the holy war. The very passivity of the spies belongs here, for it allows the hand of Yahweh to appear all the more clearly. Then there is the factor of panic because Yahweh has given the land into Israel's hand, which is recognized as central to holy war theology. This is expressed in a number of ways, and some of the expressions, such as "give into the hand of" or "the spirit did not stand firm," are well enough known, but there are some individual words which repay closer study.

1. *ḥāpar*. The word is used to report the spies' activity to the king of Jericho (vs. 2) and to Rahab (vs. 3). Ordinarily the root means simply "to dig"; here it means "to investigate, to spy" (note the semantically similar English "to dig out information"). The transferred sense is rare. Apart from the two verses here it occurs in Dt 1:22 in exactly the same sense: spies are sent to investigate the land. It appears to be used in this sense only one other time: in Job 39:29 to describe the eagle searching out his prey. This is not war, but it retains the note of ferocity. Perhaps the same can be said of Job 39:21, where the meaning is different—it describes the war-horse pawing the earth in his eagerness. The connotation of ferocity is there, and in close conjunction with *'êmâ*, another war and holy war expression in vs. 20: "his majestic snorting is a terror."[2] With so few data it is impossible to come to a firm conclusion, but it is suggestive that the word is so associated with things which inspire fear, one of the essential elements in the theory of the holy war. It may also not be without significance that it is used in the Book of Job since that book uses many expressions associated with the holy war to speak of the visitations of Yahweh. In fact, all the words we shall discuss from Jos 2 occur in Job and with some frequency.

[1] This is not the place for a full bibliography on the subject. Basic works are G. von Rad, *Der heiligen Krieg im alten Israel*[3] (Göttingen: Vandenhoeck & Ruprecht, 1958); R. Smend, *Jahwekrieg und Stämmebund*[2] (*FRLANT* 84; Göttingen: Vandenhoeck & Ruprecht, 1966); F. M. Cross, Jr., "The Divine Warrior in Israel's Early Cult," in Alexander Altmann, ed., *Biblical Motifs* (Cambridge, Mass.: Harvard Univ. Press, 1966) 11-30; Patrick D. Miller, Jr., "El the Warrior," *HTR* 60 (1967) 411-431.

[2] Interpretation of E. Dhorme, *Bible de la Pléiade* (Paris: Gallimard, 1959) II, 1337.

It seems that the expression in its transferred sense is predeuteronomistic, for it was part of the original story of the spies and Rahab which was incorporated into the history work, not composed for it. This is pointed up by the contrast between the direction to look at (*rā'āh*) the land and the city in Jos 2:1, an introduction added to the story, and the actual use of *ḥāpar* immediately after in the story itself. However, the deuteronomistic school was able to incorporate the term as we have seen in Dt 1:22. This may be taken as a sign that the term is an older usage from the time when the theology of the holy war was really alive. In any case, one suspects that, if we had more accounts of spying in connection with Yahweh-directed war, *ḥāpar* would be part of the vocabulary.

2. *'êmâ.* In Jos 2:9 this word describes the terror that overshadows the Canaanites when they have heard of Yahweh's exploits. It is connected with the divine warrior or his agents in Ex 15:16 and 23:27. In Dt 32:35, Job 20:25, and Jer 50:38 it occurs in descriptions of castigations visited by God upon sinners, and always in connection with weapons. In the passage from Jeremiah the general context is an attack by the sword, in that from Dt the word is strictly parallel to "sword," and in Job with bronze and iron weapons. We have already seen that it is found in Job 39:20, where it is an aspect of the war-horse.[3]

Other passages use the word in connection with Yahweh's visitations upon men: in Gen 15:12 in connection with a (terrifying?) darkness in which Yahweh is revealed, in Job 9:34 in parallel with the rod of divine wrath, in Job 13:21 in parallel with the punishing divine hand, and in Ps 88:16 in parallel with the divine wrath itself. These are not theophanies in the strictest sense, but they obviously recall the terrifying coming of the divine warrior—hence the name I have applied, "visitations." This seems to be emphasized by the fact that *'êmâ,* though usually translated by "terror," is in almost every one of its uses concerned not with the *emotion felt* but the *panic which causes emotion.* It is not something subjective. Rather it is a force objective enough to be used in parallelism with darkness, weapons, rod, and hand. Only in Ps 55:5 and Isa 33:18 does it refer quite clearly to internal feelings: "fear of death falls on" one, or one "mulls over his fear."

3. *māsas.* The word used in Jos 2:11 to describe the melting of the Canaanites' hearts at the report of the might of Israel's God. Jörg Jeremias has discussed the word,[4] and we need not repeat the work. It is sufficient to

[3] This passage about the war-horse is simply imitated in description of the crocodile in 41:6 so that this second passage has little to say about the primary meaning of the word.

[4] *Theophanie* (*WMANT* 10; Neukirchen: Neukirchener Verlag, 1963) 29.

note that theophany and the terrible coming of the divine warrior have much in common, if they are not identical, and this word is typical of the theophany. The connection with the war aspect is illustrated in Ps 97:5, where the effects of Yahweh's coming on nature are due to his characteristic weapons of fire and lightning. Hence it is entirely appropriate that the effect of Yahweh's warlike coming as felt by man be described by a word appropriate to theophany and to war.

4. *môg*. In Jos 2:9 this word is used in much the same sense as *māsas*: the hearts of Yahweh's enemies melt. The word is connected with the divine warrior in Ex 15:15. In 1 Sam 14:16, Isa 14:31, Jer 49:23, Ezek 21:20, and Nah 2:7 it describes the terrors felt in war. In Am 9:5, Ps 46:7, and 75:4 it is connected with the effects of theophany. Job 30:22 uses it of a divine visitation. Am 9:13 is probably a conscious reversal of 9:5: the melting mountains will run with wine under the kingdom of peace. In Ps 105:26 the word describes the terror men feel during a storm at sea. This seems to have no direct association with war or warrior, but it is hard to read the passage without recalling that the waters are a weapon of the divine warrior, for instance, in the Song of Deborah and Ps 18. Thus the only entirely neutral use of the word seems to be Ps 65:11, where the rains soften the earth. Otherwise the word is definitely tied up with war and the coming of the divine warrior to describe the reaction of fear they induce.

To sum up, *ḥāpar* in its transferred sense of "spy out" may well be a word from the vocabulary of war and particularly holy war. It is associated with ferocity, things which cause fear, and this is appropriate, for the fifth column is one of the surest ways to create panic, the operative weapon of the holy war. *'êmâ* is clearly a word from the vocabulary of war and holy war. It describes not subjective fear but the outside force which causes it. Etymologically "panic" would be the best translation, but this word too has come to imply the subjective, and I can find no suitable English equivalent. *māsas* and *môg* are also clearly connected with the war and the visitations of Yahweh. These are words which do describe the subjective side of things, the interior feeling of fear created by panic from outside. There is here a nicety of psychological distinction we often fail to associate with biblical Hebrew. And these few words from a single chapter of the Book of Joshua show clearly the intertwining of the vocabularies of the holy war and of the theophany, or perhaps better because broader, the divine visitation.

DENNIS J. MCCARTHY
Pontifical Biblical Institute
Rome

FURTHER NOTES ON THE SYMBOLISM OF BLOOD AND SACRIFICE

DENNIS J. McCARTHY, S.J.
PONTIFICAL BIBLICAL INSTITUTE, ROME, ITALY

IN an earlier article in this journal[1] I surveyed ancient evidence to see whether it indicated a widespread belief in the sanctity of blood, a belief summed up in the biblical phrase, "in the blood is life." It has been claimed that some such belief is the universal explanation of bloody sacrifice, and the appeal to ancient evidence was the strongest support of the claim. The conclusion from the evidence studied was that no such general belief is attested in the ancient world. Apart from the OT, when given an explicit role in sacrifice, blood is associated with death and not life, with the powers of the underworld and not with the upper. Since 1969 more evidence has come to my attention, and it may be worthwhile to add it to the dossier.

(I) *Blood is Associated with Unpleasantness.* Israel itself knew the darker symbolism of blood. It might be vitalizing, but it could also be dangerous and uncanny. It could have *unheilvolle Wirkung.*[2] To be sure, this is true of the blood of a murdered man, not sacrificial blood, but it is said to be due to something inherent in the blood itself. Thus blood was equivocal, and we are not imposing modern attitudes when we see blood as meaning both strength and death. In fact, the attitude is explicit in very early documents from outside Israel. Hittite texts usually equate "blood" with "bloodshed, death," but in the Bilingual Edict of Hattusilis I it stands for the source of life.[3]

Blood plays an important role in Hittite rituals for communicating with the underworld, where it is the preferred drink of its denizens.[4] The Hittite rite seems to have had congeners in Mesopotamia, Syria, and Palestine. Each area had a rite involving a pit with a name cognate to the Hittite *a-a-bi.* However, the Mesopotamian texts do not mention blood, though they describe the rite in some detail. That is, though there is some evidence from Mesopotamia connecting sacrificial blood and ghosts,[5] the texts which treat directly of ways of dealing with ghosts do not concern themselves with blood. Is this an indication that there was no serious attribution of special magic powers to blood in this area?

[1] "The Symbolism of Blood and Sacrifice," *JBL* 88 (1969) 166-76.

[2] K. Koch, "Der Spruch 'Sein Blut bleibe auf seinem Haupt,'" *VT* 12 (1962) 414.

[3] *KUB* I, 16: III, 11-12. References courtesy of Harry A. Hoffner, Jr.

[4] See Harry A. Hoffner, Jr., "Second Millennium Antecedents of the Hebrew *ʾôb*," *JBL* 86 (1967) 385-401.

[5] In the Etana myth; see *JBL* 88 (1969) 171-72.

Does it indicate that the mention in Etana story is only a sort of "common sense" observation: the blood of the sacrifice goes into the ground, the place of ghosts, and so naturally belonged to them? In any event, the contrast with the Hittite practice is noticeable: Mesopotamian necromancy neglected blood and Hittite emphasized it. If this is not simply owing to accidents of transmission, it is another sign of the disassociation of belief about the powers of blood from ideas of sacrifice,[6] for Hatti and Mesopotamia shared a common view of sacrifice as a provisioning of the gods but had different views about the importance of blood in its sphere.

The texts from Ugarit and from the Bible to which Harry A. Hoffner, Jr. has referred are not ritual. They simply allude to rites without describing them. Nevertheless, he thinks it not unreasonable in view of the Hittite parallels that blood was involved in Israelite dealings with the powers of darkness.[7] The practices associated with the *ʾôb*-pit in Israel then would point in the same direction as Ps 16:4, which may be translated: "(Those who) pursue another (god) multiply their pains, but I do not pour out libations of blood to them, nor do I take their names on my lips." The point is that the psalmist is contrasting his orthodoxy with the conduct of those who in time of illness turn to the powers which control disease with the customary blood rites, only to be confounded.[8] One must not press an argument from analogy and the interpretation of a single difficult text too far, but they do support one another and they march with other evidence indicating a sort of cultural community involving Greece, Asia Minor, and the Levantine coast.

This is important because of the light which the relatively well-documented practices of the Greeks can throw on questions of ritual, and specifically on the meaning of blood in it. It is customary to say that the Greeks distinguished between offerings by the use of the verb *thyein*, "to make an offering by fire," for those to the Olympians, and of *enagizein*, "to put under a religious ban which inspires awe," for those to chthonic deities.[9] As a matter of fact, this can be made more specific. *Enagizein* is not used for chthonic rites in general but for the grimmest of them, the rites of death.[10] I had argued that the Boeotian dialectic equivalent for *enagismata*, *haimakouriai*, points to the importance of blood in these rites. An exhaustive study shows that it did indeed have pride of place.[11]

[6] Ibid., 171-73, 175.

[7] *JBL* 86 (1967) 395. Note that the case is unlike that of Mesopotamia, where we have texts which avoid mention of blood. Here there is no evidence against its use to prohibit an argument from analogy.

[8] See *JBL* 88 (1969) 173. Ps 50:13 may also point to popular belief equating Yahweh with chthonic powers.

[9] See W. K. C. Guthrie, *The Greeks and Their Gods* (London: Methuen, 1950) 221; E. des Places, S.J., *La religion grecque* (Paris: Picard, 1969) 136, 138. The translations are those of J. Casabona (*Recherches sur le vocabulaire des sacrifices en grec* [Paris: University of Paris, 1967] 154, 197), whose word for "awe" is "horreur."

[10] Casabona, *Recherches*, 207.

[11] *JBL* 88 (1969) 172; Casabona, *Recherches*, 206.

This identification of blood with death rites is all the more striking when we note that Greek sacrificial ritual was complex and that there was a strong tendency for usages and their names to move from one rite to another.[12] In the face of this tendency blood rites were the ones which tended to keep their identity. The tradition associating blood and death was more tenacious than most in Greek religious practice. This seems natural enough. Blood rites impressed the imagination more deeply than more innocuous actions, as poetic passages about the horrors of the blood rites attest.

There is further evidence of the same kind. In the welter of their cultic terminology the Greeks had a term, *sphagiazesthai*, for an offering of blood without a communal repast which was commonly performed on the eve of battle. Once more the association is blood with death and danger in the form of war. Moreover, the noun *sphagia* was the designation for blood offerings in which there was no communal meal: blood is associated with the joyless rite.[13]

(II) *The Oath Sacrifice*. The explicit role of blood in this rite merits special notice. In its Greek form the rite was a conditional curse, and the victim which embodied the curse was destroyed, never eaten.[14] Blood is emphasized in the rite: *sphagia temnein*, "cut bloody offerings," is a synonym for *horkia temnein*, "cut oaths."[15] We actually have descriptions of the manipulation of the blood:

> Seven men, fierce captains, slaughtering a bull (*taurosphagountes*) and dipping their hands into its blood, swore by Ares, Enyo, and blood-thirsty Panic either to tear down the city of the Cadmeians and plunder it by force or to die and mix the earth with their blood (Aeschylus, *Seven against Thebes*, 42-48).
> They swore these oaths, after they had slaughtered a bull, a boar, and a ram over the shield. The Greeks dipped a sword and the barbarians a spear into the blood (Xenophon, *Anabasis* 2. 2,9).[16]

The rite is clear and clearly traditional. The poet and the pious historian are describing the same thing. It involves sacrifice, the use of a shield, and contact with blood. Aeschylus makes the symbolism clear: either the parties are to accomplish what they commit themselves to or they are to die. This is a conditional self-curse in which the curse is re-inforced by a symbolic action. The general idea of such an action is, of course, widely known, but the Greek form is special

[12] See S. Eitrem and J. Fontenrose, "Sacrifice," *Oxford Classical Dictionary* (2d ed.; Oxford: Oxford University, 1970) 944; W. K. C. Guthrie, *The Greeks and Their Gods*, 221: the distinctions are true "for the most part"; cf. especially the study of Casabona (*Recherches*) with the complexity and nuances it demonstrates in the ritual vocabulary.

[13] Casabona, *Recherches*, 188-90.

[14] Cf. J. Priest, "ὅρκια in the *Iliad* and Consideration of a Recent Theory," *JNES* 23 (1964) 55; *Oxford Classical Dictionary*, 944-45.

[15] Priest, *JNES* 23 (1964) 48.

[16] The passage from Xenophon is to be treated from the point of view of Greek practice, though Persians are also involved. Herodotus says that Persian oath ceremonies were like those of the Greeks, but he distinguishes them from sacrifices, and these rites are sacri-

because it is explicitly a sacrifice (note the root *sphag-* in both texts) and blood is the symbol of death.

The OT too associates sacrifice, blood, and covenant in Exod 24:5-8, but it does not adopt the darker symbolism of blood. The external form of the rite is much like the Greek. Animals are slain, the blood is collected, and the participants are joined by contact with the blood. However, the significance is different in the two cases because of the kinds of sacrifice involved. The Greek was not *thysia*, a feast. It could not be, for it invoked death symbolized by blood. Such things belonged to the nether powers; they made the sacrifice tabu, not the center of feasting.[17]

On the other hand, in Exodus the sacrifice is a *zẹbaḥ*, the Hebrew rite homologous with *thysia* and so involving the participants in a sacrificial banquet. It was literally a feast, and because of this the association with death characteristic of the Greek parallel is broken. Hebrew practice is like the other in its externals, but the connotations of blood are, as far as the evidence goes, peculiarly its own, because it is associated with a sacrifice which could be consumed. That is, it was salutary and not, as in Greece, tabu. It was a symbol of something with which one sought association, not, as in the Greek parallel, of death with which one did not seek communion.

This is an especially clear case of the separateness of Hebrew attitudes to blood and sacrifice. The similarities are so close that the divergences stand out. Both Israel and Greece knew the oath as a conditional curse which could be acted out in ritual.[18] The oath-taker identified himself with the slain animal if he were to violate his oath. This sort of thing is also found among Arameans and Assyrians, but it is not identified with sacrifice. In fact, in one case it is explicitly denied that the rite is a sacrifice.[19] In contrast, the Greek and Israelite rites are alike in being sacrifices. Yet only the Greek employs the darker symbolism of blood. Hence the Greek oath-sacrifice is consistent. It is an acted-out oath in which the parties identified themselves with the death of the victim through contact with its blood. However, when blood and sacrifice are given an explicit role in Israel's covenant ritual, the connection with death disappears. Perhaps this happened because Israel always associated blood with life in a ritual context. Perhaps it was because Yahwism allowed no sacrificial usages parallel to the

fices as well as oaths (1.74). Furthermore, the ceremony is very like the one described in Aeschylus. Thus there is reason to see it as Greek and not especially as Persian in form.

[17] On the *thysia*, the sacrificial feast as such, see Casabona, *Recherches*, 134; also D. Gill, "*Thysia* and *šᵉlāmîn*: Questions to R. Schmid's *Das Bundesopfer in Israel*," *Bib* 47 (1966) 255-62.

[18] This, of course, is the significance of *krt bᵉrît*, which does not of itself refer to a sacrifice. Cf. D. J. McCarthy, S.J., *Treaty and Covenant* (AnBib 21; Rome: Biblical Institute, 1963) 52-57; E. Kutsch, "Gesetz und Gnade," *ZAW* 79 (1967) 20-21. An oath rite analogous to *krt bᵉrît* is attested for Greece in Plato, *Laws* 753d.

[19] See *Treaty and Covenant*, 52-57. The Assyrian treaty with Mati-ilu of Arpad denies that the rite is a sacrifice: "This spring lamb has been brought from its fold not for sacrifice . . .; it has been brought to sanction the treaty . . ." (*ANET*³, 532).

sphagia, no association with darker powers, but only a sacrifice associated with life because it belonged to the living God. But whatever the explanation, the fact is clear. Covenant blood had a different meaning in Israel from what it had in Greece. The contrast between the gloomy character of the *sphagia* and the festal *zębaḥ*, associated as they both were with blood in otherwise similar circumstances pointed up the special character of the Hebrew attitude: blood is life.[20]

(III) *Blood and Oaths without Sacrifice.* The blood oath did not always explicitly involve sacrifice. This is true in three examples from Herodotus. He remarks that the Persians and the Scythians made oaths in a ceremony in which the parties partook of one another's blood. He also mentions Arabs who pledged themselves in a ceremony in which the blood was smeared on seven stones while the gods were invoked.[21] It is argued that the latter ceremony is to be equated with the others and that the drinking of blood implies an actual sharing in divine life symbolized by blood.[22] This is then connected with sacrifice or perhaps with conditional curse rites.

However, it must first be insisted that the texts do not speak of sacrifice; this is clear in Herodotus. Smith speaks of Arab rites involving a victim and a sanctuary, in sum, a sacrifice; but the texts he cites deal with the dipping of hands in blood and the touching of sacred stones. There is no mention of sacrifice as such, and in fact oils and perfumes, symbols of power, can be used in the same way, and they are not the products of sacrifice.[23]

Neither does there seem to be a question of an acted-out conditional curse as in the Greek rite. For one thing the parallel breaks down over the fact that the Greek rites are explicitly sacrifices; these are not. Further, the blood and the other substances — to be noted because they can be associated with death only with difficulty — are rubbed on sacred stones while divinities are invoked. This is not like the Greek rite. It can hardly mean that symbolic death is being called down on the gods who are in contact with the blood, as is the case with the Greeks

[20] Hence the rite in Exod 24:5-8 is not a *Fluchhandlung*, as E. Kutsch, in a communication to the International Organization for the Study of the OT Congress (Uppsala, Aug. 12, 1971) argued from the analogy with the passage from Aeschylus referred to earlier in this article. The comparison with the Greek is correct, but it fails to note the consistent Greek association of sacrificial blood, oath, and death (cf. Xenophon as well as Aeschylus), and the sharp contrast of this to the Hebrew rite. Explicit connection with the *zębaḥ* breaks the association with death characteristic of the conditional curse rite. Even when the curse rite is central in the OT, a remote allusion to sacrifice can tone down the grimmer aspect: see the interpretation of Gen 15:9-18 by E. Loewenstamm, "Zur Traditionsgeschichte des Bundes zwischen den Stücken," *VT* 18 (1968) 500-6.

[21] 1. 74 (Persia); 4. 70 (Scythia); 3. 8 (Arabia). Consuming blood in fellowship rites among Semites on the border of Egypt may be attested in an Egyptian text from the 12th century B.C.; see J. Černy, "Reference to Blood Brotherhood among Semites in an Egyptian Text of the Ramesside Period," *JNES* 14 (1955) 161-63.

[22] W. Robertson Smith, *Lectures on the Religion of the Semites* (2d ed.; London: Black, 1907) 315-20; cf. J. Černy, *JNES* 14 (1955) 161.

[23] See *Kinship and Marriage in Early Arabia* (2d ed.; London: Black, 1903) 56-60. The Egyptian text published by Černy does not mention sacrifice either.

who touch it. At the most one might think that the gods are being invoked as witnesses.

However, even this is improbable in view of all the material cited by Smith. It indicates that the dominant concept connected with blood among the ancient Arabs was community. It would appear that in these blood ceremonies a new member was being taken into the clan, of which the god was the first member and protector. This may be hinted at in the rest of the passage from Herodotus about the Arabs, for it emphasizes that they thought of themselves as being and acting like their gods. As they cut their hair in the manner of their gods, so they admitted members into their clan in the manner of their gods. In thus conceiving of alliance as symbolic union with the clan, the Arabs were like the Persians and the Scythians (and pretty much all the world!). Sharing blood (and other things) created kinship. This belief was not particularly associated with sacrifice, but it did connect blood with the clan, and so with life.

The further examination of the evidence leads to conclusions like those of the first survey:

(1) Similarities in externals in Greek and Hebrew covenant rituals are further evidence for some kind of community between Greece and the Levant in this as in other aspects of culture.

(2) When there is question of dealing with the numinous, blood is especially attractive to unpleasant powers.

(3) Nomadic (Arab) oath rituals do not explicitly associate blood and sacrifice, nor do they see blood as life; but they do practically identify the sharing of blood (and other things) with a community of life.

(4) The Hebrew treatment of the oath sacrifice points up the symbolism of blood peculiar to OT texts. This is so because it resembles Greek usage in external form, but it gives blood a very different meaning — life and not death.

The purpose of this survey has been to summarize the actually attested attitudes toward blood in ritual. Its conclusion: careful regard for the evidence indicates that the Hebrew attitude toward blood is unique. This attitude should not be extrapolated to explain other rites which are described without an explanation of their meaning or which imply another explanation. The principle should be applied within the OT as well; that is, one should not assume that OT sacrifice throughout its history was based on a belief that blood was life. The actual statements to this effect are deuteronomic and priestly; if the *opinio communis* that Exod 24:5-8 is predeuteronomic is correct, that text would be evidence that the belief was operative at an earlier stage.

Beyond this present evidence permits only hypothesis. It is perhaps permitted to think of several factors at work. The rather inexplicit blood rites of nomadic ancestors may have been connected with adopted Canaanite sacrificial ritual. Yahwism may have ruled out a connection with chthonic rites and directed development of the undifferentiated symbolism of blood toward the idea of life, not death.

The Inauguration of Monarchy in Israel

*A Form-Critical Study of I Samuel 8—12**

DENNIS J. MCCARTHY, S.J.
Pontifical Biblical Institute

The kingship has been integrated into the fundamental relationship between Yahweh and the people and that relationship reaffirmed. A crisis has been described and resolved in narrative and theological terms, and a new era can begin.

Structure

I. Introductory report: problems with Samuel's judgeship (8:1-3)

II. Report of an assembly: the demand for a king (8:4-22)

A. Dialogue: demand and rejection (4-9)

B. Discourse against kingship (10-18)

C. Dialogue: repeated demand and rejection (19-22)

* On the interpretation of this text see further: W. F. ALBRIGHT, "Reconstructing Samuel's Role in History," *Archaeology, Historical Analogy, and Early Biblical History* (Baton Rouge, University of Louisiana, 1966) pp. 42-65; B. C. BIRCH, "The Development of the Tradition on the Anointing of Saul in I Sam 9:1—10:16," JBL 90:55-68 (1971); HANS JOCHEN BOECKER, *Die Beurteilung der Anfänge des Königtums in den deuteronomistischen Abschnitten des I. Samuelbuches,* WMANT, XXXI (Neukirchen-Vluyn, Neukirchener Verlag des Erziehungsvereins, 1969); H. M. CHADWICK and N. K. CHADWICK, *The Growth of Literature,* 1932-1940, 3 Vols. (Reprint. Cambridge, Eng., The University Press, 1968); E. A. HAVELOCK, *Preface to Plato* (Oxford, Basil Blackwell, 1963); ROLF KNIERIM, "The Messianic Concept in the First Book of Samuel," in F. T. Trotter, ed., *Jesus and the Historian. Written in Honor of E. C. Colwell* (Philadelphia, Westminster Press, 1968), pp. 20-51; ALBERT B. LORD, *The*

III. Story: the secret anointing of Saul (9:1—10:16)
   A. The meeting with Samuel (9:1-14)
   B. The consecration (9:15—10:8)
   C. Confirmation and return home (10:9-16)
IV. Report of an assembly: public selection of a king (10:17-27)
   A. Discourse against kingship (17-19*a*)
   B. Anecdotes about Saul's selection (19*b*-27)
V. Story: Saul's first exploit (11:1-13)
   A. The inspired exploit (1-11)
   B. Result: exercise of a royal function (pardon) (12-13)
VI. Report of an assembly: renewal of kingship and denouement (11:14—12:25)
   A. Introduction: festive coronation gathering (11:14-15)
   B. Denouement: resolution of the theological problem of kingship (12:1-25)
      1. Dialogue: Samuel renounces the judgeship (1-5)
      2. Discourse: kingship and salvation history (6-15)
      3. Dialogue: reproach and reconciliation (16-25)

This section stands between the formal closing of one unit, 7:13-17, echoing the formulae which mark the end of the story of a judge (cf. Judg. 3:30; 8:28), and the formal opening of another unit, 13:1, a formula for beginning the report of a reign. Thus extrinsic elements

---

Singer of Tales. Harvard Studies in Comparative Literature, XXIV (Cambridge, Harvard University Press, 1960); DENNIS J. McCARTHY, S.J., "The Wrath of Yahweh and the Structural Unity of the Deuteronomistic History," in J. L. Crenshaw and J. T. Willis, eds., *Philip Hyatt Memorial Volume* (New York, 1973); JAMES MUILENBURG, "The Form and Structure of the Covenantal Formulations," VT 9:347-65 (1959); MARTIN NOTH, *Überlieferungsgeschichtliche Studien,* I (1943 Reprint. Tübingen, Max Niemayer, Verlag, 1957); GERHARD VON RAD, "The Provenance of Deuteronomy," in *Studies in Deuteronomy,* SBT, IX (London, SCM Press, 1953), pp. 60-69; GOTZ SCHMITT, *Der Landtag von Sichem,* AzTH, I, 15 (Stuttgart, Calwer Verlag, 1964); HORST SEEBASS, "Die Vorgeschichte der Königserhebung Sauls," ZAW 79:155-71 (1967); MATITIAHU TSEVAT, "The Biblical Narrative of the Foundation of Kingship in Israel," *Tarbiz XXXVI* (1966), pp. 99-109 (English summary, p. 116) and "Studies in the Book of Samuel, I," HUCA, 32:191-216 (1961); GERHARD WALLIS, "Die Anfänge des Königtums in Israel," (pp. 45-66) and "Überlieferungsgeschichtliche Forschung und der Samuelstoff," *Geschichte und Uberlieferung* AzTh, II/13 (Stuttgart, Calwer Verlag, 1968), pp. 67-87; MOSHE WEINFELD, Deuteronomy and the Deuteronomic School (Oxford, Clarendon Press, 1972); ARTUR WEISER, *Samuel,* FRLANT, LXXXI (Göttingen, Vandenhoeck & Ruprecht, 1962). The above are cited by name only in the body of the article.

define the limits of the pericope even though chapter 7 is in itself a direct preparation for 8ff., and the section as a whole sets the tone for all that follows.

However, the important thing is the internal articulation of the unit. Generally interest in it is concentrated on the problem of the supposed promonarchical source (9:1—10:16; 11:1-15) and the antimonarchical (8; 10:17-27; 12), their dates and their historical reliability. This is important, of course, but it has drawn attention from the careful narrative construction of the unit as such.

The most obvious element in this construction is the pattern of contrasts (Tsevat). Two genres alternate: the report and the story, and this is emphasized formally. The reports open with the explicit convening of the people (8:4; 10:17; 11:14f.) and, when a story follows, their dismissal (8:22; 10:25). Further, the reports have a similar internal structure. Each contains a solemn address by Samuel and a certain amount of dialogue. Thus the scenes are sharply etched. We move from moments of solemn "constitutional" assembly to moments of vigorous action in the stories. And it is Samuel's discourses during the assemblies which attack kingship, while the stories are positive toward it. The whole apparatus of alternations serves to reinforce the basic tension of the pericope, the problem of the proper attitude toward the kingship.

This basic element is repeated thematically. The section is not just about kingship, it is about kingship as a problem, and the reader is not allowed to lose sight of this even in the so-called promonarchical units. This is achieved by linguistic means. The first scene focuses attention on the request for a king as an evil because it is a rejection of the divinely ordained institution of the judgeship represented by Samuel. Thereafter, even when speaking positively of the king, the language is that which is familiar from the theology of the judges (cf. 9:16; 10:1 [LXX]). The associations of the vocabulary thus keep the problem present. But even when this is not the case, the problem is not entirely forgotten: in the flush of success verses 12-13 of chapter 11 remind us of the opposition to the king.

But so far we have a pattern of contrasts and recurring theme. This does not suffice for good narration by itself. There must be movement, and there is in our passage. Chapter 8 exposes the problem of kingship among Yahweh's people, but the following story creates complications. There is something good about the man Saul in spite of the problems kingship raises, problems recalled in 10:17-19*a*. This creates a tension which is released when in 11:1-13 Saul is shown to act as Yahweh's own man. This is the true climax of the narrative, and it opens the way to a final resolution in chapter 12 where, with sin acknowledged and repented, kingship can be accepted into ongoing salvation history. This resolution is emphasized by a formal device: the perfect balance between Parts I + II and VI, the reports which open and close the pericope.

Genre

The passage is a unity which tries to give a coherent account and explanation of the inauguration of kingship in Israel. That is, it is history writing. This is not to assert (or deny) that it is factual in detail, but simply that as a literary phenomenon it conforms to the definition of history: a record and analysis of past events. Like all history writing it is dependent on two factors: the evidence available to the historian about the past, and the point of view which guides him in using that evidence. One may question a historian's evidence or impugn his interpretative principles, as is commonly done when they are in part theological, as here. This is to question the quality of the history writing, not the fact of it.

And what of the antecedents of our text? How did it acquire its present shape? The classic source theory posits an older form of the history substantially the same as the present, which is simply the deuteronomistic redaction of this older history. This prototype, itself a formal history, is supposed to have been a conflation of the older promonarchical narrative with an antimonarchical narrative marked as later by its prophetic ideas. A variant of this view omits the antimonarchical narrative as such. It posits the piecemeal incorporation of the antimonarchical Samuel legends (e.g., first chaps. 8 and 10:17-27, later chap. 12) into the basic promonarchical source to produce gradually the predeuteronomistic form of the history.

Other variations on the classic theory posit separate, continuous sources which coincide in general with the supposed pro and antimonarchical strains, though they may not be defined in these terms. For example, the "antimonarchical" passages are from a history interested in the "rights of the king" (8:9; 10:25) and the others from one interested in the king as war leader (Seebass). These theories differ from classic theory because they do not assume a conflation of the sources to produce a substantially complete form of the history antecedent to our text. Rather, they assume that different histories of the beginnings of monarchy existed until they were added together by a deuteronomistic writer. In such theories the immediate antecedents of the present text were themselves a plurality of formal histories.

Or was there at least a kind of protodeuteronomistic working of the sources? Some variants on deuteronomistic language are peculiar to this section and key passages in Judges (chaps. 2, 10), and the scheme of the judges' era in 12:8-12 is not exactly that of the story as now given (for the data, cf. Schmitt, pp. 16f.). Does this point to a kind of first draft of the story within a deuteronomistic school? The slight variations in language involved may simply be special language for a special period, while variants like 12:8-12 are just what one expects in something based on traditional literature. Hence it seems unnecessary to presume an earlier deuteronomistic "edition" of the history, though this is not impossible.

A quite different view holds that there would have been an old history of Saul and David which included 9:1—10:16 and 11:1-15, but that the deuteronomistic historian himself practically composed the antimonarchical chapters and inserted them into the older history (Noth, pp. 55-61; Boecker). Thus the pericope would not be a final conflation of several sources. It would be a composition reinterpreting one older history by interpolation.

This seems to be correct insofar as it insists that the deuteronomist gave the pericope its shape. However, the Samuel sections are not really much marked by the very distinct deuteronomistic style, and they reflect older elements: prophetic ideas and the institutions of the tribal league. They are scarcely deuteronomistic compositions. Rather the deuteronomist used materials from a Samuel cycle to construct his reinterpretation of things. Or better, this is the final deuteronomistic retelling of the whole tradition.

But where does this leave us regarding the antecedents of our text? All theories based on source documents run into grave difficulties. For example, how is one to conceive the process from source to final structure? The classic view was simple. It presupposed the juxtaposition of blocks of material, whole chapters, from its sources. But the blocks will not stay separate. For example, the "promonarchical source" is contaminated with prophetic elements supposed to characterize the other source (cf. Knierim, pp. 29, 31, 34). Source-document theories must fall back on intricate fragmentations of the text, the hypothetical division of the documents into tiny pieces and their restructuring, often in a sequence different from that of the original. One is forced to think of the construction of a jigsaw puzzle.

However, this is traditional literature (often called oral—for the terminology and the whole problem see Lord) which is not constructed like a jigsaw puzzle. The problem really arises because of the assumption that the steps in the tradition are absolutes, documents which represent discrete fixations of the tradition which develops by jumping from one such fixed point to another. But traditional literature is more like an organic flow in which each telling of the tradition recreates the tradition in its own terms, and no two tellings, even by one storyteller, are exactly the same.

But to doubt unwieldy documentary source theories is not to disavow the possibility of tracing the history of tradition. It is simply an attempt to seek the limits within which it is possible. One can begin with an accepted fact: The simplest stage behind a passage like ours was a set of individual narratives of various kinds. Characteristically individual narratives acquire set traits, for example, Saul the farm-boy hero.[1] A more complex stage is that of cycles, that is, the telling of stories in groups which cluster around a person or a theme. Such cycles tend to be determined by their content. Traditional literature tends to follow the natural sequence of things, though certain connections among topics in a different order may be fixed more or less arbitrarily by tradition itself.

We have, then, stages of tradition, but these need not refer to temporal sequence. Individual narratives certainly continued to be told

1. These traits may or may not be historical. Literary study as such is not concerned with the point. It simply notes that whatever their source such traits are characteristic of traditional literature.

after cycles had begun to be recounted, and cycles are as old as the existence of a number of narratives connected with persons as interesting as Saul and themes as absorbing as kingship. Stages here are related as much to complexity as to time, and yet traditional literature exists in time in a way quite unlike written literature. It is literally always in transition because it exists only in the telling. One must forget about memorized texts. Traditional literature does not know them; it knows stories which it recreates in each telling. This combination of qualities, the tenacity of certain traits and of certain connections of topics with a constant openness to new influences as it is retold in new circumstances, means that traditional literature bears traces of the different times and places of its tellings so that we can work out some of its history.

In our example, this may be summed up as follows:

1) The formation of individual narratives.

It would be generally, if not universally, admitted that these had certain traits in their earliest forms: Saul will have appeared as the deliverer of the tribe (11:1-11) and the farmboy-hero of folklore (9:1-14; 10:23), and Samuel will have been connected with "civil" (the judgeship) and sacral institutions of the tribal league.

2) The continued retelling of these stories in cycles. In the course of this process some developments may be discerned.

a) There must have been a stage in which a pro-Saul cycle was told. Very likely this put little emphasis on royalty. Saul would be the tribal hero, the deliverer like the judges. Not that the kingship was entirely absent (cf. the old tradition of the choice of a king at Mizpah, 10:19*b*-24), but that as something new and unfamiliar it was not much developed. (There are parallels for this sort of phenomenon. For instance in Italian *märchen* the Tuscan version of a story will mention royalty without making anything of it, while the Sicilian version will have much to say about kings. Kingship was a latecomer in Tuscany, an old institution in Sicily.)

b) There seems to have been a stage in which the Saul cycle was united to the David cycle, and both were modified by concepts from royal ideology and from the prophetic movement. This stage determined the theological structure of much in the Books of Samuel (Knierim).

Within our pericope this is seen in the insistence on an antecedent divine choice marked by a prophetic anointing and followed by a display of might under the influence of the spirit of Yahweh. Hence the addition of the anointing to the folktales about Saul and the sequence between them. Influence from prophetic circles appears also in the use of call-narrative motifs in the tale in chapter 9 and following.

c) Surely there was a Samuel cycle. However, the material as it has come to us has been touched by very disparate influences. There is the timeless folklore theme of the birth of the hero; there is a connection with the cult of the tribal league: the sanctuary at Shiloh and the Ark (but now connected with a narrative tied to the royal shrine, Jerusalem —cf. the continuation of the Ark narrative in II Sam. 6); there is the tradition of a judgeship; and there is a prophetic role connected with the inauguration of the monarchy and, in chapter 12, influenced by the picture of Moses the mediator found in the Pentateuch. There is a consistency in this; Samuel represents ideals and institutions of the tribal league, often as these were remembered in later times and reinterpreted to tie into later experience. However, it is hardly possible to discern a central narrative line. Apparently the Samuel narratives remained a loose cycle which never acquired a structure like that of the story of Saul and David.

3) Finally, there was the organization of the traditional elements into our history. The basis of this was the story of Saul and David. In our pericope this was restructured by the use of material from the Samuel cycle. This was the work of the deuteronomistic school. The evidence for this is considerable. First, the thematic references to kingship which are essential to the structure are precisely the passages where deuteronomistic style is clearest. Then, the internal structure of the pericope is too sophisticated to be the product of accidental growth and simple retouches; it shows a controlling conception, the mark of an author, and this conception is integrated into the intricate structure of the deuteronomistic history as a whole. The change from the era of the judges to that of the kings is one of the hinge passages recognized by Noth (p. 5), and this change to the last era of the history is given a special theological tone by our passage. Before this the key changes of era, from Moses to the conquest, from Joshua to the judges, stood under

the explicit threat of Yahweh's devastating anger. Here, despite the negative attitude toward kingship of some of the parts integrated into the pericope, the anger of Yahweh is never mentioned, a change which marks all that follows. A new and different era has opened (McCarthy).

It is perhaps well to conclude with a reminder: We are still talking about a reworking of traditions. To speak of deuteronomistic use of the Samuel cycle to restructure a history is not to be confused with source theories which work in terms of combinations of documents. It is rather to speak of a stage of tradition which absorbed much from various old streams and retold it as one whole.

Setting

The settings of the individual narratives about Saul and Samuel must have been Benjamin and the shrines of central Palestine (Weiser; Wallis). The old Saul cycle must have been at home in the north, particularly in Benjamin, the tribe whose hero he was. II Samuel 16:5-8, 19:17 testify to continued loyalty to him there. This cycle was used in the Saul-David history, which has a complex background. The sacredness of the king seen in Saul's power to release the "worthless fellows" from the punishment already divinely ordained for them (cf. 10:27*a*; 11:12f., and Knierim, pp. 33f.) is a concept from royal ideology at home in Davidic Jerusalem, though by no means unknown in the north. But Samuel must anoint the leader like an Elijah or Elisha (I Kings 19:15f.; II Kings 9:3, 6, 12). The leader must show the power of the spirit before he receives full recognition. He must be called. Such things seem to reflect ideas from the reinterpretation of kingship in prophetic circles. These flowered first in the north, but the emphasis on them in relation to David in the larger Saul-David history indicates continued interest in Judah whence prophets came (I Kings 13; Amos) and where prophetic ideas developed after the fall of the Northern Kingdom.

The Samuel cycle reflects much from the same background. The interest in the institutions of the tribal league and the prophetic touches point to northern origins. But here, too, we have developments in the larger cycle which look to Judah: the Ark belongs now to Jerusalem, the legitimate shrine contrasted with Shiloh (Tsevat, *HUCA*). This reminds us too that the Samuel cycle is especially interested in sacral institutions. It will have developed in circles with prophet ideas but also with priestly interests. Indeed, priestly and prophetic circles are not such sharply distinguished foci of tradition as is sometimes thought (Albright).

The final structuring of our pericope was deuteronomistic. This gives us a literary setting. But who were the deuteronomists? Classic criticism associated them with the prophetic movement. However, more recent studies have tried to go beyond this. It has associated the deuteronomistic school with levitical preaching (Von Rad) or with the Wisdom traditions of the scribes at the Jerusalem court (Weinfeld). The discussion continues. One suspects that several factors were at work, not one overwhelming influence.

Intention

The several stages of tradition observed in our passage illustrate much about storytelling which can be discussed in detail only when dealing with the traditional stages as such: the individual stories as individual stories, the grand cycles as larger wholes. But we can note some few points of special interest.

Stories are told to further political purposes. The Saul cycle was an element in the opposition to the Davidic monarchy. They are used to express and develop ideologies. The structuring of the Saul-David history integrated many things: the sacredness of the king as such, his election by Yahweh, the role of the prophet, the rights of the people in order to create a theology of the king as the called and anointed leader of the people.

The Samuel cycle points to a different, supremely important function of narrative in traditional societies, the encyclopedic. It is in its narrative tradition that such a society organizes and preserves the memory of the things which constitute its identity. This must, then, be more than simple story. In the absence of important use of documents it must conserve the memory of the institutions of the people and so the continuity of the institutions themselves (cf. Havelock). The institutions of prime interest in this regard are legal and sacral (cf. Chadwick and Chadwick, III, pp. 731-49, who use "antiquarian" where I have "encyclopedic" and who emphasize the "mantic" element, i.e., priest-*cum*-prophet, in this aspect of traditional literature). Just so the Samuel cycle centers around a prophetic figure and is concerned with civil and cultic institutions of the tribal league.

However, the central point to note about our pericope is the mastering of this material with its intentions to say something new and decisive. This is accomplished through the structure. The apparatus of contrast and themes is not merely formal, it is functional. The first step starts from the institutional traditions of the Samuel cycle. It introduces kingship as an evil because it is a demand for someone to be a judge in the developed sense of a war-leader and deliverer (8:20), and this is to seek of oneself what Yahweh himself has always given (8:8). An ancient background in the tribal league and a long reflection on its institutions is used here to set the problem of the pericope.

Then we are introduced to Saul in an attractive story whose relevance to the kingship is not at once apparent. The mystery is soon solved. We are told in language from the same lexicon as the attack on kingship in chapter 8 that this is the leader who will save the people (9:16). However, here it is positive, and it serves as a thematic link which integrates a favorable element from the Saul cycle into the problem of kingship opened in the earlier chapter. This is narrative complication which is theological as well. The story picks up interest and the meaning of kingship appears less clear than it seemed.

A thematic statement against kingship in the now familiar language (10:17-19*a*) introduces the next structural unit. It is this which gives the tone to the section which was not of itself antimonarchical. On the contrary, the handsome figure of 23*b*-24 clearly connects with the young hero of 9:1ff. But with the present introduction this has changed, and the "rights of the kingdom" in verse 25 are made to recall chapter 8. An anecdote without negative import in itself has been given ominous overtones. From the tone of things one might even wonder whether the opponents of Saul in 10:27 are not in the right! At the very least, the first public revelation of the king is under a cloud because the structure has tied it to chapter 8.

And then at once comes a story where Saul acts the inspired hero. In chapter 8 kingship was condemned precisely because it went against the tradition of the judge-deliverer who represented Yahweh the savior. Now the chosen king is revealed as just such a deliverer. The use of the language of the judgeship to refer to the problem of the king is seen to have special significance. The Saul cycle had shown him as a hero-deliverer. Hence he could be presented as a king *not* like those of the nations (cf. 8:20). The condemnation of chapter 8 has been met on its own terms and reversed, and this has been done by retaining the favorable picture of Saul from the old cycle and giving it more force by the contrast with the negative chapters. The people can convene and confirm Saul's kingship with rejoicing.

Or can they? With the convening of the people one is inevitably reminded of the negative parts of the narrative, and there is much in the unit to reinforce this. Samuel returns as judge and uses the thematic language of the judgeship to proclaim a history of sin culminating in the demand for a king. For, the evil attacked in chapter 8 was twofold: the conception of kingship as a substitute for the judgeship with its special theological significance and the demand seeking for oneself what Yahweh gives. By now the action (11:1-13) has made clear that the kingship can continue the judgeship. But the problem of the popular demand itself remains. The position of the people is not clear, or, rather, it is clearly a state of sin. And so 12:8-12 returns to 8:8, but not to end there. Chapter 12, verse 13 is a formal reversal of the foregoing, a step from the historical proclamation to parenesis and covenant condition; briefly, a call to renewed obedience. The fundamental thing threatened by Israel's action was the covenant relationship, and this is the formal restoration of that relationship with the kingship now explicitly included in it (Muilenburg, pp. 363f.).

The final scene of the chapter emphasizes this. The people repent their sin as required by the theology of the era of the judges here ending (cf. Judg. 10:6-16). Then the covenant relationship is explicitly reaffirmed (12:22*b*). With this the problems raised in the pericope are finally solved. The kingship has been integrated into the fundamental relationship between Yahweh and the people and that relationship reaffirmed. A crisis has been described and resolved in narrative terms and in theological, and a new era can begin.

Exod 3:14:
History, Philology and Theology

DENNIS J. MCCARTHY, S.J.
Pontifical Biblical Institute
00187 Rome, Italy

IT IS NOT DIFFICULT these days to hear that theology is in a bad way and that this is connected with biblical studies, whether it be a cry of joy at the freeing of our studies from theological bondage, dismay at the apparent meaninglessness of biblical language, or a dispassionate statement that "biblical theology" or neo-orthodoxy was really remote from what the biblical scholar actually does.[1] Or, with Childs, one can note the passing of "biblical theology" and try a new direction. The reactions to his efforts in his Exodus commentary[2] have been mixed, to say the least. It was described as a "magnificent failure" by *Interpretation,* which one would expect to be sympathetic, while *Vetus Testamentum,* in one of its rare reviews, ignores his theology, which I suspect was his chief interest, for textual details and the like.

While in entire sympathy with Childs' aims, I am inclined to agree with the reaction for I find a total dichotomy between his splendid tradition-criticism and his theological development. He has not solved the prob-

[1] For a sampling of the various views one can consult the attitudes of the various authors in *Old Testament Form Criticism* (John Hayes, ed.; San Antonio: Trinity University, 1971), and note the remarks of Walter Brueggemann in his review, *RelSRev* 1 (1975) 12-13; Langdon Gilkey, *Naming the Whirlwind: The Renewal of God-Language* (Indianapolis/New York: Bobbs-Merrill, 1969), esp. 3-106; James Barr, *The Bible in the Modern World* (London: SCM, 1973).

[2] *Exodus: A Commentary* (Old Testament Library; London: SCM, 1974).

lem of integrating historical-critical method and the theological use of the Bible. And yet this is the basic issue to which we as believing scholars must address ourselves. (I consider the problem of "making scripture real for today" a problem in homiletics, a matter of great importance, but one at one remove at least from the problem of Bible and theology, the integration of which is the first obligation of professional biblical scholars. If this can be done, the application, the "realization" for today can come; if not, it is a close to hopeless task.) In order to look at the problems more closely it seemed useful to work in the concrete, and so I have taken Exod 3:14 as a test case.

Now, when we look at such a text we can actually look at many things. In the Tetrateuch we tend first to ask about sources. In our case, of course, we see E. Then we fit the passage into the source. However, nowadays no one stops there. There is also form-criticism and tradition-criticism. That is, we seek to go beyond the documentary to oral sources. So here we would have a pre-Israelite cult etiology (the mountain of god). Then this would have been used as the kernel to the Israelite stories of Moses' call. Finally, in P (chap. 6) it is integrated into a philosophy of history. I have no quarrel with any of this—on the contrary—but we should note how much of it is speculative and how much of it depends on non-biblical material. For instance, E as a source document is under constant questioning. Then, the etiology is a construct built on the analogies supplied by folklore and comparative religion. It is so likely a construct that we hardly notice it, but it remains a construct.[3] It is really only when we get to the prophetic character of Moses' call in 3:9-15 that we are on firm, biblical ground because the story conforms so well with so many other biblical examples.[4]

Where are we in all this? Not really in history for we have no time, no place. Where was Midian? When did Israel formulate the call of Moses in the form of a prophetic call? Without time or place one cannot really

[3] Note Barr (*Bible in the World,* 163) for an example of this problem. He lists five stages of the story in Genesis 2-3 "within the total period of the creation of the OT itself." And only the first, a pre-Israelite tale is called "possible." But the second stage, an Israelite folktale, besides being inaccurate in that more than one tale is involved, is also only a possibility. One hardly dares mention it, but the third stage, J, is also hypothetical. Further, Barr wants to limit the evidence for such divisions to the OT text because to go beyond it to church tradition puts too much of a burden on the scholar. But the evidence is not merely from the OT; it involves folklore and comparative religion (cf. G. Coppens, *La connaissance du bien et du mal et le péché du Paradis. Contribution à l'interprétation de Gen II-III* [ALBO II/3; Louvain: Nauwelerts, 1948]; Karen R. Joines, "The Serpent in Gen 3," *ZAW* 87 [1975] 1-11). If the biblist is to know these things, why not theological tradition as well?

[4] Cf. N. Habel, "The Form and Significance of the Call Narratives," *ZAW* 77 (1965) 297-323; W. Richter, *Die sogenannten vorprophetischen Berufungsberichte* (FRLANT 101; Göttingen: Vandenhoeck und Ruprecht, 1970) 57-131.

speak of history but rather of sociological setting, and in fact the great pioneers of form- and tradition-criticism, though they sought the oral stage antecedent to the documents, were primarily interested in fitting the OT into the general manifestations of man's religious nature. As far as history goes, at least one point would be agreed: the claim that Israel *learned* the divine name. But when and where? At the exodus? When it became Israel? But what do the answers to any of these questions mean, if they could be given?[5] Still, I think we can speak of history in a broad sense. There is a fact, the acquisition of the new divine name, and some vague dating: the acquisition must have occurred in post-patriarchal and pre-monarchical times. This is a very broad dating indeed, but it is a relative position in time if not place.

So far we deal with certain tools of historical-critical method: source-, form-, and tradition-criticism. They have given some help, but things remain vague. So now the scholar turns to philology to ask if there is any evidence for the new name from outside the biblical sphere. Fortunately, we have excellent surveys of most of the material here,[6] and we can merely summarize suggestions. One suggestion is a connection with Indo-European Dyaus (cf. Latin Dyauspiter become Jupiter). If we assume a stage when the D and the S were lost we get YAU and the temptation to connect with *yāhû* and so Yahweh is strong. Such connections are no longer taken seriously.[7] However, there are plenty of other candidates.

There is Old Babylonian *ya(w)um-ilum,* "Yawum is god," but the word is a pronoun, not a name, and the sentence means "God is mine." Exit another candidate. There is *ya-huwa,* "Oh! Him!" an ecstatic cult cry with Arab analogies, but it is hard to see how the pronoun replaced the name of the god who aroused such enthusiasm. There is the use of *ya-* as a nominal preformative that would give Yahweh, "The Effective One," parallel with *yarîb,* "plaintiff," but the preformative is a rarity. Finally, among the simple forms there is a suggested connection with *hwh,* "covet," meaning "The Passionate One." An appropriate enough description of Yahweh, but the root is pejorative in Hebrew—not a likely origin for divine names.

Then there are the sentence-names as possible origins. Amorite names at Mari like *yaḫwi-ilu* or *y̱awi-ilu* or with other divine names like *addu* and

[5] See the discussion of the problems in S. Herrmann, *A History of Israel in Old Testament Times* (London: SCM, 1975) 56-127.

[6] R. Mayer, "Der Gottesname Jahwe im Lichte der neuesten Forschung," *BZ* 2 (1958) 26-53; R. de Vaux, "The Revelation of the Divine Name YHWH," *Proclamation and Presence* (Old Testament Essays in Honour of G. H. Davies; eds. J. J. Durham and J. R. Porter; London: SCM, 1970) 48-75.

[7] Mayer, "Der Gottesname," 32-33.

dagan occur. The suggestion that the first means "Yahweh is El" is hardly tenable unless we wish to hold for a massive syncretism in which Yahweh is Hadad, Dagan, and who knows what else. Besides, these are normal Semitic sentence names meaning "El (Hadad, Dagan) lives/makes live," or "is/makes be." The exact meaning cannot be given because the writing does not always distinguish *hē* from *ḥēth* and *tertiae infirmae* verbs are identical in the qal and hifil forms. The parallel with Akkadian names with *baši/ibašši* may be an argument for seeing here a reference to *hyh,* but it is not decisive. De Vaux objects to connecting these names with Yahweh on further grounds: the parallel is a verb and not a name, but he himself like most others eventually derives the name Yahweh from a verb form, so the objection is not very firm. Further, there are suggestions as to how the move from verb to noun could occur. Hyatt thinks the "god of the fathers" was called *yahwê-N.*, "He makes N (the patriarch) live." When the god became the god of a group, not an individual, the latter's name was dropped and the now unfamiliar verb form was used as a divine name. Cross suggests an original habit of addressing El as *ʾil ḏu yahwī ṣabaʾōt lʾereṣ* etc. in a kind of litany. As El became more of a *deus otiosus* and the name a common noun, the verb was hypostatized into a divine name. The suggestion has the advantage of a tie through Canaan with the Semitic religious world as well as explaining the enigmatic form, Yahweh Sabaoth. It became a fixed phrase with the loss of the non-Hebrew connective in the original litany, so that there is no problem with construct state, etc. Hyatt's idea offers a neat tie-in with the important "god of the fathers."[8]

Even with all this neither Mayer nor de Vaux does justice to West Semitic influence. There is von Soden's cogent suggestion that early Canaanite *yahwi,* "he is, he is known," (cf. Amorite, Ugaritic, Aramaic) is the origin of the name Yahweh. This is supported by the parallel with Akkadian *ibašši* and the emphasis on "being" in the divine name, as we shall see. Then there is much new material in the form of personal names from the Syrian region. Ugaritic *yw.ilt* may be problematic because of the broken text and a possible connection with *ym,* "Sea," a figure of evil and unsuitable for Yahweh. However, there are personal names too. *Bn ʿbdy* occurs along with *ʿbdil, ʿbdilm* and *ʿbdbʿl.* The parallelism as well as the unlikelihood of a gentilic formed from *ʿbd* surely point toward a divine name *y* in the first example. There are similar names formed on other verbs and phrases: *ḏmry/bʿl/hd* and *bdil/y.*[9] Finally, we find a syllabic text which

[8] J. P. Hyatt, "Yahweh as 'the one God of My Father,'" *VT* 5 (1955) 130-36; "Was Yahweh Originally a Creator Deity?" *JBL* 86 (1967) 369-77; F. M. Cross, *Canaanite Myth and Hebrew Epic* (Cambridge: Harvard, 1973) 68-71.

[9] W. von Soden, "Er *ist,* Er erweist sich," *WO* 3 (1966) 177-87; Ugaritic names in C.

seems to clinch things with the name *ben milkiya.*[10] We even have the consonantal value of the apparent divine name. This should reopen the question of Amarna names like Labaya, Biridya and the like.[11] It looks as though we should give serious consideration to Ya as a divine name in 14th century Canaan. And earlier? Ebla has produced a *mi-ka-ya,* "Who is like Ya?" and *en-na-ni-ya,* "Ya has mercy on me," and *ì-ṣi-ya,* "Ya has gone forth."[12] Surely, if the readings hold up, we must reckon with a Ya in the West Semitic pantheon from the earliest times, and it is hard to deny any connection with the biblical divine name.

Such suggestions are, I believe, typical of our science. They fill the commentaries and the articles. We shall return to this and the reasons for it, but now we should simply note some of the immediate problems which the habit raises. One is that most suggestions give a possible origin without meaning—the interpretations of verbal names are an exception—for though there be a Ya, we know nothing about him, though we may hope that further discoveries will bring new light. But even so, the second problem remains: we do not know how Israel came to adopt this strange name, since no plausible replacements for the defunct Kenite and Midianite hypotheses have come forth. We have no time, no place. We are back into comparative religion, the knowledge that Israel like others borrowed divine names and that it belonged to the ancient near eastern *Kulturraum,* things not seriously in doubt anyway. Thirdly, and worst of all, which of the many possible origins are we to choose? There are reasonable arguments for them all and so no special reason for excluding any. Yet they cannot all be true, and one cannot in conscience settle on one and try to develop meaning from it. To be honest one must present and develop the others as well. Historical-critical exegesis becomes a smorgasbord of hypothetical meanings.

One can, of course, avoid this by turning to the reading of the text and leaving the origins to take care of themselves. And there is plenty of such exegesis. There is the suggestion that the sentence, "I am who I am," is actually a refusal to give the divine name so as to keep the mystery of the numen. Hebrew does use such *idem per idem* contructions for this purpose, but here the construction is used to explain a name which is in fact given.

H. Gordon, *Ugaritic Textbook* (AnOr 38; Rome: Pontifical Biblical Institute, 1965) Glossary, 1801, 727, 445.

[10] C. F. A. Schaeffer, *Mission de Ras Shamra* XII (*PRU* VI; ed. J. Nougayrol; Paris: Imprimerie Nationale/C. Klincksieck, 1971) 81, line 14.

[11] F. M. Böhl, *Die Sprache der Amarnabriefe mit besonderer Berücksichtigung der Kanaanismen* (Leipziger semitistische Studien V/2; Leipzig, J. C. Hinrichs, 1909) no. 38, u.

[12] G. Pettinato, "The Royal Archives of Tell-Mardikh—Ebla," *BA* 39 (1976) 50. Much of this information about names comes thanks to my colleague M. Dahood.

It can hardly be read as a refusal. Or the sentence is taken as a true future meaning "I shall really be with you to help." No doubt it has such overtones, but the future of *hyh* always has a predicate, as it must, for "I shall be" used absolutely means that the speaker is not yet in existence, a very unstable platform from which to speak. Finally, best known, at least in the United States, is probably Albright's suggestion: *yahweh ăšer yihweh,* "He causes to be what comes into existence." This will have been the old form from which Yahweh was hypostatized into a name, while the sentence itself was altered to conform to later developments in grammar. The suggestion has the advantage of tying the name into the history of the language, but the disadvantage of demanding emendation, positing an earlier form of the text which as it is cannot be impugned on text-critical grounds.

Moreover, it makes 3:14 primary in the context when it bears every mark of being secondary.[13] Vv 14-15 are overloaded: the divine word is introduced three separate times. Moreover, 15 is the real answer to 13, for it gives the name asked for, while 14a is an explanation, and 14b a link to tie 15 to 13. One point about the expansion created by 14 is clear even before its meaning is understood: the Hebrew ear would hear the repeated assonance, *ʾehyeh—ʾehyeh—ʾehyeh—yahweh* (merely as sound the *waw* in the latter is simple dissimilation of *yod* to *waw* for the sake of sonority and does not really break the spell of the repetition[14]). The repeated sound has by mere suggestion tied Yahweh to *hyh* irrevocably.

This is emphasized by the old form of the sentence in 14a. As is well known the simple verb "to be" is not used as a copula even with "relative" clauses. The normal form would be *ʾănî hûʾ ʾăšer ʾehyeh*, but here the desire to keep drilling in *hyh* has led to the change which repeats the verb. Thus the discussion between Schild and Albrektson is really solved in terms of style. Albrektson may be right in terms of normal grammar: "I am he who is" would be *ʾănî hûʾ ʾăšer ʾehyeh,* but the need to emphasize the connection between Yahweh and *hyh* has led to altering the normal form, repeating the verb and so by the surprise of the unusual form and the repetition making the text's point all the more strongly, as Schild held.[15]

[13] See M. Noth (*2. Mose* [ATD 5; Göttingen; Vandenhoeck und Ruprecht, 1959] 30) and G. Fohrer (*Uberlieferung und Geschichte des Exodus* [BZAW 91; Berlin: Töpelmann, 1964]40) for the structure of these verses.

[14] So Noth, *2. Mose,* 30.

[15] For the discussion see E. Schild ("On Exodus iii 14—'I Am That I Am,'" *VT* 4 [1954] 296-302), seconded by J. Lindblom ("Noch einmal die Deutung des Jahwe-Namens in Ex. 3, 14," *ASTI* 3 [1964] 4-15) and attacked in B. Albrektson ("On the Syntax of *ʾehyeh ʾăšer ʾehyeh* in Exodus 3:14," *Words and Meanings* [Essay presented to D. W. Thomas; eds. P. R. Ackroyd and B. Lindars; Cambridge: Cambridge University, 1968] 15-28). It is interesting that while all the later commentaries keep the traditional "I am who am" translation, they all admit that the Schild-Lindblom case is not to be rejected out of hand.

I would add that the point of the question in 3:13, to justify Moses before the people, makes the emphasis through the repetition all the more fitting. Moses is given as that justification the very divine name; that is, in ancient thinking, the revelation of the divine personality and a share in the divine power. Hence the addition of 14 could well be the work of E itself, developing its call narrative (vv 9-15) with emphasis on the overwhelming importance of Moses' call. To him is given not merely revelation and office but the very divine name and its special explanation. Thus the form emphasizes the style: Yahweh *really* is, "I am who am," or better (see above), "he who is."

And now the fur begins to fly. This is to introduce alien, even Greek, ideas into the Hebrew. Fortunately we are rather more free now from the silly Hebrew-Greek dichotomy, but it is still well to be sure. Of course, the text is not "Greek"; it is pre-metaphysical. It seems safe to leave it at this: Yahweh *is* above all others and this means active and helping, for being and acting effectively were not separated.[16]

Beyond a doubt this is the way in which the Bible itself points. So in Hos 1:9 Yahweh will turn away from a people who deserts Him (*lōʾ-ʾehyeh lākem,* a phrase which certainly gives the meaning of the word in relation to Yahweh, whether it is a direct allusion to Exod 3:14 or not). In the sophisticated reworking of the call narrative by P in Exod 6:2-8 the divine name has a key role. Not merely is it revealed, an honor granted to Moses over the Patriarchs, but it is an essential structural feature in a passage in which Yahweh responds to Egypt's oppression of Israel with a speech of condemnation, a display of His sovereign power: He is Yahweh and so will deal with Egypt.[17] The one who is acts.

I would see something of this even in Wis 13:1, that is, in a document strongly influenced by Greek thought, for the parallelism equates "The One Who is" (*ton onta*) with the "The Creator" (*ton technitēn*). That is, Being is creator, directly active in the world without mention of the intermediaries characteristic of Greek thought.[18] Finally, the Johannine "I am" (8:58) is based directly on the prophets, particularly Deutero-Isaiah according to current opinion. Still, no one who knew the LXX could read this and fail to recall Exod 3:14 along with the great emphasis on Jesus' works in this gospel (e.g., 5:17; 9:4; 10:25, 38).

[16] See de Vaux, "Revelation of the Name YHWH," 66.

[17] M. Oliva, "Revelacion del nombre de Yahweh en la 'Historia sacerdotal,'" *Bib* 52 (1971) 1-19.

[18] Contra de Vaux ("Revelation of the Name YHWH," 70) who sees merely a contrast between God who is and creatures who are not, without an active relation of the first to the second.

My point, of course, is that the text exists in itself and can, indeed must, be read as it is. In such a reading, no matter what the possible origins of the texts or parts of it may be, the emphasis on *hyh* is there. Further, the text has a history. It remains and works on later thinking. This develops the meaning, and it can be controlled in the texts which relate to it. There is no need to fall back on hypotheses as the pre-histories of the text inevitably do. We have seen this in the biblical developments of the revelation of the divine name, but the history naturally goes much beyond this.

The passage "served as the proof text for Christian ontology," and though this may at times have led to an emphasis on static being, there was still plenty of play for the active aspect: God gave because He supremely was.[19] Indeed, as one notices the emphasis on the "economy," the works of creation and salvation, as the means by which the Greek Fathers especially developed their ideas of the divine nature, the reverse almost seems true. It was the divine activity which reveals the being. With Augustine the effort to find some light on the Trinity led almost to the claim that God was so much being that activity had to come, at least thought and love *ad intra.* Anselm in the *Monologium* develops similar ideas. For Bernard God is Active: ". . . Amat ut charitas . . . dominatur ut maiestas . . . operatur ut virtus . . . quae omnia . . . facimus et nos, sed longe inferiore modo . . . quod participamus; Deus autem hoc ipso quod est, ait enim: Ego sum qui sum." So also for Catherine of Siena: "Nostin' filia quis sim ego, quae tu? . . . Ego sum is qui sum: tu es illa quae non es. Filia cogita de me, et ego cogitabo de te, semperque curam tui geram."[20] These are largely spiritual writers, but Bonaventure, *Breviloquium* 5.2,3, is eloquent on the divine *esse* as a principle of activity, and there is the Thomist principle that *agere sequitur esse.* For later evidence, particularly from the reformers one can consult Childs (*Exodus,* pp. 85-86) to learn that they continued the patristic and medieval tradition.

Thus the church did *not* substitute a static "Greek" for an active "Hebrew" notion of God in theology or spirituality. It developed the biblical datum in the light of useful philosophical principles, e.g., being is good, and goodness tends to give of itself. The text has a history not only in the scriptures but in the Church, and this has not falsified but enriched the meaning of the text. Whether this is a result of the stimulus given by the text to independent development or of painstaking exegesis is a matter which need not concern us now. Whatever its mode of knowing, the tradi-

[19] See J. Pelikan, *The Christian Tradition* 1 (The Emergence of the Catholic Tradition [100-600]; Chicago/London: University of Chicago, 1971) 54, 53, 204.

[20] Quoted from Cornelius a Lapide, *Commentaria in Scripta Sacra* 1 (Naples: Nagar, 1854) 295-96.

tion displays an understanding of the text.

We began with various evidences for the problems in the integration of scripture and theology in our day. We have tried to examine a test case. Can we draw any conclusions? To me they would be the following:

1. Though the historical-critical method has been admirable, it is also no longer very productive theologically. This is true for at least two reasons. Its work is largely done in disabusing the church of a too-easily accepted literal reading which saw the OT as the unified and relatively simple work of a few authors. It has thus eliminated misunderstanding and opened the way to more fruitful study where it was very necessary. However, its very success has raised a second problem. Historical criticism has become an end in itself. It is a constant search for hypothetic historical referents or for sources where the material at hand is simply insufficient to allow anything but highly speculative results.[21] As a basis for theological (or other) developments it has become a foundation of sand. Contrary to what I have heard said, it is perfectly possible to understand a text without knowing whether it is E or whatever. If I insist on a documentary setting, or an historical setting in which the text was composed, I am often, even usually, tied to pure hypothesis: the connection with a source is dubious, the existence of the source (E) is in question. In any case the historical setting of the passage's composition is largely a guess. And still the text itself in its most important setting, its actual place in scripture, lies before me to study as a grammatical and literary structure that I can analyze with some confidence without beginning with a chancy guess about origins.

We can write a reasonably complete and accurate history of Israelite literature, one to keep us from gross anachronisms and the like, and this we must have. Once again, we must make use of the positive results of historical-critical investigation. Why, then, are we still trapped in this approach to our work as though it were the only one? I estimate that ninety-five percent of the books I see submitted to *Biblica* for review analyze sources, review historical problems for which the data do not allow an answer, or present historical reconstructions of events necessarily unclear to us. I suggest that one reason is that it is the easy way out; doing what one can be trained to do according to rules recognized and acceptable in academe. With increasing specialization and narrowing of training we are unconsciously following the Romantic faith in history: the original, the primitive, is somehow the untainted truth. One need only note the com-

[21] Since writing this I find the same idea expressed by "The Sensus Literalis of Scripture: An Ancient and Modern Problem," Brevard S. Childs, *Beiträge zur alttestamentlichen Theologie* (Festschrift für W. Zimmerlis 70. Geburtstag; eds. H. Donnor, R. Hanhart, R. Smend; Göttingen: Vandenhoeck und Ruprecht, 1977) 90-91.

mon attitude toward the prophets: the authentic work of Isaiah or Ezekiel is the really valuable thing; the addition is chaff often omitted in a commentator's translation. Why does a collector, an expander, an unknown poet, have to be unimportant because he is anonymous and later?

2. This is no attack on historical and critical study as such. It is necessary, though it need not overwhelm our science. However, I suggest that authors be clear about what they are doing. If they are using the Bible as one among many ancient Near Eastern sources let them say so. If they are trying to reconstruct an obscure episode within scripture or some original form of a document or oracle, again let them say so. So too when the object is to get behind the text through form-criticism or tradition-history. So too when one rewrites a text to reconstruct the original form through philological methods. All this belongs to history, an honorable study. Let it by all means go on, but let us not mistake it for exegesis pure and simple. Nor should we insist on moving from historical reconstruction to wider interpretation, a move more insecure at every step because it begins with hypothesis and adds hypotheses as it goes on.

Moreover, we should realize that the insistence on history, whether of possible events or institutions, can and does impoverish our reading of the text in many ways. For example, in our test case we found Moses' call reinterpreted in Exod 6:2-8 as a judgment oracle which Oliva, the scholar cited, sees as the immediate reply in P to the plaint in 2:23-25. No doubt, but it is this no longer. It is now reassurance for Moses after his own failure and plaint in chap. 5. The edited narrative adds to the original: Yahweh does not merely help the oppressed, he turns setbacks into triumphs, and guarantees support for his chosen.[22] If it is exciting to compare the different theologies of the sources, it is no less so to see what can be made by reworking them, and it just might be more important, for this is the text which has worked to make our world.

3. The object of exegesis, then, is primarily the text as it stands, not possible origins or historical referent. The founders of criticism could not see this. For them the one truth was truth of historical reference. They lived in an age intoxicated with the triumphs of a new scientific movement and sceptical of the literary.[23] But we have come to know again that literature has its own truth and that it can make demands on us. This is surely

[22] On the richness added by constant re-editing see D. J. McCarthy, S.J., "Personality, Society, and Inspiration," *TS* 24 (1963) 553-76.

[23] On the very limited concept of truth in back of much criticism, see H. W. Frei (*The Eclipse of Biblical Narrative* [New Haven/London: Yale University, 1974]); on diffidence in the literary, W. K. Wimsatt, Jr. and Cleanth Brooks (*Literary Criticism: A Short History* [London: Routledge & Kegan Paul, 1957] 221-51).

true of classics. The *Iliad* demands that I face human problems of war and honor though I know nothing of its setting in the Achaean colonization of Asia Minor or of its historical referent in 13-12th century Troy. Or the *Aeneid* faces me with the problems of duty and destiny whether or not I know what the poem owes to the propaganda for the Augustan settlement. Or Shakespeare: I need know little about the War of the Roses and the Tudor settlement to be faced with the problem of ambition and disorder in *Macbeth*.

In our culture the Bible is a classic and makes like demands. Further, as the book of the believing community its demands are more insistent. It was formed by and is formative of the community. It is, therefore, in whatever form is canonical for the community, normative. Its antecedents are not normative though they may help explain it; nor is its general setting in comparative religion normative, though some knowledge of this should induce humility in communities which felt unique. None of this but the text itself is normative.

Thus, from this point of view, it matters little whence the name Yahweh came. The point is the close connection with *hyh*. Or again, as we have seen, it is not the fact that Exod 6:2-8 developed as a reply to a popular complaint that matters, but that it has been integrated into a larger text that throws light on Moses' mission and God's intentions.[24] Of course, to repeat from another angle what has already been emphasized (see above, no. 1, on respecting the history we know), work on the text must use the assured results of historical scholarship. Moses, for example, is not usually a real second millennium figure but the person the writers have chosen and developed as their protagonist. However, there is little danger of forgetting this; we can presume it and get on to the text.

4. The way in which this reading took place within the Church's traditions calls for special notice. We have seen tradition developing and enriching meaning. Moreover, it means that the Bible and its traditional interpretation is somehow authoritative—even in ages rebellious to authority. Eventually they must submit to it, not it to them. This means that the exegete must be at home in the tradition.[25] Thus the fact of authority

[24] Biblists should be more careful sometimes in dealing with the author's intention as they go behind the text to "what the author really meant." The author meant what is said in the text and it is erroneous to find intentions not in the text. Cf. W. K. Wimsatt, Jr. and M. C. Beardsley, "The Intentional Fallacy," *An Introduction to Literary Criticism* (Marlies Danziger and W. S. Johnson, eds.; Boston: Heath, 1961) 246-62 (reprinted from *The Verbal Icon: Studies in the Meaning of Poetry* [Lexington, KY: University of Kentucky, 1954]). Doubtless we can know something of the mind of Paul, but doubtless he changed his mind too, and it is dangerous to argue from his "mind" when it is not derived from his immediate text.

[25] See Gilkey, *Naming the Whirlwind*, 460, point no. 1.

is there. No one wants to return to denominational quarrels or deny what has always been the case: the variety within Christian theology even within denominations. However, if theology is to have any shape, any continuity with the Christian community, it must accept the authority of scripture and theological tradition.[26] When the Bible becomes just another book, fun to interpret perhaps for a time and then just a "great book," biblical studies will be on their way to joining the ancient classics in oblivion.

Finally, I must conclude by taking note of a possible difficulty. Christianity claims to be special: it is not merely a revelation of truths but a claim that God has intervened by specific actions even unto the Incarnation within our world. Does my suggestion that exegetical work need not be historical work go against this? After all, historical-critical study was largely motivated by the desire to show that the claim and its theological development was or was not true. Well, by all means let the debate continue, but for me the problem is apologetic and not exegetic, and I leave it to the apologetic theologians, though at the moment I admit that it is hard to find them. Nor, to be honest, can I see any great problem here. Historians of the ancient world, non-biblists and non-believers often enough, usually have no problems with using the OT, including the exodus and the settlement in some form, and the NT, including the teachings of Jesus, as good historical sources. Problems arise for us biblists because we demand more history (and less theology) than the text can give. But to repeat, my concern is not apologetic. Indeed, if we could offer a more exciting and more pertinent theological exegesis, I doubt that the apologetic problem would be so acute.

[26] For a contrary view see Barr, *Bible in the World,* 28-29.

The Uses of *wᵉhinnēh* in Biblical Hebrew

Standard grammars, e.g., Meyer 89.2; 113.3a, simply present *hinnēh* and *wᵉhinnēh* as deictic particles without expatiating on their use, though the usually exiguous sections on syntax in those grammars often treat the other ancient deictics, *'im* and *kî*. This is recognition of the need to remember various possibilities covered more simply in ancient Hebrew when we try to understand and transpose so foreign an idiom into our modern minds and languages, but the problem is passed over with respect to (*wᵉ*)*hinnēh*. This is unfortunate for the student who thus has no easy means to verify an intuition, to tell whether an interpretation is possible. Even professionals have difficulties with nuances, as a comparison of parallel passages from any set of modern translations will verify.

It seems useful, then, to attempt a systematic list of the possible nuances of *wᵉhinnēh* constructions lacking in the grammars and lexica. We keep ourselves to *wᵉhinnēh* for a simple reason: the field is more limited than that with *hinnēh* so that it is possible to keep within a convenient compass a thorough survey, "thorough survey" here meaning a check of all significant uses (not all cited), significant for us, that is, which means not touching the ordinary deictic use and the use with verbs of perception which are already dealt with in grammars and lexica, e.g., Meyer 104.3b.

The limited effort is vindicated by the fact that a wide sampling indicates that the same nuances characterize the use of simple *hinnēh*. Further, C. J. Labaschagne, studying *hēn*, *hinnēh* and *wᵉhinnēh* finds no special distinction in their uses (1).

(1) "The Particles *hēn* and *hinnēh*", *OTS* 18 (1973) 1-15. Other important literature: L. Alonso Schökel, "Nota estilística sobre la partícula *hinnēh*", *Bib* 37 (1956) 74-80; J. Blau, "Adverbia als psychologische und grammatische Subjekte/Praedikate im Bibelhebräisch", *VT* 9 (1959) 130-137; B. O. Long, "Reports of Visions among the Prophets", *JBL* 95 (1976) 353-365; K. Oberhuber, "Zur Syntax des Richterbuches", *VT* 3 (1953) 5, 10; W. Richter, "Traum und Traumdeutung im AT. Ihre Form und Verwendung", *BZ* 7 (1963) 202-220.

Labaschagne's work is helpful, but it leaves room for more — hence this inquiry. For one thing, he describes only three categories with the particles, temporal, conditional and concessive (2). Further, for him the particles "...developed in the direction of full-grown conjunctions..." and "...are more than once used as conjunctions". There is no problem for me, as there is with some, about the continued use of classical grammatical terms for Hebrew. Indeed, I shall use them myself. However, I am not sure *wᵉhinnēh* ever declines to the level of a mere connective. There is an emotional overtone when it is used (3). The user is moved about the connection, not neutral toward it, and the connective colors the thing connected. English offers a useful semantic parallel. Take the sentences: "Look! Uncle Joe is coming. We'll go!". This can reassure, say a child anxious to be off, and so be equivalent to "*When* Uncle Joe comes etc." without the force of the colloquial original. It can imply doubt: "*If* Uncle Joe etc.". It can explain — perhaps Uncle Joe has the family automobile — and equal "*Because* Uncle Joe etc.". It can even express a purpose: perhaps Uncle Joe is not a favorite so that it implies: "*To avoid* Uncle Joe we'll go away!". And so on. The exclamatory expressions can imply very different things. We identify them by the tone of voice, or, in reading, from the very large English linguistic context we possess (and even so cannot always read aright) but, alas, lack for biblical Hebrew. In all this the expression remains exclamatory with an emotional note and we miss the language-user's full meaning if we simply *equate* the sentences with the suggested temporal or conditional or causal or purpose clauses. We get the meaning but not the feeling, and the two must be grasped to get the full force of the language. So it is with *wᵉhinnēh* in biblical Hebrew: it usually carries an overtone of feeling. It also keeps a connection with verbs of perception often but by no means always, and when there is a connection it is by no means always as the "noun clause" describing the thing perceived. It is as though it liked an old neighbor but insisted on new ties as well.

In classifying the uses of *wᵉhinnēh* I use the categories of traditional grammar. They are familiar and they are the categories of

(2) See also T. Lambdin, *Introduction to Biblical Hebrew* (London 1973) no. 132.2, emphasizing the importance of *wᵉhinnēh* in expressing circumstances, but without any elaboration of details.

(3) Cf. Alonso Schökel, "Nota estilística", 74.

the grammars, lexica etc. we all still use. There are problems with these categories, as everyone recognizes, but they are useful too, if for no other reason than that in struggling to fit language into these logical categories we are forced to think about what we are saying or reading or translating. However, this very logic tells us that we are not dealing with formal logical constructions but with living language in which various nuances are carried, though we perceive a principal meaning and give it a name. So we shall find ourselves discussing some passages under more than one heading or insisting on subordinate values within the main category. This does not indicate doubt as to meaning so much as richness of meaning, the nuances we have spoken of. Finally, though using the classical categories, I have avoided the catch-all term "circumstantial clause" which simply avoids the issue. *All* "subordinate clauses" deal with the circumstances of the principal! The question is: What is the precise kind of circumstance here? And now to the classifications.

1) *Excited perception.* It is widely recognized that *w^ehinnēh* introduces the "object clause" after *rā'āh* and such verbs. Here we are concerned with special cases where the emotional tone is so strong that we cannot treat the sentence as a simple statement of fact. One widespread example is the solemn divine gift of vision or dream where *w^ehinnēh* introduces the awesome sight (4).

Sometimes there is an element of wonder or the like so great that we have to supply words in translation to get the feel of the verb and simple *w^ehinnēh*. In 1 Kgs 10,6-7 the queen of Sheba tell Solomon that she could not believe the reports of his wisdom and wealth "until I came and saw with my eyes that the half had not been told (qatal? participle?) me". Seeing is believing, and the queen is saying: "When I saw for myself I was astonished, your accomplishments really are underrated!". Here the verb of perception (*rā'āh*) is expressed and we have to feel its augmented force. It need not be: the particle alone expresses deeply moving perception.

Gn 15,17b (*w^ehinnēh* plus noun sentence) is still in the area of the dream vision. Abraham is enveloped in mystic darkness "and

(4) See the long studies of RICHTER, "Traum und Traumdeutung", and LONG, "Reports of Visions", showing that *w^ehinnēh* is an essential feature of the dream or vision report, introducing the climax, the wonder seen.

actually saw (*wᵉhinnēh*) a smoking stove and a firebrand", but the elaborate structure of the dream report worked out by Richter is missing. All that remains of the genre are awesome circumstances and awed perception. There is no special reason to see here a breaking-up of the dream report form. It is rather an example of the tendency of a verb or, as here, circumstances implying perception to educe *wᵉhinnēh*.

Other examples: 1 Sm 30,3: "David and his band came to the city *wᵉhinnēh śᵉrûpâ bā'ēš*". The impact is strong: the elated victors return — to find themselves ruined. One can put this into English without using a verb: "When David and his men came to the city, there were only burnt ruins", and the bald statement is quite effective (5). However, even it implies perception, and most versions quite properly tell us explicitly that the group found something, and found it to their consternation. Jgs 3,25bβ has *wᵉhinnēh* with participles and means: "to their horror they found their lord lying dead". 1 Kgs 3,21a (with participle) expresses the same thing. 2 Kgs 7,5bβ, a noun sentence: when the lepers reach the center of the Aramaean camp to their surprise they found there no man (*wᵉhinnēh 'ên–šām 'îš*)! The emotion is emphasized when they report the experience (10aβ) with the addition "nor heard a human voice!" There is something eerie in their surprise, the emotion augments.

In this emotive use, as often, *wᵉhinnēh* has an affinity for the participle, but it also stands with noun sentences and perhaps qatal.

2) *Cause.* In Jgs 18,9 the Danite spies encourage their tribe to move "for (*kî*) we have seen the (new) land and it is really (*wᵉhinnēh*) very fine (noun sentence)". Here *wᵉhinnēh* parallels and continues causal *kî*. It is not simply because they have seen the land that the spies urge taking it; it is really *because* it is good.

In Nm 17,11-12 *wᵉhinnēh* practically replaces *kî*. Moses instructs Aaron to begin atoning action "because (*kî*)" the LORD is angry and "the plague has begun". In reporting Aaron's response the LORD's anger is passed over and it is "because (*wᵉhinnēh*) the plague has begun (qatal)" that he hurries to purify the folk. One can see the emotional aspect: Aaron acts in a hurry (*wayyārāṣ*) because

(5) E. WATERMAN in *The Bible: An American Translation*, edd. J. M. POWIS SMITH and E. J. GOODSPEED (Chicago 1939). Of the other versions consulted only *La Sacra Bibbia*, ed. S. GAROFALO (Turin 1966) avoids a verb.

of the danger, and *wehinnēh* is the appropriate particle for the tense situation.

In Gn 37,29 Reuben returns to the pit to save Joseph "and because Joseph was not in the pit (*wehinnēh 'ên-yôsēp babbôr*) he rent his clothes" in despair. Joseph's absence causes the grief. In Jgs 3,25a Ehud's courtiers wait outside his roof chamber until they are uneasy "because he had still not opened (*wehinnēh 'ênennû pōtēaḥ*) the doors": his inaction causes their feeling and consequent action. In 1 Sm 25,36 "when Abigail returned... since (*wehinnēh*) Nabal was holding a royal banquet and he was mighty drunk (noun sentences), she told him nothing...". Nabal's drunken feast caused Abigail's silence—and we notice not merely the event but also Nabal's special ability to arouse emotion, irritation.

1 Kgs 2,8aα is interesting. David is giving a series of death-bed instructions, explaining each: "You know of Joab's murders; therefore deal with him (5-6), treat Barzillai's sons well since (*kî*) they helped me when a fugitive (7), but since (*wehinnēh*) you have Shimei in your power (noun sentence) and it was he who cursed me then, deal with him (8-9)". It is not only Shimei's fault but the accident (?) of his presence (a living curse, a pollution?) which permits, nay demands, that punishment be visited upon him. This is clearly a border case. The accident of presence is hard to see as a cause in the strict sense, but it is at least an occasion *and* in the context it parallels other causes. Perhaps we are at the limit illustrated by the next category, "occasional clauses".

In all events, *wehinnēh* with noun sentence, qatal and participle does express causality.

3) *Occasion.* There is no agreed term in classical grammar for what is in question here. There is, of course, the "circumstantial clause", a term which explains everything and so nothing (6). Sentences with *wehinnēh* indicate not just time or place or motive or cause but also opportunity, an *occasion which triggers another action.*

(6) B. Gildersleeve and G. Lodge, *Gildersleeve's Latin Grammar* (Boston, New York, Chicago 31894) no. 585, Remark, dealing with "Historical *cum*" do note: "The circumstantiality often appears as causality, but sometimes the exact shade cannot be distinguished". I.e., they touch the problem, as other grammarians usually do not, but even so they offer no designation for the type of expression in question.

The ambiguity of Joab's words in 2 Sm 18,11 is a good place to begin discussion: it illustrates the complexity of the matter. Is he saying with force that *when* the soldier had the chance to kill Absolom he should have acted? Or is it *if*, with a snear of doubt not really aimed at the claim of discovery but at the soldier's courage? Or is he simply saying that he had the opportunity, the *occasion* to make his fortune and he missed? Without the tone of voice to indicate nuances to the listener or the mass of literature which provides analogous signals for the discerning reader, neither of which we can have here, it is hard to choose among the possibilities. The reader must depend on intuition. It is a moment of great importance and Joab is the supremely efficient and ruthless leader. One doubts that he is interested in the point of time or the soldier's character. He sees opportunity. He is aghast at the man's simplicity: "You actually had the chance? For God's sake, why didn't you finish the menace off?". Surely something like this is this realist's meaning.

Other examples are easier. In Jgs 7,17 Gideon's arrival (*wehinnēh ʼānōkî bāʼ*: qatal?) amid the Midianite camp is the signal which triggers his men's action. It does not simply mark the point in time or place for an action; it brings on the action. Or Jgs 9,33: Zebul tells Abimelech "...make an ambush against the city and as he (i.e., the rebel Gaal) and the people... rush toward you (*wehinnēh-hûʼ wehāʽām... yōsîm ʼēlêkā*) deal with him as best you can". Once again, it is not merely a question of when or where the conspirators act. The *way* they act opens up the opportunity for counteraction! One can hardly speak of causality, but there is more than merely temporal or local specification; there is the occasion for further action.

Gn 37,7 offers a number of different nuances of *wehinnēh* constructions: "While (*wehinnēh*) we were binding sheaves (participle) in the field, when (*wehinnēh*) my sheave rose and stood erect (qatal, two times), then (*wehinnēh*) your sheaves stood around (yiqtol) mine and bowed down (waw consecutive with yiqtol: GK, 107b) to it". Doubtless all the particles "point", but in rather different directions. The first is the common case of indicating general circumstances, and the last indicates a result. The first meaning is too common to need discussion; the third we will meet in its place. It is the second *wehinnēh* construction (7aβ) which is to the point. The elevation of Joseph's sheave is a symbol. Behind lies future reality, Joseph's greatness, but here it is still *symbol* and so it can but give the *signal*, occasion the obeisance of the others. The *cause* of their humility lies in the future; the symbol is the present occasion for their present symbolic submission. Symbols occasion things based on deeper realities to come.

A final example: 1Kgs 19,11aα, "Stand... as (*wᵉhinnēh*) I pass by (participle)". It seems a simple directive, but in fact Elijah must recognize the passing. Only when he discerns the real thing can he actually act as directed.

There are, then, situations where *wᵉhinnēh* with the participle, yiqtol or qatal indicates the occasion for further action.

4) *Condition*. Notice Lv 13,5. There is a verb of perception, but *wᵉhinnēh* does not introduce the complement, the object directly looked, at as it often does. Rather the object is a pronoun suffix: "After seven days the priest shall look at him, and if (*wᵉhinnēh*) in his view the disease is checked (qatal)... the priest shall shut him up for seven days more". There is a connection with perception, but in fact the matter introduced by *wᵉhinnēh* may not be perceived. It is a nuance on the nature of the perception: given a certain condition, do this.

The next example also concerns investigation. Dt 13,15-17 takes up the case of a city suspected of apostasy. The whole Hebrew community is to investigate with care and "if the matter is established as true (*wᵉhinnēh ʾemet nākôn haddābār*: 15)", they are to put the place under the ban. Dt 17,4-5 uses the same language of determining individual apostasy. There is a verb of perception (*ḥāqar*) connected with the *wᵉhinnēh* sentence in 1 Sam 20,12, but still the particle (with a noun sentence) introduces the condition under which Jonathan will act, not the simple object of perception.

In 1 Sm 9,7 *wᵉhinnēh* introduces a condition with yiqtol where there is no question of a verb of perception. Saul is arguing with his servant's suggestion to seek a seer's advice, asking: "If we go, what is there to bring to the man?". It might be called a concessive statement, a subdivision of the condition, but in any case it is a kind of condition, and the ambiguity points up our problem of nuances.

In all these examples, in fact, one may ask how much is due to the indirect influence of the idea of perception, what is due to the concessive-adversative element and so on. But whatever other things are at work the examples do contain a conditional element: *only if* the diseased spot is unchanged is the priest to continue quarantine; *only if* the town or person is guilty is there to be punishment; *only if*

Saul is friendly is Jonathan to act in a certain way; *only if* Saul finds the seer does the question of fee arise (7). In part this is the problem of turning Hebrew into our thought patterns; in part it is the problem of all classifications of language: they must emphasize one nuance if they are to be classes, but they do not exclude other nuances, and one must be careful to remember this in applying any categories.

In all events, there are certainly cases where *wᵉhinnēh* with qatal, participle or yiqtol can properly be called conditional.

5) *Concession.* We have noted the concessive element in 1 Sam 9,7. In 2 Kgs 7,19 the king's officer had sneared at the prediction of immediate relief from famine in besieged Samaria: "Even if the LORD were to open (*wᵉhinnēh yhwh ʿōśeh*) sluices in the heavens" the prophecy could not be true. The alternation of *hinnēh* and *wᵉhinnēh* is patent here too, for v. 19 is the narrative repetition of the original dialogue in v. 2 where the officer is made to say *hinnēh yhwh ʿōśeh.* Further, the nuanced use of the particle is emphasized by the formulation of the prophet's answer to the snear in v. 19: "Look you (*hinnᵉkā*)! You'll see it but not eat!". In another example, Ez 17,18, Judah's king is condemned: "He has despised an oath in breaking covenant even though he had given his hand to it (*wᵉhinnēh nātan yādô*)".

wᵉhinnēh is thus used with participle or qatal to express a concessive sense.

6) *Time.* The temporal use is common. Gn 24,15 has *wayᵉhî ... ṭerem ... wᵉhinnēh*: "He had not *yet* finished speaking *when* Rebekah came out (participle). *wayᵉhî ... wᵉhinnēh* in 1 Sm 13,10, "*at the moment* he had finished offering the holocaust, *right then* Samuel came (participle)" complements 10,8, "go down before me to Gilgal and then I shall go down (*wᵉhinnēh ʾānōki yōrēd*) to you to offer holocausts". Saul has sinned by acting a fraction too precipitously. In Gn 18,10 the LORD promises to return in a year's time (*kāʿēt ḥayyâ*) and by then (*wᵉhinnēh*) Sarah will have a son (noun sentence). In

(7) LABASCHAGNE (see n. 1), 5-9, deals extensively with the particles in a conditional sense. His work answers the problem raised in Joüon, 167 1, n. 1: there are too many examples of *wᵉhinnēh* with conditional meaning to be able to deny it, even though one cannot accept all Labaschagne's examples as true conditions. Joüon deals with too few cases.

all the examples the parallel with another word indicating time points up the temporal meaning of the *wehinnēh* formulation.

This is not always the case, and whether it is or not we should note the nuances which, while still temporal, are more complex. Thus Gn 24,30: "When (*wayehi*) he (Laban) saw the rings... and heard what Rebekah, his sister, said... he went off to the man (who was) *still* standing (*wehinnēh ʿōmēd*) with the camels by the well". Laban is so eager he catches his man before he had time even to change his stance! Time, place and an attitude are all marked out for us. Jos 9,13b emphasizes a new, present state brought about by a supposedly long passage of time: the Gibeonites claim to have filled new wineskins when they set out "but now (*wehinnēh*: note the parallel with 12b, *weʿattâ hinnēh*: here *wehinnēh* alone serves to give the sense) they are frayed (qatal)". Time and result march together.

Nm 20,16 is interesting. For one thing, with 15 it forms the earliest example of the "historical credo": the fathers went down into Egypt and the people suffered there (15), but they cried to the LORD who heard them and sent his angel to bring them out (16a, a series of four narrative wayyiqtol) "and at last (*wehinnēh*) we are in Kadesh... (16b). The finish of the journey to the edge of the Land is strikingly emphasized by the switch from the flowing narrative tenses to assertion: "Now we are here!" (*wehinnēh* with noun sentence). The end of the journey is marked by a rhetorical climax. This is temporal with tone of purpose, result and, especially, relief!

A real border case appears in 1 Sm 25,20. When Abigail was riding hidden by the mountain "right then David and his men were coming down toward her (*wehinnēh ... yōrdîm liqrāʾtāh*)". By accident at just the same time? The episode concludes: "and she met them", noncomitally enough. Still these are Abigail and David, a clever pair indeed, so that one inclines to see purpose. But their very cleverness would aim at keeping up appearances and so at a "chance" meeting with both just happening to be there at that time. Once again nuances: a meeting may be purposed but be made to appear a mere matter of timing.

Other examples: 2 Sm 18,31: "When (*wehinnēh*) the Cushite arrived (qatal? participle?), he said ..."; 1 Kgs 1,42: "At the very moment he spoke Jonathan arrived". The Hebrew has two independent but linked phrases: "As he (*ʿōdennû*) was speaking, then (*wehinnēh*) Jonathan came (participle? qatal?)". Contrast 1,22 where *wᵉhinnēh* simply reinforces the temporal particle *ʿôd* plus participle instead of being played off against it in a separate member to mark an exact moment. One can see the deictic moving from a subordinate to an independent role as a marker for time. Finally, 1 Kgs 13,25: "When (*wᵉhinnēh*) people came (participle), they found ...".

Normally in temporal uses *wᵉhinnēh* has a participle, but qatal and noun sentence occur.

7) *Purpose.* As anyone who struggled with *ne* and *ut non* in Latin knows, purpose and result are not easily kept apart in mind or speech. After all, our results are sometimes our purposes! So also in Hebrew: often one may argue what is purpose and what is result. Still, there are some *wᵉhinnēh* sentences clearly expressing purpose.

In 2 Sm 3,12b Abner proposes a covenant with David "so that I may work with you to bring all Israel over to you (*wᵉhinnēh yādî ʿimmāk lᵉhāsēb ʾēlêkô ʾet–kôl–yiśrāʾēl*)". The disgruntled general from the north has a purpose in mind and he is ready to work to realize it: purpose for such a man is to bring result.

2 Sm 15,32 has David at the top of the mount "where they worship God *and there came* (*wᵉhinnēh*) to meet him (infinitive) Hushai ...". The man has come there on purpose to join his fleeing king and he must be persuaded to turn to another, more useful purpose.

1 Kgs 18,7 illustrates a special difficulty about purpose in Biblical Hebrew. We can guess at human purposes, even know our own or those explained to us. But this is a book about divine dealings with mankind and the LORD's ways are not our ways. So "when Obadiah was on the road there appeared before him Elijah (*wᵉhinnēh ʾēliyyāhû liqrāʾtô*)", and Obadiah is worried. He fears the spirit may snatch Elijah away and the disappearance will cause him trouble with the king. Elijah is a mere instrument of divine forces, moved as they will have it, and there is a mighty purpose in what he does and says. The trouble is that the purpose is the mysterious aim of providence, and it may well be opaque to a mere human, even a pious one who therefore finds it haphazard and frightening. Still it is purpose, and the construction, paralleling 2 Sm 3,12b and 15,32, emphasizes this. What is a haphazard result of being on the road for the man is a purpose with God.

A final example: 2 Sm 16,1, *wᵉhinnēh sîbāʾ ... liqrāʾtô.* Siba has a clear purpose: to help David — and feather his own nest.

All these "purpose clauses" have the infinitive with *w^ehinnēh*. The deictic reinforces a standard meaning of the verb form (GK, 114 f-g). This is an example of that problem of categories. We should hardly speak of "clauses" or "conjunctions" but nuances, shades of meaning classic grammar may help us pick up but which do not necessarily conform exactly to its categories. So here: the infinitive could express purpose. *w^ehinnēh* reinforces this by adding a shade of meaning, the emotive element in the purpose: urgency (Abner, 2 Sm 3,12), fidelity (the ancient Hushai *will* join his king, 2 Sm 15, 32), awe (Obadiah's fears, 1 Kgs 18,7) and irony (Siba, 2 Sm 16,1).

8) *Result.* One sees the relation to the deictic in 2 Sm 19,37-38. The ancient Barzillai, offered a reward for his help in David's flight, prefers to remain home to die in peace. "However, here is (*w^ehinnēh*) thy servant Chimham (Barzillai's son). Let him cross over with the king" and benefit from his father's action. *w^ehinnēh* delicately points to Chimham, contrasts him with Barzillai, and suggests the results hoped for the younger man.

There is multiple meaning in 2 Sm 14,7 but the emphasis on the deictic is much weakened. One son of the woman from Tekoa has killed the other "and now the whole family has risen against thy handmaid" to punish the killer. This is not mere sequence of time, it is the result of the event, the law and the family attitude. "And now" includes "so that": one event is to follow the other in time, to be sure, but the important thing is the sequence of cause and result.

Abraham deals with the LORD less delicately. In Gn 15,3 he responds bluntly to the divine promise: "That's all very well. But look (*hēn*)! You have given me no descendants so that a *vernus* will be my heir (*w^ehinnēh ben-bêtî yôrēš 'otî*)". The result of the situation God has created is flatly stated to Him. So in Exod 5,16 the Hebrew foremen are quite clear that their being beaten (*w^ehinnēh* with participle) is the result of the Egyptian refusal to supply straw for their brick-making. Another clear case: Shimei has attacked David, apparently beaten in Absolom's revolt, and he hastens to seek pardon when David wins. He confesses his fault and goes on (2 Sm 19,21a); "therefore (*w^ehinnēh*) have I come (qatal) today, first of all the Josephites to greet my lord the king". Fault and fear *result* in placating action. In 1 Kgs 19,13, after Elijah recognizes the passing LORD and stands covered, then he hears a voice (*w^ehinnēh 'ēlāw qôl*). This is no mere point in time. Revelation is the *result* of the meeting.

We have already noted Gn 37,7b: *wᵉhinnēh* with yiqtol expresses the submission resulting from Joseph's symbolic superiority.

Ample evidence, therefore, that *wᵉhinnēh* with qatal, yiqtol, participle or noun sentence can point out results.

9) *Adversatives.* *wᵉhinnēh* is not merely a subordinating form (to use classical grammatical terms); it can coordinate adversatives. Ze 11,6 explains God's acts: "Indeed (*kî*), I shall no longer have pity on the dwellers in the land — word of the LORD — *but rather* (*wᵉhinnēh*) I am giving over (participle) the people ...". Is 22,12 calls for penance, 13 continues "but (*wᵉhinneh*) there is only pleasure and rejoicing (noun sentence)". *wᵉhinnēh* would seem to keep its emotional coloring: the prophecies find the contrast between what the people should be and are shocking.

Our point about nuance and complexity can be repeated here. We have taken the phrase introduced by *wᵉhinnēh* in 1 Sm 25,36 as the cause of Abigail's silence to her husband. One might also understand that she returned but found Nabal so royally drunk that she said nothing. The situation was so *adverse* to her purpose as to *cause* her silence. There is really no need to force the sentence into a category and exclude everything else. Rather it is rich with meaning which overlaps categories.

Once again, the adversative use of *wᵉhinnēh* stands with participle and noun sentence (8).

A careful survey, then, seems to justify the claim that the deictic *wᵉhinnēh*, like other deictic particles in Hebrew, actually perfoms what to our way of thinking and speaking is a variety of functions. One can find it in uses which parallel just about all the various kinds of "clauses" listed in the syntax sections of our Hebrew grammars. So one must always have an eye to the variety of meaning which

(8) J. BLAU's work (*VT* 9 — see n. 1, 132-33) suggests a possible tenth category: the copula, the noun sentence with (*wᵉ*)*hinnēh* functioning rather like the pronoun in the familiar noun sentence construction. However his examples like Gn 32,21; Jer 6,21; Jb 16,19 (all with simple *hinnēh*) and Is 17,14 (with *wᵉhinnēh*) all are *Excited Perception* — in the prophets often still to come — as is confirmed by his use of a dream report (Gn 40,9 with *wᵉhinnēh*), a typical instance of our category, as an example. Thus it is difficult to distinguish a function as copula from a normal deictic function and even from the simplest deictic which naturally often points out the connection of realities. So, for example, with *rāʾāh*: one usually sees that *someone/something* is or is doing *something*.

wᵉhinnēh with various complementary forms may imply. At the same time the particle does tend to retain something of its own character. It is used primarily when there is something dramatic or emotionally telling about the cause or the time or the condition or whatever it is expressing.

It is interesting to note too that this "reality" particle supposed to point to actual experience does retain this quality much of the time when it is communicating some additional meaning. It has an affinity for the participle, the form for *states*, for the "it is" of the noun sentence, for the actuality (no futures) of qatal. Yet language is fluid. So *wᵉhinnēh* can drift a bit. It can posit a condition which may never be realized. Reality moves into the world of mere possibility.

Pontifical Biblical Institute
Via della Pilotta, 25
00187 Rome

Dennis J. McCarthy, S. J.

Hero and Anti-Hero in 1 Sam 13,2 – 14,46

Source critics mostly found 1 Sam 13 – 14 a seamless whole, apart from two obvious intrusions. Tradition criticism, however, has uncovered sources.[1] Still, the final step in the tradition is the text, and it constitutes a coherent narrative with definable historical and theological objects, the only one we can study which is not hypothetical. Besides the narrative unity and meaning which we will study, the effort at unity appears at the surface level of word recurrence and the like. For example, there are key roots running through the text, *nkh* opening the action (13,3-4), at its center (14,14 [2x]), and the closing of battle action (14,30-31); *ngš* (two roots, one sound: 13,6.9; 14,24.34[2x].38) ironically attributing ultimate failure not to fear but to Saul; and various words for "muster/disperse" (13,2.4.5.11.15; 14,17.20.[21.22?].40) to articulate the whole episode. Then, especially in ch. 14, summary (a standard instrument in narrative) and dialogue alternate, the latter at high points often marked by heightened language (see note 10).

One can discern verbal articulations, key words, link words and the like, which is a kind of "rhetorical criticism" (in English, "literary criticism"!) which, though no cure-all, is here to stay in biblical study. One objects that literary critics often disagree in their results, and contemporary ones tend to indulge in literary theories or idiosyncratic reading of texts which never get near literature. But fads pass and classic methods like "close reading" (*Werkinterpretation*) retain their value for the Bible which is a *literature* first of all, even if they do not always reach the same conclusion about a text. Different *valid* methods and different *valid* points of view must reveal different things about a text precisely because it has the rich polyvalence of good literature.

[1] Some examples of tradition analysis: F. Schikelberger, "Jonatans Heldentat: Textlinguistische Beobachtung zu 1 Sam XIV 1-23a," *VT* 24 (1974) 324-333; J. M. Miller, "Saul's Rise to Power: Some Observations concerning 1 Sam 9,1 – 10,16; 10,26 – 11,15 and 13,2 – 14,46," *CBQ* 36 (1974) 157-174; D. Jobling, "Saul's Fall and Jonathan's Rise: Tradition and Redaction in 1 Sam 14,1-46," *JBL* 95 (1976) 367-376; H. Seebass, "I Sam 15 als Schlüssel für das Verständnis der sogenannten königsfreundlichen Reihe I Sam 9,1 – 10,16; 11,1-15 und 13,2 – 14,52," *ZAW* 78 (1966) 148-169; see also his "Die Vorgeschichte der Königserhebung Sauls," *ZAW* 79 (1967) 155-171. He makes some acute observations but has not been generally followed.

Here I shall attempt such a close reading by the method of looking at the text against a convention it assumes. This is in line with a number of methods. Linguists define style as variation on normal, expected speech. Formalists found literature in diversity from the normal expectations one has of a text. The New Critics found denseness of meaning in "irony," the unity of complementary elements in a text because the "complementary" is often ambiguous, unexpected and even contrary.

These scholars worked with sophisticated forms. Ours is simpler, but not all that much so, for variation from even a simple convention produces surprise and new meaning. One can see it in a simple modern art form, the Western film. The hero always wins, but in a great example like *High Noon* or *Shane* the winners also lose and we have much to ponder. Our ancient convention is the Battle Story. The convention involved a terrifying enemy, fear, false (inadequate) hero, king (who may also be hero or the wise supporter of the hero), heroic struggle (divine intervention, sign and cause of victory and defeat, is part of the convention of the human Battle Story, although this has been denied — after the *Iliad*!), destruction of the enemy, a reward (e.g., a palace or temple). Ancient tales where these occur include *Enuma elish*, *Gilgamesh*, the *Tukulti-Ninurta Epic*, the Ugaritic Baal cycle, the Story of Sinuhe, the Iliad.[2] As with most conventions not all the elements are present in every case, nor is the order absolute, as biblists know from form-criticism. But this is the convention. Does it fit and illumine our text? We will find out by reading the text in its light.

Things begin well — the crux in 13,1 does not enter into the convention — with Saul as a good king organizing a proper army of three regiments because he learned that he cannot rely on the tribal levy alone.[3] He takes a strategic position.[4] In itself, 2b is doubtless a fragment from what must have been a trove of Saul stories about wars, marriages, the birth of a son to the farm-boy of ch. 11 who is now a grown warrior. All this is of no concern to our narrator who uses it simply to show Saul as the good, wise king. V. 3 reveals the hero, Jonathan, the winner of battles. In the heroic Battle Story it is quite

[2] I owe much knowledge of the Battle Story to discussion with my student, Harry Hagan, O.S.B. Written tools on the subject include C. M. Bowra, *Heroic Poetry* (London: Macmillans, 1961), and the material on heroic literature in H. M. Chadwick and Nora Chadwick, *The Growth of Literature*, 3 vols. (Cambridge: Cambridge U. Press, 1932-1940). These include much analogous material not from the ancient world.

[3] H. P. Smith, *The Books of Samuel* (ICC; Edinburgh: T. & T. Clark, 1899) 91, thinks the dismissed muster in 13,2 is a direct follow-up on 11,14-15. This does explain the existence of 2b, which can seem to hang in the air. However, if we read it as part of the closed narrative in 13,2 – 14,46, we see its point as explained in the text. Neither does Smith explain how the direct move from Gilgal to Michmash and Bethel allow time for Jonathan's growth. Finally, if we accept the plausible argument of R. Althann, "1 Sam 13,1: A Poetic Couplet," *Bib* 62 (1981) 241-246, 13,1 is ancient poetry which implies an indefinite but longish passage of time and is not, as usually held, an unintelligible corruption of a Deuteronomistic addition to ch. 13.

[4] On Saul as strategist see C. E. Hauer, Jr., "The Shape of Saulide Strategy," *CBQ* 31 (1969) 153-169.

proper for the victory to be assigned to the good king as in 4. Being the good king, the ultimate leader, is now clearly Saul's role. An act of prowess has marked out the hero whom the good king is to support with wisdom and material. Saul does this in mustering the tribes (3b-4: MT). (3b is an ironic taunt. The despised *ʿibrîm* have turned on the oppressor.) Such a taunt fits the heroic Battle Story, but in the mouth of Saul, who is not the hero, it may be a hint of weakness for precipitous and exaggerated acts. Of course, the Philistines react. They come in imposing force and a frightened Israel runs away (5-7a). So far all accords with the convention: hero, good king, terrible foe, fear, and retreat. Then unexpectedly the good king at Gilgal [5] begins to show an anxious religiosity. Contrary to a common idea, religion and the gods are in place in the heroic Battle Story — our list of ancient examples in enough to show this — but anxiety and hastiness have no part in the religion of the good king. A wise king would control himself and his followers, not have to "pull himself together" [6] and offer useless sacrifices. Later he shows active anxiety (vow, altar) and passivity (14,2-5). Apart even from Samuel's condemnation, Saul is not showing himself a proper king. Thus 7b-15a, rightly considered a redactional intrusion, contributes to the story's development in terms of the convention.

In fact, the powerful rhetoric of the redactor points up more than the prophetic condemnation. Consciously or not, his use of the verb *pwṣ* (13,8.11) is a link-in-reverse with the four verbs for muster in 2-5. Then, the passage is built on nine and a half lines of dialogue about one incident after twelve lines of narrative summary of great event. The rhetoric of the passage is equal to its importance. It is linked by the root *pwṣ* to what went before. It uses balance in its dialogue, anxious abruptness against solemnity, assonance, and key words to reinforce its message. Such use of dialogue is, of course, an important device for emphasis in Hebrew style. Then, the dialogue is balanced, three lines by Saul, three and one-half by Samuel, each speech with eight phrases. One thinks of poetic parallelism. Still, Saul's answer to Samuel's abrupt question in 11 is verbose, full of anxiety: he is being deserted, the Philistines press, he is in doubt about God. Samuel, on the contrary, is balanced: there is an inclusion, *šāmartā ʾet miṣwat yhwh ʾăšer ṣiwwah*, (13bA.14bB) to frame his solemn proclamation of the LORD'S decision. It is of a force becoming a prophet. Then there is the coming of Samuel just as Saul has finished his useless sacrifices, brilliantly forceful in its abruptness: "and there was Samuel," emphasized by the preceding assonance, *k*^{e}*kALLOTô l*^{e}*ha*^{cc}*ALÔT hAʿOLâ*. Saul's foolish anxiety is rebuked in the very narration. Finally, there is the careful use of *kî*. Saul acts *since* he saw *that* the people were scattering (10aA) and loses every-

---

[5] Many find this location, made 1st in v. 4, impossible. Why should Saul change for a worse base? Perhaps the people could assemble there more easily than in rough hill country: Cf. H.-W. Hertzberg, *I & II Samuel* (OT Library; Philadelphia: Westminster, 1964) 105. However, a convention from another tradition may be at work here: all Saul's dealings with Samuel have some connection with Gilgal.

[6] *wāʾetʾappaq:* 12b — for the shade of meaning here cf. Gen 43,31.

thing "in *that* the LORD would now establish your kingship (13b)" but does not *since* Saul did not obey. The reasons ("since") are real: Saul "saw" and obeyed not; the results need not have been, for a good king's wisdom would have solved the people's problem and God would not have had to act. Altogether, the redactor has done much to reinforce the impression that Saul is failing in the actions and attitudes of a good king in a Battle Story, whatever other intentions he had in adding the episode.[7]

Still, anxious and rejected, Saul has not lost forever all the good king's attributes. He steadies himself (as in the Iliad gods bolster weakening heroes) and posts his pitiful six hundred to oversee the Philistines.[8] The latter raid the land — the triple repetition in 17b-18 seems to echo the marching of the terrorizers. The situation is worse because Israel is practically unarmed (19-20).[9] Even this odd, inserted, notice fits the Battle Story ironically; in contrast to the conventional splendid arming of the hero, Saul and Jonathan have no more than a sword or spear and no one else has anything. This could be related to the Holy War element, which we shall soon see introduced, by pointing up the fact that God is all in all in the battle, but within the Battle Story conventions it is a surprise.

This summary and this notice of regrouping and arming (standard narrative practice) carry the story forward but also constitute artful retardation: important news is passed on rather dryly, and Saul has recovered for a moment his role of good king, wise and supportive. But the recovery is but a lurch on legs fallen down. The man's acts cannot remain at the level of his role. Real action resumes in 14,1, and now, as we shall see, Saul is out of it. Jonathan proposes a daring exploit *which he conceals from Saul, his father* who, by contrast, is sitting and not acting. The active hero role is clearly now Jonathan's. This is emphasized by the language. There is activity in 14,1 while 2-5 are a

---

[7] There are many questions about the fault that destroys Saul's dynasty. What was his fault? He waited the due time — though just a bit of patience and Samuel's coming would have obviated his trouble. I believe much of the problem arises from our sympathy for the weak, human Saul over against Samuel's prophetic firmness. Prophets are often hard to take! Actually, Saul has disobeyed the divine (prophetic) command in 10,8 in two ways: Samuel reserved the sacrificing at Gilgal to himself absolutely in 8a, and waiting seven days did not change that. The seven days in 8b define the time at which the *prophet* will bring divine directions which the anxious Saul tries to force *himself*. He has usurped the prophetic role! The whole action has serious consequences for the on-going story of Saul. He has begun to alienate prophet and priest in the person of Samuel who was both priest (1 Sam 2 and the contrast with the Elids; 1 Sam 7) and prophet (1 Sam 3), part of the course that ruins him.

[8] Note that the number, six hundred men, means that Saul's picked regiments have broken along with the levy. Through no fault of his own, unless he picked unwisely, the king cannot give the support he should.

[9] Smith, ICC, 101, doubts the truth of this disarmament, for Israel is able to fight later. This can be explained factually: almost any club will do against a panicked enemy. However, this is an example of the constant error of historicizing what may have a factual basis but is presented as narrative and theology. It is the same error to call Jonathan's plan of attack in 14,1 "foolhardy" (ibid., 104). What is foolhardy to us is everyday stuff for heroes — and warriors guided by God!

kind of parenthesis passively describing circumstances and not action.[10] Saul sits with his priest. Is this a hint at the religiosity that has caused a problem already? Further, the very lack of need to say anything at all about secrecy of Jonathan's act calls our attention more firmly to the fact when mention of it is dragged in. Finally, the parenthesis ends with a description of the battlefield. Description is rare in Hebrew narrative. Is this used to emphasize the Saul-Jonathan contrast, a further retardation of action which shows Jonathan ready to pass the impassible, Saul passive? Both content and form are a nugget, a classic in retardation technique contrasting the active hero, Jonathan, and the passive king, Saul.

Action resumes as 14,6 repeats 14,1, the standard Hebrew method for closing "parentheses" ends inaction and begins to move the story again. First comes a dialogue, such as we know Hebrew uses for important scenes. Jonathan speaks to his squire, then to the Philistines. The speech is lively, full of voluntative verbal forms and emphatic *hinneh* as well as assonance.[11] The result is a brilliant exploit by the hero which leads to God's direct intervention in the blattle. He creates "a divinely inspired panic" [12] throughout the Philistine army, not just the outpost attacked (v. 15).

The Holy War idea is linked with the Battle Story. Weippert has taken the trouble to document what was clear in any case: the Holy War was universal in the ancient world,[13] and the Battle Story, which was not confined to that world, involves the gods. Indeed, they provoke, guide, make revelations, and cause panic: cf. the *Tukulti-Ninurta Epic* and the *Iliad* (XVIII, 202-231), the heart of the Holy War experience. Peculiar to Israel was the theological development which took all glory from the hero to give it to God as in the Gideon tale. However, our story has not reached this stage. The hero is conscious of divine aid, as in many Battle Stories, but he acts for himself with God, and he is recognized as hero by his own people.

However, in our story Saul's reaction to the enemy panic is odd by heroic or Holy War standards. He does not follow the divine lead at once. First he must find out who is missing from his army, the one who has attacked the

[10] The contrast is probably heightened by language. According to Blenkinsopp, "Jonathan's Sacrilege: 1 Sam 14,1-46," *CBQ* 26 (1964) 423-448, 14,1 and 2 are heightened by rythmic language. He finds the same heightening in 8-10 (Jonathan's challenge and attack), 15-16 (the beginning of the Holy War as such), 29-30 (Jonathan's condemnation of Saul's adjuration of the people), and 37 + 38-39 + 43-44 (God's refusal to speak, the trial and judgment of Jonathan). That is to say that key points are heightened by more solemn language. Given the difficulties of Hebrew Prosody, it is hard to affirm that in every case here we have poetic speech, but in any case the language is more solemn.

[11] Imperatives in 14,1.6.7.9.10.12; voluntives in 8.10; *hinneh* in 7.8.11.

[12] *ḥerdat ʾĕlōhîm* and simple *ḥărādâ*, an ironic reversal against the Philistines: in 13,7 Israel *harᵉdû* before the Philistines. Other Holy War vocabulary in our story: *nāmôg* (16), *ḥereb ʾîš bᵉrēʿēhû, mᵉhûmâ* (20).

[13] M. Weippert, "Heiliger Krieg in Israel und Assyrien. Kritische Anmerkungen zu Gerhard von Rads Konzept des 'Heiligen Krieg in Israel'," *ZAW* 84 (1972) 460-493.

Philistines, and learns it is Jonathan. This inactive but now victorious king is hardly worried that someone is confusing his strategy. Rather, his eagerness and Jonathan's care to conceal his plan surely indicates that Saul is troubled by his son's prowess — there is no sign he is worried about his death. With his inactivity this concern is another sign of a change in Saul: in 13,16 and 22 even after defeat and anxiety he works calmly with his son to regroup and, presumably, arms him as a king should. Here he worries about what the hero he should be supporting has got him into.

Only with this first business done does Saul turn to the battle, but he must begin with a consultation of God. This is religiosity, not religion. The "divine panic" before his eyes is as clear a sign of God's will for Israel as any divination! Once again Saul fails to be the Battle Story's good king. He is not very ready to support the hero nor wise in discerning what is to be done. His delay and later actions actually impede success. He looks more like anti-hero than good king.

We should notice the technique here. Hebrew does not psychologize much. It tells of words and acts and leaves us to decipher as we may motives and character. So here the Saul who did his duty, organized his people, and rallied them after a moment of weakness has become inactive, worried about his hero son but not on his behalf, and indecisive, and he will grow worse. Why? He had a moment of anxiety. Has this become a state? Was this likely to happen to his excitable personality (ch. 11)? Is he, who had his heroic moment (again, ch. 11), jealous or afraid of his hero son? In the actual context are we to see Samuel's condemnation gradually unmanning him? We cannot answer any of the questions certainly, as we never can know a human character perfectly. However, seeing the results we can divine that some or all of these factors are at work. We can appreciate better a central mystery of the Bible: God at work guiding destiny through fallible, changeable humanity. Perhaps one can see the point better by contrasting 13,2-4. There the narrator is simply beginning a new action with no real antecedents, and the narrator's summary manner gives nothing to allow us to speculate on character and on God and man.

When Saul does go into action Israel is aroused and the Holy War moves toward success. Still, there is a limit. Saul has vowed his army to a fast which weakens the fighters (reading MT in 24b as parallel with and explanatory of 24a). Some defend the vow. Smith thinks it is to assure continued divine favor and to protect the booty, which was God's, from the army. Hertzberg finds it a proper way to strengthen a weakened people. Blenkinsopp thinks that vows belong to Holy War and cites Jos 6,26 and Jgs 21,18 in support.[14] However, these vows (*ḥerem*, no marriage to Benjaminites) are not such as to weaken

[14] Smith, ICC, 114; Hertzberg, OT Library, 114 associating his answer with K. Budde, *Die Bücher Samuel* (KHAT 8; Tübingen and Leipzig; J.C.B. Mohr [Paul Siebeck], 1902) 96: the vow is a substitute for the abandoned oracle; Blenkinsopp, "Jonathan's Sacrilege," 428.

warriors physically, as Saul's is. Besides, vows in Holy Wars are not connected with particularly happy results — cf. the disaster Jephthah's adding a vow to divine inspiration in war caused. It is presumption to try to move the LORD by human vow when he is already in command. Nor was there need for a substitute for the missing oracle, as Budde suggests: the panic was God's sufficient message. Finally, booty was not always *ḥerem*, certainly not here: cf. 32-34 where there is no sin in using the booty rightly. The vow stands as an error.[15]

The vow thus arrests the report of the flow of the battle story, a summary full of interesting details: Philistine panic, Hebrews returning to their allegiance, new forces coming, all to produce victory, *hôšîaʿ*, through the LORD. The arresting (and arrested) scene in which all this stops, 24-31, is carefully constructed: a command, a report, a dialogue. Saul commands a vow and the people keep it in the face of tempting food. Only Jonathan, in ignorance, violates it, to be warned at once of the oath and then to condemn it in strong terms. This piece is a ring construction: *hašbēaʿ hišbîaʿ* and *ʾārûr* in 28 pick up *yōʾel* and *ʾārûr* in 24, *hašbîaʿ* and *wayyāšeb yādô ʾel-piyw* in 27 *hašbîaʿ* and *wᵉʾēn maśśîg yādô ʾel-piyw* in 26. This closes the tale of the vow in itself and sets it against Jonathan's condemnation of its folly in 29-30. A further emphasis depends on the echo of "distress" (24), "faint" (28) and the climactic "very faint" (31). The disastrous effects of Saul's religiosity are thoroughly judged in style as well as content. In fact, his religious anxiety creates further cultic problems, for this is the meaning, as Jonathan's condemning *ʿākar*, roughly "profess, cause religious trouble,"[16] says. Jonathan the hero-fighter is wiser even in the religious sphere which is the special concern of this king, but where his anxieties preclude wisdom and hinder support in the climactic battle.

The next episode confirms the folly of Saul's vow (and perhaps is the cultic problem just spoken of). Indeed, the famished people are driven to slaughter their booty and eat meat with the blood, a grave cultic crime.[17] Saul's vow produces vice, not victory. Seeing the sin, however, here at least he repairs the situation. The scene is vividly presented. The army's sin is described (32), but with the significant transition in 31b: "the army was exhausted." Saul hears

[15] P. Kyle McCarter, *1 Samuel* (AB 8; Garden City, NY: Doubleday, 1980) 248-249 sees Saul making a mistake, acting without foreseeing consequences, not sinning, but there is no sense of sin here anyway. The point is that the good, wise king *should* foresee. Besides McCarter is reconstructing Hebrew *šᵉgāgâ* from LXX and we are reading MT's story.

[16] Cf. *ʿkr* in Jos 6,18 parallel to *ḥrm*; 7,25: Achan's violation of 6,18 has troubled the whole people; Jgs 11,35: Jephthah's daughter destroyed by his rash vow; 1 Kgs 18,17-18: idolatry brings drought. In Gen 34,30 it is not clear, though possible, that the broken promise may have religious consequences. Prov 11,17.29; 15,27, the other occurences of the root lack context for any full definition.

[17] The text has the meat "on the blood," which has caused discussion, but the case is simple enough. By not letting the blood drain away on the ground but seizing the meat as it lay in the blood the men ate meat with the blood. Saul's stone altar allowed the blood to drain away from the animal slaughtered on it.

of the sin and exclaims: "You have broken faith!" He (Saul) raps out orders, 5 imperatives and 3 voluntives in 33b-34. The activity is in sharp contrast to his idleness while Jonathan acts (v. 2) and his tardiness in joining battle (17-19). He can act, but, it seems, only in the cultic sphere, while the good king should give advice and support in the crucial battles. And even here there is irony. Saul saves the situation by building a shrine, an activity of great and good kings, but he does so only because he must undo a vice his own "pious" act had led to. Even doing the right thing, Saul is under a shadow.

The final scene is a true climax in terms of confounding the Battle Story convention. The should-be good king is about to kill the hero; he is truly anti-hero now. But he begins well enough, calling for the battle to continue. This is in order: the Battle Story should include the *total destruction* of the enemy, as should the Holy War. Further, the Holy War should be over in one day and so the battle here should go on.[18] Saul shows vigor at last, three voluntive forms in v. 36. The priest suggests consulting God, which Jobling thinks may be the priest pressing Saul, urging his own prerogatives,[19] but since Saul's religiosity is a major theme of chs. 13 – 14 we may be sure that at most he was anticipating Saul's wish. They try and receive no answer. Saul at once senses a cultic fault in the army, and his response to a cultic problem is again vigorous. He assembles the army for judgment with an oath by the LORD, "*hammôšîaʿ* of Israel," which is truly ironic in his circumstances. He picks out Jonathan. He is ready to kill his son to purify the army.

A question arises at once. Why the mention of Jonathan and why the division only between royalty and people to determine guilt? Why not the priest, for instance? Perhaps the mention of Jonathan's possible guilt merely emphasizes Saul's readiness to give up anything for his people. However, I find it suspicious. Some tension led Jonathan to conceal his activity from Saul and Saul to be concerned first with who began the Holy War battle — one must believe he knew it had to be his hero son — and not to complete the LORD's work. Further, setting himself and Jonathan over against the people for judgment is close to condemning the hero in advance. The guilt might lie among some of the people, for Saul had enforced a painful abstinence on them, but this possibility is not even considered.[20] As for himself, no one can be sure in such matters, but Saul, so careful of the liturgy, can be as confident as anyone could be that the fault was not his. Jonathan is close to standing forth for sentence, not judgment. Finally, consulting the LORD at this point was meaningless (one more reason for suspecting the scrupulous Saul of wanting it). One knew that Holy War or heroic battle had to end in *total* destruction of the enemy in one day. The LORD does not answer Saul's question because he *is*

[18] On the one day Holy War see Blenkinsopp, "Jonathan's Sacrilege," 426, and Jobling, "Saul's Fall," 367.

[19] "Saul's Fall," 369.

[20] The problem must be with the vow to fast, the only cultic matter the *narrative itself* offers, the "meat with blood" fault having been repaired.

speaking in his saving acts. He need say no more, and it is presumption to ask for more, and false interpretation to attribute the lack of reply to a foolish question to an impeding sin. As so often in Hebrew Narrative, we cannot be sure of Saul's motives, but they are surely suspect here. In any event, they may destroy the divinely blessed hero.

Again, the artistry of this important scene is careful. It makes the usual use of dialogue. Various forms of *mwt* are used brilliantly as a kind of refrain: in 39 *mwt* expresses Saul's resolve to judge, in 43 Jonathan's readiness to die, in 44 Saul's decision that he shall, in 45 (2x) the people's determination that he shall not and the fact that he does not. So throughout the scene one feels the weight of danger over Jonathan. The people (army) plays a strong role. They consent to Saul's wish to get on with the war, but they are grimly silent when its cultic sequel threatens Jonathan, preparing the way for their rebellion when he is condemned.[21] They recognize that he is the LORD's instrument: *ʿāśâ hayᵉšuʿâ... kî-ʿim-ʾĕlōhîm ʿāśâ*. Through him came the very *môšîaʿ* Saul invoked when he swore to judge the guilty. Thus an inclusion with *yšʿ* ties the judgment scene together and links it with the successful part of the war (cf. *wayyôšîaʿ yhwh* in 23). However, it took the army to see this and save the hero from a king who should himself have seen this in his wisdom. Instead he has almost destroyed Israel's hero.

To sum up, we have enough to see the Battle Story conventions at work in our narrative. Saul begins by acting the *good king*, thinking strategically (*wise*) and marshalling his forces (*support*). Jonathan is the *hero*, the mighty warrior, but Saul remains the good king, providing force to support the action begun by the hero's prowess. Then comes a lapse: instead of patient wisdom Saul succumbs to hasty anxiety and receives a terrible rebuke. Still he regroups the forces broken by *fear* before a *terrible enemy*, works with Jonathan and even *arms* him. Then the hero presses on, but Saul falls into a lethargy and apparently a jealousy of the hero who is the instrument for *destroying the enemies* of the LORD.[22] Saul seems not to grasp this or help in it, hardly the attitude of the wise, supporting king. Finally he joins the battle, but his anxious religiosity (and fear of the hero?) weakens the army, leads to sin, and almost destroys the hero. The Battle Story conventions are indeed there, and they have been ingeniously used to depict a king and a man's decline. He cannot complete his duty according to the convention and destroy the enemy and so bring order out of (political) chaos.

Saul, then, is neither hero nor good king. He is not, therefore, the one who can "save (*yšʿ*) the people from the Philistines," his commission in 9,16 as 14,52 makes clear: after four verses outlining his royal trappings it is em-

[21] Budde, KHAT 8, remarks perceptively: "Die Totenstille, die auf diese Anrede folgt [v. 39], kennzeichnet die gedruckte Stimmung, dient zugleich, dem Heere den Einspruch in v. 45 offen zu halten."

[22] Saul even builds a shrine, a surrogate for the *temple* found at the end of many Battle Stories.

phasized that they are trappings. The man at the center is not the kind of material God can work with to achieve his purposes. We may believe that Jonathan might have been, but in the present text we know that he will not be it, for Saul will have no dynastic succession (13,13-14). Can the hero without a future legitimately turn over the royal prerogatives to another family, as Jobling has argued on structural grounds: Jonathan has taken Saul's role.[23] Our Battle Story conventions supply no answer to this, but common sense would suggest that in the circumstances not only can he, and he alone, but he must for his people's sake. Even the *picture* of Saul's "court" in 14,47-51 takes on an ironic cast: Saul does not get the conventional palace. He gets a family but no order — the war goes on.

Clearly my conclusions mean that these chapters are in some sense anti-Saul, contrary to a fairly common opinion. [24] Perhaps it is a question of the sense of the phrase. The story does not condemn the man as such at once and forever. Except for his seeming jealousy of Jonathan it presents the tragic or pathetic figure of a man trying but pressed beyond his resources. Rather than making one feel anti-Saul it tends to create sympathy for him, as always for one in such a situation. At the same time, hard realities must be faced, and Saul is not the man for the times. In modern terms I would be anti-Saul in that I could not vote for him though I sympathize with him. Perhaps this negative element is due to the pro-Davidic redaction so often posited for the Saul stories, but beyond any hypotheses about redaction history the redaction before us is a fine exercise in the use of a literary convention to tell a good story and to show us a man sincere enough himself and yet inadequate for the circumstances in which God wishes to use him.

[23] D. Jobling, "Jonathan: A Structural Study in 1 Samuel," in D. Jobling, *The Sense of Biblical Narrative: Three Structural Analyses in the OT* (JSOT Suppl 7; Sheffield: Univ. of Sheffield, 1978) 4-25.

[24] "Saul's Fall," 367, cites the literature (with which he disagrees).

[illegible]

[illegible] the conventional [illegible]

Ultimately [illegible] conclusions [illegible] that most [illegible] to a fairly common [illegible] Perhaps it is a question of [illegible]

[illegible]

PART III

Biblical Theology

Reprinted from THEOLOGICAL STUDIES
Vol. 24, No. 4, December, 1963
Printed in U.S.A.

PERSONALITY, SOCIETY, AND INSPIRATION

DENNIS J. McCARTHY, S.J.
St. Mary's College, Kansas

MODERN CRITICAL study enables us to reconstruct to a certain degree the process by which our Bible came to be and thus develop a kind of phenomenology of inspired writing which may be able to enrich our somewhat abstract notion of inspiration. The Old Testament offers an especially hopeful field for this kind of investigation, since it contains a greater variety of literary forms and shows on a larger scale the processes of development. Thus the growth of the Old Testament is easier to investigate and the results may be more broadly applicable than such as depend on the study of the more restricted gamut of forms used in the New Testament. Moreover, there has been proportionately less attention devoted to the problems of Old Testament inspiration, though the Old Testament too is the word of God.[1] There seems, then, reason enough for studying certain of the processes which produced the Old Testament with a view to the light they may throw on the problem of inspiration. Obviously, it is possible to treat only a few of the many different processes involved, and we shall concentrate on certain of them which concern the relation of Scripture to the community of God's chosen people.

This social aspect of the inspired books has been a matter of increasing interest.[2] We realize that the Bible was formed in, by, and for a society. First Israel and then the Apostolic Church were communities of a special sort and subject to a special influence from God. Surely this influence extended to the writings which were formed in and in turn formed the communities. Thus the social dimension in the formation of the Scriptures may offer us the way to a fuller understanding of the divine element which we affirm when we say that God is their author.

[1] So K. Rahner, *Inspiration in the Bible* (Edinburgh–London, 1961), is almost entirely concerned with the New Testament.

[2] Cf. Rahner, *ibid.*; P. Benoit, O.P., in A. Robert and A. Tricot, *Guide to the Bible* (2nd ed.; New York, 1960) pp. 12 ff., and "Les analogies de l'inspiration," in J. Coppens, A. Descamps, and E. Massaux, *Sacra pagina* 1 (Paris, 1959) 86 ff.; J. McKenzie, S.J., "The Social Character of Inspiration," *Catholic Biblical Quarterly* 24 (1962) 115 ff.

However, it is essential to avoid the danger of too rapid a generalization. We feel that the first modern analyses of inspiration fell short in that they took a modern concept, that of the self-conscious individual author of modern times, and applied it univocally to a body of literature produced in another time and in different ways, in the attempt to understand something of what went on in the sacred writer's mind. The problem, however, is not only that the processes of ancient authorship were somewhat different from the modern; those processes also differed among themselves. This remains true when we add the indispensable social dimension, and to subsume all the various forms of inspired writing under an anonymous social form of production is to apply a univocity with its own dangers of distortion.

Thus it would be oversimplifying to take as absolute the statement that the ancient author was in all instances the spokesman of society, and society was the real author of his book.[3] The basis for such a statement in regard to the Old Testament literature is the peculiar relation of individual and society in the ancient world. Beyond doubt, the ancient lost himself in identification with his society in a way strange to us. Beyond doubt, ancient literature was a part and a product of tradition, that is, the fund of beliefs, forms of expression, and so on, held and passed on by the community, to a degree beyond anything we know. But I submit that this is still a matter of degree; individuals, anonymous to us perhaps, but still individuals, did the work, even though under the pressure of tradition. All literature—not just the ancient Oriental—involves an interplay of individual and a tradition carried in society.

The total submergence of the individual in a tradition of impersonal production is not, in fact, indicated by the ancient Oriental literatures. Thus in Accadian literature, the largest body of ancient Semitic literature known to us, tradition was of vast importance. The scribal schools were at once guardians and prisoners of a canonical tradition. They produced more than mere copies, but they tended to work within a traditional framework by gloss, expansion, and development. A bit of comparison between the Old Babylonian version of the Gilgamesh epic and the first-millennium form will show something of the process.[4]

[3] Cf. J. McKenzie, *ibid.*, pp. 117, 119.

[4] Translations by E. Speiser in J. Pritchard, *Ancient Near Eastern Texts Relating to the Old Testament* (2nd ed.; Princeton, 1956).

However, this is not quite the whole story. There were individuals as well, men who spoke distinctly of their own experiences. There is personal lyric. The man posted on the temple roof to observe the movement of the stars was a cog in a social machine, his observations were guided by traditional techniques and purposes. Still, his lyric reaction was his own and not a social expression.[5] To be sure, in a different society his position and his manner would have been different; nonetheless the personal element shines through the conventions. The writer is no mere mouthpiece for his group. Again, a hymn to Ishtar, most traditional of materials, could become a song with a truly personal note.[6] On another level, the author of the Era epic departed somewhat from the retailing of traditional material to produce his own poem of comment and interpretation on stirring experiences. Precisely because he was *extra chorum* he had to appeal to divine sanction to assure his acceptance.[7] This doubtless shows the pressure of the traditional forms, but it shows freedom within them as well.

Thus we cannot reduce ancient Oriental literature to an impersonal social product, nor, on the other hand, can we deny a large and largely determinative role to the social context in the production of other literatures. The medieval troubadour had to write his *chanson de croisade* on the themes and in the forms his society accepted for that kind of poem. Those violent individualists accepted the conventions and yet managed to produce highly personal expressions. So also the author of the individualistic Renaissance period was constrained to use certain forms (e.g., the sonnet) and certain conventions (e.g., the pastoral) because this was the poetry his society recognized. Yet no one misses the personal note in a Ronsard, a Sydney, a Marlowe. Even the very modern pose of the author as rebel, faithful to his personal vision in the face of an uncomprehending bourgeois society, is a convention determined by the traditions of his society. The Promethean man of the Renaissance and the romantics, the theories of the symbolists, and a host of other influences carried by society mark the limits within which the artist works.

This is not to deny that the group and its conventions were much

[5] Cf. A. Falkenstein and W. von Soden, *Sumerische und akkadische Hymnen und Gebete* (Zurich–Stuttgart, 1953) p. 274.

[6] *Ibid.*, pp. 235–37.

[7] Col. V, lines 42 ff. (P. F. Gössmann, O.E.S.A., *Das Era Epos* [Würzburg, n.d.] p. 37).

more important in the tradition-directed society of the ancient Orient, but we must keep perspective. The difference is not absolute and qualitative. All discourse, at least if it aspires to communication, is formed by an interplay of traditional and social elements with the personal. Of course, we use words for purposes other than communication, to relieve our feelings for instance, and here a perfectly private language would be sufficient. However, this hardly need concern the study of inspiration, for the inspired word is certainly communication. It is God's word, and the idea of God's needing to express Himself in human language as a form of relief or for any other similar motive is too grotesque to need consideration. Thus the inspired word is delimited by a social context just as any other form of communication, for it is a word and a literary form, that is, a matter of conventional signs which transmit ideas because and only because the usage of a human group has endowed them with meaning. If a writer—and this includes the sacred writer—were to demand complete freedom from the conventions of his society, he would have to give up language and destroy all possibility of communication. Thus, however personal may be the work of a writer, however new the trail he blazes, he must submit in some degree to traditional elements recognized in his society. The relative weight of personal and social factors will vary from time to time, from situation to situation, but these factors are always there. Hence we cannot reduce biblical literature to a social phenomenon, as though the social element appeared in it alone, and seek in this that which without qualification specifies inspired literature. The problem is rather to study the factors which produced our texts and to try to see if and how society functioned among them.

THE ORIGINS OF INSPIRED DISCOURSE

One class of Old Testament writing, indeed, might make us wonder about the special place of a social element in the origins of inspired discourse. The prophets were the recipients of an extraordinary, direct divine communication, revelation in a strict sense. Such immediate contact with the divine we conceive most easily in terms of the documented experiences of the mystics, but these are intensely personal, private experiences, not social. One might object that the bands of prophets seem to have used techniques to produce ecstatic phenomena in the whole group, as in 1 S 10:5, and thus connect the prophetic delirium with group activity. However, whatever may be the case with the bands of prophets, scholars now generally agree that the great "writing" prophets were of a different type. The great inaugural visions, for instance, can scarcely be connected with an ecstatic frenzy.[8] They impress one as personal, mystic, and private experience.

Here we must note that we cannot equate the experience of the prophetic vocation such as is recounted in Is 6, Jer 1, and Ez 1–3 with inspiration. The prophets are given a mission, but even an authentic mission, though it be grounded in direct, mystical experience, does not of itself and necessarily make human discourse the word of God. Rather, the connection between direct experience of the divine and the prophetic word is to be sought at one level in the consultation of the Lord exemplified by the activity of Elisha in 2 K 3:13–20, but especially in the divine communications which enabled the prophets to say of their speeches "Thus says Yahweh." This experience compelled the prophet to act (cf. Amos 3:8; Jer 1:6 ff.). It involved visions (Amos 7:1–9) and auditions (7:3 ff.; Jer 15:15–20). We can hardly consider this to mean a kind of dictation, in view of the very personal styles of the different prophets. The divine word did not suppress personality but was expressed through it.

In view of all this it is tempting to make some sort of direct divine communication the distinguishing note of inspiration. It is communication given in a manner transcending ordinary causes. It is, in effect, revelation, and the perennial problem, that of finding a distinct, recognizable divine element in inspiration, is solved. However, tempting though it is, the solution to the problem of inspiration does not lie in this direction. For one thing, there is a great deal of inspired writing which gives no evidence of a special, mystic contact with the divine such as is found in the prophets. Besides, the intrusion of the marked

[8] The problem of prophetic mysticism is often complicated by a confusion which takes mystical to mean ecstatic in the sense of violent seizure with external phenomena and often involving psychic abnormalities. The truly mystical may be defined as special, more direct communion with the divine, and whatever may have been the place of the ecstatic in some elements of the prophetic movement, it is the mystical which is of concern here, and it is meant whenever the word or its cognates are used.

personal characteristics of the prophets in their message raises a warning. They surely had a direct experience of the divine, an experience we understand most easily in terms of mysticism. However, the comparison of inspiration with mysticism is strictly limited by the fact that the central element of the former is a *motus ad exprimendum*. In contrast to this, mystical experience is interior, and the problems raised by the attempt to express it are a classical page in the theology of spirituality. Thus the comparison is weakest at the crucial point.

Still, we cannot get away from the fact that the origin of the great prophetic traditions lies in an amalgam of intimate personal experience of the divine and a personal reaction which marks the communication of the experience. Where in all this is the social and traditional element? It is not lacking, for the prophet's unique experience is communicated in recognized categories. Isaiah's message has a new note, but it is not expressed or understood except in terms of the traditions of Davidic kingship and the liturgy of Zion. Jeremiah presupposes Hosea. Ezekiel is clearly in a priestly tradition. With all their personal experience of the divine, the prophets are acted on and themselves act on a tradition carried in the social structures of Israel.

What has been said thus far applies in the first place to spoken prophecy. In the beginning the prophet had an oral message to his own generation. To be a prophet, to give out the word of God, did not in itself involve writing. Hence the problem of the written message, the point where scriptural inspiration lies, remains open. However, before taking this up, it will be useful to consider a different sort of coming to terms with the divine evidenced in the Old Testament documents.

There is much in the Old Testament which may be called theological history writing, reflection on historical experience in the light of revealed notions. A great and very early example would be the Yahwist document. This was, as far as we know, the first such compilation of the oldest traditions of Israel not as a more or less indiscriminate collection but as an ordered whole. The whole history from the fathers and beyond them to the beginnings of creation is organized in view of the chosen people and the Promised Land. The point is not mere record. It is a brilliant response to the question posed by the organization and expansion of Israel under David. The secure possession of the land flowing with milk and honey is seen as the term of a divinely directed historical process, the concrete evidence of the favor of Yahweh.[9]

Here we have the reaction of a writer to his own historical experience interpreted in terms of the Yahwist traditions. The Yahwist's experience of the divine (if we may be allowed these terms) was not of a mystical sort, as far as our evidence indicates; it comes in and through the experience of the historical situation reflected upon in the light of Yahwism. Once more there is experience, personal reaction, and tradition. The Yahwist thinks through his experience and explains it in traditional terms, and yet in a style sufficiently individual to permit us to distinguish his work amidst the whole in which it has been merged. Thus we have the same general factors as in the prophets. However, the experience, instead of being a mystical contact with the divine, is a kind of reflection comparable to our own theologizing. Where is there the mark of an extraordinary divine intervention of a mystical sort? We can find none; yet this is also inspired writing.

This is not the only example of theological history writing in the Old Testament. There is also, for example, the central section of Deuteronomy, chapters 6–28. The author of these chapters had apparently had an experience almost the contrary of that of the Yahwist writer. He saw not the secure acquisition but the threatened loss of the Land. However, once more there is experience reflected on and explained in the terms of the tradition. The new circumstances are part of the divine plan as much as the old, different as they are.

Then there was someone who added chapters 4 and 29–30 to the original Deuteronomic document and so gave the whole a more hopeful note. Once more tradition came into play, for each of these pericopes uses the Deuteronomic covenant form, but alters it so that it ends not with threats and curses but with the hope of repentance and return (Dt 4:29–31; 30:1–14). Surely, here again is reflection on experience, the bitter experience of conquest and exile, in which traditional doctrine is applied and new understanding achieved. We could cite the com-

[9] For the theological analysis of J, see G. von Rad, "Das formgeschichtliche Problem des Hexateuch," in *Gesammelte Studien zum Alten Testament* (Munich, 1958) pp. 58–81.

position of the Books of Kings from official records with the history judged in terms of the Deuteronomic traditions, and other examples as well.

Thus there is no lack of evidence for the effectiveness of theological reflection on history as a source of inspired writing. We may emphasize the role of the social and the traditional in all this, but there is also a very personal note. There was a Deuteronomic school, but a work like Dt 6–28 is not the product of featureless anonymity. The author may be nameless but he is a personality. And so of other examples. Moreover, these personalities make tradition. They are inconceivable apart from the tradition from which they draw the terms for their reflections on their experience. But equally and more, the tradition after them depends on them. It could never be the same after the Yahwist or the Deuteronomist wrote.

This touches on a special problem. What of the sources used by the sacred writers and their inspiration? Were the stories the theological writers used to construct the early history of Israel inspired? They often had a religious note, connection with cult centers or rites and so on, with often a profound meaning as in Gn 2–3. But what of the history of the kings? Here use was certainly made of documents from official archives. Were these inspired? One wonders just how inspiration affected a dusty chancery clerk. On the other hand, we feel sure that the writer who supplied the frame for the central Deuteronomic document was working on already inspired material. Surely also the redactor who composed the Pentateuch from J and E, and so on.

But how do we judge the inspiration of these things? From religious origins, value of the content? These will hardly do as criteria for inspiration—at least not without qualification. Value of content tends to mean value for me, for my generation, and it is simply a fact that different epochs find true religious values in widely diverse materials. We find the cultic minutiae of Leviticus dry and uninspiring; for someone they were of paramount interest, and that for their religious significance, and the author of Hebrews could develop a rich theology around the rubrics of the cult. So also for religious origins. Whose religion? For instance, we find the idea of an inspired government clerk amusing. Nowadays not even the bureaucrat himself would openly identify himself and his function with the divine. But what of a nation which was a true theocracy, its governor God's vicegerent in a covenant community? Even the census had a theological meaning (2 S 21:1–17). Dry lists and numbers take on new importance in such a context.

Here, perhaps, we can see how to apply the value criterion validly. We must seek the value which a source, an idea, had not for us but for the one who used it in composing an inspired text. He chose what he did because he found there a religious value, alien though it may be to our feeling in the matter. But this way leads us once again to the community. In many such instances a thing was selected precisely because of its relevance to a stage of Israelite society. So, for example, those so pedestrian lists and genealogies of temple functionaries in Chronicles; they were all important for the temple-centered, priest-governed, traditionalist postexilic community. Thus interest in firmly establishing his society was determinative in the inspired writer's work. He functioned within the process by which the developing community established its form and acquired its normative texts. Moreover, his own product was subject to the process. As he selected from his sources, so must the divinely guided community recognize his text among its rivals because it served the life of the community. The survival of inspired texts could not be a mere accident of history.

We cannot, of course, suppose without a gratuitous assumption of special revelation that the earlier writers, whether theologians of the stature of the Deuteronomist or the chancery drudge, foresaw and willed the exact use later made of their work and so understand inspiration in terms of such a finality. However, we need not fall back on a finality in the divine plan, in the divine mind only; for if it is inaccurate to submerge the person of the ancient author in a tradition, as though he had no creative personality of his own and the literary product were due simply to society, there is no doubt that he knew himself to be part of a society far more than a self-conscious modern, and he did turn his work over to a tradition carried in a society which would live after him. Just as he had used traditional materials, reworked them, and marked them by his own experience and reflection, so he knew his own work would become part of tradition to be used.

There is another aspect to this question of the inspiration of sources. We must allow for some sort of double divine influence, that on the author of the source of a historical narrative or the prophet in respect to his oracle, and that on the later person or persons who used these things to produce a larger whole. Preoccupied with the fascinating task of historical reconstruction or the problems of a short passage of great theological richness, we often isolate a passage from its literary context and consider it in its historical or theological context. This is valid and useful, but we must not forget that it is not merely or even primarily the sentence or the pericope which is inspired; it is the literary whole. A passage has a meaning in terms of its position in a whole, even when that whole is a mosaic constructed out of source material and not written as a unit in one sitting, so to speak. This meaning is not necessarily confined to that which it had in original isolation, and it is obviously a work of authorship to determine this new meaning.

We have looked somewhat more closely at prophecy and theological history writing, but these are only two among many diverse forms in which Old Testament literature was cast. One might add the Psalter and wisdom literature, to mention obvious cases, but even as it is, the examples cited suffice to show the difficulty in seeking the specific note of inspiration in a mystical experience or in the reception of revelation or in the pertaining to a society and its traditions. All these elements occur in the production of inspired writings, but they cannot be shown to belong to inspired works *omnibus et solis*. Our theory must cover mystic and nonmystic experience, reflection and revealed knowledge, traditional and personal production.

Moreover, so far we have been concerned with the problem of inspired discourse in general and not the specific problem, which is inspiration to write. The prophet at least was moved in the first instance to transmit an oral message. How was this related to writing? Is writing accidental, an alternative means of communication which adds no special signification of its own?

THE PURPOSE OF WRITING

Here we may ask why man writes at all. There are certainly reasons extrinsic to writing as such, social and economic pressures like conditions for academic advancement, or beliefs that writing gave words an added magic and made them more potent. Such effects can be and are obtained without writing. But there are also aspects which are bound up with the very nature of writing. The most venerable is the practical record, as in deeds and so on. This purpose of writing does not imply publication; the idea is less to make a fact known generally than to be able to confirm it if it is questioned. The aim of writing here is predominantly permanence. Another end of writing as such is the need to communicate with those who are beyond the range of the voice, either because they are in a different place or because they live in a different, future time. These two things may be separate. Writing need not imply desire for permanence in time, as, for instance, it usually does not in our personal letters. In the Bible, Jer 30:1–6 is an explicit instance of writing aimed at communication with absent persons, the exiles of Israel. In Jer 36, writing is a means of bringing the prophetic message into the royal court, where the prophet could not penetrate in person, but when the message is rejected and the scroll containing it burnt, a new writing is prepared and it is now aimed at bringing the message to the future and so vindicating the prophet.

Now, the Old Testament contains works which in their very conception demand writing and so imply its purposes. The Books of Kings, excerpts from administrative records with theological comment, are hardly conceivable except in terms of writing. The complex data, the reference to records, and the length of the treatise mean that it could hardly have been composed otherwise. Thus, when God chose to intervene and produce such a work through inspiration, the very nature of things means He would produce a writing. The same argumentation applies to the rest of theological history writing, at least insofar as the treatises are at all extensive. There may well be much shorter forms of expression which demand that they originate in writing. This would apply to complex, finely worked poetry. A sonnet of Mallarmé, for instance, is unthinkable except in terms of a written draft and long revision. A biblical instance might well be the elaborated poetic constructions of Isaiah.[10]

Such forms of discourse in the Old Testament imply an aspiration to a certain width of distribution and, what concerns us more, to a permanent existence in time.[11] When an author took the trouble to

[10] See Luis Alonso Schökel, *Estudios de poética hebrea* (Barcelona, 1963).

[11] And existence as a work to be read and known, not simply as a record. A literary text would seldom be committed to writing for use as a record alone.

write an extensive and/or carefully ordered work, deeply thought upon, we may imagine he would want his work to live on after him. This is especially true of an ancient writing, expensive and valuable in its material self and multiplied only by a painful process of copying. It did not, in fact, offer a great opportunity for wide distribution by modern standards; primarily it had the ability to endure. Thus we may be sure that the ancient writer and the One who inspired him to this sort of work willed to communicate to future generations. That is to say, there was a will to enter into a society and its tradition, a will more clearly and sharply expressed than it would be in the handing down of oral teaching. This will is confirmed by a glance at the content of these writings. They are religious in a special, social sense. They are concerned to understand the life of God's people in history, to judge the past and guide the future. So also the prophets, on the assumption that some of their discourse could have originated only as writing, condemned, advised, and promised with a view to edifying (in the root sense) God's people in the future as well as in the prophet's own era. It seems clear that such writings aimed at becoming a part of the complex of laws, stories, songs, and so on which made up the normative tradition of the chosen people.

Such divinely inspired contribution to the tradition would enter the stream of tradition in a relatively stable form. This is especially true of the long theological writings. Their bulk and complexity would be a protection. Glosses, expansions, and such could be introduced, but fundamental alterations would be less likely than in oral material or even in a written work which was shorter or more amorphous. The significance of the whole as a unit would be a protection against fragmentation, for fragments would be less valuable than the whole, and the size would leave the work relatively immune to change caused by being introduced into a new context. So we would expect, and such is in fact the case. The large theological history treatises tend to reach us glossed and augmented, but with the basic shape of the work preserved. Among the examples adduced, the J document would be an exception to this, for it has been truncated and used as a source for a later work. This is true, but even so the essential character of the work can be seen without much trouble. Nor does such a fate disprove the implication of permanence connected with such writing. Permanence for us is relative, and over a period of centuries writings must be interpreted and applied to new conditions—but because they are writings and so lasting that they are there to serve in the process.

The fate of shorter texts, single poems, or small anthologies would likely be somewhat different. The very complexity from which we argue to a written origin invites error on the part of scribes, and in fact the more poetic passages of the Old Testament are often the most difficult textually. Besides these accidental changes, short units are open to a use which can bring profound changes. A slight addition or omission can mean a great deal, but especially a short text can be given a new orientation by being made part of a new, larger whole.

In this respect such poems would approach the situation of a considerable portion of the prophetic discourses. These were short units and essentially something spoken. The writing down of such speeches adds a dimension beyond what is implied in the form and situation of the discourse. Perhaps here the specific meaning of writing as such can be seen most clearly.

We may exclude accidental writing—writing as a simple *ad hoc* substitute for speech which is impeded for some reason. A prophet with a sore throat might communicate an urgent message in writing, or Jeremiah might send a note into a place forbidden to him in person. Such writing does not imply anything more than oral delivery.

What, on the other hand, can be learned from the writing of a per se oral form in other circumstances? The prophets themselves offer some information on the point. In Is 8:1, a saying is recorded before witnesses so that it can be referred to when fulfilled. The idea seems to be to provide credentials that the prophet is a true one rather than to broadcast the message more widely in space or time. If Is 8:16 is to be taken as referring to writing rather than as a figure for the very presence of the prophet as a testimony to the nation, the meaning would be much the same: a record to show where the truth lies, over against those who follow false oracles and go to their ruin. However, the passage goes beyond the function of mere record. The purpose is to establish that Isaiah is the true prophet, just as possession of the deed establishes the true owner of a house; but there is also the object of validating the prophet's mission, showing that his words are the true guide for Israel. Thus the passage is concerned indirectly with publication, with getting Isaiah's doctrine known and accepted. The preoccupation with the validity of the prophetic office recurs in the mention of writing in Is 30:8. For our purpose it is immaterial whether the command to write refers to the name given Egypt in 30:7, as the parallel with the recording of the name Maher-shalal-hash-baz in 8:1 would lead one to think, or the condemnation of Judah in 30:9 ff. In either case the idea is to provide a proof that the prophet saw and revealed the truth, and a proof which will be realized in a short time. So it is with Jer 36:27 ff.: the prophet's recorded words will be seen to be true shortly and so vindicate him against the king and his advisers.[12] In Hb 2:2, things are more indefinite. The prophecy will be fulfilled, but the wait may be long, as v. 3 makes clear. Nevertheless, the record will be there.

Thus the prophetic words and actions gave a certain impetus to the preservation of the prophetic oracles in writing, but the concern was mostly with more or less immediate ends. Moreover, the writing was done not to be read regularly in a later time, but to vindicate the prophet when the events predicted came about. This is more record than literature.

THE WORD COMMITTED TO TRADITION

However, this was not the end of the matter. During and after the prophet's lifetime, there was a period of collection and preservation of the oracles, a period which involved writing from the first stages.[13] Insofar as this was merely recording of the master's words, this function must be thought of as purely secretarial, even if it meant recording memorized material rather than receiving dictation. Such recording of the prophet's words surely implies the wish to make it known to the future, and so began the process by which the prophetic sayings became part of the tradition. In these "prophetic schools" other parts of the tradition and the society which carried them began themselves

[12] On the shortness of time involved, see W. Rudolph, *Jeremiah* (*Handbuch zum Alten Testament* 12; Tübingen, 1958) pp. 147–49.

[13] This is denied, especially by the Scandinavian school. See E. Nielsen, *Oral Tradition: A Modern Problem in Old Testament Introduction* (*Studies in Biblical Theology* 11; London, 1954). Justification for the statement in the text is found in J. van der Ploeg, O.P., "Le rôle de la tradition orale dans la transmission du texte de l'Ancien Testament," *Revue biblique* 54 (1947) 5 ff.

to affect the prophetic words. Note, however, that even in the "schools" someone, an individual, no matter how much influenced by his community, had to do the work of writing, ordering, and so forth.

Thus committed to the hands of tradition, the prophetic words were open to development—development which was inevitable as long as they were treated as something alive, something to be used, and not a dead letter merely to be admired. Such development might be little more than a matter of grouping. Does the more or less standard order—threats against the Jews, threats against the nations, oracles of consolation[14]—which was one result of the activity of those who passed on the sayings, have no significance as to the meaning of the prophetic words? Does it not point up the reference to the future consolation, to the Messianic hopes?

Perhaps the example is too general to be entirely convincing. There are other more sharply defined cases, for instance, Deutero-Isaiah, Is 7, Is 10:5–27. Each of these is a grouping of originally separate, shorter oracles. Here one might raise a question as to who did the grouping. If it stems from the prophet himself—and there are those who would contend it does—what does this have to do with society and tradition? For one thing, the attribution of such work to the prophet is definitely a minority opinion, and in the case of Is 10:5–27 such attribution is scarcely tenable. In any event, even if one insisted that the prophet was the compiler, he would be functioning no longer as a prophet but merely as an agent of tradition. He appears as incapable of oracles delivered with regard to the immediate situation. He has been reduced to taking old sayings either from memory or from notes and arranging them to serve new ends.

The effects of such arrangement in Deutero-Isaiah may be seen in the well-known division between chapters 40–48 and 49–55. A main difference between the two parts is that Cyrus, the magnificent deliverer of the first part, is absent from the latter part. He had not fulfilled all the hopes that had been placed in him. He had ended the Babylonian mastery, but without punishing Babylon and without bringing about a triumphant return to the Promised Land. Still, the Cyrus oracles with their glowing terms were not suppressed or altered. Again, there are the descriptions of the return itself in magnificent terms of a new and

[14] So Ezekiel, Jeremiah (LXX), and to an extent Isaiah.

more wonderful Exodus. But the prophet and his followers who had experienced the Persian conquest of Babylon and its aftermath could not have missed the sorry prospects of the actual return: a trickle of stragglers so utterly unlike the new Exodus. Yet the oracles were conserved and even added to. This could not be simply due to the fact that they are prophetic oracles which promise great things to Israel. If such were the reason for keeping them as they are, why are the fine promises of the false prophets, Jeremiah's opponents, lost? Nor can such language be discounted as mere fancy and misplaced enthusiasm. Before the event perhaps, but they could continue in use and be made part of a prophetic book only on the supposition that they were seen to apply to something more than the miserable return. The poetry of the prophet was seen to imply more than the immediate historical event which was its occasion.

There is a similar sort of development to be seen through the work of the compiler in Is 7. Because of Ahaz's faithlessness, the Emmanuel prophecy has turned into a half-threat. Hence the pregnant "days" in 17b, recalling the "day of Yahweh" which in popular belief would see Yahweh avenge His people, but which the prophetic preaching had turned into a threat against that very people.[15] This word was a magnet attracting other Isaian sayings about the day (7:18, 20, 21, 23), so that now "day" serves as a link word tying the whole together, and the original story and oracle have become a larger unity. Thus the oracle must be read in the light of the rest of the chapter, for, as we have said, it is the whole structure which is the inspired word of God written for us, and not merely the isolated oracle as originally given. Now, the Emmanuel oracle referred to the Syro-Ephraimite war, while the sayings in vv. 18 ff. presumably concerned the invasion of Sennacherib some thirty years later! But if we must read the whole as a unit, the limitation of the oracle to a particular event is lifted, its significance generalized. Thus the tradition-conserving agent who not only handed the oracle on but gave it its present, final context shows a belief that the words of a prophet have a wider meaning than their first application and in consequence of this belief effectively interprets the oracle simply by giving it a place in a larger structure.

Similarly in Is 10:5–27, there are several originally separate sayings.

[15] Amos 5:18.

5–14 clearly are concerned with Assyria even apart from the present context.[16] 15–19 are also applied to Assyria, for with their condemnation of the arrogant it is impossible to read them as they now stand following the boasting of the Assyrian as anything but the divine condemnation of the enemy of Judah. But it is equally clear that the saying was first directed to the Jews: the picture of the desolate land belongs to the imagery of the prophetic *Gerichtsrede* against the chosen people, and the reference to the devastated forest fits Palestine rather than Assyria. Especially the remnant mentioned in v. 19 makes us think of Isaiah's prediction for his own people, and this is confirmed in the present text in that the word serves as a link word to the next oracle concerning the remnant of the chosen people. The result of the grouping here is even more complex than in chapter 7. The central oracle in 10:15–19 is clearly and fittingly applied to Assyria, yet is seen as appropriate to Israel. In sum, a two-pronged signification has been given the text by the tradition which preserved and used it. Once more arrangement has produced new meaning.

However, this was not the limit of the powers of those who passed on the prophetic word. Not being harassed by the demands of critics, they could collect with a large hand. After all, why did the "schools" preserve the oracles? It was more than simple piety toward the master, more even than the desire to justify him by preserving his fulfilled predictions. These motives were not absent, but Israel was pre-eminently practical, interested in history but not in historicism. The primary motive of the collectors was the feeling that the prophetic words had present and future reference for the life of God's people. Nor was this simply insofar as they inculcated useful moral and religious lessons of a general, universally valid character. They applied as prophecy to more particular things.

This is reflected in the freedom with which new oracles were added to the collections. This is easily seen in the sections devoted to the oracles against the nations. Sayings against the enemies of a day later than that of the prophetic master were freely taken into the corpus. These would hardly have been felt to be real alterations of the prophet's meaning. It was not just that an old oracle against Assyria, for example,

[16] Vv. 5–14 actually represent more than one saying, but this does not matter for our purpose.

and a newer against Babylon were placed side by side. Rather, the master had spoken out against the enemies of Yahweh, and one merely explicitated his meaning in the oracle against the present enemy.

Further, it was possible not merely to place later oracles among earlier as a kind of interpretation, but also to give new meaning to the original saying itself. This would probably be admitted most generally in the case of additions which gave an eschatological meaning to an older oracle with a historical context. This occurs, for instance, to the oracle about the sins of Samaria in Is 28 through the addition of vv. 5–6, or in Is 52:3–6, but the thing is common enough to need little discussion. Such changes are not confined to putting in an eschatological meaning; an oracle can receive a new or a wider application by addition, change, or complete reworking. One example is the extension of a saying originally directed to one of the two Jewish kingdoms, so that it applied to both, as in Jeremiah's famous promise of a new covenant in 31:31–34. From the context we see that the original destination was the kingdom of Israel, but the phrase "to the house of Judah" has been added to extend it to the other kingdom.[17]

Thus the sayings of the prophets were conserved and adapted with a view to their ever-present reality and concrete reference. They were possessions of the community to be used by it. Here we meet the social element, the group in which the tradition lived and reacted to new experience. The tradition did not just pass the prophetic word on; to a considerable extent it formed it.

It is obvious that all this has its repercussions on the problem of meaning. Indeed, inspiration can hardly be discussed apart from the problem of the sense of Scripture. It is, after all, meaningful discourse which is inspired. In our case it is clear that the Israel which produced the prophetic writings saw in them a meaning or meanings beyond a narrowly conceived *intentio auctoris* in the sense of what might be the very limited horizon of the human originator of the writing.[18] For Israel, for the "prophetic schools," the prophetic word had an applica-

[17] E. Vogt, S.J., "Textumdeutungen im Buche Ezechiel," in *Sacra pagina* 1 (supra n. 2) pp. 471 ff., gives more examples of change by interpolation.

[18] Surely the conception of authorship in a very individualistic sense has encouraged preoccupation with the intention of the first writer. If more than one person had a role in making up a text, more than one intention could be involved.

tion beyond the immediate application which seems to have been the concern of the prophet.

Further, the argument is not limited to the prophetic books. Even a well-constructed whole like the central part of Deuteronomy could and did undergo a certain amount of reinterpretation at the hands of the tradition, for the addition of chapters 4 and 29–30 definitely affects the doctrine as a whole. The consideration of the problem of the use of inspired sources to form a new whole, that is, effectively to alter and extend their meaning, points in the same direction. The effects of compilation and organization upon meaning cannot be attributed to the fact that a book was formed gradually by a "school," as though this were the only means to such results. The same results can come from the work of a single person working with sources.

In fact, we must recognize that the problem of the meaning of texts is not so simple as is often supposed. Literature—or better, discourse, for the problem is wider than the field of belles-lettres implied by the word literature—conserved in texts is not a dead thing. It has a kind of vitality of its own, a power which cannot be limited simply to what the author consciously intended. This is true of any such discourse, and the better the composition the more the meaning. This is not a mystique aimed at justifying a spiritual sense; it is simply a principle of sober scholars derived from the study of modern, secular literature and its meaning,[19] and it is clear enough on a little reflection. A text cannot be bounded by the author's conscious understanding and intention. Apparently Housman did not have anything in his head at all when, after a good lunch and a pint of beer, some of his loveliest lines popped unbidden into his head. And it was not simply a jest when Browning denied understanding some of his own work. Or consider the classicist eighteenth-century's view of Hamlet, that of the romantics, and that of the Freudian critics. Must we affirm that these are all aberrations, that the play does not mean any of these?

On another level, what of the formative texts of a society or culture? These are especially significant for us because, though there is great literature and almost everything else in the Old Testament, the central concern of its books is the life of God's people. At once history, ideal,

[19] See, for instance, R. Wellek and A. Warren, *Theory of Literature* (London, 1961) pp. 148, 156–57.

constitution, it is definitely for a community. So, for example, are the Declaration of Independence and the Gettysburg Address in America. They are documents from which scientific history can glean certain ideas about conditions and events of their time, but they are much more than that. They have an intentional and emotional resonance beyond what Jefferson or Lincoln had in mind. Must we deny that these meanings come legitimately from the texts? I think not. With luck and genius the authors made words into vital, richly meaningful entities. If this is so in the cases cited and in many others, why not in the Scriptures too?

Writings of the sort, concerned with social organisms, have a complex intention. They do not merely record facts, even though they be deeply involved in the realities of their time and place. They present an ideal and a program to a social unit which exists in time. The ideal can be attained, the program implemented, only in stages. That is to say, the ideas presented are not entirely verified in the first instance, in the social structure which exists before the author's eyes and to which he applies his words. The original United States with slavery retained, to take but one example, verified the principles of the preamble to the Declaration less exactly than it did in a later era, yet the text applied to the American social unit at both stages. So too, to take but one important example, a whole strain of Old Testament literature is concerned with the Davidic monarchy. It is concerned with the reality, the actual, defective realization. Equally and more, it is applied to a better implementation, for it aimed at the ideal. The birth of Hezekiah might fulfil Isaiah's prophecy of Emmanuel, but it did not exhaust it, for the ideal of God with His people was still not implemented as it might be.

COMMUNITY UTILITY

Here the question of scriptural meaning throws some light on the relation of inspiration and society. The conception of a social origin of inspiration in terms of an impersonal source is inadequate. The great streams of Old Testament revelation are deeply marked by personalities: the prophets, the Deuteronomist, the Yahwist. Whether we know their names or not is immaterial; the discourse they produced is theirs and no one else's, a product of personal reaction to experience, mystical or ordinary.

At the same time, these experiences and these reactions took place within a tradition and a society. Their expression, with all its personal character, reflected this. In itself, however, this is true to some degree of all literature. A traditional source in this sense is no more a specifying note of inspired writing than is mystical experience. Is it perhaps some peculiar character in the society and tradition in which the Old Testament arose that marks it off as the word of God? The society was indeed the people of God, and in our examples the Old Testament texts arose out of reactions to the historical experiences of this people. More, the interpretation and expression of this experience is in terms of Yahwist doctrine. Is it perhaps this explicit connection with Yahweh's community which specifies our inspired books?

If this is so, what are we to make of the Old Testament wisdom literature? The objection is classic: much of Israel's wisdom reflects a common Oriental tradition and universal human experience. There is no explicit reference to the people of Yahweh and its special, divinely guided historical experience.[20] Moreover, what of expressions which are incomplete in themselves and need further development? One thinks of Qohelet and even Job, which raise doubts about received ideas, yet manage to reach no solution but end questioningly or even negatively. Still, this is inspired literature. To be sure, later wisdom writing does concern itself with the people of Yahweh. The prologue of Sirach is an explicit statement of a process we have found at the origins of theological history writing, reflection on Israel's history in the light of its religious tradition. But this will not save the case; our theory of inspiration must still account for the rest of the wisdom literature, where the Yahwist reference is lacking.

It would seem that the position of such writings can be understood only in terms of the object and value they possessed, the use that could be made of them. If not explicitly from, they were certainly for, Yahweh's chosen community. They worked to edify the people, and this was confirmed in experience. Hence, if they lack an explicitly Yahwist source, they have an explicitly Yahwist end, and so a place in the tradition of Yahweh's people. This is a link to some other factors: the implications of writing as such; the meaning of texts, especially

[20] This is not to deny a de facto Yahwist origin, but as long as this is not explicit it cannot serve as a distinguishing note of the text as inspired.

those which aim to build a society; the implications of the processes through which Old Testament books were formed. All these emphasize the importance of the place the writings had in the community which existed and developed over extended time.

It is revealing to ask in this regard why the community preserved some books and not others. The fact is certain. We know from references in the Bible itself that ancient Israel had collections of songs and stories which are lost. Why these and not our historical books? Surely because these and not the others nourished the life of the community. To cite an example from another kind of writing, the words of Jeremiah were preserved, those of his opponent prophets disappeared, because his were verified in the historical experience of the Jewish community. This is not to equate inspiration and canonicity. Jeremiah's words as written and handed on were already inspired, but it was through the community's experience that this was recognized and their meaning appreciated. This was no passive assent to an experienced *adaequatio prophetiae ad rem.* The words were true and useful, precious guides for the community. This meant use and, as we have seen, development as new phases in the life of the community were met.

For us, accustomed to dogma and religious authority, this production of inspired writing, this separating out of what was valid among competing texts, may seem amorphous and insecure. Is this not, in fact, the point? Why does the divinely chosen community produce inspired writing? Is it not precisely because it is relatively unformed and unstructured? Not yet equipped with definitive norms and definitive authorities, its own life, its own utility had to be the criterion which guided the production and recognition of the inspired, and utility is defined in terms of end. As the growing community of God, Israel was subject to a special divine intervention which guided it to its end. This was a special divine work different from providence, conservation, and so on; otherwise Israel could not have been the chosen people in any meaningful sense, its history a special history of salvation, for all peoples and all history are under the control of the ordinary providence of God. Indeed, a divinely chosen society as yet lacking definitive norms and organs had need of continuous special divine intervention to urge on and guide the process which would terminate in the true Israel.

Given the nature of society, its existence over an extended period of time, one instrument of such divine guidance must surely be writing. With no regularly constituted teaching office, nothing else could provide norms and continuity, unless we want to posit constant direct revelation. And this is what analysis reveals. God nurtures His people, and it is within and for this divinely guided community, through a complex process in which the community itself is deeply involved, that the inspired books come to be.

Before concluding, it is necessary to note that some of this coincides with Rahner's theory of the inspiration of the New Testament. I believe, however, that it is simply a result of the Old Testament data. I have not had Rahner's formulations in mind, nor have I sought to verify them in the Old Testament.

Rahner himself distinguishes the Old from the New Testament. He points out that the Old Testament community was not the final, definitive object of divine choice and so could not produce and recognize a definitive collection of inspired writings.[21] This could be done only by the definitive society, as it alone possessed a definitive criterion. However, the distinction is not absolute. If not final, still the Old Testament community was the object of an extraordinary predefinition antecedent to man's acts.[22] It was thus specially chosen and it was the object of continued divine intervention to guide it. True, in one sense the Old Covenant was conditional and liable to be ended, and the old institutions were temporary. This latter is inevitable in a developing organism. Instruments needed for one stage of growth may often not be useful in another stage or in maturity. Thus old institutions had to disappear when the divinely directed growth of the people of God had no more need of them. Even the conditional and undetermined character of some aspects of the old, the possibility which was actually realized that some institutions would not bring about the desired result, even this is to be attributed to the fact that the Old Testament people of God was growing, and there is a certain tension in all developing organisms. Just because they are developing, that is, have not reached definitive form, they are open not merely to the loss of elements needed at an earlier stage, but also to divergent developments. Not yet

[21] Rahner, *op. cit.* (supra n. 1) pp. 41, 51–54.
[22] Dt 9:4–5.

fixed, they can turn out to be good or to be bad. In brief, they can fail. This tension is reflected in the Deuteronomic form of the covenant, with its threat of rejection if the demands of the covenant are not fulfilled, and the terrible rejection is shown to be actual in the prophetic preaching of judgment. However, Israel was no merely natural society, and if it suffered from the tensions of any organism, it also enjoyed the unconditioned promise to Abraham and David which guaranteed its permanence in some sense. More, the passing institutions and even the failures, like the covenant which was broken, are not mere facts of history. They have an enduring, present meaning and value, for in the constant Christian tradition they speak of Christ and His Church.

This simply repeats in a new context what we have seen, that the Old Testament texts from their very nature and mode of growth are not closed within themselves. They look to something to come. They belong to God's people, at a lower stage of development it is true, but still specially guided so that it could produce and discern God's word in the sacred texts, if not in definitive, still in significant, valid form. It is a matter of record that it did so, producing and preserving the inspired and dropping other writings.

DENNIS J. McCARTHY, S.J.

The Word of God and "Literary Embellishment"

"The Scripture scholars with their midrash and so forth have thrown out the baby with the bath as far as I am concerned. It is disconcerting to have no way of finding out how much is the word of God and how much is literary embellishment. I have simply given up meditation on the Bible." This is an actual quotation from a religious, and it is one which states the uneasiness many of us feel. It also exposes the total misunderstanding of what Scripture scholars are trying to do which is the real root of this uneasiness. There is "no way of finding out" what "is the word of God" and "what is literary embellishment" because the distinction is impossible. The literature *is* the word of God. The literary expression is not a mere material cloak for some mysterious divine thing; the expression is the divine communicating itself to man in the only terms man can grasp, human terms. We can speak of a divine humility in the incarnation;[1] so also God deigned to adapt Himself to our ways of speaking and the word prepares for the Word.[2] We have to take this seriously. Human expression is limited to the vocabulary and syntax of the various languages of man; if God uses language His word must come under these limitations. Further, different stages of society have their proper modes of literary expression which are in effect limitations on an author's choice of literary form: the era of epic is not that of tragedy and so on. Since God's word is spoken to man, it comes in time; therefore, it is limited to the literary forms of its given time.[3] To suppose otherwise, to think that God regularly used His almighty power so as to free Himself from these limitations, is to suppose

Dennis J. McCarthy, S.J., is professor of Old Testament at St. Mary's College; St. Marys, Kansas 66536.

[1] Phil 2:7: Christ "emptied himself" to become man.
[2] Heb 1:1–2.
[3] Pius XII, *Divino afflante Spiritu* (*Enchiridion biblicum*, 538–69).

VOLUME 24, 1965
771

that He indulged in a unique series of miracles to alter the mind of the sacred writer so that he could grasp words, syntax, and ideas not at all his own and therefore not intelligible to him and in a correlative series of miracles for his audience, a change of their habits of thought so that they could grasp the writer's meaning and preserve his text as something of value to them. Does such a procedure accord with the dignity of free men? As an alternative we must assume that the writer did not understand his own message and that the community to which he gave his writing[4] accepted and handed down, often for hundreds of years, a text which it did not comprehend. This makes men mere robots. Theoretically there is no problem with this; God could have done it, but in fact the evidence is that he did not do so. The various books of the Bible show forth in a marked fashion the individualities of the originators of the messages as well as the influence of the ideas and modes of expression of their time. Further, the extraordinary textual corruptions in the more archaic and the more difficult passages of the Old Testament show that the men who handed them on did not in fact understand them fully and as a result made the errors which such failures to understand normally produce in texts transmitted by copying manuscripts. In essence, this is the insight and the value at the base of modern Scripture study. The Scripture scholar nowadays is loyally following the directions of the Church given by a great Pope when he tries to read the text as it is. As far as he is able he does not read into it; he reads it, strange and difficult though it may seem. He uses the techniques which have been developed by modern research in language and linguistics, he uses the results of archeological study, he applies the principles of literary study and criticism which are used by the best students of literature of our own day. This is the method of "close reading," "practical criticism" which has vindicated itself in current study of prose and poetry. It is essentially a method proportionate to God's generosity in speaking to us in human terms, a humble method dedicated to the author's situation and the text as it is, trying to learn what he has to say and not what the reader would like it to say.

The details of these techniques are new; the general principle, the mode of action, is entirely traditional.

---

[4] All the evidence is to the contrary. The community accepted the author's work and handed it down precisely because it was meaningful, supplying understanding of the past and present and guidance for the future. See D. J. McCarthy, S.J., "Personality, Society, and Inspiration," *Theological Studies*, v. 24 (1963), pp. 553–76, especially 566–76.

Men of all eras have used the rhetorical and literary principles of their time in order to understand God's word to His people. St. Augustine applied, and applied brilliantly, the theories and techniques of late Roman rhetorical science to the interpretation of Scripture. St. Thomas approached Scripture as a schoolman of the 13th century. His discussions are full of divisions and distinctions much like those of his own *Summa* or Lombard's *Sentences*. One would think that Isaiah or the Gospels were products of the Schools.[5] And so it is with the modern. He uses what is available to him from the efforts of linguistic and literary scholars of his own period. I submit that these reasonably objective techniques are valuable techniques, at least as useful as those of older interpreters. However, we have an added advantage nowadays. The ancient and the medieval student of Scripture, the rhetorician and the logician had only the text plus the techniques of his own age. Through a hundred and fifty years of patient archeological and philological labor we have acquired a broad basis of comparison against which we can study our Scripture texts. It is perhaps this basis of comparison which has been most revealing and which has done most to produce the present-day interpretation of Scripture, the interpretation which disturbed the sister we quoted and many another cleric, religious, and layman.

What has happened? We have been introduced into a vast mass of popular literature. Some of it is written in languages far different from Hebrew, yet contains materials much like that of the Bible. Collections of folklore, fables, and the like have revealed certain ideas and images, wishes and dreams common to all mankind which appear in literature, biblical literature included. But more precisely, we have discovered ancient Near-Eastern literatures which are the ancestors or the brothers of our biblical texts. It is this which has brought on the disturbance which the sister feels. Specifically, discovery of the midrash as a form of rabbinical interpretation has led to the recognition of the midrash as a form of New Testament—and, for that matter, Old Testament—writing. If one had thought that the Scripture passages now known to be midrash were somehow unique and miraculously different, it might well create a difficulty to find that they were borrowed from the

+
+
+

[5] It is not without relation to our problem that the violent upheavals of Reformation and Counter-Reformation made it impossible to assimilate and use the insights of Renaissance humanism in the interpretation of Scripture to the extent earlier eras had done with Roman rhetoric and Aristotelean logic. This failure surely contributed to the lack of preparation of the religious mind for later developments.

cultural milieu of the sacred writer. This may be upsetting at first glance, but in the end it is enriching. By understanding and recognizing the form, by comparing it with its congeners, we learn to understand it better; and eventually we know more of what God has to say to us. For let me repeat: the sister's distinction is invalid. God's word *is* the literary expression. We do not have God's word *plus* expression, we have literary expression which is God's word. I would like here to give one example of modern interpretative technique, the kind of problem it can raise, and what is, I hope, a solution which reveals the richness which reinterpretation and comparison give to our text. The doctrine is not new. The dogma remains the same. But the understanding, the breadth, the depth are immeasurably increased.

The example is one we are all familiar with, the story of the fall in Genesis 2 and 3, more accurately Genesis 2:4b–3. God creates first the male. He puts the man in a glorious garden. He delegates him to perform God's own task of supervising and ordering the universe and making it productive. He gives him the animals to control, an office indicated by the naming of the animals which tells us that Adam was a sage, the man who could "control and subdue" the animal kingdom in the words of the first chapter of Genesis. Yet this tremendous office, this charge over God's creation, this being God's vicegerent on earth, was not sufficient. Man was alone. And so God created out of man his meet companion, woman. So far in the account in Genesis 2 we have had a steady progression, a buildup toward the climax which is reached with the appearance of Eve, whom Adam recognized at once as his equal, his partner, his joy. We know too how the story continues. The serpent tempts Eve; Eve falls; Eve tempts Adam; he joins her in sin and the pair are expelled from the garden and condemned to live a life of sorrow. This story has always deeply impressed men. It speaks to something in the nature of man. Everyone who has heard it remembers it. For centuries this tale has been considered unique; there was nothing to which it could be compared. It is still unique in its literary mastery and the depth of its theological insight. But now we know that it is not entirely unique simply as literature. It reflects materials which are the possession of the human race as a whole, as well as things which are characteristic of ancient Near-Eastern culture in particular.

+ + +

We may note first some of the elements of folklore which abound in this Genesis story.[6] Paradise, the

[6] The classic commentary of H. Gunkel, *Genesis*, Göttingen, 1964

primal home of man, is a place of gold and jewels, glittering and lovely. It is a place where man is friendly with the animals and talks to them. It is a place abounding in plants with wondrous properties. This is the universal legend of the primal Golden Age. Adam succumbs to a preternatural sleep; think here of the story of the Sleeping Beauty, one among many where preternatural sleep plays a part in folklore. Man is ruined through woman; we have only to remember the parallel Greek legend of Pandora, who opened the box through which ill came into the world. The story is shot through with what are called technically etiologies; that is, tales developed to explain the names or the shapes or the way of things, a form of tale beloved of mankind. The making of woman from man explains the mysterious and powerful force of sex attraction. The serpent's malice explains its strange way of moving by crawling on its belly. The name *woman,* in Hebrew as in English related to the word *man,* and the name *Eve,* in Hebrew related to the word *life,* are explained. The name man, Hebrew *Adam,* is related to the word earth, the Hebrew *'adamah.* The agony of human childbirth is explained. So also the difficulties of a farmer. And so on.

We can all recognize the analogues of the things in our own store of folklore, stories told around the fireside on a winter evening. We also know that essentially this same story reappears in the Bible as a trope to describe and explain an historical event. In the 28th chapter of Ezekiel, the prophet recounts the fall of the proud prince of Tyre who is pictured as an extraordinary being, wise like Adam, dwelling in a splendid paradise of gold and jewels like Adam, suffering a fall like Adam and so punished. Each story even has its mysterious cherub. There is no doubt that the story of Ezekiel 28 depends upon the same general ideas, the same general tradition as the story in chapters 2 and 3 of Genesis. This demonstrates that Israel was ready to use elements from folklore to express theological truths about historical events. Clearly the details of the story of the fall of the prince of Tyre are not direct pictorial descriptions of historical events; they give vivid expression to the larger dimension of events, the overweening pride of man, and the punishment it brings down from God. Equally clearly the events behind the story, the Babylonians' siege and eventual capture of the Phoenician stronghold, are historical.

+
+
+

The examples we have cited so far are related to folklore in general, the common property of mankind. We

(reprinted from the 1910 edition), pp. 4–40, collects a mass of comparative data.

can find things like them in the tales of African tribes, Eskimos, American Indians, as well as in European and Asiatic folktales. But there is more: the story of man's creation as it is told in Genesis is rooted in its immediate Near-Eastern environment.

Genesis 2:5b,15 make it clear that the immediate business of man is husbandry; so also it was an idea of those earliest of civilized peoples, the Sumerians, that man was made to till the soil and keep the flocks.[7] Further, it is significant that there are four rivers in the Garden of Eden. Innumerable representations from the Mesopotamian area show that the stream of water was a special sign of the divine gift of life. Even more pertinently the four streams of life-giving water flowing from the hands of the god appear in the iconography of the region. For instance, the upper Euphrates town of Mari—inhabited, incidentally, by Ammorites who were remote collateral kinsmen of the Hebrews—has yielded murals of gods holding vases out of which pour forth four, always four, streams of life-giving water.[8] Then there is the tree of life, perhaps the fundamental religious symbol in the ancient Near-East, the tree given by a god, representing of course the gift of plant life, the basis of life for man and animal. It is repeatedly depicted, usually as a tree with animals, cattle or sheep or goats, feeding on the tree, one on each side.

In the climax of the creation story in Genesis 2, the formation of woman, there is that odd business of the woman's being made from Adam's rib. Why the rib? In Hebrew it has no special significance. However, there is a Sumerian story in which a female is formed from the rib of the primeval god Enlil. Now, *rib* in the Sumerian language is TI, but TI is also the word for *life,* so that in the Sumerian story we get the sort of pun which all peoples, especially the more unsophisticated, love. The Sumerian *Lady of the Rib* (NIN-TI) is also the *Lady of Life,* (again NIN-TI), the life-giver.[9] But this is exactly what Eve is. She gets her name, Eve, in Hebrew *ḥavvāh,* precisely because she gives life, *ḥayyāh,*[10] although in Hebrew the force of the pun is lost since in that language *rib* and *life* have no relation, not even an accidental similarity of sound or spelling.

---

[7] See S. N. Kramer; *Sumerian Mythology,* New York, 1961 (reprinted from the 1944 edition), pp. 72–3. Note that the Mesopotamian idea was that man did this work to relieve the gods for whom food was a necessity; the transcendent God of the Hebrews had no such need, yet His creation, man, has the same office, though now without the same urgent reason.

[8] See A. Parrot, *Sumer,* Paris, 1960, pp. 278–80.

[9] See S. N. Kramer, *The Sumerians,* Chicago, 1963, p. 149.

[10] Gn 3:20.

Still, the woman gets a name related to *life*. Apparently the ancient idea, the naming through function, was felt to be too good to be dropped even though the related pun had to be lost. It is hard to believe that this partial similarity to the Sumerian tale is an accident in view of the fact that the explanation of Eve's name does not really arise naturally out of its place in the Genesis story but is dragged into it. Its natural place would be after Genesis 3:16 or perhaps 4:1; therefore, we have good reason to assume that a cause outside the Hebrew story itself dictated this naming, and the evidence points to the Mesopotamian background as this cause.

Then there is that snake. Why the snake? By definition before the fall the snake was not an object of horror but an attractive animal like the others. Hence he seems to be chosen not because he was a cause of instinctive horror but because he was a symbol and an attractive one. In fact he was just this in the cults of Baal, the fertility cults of Canaan, the milieu of the ancient Israelite author. Goddesses are represented holding snakes in their hands, sacred pillars are represented with snakes twined around them, in classical culture, in this matter surely related to the general background of the ancient Levant including Canaan, snakes are pictured as coming out of the ground to receive the sacrifice.[11] It has been suggested that the snake seems so close to earth that it was thought that he had a special relation to and was a special favorite of all-mother, the basic source of fertility, the ultimate mother-goddess, the earth. It seems that the Hebrew author has looked around him and seen this snake as the symbol of a cult which, as we know from the prophets and the Deuteronomic history, was tremendously attractive to the Israelites. They were tempted, and they fell. They joined these rites, they dedicated their fertility, human, animal, and agricultural, to the wrong god, to the Baal. And so the inspired author set out to warn them. He told a story in which the very symbol of this attractive cult became the origin of evil. This should move the people and brand this attractive cult as something frightening, dangerous, deadly, in their eyes. This is effective preaching in the milieu of this writer. He writes for his time. Thus the role of the snake fits in with this whole list of topics and images and ideas in Genesis 2:4b–3:24 which are appropriate to and depend upon the society of 10th-

+
+
+

[11] J. Coppens, *La connaissance du bien et du mal*, Louvain, n.d., pp. 87–117; see also J. McKenzie, S.J., "The Literary Characteristics of Gn 2–3," *Theological Studies*, v. 15 (1954), pp. 541–572 (= *Theology Digest*, v. 6 [1957], pp. 19–23).

century Israel where this story was most likely composed.

And thus we have all these "literary embellishments" in Genesis 2:4b–3; and the word of God seems to have disappeared. Where is original sin in all this? In fact, it is there with an emphasis that is far stronger than that which one finds when one confines his attentions to a few verses of chapters 2 and 3 in the effort to describe the state of man before his fall and the results of his sin, and this precisely because of the literary technique used. Chapter 2 is essentially a hymn to marriage, a prothalamium. There is a conscious building of suspense: the man is created, the man is given an august office, he is offered the animals as companions, but he finds that none of these things suffices. What can God do? He shows Himself master of the situation by producing this wonderful creature, this woman in whom man at once recognizes his fated companion, the being who makes his life complete. This sequence should conclude with a marriage hymn. But how does it conclude? Its head is cut off. Instead of the bridal chamber we have sin and the ugliness of the serpent, instead of the joys of marriage shame at sexuality. And this is but one instance among many in the early chapters of Genesis which reinforce the writer's technique.

He has taken old, familiar, honored stories and by giving a twist to each has made his intention clear and emphasized his point: man has been sinful from the beginning. Thus he continues in chapter 4 with what was originally an interesting tale, the sort of thing that men tell to pass the evening hours. Among the Hebrews there was a tribe of tinkers, wanderers such as tinkers have always been. Why were these men wanderers? Why did they have the odd and primitive habit of tattooing their faces? Well, the story went, just look at their name. They are the Cainites. Our Bible spells it Kenites, but it is the same name, Cain, made into a tribal name. They are the children of Cain, and it is because of the character of their father that they wander about and have those tattoos. An innocent and interesting story for the fireside. But in Genesis it has been made into a bloody lesson in primordial sin.[12] One of the

+
+
+

[12] The "dispute" was a standard literary form among the ancients, and we have an example in Sumerian of one between farmer and herdsman just as in Gn 4; see J. B. Prichard, *Ancient Near Eastern Texts Relating to the Old Testament*[2] (hereafter abbreviated *ANET*), Princeton, 1955, pp. 41–2. One might object to my calling the original tale "innocent" since presumably though not necessarily (a dispute without killing might lead to exile) it dealt with murder. At least it is serious; the stories of Lot and his daughters (Gn 19:30–8) and of Esau (Gn 25:27) show how Israel could descend to the bawdy and

first brothers was a murderer. Man's sin and fall begun in the garden has continued and extended itself.

Genesis 6 continues the process of reediting familiar tales. We have here a tale of the heroes of old, the sacred author's reworking and retelling in short compass of the story of the great epic hero. Typically, the hero was half god, a being of such power and majesty that he could only be the son of a divinity. Thus in Greek epic Achilles is the son of the sea-goddess Thetis by a human father. So also in the Aeneid, a literary imitation following on and illustrating the tradition, Aeneas, the hero, is the son of Venus by a human father. So also in the prime analogue of all epics in the Mediterranean tradition, the epic of Gilgamesh, the Mesopotamian hero was accounted part divine. So, when the ancient heard of the sons of god as he did in Genesis 6, he thought immediately of the heroes of old, the giants, the mighty men who had done famous deeds. But look at what has happened to them. The author of Genesis tells no tales of heroic deeds, no mighty if tragic struggles, no great conquests. No, these heroes of old, these sons of God, have become sordid and stupid sinners. Far from being mighty men, masters of their world, masters of themselves, they are the slaves of animal impulse. Once again the author has emphasized his history of sin by giving a theme already well known a sudden and surprising twist. Instead of god-like heroes, we have miserable sinners.

A final example of this technique of altering old stories to tell a new truth can be seen in the story of the deluge which also begins in Genesis 6 and continues on into chapter 9. The story of the deluge as it appears in Genesis is one of the pieces of Hebrew literature which reflects most closely an ancient Semitic prototype.[13] In the epic of Gilgamesh which was just mentioned, the eleventh tablet, or, in our terms, the eleventh book contains the story of a great flood which destroyed all mankind. Further, it tells this story with details which are very like those of the Hebrew story. For instance, the ark described in Genesis is actually the type of boat characteristic of Mesopotamian rivers and not at all of the Mediterranean seaboard where Israel lived. The survivor's sending birds from the ark to find out if any

celebrate sly underhandedness in its tales about strangers. The murder story at least has the dignity of tragedy.

[13] The very idea of a universal deluge is Mesopotamian, for the alluvial land was subject to unexpected floods of vast proportions while Palestine might suffer from local flash floods but not from a widespread deluge. For details of the relation between the Hebrew and the Mesopotamian stories see W. F. Albright in *The Journal of Biblical Literature*, v. 68 (1939), pp. 91–103, commenting on the ideas of S. Mowinckel.

dry land has appeared occurs almost word for word in the Mesopotamian and in the Hebrew story. There is no doubt that the Hebrew storyteller has made use of an ancient and honored tradition of his race in telling the story of the deluge, but again he has worked a significant change. In the Mesopotamian epic the deluge occurs simply because one evening the gods become annoyed at the noise mankind makes. In a fit of pique, a meaningless flash of irritation, they decide they will not put up with mankind any longer; and they set about destroying the race by a deluge.[14] There is indeed a human survivor, but there is no hint of his being chosen by the gods to survive because of his uprightness. There is nothing moral at all about this ancient Mesopotamian story. Thus Ut-napishtim, the Mesopotamian Noah, simply happens to be the crony of one of the gods for one reason or another; and this god plays a trick on the rest of the divine assembly on behalf of his friend and betrays their plan to the man so that he survives.

Now compare the biblical story of the deluge. The material details, the sequence of events, the general outline and thrust of the story are the same as in the Mesopotamian prototype. And yet what a difference! The motivation has been changed. What was simply an interesting tale, or perhaps on a somewhat more serious plane, a story told to illustrate the waywardness of the gods, their total lack of any moral concern, has become a story reiterating the Genesis author's point.[15] Why the deluge? In the Bible it is clear: the whole race of men is so sinful that God cannot stand their evil any longer. As a just God He must and He does punish the race. But He acts precisely as a just God; therefore, the good man cannot perish for the sins of others. And so the single just man, Noah, receives a divine revelation which enables him to survive. The motives of the gods in the original Mesopotamian story were simply trivial. They were annoyed. For the Hebrews, all is different; God is the source and guardian of morals, and He acts as a moral being. Man is rewarded according to his works. Once again a familiar tale has been given a new meaning.

---

[14] The motive is not stated in the Gilgamesh epic; but it can be found in an alternate deluge story, the Atrahasis epic; see *ANET*, p. 104.

[15] It is interesting that this point, the theological "history of sin," goes back to the earliest stages of Israelite religion. It is no product of a pessimism induced by the troubles of the later days of the monarchy or the exile. It occurs in the oldest of the sources of the Pentateuch, the Yahwist writer (J), who probably wrote in the 10th century B.C., and whose sources are still older (see P. Ellis, C.SS.R., *The Men and the Message of the Old Testament*, Collegeville, Minn., 1963, pp. 51–99, for the analysis and dating of the Pentateuch sources).

Now I submit that one of the clearest ways in which we can discern the intentions of an author occurs when we can compare an author's work with a prototype which he has used. If he has taken a prototype and altered it for a particular object, his ends and purposes become clear. We can mark his deviations from the traditional image or story and so plot the direction which his new story is taking. That is exactly what we have here in the Old Testament, in the first chapters of Genesis.[16] Note that this technique of studying an author's intentions in the light of his adaptions of already existing material is important in New Testament research. Scholars have gone beyond ascertaining the similarities among the synoptic Gospels and turned to the study of their significant variations. By seeing how a Gospel writer varies his story, often in minute details only, we can see more clearly his theological purposes. So here in Genesis we have theological writing, the purpose and meaning of which is made clear beyond all shadow of a doubt precisely because the author has taken old stories and directed them to a new and deeply theological end.

In the second chapter he has taken an prothalamium and turned it into a tragedy. From the very first men could do nothing right. They sinned. He has shown that the first brothers were jealous and murderous. He has shown that the heroes of old were vicious sinners. He has shown that the whole human race deserved punishment. In each instance, he has reversed or altered an ancient tale to make a new point; and the heroes have become villains. This has very correctly been called a history of sin.[17] All men are indeed touched by sin.

---

[16] This should not be understood to mean that the Hebrew writer had before him the same versions of the tales as those we have used in order to make comparisons; doubtless we are dealing with developments from common sources, not direct borrowing.

[17] The word "history" is in place here, though I do not wish to discuss the problem of historicity as such. We know there is history in Genesis (Pius XII, *Humani generis* [*Enchiridion Biblicum,* 618]) but it is history of its own peculiar kind. It is not scientific history, nor humanistic history. It is not even history in the sense of the stories of the patriarchs where the details reflect the circumstances of the early second millenium, the era they claim to describe, even though there are lacunae, problems about the sequence of things, and so forth. (See R. de Vaux, O.P., "The Hebrew Patriarchs and History," *Theology Digest,* v. 12 [1964], pp. 227–40.) In contrast, much in Gn 1–11 resembles things which are not history at all. There are hints of ancient Semitic cosmogonies, folklore elements, allusions to Canaanite cults, and use of Mesopotamian tales. The text reflects the Near-East of 3,000 years ago, and it would be remarkable if the first steps of creation followed the schemes excogitated by that culture even to indulging in Hebrew puns. More, how could we explain the transmission without change of detailed descriptions of these events over millions of years of time? Only by positing miracles which all the evidence indicates did not occur. Still, we have something historical.

+
+
+

I believe that this point is clinched by a final observation from comparative literature. We have a form of history writing from ancient Mesopotamia, the king-list, which originated with the Sumerians. Their traditional list opened with the assertion that "kingship came down from heaven." Kingship, like all the other good things of life, all the arts and crafts of government and civilization, was but a pale human copy of a primordial divine model. This type of thinking in which a people sees everyday realities as but pale reflections of the true heavenly reality, this seeking of the true being of man's institutions *in illo tempore,* the divine epoch, is typical of much of mankind.[18] So in these Sumerian king-lists, we begin with something divine. Kingship comes down from heaven. Then are listed the mythical kings of old, the great heroes whose reigns are superhuman. They reign literally for hundreds of thousands of years. And so it goes for several long, long generations. And then the sequence is broken by the story of a deluge which practically destroys civilization. With this the model has ended and there follows the miserable human reality, the failing attempt to imitate the truly heavenly. Now begins the list of kings with more normal lengths of reign and the changes of dynasty and mastery which hint at war and suffering. Notice the sequence: first the model period, the time when all was heavenly. Then the flood. And then the miserable human reality begins. We have much the same sequence in Genesis. There is the time of remote beginnings, a time which is described and described truly in its essential meaning, but it is no longer the ideal, the model time; all has been reversed. What God had designed as paradise, almost something of heaven, has been turned into a miserable history of failure because man has sinned from the beginning. Instead of a model of perfection, our first parents and our earliest ancestors provide us with a model of and a tendency to sin. Only after the story of the deluge do we have the beginning of the time of grace. Abraham appears, and in Abraham a people is chosen and all mankind is blessed.[19] Here we have the ultimate reversal. The ancient human dream of the Golden Age at the beginning of time has been reversed and made a tale

+
+
+

Currently, theologians discuss Genesis 1–11 in terms of "etiological history"; that is, these chapters explain a fact of history, man's sinfulness, in terms of causes which themselves act within history (see *Theology Digest*, v. 13 [1965], pp. 3–17).

[18] See Mircea Eliade, *Cosmos and History. The Myth of the Eternal Return.* New York, 1959.

[19] Gn 12:1–3.

which explains man's sorry state in terms of primeval sin, the true terms and the true explanation of his lot. This is taught forcefully, it is taught with great vividness by a writer of talent. And we are able to see the depth and thrust of this terrible history of sin precisely because we are able to see the literary techniques which he has used against their background in the ancient world. Here is no literary embellishment concealing the word of God. It is rather a literature which is the very word of God.

I submit that this reading of the beginning of Genesis is far richer and far more meaningful than a reading which confines itself to a few verses of the third chapter of Genesis. Instead of treating the Bible as though it contained but Genesis 1:1–2 and Genesis 3, we are able to see it as a whole. The truths are not changed. The dogmas, the doctrines of the Church, and here of course the pertinent one is original sin, remain quite the same. But we understand it better, and we feel it more, and we should be able to preach and teach it with more force because we understand it, not only in a bald, doctrinal statement, but with many of its human nuances and many of the fine meanings which God has deigned to reveal to us. Man begins indeed with a history of sin, even a blacker history than we thought. Sin is not an isolated act, it is something man has acted out in every way he can. Sin permeates his whole history and afflicts all his relationships. The union of man and woman, God's climactic gift in Genesis 2, can turn to bitterness because of sin. Brother can turn against brother and man's basic and most fitting activity, making our world fruitful, productive, can lead to the most vicious conflict. Heroism is inadequate, and lest we think that sin is the work of the exceptional man the flood story makes clear that the race is infected. But the picture is not pure darkness; God does not desert man entirely. He clothes the refugees from Eden;[20] the murderer, though exiled, is spared and even protected;[21] the just man is saved and given a covenant valid for all men.[22] Thus, amid the dark history of sin, the way is prepared for the first great grace given to and through Abraham. Sin is not the end. We know that Christ will come, Christ has come. And so also the author of Genesis is no morbid soul rejoicing in the evils of mankind. He knows

[20] Gn. 3:21.
[21] Gn 4:13–5.
[22] Gn 9:8–17. Note a departure here from the Mesopotamian form of the story where the survivor is awarded eternal life but no hope is offered to anyone else.

that man is often evil, and that mankind is sinful from the beginning. Yet God is there with His grace, and the blacker man's sin, the brighter the light of His grace which began to glow with Noah and then is flashed upon us in the gift given to Abraham, that step toward the ultimate grace, that brilliant light which is Christ.

+
+
+

Reprinted from the CATHOLIC BIBLICAL QUARTERLY, Vol. XXVII, No. 2, pp. 144-147,
April 1965

NOTES ON THE LOVE OF GOD IN DEUTERONOMY AND THE FATHER-SON RELATIONSHIP BETWEEN YAHWEH AND ISRAEL

In the pages of the *CBQ* Father Moran has established with certainty the relationship of the Deuteronomic concept of love with the ideology and terminology of the ancient oriental treaty.[1] However, we can still ask whether this is

[1] William L. Moran, S.J., "The Ancient Near Eastern Background of the Love of God in Deuteronomy," *CBQ* 25 (1963) 77-87. Note also N. Lohfink, S.J., "Hate and Love in Osee 9,15," *CBQ* 25 (1963) 417, demonstrating that Hosea too knew of a covenant love expressed by *'hb* even though he usually thought of love in very different terms. Thus a word can be associated with quite different expressions of its fundamental content. Something like the reverse is also true: Ideas and images may correspond closely even though we do not find them always expressed in the same vocabulary, as I shall try to show for covenant love and the father-son relationship when they are used as analogies to express the special connection between Israel and Yahweh.

exclusive. Can we conclude that the imagery of father and son is irrelevant to or even incompatible with the Deuteronomic conception? It is the contention of this paper that it is not so, but rather that the very ancient Israelite concept of Israel as Yahweh's son[2] is very close to or even identical with the Deuteronomic conception articulated in terms of the treaty or covenant and should not be separated entirely from it.

In fact, the father-son relationship of Israel to Yahweh was conceived in terms which correspond to the definition of covenantal love as found in Deuteronomy. The point is that the love demanded from Israel in Deuteronomy has a very particular character. It is love which is seen in reverential fear, in loyalty, and in obedience—a love which, therefore, can be commanded.[3] As the ancient treaties inform us, this is indeed the love demanded from the covenanted subject by his overlord. But it is also exactly the attitude which the Old Testament demands of Israel when it speaks of the people as Yahweh's son.

If there is any tenderness in this relationship, any love of the kind which the word naturally calls to mind in us, it is on the part of Yahweh, the Father, and even this appears but rarely. Hos 11,1 is the parade text here, and the only other one, Dt 1,31, to attribute a tender concern to Yahweh is quite clearly connected with the prophetic text, with which it shares the image of the loving Father guiding His son through the desert. There is a later text, Is 63,16, which might at first glance indicate an expectation that Yahweh will be tender with His son, Israel. However, His actual dealing with the son as described in the context is harsh and shows no note of tenderness. It would seem, then, that the idea of a tender relationship between Yahweh and His son Israel, a loving relationship according to our way of looking at these things, is a special Hosean concept.

The normative idea, the one which can be documented through a wide range of the Israelite tradition including Deuteronomy itself, was that the father-son relationship is essentially one of respect and obedience. It is reverence and fidelity which is demanded of the son, and Yahweh is concerned to assure this by punishing failure. A key text is Dt 8,5, where Yahweh is the father who does not spare the rod. Significantly this occurs in relation with the description of Yahweh's dealing with Israel in the desert, the very context where Yahweh's tenderness stands out in the Hosean view, but here the emphasis is on sternness. Of course, we assume that the ultimate motive for this is a careful love, but this is not explicit, much less is it in the foreground. Clearly the author is thinking of the way Yahweh disciplined His children in the wilderness, especially in the awe-inspiring experience of Sinai which called forth fear and reverence, not any

[2] Cf. Dt 32,5.19. On the antiquity of the text see W. F. Albright, "Some remarks on the Song of Moses in Deuteronomy XXXII," *VT* 9 (1959) 339-346, and Otto Eissfeldt, *Das Lied Moses Deuteronomium 32,* 1-43 (Berichte über die Verhandlungen der Sächsischen Akademie der Wissenschaften zu Leipzig, Phil.-hist. Klasse 104,5. Berlin: Akademie, 1958).

[3] W. L. Moran, S.J., *op. cit.,* 78.

sort of tender love.[4] This text is still somewhat unusual in that it concentrates on Yahweh rather than on Israel and its attitude toward God.

More characteristic are the passages which center on Israel, the son, and his obligations. Mal 1,6 parallels the son with the slave and expects the same sort of reverence (*kābôd*) from each. This is a late text to be sure, but it is in the tradition. Israel is a disloyal, disobedient son. He has transgressed (Is 1,2: *pš'*). He is faithless (Jer 3,19) even to the point of turning away from the Father to other gods (Dt 32,19-20), the supreme offence against the covenant relationship as against the father-son relationship. Yahweh comes into all this mostly as one who is angry with His children for their infidelities (Dt 32,19) and who is, therefore, ready to punish them (Is 30,1-5.8-14). Mostly, then, the emphasis is on the duties of the son to be loyal and obedient and his failure to fulfill them; Yahweh's attitude is a reaction to Israel's.

Finally, the relationship between father and son as conceived in this context is something which may be commanded. This appears in the adducing of the relationship in Dt 14,1 as a motive to obey a particular command forbidding paganizing funeral rites. This is, indeed, a particular case, but the relationship does depend on it. More, reductively the command is concerned with the very relationship itself. To indulge in the pagan rite is simply using a specific way of denying the fundamental relation to Yahweh. Jer 3,19 is explicit: The Father commands positively and apodictically that His son call Him Father and remain faithful.

These are the things, then, which are expected of Israel, Yahweh's favored son. There is no question of a tender, feeling love. It is simply a matter of reverence, loyalty, obedience, things subject to command and commanded. It is the same attitude which Deuteronomy demands on the basis of the covenant relationship. Further, it should be noted that in all this the concentration is on the attitude which the son, Israel, should display, whether it be in the way of reproaches upon his failures or commands demanding his action. This attention to the attitude of the son rather than of the Father corresponds with the situation in Deuteronomy where there is ever question of Israel's attitude toward Yahweh, not, as in the Hosean context, of His loving attitude toward Israel.[5]

More can be adduced for the argument than the fact that the picture of the father-son relationship as applied to Yahweh and Israel corresponds to the Deuteronomic definition of covenant love. There is the fact that the father-son image appears in connections which are relevant to covenant and treaty. We have already noticed Dt 14,1. It is not without significance that Deuteronomy sees nothing incongruous about basing a law safeguarding the essential relationship to Yahweh on an appeal to the father-son relationship. And for Deuteronomy the law is specifically covenant law, for all the laws in Deuteronomy are conceived to be covenant stipulations, conditions and determinations of the covenant

[4] See the remarks of S. R. Driver, *Deuteronomy* (ICC; Edinburgh: T. & T. Clark, 1951) 108 with the reference to Dt 4,36.

[5] W. L. Moran, S.J., *op. cit.*, 77.

relationship itself. Again, in Is 30 the sons, Israel, are condemned because they turn to a stranger for help. This corresponds exactly to the central element in the treaty relationship, the lord's claim to an exclusive fidelity from the vassal which forbade all serious dealing with outsiders. Again, in Jer 31,9 the restoration of Israel is restoration of the father-son relationship. This is in the context governed by 31,1, that is, by the proclamation of a new and better union between Yahweh and Israel based on a new covenant.[6] Thus, in the mind of Jeremiah the covenant relationship and the father-son relationship were not incompatible, they were essentially the same thing.

It appears, then, that the image of the relation between Israel and Yahweh as a son-father relationship covers the same ground as the covenant analogy. There is no reason why the two ideas could not work together. It is quite possible that both influenced Deuteronomy. This could be so in spite of the fact that the father-son relationship is but seldom mentioned in the book, and is not connected with the word for love (*'hb*).[7] The one fact probably explains the other. An idea seldom alluded to will not usually be connected explicitly with many other things. The rarity of its use, however, does not disprove the importance of the father-son image. There are obvious reasons why the Old Testament is everywhere very sparing in the use of the image. It could so easily be misleading in the light of pagan ideas well known in Israel. Nonetheless, the father-son concept is both old and fundamental. Israel's covenant with Yahweh was very early thought of as creating a quasi-familial relation.[8] There is no evidence that this was ever abandoned. Rather, the texts which indicate it stem from liturgies which shows that they were alive, part of the continuing cult and hence known long after they were first cast into form. Moreover, such texts were repeated often so that the ideas in them could be widespread without needing to appear in other texts. As for the general concept of covenant or treaty, it remained connected with the idea of kinship even late in the history of old Israel. Even a purely political treaty with Assyria was thought to produce a kind of dependent kinship so that in 2 Kgs 16,7 Ahaz could call himself the son even of his tyrannical overlord.

DENNIS J. MCCARTHY, S.J.
St. Mary's College,
St. Mary's, Kansas

[6] See A. Weiser, *Jeremia* (Das Alte Testament Deutsch, 20-21. Göttingen: Vandenhoeck & Ruprecht, 1955) 282-283.

[7] W. L. Moran, *op. cit.*, 77, 78.

[8] See Ex 24,11 and the remarks of J. Pedersen, *Israel I-II* (London: Geoffrey Cumberlege-Oxford University Press, 1959) 305-306.

The Presence of God and the Prophetic Word

DENNIS MCCARTHY, S.J.

IN Exodus 12. 12, it is God himself who destroys the Egyptians and saves Israel. In an even older tradition about the same event, Exodus 12. 23, it is a mysterious being, the Destroyer, who acts as the agent or power of Yahweh to accomplish the same ends. Without doubt the Destroyer is a remnant of very primitive beliefs in malevolent powers which menaced the young lambs. In the Wisdom of Solomon 18. 14–16 we read of the same event: "While soft silence enveloped all things, and the night was half gone in its swift course, your all-powerful word leaped from heaven, from the royal throne . . . a stern warrior carrying the sharp sword of your command, and stood and filled all things with death. . . ." In this very latest of Old Testament books, the word has supplanted the primitive Destroyer and made it unnecessary for God himself to come to do the task as in Exodus 12. 12. Nor was the word of God merely destructive. The best known record of the power of that word must be the magnificent picture in Genesis 1. 1–2. 4a, where the simple divine *fiat* causes the whole mighty panorama of creation to unfold. This too, though older than the Wisdom text, is relatively late in the form it has in our Bibles. So we can see some pattern of development: belief that God's power and presence were to be found in his word, and not only in himself or in personified agents.

The idea of the powerful word is, in fact, very old. In the third millennium B.C. the priests of Memphis told of the creative power of the word (literally, "tongue") of their god Ptah. Probably this ancient Oriental concept (it is by no means confined to the Memphite theology) was not entirely unknown in Israel. However, we must ask how belief in the presence of God and God's power in the word grew in Israel, for in view of the development so briefly outlined in the first paragraph it is clear that this belief was not universal and normative from the beginnings. In large part the answer to this question comes readily enough. It was through the prophets. In them the presence of God in his word became manifest. One of the first of them to give his name to a book of the Bible, Hosea, is directed to give his children symbolic names, for to the ancient the name was somehow the thing itself and portended its being and destiny. This appears very clearly when the change in what one was called meant a change in reality: ". . . instead of what was said of them, 'Not my people', it shall be said of them, '(They are) sons of the living God' " (Hos. 1. 10). Thus without a doubt God was present in his word, for that word could give life itself. The obvious problem when it is a question of the prophetic word is the difficulty of recognition. The word was and is not easy to grasp. God is present in his word, but where is his word present? That is the agonizing question, for "God spoke in many and various ways", and the very richness of this gift makes it no easy task to discern the true word of God. When Yahweh proclaims through his prophet that "my thoughts are not your thoughts, not your ways my ways" (Is. 55. 8), he is not merely separating his ways from those of wicked men, as 55. 7 might seem to imply. He is asserting that what is of God is so totally different from anything else that merely human means may well fail to understand what he says and so what he is.

This is all too easily documented. Men naturally misunderstood the promises characteristic of certain psalms and repeated in some of the words of Isaiah (29. 1–8; 37. 35) that Zion, its temple and its city of Jerusalem would be inviolable. They took this as some kind of magic formula guaranteeing of itself the presence of God and his protection, as though the presence depended on the words and not on what they might be. This is what Jeremiah found (Jer. 7. 1–15), and though he denounced it men continued to act in ways incompatible with the divine presence. The result was that the presence deserted its chosen place though not the prophet, for it is Ezekiel (cf. cc. 8–11) who sees and announces not exactly the utter disappearance of God but, as it were, his displacement. Often, if men did not more or less deliberately misunderstand the prophet, they turned from him and followed designs which were not those announced in the prophetic word as in Isaiah 8. 11–15 and so often in the life of Jeremiah. The result might be ruin, or it might well be silence in which God hides himself from his people (Is. 8. 16).

The word of God, then, is not easy to recognize so that one finds God in it and follows him. There was no simple external sign to guarantee that *this* was God's word. In the relatively unsophisticated days of Saul a condition approaching frenzy might be accepted as a sign of a true prophet (cf. 1 Sam. 10. 9–13; 19. 18–24), but this could so obviously be misleading that it soon fell into discredit. Neither was the holding of authentic office from God enough. In the great passage giving Nathan's promise (2 Sam. 7. 1–17) we have the king, the one anointed by choice of Yahweh himself to be especially close to him, his son (e.g., Ps. 2. 7) and agent on earth whose protection of justice, that is, right order, guaranteed the right order of nature, that is, rain and crops in due season (Ps. 72; cf. 2 Sam. 23. 3–4). Moreover, the very "spirit of Yahweh" could speak in him, the word of Yahweh be on his tongue (2 Sam. 23. 2). Thus the king had prophetic powers, and not just any king in this case, but the special favourite of Yahweh, David. So, in 2 Samuel 7 this man, authentic leader of God's people and endowed with prophetic traits, surveys his situation. He has achieved a united state for the people of God, put down their enemies, and brought the ark of the covenant to his capital, Jerusalem. It seems to him unfitting that he, a mere man, dwell in a palace of sorts while the ark, the special, visible sign of the divine presence in Israel, remain in a simple tent. He decides to provide something better for it. Surely this is fitting and reasonable. Moreover, the king consults Nathan, a true prophet, who immediately agrees with David, "for Yahweh is with you", as he says. Surely this decision represents the word, the wish of God as far as any man can reasonably be expected to know. Yet it is not. In the very night after the decision had been taken the word of Yahweh did in fact come to Nathan, and it flatly contradicted all that had been said. David is not to build a temple ("house") for God; God will rather build a dynasty ("house"—the kernel of the original word of Yahweh plays on the double meaning of the Hebrew word "house") for David! The whole sequence as it now stands in 2 Samuel 7. 1–17 is undoubtedly more complicated than this. It has grown under the impetus of the desire to explain why David himself did not build a temple, to show that David's dynasty had not been rejected like Saul's, to integrate David into the overall Deuteronomistic view of history, among other things, and this has been done by accumulating additions to the prophetic word. However, the heart of the story is old, and old or new, its lesson is clear. Man's best thoughts, an office from God, even possession of the spirit, none of these assures us that we have God's word. Hence the terrible uncertainty of the divine presence in the word.

That the dilemma is literally terrible is the teaching of 1 Kings 13. A man of God—this is an older designation of a prophet—has an authentic and detailed mission to Jeroboam at Bethel. He carries it out faithfully up to the point where an old prophet intervenes. This other prophet is surely sincere, for the words "he lied to him" at the end of 13. 18 seem to be a gloss, grammatically irregular in the Hebrew text and hardly in keeping with 13. 20 ff. Nevertheless, he turns the man of God aside from the directions he had originally from "the word of Yahweh". The result is destruction for the man of God. He had not been entirely faithful to the word given him. One is reminded of Galatians 1. 8: "Even if we or an angel... preach a gospel contrary to that which you have received, let him be accursed." It would surely be difficult to stand up for the word received in the face of an apostle or an angel. The man of god in 1 Kings found it impossible to resist a recognized prophet, abandoned the word, and died for it. No doubt this story has grown in the telling, but it emphasizes all the more for this that the stakes are high indeed, for God's word cannot fail of its ultimate purpose, but a man can fail to recognize or receive it to his cost.

This applies not only to the men who meet God through the word mediated by a prophet but also to the prophet himself. It was always true that the word of God made great demands on him. A common Hebrew word for prophecy means simply "burden", and it probably had connotations beyond those of a phrase such as "the burden of the message was...." It hints that the call God's word imposed on a man gave him an uncomfortable role with duties he might not want and deprivations he would normally fight against. It is easy to create for ourselves a false image of the prophet as a person full of self-assurance, secure in his possession of the word. In fact he gave up much, and he faced the same problem as others. He, too, had to discern where the true word of God was. And if he should mistake the word of God, as did the man of God who spoke to Jeroboam, might he not face a similar fate? It was desperately necessary to be certain that the word which presented itself to him was truly from the spirit of God. Yet the Old Testament (and anything else, for that matter) never supplies entirely satisfactory criteria for determining this. To be sure, a true prophet tended to foresee hard things (Jer. 28. 5–9), not to speak on the strength of dreams (Jer. 23. 25–28), to be disinterested (Mic. 3. 5), and to be orthodox (Deut. 13. 1–5). But none of these norms by themselves, nor taken all together, are absolute. They might help determine the truth of something, but they could not guarantee that it was the true, prophetic word of God. The criterion of fulfilment of a prophecy (Deut. 18. 22) is a little better, perhaps, but it is usually of no immediate use, and in any case the fulfilment of the prophetic word is often unexpected and obscure.

In view of all this, it is easy to understand the reluctance of a Jeremiah to assume the prophetic office (Jer. 1. 6–7). Even feeling assured that one had the true word of God did not offer an easy life; rather the contrary. When the word demands a total dedication forbidding even a family (Jer. 16. 2), it is no wonder that the prophet could be rebellious and in need of consolation (Jer. 15. 19–21; 20. 7–12). Even Ezekiel, a personality far tougher than Jeremiah, appears to need encouragement: "Listen to what I say; be not rebellious" (Ezek. 2. 8). Perhaps because Ezekiel was called on to do and to say things which still lead people to question his mental balance, we should not be surprised at this. We all want to look well to our neighbours and to history.

Prophet, king and commoner, then, all faced the same problem. Where was the word in which God might truly be found? Even if he should succeed in meeting that word, its demands could be great. The wonder is not that the prophet himself sometimes felt, and usually met, doubt and rebellion. The wonder is that the word was listened to by anyone at all. Yet the wonder is there; there was some listening, but this involved a stern pedagogy. In part this pedagogy is to be seen in the very hard sayings themselves. Just because they were hard, they call upon man to accept God and God's word on God's terms and not merely on human ones. That is, by drawing man from himself they point to God in his word, but they do not make the process of acceptance easy. It is well that a man recognize God in his word, but the mere fact that he does is no sign of happiness or success. An Amos hears the word, and he must leave his simple life and his home to preach in a foreign kingdom before a hostile audience (Am. 7. 10–14). Considering his message, the hostility is hardly surprising. He called for justice from those who profited from injustice. He placed Israel on a parallel with its despised enemies (1. 3–2. 3, 6–11). He goes so far as to point out that its privileged position calls for extra penalties on failure (3. 2). His demands are absolute: no compromise, obey and it may be possible to escape doom (5. 14–15). No wonder a tradition grew up that the true prophet would have hard things to say!

Isaiah contributed to this tradition. He believed in his nation, and he may have been close to court circles. At least he had ready enough access to the king. Yet he took up Amos' theme of justice and reinforced it. The justice of the chosen people must be like that of its God, whose justice is his holiness (Is. 5. 18), which made it an absolute beyond anything imaginable by a creature. This call to be just and holy as God is just and holy may be noble, but it is a terrible burden to put on men. Then there was Isaiah's insistent demand to put trust in Yahweh and not in armies and alliances. Once again, an absolute. This is no call for saying "in God we trust" while maintaining a reasonable defence establishment and a shrewd network of treaties. It is a call to lean on God alone (Is. 7. 1–13; 28. 14–15, 30–31). King and people were not ready for this, of course, not ready to see God in this word (6. 9–10) any more than they had been ready to listen to Amos and Hosea a few years earlier in the Kingdom of Israel, the northern and larger of the Hebrew kingdoms into which David's empire split after Solomon.

The simple fact is that the people of God fail to see God in the prophetic word. It is hard and they reject it and him. The results vary in detail, but they take two general directions. The more obvious is the fact that the disasters foreseen by the prophet occur. Amos spoke to the people of Israel, but they would not "seek Yahweh and live" (Am. 5. 6). They continued as before, and soon there was the destruction and exile so vividly pictured in most of Amos' oracles. Judah, too, paid a price for turning to human help instead of to the prophetic word. Jerusalem was not taken, but all the countryside was laid waste by the erstwhile Assyrian ally. This violent pedagogy fits the theory of schooling at the time. The basis was definitely the maxim: "Spare the rod and spoil the child", and people in those days might have seen this kind of history as the rod writ large. But still it must continue; the seeming failure of Amos and Isaiah is repeated in Jeremiah and beyond.

But we should look at the other direction, as seen in the prophets, taken by the divine pedagogy. This is the use of something very different from, but often as eloquent, as the word silence. Yahweh hides his face from a rebellious people (Is. 8. 17), which means in the context that he will not speak through the prophet for a while. The sovereignty of the word of God is clear. No man commands it, not even a prophet. We find silence as explicit pedagogy in Ezekiel also (3. 24–27), but as is so often the case, it is most poignant in Jeremiah. Unwillingly the prophet had been seized by the forces of a meaningless, hopeless rebellion against the Babylonians who had conquered and destroyed Judah. Some direction was urgently needed, but, though the prophet prayed, for ten agonizing days God remained silent. Only after this delay did the word come to Jeremiah (42. 10). Ironically, but of a piece with all of his experience, the word was immediately defied by the very ones who had sought it. In fact, the vignette in Jeremiah 42—43 is a summary history of the prophetic word. The whole sequence of events takes place amid the general ruin of Judah consequent upon failure to heed the prophet. The word is there, but given by God and not commanded even by the prophet. Men hear it but do not obey. And tragedy results, here for Jeremiah himself, who is carried off to Egypt against his will.

In most of what has been said we have distinguished between prophet and people. Of course we have seen that the prophet, also, had the problem of recognizing the true word of God. But beyond that we should not make the distinction too sharp. The prophet belonged to the people. He suffered with them. If this is best expressed in Jeremiah's cry: "Is there no balm in Gilead? Is there no physician there? Why then had the health of my people not been restored? O that . . . my eyes were a fountain . . . that I might weep day and night for the slain . . ." (Jer. 8. 22—9. 1), it is implicit in the tenderness of a Hosea, and the love of Isaiah for Jerusalem surely took in its countryside which he saw ravaged. Ezekiel, emphasizing the prophetic action as a means of communication parallel with the word, symbolically joined the suffering of the final siege of Jerusalem (Ezek. 4. 1–8) and the following exile (12. 1–7), though he was already in Babylonia as part of the earlier deportation (2 Kgs. 24. 15–16). Perhaps the prophet himself did not need the insistent pedagogy of ruin after disobedience, but he shared it. Neither did he need the lesson of silence as others did, unless we conjecture that this was part of the penalty and penance of Jeremiah already discussed. Rather, it must have been part of his regular, if unrecorded experience when we reflect on the relative paucity of words he received compared with the long periods of activity of a Hosea, an Isaiah, a Jeremiah, an Ezekiel.

And what is the worth of all this? The prophetic word was so hard to recognize. It was so often frustrated, and all suffered. Instead of the word there was often silence. An uneasy history at best, but still a fruitful one, for it made it possible to see something of the ways of God. His must be heard one way or another, for his word is always sovereignly effective. But it takes much time to learn to listen. Merely threatening the consequences of not listening was not enough; they had to be experienced. However, things could not stop at this, for it seems to leave us with a picture of a God characterized by his vindictive justice.

There is far more than this to be learned. This God will indeed have justice from and for every-ne, but this is a positive step from mere vindica-ion. However, it simply puts him in the category f many another divinity, for example the sun-god who was widely believed to be, and often appealed o as, a guardian of justice in the Ancient Near East. ahweh will have more, a perfect faith in himself, tter trust which seems to fly in the face of sound olitical reason, as in Isaiah 7. 9, or at least in the ace of overwhelming pressures as, for instance, hroughout Jeremiah's career. Probably such faith, hich could later on at least be confirmed by the ightness of the hard sayings of the prophets, was nd is the only means by which the justice de-manded might be gained. After all, possessions do ive such a feeling of security. It is difficult to see en giving them up, even though they had been quired by shady means, much less, in the pros-rous years of Jeroboam II during which Amos d Hosea spoke, abandoning the means them-lves. These two must have sounded like religious anks, rebels who were trying to unsettle an estab-hed order quite satisfactory to those in power. nd then there were Isaiah and Micah condemning iustice, idolatry and alliances which showed less an total trust in God. For their pains they saw eir country ruined and their capital impoverished. How much saner under the reign of Manasseh, when men compromised and enjoyed some peace and prosperity! There was still much to be learned.

But there is another kind of security even more inimical to the total trust in God demanded by the prophetic word. This is the security of being sure of one's own rightness. After all, the men of Judah had before them the lesson of what had happened to their northern brethren. Seeing their land stripped by the invader when the king failed to follow the lead of Isaiah was part of their history, too. But that was made right by a little compromise under a succeeding king. So what was learned? Apparently, when we compare Isaiah 29 with Jeremiah 7, only that the temple was a talisman securing the capital city no matter what they were in themselves. They did not need the word of a prophet to bring God into their midst; he was present and protective in his temple. They had to be deprived of this illusion that they had an abso-lutely right way to the presence of God, if they were to acquire a trust in God alone and be righteous as God wanted. Hence the lesson of exile. Learning from it if they will, they will be able to seek the word of God successfully and God in his word. Lest the lesson be lost, a favourite theme of Ezekiel was that their earlier failures and their present hardness of heart closes them to this word, even though they claim to seek it (e.g., Ezek. 14. 3, 10; 20. 3).

All this is reasonable and true as far as it goes, but there is more. If the divine pedagogy of the prophetic word working itself out in history taught so much, it also revealed the only possible source of the required justice and faith. Ultimately it can only come from God: "Behold, I am laying in Zion . . . a precious cornerstone", a basis of faith and justice (Is. 22. 16–17). For God is just, but he is also loving and his love includes, or in the strong imagery of the prophet, overpowers, his mere will to justice: "I will not execute my fierce anger, I will not destroy Ephraim; for I am God and not man, the Holy One in your midst . . ." (Hos. 11. 9). So speaks one of the earliest of the classic prophets. He is echoed in one of the latest, Deutero-Isaiah during the period of the exile, when he assures us that Yahweh will have mercy because his word is always effective, and it promises an eternal covenant (Is. 55. 6–13). However, these are the words of a prophet who can and does reflect the story of the prophetic word which took place during the two hundred or so years between him and Hosea. For two centuries men had expected salvation from God, a salvation more or less in accord with their own ideas, which usually meant (and means) possessions, protection and victory. There had been the prophets to protest against this, to say that God was not to be found in these things but in trust and justice, but they had not been listened to. Now, after all these years and all this confirmation of the prophetic message, the remnant of Israel could understand that indeed God's ways are not man's, God's ideas not man's. They must accept salvation on his terms which means righteousness based on trust in God's overwhelming love.

The lesson would seem to have been clear enough, and it had been driven home with overwhelming emphasis. Still it had to be repeated and in explicit terms. We learn this from some post-exilic texts. After the return it was necessary for another prophet to point out that God had indeed spoken through the prophets, but he had been disregarded, and it was this which had brought upon the people the horrors of the conquest and exile (Zech. 7. 8–14). It is true that these verses are the prelude to a hopeful picture of the new situation, but the very need to say them, and to say them so explicitly, hints that all is not as it should be in Jerusalem, a point which the history of the time shows to have been indeed the case. But really, it is superfluous to corroborate a prophet from history in this way, for one thing about the prophetic word is its immediacy. In it God is present now, and while a prophet may draw on history for some reason or another, it is always with a view to bringing God to his hearers now, not to recalling the past for its own sake. Still in the post-exilic period, Malachi is even more clear. With all its concern about worship—no mean thing in itself—a set of verses like Malachi 3. 1–10, sounds like the earliest prophets in its insistence on justice and its emphasis on judgment.

It is worth our while to note passages like these last two, if for no other reason than the universal tendency to treat the later prophets as epigone who have nothing to offer. On the contrary, they carry on the message, admittedly with different emphases and less verbal skill. We should expect the change of emphasis, for, as we have said, the prophetic word was meant to bring God's presence to the prophet's own time, and he would hardly be a prophet who ignored the concerns of his own audience, different though they may have been from those of earlier or later generations. There is a real value in all this. On the one hand, it brings out the divine will to have his word heard and so present to his people. If their situation demanded a new emphasis, new areas of interest, the word could accommodate itself to these so that it could be heard. It could also accommodate itself to lesser linguistic skills.

This teaches us a little more about how God i to be met in his word. To demand that the wor conform to the taste or interests of any epoch, a though that were the normative time (and this is great temptation, for every age thinks of itself a the mature one and would measure everything b its own concerns) is once more to demand that Go and his word conform to man's ways and man ideas. So also with the quality of expression. Th word need not be great poetry, any more than need promise security or success or conform to particular epoch's concept of what is important. I fact, whenever we seek these things in the word expect them from it according to our own unde standing of them, we seek to judge the word c our terms. God is not to be found that way. If t prophetic word has anything to say about t presence of God, it tells us this. God is to be foun in his word when we accept it in trust, faith in t word of a just and loving God which can enable to share some of that justice and love if we perm This ability to find God in the word is perha especially evident when the word is a hard one f us, hard to believe or hard to execute. The ve difficulty can be a sign; God's word brings us him, but he is always something other than wh we expect and as strange and difficult as the u expected. It must be so when the otherness is tot as it is in God. But it is in meeting God, even though it be difficult, that we are saved. Ultimately the prophets teach us that the difficulty is but a passing moment, and God in his union with his people confers a peace and security beyond our imagining (e.g., Ezek. 34. 11–16).

WHAT WAS ISRAEL'S HISTORICAL CREED?

DENNIS J. McCARTHY, S.J.*

THE "LITTLE HISTORICAL CREED" of the Old Testament—Deut. 26:5-10 is its classic statement—has aroused controversy because it omits any reference to the events on Mt. Sinai, and it has been concluded from this that the traditions of the exodus and of Sinai were originally separate. However, the creed itself has received remarkably little study for its own sake.[1] Yet it has become the basis for much Old Testament theology. Indeed, the dean of theologians of the Old Testament, Walter Eichrodt, has had to explain himself at some length in relation to it.[2] Beyond this, the creed has been used in the study of the earlier forms of Israelite worship and much else. It is even true that von Rad's work has stimulated study of the editorial work done in composing the Gospels *(Redaktionsgeschichte)*. It would seem that something so influential deserves more attention for its own sake.

One may approach this in a number of ways. Leonard Rost's study, referred to above in note one, examines the vocabulary of the creed. He finds that most of its characteristic words are Deuteronomistic. This indicates to him that the original form of the text contained merely the statement that Israel began as a poor nomad and gained a land. All the rest would be material added at the time when Josiah put Deuteronomy at the basis of his reform, and it would stem ultimately from Hosean influence. The

*Professor of Old Testament at St. Louis University Divinity School, St. Louis, Missouri. This article is based on a lecture delivered at the Seminary February 21, 1969.

1. For the controversy, see H. B. Huffmon, "The Exodus, Sinai and the Credo," *The Catholic Biblical Quarterly* XXVII (1965), 101-113; notice of the inattention to the creed itself in L. Rost, *Das kleine Credo und andere Studien* (Heidelberg: Quelle and Meyer, 1965), pp. 11-25. The basic study is now available in English: Gerhard von Rad, *The Problem of the Hexateuch and Other Essays* (New York: McGraw-Hill Book Co., 1966), pp. 1-78.

2. *Theology of the Old Testament* (Philadelphia: Westminster Press, 1961) I, pp. 512-520.

object would be to encourage faith by fuller reference to the saving acts of Yahweh.

Be this as it may, the fact remains that the essential elements of the creed are ubiquitous. These would be some sort of reference to the patriarchs, or at least to the origins of the nation, to the Egyptian-exodus experience, and to the acquisition of the promised land. Moreover, it is not normal that these references remain isolated. We find them fitted together, most often in some sort of speech. We may profitably examine this more closely. When are the elements combined? How are they treated, and especially, how expanded? Is there a fixed vocabulary for their expression? If this is a creed in our sense, or even if it can be called a creed by an analogy which is not misleading, there should be some stability in the materials which answer these questions.

It is, of course, impossible to study all the cases in question since the mass of material would demand a book, not an article.[3] The method used here will be to examine certain key uses of the material and the purposes at which it is aimed in order to see if its actual function in the Bible has anything to say about its fundamental nature.

The first example which will occupy us is the speech of Samuel in its context in I Sam. 12:6-25. It is useful to begin here because the opening of Samuel's speech has been a crux for interpreters, and, as so often, such difficult passages can supply key insights when we look upon them in a fresh light. The problem arises from the seeming incompleteness of the Hebrew text in v. 6. Most modern translations have: "The LORD is witness," or the like. In this they follow the ancient Greek text. This latter may be correct, but it may also be that even in those early days when the Greek translation was made the text was no longer understood so that the translator supplied "is witness" to make the text intelligible, for the Hebrew presents Samuel as crying out: "The LORD, who etc." This is indeed not self-evident in meaning.

3. A list of basic texts may be of use and interest. They are Gen. 15:7, 13-16; 28:13-15; Exod. 3:10-13; 6:2-9; 19:3-6; 20:5-6; Num. 20:15-16; Deut. 6:20-24; 26:5-10; Josh. 24:1-28; Judg. 6:8-10; I Sam. 10:17-19; 12:6-25; Neh. 9-10; Jer. 16:14 (=23:7); 51:10; Ezek. 20; Zech. 4:7; Pss. 78; 81; 105; 106; 135; 136. This is not exhaustive, but it illustrates the vast areas in which the "creed" or its elements are used: history, prophecy, and poetry in many forms.

However, recent gains in knowledge do give a meaning for the difficult expression. It seems to be the case that the presence of Yahweh (the LORD) at certain of the worship services of ancient Israel was symbolized by the cry "Yahweh," or "I am Yahweh."[4] I submit that this is what is taking place in I Sam. 12:6. The situation is cultic, though not part of the regular cycle of festivals which made up the normal Israelite cult, and Samuel is simply following a regular practice by making this clear in his proclamation: "Yahweh!" He then proceeds, not, as we might expect by emphasizing the presence of God through some symbol or sacrifice, but by giving a text and developing it in a sermon. The text is contained in v. 8 which is a complete statement of the "creed." The development comes in the rest of Samuel's speech, that is, through verse 15. It is appropriate to the occasion, which is clearly marked by Samuel's aversion to the newly instituted monarchy. His remarks continue the review of the history of Israel through the period of the judges. He shows that God has regularly intervened to save His people. This is in entire accord with the basic idea: to encourage faith by recalling the saving acts of God. However, the matter is different because it treats the period of the judges. The point, of course, is to emphasize that Yahweh has always been ready to respond to His people's needs even after the "canonical" events of the patriarchal, Egyptian, and conquest periods. Hence the demand for a king "like the nations" is to show a lack of true faith in Him. This is what Samuel wants to draw from his text, and he does so.

This is not the whole of the episode. Having given his sermon, as it were, Samuel continues the ritual action. He began with a proclamation of Yahweh, a kind of theophany through words. Now he goes on to more explicit and emphatic demonstration of the presence of the Lord who controls all things. This occurs in the

---

4. Note Exod. 33:19; 34:6. In teh latter text it is not by any means certain that Yahweh is speaking as the RSV would have it; Moses may well be making the proclamation. The basic studies of this form of cultic theophany are in German. W. Zimmerli, "Ich bin Jahwe," *Gottes Offenbarung* (Munich: Kaiser, 1963), pp. 11-40; J. Scharbert, "Formgeschichte und Exegese von Ex 34.6f. und seiner Parallelen," *Biblica* XXXVIII (1957), 134-150. A study of the material surveyed in the latter article reveals that the proclamation of the divine name can be separate and accompanied by a variety of epithets.

verses, 16-18, in which Samuel really does call upon Yahweh as a kind of witness. At the demand of the prophet God sends a thunderstorm at a season when such things are unheard of in Palestine. This too is a recognized form of theophany, the coming of the weather god well documented in the literature of the ancient Near East, and perhaps best expressed in the Bible in Ps. 29.[5] The service, if we may be allowed this weak term for such an event, ends where it began, with a theophany, now one visible and impressive. This gives a specific context to the "historical creed" and its development in vv. 8-15. It is indeed cultic if we allow that the special presence of God, preaching His word, and intercession (cf. vv. 20-24) constitute something cultic, but it is cultic in a special way. It is certainly not a regular part of the calendar of feasts in Israel, for that calendar, whatever the date of the antimonarchial sentiment expressed in the first book of Samuel—and this is disputed, some holding that it is actually very late, others that it represents an ancient feeling dependent not on the experience of Solomon and other kings who were failures but on the doctrines of Yahwism and the experience of kingship which was easily visible among the Canaanite neighbors of Israel—hardly contained a regularly recurring feast in which the very institution of monarchy was condemned. If nothing else, the kingdoms could not have allowed such a thing.

This is a cultic action for a special occasion. We have pointed to some of the things which mark it as cultic. What is of special interest to us is that it contains a statement of the "historical creed" and a development of this statement in the form of a speech or sermon within this cultic context. It should be noted that the development uses a certain amount of terminology which is often used in the "creed" itself. Thus in verse 10 the people "cry out" to the LORD, in 11 He "sends" saviors, and in 13 He "gives" them a king. "Cry out" is often used of the call for deliverance from Egypt and the like in the "creeds"; in them Yahweh often "sends" Moses and Aaron to save the people, and He "gives" the people the promised land. Other expressions are used for these things, but "cry out," "send," and "give" occur often enough to give the impression that this is habitual, if not quite technical

5. On the theophany see Jörg Jeremias, *Theophanie* (Neukirchen-Vluyn: Neukirchner Verlag, 1965).

terminology. Moreover, these and other characteristic words come up with slightly varied meanings so often in the contexts of the "creeds" that one gets the feeling that they were associated with them to an extent which called them to mind regularly when the "creed" itself was called to mind. This would establish certain things. The "creed" had a certain fixity but not a rigidity of vocabulary. It was associated with the cult, but not necessarily with any specific cultic occasion. (This is not a denial that it may have been associated with such an occasion; it simply affirms that such an association is not demonstrated in the passage from I Samuel.) Finally, the "creed" has a clear functional use, at least in this text. It is not a confession of faith but a text for a sermon which is aimed at renewing faith.

This impression may be confirmed by a study of another text. This is Exod. 6:2-9 which is presented as a speech put into the mouth of Moses by Yahweh, but delivered to the people. The cultic atmosphere is maintained by the repetition of the words "I am Yahweh," which we have seen to be associated with the representation of God's presence in the cult. The speech itself recounts what Yahweh will do, rather than what He has done, but this slight variation is governed by the situation: the speech is to be made before His great saving intervention rather than to recall it. However, it conforms to the pattern. It has a cultic context or association. It has a vocabulary which recurs in connection with the "creed." In fact, while Exod. 6 has certain peculiarities, such as "groaning" (v. 5) for "cry out," it contains many more words associated with the "creed" than the Samuel speech. It uses "give" with its normal object, "land." It has the standard "bring out" for the escape from Egypt and "bring into" for the coming to the promised land. It speaks of "outstretched arm" and "bondage," which are common to the "creed" context. And again, it is not a confession of faith but a speech designed to encourage faith (which incidentally it fails to do, as Exod. 6:9 makes clear).

Technically, this last speech is somewhat different from that of Samuel. It does not set out the "creed" as its text and go on to develop it. Still, the whole is an expansion of the basic motifs: the patriarchs, the Egypt-exodus experience, and the possession of the land. No doubt these are things believed, but the question is: How do they function here? The answer is that they are material for a speech given the externals of prophecy (one can hardly speak of a sermon in this case).

I find this function of the so-called creedal materials confirmed by what is probably the best known of the "creeds," the speech in Josh. 24:2-13. It is essential to von Rad's whole argument about the form of the Hexateuch (or Pentateuch or Tetrateuch, that is, whatever one decides is the limit of the account of Israel's early history) that the speech had been originally separate from the dialogue with its pledge of renewed fidelity to Yahweh which begins with v. 14.[6] If this were mere a priori reasoning about what must have been, one would be inclined to dismiss it. In fact, it is supported by close examination of the text. The speech is not really integral to the conclusion drawn from it, for its picture of the terrors visited upon Egypt and the overwhelming conquest scarcely allows the gods of Egypt or the Amorites to be taken seriously as objects of temptation. The real problem is that of "the gods your fathers worshipped beyond the River (i.e., the Euphrates)." Even though Abraham had been weaned away from them, they retained (or had regained) the prestige of ancestral deities.

If this is so, why the insertion of all the intervening history? It is easily explained as an habitual rhetorical development occasioned by the initial reference to the fathers. They started the pattern: patriarchs, Egypt-exodus, and conquest. The familiar vocabulary, "send," "bring out," and "cry out," for instance, appears, along with some other words common in the creedal context: "give (the) land," and "take possession (of the land)." Once again, here is the technique: the use of the "creed" or some aspect of it as the basis for a speech or sermon in a religious or cultic context.

We can glance at one last example. In Gen. 15 there is a series of oracles, divine words to Abraham, about his progeny and their possession of the promised land. For us v. 7 is important: "I am Yahweh, who brought you out of Ur of the Chaldees to give thee this land as a possession." Much is familiar here: announcement of the divine presence (theophany), "bring out," "give the land," and "possession." However, the picture is incomplete. There is a

6. G. von Rad, *The Problem of the Hexateuch,* p. 15. In his fundamental study of the organization of the twelve tribes made in the 1920's Martin Noth had already called attention to the fact that Josh. 24:14ff. goes with Josh. 24:2 so that the intervening verses are some kind of intruison *(Fremdkörper).*

patriarch and the land. But where are Egypt and the exodus? Just a little further on in Abraham's dream (Gen. 15:13-15). In fact, the dream sequence interrupts the flow of the action and spoils the symmetry of the oracles. This gives us all the more reason to believe that it has been inserted to fill out the details missed in v. 7. In this way all the elements of the "creed" are present, if not exactly in the normal order, and the first short statement is expanded into a little speech or oracle.

One could go on multiplying examples and developing other arguments. Most telling of these latter, different arguments, it seems to me, is the vocabulary. It is relatively fixed but far from rigid. The same words tend to appear, but with some variation in use and meaning. For example, "serve" can mean "serve God," "serve idols," or "serve as a slave." God "sends" Moses to save, or He "sends" (i.e., puts forth) "His hand" to strike down, and so forth. Certain words float around the complex of ideas known as the "historical creed." On the other hand, similar ideas receive varied expression. Sometimes it is Yahweh Himself who "brings Israel out" of Egypt, sometimes it is Moses and Aaron. Sometimes the word is not "bring out" but "bring upwards," sometimes Israel "settles," sometimes it "dwells," and it does so in the "land" or in "this place." Or it has its bit of "plowland." The land is an "inheritance," but it is also a "possession gained from another." Sometimes the whole movement is expressly governed by a compact with a patriarch or patriarchs and its fulfillment. Sometimes nothing of the sort is mentioned. These are but a few of the examples of the variations in meaning or in vocabulary. They and the others might be explained in terms of variant traditions, different tellings of the same basic tale. To an extent this is surely the case, but the explanation leaves some things uncovered. Why, for instance, does Samuel say the same thing in I Sam. 10:17-18 and in I Sam. 12:8 for the same purpose but in slightly varying words? Examples could be added until we ran out of space.

Let us put the question once again. What was the "little historical creed?" For one thing, it was often a plea for faith, not an affirmation of it, and one can multiply the ends for which it serves: hymns to praise God, words of thanksgiving, the basis of pleas for help, motivation for obedience to the law of God and so forth. Just what is a topic on which one can ring various but limited changes of expression for a variety of purposes? Perhaps we can call this a creed, but I would suggest that the data are more accurately described or categorized by the word "commonplace" with which the rhetoricians of the Renaissance translated the Greek rhetorical term *topos*. That is to say, it is a topic accepted for certain uses in a culture, a topic which the people of that culture were trained to express in varied ways, but always within the limits of variation accepted by the culture. In simple terms, this is something like the text on which a preacher rings the proper variations (though not, of course, as fixed as our canonical texts). Such a description fits the unity within variety which we find in the "little historical creed" and its uses in the Old Testament. "Creed" implies real fixity. Men have fought over verbal changes in creeds because they express basic beliefs. We have no evidence that they did so over the variations in the speeches called "creeds" in modern Old Testament scholarship. Indeed, these speeches seem to have tried to build or restore faith, not express it.[7]

7. I do not mean to disagree with von Rad's fundamental thesis that the "creed" gave shape to Israel's early traditions. However, the flexibility within fixity of the rhetorical "commonplace" would perform the same function, and probably more easily precisely because flexible for the mass of stories, law and so forth which made up these traditions. Moreover, it would separate the problem of the "creed" and its use in this way from the vexed question of a cultic locus for the "creed." One could speak at Schechem or Gilgal or where and whenever it seemed appropriate. And one could leave out or emphasize an element as it suited his aims, his audience, and other factors.

DENNIS J. McCARTHY, S.J.

Theology, freedom, and the university

The task of Catholic theology is the ongoing search to understand the whole of Catholic religious experience in a systematic or at least a relatively satisfying way. Its interpretation must not only explain past and present experience but also encourage its advancement and look to the future. To do this, as Father McCarthy shows, theology must be free to elaborate and test new hypotheses with the same freedom as any other academic discipline. The normal place where this freedom can be safeguarded and at the same time be fully responsible is the Catholic university. There the theologian must answer to his professional colleagues and through them to the whole Church.

Lecture given at St. Louis University, September 30, 1970. Father McCarthy, formerly of St. Louis University, is now Professor of Old Testament literature at the Pontifical Biblical Institute in Rome.

At the outset we must admit that freedom is not the first word we associate with Catholic theology. Why do we insist on it now? And how, in view of our traditions, do we justify the insistence? To answer these questions we have to consider what theology is or should be. It is the effort to expand one's understanding of his religious experience, which in our case is Christian revelation as mediated to us through the Catholic community. Unless it is concerned with the actual religious experience of the theologian and the present day community, theology loses contact with reality and becomes a mere word game. We must insist on this because this is not the way we have been accustomed to look at theology. The stress has rather been on doctrine; and in doctrine, on orthodoxy. It is important to note this limitation, for in itself doctrine might have a broader sense. It might be teaching, which need not be the formal exposition of propositions. In its most effective form it is the whole life of the community which forms habits and educes ideas. There is real meaning in Henry Adams' calling his autobiography *The Education of Henry Adams*; life is the great educator.

Theology vs. orthodoxy

However, the stress on orthodoxy turns doctrine into something more abstract and intellectual. It is concerned with right believing, with something that goes on strictly within our heads.

Overemphasis on orthodoxy in this way can distort theology in a number of ways. For one, it makes us confuse theology with what we believe, when it should be the attempt to understand the given which we believe. The two things are not really the same at all. Faith as firm as a rock can be combined with the most daring speculation. One might point to Teilhard de Chardin as an example of this.

Another distortion that arises from the limitation of theology to orthodoxy is that orthodoxy implies a set of propositions in which right belief is stated. If theology is essentially an affair of orthodox doctrine, in these circumstances it will concentrate on these statements of belief. Theology becomes in large part the work of exegesis of ecclesiastical documents, a procedure all too familiar in the most recent past. This has led it away from its full task, which is to wrestle with the realities of Catholic religious experience in their totality insofar as it can grasp this totality. No theology can do this exhaustively, which is the reason why it must change and why no single system has ever been entirely satisfactory.

A further problem is the assumption that orthopraxis, the actual experience of religion in life, follows from orthodoxy or, more broadly, from the complexus of one's articulated beliefs. Our religious life is thought to follow from our theological stance. If I understand correctly, this is what many are using the word "orthopraxis" to describe these days. It is of course true that belief systematized into a theology does to some extent determine the way we act, but it is far more useful to concentrate on the opposite truth: the overriding impact of our lives, our religious experience and practice, on the formulation of our theologies. This is the way it should be. Theology must be conditioned by our real experience of faith and of the way faith works in our lives. Unless it is constantly in touch with this experience, theology must become unreal.

Theology as ongoing search

I think that this is simply to repeat the classical phrase defining theology: faith in search of understanding. Customarily we have limited faith here to statements, to authoritative propositions. But faith is a personal act and an experience. It is something concrete, and this is what theology should be seeking to understand. It is useful also to remember that, in the original Latin form of the phrase "in search of" is a present participle, *quaerens*. That is, it is a form which expresses action without limit in time. It is something going on and ongoing. The classic phrase, then, indicates that faith has not found and will not find a fully sufficient understanding.

Theology must be an enterprise in perpetual movement. It could be nothing else. No human understanding is really complete. How much more is this true when by definition its object is mystery, something necessarily beyond us, not totally opaque, but not our natural intellectual field either! And then this mystery is tied into the multiplicity of human life, indeed of all creation. Theology should be the most restless of all disciplines! How it came to be conceived of as a defense of eternal truths embodied in timeless propositions is a matter of history which can be explained in terms of historical circumstances. I believe that this conception of theology can even be defended as the appropriate stance in a certain time and place because it did speak from, and for a real phase of Catholic religious experience.

To avoid misunderstandings here, I would emphasize that giving this overriding importance to our religious experience as a controlling factor in theology is not to assert that a concern for the propositions in which elements of the faith have been stated in the past has no place in theology. On the contrary, I shall affirm that such a concern is necessarily part of Catholic theology because it is part of Catholic experience. Neither is it to assert that there can be no fixed formulations of matters of experience. Nor is it an attempt to reduce religion to a subjective feeling, a certain concern for ultimate values, or the like.[1] Finally, it is not to claim that there can be no fixed formulations of matters of faith.

Old formulas meaningless?

It is easy to say that the formulas of Chalcedon, for example, belong to a past context and have no meaning today. But, though easy to say, it is hardly true in either of the customary meanings of this claim. In one sense the claim simply asserts that these formulations belong to a past context and have no moving force on men of today. It is probably true that they do not move us much *before* we have done the work necessary to appreciate their significance by understanding them in their historical context. They are not attractive upon a superficial acquaintance.

A more serious problem is the claim that these statements out of the past are literally meaningless to us. On the contrary, one *can* recover the past. One can understand what "person" and "nature" meant in the fourth and fifth centuries. To deny this is not simply to deny the possibility of recovering theological concepts of the past. It is to deny that we can recover the past at all. In this respect the decrees of the councils are no different from Justinian's Code. This is not the place to go into the epistemology of history, but there is good reason to assert that we can know historical truth. If nothing else, the assertion is backed by enough authorities to make it intellectually respectable.

Relevance of history

Whether our interest in the past is sufficient to draw us to the labor involved in its recovery is another matter. It may well be that such an interest is commonly lacking, and this has something to say about the significance of the past as part of religious experience and so a concern for a vital theology. As Benedetto Croce pointed out, all history is contemporary because we only bother with those aspects of it which are important for our lives. Our actual state of mind conditions our interest in the past and consequently our ability to recover it. This is true, but we are far too inclined these days to assume that the past has nothing to say to us and so to ignore it. A recent survey of students produced the information that they found history the most irrelevant subject required of them. But to say that all history is contemporary is not to say that all meaningful history will impress one as such at first glance. To take this attitude is dangerous and terribly con-

---

[1] For an attempt to define religion in this sense, see Frederick Ferré, "The Definition of Religion," *Journal of the American Academy of Religion* 38 (1970) 1-16. This is an attempt to produce a definition which will include all manifestations which can be labelled religious. Since I am concerned here with the Catholic experience of religion and its theological interpretation, I do not think it necessary to go into this problem. Catholic experience has always insisted on an objective correlative of human religious experience.

fining, a point which can, perhaps, be best shown by an example.

Relevance of Vatican I

A salient aspect of Catholic life in the past hundred years has been the definition of papal infallibility at Vatican I. It has dominated attitudes and structures in much of our life and thought. It is, therefore, very much a part of Catholic religious experience (even for those who now seem to be dominated by a reaction against it). Still, I doubt that I arouse immediate interest by a mention of Vatican I. It is not "relevant." There may even be an aversion to the mention of a defined article of faith. But if I have the imagination to realize that the religious structure (not just institutions but a whole way of life) in which I live and the experience mediated by it are conditioned by this definition, it should be a matter of the greatest interest. Studying it I am studying my own life!

It should be a matter of interest, and it is if we can bring ourselves to study it closely. If we do, we will find that it defines a fact, not an essence. That is, it teaches the fact that the pope is, in certain conditions, an unerring guide in matters of faith and morals. But just what does this mean? According to the Council, the pope enjoys that infallibility which Christ wished his Church to enjoy.[2] However, the Council adjourned *sine die* without telling us just what that infallibility is which Christ wished his Church to enjoy. The fact is defined plainly enough. Its exact meaning and its implications are something else again. Yet this conciliar decision and a certain interpretation of it has had an impact on Catholic life which has made it as real a factor as any in our religious lives. How are we to react to it now? I suggest that a careful historical study of the definition and of the intentions of the Council with regard to the infallibility of the Church would be most pertinent and would prove to be most enlightening.

The example illustrates a number of things. For one, there is the importance of the past and the study of the past in our own lives. Noting the qualifications which the Council put on its definition of infallibility should show what careful attention to this kind of source can produce. Then there is the obvious conclusion that a statement of doctrine can be true but far from exhaustive. The pope is infallible by definition, but the nature and extent of this infallibility are not defined. In other words, without need for any subtle argumentation about the nature of conciliar teaching it is clear that the teaching is open to further understanding, and this will not necessarily be the understanding first put upon it. The teaching does not close discussion. On the contrary, it should stimulate it. Perhaps the propositions of the faith are not open to change, but they are open to further elucidation and explanation. Finally, and this is my main point at the moment, it seems obvious that the teaching on infallibility is far more real to us, far more part of our lives, and consequently a far more important object of theological investigation than what the Fourth Lateran Council had to say about creation against the Cathari.[3]

Why is creation in the Creed?

Yet the paradox is that one way to emphasize the place of practice and experience in the formation of theology is precisely to study it historically. We should ask ourselves why certain things were important enough to become the object of theological or polemical discussion and even at times to be embodied in solemn ecclesiastical pronouncements. In this respect the doctrine of creation is literally primary. Our creeds begin with it, the Bible begins with it, and in some ways the whole Christian attitude toward the world is conditioned by the fact that it came from the hand of God and he saw that it was good. And yet, in spite of this primacy, the doctrine of creation has seldom been a burning theological issue or the object of solemn Church teaching. It has come to the fore only when there has been an upsurge of dualist ideas.

In the earliest ages the Church was confronted with Gnosticism and Manicheanism teaching that of its nature matter is evil. The Church responded with the creeds, insisting that God is the creator of all things, whatever they may be, material or spiritual. This dualism submerged for a thousand years to reappear in the Western Church in the Albigensian heresy to which Lateran IV addressed itself. Once again, faced with the claim that matter was evil and so did not come from God, the Church solemnly asserted that all things, matter included, came from God the creator. When something became an object of discussion, and, more important, when it claimed to be a basic element in Christian life, Christians reacted and ultimately the Church spoke in a formal manner.

But once more a closer study of the case is enlightening. The central issue was the uniqueness of the Creator. The existence of separate spiritual substances (angels) was assumed by all parties. It was not the direct object of discussion nor of definition. In effect, what was said was: Whatever exists, or whatever you think exists, has been made by God.

Defiant self-affirmation

The definition of papal infallibility, too, was historically conditioned. Why did it come in 1870? The background is complex, and we must content ourselves with only a few points. There was the whole history of the attempts to assert the powers of national churches, particularly the Gallican claims. The idea is very old, but it grew stronger with the growth of the power of the nation-state in modern times. In particular there was the situation in which the papacy found itself at the time of Vatican I. For the first time in a millenium and a half it was practically certain of a complete loss of its familiar temporal power base. The specter of the national church and the nation-state became very vivid. The Church might have responded differently to the situation, but this remains pure speculation. Given the habits, the mental set, of the men of the time, it was natural, if not necessary, humanly speaking, that the Church respond with a defiant, decisive affirmation of its rights and powers in matters spiritual. And so we have infallibility defined.

However, all this is to look at matters theological in the large and to concern ourselves precisely with those questions which have become matters of orthodoxy, of formal church teaching, and I wish to avoid too much emphasis on this because, as we have seen, orthodoxy and theology, while closely related, are not the same thing. I have dealt at some length with these matters in the last several paragraphs to show that, even on this more abstruse level, practice, actual religious experience, forms the framework for theological thought. It is also important to note

---

[2]Denzinger-Schönmetzer, 3074.

[3]Denzinger-Schönmetzer, 800.

that the past is actually part of our own religious experience, as the example of Vatican I especially makes clear. Now, if even the massive institutional aspect of Catholicism is so sensitive to the give and take of history, how much more so is the individual theologian or Christian, reflecting more or less alone on his faith! This is, of course, a good thing. It is such a sensitivity to real experience which makes theology itself real and vital. Further, it seems to me that it has been a great strength of Catholicism that it has provided such a complete framework within which religious experience could be encouraged and in which it has been recorded. This should have provided an ideal milieu for the work of theology.

Religion gives life meaning

Since this is all at the level of day to day living, it seems more profitable to discuss it less in terms of learned studies and more in those which show popular attitudes and impressions. Thus it is significant that in a novel like *Airport* or the works of Jacqueline Susann, of all things, it is taken for granted that the Catholic has a way of life, a framework which defines his actions and gives them a religious dimension. Whether this is still so clearly the case I am not sure, but surely books of this sort are not interested in speculations on what is going on within Catholicism. They simply record their authors' observations of how people act. In certain circumstances the Catholic would act in certain ways. There was a framework to guide him, and this is not merely an external force. It gave or could give a religious meaning to his life.

I do not find this impression of any other religious tradition recorded in popular writings of this sort, but there is a parallel example, that of Orthodox Judaism. Once more I refer to a popular article, an exposition which reflects the way ordinary people are thought to see and understand things. One of those airline magazines which one finds in the pockets on the backs of airplane seats last year carried an article on Orthodox Judaism in the United States. It pointed out that it is the healthiest branch of American Judaism in terms of appeal to the younger people. Young Jews are actually turning to Orthodoxy with its apparent restrictions. The explanation given is that Orthodoxy involves the whole man and all he does. Its practices determine what he eats and how he makes a living, not merely how he prays and where he worships. From waking to sleeping there is a law to guide his every action. Thus all experience can become religious experience, and a man's life has a real meaning in all its aspects. This is something enviable in our age, and it is something which has been available to the Catholic too.

Theology and practice

Such a rich body of experience should be fertile ground for theology, but it does not automatically produce a theology. The actual use of such material in theology is a delicate process. For one thing, the practice can become all-absorbing so as to leave no time or interest for the search for understanding. For another, such a defined, densely religious life involves many arbitrary practices. It could not be otherwise because religion and religious experience claim to deal with the absolute, and men can express a relation to the absolute only in signs even more arbitrary than those he uses for more ordinary communication. How else can he point to the inexpressible? Religion therefore tends to set up certain practices which in themselves can claim no special holiness, but which, because of their association with the absolute, acquire a kind of sanctity and become vehicles for encouraging and expressing religious experience. A theology concentrated on such signs would itself be arbitrary and shallow because its attention would be absorbed by arbitrary externals to the detriment of the experience and its meaning.

Tension is inherent

Nor is this the only problem. If there is a value in religious experience both encouraged and directed by a pattern of religious practices, we must admit also that a tension is also inherent in all this. As we have seen, practices and more or less peripheral ideas enshrine some contact with the absolute. The next step is to take these things themselves as a kind of absolute. There will be tremendous pressure not to change these practices. At the same time man lives in time and so is always meeting a new situation. He and his life-style, including its religious elements, must change under pain of not meeting the demands of the new situation and so being shunted aside from the center of things. Hence the tension between old and new. There is the familiar practice which for many represents the focal point of their experience of God. On the other hand, there are those living with and accepting change who find that long established practices have lost their meaning.

Karl Barth has stated it beautifully: "Historical relationships as a whole are found to be in perhaps a slow but at any rate a continual state of flux. And that means that religions are continually faced with the choice: either to go with the times, to change as the times change, and in that way relentlessly to deny themselves any claim to truth and certainty; or else to be behind the times, to stick to their once-won forms of doctrine, rite and community and therefore relentlessly to grow old and obsolete and fossilized; or finally, to try to do both together, to be a little liberal and a little conservative, and therefore with the advantages of both options to take over their disadvantages as well. That is why religions are always fighting for their lives. That is why they are always acutely or chronically sick."[4]

Radical action ineffective

One result of this state of affairs is the split between a steely insistence that we retain what we have just as it is, and its antithesis, the demand that we simply abandon the past and embrace a total novelty. Such oversimplifications relieve tension by simply dropping one or the other essential of all religious experience. Obviously neither choice is acceptable, and this puts limits on what we can do. For one thing we cannot simply throw over significant practices from the past and still hope to retain a position of influence within the community whose experience has been defined in part by these practices. This seems self-evident. If it is not, it is confirmed by experience.

In one of those articles summing up the state of religion in the sixties, a newspaper writer took notice of the turmoil in the churches, including the Catholic Church. The writer was obviously inclined toward many of the ideas classed as liberal. She noted with seeming approval that Bishop James Shannon was among the Catholic leaders who had made national news by a courageous stand on the birth-control issue. She was saddened, then, to note

---

[4] *Church Dogmatics*, vol. I, part 2 (Edinburgh: T. & T. Clark, New York: Scribner's, 1956), §17, p. 316.

that his influence was lessened by his wedding.[5]

Whether we like it or not, western Catholic experience has included the fact of a celibate clergy, and this has an important symbolic value for many. We all know that the law of celibacy is an ecclesiastical law and could be changed, but in fact it obtains now and, more important, it is still demanded by a large part of the community. You must not think that I am questioning the sincerity of the motives of Bishop Shannon and others when I point out that a witness can hardly be accepted by the Catholic community when it so flies in the face of its current religious practice and experience.

This is not to say that change is impossible. On the contrary, it is part of the tension in any religion between retaining something of the past and moving into the present. The tension is certainly there, but it cannot be relieved by denying change any more than by denying the past. The problem is to turn the tension into a source of development rather than conflict, so that there can be a growth which is a continuity with the past and yet can carry us into a future which is very unlike that past. Move too fast and the shock renders our move ineffectual; move too slowly and it is not tradition which is endangered but life itself. Hence some of the terrible human problems which arise in religion and in its translation into theology (for theology is one of the important means by which religion can adapt to new circumstances). We cannot ignore the fact that religious experience does not occur in the abstract. It is historical; that is, it is marked by its time and place. It has specific characteristics, and one of these is strong ties to the past.

This is one aspect of the relation between practice and theology. It is perhaps an extrinsic factor, and it is a limiting one, but it is very real. It means that one can clash with custom only so far and still remain an effective spokesman within a religious community. However, this element of custom makes up a large part of the framework of religious experience, especially Catholic experience, and I have insisted that this experience should be useful to theology. It should, therefore, offer something more than limitations, and it does.

Priesthood in our experience

I have insisted that a close relation with this experience is necessary if theology is to be something more than words. It is its connection with the experience which gives it body, reality. But perhaps this can be made more clear in an example, the theology of the priesthood. I have no intention of giving a theology of the priesthood here but simply to refer to some things one often hears about it nowadays.

It seems as though someone is always about to produce an adequate theology of priesthood, or that he would like to do so, or that he wishes someone would do so. Frankly, this sort of thing makes me shudder. Not because it is a question of the priesthood as such. On the contrary, one of the many areas where we need vigorous thought is that of the nature and position of the priesthood in our rapidly changing society. It is not that in touching the priesthood one is touching a sacred cow. No, the problem is the insistence on "adequacy" and the usual concomitant demand to return to the primitive concepts of the thing.

As for adequacy, I think that I would shudder intellectually with equal vigor if it were a question of an adequate theology of the anointing of the sick or of indulgences. The problem here is not the priesthood or indulgences or whatever but the fact that by definition Christian theology is concerned with mystery, and mystery is something which the human intellect cannot in any circumstances *adequately* comprehend. If theology is in any way a matter of understanding, then to speak of an adequate theology is to speak of an adequate understanding of mystery, that which cannot be understood adequately. One need not be a professional logician to be troubled by such a proposition.

But of course in the human context the desire for an adequate theology of priesthood or of the laity or of anything else which is important to us is really a desire for a *satisfying* theology. It is a demand for a theology which gives me sufficient intellectual satisfaction not merely to live with but to enjoy Christianity as I experience it. The problem with most "adequate" theologies, as far as I have seen them, is that they fail to include the indispensable element of present religious experience. They fail to take into account – or even worse, they explicitly reject – that historical agglomeration of usages which delivers the mystery to us and expresses it in our lives.

In regard to the priesthood this means celibacy for Roman Catholics of the West. It is also a priesthood which has always been something more than the simple dispensation of the sacraments. It has always involved teaching, administration, and many other activities. Once again, whether or not these are necessary corollaries of the Christian priesthood, this is in fact the way in which we have met it in our lives. Once again, we need not say that it has to be this way, but this is how it is here and now, and any theologizing about it should begin with the admission of the extreme complexity and the conditioned historicality of this aspect of religious experience.

One might respond that what is really needed is to clear away the accumulations of the past which mark our present situation to get back to the real thing. The view is common enough, and it has always been true that in times of renewal the Christian community has gone back to the Bible, particularly the NT. It is also true that, while we can understand something of the past, we can never return to it. Just as we cannot literally reconstitute ourselves citizens of the Roman Empire of the first century, we cannot reconstitute ourselves primitive Christians in all the aspects of their experience and psychology. We cannot escape our present selves any more than we can escape our past.

Cannot ignore experience

Inevitably, no matter how careful we are in the matter of scientific exegesis, when we turn from this to theological elaboration we are influenced by our own special experience. We would not have it otherwise, for theology should always be an interpretation of what is real, and that is our total religious experience, not merely past propositions, even biblical ones. The paradox is that part of this experience is the accumulation of two thousand years of living and reflecting. Some of this accumulation may well include practices and ideas which have had their day, but if we believe, as we Catholic Christians must, in a truth given by God and mediated to us by generation after generation of the Christian community, it is inconceivable that this accumulation of experience will not have brought out values only

---

[5] *Kansas City Star*, December 27, 1969.

obscurely expressed or implied in earlier practices and formulations. Once again we must distinguish between petrified and out-dated practices and those which cast real light on our problems or offer solid data for our theologizing.

I imagine that most of this sounds like a plea for the past. In reality, I am trying to emphasize the fact that the matrix which makes Christianity a real experience for us must form the starting point of all valid theology. Since the past is part of that experience and since there seems presently to be a tendency to ignore this or even rebel against it, I have been stressing this aspect. If this is taken as a plea that we stay where we are or, more accurately, that we go back a decade or more, I have been misunderstood.

Facing the fact of change

There is the other aspect of the necessary tension within religion, the tension between continuity with the past and growth into the future. Theology must reflect this tension, and it is implied in its definition: it is always seeking. It is always trying to go forward, to develop a deeper and more comprehensive understanding of faith. But the faith it is trying to understand is or should be the faith we actually live, that is the life of the Church in the large and in ourselves. Reflection on this forces us to the conclusion that we must come to terms with change. This means, not merely with new facts but with the fact of process as such. This is surely one of the principal objects of our experience, whether we observe our own personal experience or the experience of the Christian community.

Now, a satisfactory theory of development in theology would be interesting, and there has been considerable effort directed toward developing such a theory. Generally, this has taken the direction of seeking to explain how apparently radically new and different doctrinal formulations have been possible without their constituting a real break in continuity with the past. No one, as far as I know, thinks that all this effort has produced a satisfactory theory of development. Perhaps this is due in part to the concentration on doctrine rather than on the whole of Christian life as the context of growth and itself a growing context. Perhaps it is because it has some of this breadth that Newman's *Development of Doctrine* remains one of the most satisfactory efforts in this field. However, all this remains largely speculative. It may be an interesting problem, but I would not call it a pressing problem right now. We need to work toward a Catholic understanding of a mass of new facts and attitudes of precisely those things which are frightening to so many, stimulating to some, and in any case part and parcel of our present religious experience.

The pressing problem

Once more let me explain by an example reported popularly. It is an interview of the well-known Italian journalist, Oriana Fallaci, with Archbishop Helder Camara.[6] It seems to me a remarkable expression of some of the facts and attitudes which we must confront and in large part assimilate. There is the passion for justice which goes so far as to accept in theory the peculiar violence of our times, the kidnapping of diplomats, physical attacks on the machinery of the law, and the rest. I say, accept in theory, because in fact the violence is rejected for tactical reasons. The thing that vitiates it is its counter-productivity.

Then there is the acceptance of Marxism, at least in part. The Archbishop accepts Marx's analysis of capitalism but not his conclusions. It is not clear what these conclusions are. One supposes that atheism is one. One hopes that the totalitarianism, the dictatorship of the proletariat, is another.

Again, there is the criticism of actual institutions and particularly of the Roman Catholic Church. It has been too much preoccupied with the problem of maintaining order and too little with justice. So its order, or the order of which it is part, is in fact no order at all because it is injustice. If the Church is to regain respect, it must find again a passion for justice, and it can no longer preach resignation.

The views are familiar enough, though not from the mouths of archbishops. There are not many Helder Camaras! But coupled with all this is a quite traditional statement of spirituality. The Archbishop shows a personal devotion to Christ. The Mass is a perpetual joy because it is a reliving of the Passion and Resurrection. There is even meditation and recollection, for one can carry his monastic cell in his heart. To me it is this juxtaposition of views which is interesting and, I think, of some use for theology. It is a statement of the tension between old and new which is inevitable in religion. However, this is no theory expressed by an intellectual authority, no abstract statement. This is a tension alive in the experience of a single person.

Live with tension

We all know that such tensions exist, and I suppose we know the usual results in an ordinary personality. Either the spirituality is dismissed as irrelevant (I am reminded of the ex-priest who left Cesar Chavez's movement because of that remarkable man's personal emphasis on religion), or the passion for justice is condemned as immoral because of its unconventional expression. Neither of these solutions will do. They are instances of the either-or mentality, which reduces experience to simple parts which can then be accepted or rejected absolutely.

The trouble is that this distorts the experience so that it becomes false. It becomes a fruitless object for theological reflection. It is Helder Camara who is expressing what may be the essential Christian experience of our time. This is what theology must grapple with. This is the immense opportunity which lies before it: to help toward a reasonable intellectual integration of the experience so that we can overcome the impatience and fear which make it so hard for so many to live with the experience.

This is an opportunity. It is also a difficult task. For example, I would insist on the validity of the passionate involvement with justice. I cannot agree with even a conditioned acceptance of violence. It is indeed an uncertain tactic. But it is more than that. It will destroy the social machinery which is the only hope for betterment for the deprived. Worst of all, it can hardly be justified in itself. It is just as wrong to wound or kill the bystander in Marin County or Colombia or Uruguay as in Vietnam. Of course, Archbishop Camara recognizes this. He has deplored the attacks on diplomats as "inhuman and absurd," an offense to Christian and human sensibilities, while still calling for general conditions of justice, a society which will no longer drive men to such actions.[7] I

---

[6] *L'Europeo*, August 20, 1970.

[7] Quoted in an editorial of the *New York Times*, reprinted in the *International Herald Tribune*, August 20, 1970, p. 6.

suppose that he can express these rather different views because he is expressing immediate Christian experience, the reaction of a believing and outraged conscience to injustice wherever it finds it. Once again, it is the task of theology to help toward an integrated understanding and expression of all this.

But to take up another point, though socialism is defensible purely on the intellectual level as an analysis of capitalism, Marxism as such is not. This analysis is a theory of history predicting the uprising of the industrial masses. The fascinating irony is that this uprising has never occurred, and Marxism in some form or other has proved a convenient doctrine for the development of non-industrial areas. But we should ask why a passion for justice turns to such irrelevant means of expression. Surely it is because it has been offered no others which come close to satisfying.

Understand – and let grow

But enough of examples. By now I hope that it is clear that I have been trying to establish something about the nature of theology because without this we cannot approach the question of the freedom of theology. It may help to sum up, to see where we are at this point. For one thing, theology is not simply to be identified with orthodoxy. It is indeed concerned with the authoritative statements of faith. However, this is but one aspect of the material with which it has to work. It is concerned with the whole of Catholic religious experience as it now exists, and its task is to understand it in as systematic way as possible, or at any rate, systematic or not, to provide some sort of relatively satisfying understanding of this experience. To be satisfying in any way, the interpretation must not only explain the fact of experience but also encourage its advance. To put it another way, theology must be concerned not simply with records of the past nor even with present experience. It must also look to what is to come.

If it is to accomplish anything of the sort, and if it is not identical with the creed, we must allow it to take the chance of error because we must allow it the opportunity for development. Hypothesis and experiment are the conditions for growth. This is necessary because the theologian must confront new issues. He does this from a context of tradition, but precisely because the traditions have grown out of past conditions they do not provide instant and automatic answers to problems which are really new and which make up a major part of actual experience.

We must recognize that in such circumstances the theologian may be daring. He can even be in error and still be in the best of faith. If there is a single truth which we have failed to take account of in our history, this may well be it. The tendency to equate theology with orthodoxy *toute simple* has led us to equate error with unorthodoxy and so lack of faith. This will not meet the case, for theology is concerned with something far broader than articles of belief. It is perfectly possible to remain attached to orthodoxy – among other things because the actual number of formal statements of what has to be believed is remarkably small – and still do a great deal of daring investigation. One must run the risk of some error in the attempt to explain how these truths and others, which are only part of Catholic life, enter into the whole fabric of Catholic life here and now. It would be miraculous if all responses to new experiences, to new and pressing needs, were unerring. That is not the way the Spirit works. It allows more scope for humanity, and this means the excitement of the search and includes the danger of going astray.

The value of hypotheses

We must, then, recognize the value of the technique of the hypothesis, the tentative explanation of the phenomena of Christian experience which is offered for further investigation and debate. This is the common way in which science and even the humanities have progressed, and theology should not be deprived of this valuable instrument. However, in the very nature of the case there will be hypotheses which will be rejected. They are offered in good faith. They may be accepted for a time, but in the course of further study it will be discovered that they do not cover the facts. They may be found to be in subtle disaccord with the tenets of the religion they aim to elucidate. If so, obviously they do not do what they set out to do. They do not further understanding of their object, but in a complex field this may not be seen at once. Or it may be that there is nothing wrong with a hypothesis in terms of doctrine, but that it simply does not explain the actual state of faith, or perhaps better, of the faithful. Once again, the hypothesis must be rejected, even though it be cast in the most familiar of terms. In any case, we should not be too ready to see harm in an unfamiliar or an unsuccessful hypothesis. On the contrary, at the least it shows that one apparently inviting avenue of approach is closed. Often, even usually, the hypothesis, though rejected in its first form, will have more than this merely negative value. Apart from its usefulness in stimulating thought, it itself is likely to be refined so that it becomes a useful theological instrument.

Does this mean unlimited freedom? Of course not, because among other things such freedom is impossible to man who is always limited. Apart from this, though, we are dealing with Catholic theology and the Catholic experience behind it. If this means change, because theology is always seeking, it must somehow be Catholic change. That is, it must somehow join and continue the religious experience which is recognizably Catholic. Thus one must disagree with a writer like John Cogley in another of those articles summing up the Sixties, when he says, "The distinction between Protestant and Catholic will become less sharp. It is already true that for progressive theologians there is only Christian theology rather than sectarian branches of theology."[8] It is true that we have learned much from non-Catholic theologians, but too much of this kind of "progress" seems to me to be the way to ruin.

Robert Rodes is closer to the mark: "The facile ecumenism of the Underground Church is part and parcel of its failure to bear witness to the transcendence of God. True ecumenism requires every denomination to bear an uncompromising witness before others to its own experience of the inexhaustible reality of Jesus Christ."[9] This is talk about religion as it has always been lived by Christians, while the background of the Cogley article seems to be a strong tendency to turn from religion to humanism.

Mr. Cogley has the idea that the Catholic Church will give up its specifically Catholic schools, social agencies, and the like so that Catholics may serve in secular agencies "not as religious 'pro-

---

[8] *Milwaukee Journal*, January 3, 1970.

[9] "The Last Days of Erastianism–Forms in the American Church-State Nexus," *Harvard Theological Revue* 62 (1969) 348.

fessionals' but as men and women of the world motivated by humanistic ideals."[10] This may indeed be the shape of the future for many, but it simply is not Catholic, let alone religious, in any recognizable Christian form. It can hardly be so because it is based on the odd belief that man can save himself by his own efforts. I know that this is indeed a popular idea, but it still seems to me odd that this relic of the sunny eighteenth century can be so "relevant" in an age marked by mushroom clouds and exhaust fumes.[11]

Specifically Catholic experience

To a certain extent it is unfair to treat Mr. Cogley's position in this way, for he seems to be talking about theology under one of its transient forms. That is, he is talking about "sectarian" in the polemic sense rather than in the sense of a theology formed within the framework of a particular religious experience. Certainly there is little future in a return to polemics among Christian groups or among various religions. However, there really is as little future for a mishmash in which all the old signs of religious life have been beaten into a featureless gruel so uninspiring that not even the boys of Hardship Hall would want a second helping. Rather we want to emphasize those particular Catholic values which may be lacking or less emphasized in other traditions and other experiences. The question is, what is this special Catholic value? What is special about Catholic experience? The full answer would be the twentieth-century *Civitas Dei* or *Summa theologica* – something I am not prepared to offer. However, it still seems possible to note some aspects of Catholic religious experience which would have to mark Catholic theologizing and which would give that activity a value not just for Catholics but for the whole Christian community.

One aspect which presents itself at once is the emphasis on the sacramental or ritual in the widest sense. This means something more than the Mass and the sacraments as defined in the catechism. It means that fact that Catholic life has emphasized the use of ritual (words and practices) to mark all of life as something of supreme religious value. We have already discussed the importance of this as a means of encouraging and expressing religious experience.

Now it may well be that much in the forms which have been used to consecrate the whole of living is no longer viable. The forms may be connected with attitudes and institutions which are things of the past. There are things like clinging to temporal power, a relic of an age when men could hardly recognize a spiritual force unless it was accompanied by material power. There is the continuation of styles in art and life which reflect a triumphalism we no longer feel. There are attitudes left over from the time when a person was the subject of a paternalist state conceived in the image of the family, attitudes quite unacceptable to a free and equal citizenry.

Expressions of religion which insist on things like this, relics of a past when they were valid vehicles for religious experience, discredit not only the relics but the faith linked to them, for they create an unbridgeable gap between the actual experiences of life and the forms in which one would be compelled to express the experience. Nothing could be emptier. What is important in all this is not the particular ideas or practices but the attitude, the sacramental view which constitutes all of life an expression of man's relationship to God, a commitment to him.

Using the whole past

Another mark of Catholic experience should make us insist that we cannot ignore large areas of Christian experience in our theological work. Christian experience is a continuous one, and we cannot ignore the past or skip over parts of it to return to those we like. The past, all the past, colors our experience, as our experience colors our interpretations of the past. However, it is unfortunately possible to act as though the past were not really with us.

The message of Catholic Christianity to theology here is that we simply cannot do what is done, for example, in the article on Christology in the second volume of *Twentieth Century Theology in the Making.*[12] There the period from Augustine to Luther is dismissed as having practically nothing to offer. Once again, the study of medieval philosophy and theology is out of fashion, but fashionable or not, it is important and we should use it. For instance, in Christology even the Protestant has much to learn from a study of Cistercian-Franciscan spirituality, for it has a good deal to say about the Christology of Luther and the reformers in general. In any case, the Catholic insistence on the continuity of tradition, which is nothing else than the continuity of Christian experience, is something which should contribute to our theology and complement other Christian theologies.

Failure to be theological

Finally, although it is not really a specifically Catholic concern, it is something we should be most concerned about, namely, that theology be theology. It must be concerned with God – the *theos* who appears in its very name. I will be accused of belaboring the obvious, perhaps, but the point needs to be made in view of some of the facts already noted. There have been attempts at theologies without "God-talk." It is a fact too that many priests and nuns turn or wish to turn from their "professional" religious roles to humanitarian social work. Precisely on these terms, not as religious but as humanitarian, not as an extension of Christian love but as an expression of purely human solidarity, we are dealing with something which in no way distinguishes the Catholic from the non-Catholic or the non-Christian or the non-believing practitioner. This good and necessary work cannot, then, be said to sum up Catholic life or to be a matrix for the development of Catholic theology.

It may well be that in fact interest in social betterment will increase and interest in theology and religion in general

---

[10] Article cited in note 8.

[11] I am, of course, aware that not long ago it was fashionable to say that "God-talk" had lost its meaning for modern man and that religion was a form of idolatry erecting human institutions to the sacred level on which they did not belong. And still I insist on religion and religious experience. In part I feel justified in doing this because the fashion had its brief moment in the sun and is no longer much with us. As for the problem of the religious, I have emphasized that it is essential to distinguish between forms and their essential meaning which is given in the experience of faith. There is no real religion without some such experience, and with it there is no real problem in talking about religion because one is talking about something real, though the Christian knows that it is an experience not given to everyone.

[12] Edited by Jaroslav Pelikan, London, 1970. The book is a translation of significant articles from the second edition of the German reference work, *Die Religion in Geschichte und Gegenwart*, which is thirty years old, but definitely a landmark in modern theology.

will continue to decline. Whether it happens or not, we should at least be clear that social work is not religious, let alone theological. Nor is there any reason to assume that there must always be a widespread interest in theology, so that what just happens to be going on must somehow be theological. One of the lessons of centuries of Christian experience is that there are times when theology is not a very lively discipline. In some ways this was true of the so-called Dark Ages. It was true for very different reasons during the high Renaissance in Italy. It certainly was true of the eighteenth century Enlightenment era. One might argue that these were not the peaks of Christian living either, and there may be some relation between a lack of interest in theology and a decline of Christian life and a widespread weakening of faith. Still, it is dangerous to judge Providence, and it is true that Christian experience has managed to continue beyond these low points. A lack of interest in theology is certainly not fatal. It may even be an important part of the mysterious process of Christian history.

However, such speculation does not absolve the theologian from his task of trying to make faith more intelligible and more real. Even the believer who is not a professional theologian cannot shirk a part in this task. The problem of social improvement, therefore, becomes something which must be a concern of the theologian and the Christian. This is so because a passion for justice seems to be a characteristic of our times, and this is something closely related with ultimate Christian concerns. This being the case, I suggest that simply turning to secular expertise in the field of social work and the like is a failure to be fully Christian. We do not enlarge Christian experience in this way, let alone expand our understanding of this experience in a theology. On the other hand, by simply taking over secular expertise without giving it a Christian and a Catholic dimension, we may be failing to enrich the expertise and the discipline with something it could use. In many ways this is parallel with the sort of ecumenical theologizing which aims at a nice, bland mixture acceptable to one and all because it is tasteless, and uninteresting to the same degree.

It is, then, my contention that the task of theology is to provide a reasonably integrated understanding of religious experience. As Catholic theology it must have its special characteristics. To have any solidity it must be real, and this means that it must deal with real experience, the life of faith as it is lived here and now, not as we read about it or imagine it might be, and the experience which it is concerned with must be truly religious. To be all this, theology must have freedom.

Theology and its freedom

This need for freedom, freedom of inquiry and freedom of debate, grows out of the whole analysis of theology in which we have been engaged. For one thing, we have insisted that theology must be firmly based in experience, and Christian experience takes in so much. It is extended in time and in space for the community, and it is complex, even for the individual. The only hope we have of dealing with such experience is to allow free-ranging investigation and interpretation. Restrictions on investigation and interpretation can only mean that elements of this experience will be passed over, and until they have been subjected to the light of investigation and interpretation we can never know what elements of experience are most important in life and most fruitful for theology. Restriction can only mean lack of breadth, which is obvious, but it may mean lack of depth and vitality as well. Hence the need for ever new, ever more searching hypotheses.

Then, we have to face the problem raised by the ritual element as we have defined it. That is, we must preserve its virtue, the capability of giving meaning to all living, but we must avoid tying ourselves to empty forms from the past. This certainly demands unhampered investigation of the forms to find their essential meaning. It also must imply hypothesis and experiment to test what forms are still viable and what new things are needed.

Threats to freedom

If freedom is so necessary, it is necessary to consider some of the sources of danger to it. They are many, and they are in part inherent in the nature of theology and its relation to religious experience. Catholic experience especially includes a strong involvement with practices from the past. If one offends too much against this he loses his freedom because he loses his effectiveness as a spokesman interpreting religious experience. There are circumstances when something like this may be needed. It may be necessary sometimes to emphasize that a devotion to St. Jude is less important than a devotion to justice and charity even when this emphasis offends some. However, in most cases this is not so much the concern of theology as of preaching, and when, as with Archbishop Helder Camara, this preaching obviously retains its religious dimension, one wonders whether the offense given does come from an unadmitted realization on the part of the offended that he is in conflict with authentic religion.

However, we should not identify theology with preaching, though the two should not be entirely divorced one from another either. Much less should we demand that theology assume what the current mode calls the prophetic office. One should note that the biblical prophets were generally reluctant dragons, often unsure of themselves and unwilling to act until forced by God's overwhelming urgency. This should give us pause when someone is very ready to take on the prophetic role (we have even had a prospective beauty queen in Arizona who essayed it!). Still, I do not deny that there is such a role and that the theologian may sometimes be called to it. Nevertheless, it seems to me that theology is normally concerned with understanding the prophet, not in being prophetic. The role is humbler, but it remains necessary, and it should not be too readily absorbed into another, even that of prophecy.

Problem of rapid exposure

This is one danger to the freedom of the theological enterprise. Another is raised by the speed and ubiquity of modern means of communication. Theology is concerned not merely with propositions and statements of faith but with life itself and with its ultimate meaning. Therefore, its hypotheses can be immediately applicable to the lives of many people. This means they can have great interest, and they become news. And so we have the appearance of theology in the daily and weekly journals.

There certainly is nothing wrong with publicizing theology. On the contrary, I suppose that religion, theology included, can use all the publicity it can get. However, if work by means of hypothesis is a necessary procedure in theology, this rapidity of public exposure creates a problem. An exciting hypothesis becomes public property before it has undergone the debate and investigation needed to determine its value. I do not want to overrate this problem, but we must realize that herein lies one reason for the nervous fears of so many of our fellows. They seem to find so much which for them is literally a matter of the meaning of life and death called in question that they react with recriminations which are a danger to the freedom of theology and, worse, to charity.

There is, of course, another source of problems for freedom in theological work, repression. Just now, outright condemnations of men or positions are rare. However, there are other ways in which repression can be brought to bear. There is the exercise of pressure in one form or another. There can be the quiet or not so quiet withholding of funds. There can be the threat to job security or to advancement. There are the myriad forms of pressure brought to bear by *ad hoc* committees, gatherers of petition signatures, and organizations without number, all the apparatus and techniques with which we have become familiar and which many have learned to use with great skill. All this pressure to conform, to align oneself with a predefined position, whether it be the extremist right or the extremist left, is always an attack on the dignity of the person, and it can hinder or destroy his ability to work. This is as true for the theologian as for anyone else.

These are some of the concrete ways in which the freedom of the theologian can be hindered. They are not all new by any means, but sometimes they seem more than ordinarily pressing in our day. One reason is that this is not a patient age. It wants results, and it wants them fast. Considering the speed of change with which it has to live, this is understandable. Still, it threatens to destroy the calm needed for the study and contemplation which are so necessary if theology is to be what it should – not a technical exercise but a search for wisdom, for ultimate meanings. In fact, as we come to realize the effects of increasing knowledge, it is evident that all disciplines need this opportunity for reflection.

The other side of this problem is the simple fear of change. This is perennially human, but it is probably accentuated by the speed of change in our time. Hence the reaction, the desire to halt change and even to go backwards. Ours is a time when a demand for a petrified status and a demand for over-rapid change both seem especially dangerous to contemplation and study and so to real freedom of the mind.

Freedom and the university

The basic problem, deeper than the psychological and far more important in the long run than the concrete threats to freedom, is the problem of authority; for theology, though it must be free, must also be recognizably religious and recognizably Catholic. How is it to be decided whether a given theological expression is this? Or, since this is a human problem not subject to physical tests, who decides? I think that the Catholic answer must be that the Church decides. But the problem is, what church? A simple appeal to hierarchical authority will no longer do. It is here that an appeal to the university tradition may help. At the shallowest level, but a very real one, we must be honest and admit that to be free, the theologian must have a base from which he can operate, while remaining relatively safe from the threats we have alluded to. As far as I can see, such a base can normally be nothing but the university. Hence the close relation between the possibility for freedom and the university which can guard the freedom of theology as it guards the freedom of its other disciplines. At the same time, we are speaking of Catholic theology, and this means that the university protects the freedom of Catholic theology, the freedom to interpret Catholic experience. I think this gives or could give the role of the university in theology an extra dimension.

The university should be the ideal ground for such experience. This is so because the university should be the closest to what is vital in the modern world, meeting and interpreting its various facets before other communities or individuals do. Hence my concern that the university be really Catholic: that is, a university with the advantages that it implies, and at the same time a focus for Catholic Christian experience and a place developing specific Catholic Christian responses to the modern world.

Parenthetically, if the conclusions of Jencks and Reisman,[13] recently confirmed by a Carnegie Foundation report, are correct, one wonders whether this ideal situation is realizable. I refer, of course, to the fact that the American universities are being so thoroughly homogenized. Quite apart from the problem of the Catholic school, to anyone familiar with the monotony of the European university scene, it is a sad thing to lose the variety which could embrace everything from Bennington to Bob Jones.

A Catholic view of history?

As for the Catholic university, when it is said that it is much like any other, this means a number of things. For one, there is the relaxation of enforced religious practice, attendance at a student Mass and the like. More pertinently to our problem, it means that there is no specifically Catholic sociology (the example is from Jencks and Riesman) or history as well as no Catholic physics. Perhaps this is as it should be, but if we accept revelation as a source of knowledge, one might speculate about the impact of the fall of man, his redemption, and the existence of a sacramental, that is, a visible religious community on our theories of human conduct and human society. At least in history doctrinal positions are still very much with us. A glance at the paperbacks in our college bookstores – and paperbacks are by far the most important form of printed communication – will demonstrate that the Whig interpretation of history is very much with us. The revisionism now fashionable in American history writing is an example of the continued influence of Marxist dogma. If these old warhorses can still move, why not a Catholic view of history?

Even in the realm of the physical sciences one wonders why Catholics in the universities were not the first to raise the moral questions which have seemed so acute with the atomic bomb and now in ecology. Or might there not even be a Catholic or Christian slant to these questions? If all creation is redeemed, it is all a specifically Christian concern. Or more pointed still: Where is the Catholic viewpoint on "rational" abortion laws? Of course, we are now very shy of appearing to be a pressure group (though ready enough to join other pressure groups). It is not really so much the failure to act as a pressure

---

[13] Christopher Jencks and David Riesman, *The Academic Revolution,* Garden City, N.Y.: Doubleday, 1968.

group that is fascinating; it is a set of opinions like those reactions to the New York abortion law reported in the *New York Times*. With one exception the Catholic voices could not be distinguished from the others. It may be that a careful application of Catholic principles to the problem yielded a result no different from agnostic or other principles, but I suspect we have abandoned old positions to take up the current idols of the intellectual marketplace.

A substitute for magisterium

In other words, we have abandoned old certainties largely based on a concept of the ecclesiastical magisterium which is no longer effective for many Christians, and we have found no specifically Catholic substitute. I believe that there can, should, and will be such a substitute, and one of the functions of theology is to produce it. Not of theology alone: it can work only with the help of other disciplines. This could best be done in the university community. And it is not a demand for the subordination of the other disciplines to theology. On the contrary, if I have stressed anything, it is the dependence of theology on Catholic experience. In this case it should be Catholic intellectual experience. Perhaps it is mere dreaming, but I imagine that a truly Catholic university would help theology and safeguard its freedom by providing a milieu so rich that the theology which developed in it would be its own defense.

Putting aside speculation on ideal conditions, one can offer the university as a useful model for the protection of freedom within an academic discipline. The university already guarantees the freedom of inquiry for its community. There is a recognized and reasonably effective machinery for protecting freedom. This, of course, is the process which allows the professionals within a discipline to be the judges of the competence and suitability of a colleague. The machinery protects academic freedom from outside interference. At the same time it is designed to protect the discipline. The procedures regarding academic freedom insist on freedom, but they also insist on professional competence by putting the judgment of this competence in the hands of recognized professors of a discipline. It is hardly a radical proposal to ask that theology be treated in this way. The professional corps of theologians at the university should be the judges of the competence of a colleague as well as the custodians of their discipline.

Such a proposal is far from untraditional. In the Middle Ages, when the university originated as an institution, it was normal to call on the theological faculties to perform this function. I do not advocate a return to their style, which could be rich with invective. I simply point to the fact that then professional competence was recognized as a guide in the theological disciplines. To return this duty to the theological faculties would so far forth be a return to a tradition.

This is not a matter of jumping back in time either. In more recent times theologians have exercised something like this function in a different way. We have been accustomed to speak of the ecclesiastical magisterium as though it were a kind of impersonal power, but in fact we know that it relied on its circle of theological experts. Turning more widely to Catholic theological faculties would simply extend this reliance and make it more public. The accumulation of expertise would surely be to the good, as would be the possibility for something like checks and balances. This and greater openness would certainly mean a system more in accord with present day feeling.

Answers to whole community

Nor does such a role for theological faculties call for their complete autonomy. The Church as a whole is the subject of Catholic experience and the judge of the validity of its interpretation. Theological faculties, expertise and all, are not the Church entire. Therefore they are not the sole custodians of theology. Ultimately they must answer to the whole community. But even here we are not without an analogy within the processes of the university regarding academic freedom. The faculty is the custodian of its discipline, but not in complete autarchy. It must, for instance, answer to the standards of professional organizations. In a way less clearly defined but nonetheless real it must answer to the interested community at large. Applying this to the theological faculty, we have the obvious parallel in relationships with other faculties through professional organizations.

The relationship to the larger community is more difficult. It exists and it operates. However, we are still close to a time when the community voice was defined in an overly simple way and exercised in an authoritarian manner. It cannot be the same now, but we have not yet developed a new mode for its exercise. In fact, this is surely the crucial example of a changing religious experience which must be interpreted in freedom and in a Catholic way so as to be real in our times.

THE WRATH OF YAHWEH AND THE STRUCTURAL UNITY OF THE DEUTERONOMISTIC HISTORY

DENNIS J. MCCARTHY

Professor of Old Testament
at The Pontifical
Biblical Institute, Rome

The deuteronomistic history is divided into sharply marked eras. This is obvious from the content: the smooth flow of the conquest is contrasted with the troubled time of the judges, and the monarchical era is something else again. There are said to be deep divisions too: in Judges a cyclic view of history, in Kings a linear one. Then, the tone of the narrative is different in different eras: there is an optimistic note in parts of Kings which is felt to accord ill with the general tone of the history.[1] Finally, divisions are clearly marked by a formal device: speeches and historical essays are used as structural keys.[2]

Naturally, these diversities have given rise to explanations based on a diversity of sources or of redactions. Such explanations are inevitable, though it is exaggerated to insist that diverse attitudes in different sections mean completely different sources.[3] Surely they can be explained more directly as resulting from the different aspects intrinsic to the stories of different periods. The idea of successive redactions in periods of hope and despair is more attractive.[4] However, hypotheses of diverse origins are not the only possible nor necessarily the most fruitful ways to approach the problems. One can also consider the fact of the deuteronomistic history as a rhetorical whole. By this I mean a unified structure of effective verbal expression, which the history certainly is, however it came to be. Study of the relationships within that structure and of the rhetorical devices which produce them can throw light on meaning, for, of course, the essential meaning of a text grows out of its structure as a present (synchronic) whole, not out of its diachronic aspect, its history in terms of its antecedent parts and their adaptation to form the present whole. This latter aspect is a legitimate object of study—indeed is overwhelmingly the most common one in biblical studies—but it is not my concern here. This is rather the former aspect. Consideration of it can usefully look to the problems already noted. They draw attention to questions caused by apparent difficulties in over-all coherence, that is, crucial questions of meaning. However, the immediate means will be the study of some significant means of expression, namely, the mentions of the wrath of Yahweh.

The deuteronomistic history has two basic phrases to speak of this wrath. In one "the anger of Yahweh blazes" (*ḥarah 'aph yhvh b^e*) or, simply, "Yahweh is angry" (*hith'annaph yhvh*). These are not merely cognates; rhetorically they are interchangeable. Over against this stands another phrase: "one provokes Yahweh to rage" (*hikh'îs 'eth yhvh*).[5]

Each formula has its own immediate associations. The anger formula is typically the climax of a stylized description of Israel's desertion of Yahweh; for example: "And the people of Israel did what was evil in the eyes of Yahweh, and served the Baals and the Ashtaroth, . . . and they forsook Yahweh, and did not serve him, and the anger of Yahweh blazed against Israel."[6] It is part of a formidable set-piece, and the solemnity fits the content, for this is an assertion that the covenant is broken in terms of what this involved in the concrete: breaking the relation with Yahweh and forming one with another. Indeed, the description often includes an explicit affirmation that the covenant has been broken.[7]

Given the weight of this, the second characteristic association with the anger formula is not surprising. It is always tied to a proclamation of a divine judgment announcing a penalty. This is impressive. The formula is part of the expression of a law; revelation of divine anger demands a penalty which effectively halts the proper (independent) history of the people until repentance occasions salvation.[8] So absolute is the necessity of this sequence that, if anger is mentioned, the deuteronomistic history must complete the sequence or the story will come to a stop.[9]

In contrast, the link between the provocation formula and an announcement of a penalty is not so close. The formula is ominous enough in its own right, and it may be coupled with an announcement of a penalty, but this is not inevitable.[10] Neither is it so closely tied to the stylized description of infidelity involving the whole nation (see above, n. 5). Rather it forms part of its own statement, weighty enough but not so formidable as the context of the anger formula. Its typical context is the notice of the transgressions of kings.[11]

We have, then, a pair of formulæ for the divine wrath, each a rather forceful figure of speech in its own right, and each given added weight by regular association with a reinforcing verbal and conceptual context. But, be it noted, the latter feature clearly makes the anger formula a more formidable rhetorical instrument. These are the kinds of elements out of which larger rhetorical structures can be built. How is this done?

One fact leaps to the eye. The formulæ occur in clusters. We have already noted this for the provocation formula. It is at home in the notices of the kings of Israel from Jeroboam I to Ahaziah, and to a less noticeable extent after Manasseh in Judah. But the same phenomenon occurs with the more emphatic anger formula. It is common in the framework of Deuteronomy.[12] Another group of texts with the formula comes at the end of Joshua and the beginning of Judges.[13] Then, after a long extent of text where anger is hardly mentioned, it finally reappears at the end of the story of the kingdoms.[14]

Thus the references to divine anger are concentrated at certain key points, among them the major transitions from one to another of the eras which characterize the deuteronomistic narrative. But "transition" and "era" have an abstract sound. In fact, they are made very concrete, for it is the passing of a man, a leader, which marks the transitions.

This occurs in Deuteronomy. Simply because they are there the mentions of Yahweh's anger are associated with Moses's last discourses. But there is more here than simple association. The wrath motif is explicitly tied to Moses's death in Dt. 31:16-19. The dying leader knows that the people will fall away from Yahweh when he is gone. In a way there is a paradox in this, for the danger is not really immediate. The penalty which makes the threat of the anger so real is the exile, so far distant in fact from this literary context.[15] All the clearer for this is the intention to link the anger with the passing of the leader which marks the transition to the conquest era.

Again, the aged Joshua's admonition to fidelity (Josh. 23:16) and the editorial description of what followed upon his death (Jgs.

2:14, 20; echoed in 3:8) connect mention of Yahweh's anger and the departure of a leader. And now the danger is immediate, not something foreseen for the distant future. This offers the opportunity for a different rhetorical effect from that achieved in different circumstances in Deuteronomy. Because the death of each judge is a new, explicit occasion for danger (Jgs. 2:19-20), the threat of divine anger hangs over the whole period. However, the concentration of explicit mention of the anger attaches it emphatically to the major transition opening the era. All transitions are said to be dangerous, and the major transition is made to appear most dangerous of all.

In view of all this emphasis on the connection between the threat of divine anger and major transitions, it is all the more striking when the next such point is reached and anger is not mentioned. The climax of the story of the introduction of the kingship, Samuel's address and dialogues in 1 Sam. 12, should, according to its parallels in Deuteronomy and Judges, be full of references to divine anger, but it is not. This is all the more notable because 1 Sam. 12 has such unpropitious immediate antecedents, connecting as it does with the condemnation of the people for deserting Yahweh to seek a king "like the gentiles." One would expect this to reinforce the tendency to associate key transitions with the anger of Yahweh. Yet the text speaks not of anger and ruin, but of renewal. In spite of an express reprobation of the self-willed demand for a king (1 Sam. 12:8-12), it turns into a reaffirmation of covenant.

Here there are three points to note. Firstly, v. 13 marks the climax of the formulation, and it reverses the history of sin. The king is no longer the sign of a great infidelity; he is Yahweh's gift.[16] Secondly, vv. 14-15 place the people (and the king) under a renewed possibility of blessing or curse, which is the equivalent of the renewal of the covenant state.[17] Thirdly, this reaffirmation is confirmed explicitly in v. 22, an allusion to the so-called *Bundesformel*.[18] Reconciliation is complete.

This major transition to the monarchical era, then, is at once similar in genre and diverse in tone and content from the parallel earlier passages. Like them it is marked by an admonitory address from the leader in the old order. But in contrast to them it avoids the rhetoric of the anger of Yahweh.

So far the use of the anger formula marches to a considerable degree with Noth's observation about structure in the deuteronomistic history and with von Rad's point about the diversity between the story of the judges and that of the kings. That is to say, the emphatic clustering of the formula serves to reinforce some of the key speeches and essays in their function of structuring the narrative. Thus it contributes to the impression of over-all unity. In addition, the breaking of the established connection between the danger of divine anger and key transitions makes one notice the transition to the monarchy. Thus it too works toward defining structure. Further, the absence of reference to anger here contributes to the notable difference in tone between the era of the judges and that of the kings. This is *what* happens, but in it all is a clue as to *why* it happens, and this is in terms of leadership.

Now, the kind of leadership involved in an era is clearly one of the factors which characterizes the era in the deuteronomistic history. A Joshua makes things different from a series of judges, and a succession of kings is something else again, but the use of the anger formula in conjunction with this points to something more than the vagaries of empirical political structures. There is a religious dimension involved. The changes of leadership, even if it is a question of transfer from a Moses to a Joshua, are occasions of danger associated with the anger of Yahweh. However, with Saul's accession this changes, and not merely at the point of accession. The story of the kingdoms is organized in terms of regular successions to power. So far it is not unlike the era of the judges and, as von Rad argues, the whole story might have been constructed in terms of ups and downs or troubles, but it is not. Not just one change but the changes in general are out from under the sign of the divine anger. No doubt this is not uninfluenced by the fact that the sources, royal annals, archives, and, especially important, king lists,[19] were already organized in an unbroken sequence. Influence from this direction may have worked on the formal factor of the sequence, but it does not account for the omission of the anger formula and announcement of troubles it brings. Rather the reverse is true, for mention of divine anger is royal style![20]

To understand what is going on, one must consider the leadership factor, for we are confronted with a change not of leaders, but of the form of leadership. The monarchy is per se an ongoing institution. The sequence of kings goes on without break. This is true even without smooth dynastic succession. A usurper of seven days, a Zimri, can keep the sequence going as well as a legitimate prince. Hence, in the deuteronomistic presentation of the monarchy the dangerous crisis represented by a change in leadership is no longer acute.

The force of this fact, sequential presentation, is enhanced by explicit reference to continuity. 1 Sam. 7:1-16 is part of the pattern of key texts which set up and explain the monarchical era.[21] This text looks directly to continuity, for it is the charter not of a king but of a royal line. Its effectiveness is reiterated even in the face of difficulties (1 Kgs. 11:13). And the same point is made for the kings of Israel in the person of Jeroboam I (1 Kgs. 11:38).[22] In this way attention is focused on the kingly line. God deals directly with it so that a gift to it affects the people, and this is another new element relating to leadership. Contrast the situation with previous leaders: the gift (the word of God, victory in war) goes to the people through them. They do not receive for themselves; they are the means through which others receive. This difference is pointed up by the way prophetic activity is represented. In Kings, prophets characteristically speak to kings. What they have to say concerns them, and especially their threats which allude to penalties affecting the royal family. Contrast Jgs. 6:7-10, where the people, their conduct and their fate, is the direct object of prophecy.

And here we can return to the wrath of God theme, for it too works to the same effect. Notice the most striking cluster of the provocation formula—half of the eighteen examples concentrated in only eight chapters—in the reports of the kings of Israel from Jeroboam I to Ahaziah. These kings provoke Yahweh, but when a penalty is mentioned it normally affects royalty itself.[23] This is the case in the series of prophetic trial speeches and fulfilment notices in I Kgs. 14:9-10; 15:3; 16:2, 13; 21:21-22. The mention of wrath and its effects thus ties in to the actions of the prophets in marking out the special role of royal leaders. In this perspective the fact that mention of wrath stops with Joram becomes meaningful. His is the first regnal notice which mitigates the condemnation of a king of Israel, and after him one never again finds the extended condemnations characteristic earlier. Neither does one find the sort of prophetic text which we have just discussed and which the history associates with the earlier reigns. Improved leadership is accompanied by diminished insistence on the danger of wrath.[24]

A further device in connection with these provocation formulae helps focus attention on the royalty and turn it away from the people. The provoking sin, the worship at Jeroboam I's shrines, is bad enough in deuteronomistic eyes. Still, it never turns into the stereotyped description of the destruction of the covenant relationship by "forsaking Yahweh and going after other gods," despite the fact that the phrase which so often triggers this description in other contexts, "do evil in the eyes of Yahweh," is always present in the regnal notices where the sin is mentioned. Given deuteronomistic writing habits, this is striking. One feels in a positive way the avoidance of the allusion to the covenant with its direct (though in this context threatening) reference to the people as such. The focus on the kings tempers the danger for the people.

But we have not yet said the last word on the function of the wrath formulae. An era ends when finally the royal leadership is hopelessly corrupted. This is the significance of the last cluster of wrath texts in the reports of the last reigns. The kings provoke Yahweh, they insistently lead the people to provoke him, and the result is the anger of Yahweh and the inevitable penalty. The combination of the two expressions emphasizes the gravity of the situation and the failure of the monarchy. The office seems to have held off divine wrath, but its ultimate failure becomes the ultimate failure of the people.

It is thus that the threats in Moses's last discourses are finally realized. Once more the theme of wrath functions structurally to round off the story, tying beginning to end. This works in several ways. There is a recurrence of atmosphere, a brooding opening and a gloomy close. There is intentional direction: the beginning looks directly to the end. And there is an echo effect: even without explicit reference back to the beginning, in fact the reader "hears" it unreflectively when the wrath theme returns.

To sum up, we find that the wrath theme works in the formation of a well-knit structure in the deuteronomistic history. In Deuteronomy it helps create a troubled atmosphere of foreboding at its beginning, and its intentional direction points to the final catastrophe. Between these limits it helps distinguish eras in the story. Before the monarchy, transitions in leadership are points of threat; afterwards, this threat is deflected and a new era is marked out. At the last, it serves to characterize the final corruption of royal leadership and the consequent final catastrophe. This is an intrinsically coherent structure. It is differentiated, not as a haphazard collection, but as a meaningful, nuanced construction. It speaks directly to our original problems. The use of the wrath formulae emphasizes leadership as a central factor. It points to a coherent explanation of the diversities that have troubled scholars. Differences in the kind of leadership are in back of the cyclic view of a troubled era and the linear view of a more settled one. They also work toward producing a difference in tone, now of gloom and now of hope.

The "rhetoric of wrath" itself even points to a final hope. The cycle: anger, penalty, repentance, salvation, is not an accidental element in the story of the judges. It is an iron law which must take its course. Hence anger cannot be mentioned in connection with an era where a penalty is not applied, so much so that if it is, the cycle must be completed at any price, as we have seen in the case of 2 Kgs. 13:4-6 (see above, n. 9). But is this law not also an opportunity? Precisely because it is a law whose parts *always* hang together it means that salvation on condition of repentance is still an open possibility after 587 B.C. If it had to run its course, so much so that it forced intrusions into the story before that, it should run its course after that.

So all the deuteronomistic history becomes a call to hope and repentance, as Wolff (see above, n. 1) has argued on somewhat different grounds.

NOTES

1. See G. von Rad, *Old Testament Theology,* I, 1962, 347, 345, and "The Deuteronomistic Theology of History in the Books of Kings," *Studies in Deuteronomy,* 1953, 74-91, on these problems; for the note of hope in the history, see H. W. Wolff, "Das Kerygma des deuteronomistischen Geschichtswerkes," *ZAW,* 73 (1961), 171-186.

2. Cf. M. Noth, *Überlieferungsgeschichtliche Studien,* 1957, 5-6; D. J. McCarthy, S.J., "II Samuel 7 and the Structure of the Deuteronomic History," *JBL,* 84 (1965), 131-138.

3. Cf. G. Fohrer, *Introduction to the Old Testament,* 1968, 194: ". . . . it is impossible to think of the books Judges-Kings as parts of a work composed by a Deuteronomistic author or redactor." This is because Judges has a cyclic course of history, Kings a linear.

4. Cf. F. M. Cross, Jr., "The Structure of the Deuteronomic History," *Perspectives in Jewish Learning,* III, 9-24, accepting a basic over-all unity, and positing an "optimistic" redaction under Josiah and a "pessimistic" exilic redaction.

5. For convenience I call phrases with *hikh'îs* provocation formulae, those with *ḥarah 'aph/hith'annaph* anger formulae, and the two together constitutes the wrath formulae or theme. This refers strictly to the literary facts: the usages are stereotyped, formulaic, in the deuteronomistic history. It does not claim (or deny) that we are dealing with technical formulae from other spheres, e.g., law or cult.

6. Jgs. 10:6-7. The description varies in details (the addition of phrases, "go after other gods," "bow down to them," e.g.) but it is clearly a set-piece associated with the divine anger. It occurs ten times with the anger formula (Dt. 6:12-14; 7:4; 11:16; 29:24-26 [25-27]; 31:16-17; Josh. 23:16; Jgs. 2:19-20; 3:7-8; 10:6-7 with *ḥarah 'aph,* 2 Kgs. 17:15-18 with *hith'annaph*), it is alluded to in connection with the formula twice (Dt. 9:7-21 [note vv. 7-8, 18]; 1 Kgs. 11:9-11, both with *hith-'annaph*), and it is used with the anger and provocation formulae together once (Jgs. 2:11-14). There is one baroque expansion of the description with the provocation formula (2 Kgs. 21:2-6), and three allusions to it with that formula (Dt. 4:25; 31:29; 2 Kgs. 22:17).

7. Dt. 29:24 (25, *'azabh b^e^rîth*); 31:16 (*parar b^e^rîth*); Josh. 23:16; Jgs. 2:20 (*'azabh b^e^rîth*); 2 Kgs. 17:15 (*ma'as b^e^rîth*).

8. Deuteronomy itself is an apparent exception: anger is often mentioned, but there is no interruption of history. However, the anger *cum* penalty is really the object of prediction. When it actually blazes much later, the penalty, the exile, does interrupt the history!

9. Cf. 2 Kgs. 13:3-6 where the application of the law explains the intrusion of vv. 4-6, which puzzle commentators because they break the narrative flow and have no historical referent. They are not historical narration but theological explanation of the fact that the history continues. Cf. D. J. McCarthy, S.J., "2 Kings 13:4-6," *Bibl,* 54 (1973), for full discussion.

10. See 1 Kgs. 16:26, 33; 22:54(53); 2 Kgs. 21:6 for the provocation formula with no mention of a penalty. The omission is especially striking in the case of Ahab. Even though the author evidently loathes him, he does not mention a penalty. And note the case of Manasseh also.

11. 1 Kgs. 14:9; 15:30; 16:2, 13, 26; 21:22; 22:54(53); 2 Kgs. 21:6; 23:19. Of course, the formula occurs in other contexts too. It is occasionally tied to the description of covenant breaking (see above, n. 6) and to the sins of the people (1 Kgs. 14:15; 2 Kgs. 21:15; 22:17; 23:26). However, these latter examples are all

tied closely to the sins of the kings. Thus twelve of nineteen examples relate to kings so that in terms of frequency as well as repetition within a relatively short compass of text the royal connection of the formula stands out.

12. Dt. 4:21; 6:15; 7:4; 9:8, 19, 20; 11:17; 29:19, 23, 26, 27(20, 24, 27, 28); 31:17.

13. Josh. 23:16; Jgs. 2:14, 20; 3:8.

14. 2 Kgs. 17:18; 23:26; 24:20, and include here also 22:17 on the basis of the use of *ḥamah* which is a rhetorical equivalent for the anger formula (cf. Dt. 29:27 [28]).

15. The reference to exile is explicit in Dt. 29:24-27 (25-28); it is implicit in 6:15; 7:4; 31:16-19, which use the same language as 2 Kgs. 23:26-27; 24:19-20, texts where the exile is explicitly in question. The import of Dt. 29:19 (20) is obscure, but it could refer to individual exile. There is no question of exile in 4:21; 9:14, 19; but these are reports of the past, not threats with either present or future reference. This leaves 11:16-17 (drought) as the only threat which is clearly not connected with exile.

16. For the force of v. 13, see J. Muilenburg, "The Form and Structure of the Covenantal Formulations," *VT,* 9 (1959), 363. For the literary (not historical) analysis of the whole chapter showing its positive import, see A. Weiser, *Samuel, FRLANT,* 81, 1962, 79-88; also H. J. Boecker, *Die Beurteilung der Anfänge des Königtums in den deuteronomistischen Abschnitten des I. Samuelbuches. WMANT* 31, 1969, 60-88; M. Tsevat, "The Biblical Narrative of the Foundation of Kingship in Israel," *Tarbiz,* 36 (1966), 99-109 (Hebrew, English summary) is good on the *sic et non* structure which ties chs. 8-12 together, but fails to note the resolution of the tension in ch. 12.

17. V. 14 is to be read as a full benediction: *vihyithem . . . 'aḥar yhvh* is the apodosis which is to be interpreted "you will be of the party of Yahweh." For the sense of the phrase see the analysis of Boecker, *Beurteilung . . . ,* 79-81, but note that the parallel passages point especially to the attachment of followers to a chief, not vice versa as he argues.

18. See R. Smend, *Die Bundesformel. ThSt,* 68, 1963; N. Lohfink, "Dt. 26, 17-19 und die 'Bundesformel'," *ZkTh,* 91 (1969), 517-553.

19. On the special importance of the lists as such in forming the deuteronomistic history, see S. R. Bin-Nun, "Formulas from Royal Records of Israel and of Judah," *VT,* 18 (1968), 423.

20. Cf. the Mesha Stone, 11:5-6; discussion in McCarthy, "2 Kings 13:4-6," *Bibl* (1973).

21. Cf. McCarthy, "II Samuel 7 . . . ," *JBL* (1965).

22. Of course, it is commonly held that the dynastic principle was not easily admitted among the Hebrews and that this fact has left its traces in the deuteronomistic history. This may be so, but here one must not confuse historical background with literary fact. The problems with dynasty belong to the reconstructed background. In the text, the direct assertion of the deuteronomistic history, the monarchy is dynastic.

23. One exception: 1 Kgs. 14:15, but note also the further evidence for the connection of anger and penalty with dynasty: the condemnation of Solomon, 1 Kgs. 11:9-13 (with *hith'annaph*).

24. H. Weippert, "Die 'deuteronomischen' Beurteilung der Könige von Israel und Judah und das Problem der Redaktion der Königsbücher," *Bibl,* 53 (1972), 301-339, sees the change in the use of the provocation formula as part of the evidence

for successive redactions of Kings. I am not directly concerned with such questions of origins, but I would like to suggest that the interpretation of the change noted here points up a meaning for the differences between the two sets of passages built on the logic of the immediate narrative context. In addition, the differences are functional in a larger narrative structure. Should not such considerations modify our eagerness to see change always in terms of sources?

BE SOBER AND WATCH

By DENNIS J. McCARTHY

Hear, O heavens and give ear, O earth;
for the LORD has spoken:
Sons have I reared and brought up,
but they have rebelled against me.
The ox knows its owner
and the ass its master's crib;
but Israel does not know,
my people does not understand.[1]

THIS ORACLE was selected to open the collection of Isaiah's words because it states a basic theme of the book: the ungrateful infidelity of God's people. The sin is the more striking because it is unnatural. It goes against the proper order of things. Simple observation shows that the brute beast knows its master, as the birds know the paths for their mysterious migrations.[2] All the more, then, should superior creatures, a people chosen by special divine favour, acknowledge their God and follow his ways. The force of the argument, and especially of the implied condemnation, lies in the unquestioned experience of an order which should obtain in the human sphere as it does everywhere else.

This fundamental conviction that there is an order in the world which can be discerned by experience and to which life should conform is a central doctrine of ancient wisdom literature. This same tradition is reflected in the prophet's vocabulary: 'know' and 'understand, was the aim of the whole enterprise of the ancient schools of wisdom. The form of the prophet's utterance, a parable drawing a lesson from homely experience, is part of the same tradition. Nor is this the only use of elements from wisdom in the prophet. The Lord's judgment on his people can be expressed in the workings of history whose meaning is revealed to the prophet: the assyrian army comes, 'with all their arrows sharp, all their bows bent, . . . roaring like a lion', to smite the people which has aroused the anger of God.[3] This is what we expect from a prophet; but he also conveys the divine judgment in the words of a wise man condemning those who

1 Isai 1, 2–3. Quotations are from the *Revised Standard Version* unless otherwise indicated.
2 Jer 8, 7.
3 Isai 5, 25–30.

contravene a proverbial maxim: 'Woe to those who are wise in their own eyes'.[4] Or again, the Lord condemns the 'practical atheists', those who act as though there were no God to see and punish. The ideas and the words put in the mouth of the Lord himself are taken directly from a major wisdom theme.[5]

The prophet does not seem to have drawn a distinction between his visionary experiences and the teachings of wisdom as a source of knowledge of God. He had seen the glorious king of the universe enthroned, and he learned about the same God from the contemplation of the order in that universe. Now one experience, now the other, now vision, now wisdom doctrine, provides the content for an authentic prophetic word.

The wisdom tradition, then, is not alien to prophecy. But is the point worth making? After all, wisdom contributes whole books to the bible. Why should one expect the tradition to be incompatible with another major part of scripture? The question is sensible enough, but in fact standard scholarship has tended to see the prophetic tradition as central and to treat wisdom as a mundane late-comer without real theological relevance. In part this has been so because it has been fascinated by the personality, the doctrine and the poetry of the prophets, or, more recently, by the idea that the special character of biblical revelation comes from the fact that God reveals himself through his actions in history. The wisdom tradition is often a bit prosy, and it is not much concerned with history. Wisdom, then, has been treated as a theological step-sister because it has seemed less exciting than other aspects of the bible.

We know now that this is unrealistic. Prophecy used wisdom.[6] In the historical books it turns up in the Joseph story in the Tetrateuch, and the whole of the later complication from Deuteronomy to Kings – the deuteronomistic history – was affected by wisdom ideas. Wisdom turns out to be ubiquitous, and this is really what one would expect. Wisdom was not a special thing, the property of a separate group in Israel. In its fullest meaning it was the traditional practical lore of ancient society and of each important group within that society. Any technical skill – that of the farmer,[7] of the housewife,[8]

---

[4] Isai 5, 21; cf Prov 3,7: 'Be not wise in your own eyes' (*The New American Bible.* (NAB)). The condemnation in the form 'Woe to . . .' had its origins in wisdom teaching. Cf J. W. Whedbee, *Isaiah and Wisdom* (Nashville and New York, 1971), pp 80–110.

[5] Isai 29, 15–16; cf Ps 94, 7–8; Prov 20 ,12, for the wisdom parallels.

[6] For a full study of this important point see Whedbee, *Isaiah and Wisdom*, pp 149-153.

[7] Isai 28, 23–29.

[8] Prov 31, 10–31.

of the craftsman,[9] of the king,[10] was considered to be true wisdom. Especially important, kings needed counsellors, and it was the wise man 'who has entrance to the ruler'.[11] Hence the emphasis in wisdom on a good address: 'A man may live by the fruit of his tongue',[12] and even table manners: 'Eat what is set before you like a gentleman'.[13] Priests had the wisdom proper to their class, but they were also royal counsellors.[14] Men from a priestly background like Jeremiah and Ezekiel must have learned some forms of wisdom. So had anyone who had learned writing, as did, apparently, Isaiah and Habakkuk.[15] Thus anyone who was likely to preach, to teach, to lead, to produce a book in ancient Israel had been touched by wisdom traditions. Vision was a glory granted occasionally to a few prophets during a particular epoch. The truisms of Proverbs and the like were the stuff of ordinary living.

Wisdom, then, must not be treated as a side-issue in any effort to use the bible according to the perspectives of the bible. In a very real way wisdom was the life-setting of much of the Old Testament, not just those books classed as wisdom literature. This is not to say that the profoundest insights of a Job were there from the beginning and known to all. Nor were the most exalted prophetic states or theological insights always operative. No doubt wisdom evolved within Israel over the course of a long history. However, the basic attitude and the major themes were there from the beginning, for wisdom did not develop *ab ovo* in Israel. Rather, Israel took the tradition over from its neighbours, probably beginning when the administration of the kingdom under David and especially Solomon began to demand trained scribes. They could not come from the rural tribes which were Israel. They came from without, and they brought their training in the wisdom tradition with them. These wisdom traditions of Mesopotamia and Egypt had long since raised the great questions about the meaning of life, including the classic problem of the suffering of the good man and the justice of God. Israel's wisdom started out full-grown. Its oldest expression, the Joseph story, can already state one of the insights of developed wisdom: there is an order in things directed by the will of God, though men often cannot see it.[16]

We are well advised, then, to consider this fundamental element of biblical revelation on its own terms, even though these terms can

---

9 Exod 31, 2–3. 10 Prov 31, 1–9. 11 Sir 39, 4 (NAB).
12 Prov 18, 20 (*The New English Bible* (NEB)). 13 Sir 31, 16 (NEB).
14 Cf 2 Kg 12, 2. 15 Isai 8, 1; Hab 2, 2. 16 Gen 50, 20; cf Prov 19, 21.

seem so much less exciting than the exaltation of visions or the fear and fascination of theophanies on trembling mountains. If wisdom can rise to the lofty poetry in Job and elsewhere, this is not its characteristic form, the thing which makes it a valuable complement to the more spectacular presentations of revelation. But what is characteristic of wisdom? What are the attitudes and the themes which made it so acceptable as a basis for life in old Israel and might commend it to us? Generally commentators insist on two points. The central wisdom doctrine is that which we have already seen: the world is an ordered place. The basic attitude is empirical: the belief that men can come to know this order through experience. Here one can see at work the practical and empirical character of the origins of wisdom. The proper workings of a trade or of a farm or of an administration depend upon orderly procedures; and in the ancient world these were learned from those in the previous generation who had practised them: that is, persons whose experience confirmed their knowledge of the orderly art they taught.

However, while it never denied nor wished to deny its connection with practical particulars, wisdom goes far beyond this. It affirms an order in the whole of creation. This is implied in its analogy between human behaviour and the ways of nature on which the prophet based his condemnation of a faithless people. The order observed in part of nature should obtain in all of it. This order is no impersonal rule of law either. Creation works according to the plan of a personal God.[17] He directs it, and the wise man can see him in it. Indeed, in one of his incarnations, the wise man moves beyond simple observation to ardent contemplation:

> I will call to mind the works of the LORD,
> and will declare what I have seen . . .
> How greatly to be desired are all his works,
> and how sparkling they are to see!
> All things are reciprocal, one opposite the other,
> and he has made nothing incomplete.
> One confirms the good things of the other,
> and who can have enough of beholding his glory?[18]

This wise man looks upon the world and sees that it is good. He accepts it and is moved to praise his creator.

---

[17] Sir 43, 24, (23): 'His is the plan which calms the deep' (NAB). The 'deep' is the 'abyss' (Gen 1, 2), the primordial watery chaos whose conquest was the basis of all creation in the ancient near eastern concept.

[18] Sir 42, 15. 22. 24–25.

However, one should have no illusions. This was not a state one could acquire easily. The proponents of wisdom knew otherwise. There was always that practical background. One does not learn a trade in a day or a year. How much less could one learn this fundamental wisdom in a hurry and alone. It required application and submission to authority: 'Hear, my son, your father's instruction, and reject not your mother's teaching'.[19] Any single individual, after all, is 'but of yesterday'. How can he know anything unless he turns to those who can open out larger vistas than those his narrow span of life affords?[20] He must turn to the elders who have had experience and, more important, the instruction which enabled them to interpret experience. They could direct experience into the proper paths. The beginner is sure to err. The important thing is that he learn from his errors, and to do this he must be prepared to listen: 'he who heeds reproof is honoured', but 'he who hates it will die'.[21] This is experience speaking already. Anyone who ignores the past must repeat its mistakes. He must rather learn from it, and this means he must listen to the authorities, those who know the tradition in which the experience of the past is stored so that it can be applied. Only thus can one move forward from the past.

Wisdom, then, is open to those who will learn, 'those who seek her'.[22] They must have self-control.[23] They must accept their limitations and take things in order:

> Seek not what is too difficult for you,
> nor investigate what is beyond your power.
> Reflect on what has been assigned you,
> for you do not need what is hidden.
> Do not meddle in what is beyond your tasks.[24]

One can almost smell the dust of the school-room! Surely this is enough to cool over-generous enthusiasm. But we are reminded of more; a little adversity helps too: 'before I was afflicted I went astray'.[25] However, one must not be misled by this. So much of this wisdom instruction is directed against various forms of ardour that we are likely to see the wrong thing. Ardour is not condemned nor suppressed; it is presupposed. It is the truly eager seeker who can submit to tough discipline without discouragment. It takes strength

---

[19] Prov 1, 8. [20] Job 8, 8–10. [21] Prov 13, 18; 15, 10.
[22] Sir 4, 11. [23] Prov 14, 29. [24] Sir 3, 21–23.
[25] Ps 119, 67. This psalm, a meditation on the law, is dominated by wisdom ideas and wisdom vocabulary, as are other psalms.

and ardour to learn from reproof and affliction, and so come back to the task again and again. The danger is not felt to be that energy will be destroyed by too much discipline, but that it will be dissipated through misdirection. A powerful drive must be channelled, conformed to reality. Wisdom means control, but controlled power.

This is still austere enough. What results can it promise? Wisdom could hardly be content with the search as such, not if it saw it as difficult and restrictive as this. In any case, the idea of the search being its own justification is a romantic one which would hardly have occurred to an Old Testament thinker. The disciplined search for wisdom must take the seeker somewhere. But where? When we look for the answer we meet the problems of plurality and lack of system. Wisdom simply presents the results of its experience in aphorisms, not in any logical whole. So we are confronted with a number of ideas on the results of the search for wisdom. They do not seem to agree with one another, and we are not told how to relate them among themselves. We can only notice a number of ideas which are relevant to our problem and which are emphasized because they recur or because they are discussed at length. Then we can see if they hang together in any way.

Wisdom claimed that it came to know from experience an ordered world which proclaimed a wise God. But it also knew from experience that there is much in the world which it could not understand. Man is a mystery to himself: 'It is the Lord who directs a man's steps; how can mortal man understand the road he travels?'[26] Much in the world is beyond him, and God himself is the greatest mystery:

> Let us praise him the more, since we cannot fathom him,
> for greater is he than all his works.
> Beyond this many things lie hid;
> only a few of his works have we seen.[27]

This is a splendid profession of faith which is ready to praise what it cannot understand. But it is also an affirmation of the inadequacy of the methods of wisdom, for it admits that experience really cannot perceive the total order of things.

This may be described as a kind of theoretical failure, an experience of the limits on what wisdom could contemplate. It is more serious when wisdom has to admit practical failure. It wanted to know and understand primarily that the order it learned might be a

---

[26] Prov 20, 24 (NEB).

[27] Sir 43, 29 (28). 34 (32) (NAB).

guide to conduct. But here too it ran into limits. A man can plan, but God may determine that things go otherwise. The divine order is a mystery and therefore with all the good will in the world a man may fail to follow it. The wise Joseph had already affirmed this, though without any emphasis on man's good will in the case involved![28] Proverbs repeats it: 'Many are the plans in the mind of man, but it is the purpose of the Lord which will be established'.[29]

Thus wisdom confesses its own limitations. Much stands outside any order that man can see by ordinary experience. How does it come to terms with this? To repeat, 'it' does not. There is no one solution. Instead, one finds a number of reactions to this drastic experience of limitation. We meet one mood in Proverbs:

> Two things I ask of you;
> Put falsehood and lying far from me,
> give me neither poverty nor riches;
> provide me only with the food I need;
> Lest, being full, I deny you,
> saying, 'Who is the Lord?'[30]

This is all that the wise man asks of life. If he just has enough sometime in his life, it is enough. The limits are seen to have positive value. They keep a man from rising above himself or falling beneath the human. They keep him properly subject to the Lord. This abnegation, this readiness to accept and exploit the possibilities of a narrow life, is admirable though it is not very exciting. It does keep the old faith in a world ordered by God. It finds it good to conform to this order, restricted as it is.

This is one possible response to the recognition of limitations. There is another: 'I have seen all things that are done under the sun, and behold, all is vanity and a chase after wind'.[31] This is the central thought of a whole book which, without being a logically constructed system, forms a rather complete survey of the major wisdom themes. It considers power and pleasure, work and reward, friends and family, and the value of wisdom itself. One by one the topics are pondered and the conclusion is always the same: the efforts of man to understand and guide his life are all vain. And so 'I thought the dead more fortunate than the living . . . but better than both he who is not born'.[32] This is a denial of life parallel to

---

[28] Gen 50, 20.
[29] Prov 19, 21.
[30] Prov 30, 7–9 (NAB).
[31] Eccl (Qoh) 1, 14.
[32] Qoh 4, 2–3.

the worst pagan pessimism. However, it is the low point of a collection of *pensées*, not a final logical solution. More frequently Ecclesiastes offers a glimmer of pale light: 'it is God's gift to man that everyone should eat and drink and take pleasure in his toil'.[33] He too, with all his scepticism, can finally accept life with all its limits as something from God.

The wisdom tradition is not yet exhausted. Indeed, it seems at one point to take issue with Ecclesiastes. He had offered a magnificent poem about the seasons of things with a conclusion sceptical of man's ability to know and meet them.[34] Sirach returns to the theme. It too recognized the limits of wisdom,[35] but found there a reason to praise the God whose greatness and goodness exceeds human understanding. It has the same message on this theme:

> The works of God are all of them good;
> every need when it comes he fills.
> No cause then to say, 'This is not as good as that';
> for each shows its worth at the proper time.[36]

This is no doubt true, but Ecclesiastes' point is that the wise man does not experience this worth. Hence his melancholy. Nor does Sirach deny the fact. It simply reacts differently to it.

This seems to be the key to the different conclusions we find drawn from the experience of the limitations of wisdom. They meet the same problem from the point of view of the same tradition, but experience and training – wisdom – are not the whole story. There is the person who experiences too. In one mood he can accept limitation as a positive value. In another he finds it negative, something against which he chafes. In another, he is moved to exult in the power of the supreme mystery. Each state is very human. Each is something most of us must come to terms with sometime or other. We would be the poorer without the record of Proverbs' resignation, Ecclesiastes' revolt or Sirach's confidence. In proper wisdom fashion we can turn to the experience of those who have been there before. The elders offer guidance, or at least the knowledge that we are not alone. It is wisdom as a way, a method, which offers help; for the difficulty is that, in the end, enlightenment comes only from God:

> Whence then comes wisdom?
> and where is the place of understanding?

---

[33] Qoh 3, 13. Cf also 2, 24; 7, 14; 9, 7; 11, 9.
[34] Qoh 3, 1–15.
[35] Sir 43, 28.
[36] Sir 39, 33–34 (NAB).

> It is hid from the eyes of all living . . .
> God understands the way of it,
> and he knows its place.[37]

All man can do is wait patiently in the service of God: 'Behold, the fear of the Lord, that is wisdom'.[38] Of course, he may grant insight to the persistent seeker, but the success of the search does not depend on the man himself. Confronted with mystery and his own impotence, all he can do is possess his soul in peace and wait upon God.

It is here that the discipline of wisdom assumes its real importance. It turns out to be insufficient to bring one to enlightenment. This is the paradox of wisdom. It demands long practice in patience and control to prepare oneself to learn from experience. Then experience reveals that man cannot penetrate the mystery of his own life, let alone that of God. It is then that its emphasis on humility, on self-control, on persistence, is really needed to enable one to live with the limited results of all effort. And it is comforting to be ready to learn from those who have gone before: Sirach shares our moods of confidence, Ecclesiastes our need to endure in times of discouragement.

Nor can one say that things are very different in the new dispensation. True, the New Testament emphasizes prophecy. The Church was heir to the prophetic gifts of gold.[39] But, as in the Old Testament, this must be balanced with other factors. 'Be sober and watch', we are admonished.[40] That call to be sober is surely the voice of wisdom calling for patience and self-control, and this before a mystery far deeper and more terrific than that which the limitations on human experience presented to the wise men. We must be on the alert, sentinels ever on the watch. We are waiting for something. What? In the New Testament era one cannot think of waiting without thinking of the coming, the ultimate victory,[41] when 'God will be all in all'.[42] But 'that hour no one knows but the Father'.[43] Like the wise men of old we can but wait upon the Lord.

---

[37] Job 28, 20–21. 23.
[38] Job 28, 28.
[39] Cf Acts 2, 17–21; 1 Cor 12, 10.
[40] 1 Pet 5, 8.
[41] In 1 Pet 5, 9 it is true that the immediate object of watchfulness is the devil prowling 'like a lion' to catch the christian here and now, but ultimately it too looks to the final intervention of God in Christ.
[42] 1 Cor 15, 28 (NEB).
[43] Mk 13, 32.

LAW AND RELIGIOUS EXPERIENCE: THE OLD TESTAMENT

By DENNIS J. Mc CARTHY

ABOUT A generation ago a sensitive student of religions, a specialist in the beliefs of the ancient Romans, W. Warde Fowler, could speak of psalm 119 as a high-water mark of religious poetry. It is an idea most of us would find hard to understand now. For us the psalm is more likely to seem a laboured exercise in ingenuity, seeking to find every possible synonym for law and fitting the whole into an artificial framework. We may admire the industry and the ingenuity which was needed to produce a work of the sort, but it tends to be something of the feeling we extend to the person who builds model cathedrals from match-sticks. It would probably be difficult to find someone for whom this repetitious collections of praises of the law, without a truly organic structure, is a favourite psalm.

A good deal of history has contributed to the change of attitudes illustrated by diverse evaluations of the psalm. The specialist in ancient roman religion was dealing with something where the native gods were at once without number and without personality; the punctilious observance of a ritual, often grown unintelligible and quite without moral significance, was the essence of religious observance. In the circumstances, admiration for a psalm which honours divine concern for morality and justice is understandable enough. Further, Warde Fowler was living in a time when the phrase 'ethical monotheism' could be held to express all that was good and true in religion, and psalm 119 certainly does express ethical monotheism. However, the phrase has long since lost its lustre. For us true religion must somehow be a personal encounter with a Person come to us in Christ. All too often law has been presented to us as an absolute in its own right. Follow the law, keep the usages, do as one is told: this was religion; and of course it was impersonal, mechanical and empty. It is not the subject we choose for hymns we want to write. And yet, quite apart from the fact that no religion has existed without some rules of conduct, if not moral directives, law is central to the bible and to the religious life and experience based on it. If we are to integrate the total biblical view of religion and not merely select tit-bits which happen to please us, we must come to terms with law.

Perhaps we can begin with the law-giver, or, more accurately, with the mediator of law. For while there is no doubt that Israel actually picked up the details of its law from many sources, the final formulations of the legal traditions in Deuteronomy (seventh century B.C.) and the priestly writings (sixth to fifth centuries B.C.) made all law the direct gift of God through one exceptional man, to whom the law was revealed for the people. Even in earlier formulation, when the people hear some of the law directly, at their own urgent request Moses must face God alone and receive the bulk of the law for them.[1]

The mediator of the law must approach the 'wholly other', the Person who is entirely awesome and entirely fascinating. There may be a danger of our losing sight of this. The God who comes to give his law is accompanied by fire, smoke, clouds and roaring. It is not the way we would picture the nearness of God in ordinary circumstances, and it gives scholars a field day. They can argue whether this is a representation borrowed from the attributes of a storm god or the god of a volcano. It is fairly clear that elements of both descriptions have contributed to the picture as drawn.[2] It is the preoccupation with such questions which marks the concentration on the minutiae of historical reconstruction characteristic of so much of our scholarship. The question asked tends to be: what lay behind the present biblical picture, what kind of god was Yahweh originally and whence came the language used to describe him. These are doubtless important questions, but overriding interest in them tends to obscure the message itself. Approaching God is aweful in the root meaning, an experience like fear and yet not terrorizing, not to be undertaken lightly nor without due preparation. The book of Exodus is no treatise on higher prayer or the degrees of mysticism, but it is an old testament statement of the fact that one approaches God only through the night.

However, there is one great difference. Here the approach is not

---

[1] Exod 20, 18–21.
[2] Exod 19, 9–20.

simply that of the individual coming to meet the person, but of the representative of the community coming to hear his will. Or is the difference so great? How often does the experience of the divine include demands which are quite startling in their unexpectedness? Here the difference would simply be that the demands were not unexpected. In any event, the will expressed by God on the mountain was the law. Perhaps somewhat to our disappointment this is not a simple and lofty set of ideals. That had already been given the people.[3] What Moses alone amid the terrors of the mountain receives is an elaborate collection filled with minutiae which to us often seem anticlimactic. It tells us how to deal with vicious oxen, who is liable to military service, how one is to construct a variety of liturgical paraphernalia. Later, in revelation given no longer on the mountain but still in a sacred place of mystery, the Tent of Meeting, this law is expanded: we are given the details of various bloody sacrificial rites, of tithing, of priestly privilege; in sum, law in just the form we have come to suspect. It is an absolute which enters into every nook and cranny of life, an object which seems to stand between the people and the Person, whose directives were supposed to express a direct response to himself.

It is partly the sheer mass of law attributed to Moses which gives one this feeling. There is so much of it that it would hardly seem to leave time for other concerns. Then, we have been given certain ideas about how law was used which point in the same direction. We are told that a hair-splitting legalism did become the essence of old testament religion. However, the mass really *is* the accumulation of centuries during which the law was a living thing, developing and changing, and the supposed pettifogging was a late development, whose intention at least was to adapt the mass of the law to the realities of changing human life. If we miss these points and only pay attention to the sheer quantity of old testament law and the extravagancies of detailed application, we miss a central point of old testament theology. This is the experience of the mediator who brought law to the people. He was able to do this precisely because he was in communion with God on the mountain and in the Tent. He experienced a personal encounter with the Lord because he had faced the terrors of the mountain theophany and so won through to the presence of the living God, the God for whom

[3] Exod 20, 1–17.

Israel longed, so that he came to know the counsel of God which is the unique assurance of life.[4]

For the law was wisdom: 'the book of the covenant of the most high God, the law which Moses commanded . . . filling men with wisdom'.[5] Indeed, the very name, *torah*, which we translate 'law', means 'teaching', and so is dependent on wisdom: dependent, because in the ancient world wisdom was accumulated experience, and one went to the priest or the elder because he was the reliable custodian of the wisdom of clan or class, all that experience had shown to be proper in dealing with God or man.

But whence came wisdom ultimately?[6] How did a mind arrive at that first insight, that first wise decision which contributed to the accumulated tradition of wisdom? Who preserved the tradition? For the Old Testament only one answer was conceivable. God was the source of all teaching, all wisdom,[7] as he was of all good things.

In later times this was given vivid expression. Wisdom was personified:

> The Lord created me at the beginning of his work, the first of his acts of old.
> Ages ago I was set up, at the first, before the beginning of the earth . . .
> When he established the heavens I was there . . .
> when he marked out the foundations of the earth,
> then I was beside him, like a master workman.[8]

This does not speak of a being distinct from God; it is rather a striking affirmation that wisdom is in God and governs all his creation. It is but a step from this to the identification of this divine wisdom with the form in which it was best known among the chosen people:

> From eternity, in the beginning, he created me, and for eternity I shall not cease to exist.

---

4 Cf Psalms 42 and 1. 5 Sir 24, 23, 25.

6 Note 'ultimately', for the Israelite was well aware that wisdom was to be learned from the elders (Prov 6, 20), not divinely infused. Further, from the aspect of historical sources, it is clear that most of israelite wisdom was originally taken from ancient near eastern traditions which parallel it closely. This was once thought to be a major problem because the wisdom was not 'revealed' and was even secular in character. We know now that divine direction was highly thought of even in non-israelite wisdom, but in any case the to-do we make about historical sources meant nothing to Old Testament thought. It leapt to first causes.

7 Job 28.

8 Prov 8, 22–23; 27, 30–31.

> In the holy tabernacle I ministered before him, and so was I established in Zion . . .
> All this is the book of the covenant of the most high God, the law which Moses commanded us . . .[9]

Thus when Moses received the law he was in closest touch with wisdom, with God himself. The consequences are manifold.

For one, there is the effect on the mediator himself. One cannot come so close to the divine and remain unchanged. After Moses' unique experience he was touched by the very holiness of God. The later description puts this most vividly: holiness literally shone forth from him so strongly that the people could not face him.[10] One might expect more attention to have been given to this remarkable figure. In its way it is the closest thing to an 'incarnation' in the Old Testament, though, of course, an incarnation in a very old testament manner. It is the otherness, the awesomeness of God, which shines forth in the one who has been closest to him; not the fascination, but love. Even so, the basic fact is striking. To approach true wisdom, God himself, was an experience so awesome that it changed Moses so that his very presence communicated the divine majesty. For old testament theology, mediating the law and the most intimate experience of God are one.

However, this is far from the end of the matter. There is also the effect on those who receive the law so mediated. They were, of course, over-awed, but at the same time, precisely because they shared the experience of the divine, they were put in touch with wisdom itself, wisdom expressed as law, but still wisdom, the very source of life.[11] Thus the law could be presented as life itself.[12] This is not the language of rigid conformism to an impersonal set of rules. In Deuteronomy this is a cry from the love which has chosen and saved a people, calling for the expression of love in return. And this was a cry regularly repeated, for the speaker in Deuteronomy 30 is not really Moses himself but his representative in the ever-renewed liturgical services, urging the people to respond to God's offer of union with him which was worked by following his will, the law.

This is another important aspect of biblical law. If it came from God through a mediator who in the normative tradition was always Moses, it came to the people over the centuries and in varying

[9] Sir 24, 9–10. 23. [10] Exod 34, 29–35.
[11] Prov 3, 16; contrast 1, 18. [12] Deut 30, 19–20.

circumstances through the agency of those whose office it was to hand on the traditional wisdom. In fact, this made the torah the special responsibility of the priesthood,[13] for the priests were the custodians of the shrines about which a large part of the life of the people, as the people of God, was centred. This meant that they were custodians of the traditions, stories, rituals and wisdom connected with the shrines, but it seems that they were responsible for more than merely preserving wisdom and law. They were to solve the people's problems as judges in difficult cases;[14] and most important for our present concern, they were to make the law known, to proclaim it.[15]

To be sure, this would seem to provide a very different experience from the tremendous person-to-person meeting of Moses with the divine law giver. It sounds like equating the higher mystical elevations with the effects of a mediocre sermon; human nature being what it is, the presentation of the law by the priests doubtless often resembled a poor sermon. Still, this was not the ideal, the norm aimed at in the service. It was a falling away from what a true priestly mediation should be; it is the difference between successful and unsuccessful liturgy. What the effect could be is reflected in the poem in Sirach 45, 6–17, the reaction of a sensitive observer to the high priest in all his glory. It is not our style, perhaps, but rather than rush to apply our standards and cry 'Triumphalism!', we must try to understand what was expressed to the feeling of the era. All that gold, the precious stones, the costly stuffs were there to represent the glory of the Lord, just as similar materials have a similar function in the heavenly Jerusalem of the Apocalypse. The style and the effect can perhaps be compared with those of a truly fine byzantine mosaic. Further, whatever we may think of it, it worked on the poet, Jesus-ben-Sirach, and, in fiction which strives to represent reality, on an Esther fainting at the mere sight of the king, God's instrument, in all his splendour.[16]

---

[13] Deut 33, 10. [14] Deut 17, 9; Isai 2, 3–4; Hag 2, 11.

[15] Deut 31, 10–13. The actual directive, reading aloud the entire law during a service, is utopian, to say the least, but it is a theological application of a usage in which manageable summaries, something like the Decalogue, were actually proclaimed. Note too that law was not the exclusive concern of the shrines. Much traditional legal wisdom was preserved and applied by the 'elders at the gate' (cf Ruth 4, 1–12; Deut 25, 7–9). However, this is outside our purview because it was secular, no direct factor in religious experience. It could and did become such when and in so far as it was ultimately integrated into the body of law proclaimed as the will of God. [16] Est 15, 6–7 (LXX).

So we have one important aspect of the experience of the hearer of the law. It was proclaimed in shrine and liturgy: that is, in a holy place and a holy action; and the holy, the *mysterium tremendum et fascinans*, is the essence of the divine in human experience. In fact, in the liturgy, with its vestments, its incense, its music, the hearer of the law was supposed to experience something of that contact with the divine law-giver which the supreme mediator, Moses, had possessed amid the fire and smoke and turmoil on the mountain and in the darkness of the cloud which came over the Tent of Meeting.

However, the later Temple in Jerusalem was a unique place of worship, inaccessible to most of those who were to hear the law; and in earlier times it was but one of many shrines, which, as we have seen, did not necessarily guarantee an especially effective liturgical experience. One doubts whether many striking poems or fainting fits were inspired by it all. Nor was this the point in any case. The experience of the law was not present unless the immediate reactions which they represent so vividly could be made to endure. It was the lasting response of the hearer, his commitment to the God made known to him in his holy word, the law. This is what made it so important to impress on the participant that in meeting the law one was meeting the very wisdom of God.

Thus the law is not merely proclaimed with more or less effective formality, but urged on the hearer in such pressing terms. It is literally a matter of life and death, for God is the living God and apart from him there is really only the dusty realm of death. In the presentation of the law God was offering himself and therefore life. The primary response was not to learn the law and act out its details; it was to accept God and life through total response to the offering made by his mediators in the holy, liturgical gathering. Such a response meant the readiness to love and serve him with one's whole heart and one's whole strength, whatever particular form this loving service might take. The law was the way in which the commitment to the living God could be lived out in the concrete circumstances of life. It was, therefore, a gracious gift which defined life with God, so that even in the details of everyday life one could express and feel this union.

Once more the law was essentially wisdom, since wisdom meant knowledge of how true life was to be had. When, as we have seen, later development saw true wisdom in its ultimate form as an attribute of God, the connection with true life was even more obvious.

This was the living God, so that he was literally the word of life.

However, we must be careful to understand just what this means. Late tradition tended to emphasize the law as a direct expression of the mind of God, his immutable wisdom solemnly and unalterably revealed as a whole to a chosen people. To be sure, it is the canonical word of God, but to take this as an absolute in isolation from its origins, its development, its applications, and to treat it as an undifferentiated whole, would be to falsify its origins, its constant use in old testament times, and its essential historical character as a developing tradition defining and directing one's basic commitment to God.

To avoid such falsification we can profitably look at the historical origins of the law. What has been gathered into the great mass of directives put into the mouth of God in Exodus through to Deuteronomy is essentially the collection of verified results of experience. Once again there is a direct connection with wisdom tradition, since ancient wisdom was simply codified experience. Experience came first. What did it mean to live as a devotee of Yahweh? Of course, it was not so difficult to conclude that one could not be faithful to Yahweh and at the same time a devotee of other gods, though, as a matter of fact, this conclusion was drawn with surprising rarity and difficulty. And what of others who were fellow members of the people of this God? Did one's commitment to him affect one's relations with them? Of course it did, though once again this was not an easy lesson to learn; according to the prophetic witness it was generally forgotten or scorned. Even so, one could not treat the other person as an outsider. He was a member of the same worshipping community, a brother. Hence, stealing, killing, lying, adultery, were obviously prohibited. Hence the more complex developments, where these generalities were applied to difficult cases, or where the wise decision of the prince became the norm for handling similar cases. Such procedures are in many ways common practices easily parallelled in non-biblical societies. They are simple necessities if a group is to live together, and Israel did not hesitate to borrow from the customs of the gentiles; all of which tells us that the principles and their development are the sifted experience of many societies, whose ideas had proved useful in guaranteeing some kind of order. They were the remembered wisdom of the clan, the town, the class.

But in the bible they became more than that. This is the record of no ordinary social grouping, but of the people of God. So we have psalms 15 and 25, the torah psalms. That is to say they propound questions used by a priest to teach those who wanted to become active members of the group, participants in the cult which was the high point in the life of the people. Given such circumstances, one might well expect some rubrical demand, some liturgical nicety concerned solely with ritual purity. But no, the answers are that the one who can join the worshipping community is 'he who . . . speaks truth from his heart, who does not slander . . . and does not take a bribe against the innocent'. The merely practical norms for getting along in a group with a reasonable reduction of friction have been taken into the divine sphere. If one is to choose to remain with the people of God and so choose life, he must consider his neighbour, his fellow in the community devoted to Yahweh, for both are committed to the same God and hearers of the same law which expresses that commitment.

One consequence of this, surely, was the extraordinary development of concern for the weak and the poor. Again, the idea is not peculiar to Israel, but the lengthy development of laws on the proper treatment of the widow, the stranger, the simple labourer who often had to borrow – those without personal power to enforce rights – is striking. The passionate condemnation by the prophets of those who forgot these laws is equally remarkable.

Surely much of the reason for this is that the implications of the theology behind the law were being more sharply realized. The law, the whole law, was the means by which the people who had committed themselves to God expressed that commitment. It was their response to him, and the response had to be on his terms, in conformity with his will. Law is wisdom, and so closely related to God who is wisdom itself. The idea that law is not merely experience or convenience lay close at hand. It was felt more and more directly as revelation and so all the more a means of living out union with the Lord.

It is here that misunderstanding becomes easy, and, in fact, some misdirection took place. When law begins to be treated as a collection of the immutable wisdom of God it is easy to begin thinking of pharisaism as it is ordinarily treated. The line is thin: on the one hand, law as a free response to a God who has granted wisdom so that his people can be close to him and to one another; on the other, law as something which exists for its own sake, rather than being the means to a personal response to God, is an end in itself. This latter idea is quite false when applied to the creative period of old testament law. Because it was a living response to a person it was itself alive, adaptable and adapted as circumstances called for a new form of detailed response in line with the basic response. Early laws reflect some conditions of nomad society. They are inapplicable in a settled peasant society and they are abandoned, while the labourer needed in the new social constellation found his place in the legal system. There is increasing emphasis on care for the weak and the poor, as simple peasant farming tends to give way to the growth of large estates and dependent workers. One could multiply examples, but the fact is clear enough: law could be and was a vital, changing response to the needs of the religious community in its efforts to respond to its God.

But then conditions changed drastically. With the Exile the community was scattered, and the great need was to preserve its traditions if it were to maintain any identity at all. So we have the great codifications, canonized tradition, which could not grow and change as the old law had. The creative period is over. Yet, paradoxically, this new absolute, this unassailable text, could still be used to serve the needs of a community which could never be static. It did not necessarily become an object in itself, standing between the people and its Lord. On the contrary, when specifically israelite modes of worship became impossible with the loss of the Temple, fidelity to the law was an even clearer sign that one was committed to the God to whom the law belonged. Thus from the very beginnings of the formulation of the law as an absolute text, it was made to serve a real need; it firmly established the identity of the restored people. For example, they were the ones who stood resolutely by the sabbath rest when an easy and corrupting syncretism was a danger.[17]

It may be also that the following verses in Nehemiah, harsh though they sound especially in condemning mixed marriages, represent a necessary response to a real danger.

[17] An interesting contrast arises here. In many ancient societies (Athens, Rome, for example) law was the property of a class because it was sacred. So it remained secret from the ordinary man, for only the noble could touch the holy. The weak won some measure of protection only when law was secularized and so made public. Even so they did not have the protection of a law like the biblical one, which was always public and sanctioned by the equality of all before the one divine source of law. Only in the christian era did stoicism introduce some ideas of universal brotherhood, and so give roman law the beginnings of the concern for the person as well as for property and institution, which characterized Old Testament law from its beginnings because it was the expression of response of a person to a person.

> . . . all those who have broken with the natives of the countries to adhere to the Law of God; as also their wives, sons and daughters, all those who are old enough to understand, join with their kinsmen and leaders and undertake, under curse of oath, to walk according to the Law of God given through Moses, the servant of God, and to observe and practise all the commandments of Yahweh our Lord, his customs and his laws. In particular: we will not give our daughters to the natives of the land nor take daughters for our sons. If the natives of the land bring goods or foodstuffs whatever to sell on the sabbath day, we will buy nothing from them on sabbath or holy day.[18]

We also have to admit that this passage could be an example of the danger of over-stepping the line between the law as wise guidelines delineating the committed service of God and the law as an end in itself. Then it could come to stand between the people and its Lord rather than being a means of direct response to him; for the letter could appear to demand inhumane and divisive acts which were contrary to the original unifying genius of the law. But to repeat, this was not a necessary consequence of codifying the law. It was to substitute mechanical execution for wise application. It was to turn the law away from its sources in wisdom and its base in God, the fount of all wisdom.

This was certainly a danger, as there is danger in absolutizing any institution or usage, but it should not be thought of as inevitable or typical. The devoted hearer of the law continued to see it as the means of expressing a special union with God. This did not simply mean showing others that one belonged to the community, though it did include this so that the high moral character of later judaism became a source of attraction among pagans. Much more important was the fact that living the law was itself a response to God, the life promised by Deuteronomy.

Moreover, though the process of reforming law to meet changing needs had to stop with the fixing of a canonical legal text, the actual process of adaptation went on, so that one could continue to respond to the presence of God in an ever-changing world. This now had to be done by a process of interpretation of the fixed law. Thus the teachers, including the maligned scribes and pharisees, continued the ancient tradition in a new mode. They applied learning and wisdom to teach the people, the hearers of the law, the proper response in every circumstance. No doubt this was often overdone and the

---

[18] Neh 10, 29–31.

spirit was lost in the minutiae of mechanical observance, but this was the failure of the system to function and not the nature of the system. The life of the law was not a life of mechanical observance; attached to true wisdom and revelation, it aimed at living out unswerving fidelity to the true God and constant regard for one's neighbour. It was life itself, an experience of response to and union with the Lord, who had chosen this community and made his will known. From this it is not a long step to the ultimate offer of divine life in union with wisdom incarnate.

God as Prisoner of Our Own Choosing: Critical-Historical Study of the Bible, Why and Whither

by

Dennis J. McCarthy S.J.

"Criticism," Edgar Krenz writes in **The Historical-Critical Method**, "sets the Bible squarely in our history and makes the 'full brightness and impact of Christian ideas' shine out."

Enthusiastic praise this, but not a startling expression of an eccentric position. On the contrary, too much of the world of biblical scholarship concerns itself with the recovery of the *Urtext* and its *Ursitz,* since the essential task of such scholarship is seen to be reconstruction by recognized techniques of "origin," the words and situation lying behind, often far behind, our present biblical text. That is, explanation, interpretation *is* the reconstruction of the (hypothetical) historical form and locus of a text. Thus, what is important in 1 **Col.**: 12-20 is not Paul's words but the Christian hymn lying behind them or, in the Old Testament, a 9th century Israelite story urging a polemic against fertility cults and their symbolic snakes and trees of life is real stuff of **Gen.** 2: 4-3, 24 (not to mention other, independent strains which may be sifted out of the narrative), and all this business about an *Ursunde* is mere secondary accretion and, worse, later interpretation.

My examples are deliberately sharpened to make a point: the overwhelming preoccupation with history in exegesis, the concern for the "original," the source, and its external factual referent. "The historian," Krenz says, "interrogates documents to determine their precise significance" and so learn the *truth.* And it is but a step from this excessive focus on a particular kind of historical truth (that is, factual reference) to the paean of historical criticism as *the* royal road to find and feel Biblical truths with which we began.

■ *Dennis McCarthy, S.J., teaches scripture at the Biblicum in Rome.*

One might wonder what bright light a precise location of the land of Uz and a dating of the visit of Eliphaz, Bildad, and Zophar would throw on the overwhelming poetry describing basic religious experience in **Job**. Or, whether, if we really could learn a knowledge of what inspired whom to utter the basic structure of the tremendous hymn to Christ Jesus in **Phil.** 2: 5-11, it would shine brighter. To be sure, being able to place the utterance in some dramatic historical or polemical situation might throw light on the meaning of the present text. However, experience warns us not to expect too much from this direction. For example, a reading of Bandello's **Romeo and Juliet,** Shakespeare's attested source, far from revealing the true significance and beauty of the story or at least throwing real light on Shakespeare's meaning, simply makes us marvel at his originating genius.

These examples raise basic questions which somehow never seem to affect the central thrust of modern exegesis. One searches for the milieu which produced the speeches in our texts or even produced the persons made to speak in them (as the milieu of Hellenism and persecution, not necessarily the milieu of Hellenist persecution, produced the personage of Judith as well as her words). When one has found the milieu to his satisfaction, he explains the words and the persons in its light -- with particular attention to the antecedents in that milieu which led up to the particular form of words and the conception of the persons as they are found in our texts. This *is* interpretation, exegesis. In the course of this process, the historicity of the texts (i.e., their reference to real external events) may well come into doubt. The texts are the result of a process in which a community responds to various discernable external or internal pressures, expresses known psychological needs, uses the words and images certain situations evoke from certain people in definable historical and sociological contexts, and so on. This is by no means always erroneous. To return to Judith: the book *is* the product of a brilliant Hellenic-Jewish short-story writer reacting to a persecution problem.

For the moment, however, I do not want to dwell on this aspect of the problem, that is, any tendency there is for historical exegesis to minimize historical content. There is a deeper problem: that fascination with historical critical study as though it were the philosopher's stone to turn all interpretative dross to exegetical gold so that "Christian ideas" can "shine out." Historical interpretation of text, the attempt to reconstruct the actual world of events to which the text refers, is just one possible kind of interpretation. Why must we always ask: "What is the factual reference of this text?" Why not: "What does this text mean?" Apart from other things, a great deal of the Bible is poetry and doctrinal discussion, and our first question to these kinds of texts in other contexts is not "To what events do they refer?" but "What do they mean?" Why is the Biblist, in other words, trapped within historical questions, patient so often only of hypothetical, probable responses, therefore, always open to new hypothetical, probable objections so that he gets locked into an academic squirrel cage returning on itself, ever renewing the same essential problems and answers?

The answer goes back surely to the famous *crise de conscience europeenne* which we can, for convenience, locate around the beginning of the 18th century. Almost two centuries of religious quarrels had tired men of theology. A full century had been trumpeting the claim that reason with the right method --that "right method" being a matter of dispute -- could solve all problems. *We* may have our doubts these days, but, in fact, the 17th century with its emphasis on quantification, on experiment, on accumulation of data had produced magnificent results with its (apparently) all encompassing Newtonian synthesis in physics. Other fields had, perhaps, not moved as fast, but, if we try to imagine how it looked to a man of middle age in 1700, fantastic changes had occurred. Timepieces had become accurate. There were thermometers, barometers, microscopes, and a thousand practical improvements from mining techniques to navigational equipment. Remember, as an impressive example to a world that had lived with the plague endemic and often epidemic for centuries, that the disease disappeared from Europe after a last flair-up in Marseilles in 1720-21. It was as though one were to give our age a "cure" for the atom bomb. And the introduction of the humble turnip was about to end the leaving of one third of the land fallow every year. It could be grown in an otherwise fallow field and the field still brought rich grain the next year. A trivial example? Hardly, when it showed the experimental method pushing farther away the spectre of famine that had literally always been at the door.

Reason, observation, collection had had a long run of good press, and they had given results. The "knowledge explosion" was well under way. People of any education knew so much more, and not just in the physical sciences. The "moral sciences" were flooded with knowledge of an earth that was gradually being filled in with the outlines of new lands and with inhabitants of diverse cultures. No more could one picture Dante's empty southern hemisphere as real, however glorious its symbolism remained. Nor were the outlanders fantastic creatures met in tales. One traded with the Chinese for tea and porcelain, and, for the men of the age, trade gave a very real consistency, a three-dimensional density, to their feeling of the reality of these others.

For one reason or another, then, the age faced and wanted to face a host of new facts. Missionaries from China reported a race whose chronology antedated that of the Hebrews. The immensity of the earth now was not just known but realized -- felt by everyone who touched tea or tobacco, coffee or china; it suddenly became hard to visualize a global flood. And such a diversity of races! Their differences and their chronological spread make it hard to fit them into the geneologies of **Genesis** 10.

The situation was simple enough. A vast accumulation of knowledge had become too large to fit into the "six ages of history" which were part of the habitual mental equipment of the European mind since Augustine. The situation was the historical and sociological analogue to the Ptolemaic world view of physics. It had simply become too crowded and it burst its boundaries.

Surely, this need not have created a problem. The Bible is not a universal history nor a textbook in geology. If it had been so used for ages in Europe, it was because there was nothing else at hand to cover these areas. Neither was much *noticed* which interfered with the data thus delivered. The pre-modern man could, as *man*, delight in the lovely balance of a world map centered on Jerusalem with all the parts centered around it and as a sailor be very aware of the unbalanced nature of winds and headlands off Brittany and Finisterre! But now things were very much noticed and instead of fitting his historical world view into the biblical picture, man had to fit his picture of the biblical world into the larger frame of a new world view -- and this not long after Archbishop Ussher had nailed the date of creation down tightly at 4004 B.C.!

Now this change in the ordering of a commonly held historical view may have been shock enough. Change of habit is usually difficult. However, it was really no more than a recategorizing of general knowledge. It did not affect the *theological* vision of history which was the common possession of the western mind from the spread of Christianity until after Shakespeare: the scheme of the fall of the angels, creation, temptation-fall, the incarnation, the redemption and rebirth in Christ. This had been everyone's view and still was the view of the vast majority, whatever some intellectuals said more or less on the quiet. This scheme is no catalogue for ordering knowledge like the six ages scheme with its Adam to Noah, Noah to Abraham, Abraham to David and the rest. This is the heart of Christian doctrine. Christianity could survive the shock to slovenly intellectual habits by the substitution of a new cataloguing scheme forced by the accumulation of new facts. The history of sin and redemption is something else again. It *is* Christianity. And yet, how was one to make distinctions? On an external, even frivolous level, our summary of redemption has 6 stages as Augustine's history had 6 stages. The comparison is not deliberately created *ad hoc* -- the six stages are not mine but E.M.W. Tillyard's in his survey of the Elizabethan world picture -- and it is easy enough to move imaginatively from the loss of the 6 historical ages to the loss of the 6 doctrinal stages. I do not know if something like this ever happened, but it illustrates the problem. New content burst the boundaries of a purely historical scheme primarily biblical. What next? Can other biblical meanings remain true or are they too "out of date"?

The problem was the worse because the theological story of sin and redemption does touch history. It is historical, sinful man who is redeemed by an event. This is a serious problem, but I wish to touch on only one aspect of it for a moment, that is, the way this theology came to the European of the *crise de conscience.* It was tied to all kinds of stories, foretellings in the Old Testament, assertions in the New, post-New Testament miracles. It was emphatically tied to the 6 age view of world history: Christianity was the age of maturity. None of this interweaving in detail is necessary in logic or doctrine, but it is in fact open to easy confusion and big with consequences at the beginning of the modern age.

There was this passion for exact measurement, for facts. This was the era that equated truth with reference to external thing and ruled out imagination and symbol. The former was the proper province of man, of reason. The latter supplies "decorations" to doll up the truth or to while away idleness. There was also the Protestant principle of *sola scriptura* as the unique source of saving truth and its corollary idea that the believing reader will find the truth for himself. Among other things, such principles ruled out other sources of theological knowledge such as tradition and traditional development. Most important for us, it ruled out all interpretation of scripture except the literalist. Indeed, many contemporary proponents of the historical critical method proudly proclaim that its ruthless search for truth, i.e., demonstrable fact, in scripture, is the proper development of the Protestant principle. It may be, but not that part of it which, supposedly, gave the Bible into the hands of the people. It has finally given it rather into the hands of a very limited band of professors!

But the "Protestant principle" was not a single-minded ally of criticism. Indeed, Protestant doctrine of literal interpretation as the dictation of God was a serious impediment. Could God have dictated untruths? Scarcely! Eventually, inspiration so understood had to go, and, since in the minds of modern theologians inspiration tends to be identified with this old Protestant dictation view, when it went, inspiration as such went. There is available a far more nuanced view in Catholic theology leaving the human instrument free and emphasizing the role of the community from which the scriptures arose, to which they are addressed, and which finally received them. So far I see little done to exploit this treasure we can offer the Christian community. It would be a service to ecumenism. It would be an even greater service to exegesis if theologians would give us an adequate, supple presentation of the doctrine of inspiration and revelation. Without it we tend to accept without question the negative results of the old Protestant idea. But we must return to the problems of our time of crises.

The 1700 covert enemies of Christianity, the Bayles and later the Voltaires, who believed that the religious wars proved religion a dubious blessing or felt that it was a curb on free investigation (not to mention free exercise of faculties and urges generally held to be less noble) could make use of the insistence on fact to foster doubt. If all in the Bible was literally true -- and it was so often urged that it was -- what then? Where of the genocide commanded in God's name in Deuteronomy? And so it goes. The snipers agreed with the pious that God's word must be true fact (truth here to be judged by one's own common sense standards, for the Bible was open to all!). Then they seized on some choice "fact" and turned the argument: Could this enormity be from God? Later Tom Paine's **Age of Reason** summarized this often crude argument, and his work had a long run: it was still the source book for the working class sceptics in Mrs. Humphry Ward's **Robert Elsmere** a century later. A passion for narrow fact, an insistence on literalness, the overthrow of an accidental but time-honored historical scheme plus positive attacks on the believability -- even the morality of certain events recounted in the Bible -- all this was indeed a blow at the foundation.

It remains a real problem. The ordinary man in the street lives by intuitions and symbols -- some, we hope, given by natural insight and sound tradition, others we fear, by TV and advertising industry. But when he reflects he does not see it so. He thinks he lives by "facts," and it is dangerous to give what he has taken as a fact in a simple, straightforward reading of the Bible another value. Tell him that Cain and Abel is a tale reflecting pastoral and agricultural rivalry used to illustrate the sin pervasive in human history and he is bothered. If Cain and Abel are not historical persons who, in scripture, are? So the common feeling and it must be reckoned with. This is not an easy thing to do and we can sympathize to some extent with those who chose to meet the enemy on his own ground centuries ago.

Hence the rush to supply evidences to establish the facticity of biblical narrative. It must be so. "Dogma" said this was God's word in the most literal sense. It also said that the word was immediately available to the man in the street. He took it as truth and truth is reference to external fact. Thus the hunt for the necessary external facts began. It was well under way in the 18th century, and a later age gave us Edmund Gosse's father asserting that God put fish fossils on Alpine peaks to humble the learning of the wise. Our own day has been the claim to the finding of Noah's Ark right on Mt. Ararat, unfortunately too much iced in to be clearly identified, let alone approached. And so it goes.

One can respect the sincerity of this extreme literalism with its equation of truth with an external factual reference but the end result is to convince no one but the converted to the sacrifice of much of religion's credibility. Yet the hopeless effort continues in some quarters. What we really need is what was probably impossible in the 18th century but not now, viz., an epistemology and a consequent apologetic that distinguishes the various kinds of truth (separating truth of factual reference from truth of general meaning, for starters).

But again to the time of crisis. There were those who saw that a last ditch defense of a literalist reading was not the only hope, nor even the best hope. One way out was to avoid the embarrassing historical problems entirely. One could turn to Nature. This was the central word for most of the 18th century. As Basil Willey has pointed out, it covered an unperceived diversity of meanings, a fact which did not really conduce to clear or profound thought, but did allow the *philosophes* to talk without end. Pope could express the central vision in his **Essay on Man**: a perfectly ordered world with "a place for everything, and everything in its place." In the early 18th century this ordered vision was widely spread among the pace-setters of society who took this theism to be the deliverance from untrammeled reason supported by that solid argument, universal consent. Churchmen, imbued with this vision, showed that Christianity paralleled the religion of nature, teaching one God and inculcating the highest morals. True, one had to put up with many crudities in Christianity's Bible. It had its oddities, but *at least* it provided the means of bringing the common man, who was, perhaps, incapable of the deeper reasonings of the philosopher, to worship God and respect his fellow. Deism became the religion of the elite, the educated, and even of the Churchmen (Archbishop Tillotson).

The religious spirit soon took its revenge with the much deplored "enthusiasm of Wesleyianism, the Great Awakening, Pietism." It seems as though it is safer to ignore religion than feed it empty platitudes. It may die of sheer neglect, inanation, but as long as it is kept alive, it will out, and that usually in ways that affront the genteel.

The religion of nature of the 18th century looks somewhat crude and simple to us today. Why dwell on it? Well, it represents an early and clear example of what becomes, under many guises, one of the regular attempts at dealing with the historical problems of the Bible: the claim that historicity does not matter. It is not the fact of the biblical story of sin and redemption, but the general idea that counts: the idea of God and ethics, the "something not ourselves that makes for morality." It is not long before this stance produces the question: "Why such emphasis on Christianity if it is on a natural level with other cultures?" Buddhism or Confucianism can teach high moral standards, and their cultures, if not the doctrines themselves, offer divinity. For that matter, even voodooism provides a satisfying religious, sociological and emotional integration. "Nature" (i.e., a catalogue of historical human traits) produces these many religions that work in satisfying human needs. Why choose one rather than another? The 18th century, living on its unconscious Christian presuppostions, could make its choice without reflecting on the base of the presuppositions.

But other generations are not so naive. They do not equate Christianity with a universal religion "given by nature" which is really a sort of ersatz Christianity created all unknown for its partisans by a particular historical conjunction really dependent on Christendom. One tries to break loose from the relativist realm of history into some sort of absolute. So Christianity becomes the positive existential commitment to be. Or it is laying hold of true selfhood. Or seeing Jesus as the paradigm of the true self. Or it is the encounter with the Person of Christ. In the end it is all more philosophy made to refer to a particular person's attitude or self understanding. But if Jesus is not extraordinary as the biblical canon claims or, at least, is not knowable as such, why does He call me to commitment or imitation any more than Theudas or Judas (**Acts** 5, 36-37) or another? Why is the doctrine attached to Him better or more demanding than Confucius' or the Gautama's? And if one passes quickly over all but a few details of His life as historically difficult, what Person does one encounter? How can it compare with the impact of a personality I am much in contact with now or even with a sharply defined historical personage? The best one can say is that He is the paradigm my particular bit of Western culture presents me with, as another culture would offer another paradigm. We are back to relativism again. It looks as though we must face history after all.

Nor was the century of crisis at all unwilling to do this. We have seen it as a time of both scepticism and belief and of great confidence in human ability to attain truth. The sceptics looked for ammunition, the believers looked to their defenses, and it was widely believed that the truth would come out with a diligent approach and a proper methodology. This, after all, was the age that laid the bases for the four-source theory of Pentateuch, discovered the synoptic problem, invented the "science" of Introduction (the search for the real dates and authors of the biblical books, their historical interrelations, the history of the development of the canon) and biblical theology -- this later as an effort to get away from the crusty formulations of tradition to the real meat that lay in the underlying formulations of the texts read as history. It was also the heyday of the "canon within the canon." The opportunity was obvious. When the critic had decided what was oldest, original, authentic, reasonable (analogous to everyday experience) he had his measure, his canon. It might be doctrinal: ethics culled from the Sermon on the Mount for 19th century liberal theologians, a fanatic eschatology for Schweitzer, or the idea that sequential and purposive, not meaningless and cyclic, history was peculiar to Judaism. It might be historical or literary: ancient J has special value, or Mic, 4: 9-12 is from Micah himself while 6: 1-5 is probably not and so of secondary value. And so forth. Whatever the critic selected could and did become a criterion for judging what was normative. Things not in accord with it might have a passing historical interest but they are not religiously or morally exigent.

We have been living amid all this ever since and I do not want to offer another history of critical scholarship. I would simply emphasize certain of its effects. Ultimately it took the Bible out of the pew into the library, and not the public library but the professor's seminar room. A later 19th century Anglican parson was reported to have kept two large Bibles. A conscientious professional man, he kept up with his studies and noted the developing vagaries of critical scholarship in the margins of one. A conscientious pastor, he put material helpful for preaching in the other. Inevitably the split became a gap and then a chasm. And then the question had to be put: Can one preach what is shown to be factually untrue (or at least unlikely)? A conscientious man could only give one answer: No. An epoch fired by search for truth (it had, after all, among other things proved profitable in commerce, manufacturing, agriculture), which tended to equate truth with fact, could hardly have done otherwise. It was bound to test truth claims by its criteria, and that meant treating facts as facts even if, all unknown to it, seeming narrative facts were something quite else. Inevitably there was a narrowing of the religious message of such religious "facts" the Bible might be forced to deliver.

The Romantic Movement grew out of this era of rationalism. Not as a mere reaction; rationalist insistence on *politesse* helped produce a man of taste who easily became the man of feeling. The attempt of the associanist David Hartley to construct a "calculus of pleasure" to provide a basis for morals as quantitative calculus had for physics had also worked to emphasize feelings, Jane Austen's "sensibility." Whatever its origins Romanticism had a mighty impact on biblical study.

One very weighty factor was a kind of primitivism. This was the age when Percy collected his **Reliques,** Scott his **Border Ballads,** the Grimms their tales, Lonnrot the Finnish **Kalevala.** It was fooled by the Ossian forgeries because it wanted to be. Herder and Vico had seen that an early stage of human development naturally expresses itself in heroic poetry, fantastic tales and the like. The idea was not so new, but the evaluation was. These early forms were seen, not as mere crude probings toward later scientific statement but as valuable things, unspoiled, though at times lurid, insights into the heart of things without which mere reason was sapless and fruitless. The Grimms did not seek out their tales because they were quaint but because they were an unsullied fountain of truth. The application to scripture leaps to the eye. Here is the origin of that fascination with the *Urtext,* the primitive community and so on. Here in the pure beginnings lay shining truth. And still today many a professor who has long lost any romantic illusions about the primitive unconsciously values his *Urtext* for these reasons. The force of the romantic idea is still powerful, all the more because it is now unexpressed and unspecified.

Then there were the great evolutionary systems of Romantic philosophy. Their effect can hardly be overestimated. History was assuredly guided by immanent laws which might be the working out of the Absolute Spirit, the development of the ethical spirit, progress from the material to the divine, the unfolding of matter. The exact description of the immanent laws at work varied from philosopher to philosopher, but the conviction that there were such laws varied not at all! This was particularly fateful for New Testament study where the immanent dialectical laws of Hegelianism were set to work. The Christianity of Peter and Matthew was the thesis, the Christianity of Paul, the antithesis, and early Catholicism the synthesis (**Fruhkatholocismus** is still very much with us!). The scheme is F.C. Baur's and it is redolent of the spirit of its time: rational laws governed history. The Hegelian scheme had already been imposed on Christianity by D.F. Strauss of **Life of Jesus** fame, younger than Baur but an earlier bloomer. Baur's contribution lay in his "finding" it reflected in especially biblical literature. Indeed, Baur insisted on the need to evaluate the sources both for their date and their determining purpose (a polemic tells the story rather differently from a mere chronicle and the difference must be allowed for) and so their original core and *Tendenz.* In this way, he put Christianity squarely within the compass of secular history. It was subject to history's inner laws as well to its critical methods. For Baur the laws were Hegel's. Others would posit other laws but whatever happened, Christianity had become the object of profane historical study, entwined in a chain of laws, necessarily profane laws.

This was radically new. The changes at the 18th century *crise de conscience* had demanded a new cataloguing system. So many new facts had been found that the traditional Christian scheme of world ages could no longer contain them all. Biblical facts, taken as such and left in their specialness, could fit into a new scheme which contained much else that was strange. There was no change of laws of thought to which facts had to conform. Facts were accepted. An ill-advised effort to defend all these facts carried the seeds of much later trouble, but the major conflict was avoided, for the moment, by prescinding from the facts and proclaiming a "higher truth:" the correspondence between Christianity and general natural religion, at what cost we have seen.

Now the very workings out of history, the workings of Spirit, or Ethics, or Progress (whatever you choose to name it) in history, became the central source of the highest knowledge. Particulars were checked against this. If they conformed, they were true, if not, false. And Biblical religion was seen as simply one phase of this great mechanism. It conformed or it was rejected. Baur and Hegel thought it conformed; others were less sure, but in either case it did not matter. What mattered was that the biblical narrative was made to be a mere part of the workings of the great world historical scheme. That was all, and that was tremendous. There was now no way to fit the essential historical and unique sin, incarnation, redemption and eschaton scheme of classic Christianity into this. The essential theology had to go. The biblical story was subordinate to the secular scheme of a philosophy of history.

This philosophy is pretty well dead, but it has left a legacy important for our topic. The 18th century believed in unending progress in history, the 19th tried to codify the laws of this progress. Our age is less confident of history. Apart from Marxists, it does not expect to discover the laws of onrolling history, and is unsure that the onrolling will be an advance. What comes brings future shock as much as progress. However, the old views still have a powerful effect when combined with theories of method drawn from the uses of natural science. The truth *is* not, it may simply *come to be,* more likely, *approached but never attained.* Thus the chronicler of traditional historical study, Douglas Knight, can call the latest hypothesis the "truth", with which one must work until a new hypothesis replaces it.

In any event, this view of reality as becoming and not being challenges more than the factual reference of the biblical narrative. The 18th century had already done that. Now it goes on to reject its central theological meaning. Search for truth of fact, search for the historical original, the application of the philosophy of history to the biblical narrative has culminated in a wave that threatens to swamp biblical religion.

We must pause to observe much irony here. This notion of the unbroken causal chain has taken firm hold on biblical studies through the constant and triumphant use of the historical method. This 19th century theology is not its first appearance. "The Chain of Being" was already there in Pope's **Essay on Man**. But that was a chain of historical causes, and we find it gaining its first hold through the application of casual catagories derived from history by romantic philosophy. The categories would mostly be rejected now but the causal chain they brought with them still retains its hold. In any case, it has been a standard objection to historical studies from Aristotle to Lessing that they deliver only isolated facts, not the universal laws sought by reason. From almost the contrary position the historicist point of view developed in the later 19th century which, given its classic theoretical statement by Frederick Meinecke, gloried in this very individualism of the historical. It saw the object of historical study as some sort of organic individual social unit or factor largely closed within itself, only open to the influence of its unique and accidental time and place. This unit was comprehensible and so amenable to judgment only in relativist terms, the special terms of its unique growth. Just because it was individualist it denied that history exhibited general natural laws as much as the philosophers interested in the universal did!

However such warnings did not halt the *Zeitgeist* which was so full of the "laws" of history. There must be truth there, and if critics tried to use it to reduce Christianity to the level of all other history or, with Feuerbach, reduce all to the finite and material, perhaps it could be the other way around. Perhaps history might be made to ground religion -- even the specific religion of the Bible. Thus, for example, instead of being a problem to the rationalist critic, the so-called prophecies of Christ from the remote past became a positive plus. History is the history of redemption, *Heilsgeschichte,* a real development in which any particular event, even an apparent prophecy, can only be understood as a part of the whole.

The process unfolded the meaning. The coming of Christ makes clear in part the earlier accounts (even the Gentile developments) and part is not yet even intelligible. That can come only with the completion of history. There the Erlangen school led by J.C.K. von Hoffmanintroduced an idea and a word which we must still reckon with.

This use of causality can be used with great skill and appear to give comfort to what seems a relatively conservative interpretation of the Bible. Indeed, if the revealed word is seen in terms of tradition, an ongoing struggle to see the truths of religion in the light of new problems, new needs, and new ideas, it may have much to offer. However, there are problems. If one insists overmuch on the historical process, one soon meets the fact that events are dumb. Only interpretative words show their sense, as recent theology rightly insists. But whose or what word? Hardly the prophetic, which read precisely as interpretative word, is misleading if read for itself and according to the canons proper to reading all literature. It must wait on further events and on further interpretation but then this new link in the chain needs its interpretation and so on down the line literally, on the hypothesis, until the end of the world.

A great scholar and theologian of our own time, Gerhard von Rad, has attacked the problem by emphasizing the immanent laws of history and not the dialectical process. He begins with the thesis that only those who make history can write history. One wonders. if as he wrote this, he realized his debt to that wonderful old Neapolitan Papist, G.B. Vico, who early in the 18th century launched the fertile idea that only the maker really understands a product because he alone knows what or why anything went into it. So only God can really understand the world in depth for He made it; we can only use it in part. Vico saw that man does make something his own, society and history, and so these are the things he can and should try to understand. Well, if Vico stood behind the German's assertion he stands unacknowledged. Von Rad goes on to show how true history-writing develops. For it, there are no inspired figures (charismatics), no miracles. Events unwind according to their inner law. The divine is there only in the *concursus divinus,* the providence of God, which for the theist covers all history, Well enough, but then what is special about biblical history? What does it reveal that the history of England or Europe does not?

Walter Scott and Macaulay saw providence clearly in the "Glorious Revolution" of 1688 putting down Catholicism; Father Broderick saw providence in the wealth of America arriving just in time for Spain to stem the Protestant tide, and so on. The *concursus divinus* is everywhere and we seem dangerously close to making the Bible deliver one of those undifferentiated natural religions which, we have seen, have been the bane of one line of apologetics.

This discussion involving the great 19th century German philosophies, general theories of history and muchelse can hardly conclude without a remark on a phenomenon which characterizes contemporary biblical studies! Compartmentalization. Whatever else they were, the critics of the 18th and 19th centuries were people who shared the general culture of their world. They knew the classics. Indeed, Pentateuchal source criticism went hand in hand with the Homeric question. They had read history. They knew a philosophic tradition. Now, more and more biblists are specialists not particularly versed in even their own vernacular literature or well read in history. I have actually heard it argued that form-criticism is a method necessarily unique to the Bible because it is special, (though not necessarily supernatural). But, in fact, the proper use of form-criticism should treat biblical literature as it is -- closely related to literature in general, and aimed at relating biblical pericopes to their general class, and, thereby, elucidating them in the light of what literary history, ethnology, sociology, and psychology can tell us about the place where such classes are at home in the human spirit or human culture. This turnabout, this isolation of biblical literature by later scholars, came about because terms and techniques have become fossilized in manuals of biblical introduction and are not longer *au courant* with advanced knowledge.

So also with von Rad. He thought and wrote under old influences, old ideas of history, at the very moment when the new quantified history was beginning to feel its oats. We have a new classic, Pautrell on the 16th century Mediterranean, a mass of often fascinating facts cutting across all familiar historical lines. Or the Burckhardt of our age, Peter Burke, "explains" **Tradition and Change in Renaissance Italy** with the aid of birth registers, inventories, etc., plus the inevitable computer. Historical research and writing is rapidly looking away from narrative, and without a story how can we see the Absolute or revelation or whatever unwind itself before our eyes? What serious scholars call history is rapidly changing, and the biblical-critical fascination with "history" may well find itself without an object recognizable except to itself. It will catch up, of course, though how much "history" based on computer calculation of quantitative data the Bible and all that can be brought to bear on it will reveal is surely an open question. In any event, new trends will leave behind a sad debris of lost causes, forlorn hopes, theologies built on a view of history which is as strange as King Tut. Which, of course, is the basic problem: Can theology let alone religion be based on the ever-shifting ground of what is momentarily taken as history? As biblists get further away from what goes on in academic history work and the rest -- the problems become more acute.

One can, of course, avoid the problem of trying to see supreme meaning in the mere sequence of events by turning to the interpreters. The specific way this is done is to make the prophet the true voice of God because the prophet has really heard God. This is clear from the call stories of Hosea or an Isaiah. So Bernhard Stade tries to insert a unique divine element in the immanent evolutionary world of Wellhausen's reconstruction of Israelite history and religion in the light of the documentary hypothesis. This is an interesting idea, but it has its weaknesses. One has to take the call reports (e.g., Hos. 1.3; Is 6; Ezech. 1-3) seriously. Still they are often put together from different sources. Is every one of the disparate bits authentic? And even though they be sincere reports of experience, how do we know them to be *true* and not the delusions of an over-excited mind? The whole idea depends on accepting the validity of mystical experience, a phenomenon common enough to humanity, and so subject to some sort of check. However, it is a phenomenon which makes the rationalist just that least bit uncomfortable until he can get it where he can measure it. Then we get ectoplasm and statistics on long-distance card tickets which make the phenomenon look silly.

We must return to this, but first let us notice the real difficulites the idea has run into on its home ground of biblical scholarship. Let us grant for the sake of argument the divine origin of the authentic prophet. Grant he was a true seer. How do we know what his inspired interpretations were? Here we come up against all the problems of discerning the true words of a Hosea or an Isaiah. For Hosea, in fact, the problem is not so difficult. Most of the book is accepted as reflecting the original prophet. The trouble is understanding him; the text is, with Job, the worst preserved in the Bible! But Isaiah! Scholars fight tooth and nail -- and wouldn't you know it -- the passages in doubt are your favorites, the poems on the prince of peace in chapters 9 and 11 and at least the place and meaning of the Emmanuel prophecy. But words which are not from the prophet whose revelations are emphasized in his reported call cannot be accepted without cavil as divine, let alone true.

The case is positively pathetic with Deutero-Isaiah. Is.: 50-55 are not guaranteed by Is.: 6. They are the words of another man. One can scrape a sort of call report together in 40: 1-11, but it does not really conform to the formal call report. It leaves the prophet with something like the incomplete fragments of a driver's license. Try the validity of that on your nearest friendly policeman! But with Deutero-Isaiah it is the beauty and power of the message which is really felt to validate. There may be something in this, but it is no longer the criterion of the official call.

But let us grasp the nettle and accept Deutero-Isaiah without his fully authenticated call. We remain ill at ease, for amid the many wonders of Deutero-Isaiah the Servant Songs, especially 52:13 and 53: 12, shine with special brilliance. But these all-important texts are often asserted to be secondary increments to an otherwise almost entirely homogeneous book. The very fates work against the critic, even the believing one: the moment he has elaborated a theory which allows some special value to the text, the text is torn from his grasp.

Of course, a theory of inspiration which looks to the text as it is and not to (largely hypothetical) reconstructions of divisions within the text, could be of use here, but as we have seen such a theory has not been available to much of modern exegesis, even Catholic, for that exegesis is the conscious or unconscious progeny of "the Protestant principle" with its theory of dictational inspiration which was abandoned as soon as it became clear that the ordinary man took the word of God as referring to facts when the critic knew it did not. God was equivalently lying to the people to whom He gave the Book! That would never do, and having no theory of inspiration to put in its place the whole problem was dropped. One must wonder about the silent effects of this on Catholic scholars who quite properly learn and apply the technical means of biblical study largely the work of Protestant scholars, learn and apply, that is, without investigating the theoretical aura unnecessarily but *de facto* surrounding the techniques.

Indeed, a knowledge of spiritual theology would enable us to accept the visions of anonymous authors who added their bits to the work of an Isaiah or Jeremiah. We know that God speaks to the simple and the obscure. There is no need to restrict the possibility of revelation to a literary genius (Isaiah) or extraordinary personality (Ezechiel). The insights, the thoughts, the words of an unknown disciple can be as much inspired as the revelations of a great master. As with inspiration the failure to bring the rich Catholic tradition of mysticism and the theological critique of mysticism is a failure in ecumenism -- the failure to offer an insight and experience we possess to the enrichment of theology as a whole. The result of this failure is a drive to put prophecy on familiar, comfortable ground. The call report is a (properly) recognized form, a claim to office which can be read as analogous to other validating formulae used for kings or for creating officials and the like. It is freed of any eerie contact with the supernatural. The prophet is seen as a functionary paralleled in the Ancient world from second millenium Syria to classical Greece. Some Hebrew prophets just happened to be geniuses. Thus a bold (for the critical world) attempt to get the supernatural into at least a bit of the Bible has been rendered innocuous.

We seem to be at an impasse. We find critical-historical study of scripture constantly winding up at one of two dead ends: The general philosophical or the fundamentalist fideistic. The latter takes the Bible pretty much as a lump: it is all fact with little variety in the truths it has to tell. One winds up explaining the inexplicable and misses great masses of deepest truth in a desperate defense of universal facticity. The former regularly reduces it to some going philosophic system, natural religion, historical dialectic, existentialism, personalism -- you name it! To all of which the question keeps coming back: Why is the Bible our model of theism? Why are its heroes-- and especially its Hero -- our stimulus to commitment and growth? Because, to be frank, they are what "just happens to be lying around" in the West, to use Chesterton's phrase about uncritical habit.

Of course, one can claim a special place for the Bible to defend the external reference of its realistic statements. The Bible is indeed special, and from this I can build a logical case for factual reference: God could *always* make exceptions to the ordinary way of things to be sure His word pointed to external fact. But this is a logical house of cards not really supportable even from its own weight. Anyway, what would be the point? The argument convinces and converts no one, and it can cause the Bible to be subject to ridicule.

We cannot abandon criticism. It is part of the fabric of the modern world, part of the whole picture of temporal sequence and material objects and theories and ways of doing things which make the frame into which we consciously or unconsciously fit our lives and thoughts, the frame which three centuries ago replaced the "ages of the world" and the Ptolemaic universe. Like it or not, we can no more escape it than the air (which too nowadays we often do not like!). One could try a sort of isolation ward technique but that is the way of the Amish and the like -- admirable testimony in its way to fidelity and firmness -- but hardly the Church militant marching like an army with banners of truth. We must allow critical history the freedom of the Church, the stronghold of truth, for the Church is strong and the method deals with truth.

More, we cannot grow prissy and stop it when it seems to be doing messy things to texts we love. With all the failures and weaknesses of its practitioners, it is trying to add to our fund of knowledge about Israel, about Jesus, about the nascent Church. It has its successes by which we gain more of the truth, which is convertible with the good. And can any man, any Christian, turn away from the true and the good? Hardly, for this is specifically Christian: "I am the Truth. . ." The only real question is how to use criticism properly. Surely after three hundred years of struggling with it, we should be able to move some distance in this direction.

It is certainly time that we begin doing so and one necessary approach is reflection on the ancient question of the division of the sciences, defined here both in terms of the object studied and the possibilities of the human instrument of study. It is encouraging that one hears from England, France, even Germany, murmurs of dissatisfaction with the limited historical methods and objects so far dominant. Another significant sign is the decline of "biblical archeology" to affirm or deny historicity. Interest is no longer in "validating" the Bible but in the culture of history of Syria-Palestine for its own sake, as it should be. Even the use of the Bible for strictly historical purposes should have this aim: learning more about the past for its own sake. That is what history is all about, not defending non-historical ideas. However, the movement is quite new and still tentative. One cannot plot its directions as though describing actual activities; one is trying to chart future developments. This can be difficult and unclear. Still, those three hundred years of experience should help to indicate some definite need one hopes will be met.

In any case, the quasi-identification of exegesis with historical research must end. Historical investigation has done great service, disabusing us of simple-minded errors, filling in a background in history for the things said in the Bible, the sort of background the understanding of any literature demands, and supplying a general picture of the stages within biblical literature. To be sure, work on history should continue, but it should be recognized for what it is -- strictly historical research which uses the Bible as one of many documents that can help reconstruct the ancient milieu from which our culture comes. An honorable occupation, one to be encouraged, but let it do its own thing. To insist now on more history, and history primarily as the panacea for bringing biblical religious ideas to the light where they can "shine forth," is narrowing. In practice it confines the scholar to those small and often unclear bits of the Bible which seem to have reference to external fact. Since the bits and their supposed referents keep changing as hypotheses change, the scholar finds his historical ground constantly shifting as he tries to use it as a platform for affirmations beyond the historical. He never *knows* what is historical! Within a few decades we have seen the patriarch and the structure of Israel in the era of Judges doubted by criticism, then affirmed with often surprising detail, and now pushed back into the gloom of doubt and beyond. In the New Testament, honest historical criticism has gone from John as the best witness of historical fact and sequence in the New Testament (Schleiermacher and the succeeding generation) to a confidence in Mark (all those Lives of Jesus!) to a fairly confident affirmation that at least the crucifixion happened! Bibical theology based on last year's historical hypothesis must be this year's remainder in such a situation. How can history produce anything else, especially when we are dealing with a remote and poorly documented period, as we are in biblical history?

The first necessity,then, is to affirm the obvious. The Bible contains much beside history. The first task of scientific division is to discern the kind of text at hand. There is nothing esoteric about it.

It, of course, is full of poetry, and not just in the "poetical books." Images, symbols, the fanciful, the visionary and even the fantastic are scattered everywhere. It must be read in this light. What are we to do with Leviathan who is variously made to sport in free joy in the depths. (Ps.: 104,26), be the captive pet of the LORD (Job : 41,4) and to be crushed to provide food for the beasts (Ps.: 74,14)? One can provide an imaginary history here: Leviathan is the symbol of evil, (he is in the sea, always an enemy of order in the Bible) left free for its appointed time until the Messiah restrains him to be a show at his triumph and later the meal at the Messianic banquet. We can smile, perhaps, but the equation of truth with factual reference is really being carried out logically here within the real scheme of sin and redemption. The trouble is the narrow definition of truth which demands that the most real, the most meaningful scheme in the world, be given its exact temporal (historical, factual) referent which then incidentally provides a neat time frame for poor old Leviathan's career.

Of course, what is going on is the use of an image taken from Canaanite mythology. In the various passages, the greatfish show forth the joy of sheer living; illustrates the power of the God who bends so mighty a creature to His will; and, finally, is seen as the symbol of chaos which the Creator keeps in order. Leviathan is, in sum, a mythological symbol with real meaning -- but no more factual reality than Venus and Adonis had for Shakespeare. This example may seem obvious, but it was not always so. The historicizing outlined really occurred and held place for long epochs. And there are many things in the Bible which are not so obviously "poetry" and yet they are. A commentary on Judith which concentrated on its literary excellence and its message would be much preferable to the discussion of its open shortcomings as historical report and guesses about its historical origins.

The Bible also contains realistic narrative. It is important not to confuse it with history. For one thing, such confusion is open to debunking and subsequent ridicule. More positively, recognizing the "made" character of the narrative makes us focus on the meaning which is important when the facts often are not. In other words, what does the narrative *teach*? For instance, there is the tale of David and Bathsheba and the murder of her husband, Uriah, the Hittite. Personally, I think its historicity can be defended. But, if it were not so, what a picture and what a lesson! David let himself be idle and so easily tempted. Here is a man of immense energy and talent made "technologically redundant" -- a king too valuable to risk in the field -- at the height of his powers. And Bathsheba: it took a Rembrandt to perceive and express the tensions, the psychological conflict she felt while deciding her reply to the king's urging. One could go on and on. With or without factual reference, this realistic narrative is a revelation of poignant human conditions and the causes of sin. Reflecting on the general truth found in realistic narrative, it is sobering to note that modern biblical study grew up in Germany, a nation which did not develop a realistic narrative literature until Thomas Mann's **Buddenbrooks** at the beginning of this century, a hundred years after England and France had developed the literary form to the point where Jane Austen or Stendhal could use it with the mastery of familiarity, and a hundred and fifty years after its sturdy beginnings with Richardson and Fielding. It was not just insularity that kept criticism in a corner for long years in the 19th century England. There was the concrete experience that "there are more things (and more ways of expressing truth of meaning) than are dreamt of in your philosophies" -- an experience largely unavailable to, because not a part of, German culture.

In short, exegesis and historical research, the search for factual backgrounds, sources and the rest, are not identical. They can and should be separated. Not that history is to be ignored. To ascribe a meaning attested only in the 4th century to a word in an 8th century text is simple error. But as we said, historical investigation has done its job and we have a reasonable background to enable us to understand our biblical literature without too many gross historical solecisms.

In short, we should feel free to do something besides historical research on the Bible. And no matter what we do, certain elementary statements of the purpose of the work we are doing should be clarified. When we have determined the kind of text before us, we must make clear what we are doing with it. If we are using it as a mine of historical information well and good, but let us say so. If we are doing something else, we must say this clearly and justify it. There is no intrinsic reason for this -- kinds of interpretation other than the historical are surely legitimate -- but given the habitual identification of history and exegesis the professional reader will find it hard enough to understand what we are doing if it is not history unless we explain ourselves clearly -- and often not even then.

This, of course, implies a clear division within biblical studies. One is surely history. Surely enough has been said about this by now. There is no danger of forgetting what it offers, and we may even add some information about stages of oral transmission and traditional development prior to the textual record. There is geography. The Bible and other documents can help us feel the climate, the plants and animals, the shape and contours of the land which formed the texts to which they refer. There is sociology, the study of the human structures which held Israel and the early Church together, the classes and their interaction within and outside the structures, all the manifold societal aspects the Bible and other documents can reveal to us. There is comparative religion, the study of rite and shrine functionary, of doctrine and moral demands. All this is knowledge, perhaps only of men and environment and not specifically theological, but knowledge and as such good.

One could easily go on dividing the various forms of knowledge to which the Bible could contribute. But we must go on to the most obvious thing of all. The Bible is a book. It is the literary heritage of a nation and of a vital religious community. It can certainly be studied as such. We have already pointed out how historical study has given us the framework which enables us to study it diachronically without too many gross errors. And all the other sciences mentioned can do their part in interpretation. A knowledge of the community structure gives a word like "sojourner" (gēr), for example, real substance, not just a sound. Comparative religion helps understand the sacrificial rites and the prayer forms of the psalms. And geography will enable us to distinguish and understand desert, steppe, farm land and pasture land.

But the primary object of literary study is the text, its primary tools a knowledge of words and phrases and a feel for their use. A first call then: let us read the text for what it is with all the wit and skill we can bring to it. This sounds very simple, but it is not. Normally, the Biblist does not read the text. He breaks it up and reads parts. He tears out its sources. He does not explain the significance of the so-called "plague stories" in Exodus. He merely explains what the Yahwist writer or the Priestly writer thought about plagues. But it is the narrative as it stands which interests the Church or the men of culture concerned with the world's classics. This also should be the biblist's interest in so far as he is concerned with explaining the Bible.

A further proposal is even more revolutionary. The Bible is a whole, a single book with a unity. This is not simply a theological claim. It is a fact of history. The Bible was composed by the refinement of traditional elements and their collection and collocation by choice by the organs of that tradition, (synagogues, rabbis, churches, bishops), not a mere compilation of all that happened to be lying around. Therefore, its parts, though they can be read intelligently as individual chapters, have full meaning when read as integral parts of a meaningful whole.

We must go even farther. The Bible is the community's book and the community's use of it is an element in its total meaning. This is not the on-going clarification of ever obscure events by more events of *Heilsgeschichte.* It is simply the recognition that the Bible has acquired even more meaning through an on-going interpretation which can be found in the Bible itself and continued in the post-biblical Church. No one today has the training nor methodology for such total interpretation. But the ideal remains over against the fragmentation present and it must be kept alive as a hope.

I have not even touched on many basic problems, nor can I. However, one must be faced. We have seen that one "answer" to the problems raised by historical criticism is to rise above the particular to some general theological or philosophic theme. The trouble is that it is not real necessity but cultural conditioning which leads us to tie the general theme to Christianity. Have I not done just the same: called for interpretation of a basic text of Western culture just because it is there? It may only be interesting but what further claim does it have on me?

Biblical religions are, in fact, special because they are not religions of general ideas and eternal truths but historical. They claim that the divine, the Eternal Truth, has been at work in a special way in the world's events. We can discard the six twenty-four days of creation and the six ages of the world as accidental, as outmoded cataloguing schemes, but not the theological vision of *history,* i.e., of the sequence of facts of sin, incarnation, redemption and rebirth. This is Eternal Truth concretely at work in the world, and if it is "concrete," in the world, it is historical. I cannot ignore this and leave history to the historian who *will* ignore it.

However, this is not exactly an *exegetical* problem, a problem of interpretation. Such problems concern meanings. The problem of fact belongs to the historian and, in theology, the apologete, for whom the exegete as such is a mere auxiliary. Part of the confusion in biblical study in the past three centuries comes from the confusion over this distinction, the urge to make exegesis apologetics (or, in some cases, anti-apologetics). I, as a Christian interpreter, assume the reasonableness of accepting the historicity of the cardinal points of my theological vision of history (not, of course, the natural proof of the point of certitude – I want to keep the faith!) Then I go on to interpret as fully as I can the literature which conveys and expands that vision. In other words, I rely on the apologete whose methods and expertise are not mine (acquaintance with and understanding of current and ever changing problems and methods in epistemology, for instance).

With this, of course, we move from the problem of exegesis as such to looking at a larger prospect worth further consideration. Where are the apologetics for the modern world? Not, I mean, the eloquence which will bring back the faith. The loss of religion in the modern world is a matter of *Zeitgeist,* an attitude toward the world and a habit of mind which has been long developing. No, I am not appealing for persuasion looking to conversion, but for a solid intellectual basis which I can know is there though I have not worked it out myself. Knowing that it is there, I can go on with my work of interpretation with a good intellectual conscience. Perhaps good interpretation which delivers the biblical message in its rich beauty will be the converting eloquence mentioned. Still that does not obviate the need for scientific apologetics and, looking at theology as an exegete, I seem to find that apologetes are very thin on the ground these days. And oh how we need them!

As an exegete, perhaps I can help with some leading questions derived for the philosopher-apologete from these Troelschian canons of historical criticism: (1) autonomy -- the scholar must make up his own mind in light of the evidence he sees; (2) analogy -- a past event is understandable and believable only if it is similar to our own experience; (3) the causal chain -- events follow one another as an unbroken series of immanent causes and effects. Why cannot one assert that God intervenes in the causal chain without becoming a mere part in it, and remain intellectually respectable? Why can I not appeal to a theist philosophy, and though I, as a non-professional, cannot expound it, be sure I can refer to a respected philosophical community that can? As for analogy, it is simply a new way of proposing Hume's old saw about what we expect. Well, as a theist, I *can* expect the miracles which analogy supposedly forbids. A hundred years ago that entirely admirable exponent of honest doubt, Matthew Arnold, said there is no reason why the god of theist philosophy cannot work miracles, it just happens that he does not. Where is the vigorous religious philosophy which supports my belief that He can and does?

There is more epistemology. What of the validity of the insight over against mere accumulation as a source of knowledge? Why am I satisfied that Burckhardt's insight still tells me more about Renaissance art and history than all the birth-lists, inventories and account books that computers can absorb? At another level, what of insight as delivering first principles? Modern philosophy, as felt in biblical studies, has regularly denied this -- with one significant almost exception. "Almost" because Coleridge is not usually treated as a philosopher since he never succeeded in formulating his ideas very clearly. Nevertheless, the "sage of Highgate" did mighty battle for *reason* (and imagination) as opposed to *understanding* (and fancy). The latter was in the Lockean tradition, concerned with quantities and external relations. The former somehow saw deeper: its "activity" gave life to the abstractions of understanding. One may be reminded of Kant with the mind imposing order on the **Dinge-an-Sich**, but there is more to it than this. Coleridge maintains that to this activity "mysteriously, their (external things) own life is revealed. Things to it are . . . symbols characterized by a translucence of the general in the particular."

This comes close to a doctrine of a real abstraction of universals from the particular -- if it never becomes very clear. Still, it convinced many in 19th century England that a human faculty could perceive things in the moral realm which were closed to the calculating powers directed to the merely quantitative and factual. It helped theologians diverse as Newman, F.D. Maurice, and the Cambridge trio, "Westcott, Lightfoot and Hort (great biblical critics and orthodox believers). Presumably with it they could defend a solid theism and so a solid conviction in matters of doctrine and biblical interpretation allowing scripture to say the things it really says -- all its truths including even those it is the virtue of criticism to reveal.

However, there is peril here when the idea is interpreted in terms of a moral faculty separate from intellect, as Kant is often interpreted. One should not, I believe, take Coleridge in this direction, although one is easily led to doing so by his tortuous efforts toexpress his idea of a unitary power of imagination and intellectual insight. Perhaps the English were protected from going too far by the supposed national tendency not to drive any principle too far in its conclusions. In any event, not everyone is like that, and danger arises when the idea is used to lift a personal religious stance above attack, which, by definition, can come only from those who lack or do not use the faculty. It leaves things other than the moral and religious life, things like the Bible, open to the never ending work of the intellect with its canons of criticism. The religious stance becomes isolated, individual, almost a feeling, not a reasoned conviction. So the perennial problem: Why should the stance be especially Christian? This especially when remorseless historical criticism is "showing" that the basic Christian document is not really very reliable Ritschl's theology, which many in the last part of the 19th century greeted as salvation for supplying a sound basis for Christian conviction through criticism, succumbed to just this combination of problems, if I read it aright. It would seem that only an integrated view of the person, able to see, formulate and defend a full metaphysic, not just a few moral insights, will do.

Coleridge is especially important here because he puts an emphasis on the imagination not usual in the *philosophia perennis,* for we must confront the fact that we face a new epistemological situation. We *have* to accept the knowledge that comparative religion, literature and folklore have given us. In cultures, it simply is true that great people and great events attract stories to themselves. Thus the great come and go in an extraordinary way: Moses in the bulrushes is paralleled very closely by the birth legend of Sargon of Akkad; the first "world conqueror" -- Hercules -- strangles snakes in his cradle; there are heavenly portents when great Caesar dies; and so on. The great man has preternatural insight into other minds; he heals; he curses effectively. There is no need to expand. We know the argument and it is a strong one. We must face it: if there were no extraordinary stories about David, let alone Jesus, the popular mind would have supplied them, and if this is the case, how do we know which stories it did not invent?

Theoretically one might just compare the legends. Hennecke's **New Testament Apocrypha** and Ginsburg's **Legends of the Jews** and massive folklore collections are at hand. Of course, few actually do this. It is assumed that it has been done and the religious "legends" disproved. How else could Frazer's **Golden Bough** be a pillar of our intelligensia, its unexamined conclusions the basis for further speculation and literary criticism? It is the odd fellow who reads it who finds out how inaccurate is much of its information, how tendentious its reasoning. For comparative legends in general, just read the Infancy Narratives along with a mass of birth legends and it is wild diversity, not similarity, which leaps to the eye. For an even more striking case one can turn to accounts of resurrection.

However, the problem thus attacked remains unsolved. Many really cannot see the differences I say leap to the eye. Besides, popular culture's producing the occasional masterpiece does not make what that work says true to fact. **Sir Patrick Spens** does not become detailed historical narrative by being great poetry. So how can I rely on a piece of poetry, though it be splendid, to tell me the truth especially when I know that an extraordinary individual would occasion fancies about him in a popular, oral culture in any case? That the fancies reach poetic heights may well be merely the accident of a genius' presence to tell the tale, not a sign of its truth, so my case of **Sir Patrick Spens.** The accident of its being recorded in the version of a singer of great talent does not make it history!

However, the parallel is not perfect. It is quite accurate that "the hopes and fears of all the years" met in Bethlehem that night. There would seem to be a difference between those images and stories which occur everywhere and express universal longing for purity, for a savior and healer, for life, and popular poesie on lesser subjects. Do the great biblical images express the truth of what humanity has sought and expressed so often, sometimes haltingly, sometimes tellingly? I believe they do, but we need an epistemology which can confidently show they do. Cannot students of literature, psychologists, philosophers help us here? Can we not press on beyond the lines drawn in Ricouer's The Symbolism of Evil? He stops short at "the human condition" and the final step must show how that condition is tied not to *imaginative* but to *historical* paradigms. We are still at the stage when Langdon Gilkey can gently tap Karl Rahner's wrist for insisting that our sinful condition goes back to an *historic* fall. We need to show that such things must be, though the historic event be delivered to us decorated with poetic symbols (which properly seen elucidate the event but now are adduced to bring it into question). Jung, of course, went some way in this direction with his idea of primordial experiences imprinted on the mind of the race, but so far his work is too occasional, intuitive and unorganized to serve our purpose. Still, the hints are there. Can we not follow them to a conclusion which will satisfy the modern, who is doing plenty of seeking, that the Bible opens the way to his historical home?

I think some such an epistemology would be richer and more satisfying than the alternative which occurs to me. That is, to develop the earlier suggestion. Create a vital tract *de Deo uno,* the implications of revelation, of inspiration. One can answer most of the problems (probably not all) of the Infancy Narratives within this framework. The stories and poems reflect a Jewish milieu. What else? Should they reflect 20th century Chicago? They are attested by only one witness, not three or four as so much of the Gospel. Of course, they are about private matters, not the public life. But if there was such a stir, how were they forgotten and not adduced in evidence? What stir? "All the hill country of Judaea" would not be as large as many a Kansas township nor more densely populated. And any newsman knows that last week's stir is a dead issue. The stir of thirty years ago is simply nothing. What is a Shmoo? Who is Sparkle Plenty? Well, they were the stir of a whole nation thirty years ago! Still, I must admit that, as an historian, this thirty or sixty year submergence of the stories is a real stumbling block.

One can get around it, though the phrase "get around it," already raises bad implications of avoiding and not overcoming difficulties. But let it be: we accept a bad press if we must. What is the evidence for the truth as history of the events told and the poetic interpretation which is offered, as history always offers interpretation, though it is not usually such magnificent writing? No more and no less than the revelation and inspiration granted by God to those who told, developed and finally wrote them. This is what God wanted us to know *e basta.* This is so, but to use it confidently in the intellectual market-place, I need the support of philosophy and theology which convinces. It must show that the God of theism can intervene among the causes immanent in this world. It must give an account of revelation and inspiration which frees that a simplicist concept of inerrancy that respects neither psychological nor historical nor literary realities. And it must mark out the central theological citadel so that I can concentrate on this and not be dealing with a succession of outposts.

Most of all, it must respect knowledge acquired, be it from philology, literature, history, archeology, and leave the biblist free to use all this and all the new stocks that will come. A confident theistic philosophy and consequent theology should have no problem doing this. Certainly, it will be a surprise to see how much this will show that non-historical elements in the Bible, poetry tales, comments, much that seems secondary, throw light on and enrich understanding of the central theological block I have asked to be emphasized.

It really comes to one thing after all. Classic philosophy and theology must be reinvigorated and filled with confidence, so that an exegete who is neither a philosopher nor a theologian can look to and refer to them with confidence when he wants backing. One vital element in such a reinvigoration would have to be an epistemology that takes symbols seriously and demonstrates their real (not ideal or wish-fulfillment) relation to history. For this, classic methods need not be abandoned. The potential is there. In any case, we need not fear the "old," for truth has no age. Think how little has been done with Thomas' work on the integration of sense, imagination, and intellect, and how much this would help develop Coleridge's insight into the unitary imagination and reason and so into the importance of symbol. Let work like this go on so that theology, active, interesting and growing itself, will help and be helped by real exegesis. It certainly will be in no danger of giving way to an "exegesis" which absorbs it, as in many places it has, in fact, become theology *tout court.*

Human Rights and the Old Testament

It is not easy to speak about human rights in OT terms because the phrase, rich in meaning and connotations though it has become, is still abstract. The OT uses language and so ideas and images which are almost all concrete. It talks about men and women, not humanity. The words translated "law, righteousness, justice" and the like, which might seem suited to a discussion of rights, stand originally for a particular teaching on what to do in a given situation, or for a particular decision or decree dealing properly with an individual case. Even "justice", *ṣedeq, ṣ*ᵉ*dāqâ*, means "what is fitting according to the circumstances" and so a concrete act of justice or the attitude which leads to such acts but also in war "victory" or in nature "crops" or "plenty" (see Ps 72,3). Nevertheless, the OT may have something to teach us. Its description of a vast and varied and long experience may finally point to firmer, more realistic basis for human rights than any mere philosophical discussion from the Stoics, who first made rights real in the world of western law and action, to the latest speculations of ethicians.

A good place to begin to look at this record of men involved in moral action is stories, for the heart of the OT (and the Bible) is a Story: creation, rebellion and redemption (in the OT not yet acquired but passionately desired), told largely through narratives. And most useful for our purpose, given limitations of space, are those stories which show directly spontaneous human reactions or recurring human feelings. Such stories are legion in the OT. We refer to a few which show them to be a constant in OT literature and, therefore, presumably in the history which lies behind it.

In 2 Sam 15,18-28, part of what is generally held to be the oldest written history in the OT (10th century?), David, fleeing his rebellious son Absalom, releases his personal guard, Ittai and six hundred men of Gath, from their loyalty. Why should these aliens suffer in a seemingly hopeless cause? It would be far better for them to leave David and return home safely. Yet the Gittites remain loyal. Here we have a relationship, perhaps a sworn one, certainly a paid one, between master and man. However, it is not simply a matter of a contract binding without regard to circumstances. The master refuses to insist on his "rights" when the relationship becomes dangerous for the man. The man, however, equally human and generous, will have none of it; he remains. It is a splendid human scene: the master, responsible and concerned, releasing the man from a pointless relationship and the man, loyal and even reverent, helping the master, profit or not. Love and loyalty are valued above need or reward, and note, this is true of the man from Gath, a despised Philistine, as well of David, the beau ideal of Israelite kings.

Again, in a scene many think to have been composed later under the influence of 9-8th century prophecy, Nathan condemns David for adultery and murder (2 Sam 12,1-15a). In Israel even great kings are bound to righteousness! However, the method by which the prophet makes this point is what is of special interest here. He begins with the story of a pitiless rich man who took a poor man's single pet lamb to feed a guest in order "to spare" his own immense flocks. David's reaction is so human: such a man is worthy of death not for his minor crime but for his vile character. Then, as king and judge, without asking the race or status of the offended man — and David had many non-Israelite subjects — David decrees fourfold compensation to be paid. Of course, the story is only a tale to excite David's indignation and make him realize that he himself is a criminal. He is the oppressor. In Bathsheba he, the king who has all, took the only thing his servant had and loved, and murdered the faithful servant in the bargain. Much might be said about the concern for justice God manifests through his prophet, but this will be treated later. Here we want to note David's humanity, his spontaneous indignation at what he thinks a vile abuse of power against the weak.

Other early stories, the odd tale of Tamar (Gen 38) or of Joseph, illustrate the same human urge to vindicate the weak. The story of Ruth shows the feeling still alive in much later times. This is no surprise because the theme reflects a concern for the poor, the stranger, those without family, in sum the weak, those without built-in social defenses which runs through Israelite teaching (Torah) from its earliest large formulation, the so-called Covenant Code: "You shall not... oppress an alien... (nor) wrong a widow or orphan" (Exod 22,20-21). Rather one must help them, for example, by leaving something in the harvest fields for them to gather (Deut 24,19-21; Lev 19,9-10). One of the last kings of Judah is praised precisely because he "dispensed justice to the weak and poor" (Jer 22,16). The tradition is continuous and emphatic. It surely reflects a basic and admirable human trait: the feeling that favors the underdog. Other ancient literatures mention the feeling, and certainly many ancients felt it, but none, to my knowledge, makes it so central that it produced a full spirituality revealed especially in the psalms in which the weak are actually the favorites of God, the ones closest to him, precisely because, thrown on his protection, they learn faith and trust.

We shall note but one more instance to show a humane reaction to a rather different kind of unfairness. It comes from a late source, confirming the steadiness of the humane tradition. In Mal 2,13-16 we read: "This also you do:

you cover the altar of the LORD with tears because he no longer regards your sacrifice..., and you say, 'Why is it?' — Because the LORD is witness between you and the wife of your youth, with whom you have broken faith though she is your companion, your betrothed wife... For I hate divorce, says the Lord..." There is a good deal of complex controversy behind this text, but the prophet's (and expressed through him, God's) passionate feeling is clear. It is vile to repudiate the woman you have taken in youth to be your companion throughout life. Perhaps the prophet felt it more strongly than our contemporaries — which says more for OT humanity than for ours!

There is plenty of evidence, then, that Israelites reacted humanly to human situations. Indeed, we have seen that this was not left to mere chance feeling. The traditions of helping the poor and being fair were expressed as directives: see the classic formulation, "administer true justice... do not consider who a person is..." (Deut 1,16-17), as well as illustrated in stories and prayed about in psalms. The traditions were strong, but eventually old instruments for handing them on, shrines end even kingdoms, were endangered and destroyed. It was necessary to gather the traditions and one result was the codes, the Covenant Code, Exod 20,1 - 23,19; the Deuteronomic Code, Deut 12,1 - 26,15, and the Holiness Code, Lev 17-25. These were to be sources of wisdom, guides and consolers (Deut 4,6-8; Sir 24, especially v. 23). In fact, the appearance of written codes doubtless encouraged knowledge of and thought about the traditions. More, these became the canonical word of God (Deut 4,6-8 again; 30,11-14). Still, they spoke in the forms of the culture of their time and in many things are similar to other ancient laws. An important aspect of this is that it means that they were particular. They did not deal with the rights and duties of men as such but of members of the group, city, tribe or religious community. Real outsiders — there were usually provisions for proper resident aliens — seem to be outside the law, scarcely considered to have rights and duties. Even, it must be said, objects of outright hatred and attack.

One can read much in the OT codes in this fashion, but this would be to forget that underlying humane tradition expressed in the Codes' over-riding concern for the weak. Nor should we forget the stories which continued to be told. In them it is often the alien who is the model of righteousness and the one who benefits from justice and goodness: Tamar was perhaps a Canaanite, Ittai was a Philistine, Ruth a Moabitess, and the arch-infidels of Assyrian Nineveh listen to the preaching of Jonah. The influence of a basic feeling for common humanity cannot be denied, restrictive though some laws are. In fact, the thrust of the feeling for the under-dog was so strong it had to be cautioned. One should not cheat on behalf of the poor and weak, and Exod 23,3 and Lev 19,15 warn against unjust favoritism for the poor. Or consider Deut 20,19-20 forbidding the destruction of fruit trees around a besieged city, and not just an Israelite city, because they will be needed for food when the war is past. Or Deut 21,10-14 which defends the rights of a captive woman taken as a wife.

Israelite or not, she, the most helpless of creatures, is to be treated with fairness and respect.

The humane tradition, then, went on. However, humanity runs off in many directions. It can be just and generous. It can trust, saying in the face of mass armies, "we are strong in the name of the LORD, our God" (Ps 20,8; cf. Is 30,15-17). It can reach toward mystic union with God: "Whom have I in the heavens but you? And having you, I wish naught else" (Ps 73,25; cf. 84,11).

However, the David who is horrified by the despoiling of a poor man has just come from a vicious adultery and murder. Perhaps worse because it represents an attitude, a habit of mind and not a stroke of weakness, humanity can indulge in continuous rage at real or imagined oppression or sharp dealing. The cursing psalms like 109, asking that a man be erased from the book of life and his innocent family subjected to want, or 137, calling for the slaughter of enemy infants, are ample evidence of this human trait. It is, in fact, an advantage of the OT that it makes clear the force of injustice through the expression of the mindless rage it arouses. It is a sign that mere humanism will not do. There are other signs: the wish to dominate in Ps 149 or Is 49,23-26. But depriving others does not insure one's own position. Neither hate nor power is an answer to the problems of society. This is poignantly clear in Chronicle's treatment of David and Solomon. The old king, mighty warrior and cunning enemy — and the Chronicler's favorite, had shed so much blood (and not all in clean battle) to establish his power that he was not fit to build the Temple. This crowning achievement belongs to the young king, a man of peace and a wise dispenser of justice (1 Chron 22,7-10).

What is one to make of a mix like this: good-will, humanitarianism, rage, power-hunger, favoritism? Nothing without the central element of the divine. It is God who is guarantor of the law and wisdom which is his own gift. According to Lev 19 Israel is to be holy because it is the people of the holy God, and here to be holy indeed means worship and the like, but it also means fair and generous treatment of one's fellow. This is what it means to belong to a God who is ready to condemn a David or the nobles of Samaria who oppress the weak. Are there stronger words than Am 4,1-2: "Hear this word, women... of Samaria, you cows of Bashan, you who oppress the weak and abuse the needy... The Lord GOD has sworn by his holiness: Truly the days are coming... when they shall drag you away with hooks..." But Isaiah is as hard on the nobles of Judah, as is Micah (Is 5,8-16; Mic 3,1-3). The reason is clear from the mention of holiness in two of the passages, for this God "shows himself holy by his justice" (Is 5,16). Hence the violence of the prophets who speak for him. A people especially linked to this God, when they turn to injustice, are actually trying to defile him! The result can only be to destroy themselves as far as they can. A faithless people will be turned out of a land which is nothing "but sulphur and salt, a burnt out-waste, unsown and unfruitful, without a blade of grass" (Deut 29,22). So God vindicates himself. It is important to note the language here. It is certainly not strictly eschatological, but it evokes more direct apocalyptic visions like Is 34,9-10; 27,10-11 and so is a first hint of a final divine intervention, an idea which develops in relation to our theme.

Still, despite the wrath of the Holy God, the people cannot destroy themselves, misuse its privileges as it may, for its God is not merely full of rage at injustice. His rage, in fact, is but a facet of his passionate attachment, a sign of disappointment. He can be as urgent in pleading his loving care. He breaks off a condemnation with the cry: "How can I give you up, O Ephraim, or give you over, O Israel? My heart is overwhelmed, my pity stirred. I will not give vent to my blazing anger" (Hos 11,8-9a). He pleads with his people: "O my people, what have I done to you, or how have I wearied you? Answer me! For I brought you up from Egypt, from the place of slavery..." (Mic 6,3-4a). His attachment is far beyond that of a loving mother (Is 49,14-16). No doubt this is anthropomorphic and the OT God is not emotional as we are, but neither is he an aloof prime mover, a cold dispenser of justice. His concern is transposed to a higher level. It is more than, not the negation, of human feeling. Justice, then, respect for one's fellow, goes back to and is guaranteed by a God who is passionately devoted to each of his people, and especially to the weak and the poor.

But there is the rub. "His people": the codes, the fierce and loving call to treat one another as fellows under God seems to be confined to Israel. Often enough, this is express, and in the psalms, for example, the people are played off against enemies, named or unnamed, who are hardly more than strawmen, mere objects for the divine wrath. However, this is not the whole story. Quite early the prophet Amos revealed the God of Israel was concerned with rights and wrongs among other peoples and these the immediate enemies of Israel (Am 1,3 – 2,3). Nor was he concerned only with sin. He actively guided other peoples just as he did Israel: "Did I not bring Israel out of Egypt as I brought the Philistines from Caphtor and the Arameans from Kir?" (Am 9,7) — Israel's proudest boast, that the LORD had gone down to Egypt to save it, is shared by others! Or, according to a poem of disputed date, but which may be very early, Deut 32,8-9, the LORD "assigned the nations their heritage... He set up the boundaries of the peoples according to the number of the Sons of God (LXX), while the LORD's own share was Jacob..." That is, the LORD is the lord of all peoples and all supernal powers (early Israel did not have the conceptual or verbal equipment to separate mysterious powers from something divine; it simply knew that the LORD was superior to any other power). The LORD is supreme and he cares about the nations, even assigning them protectors (the forerunners of the guardian angels of nations?).

It might not center on the idea, but early on the OT thus proclaims a divine concern for all men. When it realizes clearly that the LORD "is God, there is no other" (Is 45,22b etc; Ps 115,4-7, with a sneer at idols), the consequences are near at hand, though perhaps all Israel did not see them. Like most of us, Israelites were not governed by logic alone. Nevertheless, it is clear that the one God must be sovereign of all peoples. Often enough this insight is used to emphasize that God will punish these peoples, but some realized that all have an access to him: "All the nations you have made shall come and worship you, O LORD, glorify your name, for you are great and do wondrous deeds; you alone are God" (Ps 86,9-10). Finally Wis 9,1-3 can assert: "You have made all things by your word and in your wisdom have established man to rule the creatures produced by you, to govern the world in holiness and justice, and to render judgment in integrity of heart." Thus all are raised to the holiness of God which is justice, all are guided by him, all are subject to him, the passionate defender of justice and punisher of the unjust so well known to Israel.

Practically this means the submission of all peoples to the God of Israel. But how is this to come about? Most often the reunion of peoples under God is simply proclaimed. He wants it and it will be. Is 19,19-25 is truly startling here, for it proclaims the ancient and permanent enemies of Israel, the images of all her troubles, Egypt and Assyria, are to be one with her. All three nations are given the proud title "My people." If such enemies can be reconciled, anything can be done. Then there is the beautiful passage Is 2,2-4 (= Mic 4,1-3): "In days to come the mountain of the LORD's house shall be established... All nations shall stream toward it; many peoples shall come and say, 'Come, let us climb the LORD's mountain..., that he may instruct us in his ways, and we may walk in his paths.' For from Zion shall go forth instruction, and the word of the LORD from Jerusalem. He shall judge between nations... They shall beat their swords into plowshares and their spears into pruning hooks; one nation shall not raise the sword against another, nor shall they train for war again." Because of its appearance in two prophets and its unusual language many think this is a quotation from a liturgical piece. If so, it would mean that the hope of reunion was proclaimed to a far wider audience than any prophet or writer could hope for. In any case, the peoples are to come together. They are to learn the LORD's ways, the ways of right and justice. Then perfect peace will reign, once again a hint at the eschatological, for a standard image of the final reign of God was a return to the peace of the original paradise (see, for example, Is 11,1-9). Not just society but the cosmos is in travail: "How long must the earth mourn, the green... wither for the wickedness of those who dwell in it?" (Jer 12,4; cf. 23,10; Gen 3,17). A disturbed world cries out for order (Rom 8,22).

However, we have insisted on the concreteness of the OT. One may proclaim that God is the God of all peoples, but what concrete means will bring them to him? Well, "salvation is from the Jews" (John 4,22). In Amos God is concerned about other peoples and speaks about them; Israel he addresses directly. So, in some texts, it is through the example of Israel that God obtains the submission of all. The nations seeing the LORD at work among them, for example, bringing Israel back from the Exile, will see that he is the true God (e.g., Ezek 36,23). At times the lesson is harsh. God is to strike the heathen, "pour out his wrath," and then they "will know... that there is no other God" (see Sir 36,1-13). It is not always so. According to Tob 13 so mighty an act as the return from Exile will be a "bright light to all the earth" so that "many nations shall come to you (Jerusalem)" "bearing gifts," and Jerusalem will be built of gold and precious stones, the Book of Revelation's symbol for the end of alienation (time). Once more the eschatological note creeps into our context.

There is a problem with all this. Universal restoration is proclaimed. The Israelites are to lead it. But it turns out that this seems to be universal integration into old Israel. Other peoples share the covenant and especially worship on Zion (Ps 86; Is 2,2-4, etc.). But note that much of this is imagery which proclaims that all will join the Temple worship. No doubt some of this was taken literally, but if pressed too hard it leads to an absurdity: numberless hordes in one tiny place. This was realized: Ps 87 praises Zion as the native place of all peoples, an obvious trope. One could go to the God of Zion without going to Zion. (This gap between imagery and a larger reality conceivably could leave room for the non-believer, the ignorant man of good will too, but this is not really an OT question. The outsiders of good will seem eventually to acknowledge the LORD: see Rahab [Jos 2], Nebuchadnezzar [Dan 2,47, etc.], Achior the Ammonite [Jdt 5,5-24 + 14,10]).

However, there was something more basic than worship and its imagery in Israel. The Israelites did not worship simply as the natural subjects of a Supreme Lord. They worshipped as a community covenanted with God. This means that the nations too must have a covenant, the central OT statement of a relation to God, to belong to the true God. One solution within the OT itself was the Noachic covenant (Gen 9,1-17). It had its rainbow sign and developed a simple code expressing God's will for all. According to Acts 15,20 it was remembered and believed in. However, it is thin, over-simple, and despite Acts it hardly was universally known or accepted. The covenant as developed in Deuteronomy, actually a document recording Israel's covenant with God, is more fruitful for us. We cannot deal with all its riches. The major point, I think, is that covenant is a free association: one may choose it (life) or refuse it (death) (Deut 30,15). God offers himself to the people and they to him. "This very day *you have confirmed the LORD's declaration that he will be your God* since you will walk in his ways and observe his statute... and hearken to his voice, and *he has confirmed your declaration*, since you are ready to be made his people, a special possession..., *that you will keep his commandments* as he sets you over all the nations... so as to be a holy people to the LORD your God..." (Deut 26,17-19). God and the people exchange pledges and "he is their God and they are his people," the covenant formula which becomes ubiquitous after Deuteronomy. This element of choice by God and by man is rich with endless possibilities.

Rich possibilities, moving imagery, great hopes, free will, access to God: there is much here that relates to the question of human rights, but one cannot claim that it adds up to a complete doctrine of rights nor even an orderly whole. Nor should we expect it to. As we said at the beginning, the OT is not the expression of a neat theory nor even of an orderly doctrine. It is the story of long experience and much learning with the untidiness, the loose ends, the unclarity and incompleteness of all earthly experience, especially when that experience is seen through the tunnel of a thousand years of violent history. Still, this has advantages: its has the reality of experience, untidy though it may be, not the lifelessness of a set of clear and distinct ideas. Moreover, this immense experience does allow us to sum up with some points which the OT can contribute to any thinking about human rights.

First, they are a prime concern of God. He will defend his creatures against abuse of power (Nathan against David; Amos against the Samarian nobles, etc.) or against infidelity (Elijah against Ahab; Malachi against divorce). That is, he will do so if we will let him, listen to his directions and his spokesmen.

Secondly, God will do this concretely. By this I mean that not some idea but some person or persons will stand up for the right under God. This was the role of the prophet, of the priest (2 Macc 3,10), the people Israel whom God addressed directly while he spoke about others and who were to be a sign to reunite all peoples under God. This work of reconciliation is the role of the instruments God chooses to guide people throughout history.

Thirdly, all are called. All have access to God. All should be able to find him and having found him remain with him forever. This is the importance of the use of quasi-apocalyptic language in so many of the texts we have seen. True universal reconciliation is to be final, a reunion of peoples and a reintegration of the cosmos.

But how is all this to happen? Quite simply, by submission, by acknowledging God for what he is, supreme and absolute Lord. In OT terms this means offering oneself in response to God's offer of himself in convenant so that this submission really means the freedom of the household of God: *ama et fac quod vis!* This is the fundamental meaning of the Deuteronomic covenant with its offer of life, a life of union with God in the community of his people, for "he will be your God and you will be his people." Indeed, 1 Sam 12,14b affirms that a people responsive to him "will belong to the household of the LORD." One could substitute, or better, add "retinue" and "family" to "household" — I know no single modern English word which catches the full force of the Hebrew phrase here. "Team" would come close except of its slangy and, largely from use in politics, humorous overtones.

Alas, modern translations are no help here. They miss the meaning completely. Some include 14b with 14a as part of a protasis, "if you and your king follow me..." and make 1 Sam 12,14 an anacoluthon; some conjecture an apodosis such as "it will be well with you" to produce a complete and colorless sentence. To be fair, one must note that *La nueva Biblia española*, "viviréis siendo fieles al Señor," does give the nuance of fidelity, but it seems to lack that of the family. Perhaps the venerable AV, "then shall ye and also the king... continue following the LORD," remains the best, if we can take "continue following" as "continue in the retinue, the loyal followers of the LORD."

In any event, this proper meaning of the Hebrew phrase *hāyâ ʾaḥar (yhwh)*, literally, "to be after the LORD (or someone else)," is no new discovery (cf., for example, K. Budde, KHAT VIII: *Die Bücher Samuel*. Tübingen, 1902, 80: "[eine] gute alte Wendung"). It is a standard idiom applying to one who faithfully attaches himself to a proper leader like a king and is accepted into the leader's group of regular followers.

To be members of the LORD's household. It means to be a full person truly and immediately ordered to God. No one may interfere with this relation and its consequences. Here is the one inviolable basis for human rights.

Errata corrigenda

P. 3, line 2: read Gn 21,22-34 instead of Gn 21,22-24.
P. 3, line 3: read Gn 31,44-54 instead of Gn 31,49-54.
P. 5, note 5: read Dt 7,12 instead of Dt 7,11.
P. 6, note 10: read 2 Kgs 16,7-8 instead of 2 Kgs 14-15.
P. 7, line 26: read Gn 21,30 instead of Gn 21,25-26.
P. 8, line 19: read Gn 21,25-26 instead of Gn 21, 25-25.
P. 9, note 16: read 2 Chr 13,5 instead of 2 Chr 13,15.
P. 12, line 7 from bottom: read Dt 26,17-18 instead of Dt 26,17.
P. 16, line 4: read *šōḥad* instead of *šōḥād*.
P. 20, line 13: read Is liii 10 instead of Is lii 10.
P. 20, line 18: read Jer xxxi 9a instead of Jer xxi 9a.
P. 22, line 8: n. 23 refers to note 1 on. p. 75 of the original pagination and p. 31 of the present reprint.
P. 22, note 3 of notes: the page numbers of the review article in *Biblica* are 110-121.
P. 22, note 2: read Hos x 4 instead of Hos ix 4.
P. 23, note 2: n. 14 refers to note 3 on p. 70 of the original pagination and p. 26 of the present reprint.
P. 25, line 11: read 1 Sam xx 8 for 2 Sam xx 8.
P. 25, line 18: read 1 Sam xvii 13 instead of 1 Sam xvii 3.
P. 26, line 12: read 1 Sam xviii 1-4 instead of 2 Sam xviii 1-4.
P. 26, line 18: read 1 Sam xx 7-8 instead of 2 Sam xx 7-8.
P. 26, line 10 from bottom: read "Roland" instead of "Rolan".
P. 26, note 3: read 1 Sam xx 8b instead of 1 Sam xx 7b.
P. 27, line 21: read 1 Sam xx 10-17 instead of 1 Sam xx 11-17.
P. 28, line 5 of note 1: read "MT" instead of "Mt".
P. 29, line 4: read 1 Sam xx 10-17 instead of 1 Sam xx 20-17.
P. 30, note 3: read Hos x 4 instead of Hos ix 4, and Hos x 3 instead of Hos ix 3.
P. 31, line 3 from bottom of text: read "reversed" instead of "reverses".

P. 31, line 16 from bottom: read Gn xxi 31-32 instead of Gn xx 31-32.
P. 34, line 15: read 2 Kgs xi 17b instead of 2 Kgs xx 17b.
P. 37, note 1: read 1 Sam xxiii 16-18 instead of 1 Sam xxiii 16-16.
P. 37, note 1: read 2 Sam iii 12-21 instead of 2 Sam iii 21.
P. 37, note 1: read 2 Sam iii 21 instead of 2 Sam iii 12-21.
P. 37, note 1: read Hos x 4 instead of Hos ix 4.
P. 37, note 1: read Hos xii 2b instead of Hos xii 12b.
P. 38, line 6: read Hos x 4 instead of Hos ix 4.
P. 38, line 15: read Gn xxxi 23 - xxxii 3 instead of Gn xxxi 32 - xxxii 3.
P. 38, line 16: read "This" instead of "it".
P. 38, line 23: read Hos x 4 instead of Hos ix 4.
P. 38, line 24: read "and in Hos. xii 2b Ephraim's obligation must" instead of "and in Hos xii 12b, and Ephraim's obligation must".
P. 38, note 1: n. 34 refers to note 1 on p. 81 of the original pagination and p. 37 of the present reprint.
P. 39, line 5: n. 33 refers to note 4 on p. 80 of the original pagination and p. 36 of the present reprint.
P. 39, line 10: read 2 Kgs xi 4 instead of 1 Kgs xi 4.
P. 39, line 22: read Hos x 4 instead of Hos ix 4.
P. 39, line 23: read 2 Sam iii 21; v 3 instead of 2 Sam iii 21-v3.
P. 40, lines 23-24: read 2 Sam v 3 instead of 1 Sam iii 5.
P. 40, note: read 1 Sam xx 8 instead of 1 Sam xx 16 and rules instead of tules.
P. 49, line 16 from bottom: read Ex 34,27 instead of Ex 34, 37.
P. 51, line 12: read Ezra 10 instead of Ex 10.
P. 58, line 12: read Gn 21,27 instead of Gn 21,27.
P. 60, note 17: read 2 Sam 3,18 instead of 2 Sam 3.li.
P. 60, note 17: read 2 Sam 5,2 instead of 2 Sam 52.
P. 72, line 18: read 1 Kgs 5,26 instead of 1 Kgs 5,22.
P. 72, line 23: read *l*^{e}*šālôm* instead of *b*^{e}*šālôm*.
P. 72, note 18: read *ʿălēkem* instead of *ålēkem*.
P. 73, line 4: read *wayyaʿ ab*^{e}*dûm* instead of *wayyaʾ ab*^{e}*dûm*.
P. 77, line 19: read Joshua 9 instead of Joshua 8.
P. 77, last line of text: read 1 Sam 11:2 instead of 1 Sam 11:12a.
P. 77, last line of note 13: read Joshua 9 instead of Joshua 8.
P. 78, line 7: read 2 Sam 3,12 instead of 2 Sam 2,12.
P. 78, last line of text: read 1 Sam 8,11-12.14 instead of 1 Sam 8,11-12,14.
P. 79, line 10 of first note: read 1 Sam 20,8 instead of 1 Sam 20,5.
P. 79, line 4 from bottom of note 18: read 1 Sam 10,1 instead of 2 Sam 10,1.
P. 81, line 5 from bottom of text: read 1 Sam 24,7 instead of 1 Sam 24,4.

P. 81, line 5 from bottom of text: read 1 Sam 26,9 instead of 1 Sam 28,9.
P. 81, line 4 of note 24: read 2 Kgs 12,5-8 instead of 2 Kgs 12,13-16.
P. 83, line 3 from bottom of text: read Ex 22,24 instead of Ex 22,21.
P. 85, last line of text: read Jer 27,3 instead of Jer 27,2.
P. 87, line 3: read 2 Sam 23,3b-4 instead of 2 Sam 23,3b.
P. 89, line 7 from bottom of text: read 2 Kgs 12,21 instead of 2 Kgs 12,20.
P. 94, line 9: read 1 Chr 22,10 instead of 1 Chr 22,9.
P. 94, note 6: read Ex 34 instead of Esra 3,4.
P. 95, line 2: read 2 Chr 15,3 instead of 2 Chr 15,5.
P. 96, line 10: read 2 Chr 29,5-11 instead of 2 Chr 29:5:11.
P. 96, line 12: read 2 Kgs 23,2 instead of 2 Kgs 23,3.
P. 96, line 7 from bottom of text: read 2 Kgs instead of 1 Kgs 23.
P. 97, line 2: read Chr 25,5-6 instead of 1 Chr 25,3-4.
P. 97, line 12: read 1 Chr 16,22 instead of 1 Chr 16,25.
P. 97, line 19: read 1 Kgs 18 instead of 1 Kgs 8.
P. 97, note 12: read 2 Chr 12,2-7 instead of 2 Chr 12,2-4.
P. 97, note 12: read 2 Chr 16,7 instead of 2 Chr 16,4.
P. 97, note 14: read 2 Kgs 20,1 instead of [Is] 20,1.
P. 97, note 14: read "Cyrus" instead of "Darius".
P. 98, line 14 from bottom of text: read 2 Chr 24,20 instead of 2 Chr 24,3.
P. 99, line 20: read 2 Chr 31,21 instead of 2 Chr 32,21.
P. 99, line 6 from bottom of text: read Dn 9,10 and *1 Esdras* 8,79 instead of Ezra 8,11.
P. 100, line 14: read Gn 31,44.33 instead of Gn 31,44.54.
P. 100, line 14: read 2 Chr 15,12.14 instead of 2 Chr 15,11.14.
P. 120, line 2: read Ex 7,15 instead of Ex 8,15.
P. 122, note 17: read *ʾănî* instead of *ʾaenî*.
P. 125, line 9: read Ex 8,18 instead of Ex 8,19.
P. 125, line 7: read "first" instead of "second".
P. 125, line 8: read "second" instead of "third" and "fourth" instead of "fifth".
P. 125, line 12: Read Ex 9,29 instead of Ex 9,19.
P. 128, line 9: read "as in the words" instead of "in the words".
P. 128, line 24: read 2 Sam 8,9b instead of 2 Sam 7,9b.
P. 128, line 1 of note 5: read p. 223 instead of p. 233.
P. 140, line 21: read Ex 12,51 instead of Ex 12,54.
P. 141, line 24: read Ex 5,1 - 6,1 instead of Ex 5,1 - 6,2.
P. 142, line 3 of note 13: read Ex 7,8 - 10,27 instead of Ex 7,8 - 10,10.
P. 144, line 5 from bottom of text: read Ex 12,27b-28 instead of Ex 12,27b-29.

P. 145, line 25: read Ex 7,8 - 10,27 instead of Ex 7,8-27.
P. 146, line 4 from bottom of text: read Ex 12,30 instead of Ex 12,29.
P. 150, bottom line of text: read Ex 14,27 instead of Ex 14,28.
P. 154, line 8: read Ex 5,1 - 6,1 instead of Ex 5,1 - 6,6.
P. 155, line 7 from bottom of note 38: read Ex 11-13 instead of Ex 11-12.
P. 174, line 1 of note 14: read Lv 4,12 instead of Lv 7,12.
P. 183, line 3 of note 5: read 1 Chr 22,13; 28,20 instead of 1 Chr 22,13.
P. 186, line 16: read Am 2,14 instead of Am 2,4.
P. 198, line 14 from bottom of text: read v. instead of vv.
P. 199, line 3: read Jos 2,18 instead of Jos 2,17.
P. 202, line 10: read v. 1 instead of v. 2.
P. 206, line 15: read Ps 107,26 instead of Ps 105, 26.
P. 245, line 10: read Jos 9,13a instead of Jos 9,13b.
P. 246, line 15: read *'ēlêkā* instead of *'ēlêkô* and *kol* instead of *kôl*.
P. 271, line 2: read 2 Sam 24,1-17 instead of 2 Sam 21,1-17.
P. 294, bottom line of note 12: read Gn 27 instead of Gn 25,27.
P. 303, line 7: read Jer 3,20 instead of Jer 3,19.
P. 303, line 8: read Dt 32,17-18 instead of Dt 32,19-20.
P. 307, line 16 from bottom of column on right: read Am 7,10-15 instead of Am 7,10-14.
P. 308, line 2 of column on left: read Is 5,16 instead of Is 5,18.
P. 308, line 12 of column on left: read Is 28,14-15; and not Is 28,14-15,30-31.
P. 308, line 9 of column on right: read Jer 42,7 and not Jer 42,10.
P. 309, line 9 from bottom of column on right: read Is 28,16-17 instead of Is 22,16-17.
P. 313, line 4 of note 3: read Zech 87 instead of Zech 4,7.
P. 314, line 1 of note 4: read "the" instead of "teh".
P. 347, line 14: read 2 Sam 7,1-16 instead of 1 Sam 7,1-16.
P. 348, line 3: read 1 Kgs 16,2-3 instead of 1 Kgs 16,2.13.
P. 351, line 3 of note 6: read Dt 6,12-15 instead of Dt 6,12-14.
P. 351, line 4 of note 6: read Dt 11,16-17 instead of Dt 11,16.
P. 351, line 1 of note 7: read *ʿabhar* instead of *ʿazabh*.
P. 362, line 1 of note 41: read 1 Pt 5,8 instead of 1 Pt 5,9.
P. 366, note 5: read Sir 24,23.25 instead of Sir 24, 23, 25.
P. 366, note 8: read Prov 8,22-23.27.29-30 instead of Prov 8,22-23; 27,30-31.
P. 368, note 16: read Est 5,1c-1d.2a-2b instead of Est 15,6-7.
P. 373, note 18: read Neh 10,29-32 instead of Neh 10,29-31.
P. 375, line 1 of text: read "Krentz" instead of "Krenz".

P. 375, line 11 of text: read Col 1 instead of 1 Col.
P. 375, line 15 of text: read Gen 2,4 - 3,24 instead of Gen 2,4 - 3,24.
P. 382, line 20: read "the deliverance of untrammeled reason" instead of "the deliverance from untrammeled reason".
P. 385, line 3: omit "quite".
P. 385, line 9: read "associantionist" instead of "associanist".
P. 386, line 11: omit "especially".
P. 387, line 5 from bottom: read "But now it was a chain" instead of "But that was a chain".
P. 387, bottom line: read "Of course it has" instead of "In any case, it has".
P. 388, line 16: read "to use them to reduce" instead of "to use it to reduce".
P. 390, line 18: read "and specialists are no longer *au courant*" instead of "and are not longer au courant".
P. 390, line 18: read "and are specialists no longer" instead of "and are no longer".
P. 390, line 22: read "Braudell" instead of "Pautrell".
P. 391, line 3: read "The specific way this is done is to take the prophet out of history, to make the prophet the true voice of God" instead of "The specific way this is done is to make the prophet the true voice of God".
P. 391, line 10: read Hos 1-3 instead of Hos 1.3.
P. 391, line 18: read "tricks" and not "tickets".
P. 391, line 2 from bottom of text: read Is 40-55 instead of Is 50-55.
P. 392, line 10: read Is 52,13-53,12 instead of 52,13 and 13,12.
P. 393, line 4 from bottom: read "even against its own" instead of "even from its own".
P. 397, line 17: read "in 19th century England" instead of "in the 19th century England".
P. 398, line 14 from bottom: read "sacrificial rites" instead of "the sacrificial rites".
P. 399, line 12 from bottom: omit "only".
P. 402, lines 3-4 from bottom: read "of Sargon of Akkad, the first 'world conqueror'; Hercules strangles snakes" instead of "of Sargon of Akkad; the first 'world conqueror' — Hercules — strangles snakes".
P. 405, line 9: read "which frees from a simplicist" instead of "which frees that a simplicist".

Index of Biblical Passages

An asterisk (*) indicates that the *Errata corrigenda* should be consulted in connection with the passage in question.

Passages of greater moment are indicated by the use of boldface type.

DEUTERONOMY

2 SAMUEL